Lecture Notes in Computer Science

Lecture Notes in Artificial Intelligence   13900

Founding Editor

Jörg Siekmann

Series Editors

Randy Goebel, *University of Alberta, Edmonton, Canada*
Wolfgang Wahlster, *DFKI, Berlin, Germany*
Zhi-Hua Zhou, *Nanjing University, Nanjing, China*

The series Lecture Notes in Artificial Intelligence (LNAI) was established in 1988 as a topical subseries of LNCS devoted to artificial intelligence.

The series publishes state-of-the-art research results at a high level. As with the LNCS mother series, the mission of the series is to serve the international R & D community by providing an invaluable service, mainly focused on the publication of conference and workshop proceedings and postproceedings.

David S. Warren · Veronica Dahl · Thomas Eiter ·
Manuel V. Hermenegildo · Robert Kowalski ·
Francesca Rossi
Editors

Prolog: The Next 50 Years

 Springer

Editors
David S. Warren 🆔
Stony Brook University
Stony Brook, NY, USA

Thomas Eiter 🆔
TU Wien
Vienna, Austria

Robert Kowalski 🆔
Imperial College London
London, UK

Veronica Dahl 🆔
Simon Fraser University
Burnaby, BC, Canada

Manuel V. Hermenegildo 🆔
Universidad Politecnica de Madrid/IMDEA
Software Institute
Madrid, Spain

Francesca Rossi 🆔
IBM Research
Yorktown Heights, NY, USA

ISSN 0302-9743   ISSN 1611-3349 (electronic)
Lecture Notes in Artificial Intelligence
ISBN 978-3-031-35253-9   ISBN 978-3-031-35254-6 (eBook)
https://doi.org/10.1007/978-3-031-35254-6

LNCS Sublibrary: SL7 – Artificial Intelligence

This Springer imprint is published by the registered company Springer Nature Switzerland AG
The registered company address is: Gewerbestrasse 11, 6330 Cham, Switzerland

Preface

The Year of Prolog

This book is an outcome of the Year of Prolog[1] effort celebrating 50 years of Prolog and looking to the future. The Year of Prolog was organized by the Association for Logic Programming and the Prolog Heritage Association.

In the summer of 1972, Alain Colmerauer and his team in Marseille developed and implemented the first version of the logic programming language Prolog. Together with both earlier and later collaborations with Robert Kowalski and his colleagues in Edinburgh, this work laid the practical and theoretical foundations for the Prolog and logic programming of today. Prolog and its related technologies soon became key tools of symbolic programming and Artificial Intelligence.

The Year of Prolog celebrated the 50th anniversary of these events and highlighted the continuing significance of Prolog and logic programming both for symbolic, explainable AI, and for computing more generally. It also aimed to inspire a new generation of students, by introducing them to a more human-friendly, logic-based approach to computing.

The initiatives of the Year of Prolog included:

- The inaugural edition of the ALP Alain Colmerauer Prolog Heritage Prize (in short: the Alain Colmerauer Prize) for recent practical accomplishments that highlight the benefits of Prolog-inspired computing for the future.
- A Prolog Day Symposium,[2] celebrated in Paris on November 10, 2022, in which the inaugural edition of the Alain Colmerauer Prize was awarded. Subsequent editions of the prize will be awarded at the corresponding year's International Conference on Logic Programming, starting with ICLP 2023.
- A survey paper on "Fifty Years of Prolog and Beyond," which was published in the 20th anniversary special issue of the ALP journal Theory and Practice of Logic Programming (TPLP), Vol. 22(6), Cambridge University Press. This paper, complementary to this book, covers the evolution of Prolog systems, up to the most relevant ones today, and their future directions.
- A Prolog Education initiative, which will use Prolog to introduce schoolchildren and young adults to logic, programming, and AI and also map and provide Prolog education resources for educators. This is a long-term initiative which will be continued in future years.
- There were also special sessions and invited talks at several events and conferences, including ICLP 2022, at FLoC.
- Finally, ICLP 2023 marked the closing of this Year of Prolog celebrations. It included the award of the 2023 ALP Alain Colmerauer Prize and presentations of this Prolog

---

[1] https://prologyear.logicprogramming.org.

[2] https://prologyear.logicprogramming.org/PrologDay.html.

Book, progress on the education initiative, the online Prolog community, and other related activities.

1 The Idea of This Book

This volume, part of the Year of Prolog celebrations, represents both the State of the Art and Visions for the Future of Prolog. The goal for the volume is to be accessible to a broad audience, being as self-contained as possible and containing a minimum of technical details. An open call to authors encouraged them to write "position papers" aimed at a wide audience.

Papers were solicited in an open call, and members of the Prolog Year Scientific Committee reviewed all the papers. The reviewers were: Veronica Dahl, Thomas Eiter, Gopal Gupta, Manuel Hermenegildo, Bob Kowalski, Francesca Rossi, Marie-Christine Rousset, and David S. Warren. This book contains the papers that were selected in this process.

The editors of the volume, a subset of the Scientific Committee, are: Veronica Dahl, Thomas Eiter, Manuel Hermenegildo, Bob Kowalski, Francesca Rossi, and David S. Warren.

The papers included here exhibit a wide variety of views on the role, meaning, goals, and impact of the Prolog language and its applications. One of Prolog's strengths is its great generality and its ability to be used and extended in a wide variety of ways. Because of the broad collection of different opinions included here, clearly not all the views are endorsed by all the editors. But a strong attempt has been made to ensure that everything included correctly represents considered and interesting views from the Prolog community.

The volume also includes papers from all of the five finalists for the 2022 Colmerauer Prize for applications of Prolog that describe their applications.

2 The Contents of This Book

The papers in this book are grouped by subject matter and organized as described in the following.

1. **Background**

   This paper introduces the Prolog programming language.

   (a) **Introduction to Prolog** by David S. Warren
   This paper provides a gentle introduction to the Prolog programming language through examples. It is intended to provide background that may be necessary to understand many of the other papers in this volume.

2. **About Prolog, Present and Future**

   These papers discuss general aspects or views of the Prolog language and its possible extensions for the future, and how it can generally be used to solve problems.

   (a) **Types, Modes and So Much More – The Prolog Way** by Manuel V. Hermenegildo, Jose F. Morales, Pedro Lopez-Garcia and Manuel Carro

The authors present in a tutorial way some ideas from Ciao Prolog that they believe could be useful for the future evolution of Prolog, including the use of assertions with types, modes, and other properties, and other extensions to the expressiveness and functionality of the language. They also argue that the unique characteristics of Prolog facilitated many advances in the area of combining static and dynamic language features.

(b) **Prolog as a Knowledge Representation Language the Nature and Importance of Prolog** by Michael Genesereth

In this paper Michael Genesereth takes the viewpoint that classifying Prolog primarily as a programming language is a disservice to it, and argues for its use as an excellent language for knowledge representation, which may be even one of its main assets. He compares it to First-Order Logic as another popular language for knowledge representation, and points out the versatility of Prolog for enabling a multiplicity of uses from a single representation.

(c) **Prolog: Past, Present, and Future** by Gopal Gupta, Elmer Salazar, Farhad Shakerin, Joaquín Arias, Sarat Chandra Varanasi, Kinjal Basu, Huaduo Wang, Fang Li, Serdar Erbatur, Parth Padalkar, Abhiramon Rajasekharan, Yankai Zeng, and Manuel Carro

This paper discusses a variety of additions and extensions to Prolog made over the years to extend its applicability. It describes a system, s(CASP), which combines many of these features, and then proposes how it can be used to attack the problem of general Artificial Intelligence.

(d) **Writing Correct Prolog Programs** by David S. Warren

Warren presents, by example, a methodology for writing Prolog programs that proposes the primary use of bottom-up thinking. He argues that this methodology will more likely result in correct programs due to the fact that most proofs of logical correctness involve bottom-up thinking.

(e) **Demonstrating Multiple Prolog Programming Techniques Through a Single Operation** by Nick Bassiliades, Ilias Sakellariou and Petros Kefalas

Bassiliades, Sakellariou and Kefalas illustrate the power of the full Prolog language, by showing alternative implementations of a single list operation, thus demonstrating a good number of Prolog programming aspects and techniques, and some related issues such as efficiency or readability of the code.

(f) **A Better Logical Semantics for Prolog** by David S. Warren and Marc Denecker

This paper proposes that positive Prolog programs can be productively understood as inductively defining predicates. It informally develops a compositional semantics that gives a precise meaning to components of full programs.

(g) **The Janus System: A Bridge to New Prolog Applications** by Carl Andersen and Theresa Swift

This paper presents the Janus system, an integration of Prolog and Python, with the goal of making Prolog more accessible to large-scale industrial applications. Janus makes the large number of libraries present in Python available within Prolog. The paper also discusses the use of the Janus system for several large, real-world applications.

3. Teaching Prolog

These papers explore various ideas and experiences of teaching Prolog programming.

(a) **Some Thoughts on How to Teach Prolog** by Manuel V. Hermenegildo, Jose F. Morales and Pedro Lopez-Garcia

The uniqueness of the programming paradigm represented by Prolog is a strong motivation for teaching the language, but also demands a specific approach for success. Hermenegildo, Morales, and Lopez-Garcia present a good number of ideas for teaching Prolog, from how to show the beauty and usefulness of the language to how to avoid some common pitfalls, misconceptions, and myths.

(b) **Simultaneously Teaching Mathematics and Prolog in School Curricula: A Mutual Benefit** by Laurent Cervoni, Julien Brasseur and Jean Rohmer

Thanks to its logical nature, the use of Prolog in mathematical fields that build on axiomatic systems and decomposition-based problem solving was explored early on. In this paper the authors argue that Prolog is a useful tool to aid high school students in developing skills for properly modeling mathematical problems. They report on case studies in geometry and algebra, and reflect on advantages and the potential of using Prolog for education in mathematics.

(c) **Logic Programming at Elementary School: Why, What and How Should We Teach Logic Programming to Children?** by Laura Andrea Cecchi, Jorge P. Rodríguez and Veronica Dahl

This paper explores the use of Logic Programming to teach computer science to elementary school children and help them develop computational thinking skills. A specific teaching method is described, supported by projects of different complexity to make this type of knowledge accessible to children in a collaborative learning environment. The paper also describes a pilot experience in elementary schools in Argentina.

(d) **Prolog Education in Selected High Schools in Bulgaria** by Veneta Tabakova-Komsalova, Stanimir Stoyanov, Asya Stoyanova-Doycheva and Lyubka Doukovska

In this paper the authors present their experience of teaching Prolog programming in secondary schools in the Plovdiv region of Bulgaria. They also introduce their new project, called "Digital Bulgaria in Prolog", which will use Prolog to model the cultural and historical heritage of Bulgaria in a national network of STEM centers.

(e) **Introducing Prolog in Language-Informed Ways** by Veronica Dahl and Laura Cecchi

This paper argues for leveraging children's language and grammar skills, and our knowledge of how children acquire language, to teach them Prolog while helping them develop their computational and logical-reasoning skills. The paper advances the concept of "doughnut computing" as a method to help children learn Prolog while understanding issues involved in remedying societal and ecological breakdown such as global warming.

4. **Tools for Teaching Prolog**

These two papers discuss technology that has been developed for help in teaching Prolog.

(a) **Teaching Prolog with Active Logic Documents** by José Morales, Salvador Abreu, Daniela Ferreiro and Manuel V. Hermenegildo

Morales, Abreu, Ferreiro and Hermenegildo present their Active Logic Documents approach and tools, for easily developing Prolog teaching materials with embedded runnable code and interactive components. In this approach, the materials are self-contained, can be developed with standard tools, and run locally on the student's browser, not relying on a server infrastructure or notebook facility. They argue that this offers advantages in scalability, ease of maintenance, security, etc.

(b) **Simply Logical—The First Three Decades** by Peter Flach, Kacper Sokol and Jan Wielemaker

This paper traces the evolution of the Prolog textbook "Simply Logical – Intelligent Reasoning by Example" from print (with a 3.5″ diskette containing runnable programs) published in 1994 to the fully interactive online edition based on SWI Prolog's SWISH interface available today. The authors describe the philosophy behind the original book, along with how contemporary web programming eventually enabled a versatile authoring toolkit that underlies the book's interactive edition.

5. Prolog-Based Languages and Systems

These papers describe new languages firmly based on Prolog which show future directions for logic programming.

(a) **Dynamic Logic Programming** by Michael Genesereth

Genesereth describes an elegant extension to a subset of Prolog aimed at supporting the representation of knowledge about dynamic worlds. The resulting language allows the definition of operators that update the state of the extensional database (by moving between worlds which are such extensional database states), as well as reasoning about the evolution of such worlds.

(b) **Combining Logic Programming and Imperative Programming in LPS** by Robert Kowalski, Fariba Sadri, Miguel Calejo and Jacinto Dávila Quintero

The language LPS (Logic Production Systems) combines the logic programming and imperative programming notions of computing, by using logic programs to represent an agent's beliefs, and using reactive rules and constraints to represent the agent's goals. An agent program in LPS computes by generating actions, to satisfy its goals in a model that is defined by its beliefs extended by its actions. The paper describes a Prolog implementation of LPS, which displays the model that is computed, either as a timeline or as an animation of the destructively changing state of computation.

(c) **Ergo: A Quest for Declarativity in Logic Programming** by Benjamin Grosof, Michael Kifer, Theresa Swift, Paul Fodor and Janine Bloomfield

This paper describes the Ergo system, a declarative, logic-based, object-oriented system based on the well-founded semantics that includes defeasible rules, fully logical updates, and explanations. Applications that represent tax laws and banking regulations are presented.

6. Prolog Applications: Finalists for the Colmerauer Prize

These next five papers describe the applications that were the finalists for the 2022 Colmerauer Prize. The first one, by Michael Leuschel on **ProB**, was the winner of the prize.

(a) **ProB: Harnessing the Power of Prolog to Bring Formal Models and Mathematics to Life** by Michael Leuschel

Leuschel presents the ProB system, an animator, model checker and constraint solver for high-level formal models, implemented in Prolog, making significant use of constraints. It has been developed for over 20 years and has been used extensively in both academic and industrial applications, e.g., by several companies (Siemens, Alstom, ClearSy, Thales) to validate train system configurations worldwide. ProB was the winner of the first edition of the Colmerauer Prize.

(b) **Pacioli: A PROLOG System for Financial Report Processing** by Miguel Calejo and Charles Hoffman

Pacioli is a logic and rules engine toolkit implemented in Prolog, which validates financial information reported by public companies to regulators worldwide using a standard, rich structured, data format, the "Extensible Business Reporting Language", or XBRL. At the time of writing, a dozen Pacioli instances, operated by different entities around the world, have validated thousands of financial reports in different jurisdictions. The authors argue that the wide range of capabilities needed for Pacioli would be hard to implement in a mainstream language such as Python or Javascript.

(c) **Logic Model Processing** by Pierre Dissaux

This paper describes the application of Prolog to Model Driven Engineering, that refers to the use of software models to standardize and ease industrial engineering processes. It includes the description of the methodology, the implementation, the tools, and the Prolog libraries that have been developed over many years and deployed worldwide for industrial usages, with examples of its practical use and its most recent developments.

(d) **Symbium: Using Logic Programming to Streamline Citizen-to-Government Interactions** by Tristan Krueger, Abhijeet Mohapatra and Michael Genesereth

This paper describes an interesting, useful real world application, offered by the US company Symbium, that helps homeowners, architects, and contractors comply with the regulatory aspects of residential construction. Logic Programming is used to facilitate and, in some cases, automate regulatory processes involving permits, inspections, and rebates. Interestingly, uses of this application in interaction with municipalities have uncovered contradictions and omissions in the law, suggesting that further applications in this regard might also bear good fruit.

(e) **PROLEG: Practical Legal Reasoning System** by Ken Satoh

The PROLEG system is possibly the largest legal rule base in the world, having been used since 2009 to build a rule base of approximately 2500 rules and exceptions consisting of civil code and supreme court case rules in Japan. In this paper, Ken Satoh presents the PROLEG system, which is based on Prolog, but which represents rules and exceptions without negation as failure. He argues that the PROLEG representation of rules and exceptions corresponds better than negation as failure to the way that lawyers reason with such concepts as "burden of proof".

7. **Contributed Prolog Applications**

These papers describe some additional, contributed applications developed using the Prolog language. They illustrate further the range of applications for which Prolog is well-suited.

(a) **Logical English for Law and Education** by Robert Kowalski, Jacinto Dávila Quintero, Galileo Sartor and Miguel Calejo

This paper convincingly argues, supported by a variety of tested applications, for the benefits of Logical English, an ambiguity-resilient, paraphrase-based variant of LP with interesting applications in, for example, law and education. It can also serve as interface to languages such as Prolog, Its expressions are closer to natural language than Prolog proper, and hence easier to understand, thus making Prolog—and logical reasoning in general—more accessible to younger students in particular.

(b) **Exploiting Logic Programming for Runtime Verification: Current and Future Perspectives** by Davide Ancona, Angelo Ferrando and Viviana Mascardi

This paper describes a Prolog application that performs runtime monitoring and verification. It uses Prolog to allow users to specify complex parameterized patterns that are matched against system runtime event sequences to flag erroneous or suspicious activity.

(c) **Prolog Meets Biology** by Alessandro Dal Palù, Agostino Dovier, Andrea Formisano and Enrico Pontelli

This paper describes the use of Prolog and its derivatives to support research and development in bioinformatics and computational biology. The declarative nature of Prolog and the combinatorial nature of several applications in computational biology have allowed significant applications. The paper also includes a description of potential directions that the Prolog community can continue to pursue in this domain.

(d) **Prolog in Automated Reasoning in Geometry** by Vesna Marinkovic

This paper briefly overviews various Prolog systems for solving problems in geometry. It then concentrates on one Prolog system that solves geometric construction problems, focussing on constructing triangles given various related points.

(e) **Logic-Based Explainable and Incremental Machine Learning** by Gopal Gupta, Huaduo Wang, Kinjal Basu, Farhad Shakerin, Elmer Salazar, Sarat Chandra Varanasi, Parth Padalkar, and Sopam Dasgupta

This paper presents several machine learning methods that exploit the knowledge representation advantages of default rules in logic programming. It shows that these can be competitive with mainstream machine learning methods in terms of accuracy and execution efficiency, while providing advantages of interpretability, explainability, incrementality, and data economy.

(f) **Reflections on Automation, Learnability and Expressiveness in Logic-Based Programming Languages** by Paul Tarau

This paper addresses the question of what features need to be improved or added in logic-based languages to compete with current languages that have adopted latest innovations in usability, robustness, and ease-of-use. The paper illustrates some of the language constructs it proposes via definite clause grammar-based prompt generators for today's generative AI systems.

(g) **Prolog for Scientific Explanation** by Jean-Christophe Rohner and Håkan Kjellerstrand

This paper describes how abduction in Prolog can be used to generate scientific explanations. It shows how abduction and constraints can be used effectively to produce explanations for scientific theories described by simple rules. Darwin's theory of natural selection is used to exemplify the approach.

(h) **Machines as Thought Partners: Reflections on 50 Years of Prolog** by Gregory Gelfond, Marcello Balduccini, David Ferrucci, Adi Kalyanpur and Adam Lally

This paper describes the introduction of Prolog as a revolution that enabled us to think previously impossible thoughts, by leveraging the paradigms of logic programming and declarative programming. It then shows examples of this revolution by discussing the important role of Prolog in the landmark IBM Watson AI system and its successors, and introducing the readers to a new member of the Prolog family of languages—the logic programming language Cogent.

Acknowlegdements. The Year of Prolog celebrations were initiated by the Prolog Heritage Association, under the leadership of Colette Colmerauer, Guy Alain Narboni, Jean Rohmer and Célestin Sedogbo, and the Association for Logic Programming, under the leadership of Thomas Eiter and Manuel Hermenegildo.

The scientific content of the Year, including the preparation of this volume, was overseen by a Scientific Committee, consisting of Veronica Dahl, Thomas Eiter, Gopal Gupta, Manuel Hermenegildo, Bob Kowalski, Francesca Rossi, Marie-Christine Rousset, and David S. Warren, and was initially chaired by Bob Kowalski, and later by David S. Warren.

The Scientific Committee was supported by an honorary membership consisting of Krzysztof Apt, Maurice Bruynooghe, Keith Clark, Jacques Cohen, Stefania Costantini, Mehmet Dincbas, Hervé Gallaire, Maria Garcia de la Banda, Michael Genesereth, Seif Haridi, Gerda Janssens, Evelina Lamma, Annie Liu, Paola Mello, Luis Moniz Pereira, Fernando Pereira, Enrico Pontelli, Philippe Roussel, Fariba Sadri, Taisuke Sato, Torsten Schaub, Peter Stuckey, Theresa Swift, Peter Szeredi, Paul Tarau, Francesca Toni, Mirek Truszczyński, Pascal Van Hentenryck, and Jan Wielemaker.

The Jury for the 2022 ALP Alain Colmerauer Prolog Heritage Prize, which selected the finalists and the winner, consisted of Gopal Gupta, Annie Liu, Manuel Hermenegildo, Francesca Rossi (chair), and Marie-Christine Rousset.

We are grateful to the Springer Computer Science team for their welcome encouragement and support to publish this book, and to Randy Goebel as responsible editor for shepherding the publication in Springer's LNAI series. We thank the providers of EasyChair for making the generation of the necessary files easy.

May 2023

David S. Warren
Veronica Dahl
Thomas Eiter
Manuel V. Hermenegildo
Robert Kowalski
Francesca Rossi

Contents

Contributed Prolog Applications

Background

Introduction to Prolog

David S. Warren[(✉)](iD)

Stony Brook University, Stony Brook, USA
`warren@cs.stonybrook.edu`

Abstract. This first chapter of the Prolog50 book is brief introduction to the Prolog programming language. It is intended to provide background knowledge that will help in the understanding of many of the papers here. It covers basic Prolog definitions, their procedural interpretation, the idea of predicate modes, bottom-up evaluation of definitions, negation including stratified and nonstratified definitions, tabled evaluation, Prolog's use of operators, program meta-interpretation, Definite Clause Grammars, and constraints. All topics are covered only briefly, and through the use of simple examples. For each topic there is much more to be said, some of which will be said in the papers in this volume.

1 What is Prolog?

Prolog is a logical language for making true statements about a world, whose statements can be interpreted as a program and thus evaluated to conclude an answer to a question. Functional programs are understood as defining functions whereas Prolog programs are generally understood as defining relations.

Various family relationships can easily be defined in Prolog. For example, a grandparent is the parent of a parent. We can define a `child_of` relation by providing a set of *facts* giving child-parent pairs, for example, some recent relationships of the House of Windsor, as follows:

```
childOf(charles,elizabeth).
childOf(william,charles).
childOf(harry,charles).
childOf(george,william).
childOf(charlotte,william).
childOf(louis,william).
childOf(archie,harry).
childOf(lilibet,harry).
```

And we can define the grandparent relation, containing person-grandparent pairs, using the `childOf` definition by the rule:

```
hasGrandparent(X,GPofX) :- childOf(X,ParX), childOf(ParX,GPofX).
```

This rule states that X has grandparent GPofX **if** X is a child of ParX **and** ParX is a child of GPofX. Prolog uses the token `:-` to mean *if*, and the comma to mean

D. S. Warren et al. (Eds.): Prolog: The Next 50 Years, LNAI 13900, pp. 3–19, 2023.
https://doi.org/10.1007/978-3-031-35254-6_1

and. Symbols starting with uppercase letters are variables, which can take on any value, and those starting with lowercase letters are constants. The atomic formula before the :- is known as the *head* of the rule; the sequence of formulas following that token form the *body* of the rule. For every assignment of values to the variables of a rule, if its body is true, then its head is true.

If we consistently substitute constants for variables into a rule, we obtain an *instance* of this rule. For example, substituting `harry` for `X`, `charles` for `ParX` and `elizabeth` for `GPofX`, we get the rule instance:

```
hasGrandparent(harry,elizabeth) :-
    childOf(harry,charles), childOf(charles,elizabeth).
```

Since our database of `childOf` facts includes the two facts in the body of the rule, then we (and Prolog) can conclude that `hasGrandparent(harry,elizabeth)` is true, i.e., that `harry` has a grandparent `elizabeth`. Similarly we can conclude that `archie` has grandparent `charles`, `george` has grandparent `charles`, and a number of other grandparent pairs.

Prolog accepts such rules and facts and then answers certain queries about them. For example, given the rules and facts above for `hasGrandparent`, we can ask Prolog who are the grandparents of Lilibet:

```
?- hasGrandparent(lilibet,GP).
GP = charles;
no
```

Here (after loading the `childOf` facts and the `hasGrandparent` rule to Prolog's memory) we have asked at Prolog's prompt "?-" for the variable `GP` to be given values that make the `hasGrandparent(lilibet,GP)` atomic formula true. Prolog responds that such a value is `charles`, to which we respond with a ";", requesting another answer. And Prolog responds with "no" meaning that it failed to find any (more) answers. If a query has no answers at all, its execution is said to `fail` and "no" printed. We could ask for all of Elizabeth's grandchildren with the query: `hasGrandparent(GC,elizabeth)`.

We can then use `hasGrandparrent` to define `hasGreatGrandparent` with the rule:

```
hasGreatGrandparent(X,GGPofX) :-
    hasGrandparent(X,GPofX), childOf(GPofX,GGPofX).
```

and then infer `hasGreatGrandparent(lilibet,elizabeth)`, among others. And now, with this rule added, we can ask queries involving `hasGreatGrandparent`.

We can also use recursive (a.k.a. inductive) rules. For example, we can define the relation `hasAncestor` as follows:

```
hasAncestor(X,AncX) :- childOf(X,AncX).
hasAncestor(X,AncX) :- childOf(X,ParX), hasAncestor(ParX,AncX).
```

This relation requires two rules for its definition. The first says X has ancestor AncX if X is a child of AncX. The second says X has ancestor AncX if X is a child of ParX and ParX has ancestor AncX. I.e., a parent is an ancestor, and an ancestor of a parent is an ancestor. With this definition, Prolog will infer many ancestors from our definition of childOf, including hasAncestor(charles,elizabeth) and hasAncestor(lilibet,elizabeth).

In addition to defining relations over constants, Prolog can define relations over complex data structures, for example lists. A list is a sequence of terms (constants or lists)[1], and is written within square brackets with its elements separated by commas. For example, [charles,harry,charlotte] is a list, and so is [], the empty list. The **head** of a (nonempty) list is the first element of the list; the **tail** of a (nonempty) list is the list that remains when the head is removed. We can write a pattern [H|T] to match a list, in which case H is matched to the head of the list and T is matched to the tail. So for example, matching [H|T] to the list [charles,harry,charlotte] results in variable H getting the value charles and T getting the value [harry,charlotte]. With this understanding, we can now write a relation of pairs of elements and lists for which the element appears in the list, which we call member:

```
member(E,[E|L]).
member(E,[X|L]) :- member(E,L).
```

The first clause says that a item E is a member of any list that has E as head. The second clause says that E is a member of a list, if it's a member of the tail of the list.

2 Procedural Interpretation

Now we turn to considering how Prolog actually carries out the necessary inferencing to be able to answer queries using a process formally called *resolution*.

Each clause in a Prolog program can be understood as defining a procedure: the head of a rule provides the name of the procedure and the body of the rule provides the procedures to call, in order, to carry out the execution of the head procedure. For example, the rule:

```
hasGrandparent(GC,GP) :- childOf{GC,P}, childOf(P,GP).
```

is understood to define a procedure named hasGrandparent. When hasGrandparent is called, it is evaluated by first calling childOf with the indicated arguments, and then calling it again with different arguments (noting the calls do share the variable P).

Variables in Prolog are assign-once variables, they either have a value or not, so once they get a value that value cannot change during procedure execution. When hasGrandparent is called, the variables GC and GP are bound to the arguments of the call. Let's assume GC has a value, say lilibet, and GP

---

[1] We will see later that there may also be record structures.

does not have a value. I.e., the call to `hasGrandparent` gives a person and asks for a grandparent of that person. Then `childOf` is called passing the indicated arguments. The variable `P` will not have a value when the first `childOf` is called, but will be assigned a value during the execution of the `childOf` procedure, say `harry`, so when `P` is passed to the second call to `childOf` as its first argument, it will have that value. This call to `childOf` will bind variable `GP`, say to `charles`, which will be returned as the value of the second parameter to the original `hasGrandparent` call. In this way every rule can be understood as defining a procedure whose execution will take some variables and further bind them (i.e., give them values) as it executes the procedures in the body of the rule in order. Facts, like those for `childOf` just bind variables in their call and directly return. Thus, if we assume only one rule per relation, we can think of a call to a relation definition as being carried out by a machine that carries out that sequence of procedure invocations and returns.

2.1   Prolog as Multiple Procedural Machines

However, Prolog is a relational, or nondeterministic, language, meaning that a procedure may return multiple different values. This happens when there are multiple clauses with the same predicate symbol in their heads, i.e., multiple ways to compute values are provided for the same procedure. For example, our `childOf` predicate symbol has multiple ways to compute it, and `member`, too. In this case, we can think of procedure evaluation as being done by multiple machines, one for each alternative deterministic evaluation. When a call is made to a procedure with multiple ways to compute it (a choice point), the executing machine duplicates itself as many times as there are alternative ways and for each way sends one machine instance off to compute it. So we envision a set of deterministic machines executing procedures, increasing in number whenever a choice point is encountered and decreasing in number when a particular machine encounters failure, i.e., attempts assignment of a different value to a variable that already has a value, which means the computation cannot be consistently continued and thus must fail. The machines that survive to return from the initial call simply stop executing and provide answers to that call. Every deterministic machine either fails or succeeds to return an answer to the initial call.

An example of a nondeterministic query is `hasGrandparent(CG,elizabeth)`. To evaluate this query at the point that the subquery `childOf(X,elizabeth)` is posed there is only one fact that matches (in this reduced Windsor family) (i.e., all but one of the forked machines fail immediately), but when the later subquery `childOf(GC,charles)`, is posed, there are two facts that match, so at this point there will two executing machines: one proceeding with `GC = william` and one with `GC = harry`. Both those machines will eventually return giving those two answers for the grandchildren of Elizabeth.

To execute Prolog programs in a single process, we must simulate this set of machines in some order. Prolog uses a stack to save and restart machines: When Prolog encounters a choice point, it pushes machines created to execute the various alternatives onto a stack (in reverse order so they will be popped in the order their clauses appear in the program) and then executes the top (first) one. When a machine fails, the machine on the top of the stack is removed and executed. In this way, Prolog uses a depth-first, backtracking (to restore the state to that of the top machine on the stack) strategy.

The metaphor of "deterministic machines" is used here for didactic purposes. In practice Prolog systems implement this strategy extremely efficiently, using techniques very similar to traditional procedural languages for forward machine execution, and essentially constant time backtracking techniques for restoring a previous state.

Alternative strategies are possible, but this depth-first strategy is generally the most efficient, and it is the one adopted, at least by default, by Prolog engines.

2.2   Recursive Programs

Notice that if we pose a query to our `hasAncestor` definition, the evaluation of its second rule will involve a recursive call to the procedure `hasAncestor`. And similarly, the query:

```
?- member(3,[1,2,3,4,5]).
yes
?-
```

causes the `member` procedure to be called recursively, searching down the list until the constant 3 is found, at which point Prolog can answer "yes", the query is true.

And consider the query:

```
?- member(X,[1,2,3]).
X = 1;
X = 2;
X = 3;
no
?-
```

which asks Prolog what values of X are in the list [1,2,3]. For this case three deterministic machines succeed, each returning one correct answer.

3   Modes

Procedures, as noted, can be called with some arguments having values and with other arguments being variables without values. Variables that have values are said to be *bound*[2], and variables that don't (yet) have values are said to be *unbound* or *free*. In our first example, evaluation for the `hasGrandparent` procedure we assumed the first argument to `hasGrandparent` was bound to

---

[2] Note this is a different meaning for a *bound* variable than in first-order logic.

lilibet and the second argument was free. This particular "value pattern" (or "instantiation pattern") is known as the *mode* (+,-). A mode is a sequence of the symbols such as: +, -, and ?, and indicates the binding pattern of a sequence of arguments, for example, + meaning bound, - meaning free, and ? meaning either (or other). In our first hasGrandparent example, finding the grandparents of Lilibet, the mode for hasGrandparent goal was (+,-), and the mode for (both calls to) childOf was also (+,-). The modes at success of all three of those calls was (+,+). In the example to find the grandchildren of Elizabeth, the corresponding modes were (-,+) for hasGrandparent, then (-,-) for the first childOf subquery, and (+,+) for the second.

Because variables get values by *unification*, a generalized matching operation, many procedures can be called in multiple different modes, as we see for hasGrandparent and childOf. Indeed the hasGrandparent procedure may also be called in (+,+) modes, in which case Prolog will check whether the names provided indeed stand in the grandparent relation. It may be called in (-,-) mode, in which case Prolog will generate *all* pairs of names in the grandparent relation. And as we saw before, member can be called in modes (+,+) to check membership and in mode (-,+) to generate all members.

It is useful to know the modes of calls (and returns) since many Prolog predicates can be called effectively only in certain modes. For example, in other modes the computation may loop infinitely or may generate infinitely many answers, as would member called in (+,-) mofe, and so calls in such modes to those procedures should generally be avoided.

Sometimes modes are combined with type information, so that, e.g., mode (-,+list) for member/2 means that it is called with the second argument bound to a list.

Modes are used in most Prolog systems as program documentation, and as an aid for discussing the uses of a predicate, as we do here. There are however some Prolog systems that can check the modes and other properties declared for a given predicate and detect if such modes and properties are violated. This can be done either at compile time (when loading the program) or at run time (when executing a query).[3]

4   Bottom-Up Evaluation

The procedural interpretation of Prolog programs presented before is known as top-down evaluation, since it starts at the top with a query (or goal) and computes down to the facts. Prolog programs may also be evaluated bottom up, starting with the facts and generating implied atoms.

For example, consider the hasGrandparent and childOf definitions above. We can start by seeing that we know that all the facts are true, so we can initialize our set of atoms we know to contain these facts:

---

[3] See Chapter "Types, modes and so much more – the Prolog way," in this volume.

```
childOf(charles,elizabeth).    childOf(william,charles).
childOf(harry,charles).        childOf(george,william).
childOf(charlotte,william).    childOf(louis,william).
childOf(archie,harry).         childOf(lilibet,harry).
```

Next we can look at each rule, here

`hasGrandparent(X,GPofX) :- childOf(X,ParX), childOf(ParX,GPofX)`

and see what instances of the body of the rule are already in our set of known atoms. And we add them to our set. So here, we see that since `childOf(william,charles)` and `childOf(charles,elizabeth)` are both in our known set, and these facts make up an instance of the body of our rule, then we can add `hasGrandparent(william,elizabeth)`, the rule's corresponding head instance, to our known set. And there are many more we can add, such as `hasGrandparent(archie,charles)` because we already have `childOf(archie,harry)` and `childOf(harry,charles)`, and `hasGrandparent(harry,elizabeth)` since we have `childOf(harry,charles)` and `childOf(charles,elizabeth)`, and so on. For this definition, we need only two steps to get all the known atoms: one for the known `childOf` facts, and then one more for all the known `hasGrandparent` facts. After two rounds, we will never get anything new, so we can stop. If we include our rule for `hasGreatGrandparent`, then we would have needed three rounds in our example. This is because the first two rounds would be identical to above, and then `hasGreatGrandparent` facts can be added only at the third round.

This bottom-up computation, starting with facts and then iteratively adding more facts by using the rule instances, is also known as forward reasoning. For some rule sets it may take many rounds to infer all facts that can be known; in fact, there may be infinitely many rounds, and so this computation may not terminate. Also note that bottom-up computation computes, for example, *all* `hasGrandparent` facts, not just those, say related to being grandparents of Lilibet, as top-down evaluation can. On the other hand, for rules that contain only constants (i.e., no lists), bottom up is guaranteed to terminate, whereas (simple) top-down is not. So, bottom-up evaluation is more used in database contexts, where rules contain only constants (and variables, of course.) Such Prolog programs, those with only constants, are called `Datalog` programs, and they are traditionally implemented using bottom-up methods. (But see the discussion of tabling below.)

We note that, in theory, top-down and bottom-up evaluation of a query produce the same results, when infinite loops in each are considered appropriately. In practical computations of a given query, however, they may encounter infinite loops in different ways. So while they are logically equivalent, they are not computationally equivalent.

5   Negation and Stratification

The example Prolog programs we have seen thus far have had atomic formulas, or subgoals, in their bodies, which are interpreted as procedure calls. But Prolog supports negative subgoals, as in:

```
bachelor(P) :- male(P), not married(P).
```

```
male(walter).        married(walter).
male(bill).          married(sarah).
```

The intuitive meaning of this is clear. We define bachelor as a person who is male and is not married. When the subgoal `not married(p)`, for some constant p, is encountered in procedural evaluation, the `married(p)` subgoal is called and if it succeeds, then the `not married(p)` subgoal fails, and if it fails the not subgoal succeeds. And we can see Prolog's evaluation:

```
?- bachelor(Person).
Person = bill;
no
```

which gives the expected answer that `bill` is a bachelor, but `walter`, who is married, is not.

It turns out that, for this treatment of negative subgoals, the mode of the subgoal is important; it must not have variables in it. In our example the first subgoal `male(P)` in the body of the bachelor definition will always bind P to a value, so `married(P)` will always be called in mode $(+)$. Notice that if the body literals in `bachelor` were reversed, then our query to `bachelor(Person)` would invoke the subgoal `married(Person)` (with `Person` still a variable), and this would succeed, since there are two married persons, so `not married(Person)` would fail, as would the original query; this is clearly is *wrong*. The moral is that the mode of a negative subgoal when called is critical for Prolog's procedural interpretation of `not` to be intuitively correct. If a negative subgoal is called with a variable, the computation is said to *flounder*.

5.1 A Subgoal Depending on Its Own Negation

Another interesting issue with negative subgoals in Prolog is shown in the following example of a barber in a (very) small town:

```
shaves(barber,X) :- person(X), not shaves(X,X).
shaves(butcher,butcher).
```

```
person(butcher). person(baker). person(barber).
```

In this tiny (male populated) town, the barber shaves any person who doesn't shave himself. So, he clearly shaves the baker, since the baker doesn't save himself, and clearly doesn't shave the butcher, since he does shave himself. So, who shaves the barber? We have the rule instance

```
shaves(barber,barber) :- not shaves(barber,barber).
```

Since normally for a single rule the ":-" is informally understood as "if and only if," this means `shaves(barber,barber)` is true if and only if
`not shaves(barber,barber)` is true. And this is a contradiction. We note that Russell's paradox is another example of this phenomenon.

5.2 Stratified Programs

This issue arises when a subgoal depends, in some way, on its own negation. For example, shaves(barber,barber) depends directly on
not shaves(barber,barber). There have been many suggested approaches for resolving this issue. We can simply avoid this possibility by allowing only programs that are "stratified." A program is *stratified* if we can assign each predicate to a stratum (a natural number) where for every rule, (1) each predicate of a positive body subgoal has stratum the same or lower than the stratum of the head predicate, and (2) each predicate of a negative body subgoal has a stratum that is strictly less than the stratum of the head predicate. This ensures that no subgoal can depend on its own negation. Stratified programs have their expected meanings.

5.3 Non-stratified Programs

But what about non-stratified programs? After much work and discussion, the Prolog community has (mostly) come to the conclusion that there are two distinct, and reasonable, ways to give meanings to non-stratified programs. They go by the names of the Well-Founded Semantics (WFS) and the Stable Model Semantics (SMS). We note that both semantics give the same meaning to stratified programs; they differ *only* in their treatment of non-stratified programs. We give only a cursory introduction, by example, to these two approaches.

Consider our shaves example above. The WFS uses a 3-valued logic with truth values of *true*, *false*, and *undefined*. It gives the value *true* to shaves(barber,baker), the value *false* to shaves(barber,butcher) and the value *undefined* to shaves(barber,barber). The WFS always associates a unique (3-vaued) model to a program. The SMS uses multiple 2-valued models to give meanings to (non-stratified) programs. The shaves program has *no* such stable model, so that program is said to be inconsistent in SMS.

Consider another unstratified program, describing how the "Programming Languages" course is taught in our department:

```
teach(david,progLang) :- not teach(annie,progLang).
teach(annie,progLang) :- not teach(david,progLang).
```

So, in our department, David teaches programming languages if Annie doesn't teach it; and Annie teaches it if David doesn't. This program is not stratified since teach(david,progLang) depends on teach(annie,progLang) which depends on not teach(david,progLang), so there is no stratification. For this program, the WFS assigns both teach subgoals the *undefined* truth value. On the other hand the SMS assigns two different models to this program: in one teach(david,progLang) is true and teach(annie,progLang) is false; in the other teach(david,progLang) is false and teach(annie,progLang) is true. I.e., there are two possible states of affairs, one with David teaching and one with Annie teaching.

The computational complexities of these two semantic approaches differ. For propositional programs (those without any variables or constants), finding the WFS is at worst quadratic in the size of the program, whereas finding the existence of a model in the SMS is NP hard, i.e., (most likely) exponential. We note that SMS has led to *Answer Set Programming* (ASP), a programming paradigm like that of constraint solvers and SAT solvers.[4]

6   Tabling

Tabling is an alternative evaluation strategy for Prolog, based on the idea of saving calls and results from procedure invocations in a table, and then using those results for future identical (or subsumed) calls. Implemented correctly, it is easy to see that with tabling Prolog programs that use only constants and variables (no lists or other data structures), the so-called Datalog programs, will always terminate. Such programs have finitely many possible calls and finitely many possible returns, so if none is done more than once, their processing must eventually terminate.

This has far-reaching consequences for Prolog programming. Consider for example, the rules that define transitive closure for an arbitrary directed graph, edge:

```
transclose(X,Y) :- edge(X,Y).
transclose(X,Y) :- transclose(X,Z), edge(Z,Y).
```

Given any definition of an edge predicate representing a directed graph, this defines its transitive closure, and every call to it will terminate under tabled evaluation. Notice Prolog will not terminate for any call, since the immediate call to transclose in the second rule will always lead to an infinite loop.

Notice that we could also write the second transclose rule as right recursive, with a call to edge first and then a call to transclose. In this case execution without tabling will terminate if the graph is acyclic, as seen in the earlier hasAncestor example, which is a special case of transitive closure, in which the edge relation is childOf, and it necessarily defines an acyclic graph.

To understand how tabling works, consider again the multiple machines view of procedural Prolog evaluation. For tabling, there is a global table of calls and results that is accessed by every executing machine. Before a subgoal is called, the table is consulted to see if it has been called before. If not, then the call is entered into the table, the machine suspends on the entry to wait for answers, and a new machine is created to actually call the procedure; each time a machine returns an answer to a call, that answer is added to the corresponding table entry (if it's not already there) and the machine fails. If an executing machine finds its call already in the table, then the machine forks a new machine to return each

---

[4] See chapter "Ergo: A Quest for Declarativity in Logic Programming" for more on unstratified programs, and chapter "Prolog: Past, Present, and Future" for more on ASP and SMS.

answer currently in the table and suspends on that table entry. Whenever a new answer shows up for an entry, the suspended machine forks off another machine to continue with that answer. The implementation is complicated by the fact that full asynchronicity of returning answers to suspended calls is indeed required because there may be two distinct calls with each one alternately producing a new answer for the other to consume.

Tabling does, of course, take time, to add entries to a table, and space, to store it. In many, but not all, cases that time and space is more than recovered by the savings from redundant computation that is avoided. For this reason, tabling is generally optional and can be turned on, or off, for any given predicate.

A number of Prolog systems now include the tabling options. Some of them use tabling to implement the WFS for non-stratified programs. They maintain information to distinguish between successful derivations that indicate true answers and those that indicate undefined answers.

7 Operators

Prolog has a flexible syntax. We've mentioned lists, but Prolog actually supports a more general structured data type, called the term. (A list is just a special kind of term.) A term is a labeled, ordered, tree. The fundamental type is the labeled record. A record is written as, e.g., `employee(david,2020,programmer)` which indicates a record with label `employee` and three fields, the first and last populated by string constants and the second by an integer constant. Records may be nested. For example, `cons(a,cons(b,cons(c,[])))` is a nested record structure, made up of binary `cons` records, and the constant symbol `[]`. Another example is `+(1,*(2,3))` where we have two binary records, one a +-record and one a *-record nested in the first. Such record structures are heavily used in Prolog programming.

This last record structure can also be seen as representing an arithmetic expression. In fact, it is used in Prolog (in some contexts) for precisely this. But this record notation for expressions is not what is normally used in mathematics. One would rather represent it as 1 + 2 * 3, in what is known as *infix* notation. Here the record symbols + and * are *infix operator symbols* and thus are placed between their operands. Prolog supports such infix operators for binary record symbols, as well as prefix and postfix operators for unary record symbols. For example, - is both an infix operator (normally interpreted as subtraction) and a prefix operator (normally interpreted as the additive inverse). While the basic nested record notation, known as canonical form, is unambiguous, infix notation can be ambiguous. E.g., does `1+2*3` mean `+(1,*(2,3))` or `*(+(1,2),3)`? The convention we learn early on is that it means the first, but the Prolog parser must be told that. This is determined by the relative *precedence* of the operators.

In fact, a Prolog rule itself is actually a record structure. It is clear that subgoals can be directly seen as record structures. And the conditional symbol ":-" and the conjunction symbol "," of Prolog rules are infix operators (with appropriate precedences) so that a rule is read as a set of nested records. For example, the rule `p :- q,r.` is in fact a record structure of the form `:-(p,','(q,e))`.

Prolog supports user-defined operators, prefix, infix, and postfix, allowing the programmer to declare them and their precedences. This means that with proper operator declarations, Prolog syntax can be very flexible. With simple operator declarations Prolog can be made to process programs that look like natural language expressions.

For example, with appropriate declarations of `like` and `and` as infix operators, and of `a` as a prefix operator, all with proper precedences, "`john and mary like bill and a woman`" will be read as the record structure:
`like(and(john,mary),and(bill,a(woman)))`.

8   Meta-interpretation

One strength of Prolog is that, as we saw, its programs are expressible as simple data structures in the language. This allows Prolog to easily manipulate its own programs.

A subgoal looks exactly the same as a record structure. Prolog has a builtin predicate, named `call`, that allows a program to treat a record structure as a subgoal. Consider the situation in which the Prolog programmer wishes to make it easier for non-experts to invoke specific complex Prolog queries by simply entering the query name. The programmer creates a relation that associates a name with a query. E.g.:

```
queryName(allGrandparents, hasGrandparent(X,Y)).
queryName(memberTest, member(X,[1,2,3,4])).
```

Then the programmer can define a relation: `query` as follows:

```
query(Name,Res) :- queryName(Name,Res),call(Res).
```

Then the non-expert can find all grandparents by simply invoking:

```
?- query(allGrandparents,Res).
Res = hasGrandparent(william,elizabeth);
Res = hasGrandparent(harry,elizabeth);
Res = hasGrandparent(george,charles);
Res = hasGrandparent(charlotte,charles)
yes
```

Prolog prints out the query with the variables instantiated to child-grandparent pairs. Since ";" was not entered after the fourth answer, Prolog stops generating answers (and just prints "yes").

This simple example shows how Prolog can build a goal as a record structure during execution and then invoke it. This `call` facility supports higher-order programming in Prolog.

Another implication of the easy reflection of Prolog programs as data structures is that one can write a "meta-interpreter" in Prolog. A meta-interpreter is a program that takes another program and goal as input and evaluates that query with respect to the program. For example, we could store the clauses of a program as facts of a binary predicate we call `rule`, with the head as the first argument and the body as the second. For example,

```
rule(member(X,[X|L]),true).
rule(member(X,[Y|L]),member(X,L)).
```

is our `member` program from back in the first section. Now we can define a predicate, say, `interp` that takes any subgoal and determine its instances that follow from the rules defined in `rule`:

```
interp(true).
interp((X,Y)) :- interp(X), interp(Y).
interp(X) :- rule(X,B), interp(B).
```

The first rule (a fact) says that if the query is `true` we should just succeed. The second rule says that if we have a query that is a conjunction, we just need to interpret each conjunct in turn. The unusual double parentheses in the head of that rule are to indicate that `interp` takes a single argument, and that argument is a record structure with two subfields that has the record name of "," (comma) and is represented in infix notation (with the comma between the two operands). The final rule says what to do if the query is a subgoal: see if there is a rule with the query as its head, and if so, interpret the body of that rule. (Actually, do this, nondeterministically, for every rule that has a matching head.)

And evaluating `interp` goals, we see:

```
?- interp(member(0,[3,2,1])).
no
?- interp(member(X,[3,2,1])).
X = 3;
X = 2;
X = 1;
no
```

These three clauses are all that are needed to execute many Prolog programs, e.g., almost all we have seen so far. (What rule should be added to handle negative subgoals?) This simplicity never ceases to amaze. Compare this with the complexity of a metainterpreter for Java written in Java, for example.

The importance of this simple metainterpreter is not that it can execute Prolog programs; we have the Prolog engine itself to do that. The importance is that we can add arguments to this metainterpreter to carry along debugging or other analysis information; we can add logging subgoals (built-ins of Prolog) to provide a trace; we can modify it to perform different kinds of evaluation.

For example, we can write a Prolog meta-interpreter that will only invoke procedures up to some fixed depth, and thus will always terminate, albeit sometimes incorrectly:

```
interp(true,Depth,Max).
interp((X,Y),Depth,Max) :-
    interp(X,Depth,Max), interp(Y,Depth,Max).
interp(X,Depth,Max) :-
    Depth < Max,
    NewDepth is Depth + 1,
    rule(X,B),
    interp(B,NewDepth,Max).
```

Here Max is the maximum predicate nesting depth to be searched; Depth is the current nesting depth. The first subgoal of the final rule is a Prolog builtin, the infix operator "<", that compares the two integers, and so only succeeds if the limit is not reached. The second subgoal, using builtin infix operator "is", computes the new depth when a rule is used. So, for example, a query of interp(member(5,[1,2,3,4,5]),0,3) will fail since finding 5 in the list requires making more than 4 nested subgoal invocations.

Of course we can extend this interpreter to indicate "depth limit exceeded" instead of simply failing. Similar techniques can be used to implement other forms of search through the tree of executing virtual deterministic machines. For example, breadth-first search, or iterative deepening strategies can be implemented when useful in educational and other contexts.

9   Definite Clause Grammars

The original motivation for creating Prolog was to process natural language. Thus, Prolog is ideal for representing grammars and processing sequences of tokens. Prolog even has a special notation for representing grammars, known as Definite Clause Grammars (DCGs).

Let's first consider how we might represent a context-free grammar in Prolog. Consider the example context-free grammar in a BNF-like notation:

```
sentence --> subject, verb_phrase.
subject --> noun_phrase.
noun_phrase -->  det noun ; [john] ; [sarah].
det --> [a] ; [the].
noun --> [woman] ; [man].
verb_phrase --> transitive_verb, noun_phrase ; intransitive_verb.
transitive_verb --> [loves].
intransitive_verb --> [walks].
```

This is a grammar that represents a small fragment of English. The syntax we've used is similar to BNF, with nonterminals represented by constant symbols, and terminals represented by the symbol surrounded by square brackets. We've separated symbols in the right-hand-sides of rules by commas, and alternate right-hand-sides by semicolons. The language of this grammar includes such sentences as "sarah walks" and "the man loves a woman."

We can represent this grammar in Prolog by introducing for each non-terminal a Prolog predicate with two arguments; the first argument is a list of tokens and the second a tail of the first list that remains after removing a sequence of tokens generated by the non-terminal. So, for example, the predicate noun_phrase should take the list ['a', 'man', 'walks'] and, removing the noun phrase, "a man", return the list ['walks']. The following Prolog program represents this grammar:

```
sentence(S0,S) :- subject(S0,S1), verb_phrase(S1,S).
subject(S0,S) :- noun_phrase(S0,S).
noun_phrase(S0,S) :-  det(S0,S1), noun(S1,S) ;
                      S0 = [john|S] ; S0 = [sarah|S].
det(S0,S) :- S0 = [ a |S] ; S0 = [the|S].
noun(S0,S) :- S0 = [woman|S] ; S0 = [man|S].
verb_phrase(S0,S) :- transitive_verb(S0,S1), noun_phrase(S1,S) ;
                     intransitive_verb(S0,S).
transitive_verb(S0,S) :- S0 = [ loves |S].
intransitive_verb(S0,S) :- S0 = [ walks |S].
```

Here we have used the Prolog "or" operator, represented by the semi-colon (;), which we haven't seen before. The translation of the context-free grammar to a Prolog program is clear. Each rule has a clear meaning: if the right-hand-side non-terminals (and terminals) of a grammar rule generate a sequence of strings, then their concatenation is a string generated by the left-hand side of the rule. We can query these predicates to recognize sentences in the grammar.

```
?- sentence([the,man,loves,sarah],[]).
yes
?- sentence([the,man,loves,walks],[]).
no
```

as expected. Looking at the execution of this program, we see that Prolog is carrying out a recursive descent recognition algorithm. We note that if all the predicates are tabled, then Prolog would carry out a variation of the efficient Earley recognition algorithm.

We now point out that the syntax for the context-free grammar we used to introduce it above is actually accepted by Prolog and converted into the Prolog program we just presented. This is done automatically by the Prolog reader using a built-in Prolog facility called *term expansion* which supports very powerful macro capabilities[5]. Grammars in this syntax are called Definite Clause Grammars or DCGs. So, DCG syntax uses the "-->" symbol instead of the ":-" symbol to separate head and body of rules. It requires terminal symbols of the grammar to be placed in lists. Then the DCG processing of Prolog translates such rules to predicate definitions by adding two extra arguments to each nonterminal symbol, and threading the variables through the body subgoals, including the terminal lists, as illustrated above.

---

[5] Term expansion and other related facilities such as "attributed variables" have been used to add many other syntactic and semantic extensions to Prolog, such as functional programming and constraints. We discuss the latter in the following section.

The Prolog program of this example is a recognizer. We could easily write a parser by adding an argument to the nonterminal predicate symbols to construct the parse tree (as a tree of records). The DCG notation includes this by allowing the nonterminal symbols to have arguments: in which case the string variables are added to those arguments, at the end. Thus, a nonterminal symbol with n arguments will translate to a Prolog predicate with $n + 2$ arguments.

In fact, this same DCG can be used to generate sentences of the language simply by providing a variable in the query in place of the first list.

This DCG notation makes it extremely easy to write string processing predicates.[6]

10   Constraints

As we have seen, Prolog has basic arithmetic builtin predicates, such as `is` for evaluating expressions, e.g., `X is Y + 1`. This builtin requires that the expression has no variables, i.e., in this case that `Y` must have a value. But it may be the case that `Y` doesn't have a value at the point of evaluation, but will be given a value by the evaluation of a later subgoal. So, waiting until `Y` has its value would allow the builtin `is` to correctly evaluate to give `X` a value. For this situation, many Prologs have a `wait` operation, which allows the programmer to specify that a particular subgoal, say `X is Y + 1`, should be delayed until certain variables, say `Y`, are given values, at which point it will be evaluated. The `wait` facility allows more flexible evaluation strategies, or what gets done when, driven by various modes.

But there are cases for which waiting for variables to get values may still not allow some seemingly reasonable programs to be evaluated. Consider a simple example of a compound goal: `X is Y + 2`, `Y is X * 3`, where neither X nor Y have values. But we can solve these two simple equations in two unknowns and determine that `X` must be -1 and `Y` must be -3. Many Prolog systems support such constraint solving.

The general idea is for the Prolog system to accumulate the set of constraints imposed by evaluated constraint subgoals, and then to solve those constraints, using some solver methodology, to bind variables to values that satisfy the constraints. In many Prolog implementations the constraints are stored in the attributes of *attributed variables* and incrementally solved as soon as enough of the variables involved are known. This improves efficiency by both detecting inconsistent constraints early and binding variables to constants as soon as possible, thus avoiding unnecessary search. For example, if the constraints are linear constraints over the real numbers, one could use an incremental version of the method of Gaussian elimination to solve them.

This constraint framework is known as Constraint Logic Programming (CLP). CLP systems may support constraints over a variety of domains, such as real numbers (as we've seen here), rational numbers, booleans, or finite domains.

---

[6] See chapter "Introducing Prolog in Language-Informed Ways" for more uses of DCG's.

Each domain will have a specific solver that solves sets of constraints of some specified forms. And there may be multiple solvers for some specific domains, depending on the form of the constraints. There has been significant research into CLP, and many powerful constraint systems have been developed. For example, see the chapter "ProB: Harnessing the Power of Prolog to Bring Formal Models and Mathematics to Life."

11   Conclusion

We hope that this brief introduction to Prolog has provided some insight into Prolog's capabilities. But we have only scratched the surface of what Prolog can do. Fifty years of research and language extensions have created extremely powerful systems.[7] Perhaps now you can begin to see that Prolog is a logic language, and how Prolog can be understood as a "declarative language" in which programmers describe *what* they want, and not so much *how* to compute it; yet also write very efficient recursive algorithms if desired. The rest of this book will further explore what has been done, and what can be done, with Prolog programs.

---

[7] See *Fifty Years of Prolog and Beyond* by Korner, Leuschel, Barbosa, Santos Costa, Dahl, Hermenegildo, Morales, Wielemaker, Diaz, and Abreu in TPLP 22(6).

About Prolog, Present and Future

Types, Modes and so Much More – The Prolog Way

Manuel V. Hermenegildo[1,2(✉)], Jose F. Morales[1,2], Pedro Lopez-Garcia[2,3],
and Manuel Carro[1,2]

[1] Universidad Politécnica de Madrid (UPM), Madrid, Spain
[2] IMDEA Software Institute, Madrid, Spain
{manuel.hermenegildo,josef.morales,pedro.lopez}@imdea.org
[3] Spanish Council for Scientific Research (CSIC), Madrid, Spain

Abstract. We present in a tutorial way some ideas developed in the context of the Ciao Prolog system that we believe could be useful for the future evolution of Prolog. We concentrate primarily on one area: the use of assertions with types, modes, and other properties, and how the unique characteristics of Prolog have made early advances possible in the area of combining static and dynamic language features. However, we also address briefly some other issues related to extending the expressiveness and functionality of the language.

Keywords: Prolog, Static Languages · Dynamic Languages · Types, Modes · Assertions · Verification, Testing · Test Generation · Language Extensions

1 Combining in Prolog the Best of the Dynamic and Static Language Approaches

Prolog is a dynamically-typed language and this aspect, combined with the intrinsic power of the language, has arguably contributed to its continued relevance and use in many applications. In fact, the environment in which much software is developed nowadays, aligns well with the classical arguments for dynamic languages, and many of the currently most popular languages, such as Python, JavaScript, Ruby, etc. (with Scheme and Prolog also in this class) are dynamic.

At the same time, detecting errors as early as possible at compile time, and inferring properties required to optimize and parallelize programs are clearly important issues in real-world applications, and thus, strong arguments can also be made for static languages. For example, statically-typed logic and functional languages (such as, e.g., Mercury [37] or Haskell [17]) impose strong type-related

Partially funded by MICINN projects PID2019-108528RB-C21 *ProCode*, TED2021-132464B-I00 *PRODIGY*, and FJC2021-047102-I, by the Comunidad de Madrid program P2018/TCS-4339 *BLOQUES-CM*, and by the Tezos foundation. The authors would also like to thank the anonymous reviewers for very useful feedback.

D. S. Warren et al. (Eds.): Prolog: The Next 50 Years, LNAI 13900, pp. 23–37, 2023.
https://doi.org/10.1007/978-3-031-35254-6_2

```
:- module(_,[qsort/2],[assertions,nativeprops,modes]).

qsort([], []).
qsort([First|Rest],Result) :-
    partition(Rest,First,Sm,Lg),
    qsort(Sm,SmS),
    qsort(Lg,LgS),
    append(SmS,[First|LgS],Result).

partition([],_,[],[]).
partition([X|Y],F,[X|Y1],Y2) :-
    X =< F,
    partition(Y,F,Y1,Y2).
partition([X|Y],F,Y1,[X|Y2]) :-
    X > F,
    partition(Y,F,Y1,Y2).
```

Fig. 1. With no entry information, the system warns that it cannot verify that the call to =</2 will not generate a run-time error.

requirements such as that all types (and, when relevant, modes) have to be defined explicitly or that all procedures have to be well-typed and well-moded. An important argument supporting this approach is that types clarify interfaces and meanings and facilitate programming in the large by making large programs more maintainable and better documented. Also, the compiler can use the static information to generate more specialized code, which can be better in several ways (e.g., performance-wise).

In the design of Ciao Prolog we certainly had the latter arguments in mind, but we also wanted to retain the usefulness of standard Prolog for highly dynamic scenarios, programming in the small, prototyping, developing simple scripts, or simply for experimenting with the solution to a problem. We felt that strong typing and other related restrictions of statically-typed logic languages can sometimes get in the way in these contexts.

The solution we came up with –the *Ciao assertions model*– involves the combination of a rich assertion language, allowing a very general class of (possibly undecidable) properties, and a novel methodology for dealing with such assertions [3,13,14,29,30], based on making a best effort to infer and check assertions statically, using rigorous static analysis tools based on *safe approximations*, in particular via abstract interpretation [7]. This implies accepting that complete verification or error detection may not always be possible and run-time checks may be needed. This approach allows dealing in a uniform way with a wide variety of properties which includes types [33,41], but also, e.g., rich modes [24,25], determinacy [19], non-failure [4,9], sharing/aliasing, term linearity, cost [20,26,35], etc., while at the same time allowing assertions to be *optional*. The Ciao model and language design also allows for a smooth integration with testing [21]. Moreover, as (parts of) tests that can be verified at compile time are eliminated, some tests can be passed without ever running them. Finally, the model supports naturally assertion-based test case generation. In the following we illustrate these aspects of the model through examples run on the system.[1]

---

[1] The examples are runnable in the Ciao playground ▶; they have been developed with version 1.22 of the system. Screenshots are from the Ciao Prolog Emacs interface.

```
partition([],_,[],[]).
partition([X|Y],F,[X|Y1],Y2) :-
 ► At literal 1 could not verify assertion:
      partition(Y,F,Y1,Y2).
partition([X|Y],F,Y1,[X|Y2]) :-
```

Fig. 2. Hovering over the clause the system shows a popup saying that it cannot verify the assertions for =</2 (present in the library!).

```
:- module(_,[qsort/2],[assertions,nativeprops,modes]).      ►

:- pred qsort(+list(num),_).

qsort([], []).
qsort([First|Rest],Result) :-
    partition(Rest,First,Sm,Lg),
    qsort(Sm,SmS),
    qsort(Lg,LgS),
    append(SmS,[First|LgS],Result).

partition([],_,[],[]).
partition([X|Y],F,[X|Y1],Y2) :-
    X =< F,
    partition(Y,F,Y1,Y2).
partition([X|Y],F,Y1,[X|Y2]) :-
    X > F,
    partition(Y,F,Y1,Y2).
```

Fig. 3. Adding information on how the exported predicate should be called the system can infer that =</2 will be called correctly, and no warnings are flagged.

1.1   The Assertions Model in Action

While there are several ways to use the system, we will show screenshots of one of the most convenient, which is to have the system running in the background giving instant feedback as a program is opened or edited –we refer to this as the "verifly" ("verification on the fly") mode (see [34] for more details).

A First Example. Consider the classic implementation of quick-sort in Fig. 1. If no other information is provided, the exported predicate qsort/2 can be called with arbitrarily instantiated terms as arguments (e.g., with a list of variables). This implies that the library predicates =</2 and >/2 in **partition/4** can

```
:- pred qsort(+list(num),-list(num)) + semidet.      ►

qsort([], []).
qsort([First|Rest],Result) :-
    partition(Rest,First,Sm,Lg),
    qsort(Sm,SmS),
    qsort(Lg,LgS),
    append(SmS,[First|LgS],Result).

:- pred partition(+list(num),+num,-list(num),-list(num)) + det.

partition([],_,[],[]).
partition([X|Y],F,[X|Y1],Y2) :-
    X =< F,
    partition(Y,F,Y1,Y2).
partition([X|Y],F,Y1,[X|Y2]) :-
    X > F,
    partition(Y,F,Y1,Y2).
```

Fig. 4. We add more assertions expressing various properties.

also be called with arbitrary terms and thus run-time errors are possible, since =</2 and >/2 require their arguments to be bound to arithmetic expressions when called. Even though there are no assertions in the program itself, the system is able to warn that it cannot verify that the calls to =</2 and >/2 will not generate a run-time error (note >> symbol and code underlining in orange). This is the result of a modular global analysis and a comparison of the information inferred for the program points before the calls to =</2 and >/2 with the assertions that express the calling restrictions for =</2 and >/2. Such assertions live in the libraries that provide these standard predicates. Further details can be obtained by hovering over the literal (Fig. 2).

In Fig. 3 we have added an assertion for the exported predicate qsort/2 expressing that it should be called with its first argument bound to a list of numbers.[2] Assuming this "entry" information, the system can verify that all the calls to =</2 and >/2 are now correct (with their arguments bound to numbers in this case), and thus no warnings are flagged. Note that in practice this assertion may not be necessary since this information could be obtained from the analysis of the caller(s) to this module.

Let us now add more assertions to the program, stating properties that we want checked, as shown in Fig. 4. The assertion for predicate partition/4 (eighth line of Fig. 4) expresses, using modes,[3] that the first argument should be bound to a list of numbers, and the second to a number, and that, for any terminating call meeting this call pattern: a) if the call succeeds, then the third and fourth arguments will be bound to lists of numbers; and b) the call is deterministic, i.e., it will produce one solution exactly, property det in the + field (as in Mercury [37]), which is inferred in CiaoPP as the conjunction of two properties: 1) the call does not (finitely) fail (property not_fails as in [4,9]) and 2) the

```
:- pred qsort(+list(num),-list(num)) + semidet.

qsort([], []).
qsort([First|Rest],Result) :-
    partition(Rest,First,Sm,Lg),
    qsort(Sm,SmS),
    qsort(Lg,LgS),
    append(SmS,[First|LgS],Result).

:- pred partition(+list(num),+num,-list(num),-list(num)) + det.

partition([],_,[],[]).
partition([X|Y],F,[X|Y1],Y2) :-
    X =< F,
    partition(Y,F,Y1,Y2).
partition([X|Y],F,Y1,[X|Y2]) :-
    X > F,
    partition(Y,F,Y1,Y2).
```

Fig. 5. All the added assertions get verified by the system.

---

[2] Due to space limitations we present the assertion language through –hopefully intuitive– examples. More complete descriptions of the assertion language can be found in [2,12,29].

[3] See, e.g., [43] in this same volume for an introduction to modes.

call will produce one solution at most (property `is_det` as in [19]). Similarly, the assertion for `qsort/2` expresses the expected calling pattern, and that the call can have at most one answer, property `semidet`.

In the assertion model, modes are *macros* that serve as a shorthand for assertions, in particular *predicate-level assertions*. These are in general of the form:

:- [*Status*] pred *Head* [: *Pre*] [=> *Post*] [+ *Comp*].

where *Head* denotes the predicate that the assertion applies to, and *Pre* and *Post* are conjunctions of *state property* literals. *Pre* expresses properties that hold when *Head* is called. *Post* states properties that hold if *Head* is called in a state compatible with *Pre* and the call succeeds. *Comp* describes properties of the whole computation such as determinism, non-failure, resource usage, termination, etc., aso for calls that meet *Pre*. In particular, the modes for `qsort/2` in Fig. 4 are expanded by the `modes` package (see module declaration in Fig. 3) to:

:- pred qsort(X,Y) : list(num,X) => list(num,Y) + semidet.

All the assertions in Fig. 4 indeed get verified by the system, which is shown by underlying the assertions in green (Fig. 5), and again further information can be obtained in a popup (Fig. 6).[4] Figure 7, shows again `qsort/2` but now the assertions are written as machine readable comments enabled by the `doccomments` package. Such comments can contain embedded assertions, which are also verified. Here we use again modes and determinacy. This format is familiar to Prolog programmers and compatible with any Prolog system without having to define any operators for the assertion syntax.

In Fig. 8, we have replaced `=</2` with `</2` in the second clause of `partition/4`, and the system warns that this predicate may fail. This is because the case where `X=F` is not "covered" by the "tests" of `partition/4` [4,9]. Conversely, if we replace `>/2` with `>=/2` in the second clause of the original def-

```
:- pred partition(+list(num),+num,-list(num),-list(num)) + det.
 ► Verified assertion:
:- check calls partition(A,B,_,_)
   : ( list(num,A), num(B) ).
 ► Verified assertion:
:- check comp partition(A,B,C,D)
   : ( list(num,A), num(B) )
   + det.
 ► Verified assertion:
:- check success partition(A,B,C,D)
   : ( list(num,A), num(B) )     ),-list(num)) + semidet.
   => ( list(num,C), list(num,D) ).
```

Fig. 6. The popup shows that calls, computational/global properties, and success pattern for `partition/` are verified.

---

[4] Note that while, as mentioned before, the assertions in Fig. 4 use *modes* they are represented internally in normal form and the popup message uses syntax close to this form, where the computational properties and the state properties that must hold upon success are split into separate (`comp` and `success` assertions respectively).

```
%! qsort(+list(num),-list(num)) + semidet:
%  Y is X sorted.
qsort([], []).
qsort([First|Rest],Result) :-
    partition(Rest,First,Sm,Lg),
    qsort(Sm,SmS),
    qsort(Lg,LgS),
    append(SmS,[First|LgS],Result).

%! partition(+list(num),+num,-list(num),-list(num)) + det:
%  Partitions a list into two lists, greater and
%  smaller than the pivot (second argument).
partition([],_,[],[]).
 ► Verified assertion:
:- check calls partition(A,B,_,_)
   : ( list(num,A), num(B) ).
 ► Verified assertion:
:- check comp partition(A,B,C,D)
   : ( list(num,A), num(B) )
   + det.
```

Fig. 7. Using modes/assertions in *doccomments* syntax (which are also verified).

```
:- pred qsort(+list(num),-list(num)) + semidet.

qsort([], []).
qsort([First|Rest],Result) :-
    partition(Rest,First,Sm,Lg),
    qsort(Sm,SmS),
    qsort(Lg,LgS),
    append(SmS,[First|LgS],Result).

:- pred partition(+list(num),+num,-list(num),-list(num)) + det.

partition([],_,[],[]).
partition([X|Y],F,[X|Y1],Y2) :-
    X < F,
    partition(Y,F,Y1,Y2).
partition([X|Y],F,Y1,[X|Y2]) :-
    X > F,
    partition(Y,F,Y1,Y2).
```

Fig. 8. If we replace =</2 with </2 the system warns that partition/4 may fail.

inition of **partition/4**, Fig. 9, the system warns that the predicate may not be deterministic. This is because the analyzer infers that not all the clauses of **partition/4** are pairwise mutually exclusive (in particular the second and third clauses are not), and thus, multiple solutions may be obtained [19].

Defining Properties. The reader may be wondering at this point where the properties that are used in assertions (such as **list(num)**) come from. As mentioned before, such properties are typically written in Prolog and its extensions; and they can also be built-in and/or defined and imported from system libraries or in user code. Visibility is controlled by the module system as for any other predicate. Figure 10 shows some examples of definitions of properties. Two of them are marked as *regular types* (**regtype** directive): **color/1**, defined as the set of values {red, green, blue}, and **colorlist/1**, representing the infinite set of lists whose elements are of **color** type. The third property is not a regular type, but an arbitrary property (**prop** directive), representing the infinite set of lists of numeric elements in descending order. Marking predicates as properties allows them to be used in assertions, but they remain regular predicates, and can be called as any other, and also used as run-time tests, to generate examples (test cases), etc. For example:

```
:- pred qsort(+list(num),-list(num)) + semidet.                    ▶

qsort([], []).
qsort([First|Rest],Result) :-
    partition(Rest,First,Sm,Lg),
    qsort(Sm,SmS),
    qsort(Lg,LgS),
    append(SmS,[First|LgS],Result).

:- pred partition(+list(num),+num,-list(num),-list(num)) + det.

partition([],_,[],[]).
partition([X|Y],F,[X|Y1],Y2) :-
    X =< F,
    partition(Y,F,Y1,Y2).
partition([X|Y],F,Y1,[X|Y2]) :-
    X >= F,
    partition(Y,F,Y1,Y2).
```

Fig. 9. If we replace >/2 with >=/2 the system warns that both `partition/4` and `qsosrt/2` may not be deterministic.

```
:- regtype color/1.                                                ▶
color(red).
color(green).
color(blue).

:- regtype colorlist/1.
colorlist([]).
colorlist([H|T]) :- color(H), colorlist(T).

:- prop sorted/1.
sorted([]).
sorted([_]).
sorted([X,Y|T]) :- X .>. Y, sorted([Y|T]).
```

Fig. 10. Defining some properties which can then be used in assertions.

```
?- colorlist(X).
X = [] ? ;
X = [red] ? ;
X = [red,red] ? ...
```

or, if we select breadth-first execution (useful here for fair generation):

```
?- colorlist(X).
X = [] ? ;
X = [red] ? ;
X = [green] ? ;
X = [blue] ? ;
X = [red,red] ? ...
```

Figure 11 shows the same properties of Fig. 10 but written using functional notation. The definitions are equivalent, functional syntax being just syntactic sugar.

```
:- regtype color/1.                                                ▶
color := red | green | blue.

:- regtype colorlist/1.
colorlist := [] | [~color|~colorlist].

:- prop sorted/1.
sorted := [] | [_].
sorted([X,Y|T]) :- X .>. Y, sorted([Y|T]).
```

Fig. 11. The properties of Fig. 10 written in functional notation.

```
:- module(_,[p/1,colorlist/1,sorted/1,color/1],[assertions,regtypes,fsyntax]).  ▶

:- pred p(X) => sorted(X).
p(X) :- q(X).

:- pred q(X) => color(X).
q(M) :- M = red.
```

Fig. 12. An error is flagged in the success of **p/1**.

```
:- pred p(X) => sorted(X).
➤ False assertion:
:- check success p(X)
   => sorted(X).
because the success field is incompatible with inferred success:
[eterms] rt27(X)
with:

:- regtype rt27/1.
rt27(red).
➤ Verified assertion:
:- check calls p(X).
:- prop sorted/1.
sorted := [] | [_].
sorted([X,Y|T]) :- X > Y, sorted([Y|T]).
```

Fig. 13. Success and inferred properties (**sorted/1** and **red**) are incompatible.

```
:- pred p(X) => sorted(X).                                                       ▶
p(X) :- q(X).

:- pred q(X) => list(X).
q(M) :- M = [_,_,_].
```

Fig. 14. New definition of predicate **q/1** (and change in assertion).

```
:- module(_,[p/1,colorlist/1,sorted/1,color/1],[assertions,regtypes,fsyntax,clpq]).

:- pred p(X) => sorted(X).
➤ Could not verify assertion:
:- check success p(X)
   => sorted(X).
because
    incompatible_type_f_fixed:sorted(X)
could not be derived from inferred success:
[eterms] rt27(X)
with:

:- regtype rt27/1.
rt27([A,B,C]) :-
    term(A),
    term(B),
    term(C).
[shfr]   native_props:mshare([[X]])
```

Fig. 15. Just a warning: **sorted** could not be verified (with selected domains).

```
:- module(_, [nrev/2], [assertions,fsyntax,nativeprops]).  ▶

:- pred nrev(A,B) : (list(num,A), var(B)) => list(B)
    + ( det, terminates, steps_o( length(A) ) ).

nrev( [] )    := [].
nrev( [H|L] ) := ~conc( ~nrev(L),[H] ).

:- pred conc(A,B,C) + ( det, terminates, steps_o(length(A))).

conc( [],    L ) := L.
conc( [H|L], K ) := [ H | ~conc(L,K) ].
```

Fig. 16. An example with more complex properties, a cost error is flagged.

```
:- module(_, [nrev/2], [assertions,fsyntax,nativeprops]).

:- pred nrev(A,B) : (list(num,A), var(B)) => list(B)
 ► False assertion:
:- check comp nrev(A,B)
   : ( list(num,A), var(B) )
   + ( det, terminates, steps_o(length(A)) ).
because the comp field is incompatible with inferred comp:
[generic_comp] steps_lb(0.5*exp(length(A),2)+1.5*length(A)+1),steps_ub(0.5*exp(l
ength(A),2)+1.5*length(A)+1)
 ► Verified assertion:
:- check calls nrev(A,B)
   : ( list(num,A), var(B) ).
 ► Verified assertion:
:- check success nrev(A,B)
   : ( list(num,A), var(B) )
   => list(B).
```

Fig. 17. The system reminds us that **nrev/2** is of course quadratic, not linear.

```
:- module(_, [nrev/2], [assertions,fsyntax,nativeprops]).                      ►

:- pred nrev(A,B) : (list(num,A), var(B)) => list(B)
   + ( det, terminates, steps_o( exp(length(A),2) ) ).

nrev( [] )    := [].
nrev( [H|L] ) := ~conc( ~nrev(L),[H] ).

:- pred conc(A,B,C) + ( det, terminates, steps_o(length(A))).

conc( [],    L ) := L.
conc( [H|L], K ) := [ H | ~conc(L,K) ].
```

Fig. 18. With the cost expression fixed all properties are now verified.

In Fig. 12 we add some simple definitions for **p/1** and **q/1**, and a **pred** assertion for **q/1**, meaning "in all calls **q(X)** that succeed, **X** is *instantiated* on success
to a term of **color** type." This is verified by the system. We have also added
an assertion for **p/1** meaning "in all calls **p(X)** that succeed, **X** gets instantiated to a term meeting the **sorted** property." The system detects that such
assertion is false and shows the reason (Fig. 13): the analyzer (with the **eterms**
abstract domain [41]) infers that on success **X** gets bound to **red**, expressed as the
automatically inferred regular type **rt27/1**, and the system finds that **rt27(X)**
and **sorted(X)** are incompatible (empty intersection of the set of terms they
represent). In Fig. 14, we have changed the definition of **q/1** so that there is no
incompatibility, and now the system simply warns (Fig. 15) that it cannot verify
the assertion for **p/1**. The success type **rt27(X)** inferred for **p/1** (lists of three
arbitrary terms) and **sorted(X)** are now compatible, and thus no error is flagged.
However, **rt27(X)** does not imply **sorted(X)** for all **X**'s, and thus **sorted(X)** is
not verified (with the default set of abstract domains). In this case the system
will (optionally) introduce a run-time check so that **sorted(X)** is tested when
p/1 is called. Furthermore, the system can run unit tests or generate test cases
(in this case arbitrary terms) automatically to exercise such run-time tests.

An example with more complex properties (also using the functional syntax package) is shown in Fig. 16. It includes a user-provided assertion stating
(among other properties) that the cost of **nrev/2** in resolution steps, for calls to
nrev(A, B) with **A** a ground list and **B** a free variable, should be linear in the

```
:- module(_, [nrev/2], [assertions,fsyntax,nativeprops]).                      ▶

:- pred nrev(A,B) : (list(num,A), var(B)) => list(B)
   + ( det, terminates, steps_o( exp(length(A),2) ) ).

nrev( [] )     := [].
nrev( [H|L] ) := ~conc( ~nrev(L),[H] ).

:- pred conc(A,B,C) + ( det, terminates, steps_ub(length(A))).
 ➤ False assertion:
:- check comp conc(A,B,C)
   + ( det, terminates, steps_ub(length(A)) ).
because the comp field is incompatible with inferred comp:
[generic_comp] steps_lb(length(A)+1),steps_ub(length(A)+1)
```

Fig. 19. If we change the assertion for `conc/3` from complexity order (_o) to upper bound (_ub) then the system flags that `length(A)` is not a correct upper bound.

```
:- module(_, [nrev/2], [assertions,fsyntax,nativeprops]).                      ▶

:- pred nrev(A,B) : (list(num,A), var(B)) => list(B)
   + ( det, terminates, steps_ub( exp(length(A),2) ) ).

nrev( [] )     := [].
nrev( [H|L] ) := ~conc( ~nrev(L),[H] ).

:- pred conc(A,B,C) + ( det, terminates, steps_ub(length(A)+1)).
 ➤ Verified assertion:
:- check comp conc(A,B,C)
   + ( det, terminates, steps_ub(length(A)+1) ).
```

Fig. 20. With the cost expression fixed all properties are now verified.

length of the (input) argument A ($O(\texttt{length(A)})$), property `steps_o(length(A))` in the + field. The system can infer that this is false and underlines it in red. The popup, Fig. 17, explains that the stated worst case asymptotic complexity is incompatible with the quadratic lower bound cost inferred by the analyzer (in fact: $\frac{1}{2}\,length(A)^2 + \frac{3}{2}\,length(A) + 1$, see the `steps_lb` property). If we change the assertion to specify a quadratic upper bound, it is now proven,[5] see Fig. 18 which also shows verification of the assertion for predicate `conc/3` and determinacy and termination properties. In Fig. 19, we have changed the assertion for `conc/3` from complexity order (_o) to a concrete upper bound (_ub), and the system detects the error: `length(A)` is not a correct upper bound because, as shown in the popup, it is incompatible with the lower bound `length(A) + 1` inferred by the analyzer [8,35]. Figure 20 shows that if we change the upper bound to `length(A) + 1`, then the assertion is verified.

1.2   Discussion

We argue that this assertion model greatly enhances the power of Prolog for programming both in the small and in the large, combining effectively the advantages of the of dynamically- and statically-typed languages. It preserves the dynamic language features while at the same time providing safety guarantees and the capability of achieving the performance and efficiency of static systems [6]. The novel combination of assertion language, properties, run-time checking, testing, etc. generates many new synergies.

   We believe that a good part of the power of the approach (and perhaps why this approach was first proposed in the context of Prolog) arises from characteristics of the logic programming paradigm and the Prolog language in particular.

---

[5] An upper bound [26,35] is also inferred, equal to the lower bound (Fig. 17).

For example, as we have seen, the fact that Prolog allows writing many properties (including types) in the source language is instrumental in allowing assertions which cannot be statically verified to be easily used as run-time checks, allowing users to obtain benefits even if a certain property cannot be verified at compile time. As another example, the reversibility of properties written in Prolog allows generating test cases automatically from assertions, without having to invent new concepts or to implement any new functionality, since "property-based testing" comes for free in this approach and thus did not need to be invented. Another contributing factor is that it was in the Prolog community that formal static analysis techniques, in particular abstract interpretation, flourished first, during the 80's and 90's [10], leading quite naturally to the development in the mid-90's of the Ciao model.

The practical relevance of the combination of static and dynamic features brought about by this approach is illustrated by the many other languages and frameworks which have been proposed more recently, aiming at bringing together both worlds, using similar ideas. This includes, e.g., the work on *gradual typing* [31,36,40] and *liquid types* [32,42]. Pfenning's et al.'s early work on *refinement types* [28] and *practical dependent types* [44] was seminal in this context and also uses abstract interpretation or constraint solving, but stays on the decidable side and is thus not combined with run-time checking or testing. Another example is the recent work on verifying *contracts* [18,23,27,39]. Prolog pioneered and is continuing to push the state of the art in this area. However, although some Prolog systems have introduced run-time checks or testing, there is still much work in this area that could become more widely adopted.

2 Making Prolog Even More Extensible, to Support Multiple Features in a Modular Way

The future evolution of Prolog should arguably seek **increasing the power and expressiveness of the language** and its tools to make it even simpler to solve progressively more complex problems. This means continuing in the path exemplified by the addition of, e.g., constraints, concurrency/parallelism, tabling [38], assertions (as discussed previously), or (to name a more recent addition) s(CASP) [1,11]. As also advocated by Gupta et al. [11], it is also desirable to have systems that support all these and additional future extensions within the same implementation.

However, the syntactic and semantic elegance and simplicity of Prolog contrasts with (or may perhaps be thanks to) the implementation sophistication of state-of-the-art Prolog systems, and this can potentially complicate the task of incorporating new functionality to the language.

Fortunately, many good ideas have progressively allowed making extensions in less painful ways. For example, attributed variables, pioneered by Holzbaur and Neumerkel in SICStus [16], made it much easier to add constraint systems to standard Prologs, and in a largely portable way.

Ciao Prolog introduced **new mechanisms for language extension**, such as more principled and modular versions of the *term expansion* facilities,[6] special features in the module system, and the notion of *packages*, which offer a clean distinction between compile-time and run-time extensions [5]. This is essential for global analysis (necessary for the assertion model and optimization), separate/incremental compilation, and language bootstrapping –in fact, most of Ciao, including its abstract machine, is defined in Prolog [22]. These ideas have allowed building the complete system starting from a small kernel in a layered way into a **multiparadigm language**, while having all built-ins and extensions (*constraints, different search rules, functions, higher-order, predicate abstractions, lazyness, concurrency, s(CASP)*, etc.) as optional features that can be activated, deactivated, or combined on a per module basis. Even if for efficiency some such predicates (including for example the cut) may be implemented internally and supported natively in the virtual machine and compiler, none of them are considered *builtins* and their visibility can be controlled, including for example choosing to not load any impure ones, or to redefine them. This modular design allows moving from *pure LP*, where, e.g., no impure builtins are visible, to *full ISO Prolog* by specifying the set of imported modules, and going well beyond that into a multi-paradigm language, while maintaining full backwards compatibility with standard Prolog. Being able to travel these paths is also very useful in an educational context (see, for example, [15] also in this volume).

We believe that future systems should build further on these extensibility-oriented ideas and that the advocated *modularity* and *separation of concerns* are fundamental to Prolog's future evolution. Key features here are *advanced module systems* and the technology to *bridge the gap between the dynamic and static approaches*. They can facilitate **adding more declarative features and more advanced reasoning capabilities to Prolog**, while **providing guarantees** and **increasing performance**. This is specially relevant in a world where programs can be generated by learning systems and need to be modified and verified before use, and where they run on multi-core and heterogeneous computing devices, with complex specialized data representations to make optimal usage of the memory hierarchy. This can greatly benefit from more declarative program specifications (e.g., Prolog programs) and establishing a "dialogue" between programmers and the compiler (e.g., via the assertion language).

References

1. Arias, J., Carro, M., Salazar, E., Marple, K., Gupta, G.: Constraint answer set programming without grounding. Theory Pract. Logic Program. **18**(3–4), 337–354 (2018). https://doi.org/10.1017/S1471068418000285
2. Bueno, F., Carro, M., Hermenegildo, M.V., Lopez-Garcia, P., Morales, J. (eds.) The Ciao System. Reference Manual (v1.22). Techncial report, April 2023. https://ciao-lang.org

---

[6] See again [43] for in introduction to term expansion in Prolog.

3. Bueno, F., et al.: On the role of semantic approximations in validation and diagnosis of constraint logic programs. In: Proceedings of the 3rd International WS on Automated Debugging-AADEBUG, pp. 155–170. U. Linköping Press, May 1997

4. Bueno, F., López-García, P., Hermenegildo, M.: Multivariant non-failure analysis via standard abstract interpretation. In: Kameyama, Y., Stuckey, P.J. (eds.) FLOPS 2004. LNCS, vol. 2998, pp. 100–116. Springer, Heidelberg (2004). https://doi.org/10.1007/978-3-540-24754-8_9

5. Cabeza, D., Hermenegildo, M.: A new module system for prolog. In: Lloyd, J., et al. (eds.) CL 2000. LNCS (LNAI), vol. 1861, pp. 131–148. Springer, Heidelberg (2000). https://doi.org/10.1007/3-540-44957-4_9

6. Carro, M., Morales, J., Muller, H., Puebla, G., Hermenegildo, M.V.: High-level languages for small devices: a case study. In: Flautner, K., Kim, T. (eds.) Compilers, Architecture, and Synthesis for Embedded Systems, pp. 271–281. ACM Press / Sheridan, October 2006

7. Cousot, P., Cousot, R.: Abstract interpretation: a unified lattice model for static analysis of programs by construction or approximation of fixpoints. In: ACM Symposium on Principles of Programming Languages (POPL'77), pp. 238–252. ACM Press (1977). https://doi.org/10.1145/512950.512973

8. Debray, S.K., Lopez-Garcia, P., Hermenegildo, M.V., Lin, N.W.: Lower bound cost estimation for logic programs. In: ILPS'97, pp. 291–305. MIT Press (1997)

9. Debray, S., Lopez-Garcia, P., Hermenegildo, M.V.: Non-failure analysis for logic programs. In: ICLP'97, pp. 48–62. MIT Press (1997)

10. Giacobazzi, R., Ranzato, F.: History of abstract interpretation. IEEE Ann. Hist. Comput. **44**(2), 33–43 (2022). https://doi.org/10.1109/MAHC.2021.3133136

11. Gupta, G., Salazar, E., Arias, J., Basu, K., Varanasi, S., Carro, M.: Prolog: past, present, and future. In: Warren, D.S., Dahl, V., Eiter, T., Hermenegildo, M., Kowalski, R., Rossi, F. (eds.) Prolog: The Next 50 Years. LNCS (LNAI), vol. 13900, pp. 48–61. Springer, Cham (2023). https://doi.org/10.1007/978-3-031-35254-6_4

12. Hermenegildo, M.V., et al.: An overview of ciao and its design philosophy. Theory Pract. Logic Program. **12**(1–2), 219–252 (2012)

13. Hermenegildo, M.V., Puebla, G., Bueno, F.: Using global analysis, partial specifications, and an extensible assertion language for program validation and debugging. In: Apt, K.R., Marek, V.W., Truszczynski, M., Warren, D.S. (eds.) The Logic Programming Paradigm: a 25-Year Perspective, pp. 161–192. Springer, Heidelberg (1999). https://doi.org/10.1007/978-3-642-60085-2_7

14. Hermenegildo, M.V., Puebla, G., Bueno, F., Lopez-Garcia, P.: Integrated program debugging, verification, and optimization using abstract interpretation (and the Ciao system preprocessor). Sci. Comput. Program. **58**(1–2), 115–140 (2005). https://doi.org/10.1016/j.scico.2005.02.006

15. Hermenegildo, M., Morales, J., Lopez-Garcia, P.: Some thoughts on how to teach prolog. In: Warren, D.S., Dahl, V., Eiter, T., Hermenegildo, M., Kowalski, R., Rossi, F. (eds.) Prolog: The Next 50 Years. LNCS (LNAI), vol. 13900, pp. 107–123. Springer, Cham (2023). https://doi.org/10.1007/978-3-031-35254-6_9

16. Holzbaur, C.: Metastructures vs. attributed variables in the context of extensible unification. In: Bruynooghe, M., Wirsing, M. (eds.) PLILP 1992. LNCS, vol. 631, pp. 260–268. Springer, Heidelberg (1992). https://doi.org/10.1007/3-540-55844-6_141

17. Hudak, P., et al.: Report on the programming language Haskell. Haskell Spec. Issue, ACM SIGPLAN Not. **27**(5), 1–164 (1992)

18. Logozzo, F., et al.: Clousot. https://msdn.microsoft.com/en-us/devlabs/dd491992.aspx. Accessed 2018

19. Lopez-Garcia, P., Bueno, F., Hermenegildo, M.V.: Automatic inference of determinacy and mutual exclusion for logic programs using mode and type analyses. N. Gener. Comput. **28**(2), 117–206 (2010)
20. Lopez-Garcia, P., Klemen, M., Liqat, U., Hermenegildo, M.V.: A general framework for static profiling of parametric resource usage. TPLP (ICLP'16 Spec. Issue) **16**(5–6), 849–865 (2016). https://doi.org/10.1017/S1471068416000442
21. Mera, E., Lopez-García, P., Hermenegildo, M.: Integrating software testing and run-time checking in an assertion verification framework. In: Hill, P.M., Warren, D.S. (eds.) ICLP 2009. LNCS, vol. 5649, pp. 281–295. Springer, Heidelberg (2009). https://doi.org/10.1007/978-3-642-02846-5_25
22. Morales, J., Carro, M., Hermenegildo, M.V.: Description and optimization of abstract machines in a dialect of prolog. Theory Pract. Logic Program. **16**(1), 1–58 (2016). https://doi.org/10.1017/S1471068414000672
23. MSR: Code contracts. https://research.microsoft.com/en-us/projects/contracts/. Accessed 2018
24. Muthukumar, K., Hermenegildo, M.: Combined determination of sharing and freeness of program variables through abstract interpretation. In: ICLP'91, pp. 49–63. MIT Press, June 1991
25. Muthukumar, K., Hermenegildo, M.: Compile-time derivation of variable dependency using abstract interpretation. JLP **13**(2/3), 315–347 (1992)
26. Navas, J., Mera, E., López-García, P., Hermenegildo, M.V.: User-definable resource bounds analysis for logic programs. In: Dahl, V., Niemelä, I. (eds.) ICLP 2007. LNCS, vol. 4670, pp. 348–363. Springer, Heidelberg (2007). https://doi.org/10.1007/978-3-540-74610-2_24
27. Nguyen, P.C., Tobin-Hochstadt, S., Van Horn, D.: Soft contract verification. In: Proceedings of the 19th ACM SIGPLAN International Conference on Functional Programming. ICFP '14, pp. 139–152. ACM, New York, NY, USA (2014). https://doi.org/10.1145/2628136.2628156
28. Pfenning, F.: Dependent types in logic programming. In: Pfenning, F. (ed.) Types in Logic Programming, pp. 285–311. The MIT Press (1992)
29. Puebla, G., Bueno, F., Hermenegildo, M.: An assertion language for constraint logic programs. In: Deransart, P., Hermenegildo, M.V., Małuszynski, J. (eds.) Analysis and Visualization Tools for Constraint Programming. LNCS, vol. 1870, pp. 23–61. Springer, Heidelberg (2000). https://doi.org/10.1007/10722311_2
30. Puebla, G., Bueno, F., Hermenegildo, M.: Combined static and dynamic assertion-based debugging of constraint logic programs. In: Bossi, A. (ed.) LOPSTR 1999. LNCS, vol. 1817, pp. 273–292. Springer, Heidelberg (2000). https://doi.org/10.1007/10720327_16
31. Rastogi, A., Swamy, N., Fournet, C., Bierman, G., Vekris, P.: Safe & efficient gradual typing for typescript. In: 42nd POPL, pp. 167–180. ACM, January 2015
32. Rondon, P.M., Kawaguchi, M., Jhala, R.: Liquid types. In: Gupta, R., Amarasinghe, S.P. (eds.) Proceedings of the ACM SIGPLAN 2008 Conference on Programming Language Design and Implementation, Tucson, AZ, USA, 7–13 June 2008, pp. 159–169. ACM (2008). https://doi.org/10.1145/1375581.1375602
33. Saglam, H., Gallagher, J.: Approximating constraint logic programs using polymorphic types and regular descriptions. Technical report CSTR-95-17, Department of Computer Science, U. of Bristol, Bristol BS8 1TR (1995)
34. Sanchez-Ordaz, M., Garcia-Contreras, I., Perez-Carrasco, V., Morales, J.F., Lopez-Garcia, P., Hermenegildo, M.V.: Verifly: on-the-fly assertion checking via incrementality. Theory Pract. Logic Program. **21**(6), 768–784 (2021)

35. Serrano, A., Lopez-Garcia, P., Hermenegildo, M.V.: Resource usage analysis of logic programs via abstract interpretation using sized types. TPLP, ICLP'14 Spec. Issue **14**(4–5), 739–754 (2014). https://doi.org/10.1017/S147106841400057X
36. Siek, J.G., Taha, W.: Gradual typing for functional languages. In: Scheme and Functional Programming Workshop, pp. 81–92 (2006)
37. Somogyi, Z., Henderson, F., Conway, T.: The execution algorithm of mercury: an efficient purely declarative logic programming language. JLP **29**(1–3), 17–64 (1996)
38. Swift, T., Warren, D.S.: XSB: extending prolog with tabled logic programming. Theory Pract. Logic Program. **12**(1–2), 157–187 (2012). https://doi.org/10.1017/S1471068411000500
39. Takikawa, A., et al.: Towards practical gradual typing. In: Boyland, J.T. (ed.) 29th European Conference on Object-Oriented Programming, ECOOP 2015, 5–10 July 2015, Prague, Czech Republic. LIPIcs, vol. 37, pp. 4–27. Schloss Dagstuhl - Leibniz-Zentrum fuer Informatik (2015). https://doi.org/10.4230/LIPIcs.ECOOP.2015.4
40. Tobin-Hochstadt, S., Felleisen, M.: The design and implementation of typed scheme. In: POPL, pp. 395–406. ACM (2008)
41. Vaucheret, C., Bueno, F.: More precise yet efficient type inference for logic programs. In: Hermenegildo, M.V., Puebla, G. (eds.) SAS 2002. LNCS, vol. 2477, pp. 102–116. Springer, Heidelberg (2002). https://doi.org/10.1007/3-540-45789-5_10
42. Vazou, N., Tanter, É., Horn, D.V.: Gradual liquid type inference. Proc. ACM Program. Lang. **2**(OOPSLA), 132:1–132:25 (2018). https://doi.org/10.1145/3276502
43. Warren, D.S.: Introduction to prolog. In: Warren, D.S., Dahl, V., Eiter, T., Hermenegildo, M., Kowalski, R., Rossi, F. (eds.) Prolog: The Next 50 Years. LNCS (LNAI), vol. 13900, pp. 3–19. Springer, Cham (2023). https://doi.org/10.1007/978-3-031-35254-6_1
44. Xi, H., Pfenning, F.: Dependent types in practical programming. In: Appel, A.W., Aiken, A. (eds.) POPL '99, Proceedings of the 26th ACM SIGPLAN-SIGACT Symposium on Principles of Programming Languages, San Antonio, TX, USA, 20–22 January 1999. pp. 214–227. ACM (1999). https://doi.org/10.1145/292540.292560

Prolog as a Knowledge Representation Language the Nature and Importance of Prolog

Michael Genesereth[✉]

Computer Science Department, Stanford University, Stanford, USA
genesereth@stanford.edu

Abstract. In the Computer Science literature, Prolog is usually characterized as a language for programming computers. That makes sense. Its inventors described Prolog as a programming language [14]; and its very name is an abbreviation for PROgrammation en LOGique (PROgramming in LOGic). Unfortunately, characterizing Prolog as primarily a *programming language* may be doing it a disservice. As argued in [5,6] and elsewhere, it is also an excellent *knowledge representation language*. In fact, an argument can be made that Prolog's *main* value lies not so much in programming as in knowledge representation.

1 Introduction

In the Computer Science literature, Prolog is usually characterized as a high-level programming language. However, it also has value as a knowledge representation language. The main distinction between these two viewpoints lies in the way one thinks about the semantics of Prolog programs.

The knowledge representation point of view is purely declarative. A Prolog "program" can be viewed as simply a set of inductive definitions of higher level relations in terms of lower level relations. There is no specification for how those definitions are to be used.

The programming point of view is more procedural. Prolog programs are usually assumed to be processed by a specific algorithm (based on SLD-resolution) for a specific purpose (computing answers to queries), possibly with procedural directives to guide the process.

The practical difference between these viewpoints can be seen by realizing that the rules in a Prolog program can be effectively used in multiple ways. (1) The rules can be used to deduce answers to given queries. (In this case, the two views are effectively equivalent.) (2) The rules can also be used to abduce data that produces specified query results (constraint satisfaction). (3) The rules can be used to compare relations for disjointness or overlap or equivalence (containment testing). (4) View definitions can be "differentiated" to produce rules for computing updates to materialized views (as suggested by Orman). (5) Definitions can be automatically "inverted" to enable query folding (for purposes of

D. S. Warren et al. (Eds.): Prolog: The Next 50 Years, LNAI 13900, pp. 38–47, 2023.
https://doi.org/10.1007/978-3-031-35254-6_3

data integration). And so forth. Each of these tasks requires a different "interpreter", but *the rules are the same in all cases*. (And, incidentally, few of these tasks can be performed easily with programs written in traditional imperative programming languages.)

The point is that, by focussing on Prolog as a programming language rather than a knowledge representation language, we may be doing it a disservice. In fact, it can be argued that Prolog's *main* value lies not so much in programming as in knowledge representation. In this article, I make this argument in three stages. First of all, I explain why I think Prolog is superior to other knowledge representation formalisms, such as First-Order Logic. I then discuss the merits of having multiple interpreters for Prolog. Finally, I talk about the prospects for automatically transforming logic programs from natural but potentially expensive form into versions that execute more efficiently for specific interpreters.

2   Simplicity and Completeness

In an early paper [20], John McCarthy extolled the benefits of First Order Logic (FOL) as a framework for knowledge representation. The language of FOL provides a variety of useful linguistic features, e.g. logical operators, variables, and quantifiers. Moreover, being domain-independent, the language of FOL has no built in assumptions and thus is more general than domain-specific languages.

Unfortunately, FOL has some properties that limit its usefulness. For example, in FOL, it is not possible to define the notion of transitive closure in a way that precludes non-standard models (at least without Herbrand semantics [7]). Moreover, in defining relations, it is usually necessary to write "negation axioms" to say when those relations do *not* hold as well as positive axioms that say when those relations do hold.

One nice feature of Prolog is that it deals with these limitations in a graceful way. If one abides by a few restrictions in writing Prolog programs (e.g. safety and stratified negation) and if one uses minimal model semantics for the language (i.e. negation as failure), transitive closure can be defined precisely, and negation axioms become unnecessary.

Some might argue that this feature of Prolog is also a disadvantage. Under the conditions just mentioned, every Prolog program has a unique minimal model. This effectively prevents one from encoding incomplete information. In order to deal with this disadvantage, it might be nice to allow programmers to write rules with negations or disjunctions or existential heads. And Answer-Set Programming (ASP) [19] provides a way for programmers to blend classical negation with negation as failure.

On the other hand, in many circumstances it is often desirable to strive for complete knowledge about the application area of a program. For example, in writing specifications for runnable programs, it is desirable to know what is acceptable behavior and what is not acceptable so that a system executing the program can act with confidence. While it is possible to write complete theories in FOL, it is not always easy to determine whether or not a given theory is complete. By contrast, in Prolog (with safety and stratified negation), one knows that the theory is complete. And, when one absolutely needs to express incomplete information, ASP provides a natural extension to Prolog to express this information.

3   Multiple Interpreters

The main distinction between the view of Prolog as a *programming language* and the view of Prolog as a *knowledge representation language* lies in the way one thinks about the semantics of Prolog "programs". The KR point of view is purely *declarative*. A Prolog program can be viewed as simply a set of inductive definitions of higher level relations in terms of lower level relations. There is no regard for how those definitions are to be used. The programming point of view is more *procedural*. Prolog programs are assumed to be processed by a specific algorithm for a specific purpose (computing answers to queries), possibly with procedural directives to guide the process [10].

If one's only interest is getting answers to queries, then the two approaches are effectively equivalent. The declarative semantics specifies which answers are correct, and the Prolog interpreter computes those answers.

The practical difference between these viewpoints can be seen by realizing that the rules in a Prolog "program" can be used in multiple ways to solve different types of problems. In what follows, we illustrate this point by presenting three real world problems that can be solved by encoding knowledge in standard Prolog and applying different interpreters.

3.1   Query Evaluation - Kinship

Query Evaluation is the simplest way in which a Prolog program can be used. We start with a ruleset and a dataset and apply a query evaluation procedure to compute answers to queries. The interpreter could be a bottom-up interpreter or a top-down evaluator (like the standard Prolog interpreter [4]) alone or in combination with optimization refinements such as conjunct ordering and/or tabling [26].

Suppose, for example, we have a dataset of kinship information like the one below. The person named art is a parent of a person bob and another person bea; bob is the parent of both cal and cam; and bea is the parent of both cat and coe.

```
parent(art,bob)
parent(art,bea)
parent(bob,cal)
parent(bob,cam)
parent(bea,cat)
parent(bea,coe)
```

The following Prolog rule defines the grandparent relation in terms of parent. A person x is the **grandparent** of a person z if x is the **parent** of a person y and y is the **parent** of z.

```
grandparent(X,Z) :- parent(X,Y) & parent(Y,Z)
```

Given this dataset and ruleset, we can apply a query evaluation procedure to compute the corresponding instance of the grandparent relation.

```
grandparent(art,cal)
grandparent(art,cam)
grandparent(art,cat)
grandparent(art,coe)
```

Query evaluation is the usual way in which Prolog is used. The answers are logically entailed by the data and rules, and the standard Prolog interpreter produces these answers by some form of *deduction* (typically SLD-resolution [13]).

3.2   Constraint Satisfaction - Map Coloring

Now, consider the problem of coloring planar maps using only four colors, the idea being to assign each region a color so that no two adjacent regions are assigned the same color. A typical map is shown below. In this case, we have six regions. Some are adjacent to each other, meaning that they *cannot* be assigned the same color. Others are not adjacent, meaning that they *can* be assigned the same color.

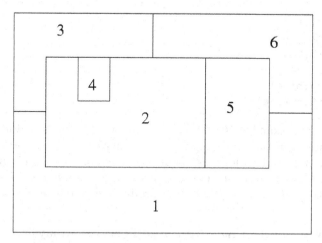

We can represent the basic facts of this problem as a set of ground atoms like the ones below. We use the unary relation **region** to enumerate regions. We use **hue** to enumerate possible colors of regions. And we use the binary relation **next to**

capture contiguity between regions. (Note that the sentences here capture contiguity in one direction. One might wish to include the sentences with arguments reversed to capture contiguity in the other direction as well.)

```
region(r1)     hue(red)      next(r1,r2)    next(r2,r5)
region(r2)     hue(green)    next(r1,r3)    next(r2,r6)
region(r3)     hue(blue)     next(r1,r5)    next(r3,r4)
region(r4)     hue(purple)   next(r1,r6)    next(r3,r6)
region(r5)                   next(r2,r3)    next(r5,r6)
region(r6)                   next(r2,r4)
```

One way to codify the constraints in this problem is to define a relation `illegal`, which is true for any assignment that violates those constraints. For example, the first rule below states that no two adjacent regions can have the same color. The second rule states that no region can have more than one color. The last two rules state that every region must have at least one color.

```
illegal :- next(R1,R2) & color(R1,C) & color(R2,C)
illegal :- color(R,C1) & color(R,C2) & distinct(C1,C2)
illegal :- region(R) & ~hascolor(R)
hascolor(R) :- color(R,C)
```

Our goal in this problem is to infer a set of ground atomic sentences that characterize the color relation. Given these definitions, it is possible to determine that the dataset below is one solution to the problem. Of course, this is not the only solution. It is possible to permute the colors in various ways and still satisfy the constraints.

```
color(r1,red)
color(r2,green)
color(r3,blue)
color(r4,red)
color(r5,blue)
color(r6,purple)
```

The point of this example is that *none* of these solutions is *logically entailed* by the definitions in the problem, and the standard Prolog interpreter will *not* produce any answers to questions about the colors of regions (given the rules as written). However, an interpreter that is capable of *abduction* (as opposed to deduction) or *constraint satisfaction can* produce answers like the one above.

3.3   Containment Testing - Insurance Portfolio Analysis

A common problem in analyzing insurance products is determining whether an insurance policy or collection of policies provides coverage for a collection of possible events. [9]

Consider the example below. Here we see the preferences of an insuree joe. In particular, he wants a portfolio of policies that covers him for hospitalizations in Japan or Korea. The binary relation `patient` here relates a hospitalization and the patient. The relation `hospital` relates a hospitalization and a hospital. And the `country` relation relates a hospital and a country.

```
covered(Z) :- patient(Z,joe) & hospital(Z,H) & country(H,japan)
covered(Z) :- patient(Z,joe) & hospital(Z,H) & country(H,korea)
```

Here we have the definition of the hospitalizations covered by a particular policy he is considering. The insuree and his relatives are covered anywhere in Asia.

```
covered(Z) :-
  patient(Z,P) & related(P,joe) &
  hospital(Z,H) & country(H,C) & continent(C,asia)
```

We also have some background information. The individuals related to an insuree include himself, his spouse, and his kids. And the countries of Japan and Korea are in Asia.

```
related(I,I)
related(P,I) :- spouse(P,I)
related(P,I) :- parent(I,P)

continent(japan,asia)
continent(korea,asia)
```

Given this information, it is easy for us to see that the policy covers the preferences of the insuree. Like the preceding examples, we have definitions of view relations. Unlike the case of query evaluation, we do not have a complete dataset. And, unlike the case of constraint satisfaction, we are not looking for a complete dataset. Instead, we are trying to determine whether a policy covers his needs for *every* complete dataset. The key to automating this determination is to use an interpreter capable of *containment testing* [1, 24] to determine whether one program produces all of the results of another program for *any* dataset, not just one particular dataset.

4   Program Transformation

One of the nice benefits of Prolog's declarative semantics is that it gives us a natural definition for the equivalence of different programs - two programs are equivalent if and only if they compute the same results. Of course, we can define the equivalence of programs with imperative semantics in similar fashion. However, it is much easier to determine the equivalence of declarative programs than to determine the equivalence of procedural programs. Moreover, there are powerful techniques for automatically transforming declarative programs into equivalent (but computationally more efficient) form and/or compiling them into procedural programs. (Yes, equivalence testing for Prolog is undecidable in general, but it is practical in many special cases.)

As an example, consider the map coloring problem described above. As mentioned earlier, the standard Prolog interpreter is not capable of finding solutions. However, this problem can be solved by transforming the program from its natural expression as a constraint satisfaction problem into a form suitable for execution by the standard Prolog interpreter.

The version below was proposed by Pereira and Porto [22] and subsequently mentioned by McCarthy [21]. Rather than defining on regions, we start by defining ok as a relation on colors, viz. the pairs of colors that may be next to each other.

```
ok(red,green)   ok(green,red)    ok(blue,red)    ok(purple,red)
ok(red,blue)    ok(green,blue)   ok(blue,green)  ok(purple,green)
ok(red,purple)  ok(green,purple) ok(blue,purple) ok(purple,blue)
```

In the case of the map shown above, our goal is to find six hues (one for each region of the map) such that no two adjacent regions have the same hue. We can express this goal by writing the query shown below.

```
goal(C1,C2,C3,C4,C5,C6) :-
  ok(C1,C2) & ok(C1,C3) & ok(C1,C5) & ok(C1,C6) &
  ok(C2,C3) & ok(C2,C4) & ok(C2,C5) & ok(C2,C6) &
  ok(C3,C4) & ok(C3,C6) & ok(C5,C6)
```

Given this version, we can use the standard Prolog interpreter to produce 6-tuples of hues that ensure that no two adjacent regions have the same color. Of course, in problems like this one, we usually want only one solution rather than all solutions. However, finding even one solution is such cases can be costly.

The good news it is possible to convert the formulation described earlier into this form; and in many cases this conversion can be done automatically [11]. The benefit of doing things this way is that the programmer can formalize the problem in its most natural form - as a constraint satisfaction problem - and the system can then transform into a version that can be executed by the standard Prolog interpreter.

But, wait, there's more! Given a program's declarative semantics, it is possible to rewrite the program into a form that runs even more rapidly. In our example, the program can be improved by reordering the conjuncts in the definition of goal, based on size heuristics and/or the Kempe transformation described by McCarthy [21], resulting in the version shown below.

```
goal(C1,C2,C3,C4,C5,C6) :-
  ok(C1,C2) & ok(C1,C3) & ok(C1,C6) &
  ok(C2,C3) & ok(C2,C6) & ok(C3,C6) &
  ok(C2,C4) & ok(C3,C4) & ok(C1,C5) & ok(C2,C5) &
  ok(C5,C6)
```

This version looks the same but runs faster due to the better ordering of subgoals. This is not something that necessarily matters to the programmer; but it does matter to the interpreter. If this transformation is automated, the programmer does not need to worry these details.

Similar examples can be found in the formulation of computationally complex problems such as the fibonacci function. The programmer can write the definitions in their most natural but computationally inefficient form, and the program can be automatically written in a form that can be executed efficiently, either by rewriting the fibonacci definition with a single recursion or by using a tabling interpreter [23].

The computer programming community has long recognized the value of Interactive Development Environments (IDEs) to help in developing and maintaining programs. Logical Interactive Development Environments (LIDEs) have similar value for Logic Programming. These systems can save authors work providing pre-existing ontologies and databases and knowledge bases. They provide tools for the verification, analysis, and debugging of legal codes. And they can provide technology for automatically translating to and from other formal languages. They can support languages that are more expressive than Logic Programming, e.g. FOL and beyond. They can support languages that are more human-friendly, e.g. controlled English, such as Kowalski's Logical English [18], thus making possible pseudo-natural language authoring without the drawbacks of general natural language.

More importantly, it is possible in many cases for such environments to transform programs into computationally more efficient versions, allowing the programmer to encode knowledge in its most natural form while the computer gets to execute a more efficient version. The cost of these transformations can be paid once, and the cost can be amortized over multiple uses of the transformed programs.

5   Conclusion

The facts and rules in the examples described above are all Prolog programs written using simple *declarative semantics*; but, in the various examples, the programs are *processed* in completely different ways. This multiplicity of uses illustrates the value of using Prolog to encode the knowledge relevant to applications rather than thinking of sets of Prolog facts and rules as programs for processing that knowledge in one specific way for all applications. Transformations to enhance efficiency can be applied by an interactive development environment. The upshot is that the user can code the knowledge in its most natural form and use the LIDE to find a suitable interpreter or a computationally tractable form for the program that can be executed by the standard interpreter or a variant like XSB [23].

References

1. Carlson, P., Genesereth, M.: Insurance portfolio management as containment testing. In: ICAIL (2023)
2. Chandra, A.K., Merlin, P.M.: Optimal implementation of conjunctive queries in relational databases. In: Proceeding of the 9th Annual ACM Symposium on the Theory of Computing, pp. 77–90 (1977)
3. Chen, W., Swift, T., Warren, D.: Efficient top-down computation of queries under the well-founded semantics. J. Logic Program. **24**(3), 161–201 (1995)
4. Clocksin, W.F., Mellish, C.S.: Programming in Prolog, 4th edn. Springer, New York (1994). https://doi.org/10.1007/978-3-642-97596-7
5. De Cat, B., Bogaerts, B., Bruynooghe, M., Janssens, G., Denecker, M.: Predicate logic as a modeling language: the IDP system. Declarative Logic Program. 279–323 (2018)
6. Gelfond, M., Leone, N.: Logic programming and knowledge representation. Artif. Intell. **138**(1–2), 1 (2002)
7. Bassiliades, N., Gottlob, G., Sadri, F., Paschke, A., Roman, D. (eds.): RuleML 2015. LNCS, vol. 9202. Springer, Cham (2015). https://doi.org/10.1007/978-3-319-21542-6
8. Genesereth, M., Chaudhri, V.: Logic programming. Synth. Lect. Artif. Intell. Mach. Learn. (2020). https://doi.org/10.2200/S00966ED1V01Y201911AIM044
9. Genesereth, M.: Insurance portfolio management. Complaw Corner, Codex: The Stanford Center for Legal Informatics (2022). https://law.stanford.edu/2022/07/30/insurance-portfolio-management/
10. Hayes, P.: Computation and deduction. In: Proceedings Second Symposium on Mathematical Foundations of Computer Science, Czechoslovakian Academy of Sciences, Czechoslovakia, pp. 105–118 (1973)
11. Hinrichs, T.: Extensional reasoning. Ph.D. thesis, Computer Science Department, Stanford University (2007)
12. Kakas, A.C., Kowalski, R., Toni, F.: The role of abduction in logic programming. In: Gabbay, D.M., Hogger, C.J., Robinson, J.A. (eds.) Handbook of Logic in Artificial Intelligence and Logic Programming, vol. 5, pp. 235–324. Oxford University Press, Oxford (1998)
13. Kowalski, R., Kuehner, D.: Linear resolution with selection function. Artif. Intell. **2**, 227–60 (1971)
14. Kowalski, R.: Predicate logic as a programming language. In: Proceedings of IFIP 1974, North Holland Publishing Company, Amsterdam, pp. 569–574 (1974)
15. Kowalski, R.: Algorithm = Logic + Control. Commun. ACM **22**(7) (1979)
16. Kowalski, R., Sadri, F.: LPS - a logic-based production system framework (2009)
17. Kowalski, R., Sadri, F.: Integrating Logic Programming and Production Systems in Abductive Logic Programming Agents (2009)
18. Logical English as a Programming Language for the Law. ProLALA **22** (2022)
19. Lifschitz, V.: What is answer set programming? (PDF). In: Proceedings of the 23rd National Conference on Artificial Intelligence, vol. 3, pp. 1594–1597. AAAI Press, 13 July 2008
20. McCarthy, J.: Programs with common sense. In: Proceedings of the Teddington Conference on the Mechanization of Thought Processes, pp. 75–91. Her Majesty's Stationary Office, London (1959)
21. McCarthy, J.: Coloring maps and the kowalski doctrine. In: Lifschitz, V. (ed.) Formalizing Common Sense: Papers by John McCarthy, pp. 167–174 (1998)

22. Pereira, L.M., Porto, A.: Selective Backtracking for Logic Programs. Departamento de Informatica, Faculdade de Ciencias e Tecnologia, Universidade Nova de Lisboa, Lisboa, Portugal (1980)
23. Sagonas, K., Swift, T.: Warren, D.S.: XSB as an efficient deductive database engine. In: Proceedings of the ACM SIGMOD International Conference on the Management of Data (1994)
24. Ullman, J.D.: Information integration using logical views. Theor. Comput. Sci. **239**(2), 189–210 (2000). https://doi.org/10.1016/S0304-3975(99)00219-4
25. van Emden, M., Kowalski, R.: The semantics of predicate logic as a programming language. J. Assoc. Comput. Mach. **23**(4), 733–774 (1976)
26. Warren, D.S.: Programming in Tabled Prolog. https://citeseerx.ist.psu.edu/viewdoc/download?doi=10.1.1.49.4635

Prolog: Past, Present, and Future

Gopal Gupta[1]([✉]), Elmer Salazar[1], Farhad Shakerin[1], Joaquín Arias[2],
Sarat Chandra Varanasi[1], Kinjal Basu[1], Huaduo Wang[1], Fang Li[1],
Serdar Erbatur[1], Parth Padalkar[1], Abhiramon Rajasekharan[1], Yankai Zeng[1],
and Manuel Carro[3]

[1] Department of Computer Science, UT Dallas, Richardson, USA
gupta@utdallas.edu
[2] CETINIA, Universidad Rey Juan Carlos, Madrid, Spain
[3] Universidad Politecnica de Madrid and IMDEA Software Institute, Madrid, Spain

Abstract. We argue that various extensions proposed for Prolog—tabling, constraints, parallelism, coroutining, etc.—must be integrated seamlessly in a single system. We also discuss how goal-directed predicate answer set programming can be incorporated in Prolog, and how it facilitates development of advanced applications in AI and automated commonsense reasoning.

1 Introduction

The year 2022 was celebrated as the 50th anniversary of the founding of logic programming (LP) and Prolog [16]. Prolog harnesses the power of logic and provides a new declarative paradigm for computing. Initially, Prolog was based on Horn clauses with some built-ins added. Over time more features were added to make the language more powerful as well as efficient. These features include constraints over various types of domains (reals, booleans, finite domains, etc.), negation-as-failure, coroutining, tabling, parallelism, etc. Prolog has been applied to many (innovative) applications. Today, Prolog is a highly sophisticated language [34] with a large user base. Over the last fifty years, as one would expect, research in logic programming has flourished in three main areas: making Prolog more efficient, making Prolog more expressive, and developing applications that make use of logic programming technology. We will focus on the first two issues, as any discussion of applications of logic programming will take significantly more space. However, one of the applications of LP that we will discuss in this paper is automating *commonsense reasoning* with the aim of building systems that can emulate the thought process of an (unerring) human [18,25,37,47]. We believe that logic programming is indispensable for this purpose. We assume that the reader is familiar with Prolog, logic programming, and answer set programming. An excellent, brief exposition is given in the introductory chapter of this book [51]. More detailed expositions can be found elsewhere [23,39,48].

1.1 Making Prolog More Efficient

Given a call, a Prolog interpreter finds matching clauses and tries them one by one via backtracking. Once a matching clause is selected, subgoals in the body

D. S. Warren et al. (Eds.): Prolog: The Next 50 Years, LNAI 13900, pp. 48–61, 2023.
https://doi.org/10.1007/978-3-031-35254-6_4

of the clause are executed. The strategy for rule selection and subgoal selection is called the *computation rule* [39]. Prolog uses a computation rule that tries clauses in textual order, while subgoals in a clause are tried left to right. A considerable amount of research has been undertaken over the past decades to improve the rule selection process. Executing Prolog programs in or-parallel—trying multiple matching clauses simultaneously on multiple processors—can be regarded as a strategy to improve rule-selection. Tabled logic programming can also be viewed as a rule-selection strategy, where rules are (optionally) selected in a non-textual order to ensure termination of left-recursive programs, for example. Research has also been undertaken over the past several decades to improve the subgoal selection process. Research in goal selection strategies includes constraint logic programming (where the *generate and test* strategy is flipped into *test and generate*), coroutining, concurrent logic programming, and and-parallelism. These efforts in improving rule selection and subgoal selection have resulted in Prolog systems that are highly effective [34].

Unfortunately, various strategies developed to make execution more efficient are not all available in a single Prolog system *where they work seamlessly with each other*. We believe that future research in Prolog must focus on building a unified system that supports tabling, constraints, coroutining, parallelism, and concurrency [27]. These enhancements must also work seamlessly with each other. Many groups have been steadfastly working towards this goal. These include, among others, efforts by Arias and Carro to integrate constraints in tabled logic programming [6] and by Rocha and Santos Costa to combine tabling and or-parallelism [44]. Research has also been conducted on adding concurrency at the user level to Prolog [3,12,17]. Some of these ideas have been incorporated in systems such as SWI-Prolog [52] and Ciao-Prolog [31], nevertheless, research to realize a system where all these advanced features are efficiently and seamlessly integrated and available in a single system must continue. Our hope is that such a logic programming system will be realized in the future.

1.2 Making Prolog More Expressive

We next consider research on making Prolog more expressive. Prolog is a Turing-complete language, so by greater expressiveness we mean the ability to represent and solve problems more elegantly, i.e., the logic program developed to solve a problem is "close" to the problem specification. A large segment of this research is dedicated to adding negation-as-failure (NAF) to logic programming, though, considerable research has been done in devising other extensions, e.g., constraint handling rules [20], functional-logic programming [29], higher order LP [14], coinductive logic programming [46], and adding assertions [30]. Due to lack of space, we will primarily focus on the incorporation of NAF and coinduction into logic programming, one of the reasons being that they help in realizing (predicate) ASP within Prolog, critical for automating commonsense reasoning. [18,37,47].

Stable models semantics [24] led to the paradigm of Answer Set Programming (ASP) [9]. Commonsense reasoning, realized via default reasoning, imposing integrity constraints, and assumption-based reasoning, can be elegantly emulated in ASP [23,42]. However, a problem faced by ASP is the following: how to execute answer set programs in the presence of predicates? ASP researchers resorted to allowing only propositional programs. Thus, ASP programs containing predicates have to be grounded first so that they become propositional and then a SAT-solver is used to find its (multiple) models. This leads to a number of restrictions including: (i) programs have to be finitely groundable, (ii) data structures such as lists are not permitted, (iii) program size blows up exponentially during grounding, (iv) real numbers cannot be faithfully represented. Thus, while ASP enhances Prolog, it also restricts it due to the choice of implementation mechanism used. While extremely efficient propositional ASP systems such as CLINGO [22] have been developed, restriction to propositions-only programs make them hard to use for knowledge representation applications, in particular, modeling commonsense reasoning, which is often *query-driven* or *goal-directed*. To overcome this, stable model semantics-based NAF must be incorporated in Prolog. The discovery of coinductive logic programming [46] led to development of query-driven implementations of ASP called s(ASP) [40] and s(CASP) [4]. The s(ASP) and s(CASP) systems allow predicates, do not require grounding, and can be thought of as extending Prolog with stable model semantics-based negation. Thus, default rules with exceptions, integrity constraints, and cyclical reasoning through negation can be elegantly supported in this extended Prolog, thereby supporting automation of commonsense reasoning. The s(ASP) and s(CASP) systems rely on many advanced techniques such as constructive negation, dual rule generation, coinduction, etc., and are scalable.

2 Emulating Human Thinking with Logic Programming

Logic programming was conceived as a language for problem-solving, AI, and emulating human thinking [37,38]. However, Prolog's inability to effectively model incomplete information limited its use for AI and emulating human reasoning, which became an impetus for significant subsequent research by various groups [18,23,25,37]. Negation-as-failure is an important component in these research efforts and ASP is an important effort in this direction. ASP extends logic programming with stable model semantics-based NAF [9,23]. ASP allows reasoning with incomplete information through NAF and defaults. ASP also supports integrity constraints, and non-inductive semantics in which multiple models (worlds) are admitted. Thus, ASP is a paradigm that comes close to supporting commonsense reasoning and emulating the human thought process [23,28]. It is our position that the path to automating commonsense reasoning in a practical manner goes through Answer Set Programming realized via Prolog-like implementations of predicate ASP such as the s(CASP) system [4,40]. By Prolog-like, we mean that predicates and first order terms are supported, and execution is query-driven, carried out in a top-down manner. Thus, the power of ASP, i.e., negation based on stable model semantics, is supported within Prolog.

We strongly believe that the best path to building intelligent systems is by emulating how intelligent behavior manifests in humans. Humans use their senses (sight, sound, smell, taste, and touch) to acquire information via pattern matching, but to draw conclusions based on this information, humans use (commonsense) reasoning. Note that:

1. Machine learning technologies are akin to human sensing and pattern matching (humans learn by observing patterns through use of various senses). Machine learning technologies have greatly advanced in the last few years.
2. Commonsense reasoning relates to human thinking. ASP and systems such as s(CASP) provide the wherewithal to elegantly automate commonsense reasoning.

Note that sensing and pattern matching corresponds to Kahneman's System 1 thinking, and reasoning to Kahneman's System 2 thinking [33]. Just as it is hard for a human to explain the information they have acquired through senses (for example, it will be very hard for someone to explain why they believe that the sound they heard is the sound of a siren), explaining their own decisions has been a problem for machine learning systems. Even understanding natural language involves sensing and pattern matching. Humans hear or read a sentence and are quickly able to understand the knowledge implicit in that sentence. Note that commonsense knowledge may also be used in this sensing and pattern matching process [53]. The knowledge acquired through sensing and pattern matching is represented in some manner in our mind. Next, to draw further conclusions, humans perform reasoning over this knowledge that resides in the mind. This reasoning may also involve using (additional) commonsense knowledge that has been acquired over a period of time and that also resides in our mind in some form. For example, once the sound of the siren is heard, its occurrence is represented in our mind as knowledge. This knowledge may prompt us to find a safe spot as we know that the siren sound is announcing a tornado in the area (commonsense knowledge for those who live in the plains of Texas).

We believe that AI systems can be built better by using (i) machine learning technologies for sensing (seeing, hearing, etc.), and (ii) goal-directed ASP systems such as s(CASP) for reasoning [28]. This is in contrast to using machine learning alone. In this framework, machine learning systems or a neurosymbolic system [53] will translate a picture, video, sound, text, etc., to knowledge expressed as predicates. These predicates capture the relevant knowledge in a manner similar to how humans represent knowledge in their mind. This knowledge gleaned from "senses" and represented as predicates is further augmented with commonsense knowledge expressed in s(CASP) as default rules, integrity constraints, etc. In real life, commonsense knowledge is learned and stored in our mind throughout our life. Next, a question that we may want to answer against this combined knowledge can be treated as a query, and executed using the s(CASP) system. This framework can be used to develop, for example, an autonomous driving system [35] or a goal-oriented interactive conversational agent that can actually "understand" human dialogs [43,55].

2.1   Deduction, Abduction, and Induction

A significant part of commonsense reasoning can be emulated with defaults, integrity constraints, and assumption-based reasoning [18,23,37,47]. ASP obviously supports deduction. Default rules can be viewed as inductive generalizations, and assumption-based reasoning can be viewed as abduction. Thus, the three major modes of reasoning—deduction, abduction, and induction [19]—are naturally supported within ASP. Consider the proposition p, q, and the formula $p \Rightarrow q$.

Deduction: Given premises p and $p \Rightarrow q$, we *deduce* q. Suppose we are given the premises that Tweety is a bird (*bird(tweety)*), and the formula $\forall X bird(X) \Rightarrow flies(X)$. From these two premises, we can deduce that *flies(tweety)* holds, i.e., Tweety can fly. Obviously, such deductive reasoning is easily expressed in ASP.

Abduction: Given the observation q and the premise $p \Rightarrow q$, we *abduce* p. Suppose we observe Tweety flying (*flies(tweety)*), and we know that $\forall X bird(X) \Rightarrow flies(X)$. From these, we can *abduce* that *bird(tweety)* holds, i.e., we assume (or advance the most likely explanation) that Tweety is a bird. Note that there may be other explanations, e.g., Tweety may be the name of an airplane. Generally, the set of abduced literals is fixed in advance. Abductive reasoning in ASP is elegantly modeled via possible worlds semantics. If we make an assumption p, i.e., declare p to be abducible, then we can assert via an *even loop over negation*:

```
p :- not _notp.            _notp :- not p.
```

where _notp is a dummy proposition. This even loop will result in two possible worlds: one in which p is true and one in which p is false. It should be noted that abductive reasoning is, essentially, assumption-based reasoning. Humans perform assumption-based reasoning all the time [18].

Induction: Given instances of p and corresponding instances of q that may be related, we may induce $p \Rightarrow q$. Thus, given the observations that Tweety is a bird and Tweety can fly, Sam is a bird and Sam can fly, Polly is a bird and Polly can fly, and so on, we may *induce* the formula *bird(X)* $\Rightarrow$ *flies(X)*. Induction, of course, relates to learning associations between data. Induced rules can be elegantly captured as an answer set program. This is because ASP can be used to represent defaults with exceptions, which allows us to elegantly represent inductive generalizations. Consider the following rule:

```
flies(X):- bird(X), not abnormal_bird(X).
abnormal_bird(X):- penguin(X).
```

The above default rule with exception, namely, *normally birds fly unless they are penguins*, elegantly captures the rule that a human may form in their mind after observing birds and their ability to fly. The list of exceptions can grow (ostrich, wounded bird, baby bird, ...). Similarly, the list of defaults rules can grow. For instance, we may have a separate rule for planes being able to fly. Explainable machine learning tools that induce default theories have been developed [49,50] that are comparable in accuracy to traditionally popular tools such as XGBoost [13] and Multilayer Perceptron [1,26].

Given that deduction, abduction, and induction fit into the framework of ASP well, it gives us confidence that ASP can be a good means of representing commonsense knowledge and reasoning over it.

2.2   Representing Commonsense Knowledge in ASP/s(CASP)

As stated earlier, a large portion of the human thought process can be largely emulated by supporting (i) default rules with exceptions and preferences, (ii) integrity constraints, and (iii) multiple possible worlds. As explained earlier, default rules with exceptions express inductive generalizations, and are used by humans for making deductions. Similarly, multiple possible worlds help in abduction, or assumption-based reasoning. Integrity constraints allow us to prune unfruitful paths in our abductive reasoning process. Unfruitful paths in the deductive reasoning process are pruned by adding conditions to rule bodies.

Default Reasoning with Exceptions and Preferences: Humans use *default reasoning* [23] to jump to conclusions. These conclusions may be revised later in light of new knowledge. For example, if we are told that Tweety is a bird, and then asked whether Tweety flies, we will immediately answer, yes, it does. However, later if we are told that Tweety is a penguin, we will withdraw the conclusion about Tweety's flying ability, labeling Tweety as an *exception*. Thus, human reasoning is non-monotonic in nature, meaning that conclusions may be withdrawn as new knowledge becomes available. Humans use this sort of *default reasoning* to jump to conclusions all the time, and if they find the assumptions made to jump to this conclusion to be incorrect, they revise their conclusion. Multiple default conclusions can be drawn in some situations, and humans will use additional reasoning to *prefer* one default over another. Thus, default rules with exceptions and preferences capture most of the deductive reasoning we perform. (More details on default reasoning can be found elsewhere [23,37]). It should be noted that expert knowledge is nothing but a set of default rules about a specialized topic [23].

Classical logic is unable to model default reasoning and non-monotonicity in an elegant way. We need a formalism that is non-monotonic and can support defaults to model commonsense reasoning. ASP is such a formalism. ASP supports both NAF (not p) as well as *strong negation* (-p), where p is a proposition or a predicate. A strongly negated predicate has to be explicitly defined, just as positive predicates are. Combining these two forms of negations results in nuanced reasoning closer to how humans reason:

1. p: denotes that p is *definitely* true.
2. not -p: denotes that p *maybe* true (i.e., no evidence that p is false).
3. not p ∧ not -p: denotes that p is unknown (i.e., no evidence of either p or -p being true).
4. not p: denotes that p *may* be false (no evidence that p is true).
5. -p: denotes that p is *definitely* false.

The above insight can be used, for example, to model the exceptions to Tweety's ability to fly in two possible ways. Consider the rules:

```
flies(X):- bird(X), not abnormal_bird(X).        % default
abnormal_bird(X):- penguin(X).                   % exception
```

which state that if we know nothing about a bird, X, we conclude that it flies. This is in contrast to the rules:

```
flies(X):- bird(X), not abnormal_bird(X).        % default
abnormal_bird(X):- not -penguin(X).              % exception
```

which states that a bird can fly only if we can *explicitly* rule out that it is a penguin. So in the latter case, if we know nothing about a bird, we will conclude that it *does not* fly. Which of the two rules one will use depends on how conservative or aggressive one wants to be in jumping to the (default) conclusion. Note that exceptions can have exceptions, which in turn can have their own exceptions, and so on. For example, animals normally don't fly, unless they are birds. Thus, birds are exception to the default of not flying. Birds, in turn, normally fly, unless they are penguins. Thus, a penguin is an exception to the exception for not flying. Defaults, exceptions, exceptions to exceptions, and so on, allow humans to perform reasoning elegantly in an *elaboration tolerant* manner [11,23].

Integrity Constraints: ASP can also model integrity constraints elegantly. An integrity constraint is a rule of the form:

$$\text{false:- } p_1, p_2, \ldots, p_n.$$

which states that the conjunction of p_1, p_2, through p_n is false (the keyword false is often omitted). Integrity constraints elegantly model global invariants or restrictions that our knowledge must satisfy, e.g., p and -p cannot be true at the same time, denoted

$$\text{false:- } p, -p.$$

Humans indeed use integrity constraints in their everyday reasoning: as restrictions (two humans cannot occupy the same spot) and invariants (a human must breath to stay alive). Note that integrity constraints are *global* constraints, in that they eliminate possible worlds. Unfruitful paths during deductive reasoning are eliminated by adding appropriate conditions to the rule-bodies. Note that in ASP, integrity constraints may also arise due to *odd loops over negation* (OLON), i.e., rules of the form:

$$p(\bar{t}) \text{ :- } G, \text{ not } p(\bar{t}).$$

where $p(\bar{t})$ is a predicate and G is a conjunction of goals. In absence of an alternative proof for $p(\bar{t})$, the only admissible model for the above rule is $p(\bar{t}) =$ false, G = false, which amounts to the global constraint that G must be false.

Possible Worlds: Humans can represent *multiple possible worlds* in parallel in their minds and reason over each. For example, in the real world, birds do not talk like humans, while in a cartoon world, birds (cartoon characters) can talk.

Humans can maintain the distinction between various worlds in their minds and reason within each one of them. These multiple worlds may have aspects that are common (birds can fly in both the real and cartoon worlds) and aspects that are disjoint (birds can talk only in the cartoon world). Unlike Prolog, ASP/s(CASP) support multiple possible worlds. (See also the example about Annie and David teaching programming languages in the introductory paper of this volume [51]).

3   The s(CASP) System

The s(CASP) system [4] supports predicates, constraints over non-ground variables, uninterpreted functions, and, most importantly, a top-down, query-driven execution strategy for ASP. These features make it possible to return answers with non-ground variables (possibly including constraints among them) and compute partial models by returning only the fragment of a stable model that is necessary to support the answer to a given query. The s(CASP) system supports constructive negation based on a disequality constraint solver, and unlike Prolog's negation as failure and ASP's default negation, not p(X) can return bindings for X on success, i.e., bindings for which the call p(X) would have failed.

The s(CASP) system is based on the earlier s(ASP) system [40], and also supports constraints over reals. The s(CASP) system provides support for full Prolog, however, in addition, it also supports coinductive (circular, or assumption-based) reasoning, constructive negation, dual rules, and support for universally quantified variables. These are explained briefly next. More details can be found elsewhere [4,5,40].

Coinductive Reasoning: Coinductive reasoning is crucial for s(CASP). Answer set programs may contain circular rules, for example:

```
p:- not q.              q:- not p.
```

If we ask the query ?-p in Prolog with these rules, execution will loop forever. This is because p calls to not q, which calls q, which calls not p, which then calls p. If we allow coinductive or circular reasoning [45,46], then the query p should succeed. Essentially, we are stating that p succeeds if we *assume* p to hold. This yields the answer set in which p is true and q false. Note also that at least one intervening negation is required between a call and its recursive descendent for coinductive success in s(CASP). This prevents *positive loops*, i.e., loops with no intervening negation, from succeeding, and allows us to stay faithful to stable model semantics (in contrast, such positive loops will not terminate under *completion semantics* as realized in Prolog). Thus, given the rule:

```
p :- p.
```

the query ?- p. will fail in s(CASP), while the query ?- not p. will succeed [4,40]. More details can be found elsewhere [40,45].

Constraints and OLON rules: Global constraints of the form

```
false :- p₁(t̄₁), ..., pₙ(t̄ₙ).
```

are suitably transformed and appended to each top level query to ensure that each constraint is enforced. Global constraints can also implicitly arise due to OLON rules. These are analyzed at compile time and the appropriate constraint generated and appended to a top-level query [4, 40].

Constructive Negation: Since s(CASP) allows general predicates that could be negated, support for constructive negation becomes essential. Consider a program consisting of the simple fact:

```
p(a).
```

If we pose the query ?-not p(X), it should succeed with answer X ≠ a. Intuitively, X ≠ a means that X can be any term not unifiable with a. To support constructive negation, the implementation has to keep track of values that a variable cannot take. The unification algorithm has to be extended, therefore, to account for such disequality-constrained values. The s(CASP) system incorporates [4, 40] constructive negation.

Dual Rules: ASP assumes that programs have been *completed* [23, 39]. To complete a program, the s(CASP) system will add *dual* rules [2] to the program. The procedure to add the dual rules is relatively simple and can be found elsewhere [4]. An additional complication in computing the dual rules is the need to handle existential variables. Consider the following very simple rule:

```
p(X):- not q(X,Y).
```

This rule corresponds to the Horn clause:

$$\forall X(p(X) \Leftarrow \exists Y \ not \ q(X,Y))$$

Its dual will be:

$$\forall X(not\_p(X) \Leftarrow \forall Y \ q(X,Y))$$

which, in s(CASP), will be represented as:

```
not_p(X):- forall(Y, q1(X,Y)).        q1(X,Y):- q(X,Y).
```

Universal quantification in the body of the dual rule is needed because, for example, for the goal not p(a) to succeed, we must prove that q(a, Y) holds for every possible value of Y. The s(CASP) system handles all these issues and produces dual rules for arbitrary programs. The execution of the *forall*, however, is non-trivial, as often times the foralls are nested.

4 Applications

Several advanced applications that automate commonsense reasoning using ASP and s(CASP) have been developed. Most prominent is the CHeF system [15] which emulates the expertise of a cardiologist to automatically generate treatment for congestive heart failure. Our studies show that the CHeF system performs on par with a cardiologist. The s(CASP) system has also been used by others to develop intelligent applications [36,41]. With respect to the framework above, where we use machine learning for sensing and pattern matching and s(CASP) for commonsense reasoning, two major strands have been pursued.

Image Understanding: A major task in AI is to understand a picture and answer questions about it. Current approaches for visual question answering (VQA) are solely based on machine learning. These approaches train on a collection of images together with the question-answer pairs for each image. Once the model has been learned, a new image along with a question is given, and the expectation is that a correct answer will be generated. Given that a generated answer cannot be justified, or may not be accurate, an alternative approach is to use machine learning for translating an image into a set of predicates that capture the objects in the image, their characteristics and spatial relationships. Commonsense knowledge about the image's domain can be coded in ASP. Next, the question to be answered is translated into an ASP query, which is then executed using s(CASP) against the knowledge (represented as predicates) captured from the image augmented with commonsense knowledge of the domain. 100% accuracy in answering questions is achieved in some of the VQA datasets [7]. The process is similar to how humans answer questions about an image, and can be leveraged to realize reliable autonomous driving systems [35].

Natural Language Understanding (NLU): A combination of machine learning and commonsense reasoning can be used for NLU as well. The idea is to generate predicates from text using large language models such as GPT-3 [10] via the use of *in-context learning* or *fine-tuning*. These predicates represent the meaning of the sentence, i.e., its *deep structure*. Commonsense reasoning can then be performed over these predicates to draw further conclusions, ask for missing information, and check for consistency of the information in the sentence. We have used this approach for qualitative reasoning, solving simple word problems in Algebra, and developing conversational agents that can interact with a human while "understanding" what he/she is saying [43,55]. Essentially, we emulate how a person understands sentences and carries on a conversation. Commonsense knowledge is also embedded in the LLM, so just like humans, commonsense knowledge is used at two levels—in "understanding" text as predicates and subsequent reasoning.

5   Conclusion

Learning/pattern-matching and reasoning are crucial to human intelligence. It is our belief that effective AI systems can only be obtained by combining machine learning for sensing/pattern-matching and a Prolog system that encapsulates ASP, such as s(CASP), for commonsense reasoning. While the applications developed so far are in narrow domains, it is our position that the path to building AI applications that perform as well as humans goes through logic programming. Machine learning *alone* cannot be used for modeling human thinking, as fundamentally it is a statistical technique. If this was indeed possible, then we believe that nature would have already produced an intelligent being—as intelligent as humans, or more—based on pattern matching and operating on instincts alone. As we move up the evolutionary chain towards more intelligent life-forms culminating in humans, reasoning abilities improve. "Lower" life forms sometimes do have better sensing capabilities, e.g., dogs can smell better, eagles can see better, etc., but a combination of instinct and reasoning puts humans on top of the evolutionary chain. Therefore, just as humans rely on both learning/sensing/pattern-recognition *and* reasoning, an AI system that aims to achieve human-level performance must follow the same path [21,53]. This is also evident in large language models such as GPT-3 and ChatGPT [10] that use pattern matching on a massive scale to generate a human-like response. Due to the statistical nature of LLMs, we can never be certain that the generated text is correct, consistent, and useful [8]. Logic is essential for producing a consistent, correct, and assuredly-useful response.

In conclusion, Prolog is an indispensable part of computing's and AI's landscape. We believe that it is an essential component in achieving Artificial General Intelligence (AGI) [32,54]—AI's purported holy grail for some—whether we agree with that goal or not. Considerable research is still needed to: (i) improve the s(CASP) system (by incorporating tabling, constraints, coroutining, etc.) and making it more efficient; (ii) develop machine learning systems that extract knowledge as predicates from arbitrary text & images; and, (iii) develop methods to automatically extract commonsense knowledge and represent it in s(CASP). We hope that these tasks will be completed in the coming years.

Acknowledgements. We are grateful to the anonymous reviewers and to David S. Warren for insightful comments and suggestions that resulted in significant improvements to the paper. Authors acknowledge partial support from NSF grants IIS 1910131, IIP 1916206, and US DoD.

References

1. Aggarwal, C.C.: Neural Networks and Deep Learning. Springer, Cham (2018). https://doi.org/10.1007/978-3-319-94463-0
2. Alferes, J.J., Pereira, L.M., Swift, T.: Abduction in well-founded semantics and generalized stable models via tabled dual programs. TPLP **4**(4), 383–428 (2004)
3. Areias, M., Rocha, R.: Multi-dimensional lock-free arrays for multithreaded mode-directed tabling in prolog. Concurr. Comput. Pract. Exp. **31**(5), 1–16 (2019)
4. Arias, J., Carro, M., Salazar, E., Marple, K., Gupta, G.: Constraint answer set programming without grounding. TPLP **18**(3–4), 337–354 (2018)
5. Arias, J., Carro, M., Chen, Z., Gupta, G.: Modeling and reasoning in event calculus using goal-directed constraint answer set programming. TPLP **22**(1), 51–80 (2022)
6. Arias, J., Carro, M.: Description, implementation, and evaluation of a generic design for tabled CLP. TPLP **19**(3), 412–448 (2019)
7. Basu, K., Shakerin, F., Gupta, G.: AQuA: ASP-Based Visual Question Answering. In: Komendantskaya, E., Liu, Y.A. (eds.) PADL 2020. LNCS, vol. 12007, pp. 57–72. Springer, Cham (2020). https://doi.org/10.1007/978-3-030-39197-3_4

8. Borji, A.: A categorical archive of chatgpt failures (2023). Preprint arXiv:2302.03494
9. Brewka, G., Eiter, T., Truszczynski, M.: Answer set programming at a glance. Commun. ACM **54**(12), 92–103 (2011)
10. Brown, T., Mann, B., et al.: Language models are few-shot learners. In: Proceedings NeurIPS, vol. 33, pp. 1877–1901. Curran Associates Inc. (2020)
11. Baral, C.: Knowledge Representation, Reasoning and Declarative Problem Solving. Cambridge University Press, Cambridge (2003)
12. Carro, M., Hermenegildo, M.V.: Concurrency in prolog using threads and a shared database. In: De Schreye, D. (ed.), Proceedings ICLP, pp. 320–334. MIT Press (1999)
13. Chen, T., Guestrin, C.: XGBoost: a scalable tree boosting system. In: Proceedings of the 22nd ACM SIGKDD, KDD 2016, pp. 785–794 (2016)
14. Chen, W., Kifer, M., Warren, D.S.: HILOG: a foundation for higher-order logic programming. J. Log. Program. **15**(3), 187–230 (1993)
15. Chen, Z., Marple, K., Salazar, E., Gupta, G., Tamil, L.: A physician advisory system for chronic heart failure management based on knowledge patterns. Theory Pract. Log. Program. **16**(5–6), 604–618 (2016)
16. Colmerauer, A., Roussel, P.: The birth of prolog. In: History of Programm Languages Conference (HOPL-II), pp. 37–52. ACM (1993)
17. Costa, V.S., de Castro Dutra, I., Rocha, R.: Threads and or-parallelism unified. Theory Pract. Log. Program. **10**(4–6), 417–432 (2010)
18. Dietz Saldanha, E.A., Hölldobler, S., Pereira, L.M.: Our themes on abduction in human reasoning: a synopsis. In: Abduction in Cognition and Action: Logical Reasoning, Scientific Inquiry, and Social Practice, pp. 279–293 (2021)
19. Flach, P.A., Kakas, A.C.: Abductive and Inductive Reasoning: Background. In: Flach, P.A., Kakas, A.C. (eds.) Abduction and Inductionand Issues, pp. 1–27. Springer, Cham (2000). https://doi.org/10.1007/978-94-017-0606-3_1
20. Frühwirth, T.W.: Theory and practice of constraint handling rules. J. Log. Program. **37**(1–3), 95–138 (1998)
21. d'Avila Garcez, A., Lamb, L.C.: Neurosymbolic AI: The 3rd Wave (2020). arXiv: 2012.05876 [cs.AI]
22. Gebser, M., et al.: Potassco: the potsdam answer set solving collection. AI Commun. **24**(2), 107–124 (2011). https://doi.org/10.3233/AIC-2011-0491
23. Gelfond, M., Kahl, Y.: Knowledge Representation, Reasoning, and the Design of Intelligent Agents: An Answer Set Programming Approach. Cambridge Univ. Press, Cambridge (2014)
24. Gelfond, M., Lifschitz, V.: The stable model semantics for logic programming. In: ICLP/SLP, vol. 88, pp. 1070–1080 (1988)
25. Gunning, D., Chaudhri, V.K., Clark, P., Grosof, B., et al.: Project halo update - progress toward digital aristotle. AI Mag. **31**(3), 33–58 (2010)
26. Gupta, G., et al.: Logic-based explainable and incremental machine learning. In: Warren, D.S., Dahl, V., Eiter, T., Hermenegildo, M., Kowalski, R., Rossi, F. (eds.) Prolog: The Next 50 Years. LNCS (LNAI), vol. 13900, pp. 346–358. Springer, Cham (2023). https://doi.org/10.1007/978-3-031-35254-6_28
27. Gupta, G.: Next generation of logic programming systems. Technical report, 2003. Dept. of Comp. Sci., UT Dallas (2003)
28. Gupta, G., et al.: Automated commonsense reasoning. In: Proceedings of the GDE 2022 (2022). https://utdallas.edu/~gupta/csr-scasp.pdf
29. Hanus, M.: From logic to functional logic programs. Theory Pract. Log. Program. **22**(4), 538–554 (2022)

30. Hermenegildo, M.V., Morales, J.F., Lopez-Garcia, P., Carro, M.: Types, modes and so much more - the prolog way. In: Warren, D.S., Dahl, V., Eiter, T., Hermenegildo, M., Kowalski, R., Rossi, F. (eds.) Prolog: The Next 50 Years. LNCS (LNAI), vol. 13900, pp. 23–37. Springer, Cham (2023). https://doi.org/10.1007/978-3-031-35254-6_2

31. Hermenegildo, M.V., et al.: An overview of ciao and its design philosophy. Theory Pract. Log. Program. **12**(1–2), 219–252 (2012)

32. Hutter, M.: Universal Artificial Intellegence. TTCSAES, Springer, Heidelberg (2005). https://doi.org/10.1007/b138233

33. Kahneman, D.: Thinking. Fast and Slow. Farrar, Straus and Giroux (2011)

34. Körner, P., et al.: Fifty Years of Prolog and Beyond. Theory and Practice of Logic Programming, pp. 1–83 (2022)

35. Kothawade, S., Khandelwal, V., Basu, K., Wang, H., Gupta, G.: AUTO-DISCERN: autonomous driving using common sense reasoning. In: Proceedings of the ICLP Workshops: GDE 2021, vol. 2970, CEUR Workshop Proceedings. CEUR-WS.org (2021)

36. Kowalski, R., Davila, J., Sartor, G., Calejo, M.: Logical English for law and education. In: Warren, D.S., Dahl, V., Eiter, T., Hermenegildo, M., Kowalski, R., Rossi, F. (eds.) Prolog: The Next 50 Years. LNCS (LNAI), vol. 13900, pp. 287–299. Springer, Cham (2023). https://doi.org/10.1007/978-3-031-35254-6_24

37. Kowalski, R.A.: Computational Logic and Human Thinking. Cambridge University Press, Cambridge (2011)

38. Kowalski, R.A.: Logic for Problem Solving. North Holland (1979)

39. Lloyd, J.W.: Foundations of Logic Programming, 2nd edn. Springer, Heidelberg (1987). https://doi.org/10.1007/978-3-642-83189-8

40. Marple, K., et al.: Computing stable models of normal logic programs without grounding. Preprint arXiv:1709.00501 (2017)

41. Morris, J.: Blawx: user-friendly goal-directed answer set programming for rules as code. In: Proceedings of the Programming Language and the Law (ProLaLa) (2023)

42. Mueller, E.T.: Commonsense Reasoning: An Event Calculus Based Approach. Morgan Kaufmann, San Francisco (2014)

43. Rajasekharan, A., Zeng, Y., Padalkar, P., Gupta, G.: Reliable natural language understanding with large language models and answer set programming (2023). Preprint arXiv:2302.03780; in Proc. ICLP'23 (Tech. Comm.) (2023, to appear)

44. Rocha, R., Silva, F.M.A., Costa, V.S.: On applying or-parallelism and tabling to logic programs. Theory Pract. Log. Program. **5**(1–2), 161–205 (2005)

45. Salazar, E.: Proof-theoretic Foundations of Normal Logic Programs. Ph.D. thesis, Department of Computer Science, Univ. of Texas at Dallas (2019)

46. Simon, L., Bansal, A., Mallya, A., Gupta, G.: Co-logic programming: extending logic programming with coinduction. In: Arge, L., Cachin, C., Jurdziński, T., Tarlecki, A. (eds.) ICALP 2007. LNCS, vol. 4596, pp. 472–483. Springer, Heidelberg (2007). https://doi.org/10.1007/978-3-540-73420-8_42

47. Stenning, K., van Lambalgen, M.: Human Reasoning and Cognitive Science. MIT Press, Boston (2008)

48. Sterling, L., Shapiro, E.: The Art of Prolog. MITPress, Cambridge (1994)

49. Wang, H., Gupta, G.: FOLD-R++: a scalable toolset for automated inductive learning of default theories from mixed data. In: Hanus, M., Igarashi, A. (eds.) Functional and Logic Programming. FLOPS 2022. LNCS, vol. 13215, pp. 224–242. Springer, Cham (2022). https://doi.org/10.1007/978-3-030-99461-7_13

50. Wang, H., Shakerin, F., Gupta, G.: FOLD-RM: efficient scalable explainable AI. TPLP **22**(5), 658–677 (2022)

51. Warren, D.S.: Introduction to Prolog. In: Warren, D.S., Dahl, V., Eiter, T., Hermenegildo, M., Kowalski, R., Rossi, F. (eds.) Prolog: The Next 50 Years. LNCS (LNAI), vol. 13900, pp. 3–19. Springer, Cham (2023). https://doi.org/10.1007/978-3-031-35254-6_1

52. Wielemaker, J., Schrijvers, T., Triska, M., Lager, T.: Swi-prolog. Theory Pract. Log. Program. **12**(1–2), 67–96 (2012)

53. Wikipedia. Neurosymbolic AI. https://en.wikipedia.org/wiki/Neuro-symbolic_AI#. Accessed Feb 2022

54. Wikipedia contributors. Artificial general intelligence - Wikipedia, the free encyclopedia, 2023. https://en.wikipedia.org/w/index.php?title=Artificial_general_intelligence&oldid=1148436187. Accessed 8 Apr 2023

55. Zeng, Y., Rajasekharan, A., et al.: Automated interactive domain-specific conversational agents that understand human dialogs. Preprint arXiv:2302.08941 (2023)

Writing Correct Prolog Programs

David S. Warren[⊠] [iD]

Stony Brook University, Stony Brook, USA
warren@cs.stonybrook.edu

Abstract. This article describes a somewhat new way of thinking about Prolog programming. It was motivated by a video and presentation by Leslie Lamport [6] in which he argued for a simple model of computation in which, to develop a program, one uses conventional mathematical language with the necessary invariants being front and center. He used as a motivating example the problem of finding the greatest common divisor (GCD) of two positive integers. I felt his model of computation was too simple to be useful for complex programs, but I liked his essential idea. I thought I'd like to apply it to the computational model(s) of logic programming, in particular to Prolog. It led to a somewhat different way of thinking about how to develop Prolog programs that takes advantage of both bottom-up and top-down thinking. This article explores this program development strategy using the GCD problem as a motivating example.

1 Inductive Definitions

Prolog is basically a language of inductive definitions. (See M. Denecker's work including [3,8].) We all learn about inductive definitions early in our mathematics education. The first definition I remember learning was of the factorial function. Factorial is described informally as a function of natural numbers where $n! = n * (n-1) * (n-2) * ... * 1$. Even though this seemed pretty clear to me (at least for positive integers), I was told that the "..." in this purported definition isn't precise enough. A better way to define factorial is needed, and an inductive definition does the job:

```
n! = 1 if n=0
n! = n*(n-1)! if n>0
```

The first clause specifies the value of factorial of 0 directly; the second clause specifies the values for all natural numbers greater than 0. It's clear how one can use this definition to find the value of $n!$ for any n. For example, say we want the value of 4!. We know $0! = 1$ from the first clause; from the second clause, we know $1! = 1*0!$, and since we've established that $0! = 1$, then $1! = 1*1 = 1$; again from the second clause $2! = 2*1! = 2*1 = 2$; again $3! = 3*2! = 3*2 = 6$; and finally $4! = 4*3! = 4*6 = 24$. In the same way we can find the value of factorial for *any* natural number by starting with 0 and computing the values of factorial

D. S. Warren et al. (Eds.): Prolog: The Next 50 Years, LNAI 13900, pp. 62–70, 2023.
https://doi.org/10.1007/978-3-031-35254-6_5

for all numbers up to and including the one of interest. This is ensured by the fact that all natural numbers can be reached by starting with 0 and adding 1 some (finite) number of times.

Here we have defined a function inductively. We can also (or more generally) defines sets inductively. To define a set inductively, one first specifies a universe of elements. Then one explicitly gives some subset of them as members of the desired set, and provides a set of rules. Each rule says that if certain elements of the universe are in the desired set, then some other element(s) must be in the set. This defines a subset of the universe: the smallest set that contains the explicit elements and is closed under the rules.

As another, perhaps slightly more interesting, example of an inductive definition, we consider GCD, the Greatest Common Divisor relation. The GCD of two non-zero natural numbers is the largest natural number that evenly divides them both. E.g., the GCD of 18 and 24 is 6. We'll want to define $gcd(n, m, d)$ to mean that d is the GCD of the non-zero natural numbers n and m. An inductive definition of this set is:

```
gcd(n,n,n) for n > 0
gcd(n+m,m,d) if gcd(n,m,d)
gcd(n,n+m,d) if gcd(n,m,d)
```

The first (base) clause says that the GCD of a number and itself is that number. The second clause, a rule, says that if d is the GCD of n and m, then it is also the GCD of $n + m$ and m. And the third is similar. We'll leave it to the reader to compute a few of these triples. For example, starting from the single basic element $gcd(1, 1, 1)$ we see that it generates pairs with GCD of 1, i.e., pairs that are relatively prime.

There are two nice properties of inductive definitions that use well-defined and computable conditions:

1. They come with a mechanism to compute their values, as we have seen, by starting with the base clauses, which give the first (unconditional) set members; and then continuing to apply the other clauses until we get the answer we want (or maybe all the answers.) This iterative process can serve as a computational model for inductive definitions.
2. They provide a ready-made structure for proving properties that hold of all members of the inductively defined sets: we just need to show that the desired property holds for the unconditional members defined by the base clauses, and that if the property holds for the set elements used in the conditions of an inductive clause and the condition itself holds, then the property holds for the newly specified member. Intuitively our reasoning for why this is true can follow exactly the process we used to add members to the set: we see that each *initial* member and each *added* member must have the desired property, so that *all* members of the set must have it. The Induction Principle guarantees that the property holds for *every* member of the defined set.

As an example of a proof, say we want to prove that if $gcd(n, m, d)$ is in the set defined inductively above, then d is indeed the greatest common divisor of n

and m. For the base clause, clearly the greatest common divisor of two identical numbers is that number itself. For the inductive clauses, if d divides n and m, then it clearly divides $n+m$. And if there were a greater divisor of $n+m$ and m, that greater divisor would have to divide n, contradicting the assumption that d is the GCD of n and m. And similarly, for the other inductive clause. So. we have proved the desired property. In fact our (perhaps implicit) recognition of this property was what led us to write this definition in the first place.

The computational model and the proof method are fundamentally intertwined. When we wrote the inductive definition we had in mind the property we wanted the set to have, and ensured that each rule preserved that property. I.e., we had the proof of correctness directly in mind when we wrote the definition.

2   From Inductive Definition to Prolog Program

We now have an inductive definition of the GCD relation, which has been proved to be correct. But we want a Prolog program for finding GCD. How do we turn this inductive definition into a correctly running Prolog program?

We take the inductive definition that was written in English using conventional mathematical notation:

```
gcd(n,n,n) for n > 0
gcd(n+m,m,d)) if gcd(n,m,d)
gcd(n,n+m,d)) if gcd(n,m,d)
```

and we directly convert it to a Prolog program. We note that there have been many extensions to the Prolog language, so it makes a difference which dialect of Prolog we are working with. For our purposes here, we will assume a relatively primitive Prolog, essentially ISO Prolog. But there are Prolog systems that support functional notation and general numeric constraints. In these Prologs different transformations, perhaps including none, would be necessary.

ISO Prolog doesn't support functional notation, so we need to introduce new variables (identifiers starting with upper-case letters) for the sums in the atomic formulas. And we can convert the sums to use Prolog's general arithmetic construct, is/2:

```
gcd(N,N,N) :- N > 0.
gcd(NpM,M,D)) :- gcd(N,M,D), NpM is N + M.
gcd(N,NpM,D)) :- gcd(N,M,D), NpM is N + M.
```

This form now is a Prolog program in that it satisfies Prolog syntax. However, to determine if it will correctly execute to solve a problem, we have to consider the queries we will ask. In our case, we want to provide two integers and have Prolog determine the GCD of those two integers. This mode of the queries we will ask is denoted by gcd(+,+,-), where + indicates a value is given and - indicates a value is to be returned by the computation. Here we intend to give the first two arguments and expect the have the third one returned. And we also need to know the mode of each subquery in order to determine if the definition can be executed by the Prolog processor.

Correct Prolog evaluation depends on subquery modes in two ways: 1) subqueries must have only finitely many answers, and 2) Prolog's predefined predicates (like is/2) often work only for particular modes and so the modes for calls to those predicates must be acceptable.

We must check that the modes of our Prolog program for GCD are correct. The first requirement for correct evaluation of a query (or subgoal) is that it must have only finitely many answers. Since Prolog uses backward-chaining, it poses a number of subgoals during its computation starting from an initial goal. We must be sure that every one of those subgoals has only finitely many answers. Otherwise, Prolog would go into an infinite loop trying to generate all infinitely many answers to such a subgoal. For example, the goal gcd(27,63,D) has only finitely many instances in the set defined by the gcd program; actually only one instance, with D=9. But the goal gcd(N,63,9) has infinitely many instances in the defined set; including all those with N being a multiple of 9. The lesson here is that we need to understand the *modes* of all subgoals generated by a Prolog computation. The *mode* of a subgoal describes where variables appear in it, and this affects whether it matches infinitely many set members or not.

We note that since Prolog calls goals in the body of a rule in a left-to-right order, the mode of a subgoal is determined by the success of goals to its left in the rule body, as well as by the mode of this initial call. We assume that the initial goal that we pose to this program will have the first two fields as numbers and the third field as a variable. I.e., we'll be asking to find the GCD of two positive integers. This mode is expressed as gcd(+,+,-).

We next explore the modes of the subgoals in our Prolog program above. Under this mode assumption, since any call to gcd will have its first two arguments bound to values, the variable N in the subgoal N > 0 in the first clause will have a value as required by Prolog so this condition can be checked.

In the second clause NpM and M will be integers (by the mode assumption), so in the first subgoal, NpM is N + M, NpM and M will have values, but N will be a variable. That means that the call to gcd(N,M,D) will have mode (-,+,-), and this subgoal will have infinitely many answers. So, this Prolog program will not execute correctly. (The third rule suffers from a similar problem.) We need N to get a value before the call to gcd(N,M,D). N appears in the second subgoal of that condition, so let's try evaluating that subgoal first. To this end we move the is/2 goals earlier and get a new program:

```
gcd(N,N,N) :- N > 0.
gcd(NpM,M,D)) :- NpM is N + M, gcd(N,M,D).
gcd(N,NpM,D)) :- NpM is N + M, gcd(N,M,D).
```

Now in the call to is/2, NpM and M will have values (because of the mode assumption for calls to gcd/3). Prolog, however, requires is to have the mode of is(?,+). (The "?" indicates either "+" or "-" is allowed.) Since N will not have a value, the second argument to is/2 will not have a value and this rule will result in an error when evaluated with the expected values. But we can change the is/2 to compute N from MpN and M by writing N is MpN - M. This imposes the equivalent constraint among N, M and MpN and is correctly modded for Prolog to evaluate it. Similarly fixing the third clause gives us a program:

```
gcd(N,N,N) :- N > 0.
gcd(NpM,M,D)) :- N is NpM - M, gcd(N,M,D).
gcd(N,NpM,D)) :- M is NpM - N, gcd(N,M,D).
```

In the second clause now, the first body subgoal causes N to get a value, so the second subgoal is called with N and M with values, and thus in the same mode as the original mode, that is gcd(+,+,-). Similarly for the third clause. Thus all calls to gcd/3 (and is/2) will be correctly moded.

However, there is still an issue with this program: Prolog computes with integers, not natural numbers, and so the subtraction operations might generate negative integers. But we want only positive integers. So we must add this constraint explicitly as follows:

```
gcd(N,N,N) :- N > 0.
gcd(NpM,M,D)) :- N is NpM - M, N > 0, gcd(N,M,D).
gcd(N,NpM,D)) :- M is NpM - N, M > 0, gcd(N,M,D).
```

Only when we generate a new integer do we need to check that it is positive. And we must do the check *after* the number variable gets a value to satisfy the mode requirement of </2; immediately after it gets that value is best. This is now a good Prolog program for computing the GCD of two integers. You might recognize this as the Euclidean algorithm for GCD. I.e., the Euclidean algorithm is the top-down evaluation (i.e., Prolog evaluation) of this inductive definition. Actually, we can make this algorithm slightly more efficient, and maybe make it look a bit more like Euclid's algorithm by noting in the second clause (and analogously in the third) that N will be greater than 0 only if NpM is greater than M, so we can make that check before taking the difference, getting:

```
gcd(N,N,N) :- N > 0.
gcd(NpM,M,D)) :- NpM > M, N is NpM - M, gcd(N,M,D).
gcd(N,NpM,D)) :- NpM > N, M is NpM - N, gcd(N,M,D).
```

(Renaming the variables in the third clause might make it look even more familiar.) Now we can see that only one of the three clauses can ever satisfy its comparison condition for a (correctly moded) subgoal, and so the Prolog computation is deterministic.

See Kowalski et al. [5] for another development of Euclid's algorithm, there in a more English-like dialect of Prolog.

Let's recap how we approached Prolog programming. We followed a sequence of steps, which we will describe in some generality here. They are a generalization of the steps we just used in our development of the gcd Prolog program.

1. Use inductive clauses to define the relation, a set of tuples, that characterizes the solution to the problem of interest. Use names for the relations to organize

and name sets of tuples. Above we used the name **gcd** as the predicate symbol to remind us that it is a set of triples that define the Greatest Common Divisor function. Use whatever mathematical notation is convenient. Similarly, define and use whatever sets of tuples are useful as subsidiary definitions.

2. Convert this mathematical definition into Prolog clauses, using the necessary Prolog built-ins.

3. Consider the mode of each subgoal that will be invoked during top-down evaluation of the clauses. Ensure that the subset of each relation required to answer each moded subgoal is finite. Ensure that all built-ins are invoked in modes that they support. Ensure that defined subgoals are all invoked in desired modes, by ordering the subgoals of rule bodies so their left-to-right evaluation is well-moded and efficient.

Notice that in developing this program, we did not consciously think about recursive programming. We thought about an inductive definition. Recursion is the procedural mechanism used to evaluate inductive definitions top-down. The procedural mechanism to evaluate inductive definitions bottom-up is iteration.

To understand the correctness of an inductive definition we can think iteratively; just iterate the application of the inductive rules, starting from empty relations. Intuitively, this is easier to understand than recursive programming. The recursion showed up in the final program because of the form of the rules of the inductive definition. We know the recursive evaluation will give the correct answer because top-down evaluation computes the same answer (when it terminates) as the bottom-up iterative evaluation.

Many others have noted the importance of bottom-up thinking. The deductive database community (see, e.g., [7]) looks at programs with only constant variable values, so-called Datalog programs, exclusively bottom up. And teachers of Prolog teach bottom-up evaluation, and sometimes provide bottom-up evaluators for students to use to understand the programs they write, [4].

3   The Claim

Let's look at what needs to be done to write a correct program. First we have to determine what it means for a correct program to be correct. For that we need to have an idea in our heads of what our program should do, i.e., a property the program should have, i.e., for a logic program a property that must hold of every tuple in the defined relation. And we must ensure that it contains every tuple it should. Then we have to write a program that defines a relation that has that property.

We could require that this whole process be done formally, i.e., do a formal verification of our program. In that case, we would specify the correctness property, a.k.a. the program specification, in some formal language. Then we would generate a formal proof that the program we created satisfied that specification. This turns out to be rather complicated and messy, and for large practical programs essentially undoable. Almost no large programs in practice are ever proved correct in this way. (See [2] for a discussion of relevant issues.)

In lieu of formal verification we might use informal methods that won't guarantee exact program correctness but might provide some confidence that our programs do what we want them to do. We argue that the informal program development strategy that we have described above does just that.

When we develop an inductive definition of a relation that satisfies our intuitive correctness criteria (what we want the program to do), we are thinking of bottom-up generation of a satisfying relation. And the bottom-up generation must generate correct tuples at every step. And seeing that rules always generate correct tuples is exactly what a proof of correctness requires. Indeed, the name given to the predicate is naturally a shorthand for its correctness property. We named our predicate gcd because of the Greatest Common Divisor property that we wanted its tuples to have. So, when generating an inductive definition of a relation, one has directly in mind the property all its tuples must have, and so writes rules that guarantee that property. This is exactly the thinking necessary to formulate a proof of correctness. In this way the thinking required to formulate the program is exactly the thinking require to formulate a proof of its correctness. Even if the proof is not formally carried out, the intuitive ideas of how it would be created have already been thought through.

Note, however, that such an inductive proof is not a formal proof of correctness for a Prolog program. That would require formal consideration of modes, occur-check, termination, and other important details of actual Prolog evaluation. Discussions of formal proofs of total correctness of Prolog programs in the literature tend to focus on these issues, e.g., [1].

Of course, most Prolog programs are more complicated than a single inductive definition. Most require multiple subsidiary relations to be defined and then used in more complex definitions. But each such subsidiary relation is also inductively defined and a similar methodology can be used for them. For procedural programs with while and for constructs, one needs to generate an invariant for each loop; the corresponding logic program requires a relation, with its own name and inductive definition, for each loop, thus laying bare the correctness criteria that may be hidden for iterative programs with loops.

4   Caveats

What is proposed here is an idealized methodology for developing Prolog programs. Of course, it won't always work this way. Prolog programmers learn (and are encouraged) to think about top-down execution and recursion in a procedural way. Indeed, to develop definitions that evaluate efficiently top-down, it is often necessary to think in this way. So almost always an experienced Prolog programmer will develop a program without ever thinking about how it would evaluate bottom up. My suggestion is that programmers should initially be taught this bottom-up-first methodology, and then as they advance and develop their top-down intuitions, they should always go back and look at the bottom-up meanings of their programs. As a practicing top-down Prolog programmer, I've found it often enlightening to think of my programs in a bottom-up way. Sometimes efficient top-down programs are infinite, or ridiculously explosive, as bottom-up programs. But experience can make them intuitively understandable, and thinking that way provides insight. It deepens an understanding of what the program defines and can sometimes uncover problems with it. It is also worth noting that bottom-up evaluation is independent of problem decomposition, which is a good development strategy, independent of any evaluation strategy.

Bottom-up evaluation is generally easier to understand not only because it is based on iteration instead of recursion as is top-down. Every state reachable in a bottom-up construction satisfies the desired correctness property. But in top-down, many reachable states may not satisfy the correctness property; they may be states only on a failing derivation path. This means that for top-down one must distinguish between states that satisfy the desired property and those encountered along a failing path towards a hoped-for justification. It's more to keep track of in one's head. Perhaps another way to say it is that bottom-up evaluation is intuitively simpler in part because it needs no concept of failure.

5   Conclusion

I would claim that mathematical induction provides the formal foundation of all algorithmic computation, i.e., computation intended to terminate[1]. Prolog asks programmers to give inductive definitions directly. The form of definition is particularly simple, being straightforward rules for adding members to sets. Since the programmer creates definitions thinking directly in terms of the mathematical foundations of computation, there is less of a distance between programming and proving. This makes for programs more likely to do what the programmer intends.

References

1. Apt, K.R.: Program verification and Prolog. In: Börger, E. (ed.) Specification and Validation Methods, pp. 55–95. Oxford University Press, Oxford (1993)
2. DeMillo, R., Lipton, R., Perlis, A.: Social processes and proofs of theorems and programs. In: Tymoczko, T. (ed.) New Directions in the Philosophy of Mathematics: An Anghology, pp. 237–277. Birkhauser Boston Inc., Boston (1986)
3. Denecker, M., Warren, D.S.: The logic of logic programming. CoRR, cs.LO/2304.13430, arXiv:2304.13430 (2023)
4. Hermenegildo, M.V., Morales, J.F.: Some thoughts on teaching (and preaching) Prolog. In: Warren, D.S., Dahl, V., Eiter, T., Hermenegildo, M., Kowalski, R., Rossi, F. (eds.) Prolog - The Next 50 Years. LNCS, vol. 13900, pp. 107–123. Springer, Cham (2023)
5. Kowalski, R., Quintero, J.D., Sartor, G., Calejo, M.: Logical English for law and education. In: Warren, D.S., Dahl, V., Eiter, T., Hermenegildo, M., Kowalski, R., Rossi, F. (eds.) Prolog - The Next 50 Years. LNCS, vol. 13900, pp. 287–299. Springer, Cham (2023)

---

[1] Clearly quantum computation has a different foundation. And infinite computations have their foundations in co-induction.

6. Lamport, L.: If you're not writing a program, don't use a programming language. In: LPOP 2020, November 2020. https://www.youtube.com/watch?v=wQiWwQcMKuw
7. Maier, D., Tekle, K.T., Kifer, M., Warren, D.S.: Declarative logic programming. Chap. Datalog: Concepts, History, and Outlook, pp. 3–100. Association for Computing Machinery and Morgan & Claypool, New York, NY, USA (2018). https://doi.org/10.1145/3191315.3191317
8. Vennekens, J., Denecker, M., Bruynooghe, M.: FO(ID) as an extension of dl with rules. Ann. Math. Artif. Intell. 58(1–2), 85–115 (2010)

Demonstrating Multiple Prolog Programming Techniques Through a Single Operation

Nick Bassiliades[1]([⊠]) ⓘ, Ilias Sakellariou[2] ⓘ, and Petros Kefalas[3] ⓘ

[1] School of Informatics, Aristotle University of Thessaloniki, Thessaloniki, Greece
`nbassili@csd.auth.gr`
[2] Department of Applied Informatics, University of Macedonia, Thessaloniki, Greece
`iliass@uom.edu.gr`
[3] Department of Computer Science, City College, University of York Europe Campus, Thessaloniki, Greece
`kefalas@york.citycollege.eu`

Abstract. Without doubt Prolog, as the most prominent member of the logic programming (LP) approach, presents significant differences from the mainstream programming paradigms. However, demonstrating its flexibility to larger audiences can indeed be a challenging task, since the declarative style of LP lies outside the mainstream programming languages most are familiar with. In this paper, we demonstrate how alternative implementations of a single list operation can prove to be a rather helpful tool for demonstrating a plethora of Prolog programming aspects and techniques, and some issues associated with these, such as efficiency, readability and writability of code.

Keywords: Logic Programming techniques · Prolog Flexibility · Prolog Efficiency · Prolog Education

1 Introduction and Motivation

Communicating the flexibility of the logic-based approach to problem solving supported by Prolog, to wider audiences, such as students, programmers and in general people less familiar with LP, can prove to be a somewhat complicated task. Thus, the motivation behind this paper is to demonstrate the flexibility of Prolog in coding a simple operation, commonly found in all programming environments supporting lists, by employing a variety of programming techniques. As educators, we have been teaching Prolog for many years, following a fairly standard approach of introducing the language constructs and techniques that differentiate it from other mainstream programming languages. By starting from pure Prolog syntax, declarative and operational semantics, then moving towards recursion and lists and concluding with extra-logical features and practical meta-programming techniques, gave us the opportunity to teach Prolog through a good number of examples of various complexity.

D. S. Warren et al. (Eds.): Prolog: The Next 50 Years, LNAI 13900, pp. 71–81, 2023.
https://doi.org/10.1007/978-3-031-35254-6_6

What was missing was a standard reference to a single operation that could be implemented in different ways, thus demonstrating the flexibility of the language which, however, may raise issues for discussion around declarative versus procedural approach, readability versus writability of code and simplicity versus efficiency. We found that `list_min` predicate could serve this purpose. We followed different approaches in our own institutions; either to present this example throughout the semester as we introduce concepts together with other examples, or to devote a revision session towards the end of the semester to summarise the language potential before the final exam. Results were encouraging in both approaches.

Therefore, we demonstrate how a single list operation, i.e. the minimum of a list, can prove to be a rather helpful tool to refer to a plethora of Prolog programming aspects and techniques. The benefits are numerous: (a) it is a simple operation, with which students are familiar with and thus presents no barriers in understanding its specification, (b) it has a surprising number of alternative implementations, (c) benchmarking of the alternatives is a straightforward task, allowing discussion of complexity issues that arise. The current paper contributes towards demonstrating Prolog flexibility, especially in audiences just getting familiar with Prolog, by:

- discussing how a single simple list operation can demonstrate a number of programming techniques, through alternative implementations,
- presenting how such simple code can expose a number of lower level issues of some techniques, such as garbage collection and tail recursion optimization.

The paper is not aimed to be a tutorial in Prolog, as this is presented earlier in this book [14]. It is assumed that the reader has some knowledge of the language. Additionally, our audience includes educators who would like to adopt this example throughout their courses on top of all existing material they teach as a single point of reference suitable for discussing the flexibility of the language.

2   The Challenges of Learning Prolog

Learning Prolog can indeed be a challenging task, usually attributed to the declarative style of LP, which lies outside the mainstream programming languages. Indeed, in CS curricula, students are exposed early to concepts such as while-for loops, destructive assignment variables, types, common functions with a single return value, etc. in the usual first "Introduction to Programming" course. This programming paradigm mindset is further deepened, for example by object oriented programming courses that although they introduce new concepts such as inheritance, still follow the well established procedural vein and the usually OO focused software engineering courses. The distance between the paradigms is further enlarged because students are normally instructed to avoid as much as possible recursion due to inefficiency issues, present in most mainstream languages that lack optimization support. Consequently, as educators we must overcome a number of obstacles and in fact "reset" the way students think about programming. Although a number of classic introductory and advanced books and tutorials exist, such as [1,3,9,10,12], the pedagogical issues faced in class remain a great challenge [6,11,13], and require novel approaches and environments [4,8].

Students often ask the question "*Why Prolog?*" Some are convinced by typical justifications that refer to foundations of the discipline as well as teaching programming principles with a minimum set of constructs. It is expected, however, that a tighter integration, both in terms of facilities and available examples, with other programming languages and tools will be sought towards the perception of students for its applicability. Additionally, the current growth of Knowledge Graphs [7] and their associated Semantic Web technologies that rely mostly on logic, raises some extra arguments in favor of learning LP.

For as long as Logic forms the foundations of Computer Science, LP, through its main representative (Prolog) will remain current. It is no surprise that Prolog is perhaps one of the few programming language that persists for many years in Computer Science curricula; while other programming languages come and go, Prolog remains as a paradigm for declarative thinking (programming) that can be used to teach a plethora of programming principles and techniques. We anticipate that this fact will also remain true in the future.

The power of simplicity (syntax and constructs) gives us, educators, the opportunity to focus on programming principles that span from purely declarative to procedural. In this paper, we attempt to demonstrate a showcase on how this is feasible through alternative implementations of a single operation that can be referenced throughout the learning process or used to summarise and revise the language abilities and flexibility.

3   Logic Programming Techniques

The term "programming technique" has been used in different contexts: we adopt the definition that a *technique* is a pattern, applied to a wide range of problems [2], as for example *failure driven loops*, *generate-and-test* and *accumulator pairs*, among many others.

A *schema* is a representation of a technique that allows developers to represent a general structure solution code to a problem, so that, given the specific context, the schema may be instantiated to executable code that solves the particular problem. The schema approach to teaching Prolog was introduced rather early, as for instance in [5], where also a single example was used. Although we follow the same approach, our focus is different, since we contend that the single task used can serve to discuss a wider number of issues, as for example efficiency and non-recursive techniques.

Probably the most widely used approach for logic programs is *recursion*. It is derived through the mathematical concept of induction [15] and assumes that a problem of a certain size, say N, can be solved if the same problem of a smaller size, say N-1, is solvable. Although a powerful approach, that provides for simple solutions of rather complex problems even when considered in a procedural mindset, it is still a skill that most novice programmers lack, or have not been exposed and exercised to a great extent.

4   One Problem - Many Solutions

The problem in question is to find the minimum element of a list of numbers, what we refer to as *list_min/2* predicate. We will show the recursive approach first, and then we will explain some more complex non-recursive schemata. In the following, in order to distinguish easily between the different implementations of *list_min/2*, we adopt a numbering in the name of the predicate, i.e. list_minX/2 with X ranging from 1 to 9.

4.1   Recursive Super-Naive Declarative Implementation

The first attempt to a solution, focuses on presenting a rather simple view of recursion, that reads as follows: "*To find the minimum of a list of N elements, assume that you know the minimum of its N−1 elements and compare with the Nth*". This leads to a (super-naive) recursive implementation of the *min_list* predicate, shown below as predicate (list_min1/2).

```
list_min1([Min],Min).
list_min1([H|T],H):-
    list_min1(T,MinTail),
    H =< MinTail.
list_min1([H|T],MinTail):-
    list_min1(T,MinTail),
    H > MinTail.
```

This implementation offers the grounds for raising a number of issues: (a) **list decomposition** in the head of the clause, (b) an introduction to the structure of a predicate definition with **recursive and terminal cases** (rules) and (c) placing **alternative choices** in separate rules, as a straightforward rule-of-thumb instead of OR (;) within the body of the clause that leads to several concerns. List decomposition on the head of the clause, provides a syntactically simple list operation, whereas alternative cases in a definition enhance readability and make the resulting code more extensible.

However, a number of other issues are eminent. Probably the one with "*what is hidden*" in the previous implementation is the fact that there is a choice point in the recursive rule embedded in the predicate; the choice between the minimum among the head of the list and the minimum of the tail of the list, that occurs after the recursive call, leads to **inefficiency issues** and provides a great chance to discuss the **execution tree** and placing checks as early as possible. The response to the obvious reaction for **subgoal reordering** in the body of the rules, leads to a discussion on the **non-logical handling of numbers** in classical (non CLP) Prolog implementations, that expects ground variables in any arithmetic expression. This discussion provides an excellent prompt to introduce Constraint LP.

4.2   Naive Declarative Implementation

The inefficiency issue manifested in the previous implementation, demands a better recursive definition, that of *"the minimum element of a list is the minimum among its head and the minimum of its tail"*, implemented as predicate list_min2/2, shown below.

```
list_min2([Min],Min).
list_min2([H|Tail],Min) :-
    list_min2(Tail,MinTail),
    min(H,MinTail,Min).


min(X,Y,X) :- X=<Y.
min(X,Y,Y) :- X>Y.
```

Although, arithmetic checks are delayed and placed "after" the recursive call, committing to the min value is delayed, i.e. variable Min is instantiated at the last call, after the arithmetic check. This leads to a *linear complexity*, albeit some memory inefficiencies. A puzzling point to novice learners is that comparisons take actually place backwards, from the last element of the list to the first, usually referred to as building the solution "on the way up".

This version offers itself to talk about the **if-then-else** construct (without explicit reference to the hidden cut) by rewriting the code for min/2 as follows:

```
list_min21([Min],Min).
list_min21([H|Tail],Min) :-
    list_min21(Tail,MinTail),
    (H>MinTail -> Min=MinTail; Min=H).
```

Although, some may find that the above presents a more readable implementation, it does contain explicit unification, i.e. the use of the "=" operator, which can be easily (mis)taken for assignment.

4.3   The "Standard" Algorithmic Implementation

Following the implementation of the "naive" program where numbers are compared in the reverse order, this predicate allows for an explanation of its memory inefficiency, due to its inability to take advantage of **recursion optimization** techniques. Having been exposed in Compiler and Computer Architecture courses to the function call mechanisms, one can easily understand that having to execute code after the recursive call, a lot of information must be kept in the *memory stack* (i.e. values of variables at each recursive step), so this implementation is memory demanding. The latter offers an excellent chance to discuss **tail recursion optimization**, and the need to place the recursive call last in the body of the predicate.

The implementation shown below (predicate list_min3/2), is based on the "standard" algorithm that is taught in programming courses. Thus, the **accumulator pair** technique [2,5], is introduced that offers a great opportunity to discuss *single assignment variables* in the Prolog programming context. The technique of introducing an **auxiliary predicate** is common in Prolog. It is interesting to notice that the auxiliary predicate may have the same functor name as well since it has different arity.

```
list_min3([H|T],Min) :-
    list_min3_aux(T,H,Min).

list_min3_aux([],Min,Min).
list_min3_aux([H|T],TempMin,Min) :-
    min(H,TempMin,NextMin),
    list_min3_aux(T,NextMin,Min).
```

Alternatively, since now the comparison is done before the recursive call, we could avoid the use of the min/3 predicate and have instead two recursive calls, without causing so much inefficiency this time, as shown in predicate list_min4/2). However, to maintain efficiency, it is needed to explicitly insert the **cut operator** leading to a **check-and-commit** technique.

```
list_min4([H|T],Min) :-
    list_min4_aux(T,H,Min).

list_min4_aux([],MSF,MSF).
list_min4_aux([H|T],MSF,Min):-
    H < MSF, !,
    list_min4_aux(T,H,Min).
list_min4_aux([H|T],MSF,Min):-
    H >= MSF, !,
    list_min4_aux(T,MSF,Min).
```

Although the cut in the code above is inserted to take advantage of the **tail recursion optimization**, since checks are mutually exclusive, the second check could be eliminated, leading to a reduced number of checks in the code. Alternatively, as mentioned above, cut can be implicitly replaced by the "more declarative" **if-then-else** construct.

4.4 A Reduction Approach

The next implementation is in fact an ad-hoc application of the **reduce** operator commonly found in functional languages and recently in many Prolog implementations (predicate list_min5/2).

```
list_min5([M],M).
list_min5([H1,H2|T],Min):-
    H1 > H2, !,
    list_min5([H2|T],Min).
list_min5([H1,H2|T],Min):-
```

```
H1 =< H2, !,
list_min5([H1|T],Min).
```

Selecting two elements instead of a single from the list supports an early arith-metic comparison, leading to an immediate **pruning of the non-successful branch**. What is left to be decided is the repeated execution of the operation for the rest of the elements, achieved by "pushing" the result (i.e. the minimum between the two) elements to the top of the list for the next recursive call.

Alternatively, an even more compact version of the predicate relies on the min/3 predicate mentioned previously (predicate list_min6/2).

```
list_min6([Min],Min).
list_min6([H1,H2|T],Min):-
    min(H1,H2,M),
    list_min6([M|T],Min).
```

The introduction of the latter provides the necessary ground to demonstrate the implementation of the *reduce* operator using **variable call**, that can work on any binary operation (e.g. min, max, etc.). The latter is achieved by simply adding one more argument to hold the predicate name of the operation and the term construction subgoal using the **univ/2** operator, as shown below:

```
list_reduce([Value],_,Value).
list_reduce([H1,H2|T],Operation,Value):-
    C =.. [Operation,H1,H2,Next],
    call(C),
    list_reduce([Next|T],Operation,Value).
```

We usually call this implementation an elegant, declarative "hack", taking advantage of the list itself to deliver the temporary result to the end. Although novice learners find this implementation rather ingenious, they rarely reproduce it in future programming tasks. This is probably due to the fact that they are not used to a *functional style* of programming; rather they prefer the more traditional "array" style of iterating the list and keeping the temporary result in a separate variable as an extra argument.

4.5   A Non-recursive Declarative Definition

A verbal description of a complete definition of list_min/2 could be *the min-imum of a list, is a member of the list such that no other member of the same list exists smaller than it.* Interestingly enough this can be directly implemented in Prolog (predicate list_min7/2).

```
list_min7(List,Min):-
    member(Min,List),
    not((member(X,List), X < Min)).
```

This is probably the most declarative version of `list_min/2`, reported here, and is in fact an application of the **generate-and-test** technique. Understanding, however, the operation of the predicate presents significant challenges. First of all, it demands a good understanding of **backtracking** and **negation**, i.e. the fact that once an element smaller than the current `Min` is found then the second subgoal fails, leading to a *re-instantiation* of the `Min` to the next element of the list. The process is repeated until the argument inside the negation in the second subgoal fails, for all instantiations of `X`, leading to the solution.

However, this elegant indeed definition suffers from high *computational complexity*. It does not take long to realize that it has $O(N^2)$ complexity whereas all other previous solutions (except the "super-naive" one) have linear complexity.

4.6   Using Solution Gathering Predicates

Another version (`list_min8/2`) mainly used for illustrating the operation of the **setof** **solution gathering** predicate, stressing that it is a clever trick, but with higher-than-needed computational cost.

```
list_min8(List,Min) :-
    setof(X,member(X,List),[Min|_]).
```

This version exploits the builtin predicate `setof` and follows the naive algorithmic thinking of sorting a list in ascending order to return its first element. However, one needs to realize that sorting has a larger average complexity $O(n \log n)$ than finding the minimum $O(n)$, so in general it should be avoided.

4.7   Using Assert/Retract and Failure-Driven Loops: The One to Avoid

No matter how simple a programming language can be, some of its features may be used to create the "unthinkable". The same happens with Prolog's ability to alter its program while the program is executed, i.e. asserting and retracting clauses on the fly. We refer to this version (predicate `list_min9`) as the "one to avoid", since it relies on a **"global" variable** implemented as a separate dynamic predicate, to simulate *destructive assignment*. It offers the opportunity to present a number of issues regarding assert/retract, as well as the necessity of **side-effects** inside a **failure-driven loop**.

```
list_min9([H|_T],_Min) :-
    assert(temp_min(H)),
    fail.
list_min9(List,_Min) :-
    member(X,List),
    retract(temp_min(TmpMin)),
    min(X,TmpMin,NextMin),
    assert(temp_min(NextMin)),
```

```
    fail.
list_min9(_List,Min) :-
    retract(temp_min(Min)).
```

We do not present this as a technique that someone should adopt. We just mention it as an extreme example of how flexible and "dirty" Prolog programming can get!

5 Evaluation of Efficiency vs. Perception

An interesting aspect of demonstrating the list_min operation in many different versions is that it leads to commenting on the efficiency of each version using automatically generated lists of random integers, best and worst case scenarios, e.g. ordered or reverse ordered lists, and Prolog statistics. Thus, a novice learner can see how each technique affects the performance.

Having completed all the classes, we requested our students to conduct experiments with all versions of list_min, with lists of various sizes in ascending, descending and random order. Having gathered the results in terms of cputime and number of inferences, they were asked to express their opinion which are the best three versions, by reconciling efficiency, readability and writability of code.

The results obtained by different lists sizes, ranging from 1000 to 100000 elements (1K, 30K, 60K, 100K), present some interesting aspects regarding the different predicate versions. All experiments were conducted using SWI Prolog. With respect to efficiency, we have found that the predicates above can be classified in three groups: The first group contains list_min1, which in fact fails to report a solution for large lists in descending order; for instance, the execution time for a list of only 30 elements is 218.6 s. Obviously, results for ascending lists are comparable with those of other predicates; however, the decision was to exclude the predicate from further testing since it would not provide any significant results with respect to random and descending lists.

The fully declarative solution (list_min7, second group), although it performs better, it still follows the generate and test strategy, yielding high execution times and a large number of inferences to reach a solution for the descending worst case: starting with 5.3 s for a list of 10K elements up to 548 s approximately for the list of 100K elements. This is expected, since in the descending case, the solution generator (member/2) produces the correct solution last, yielding the highest number of iterations. For the same reason, best results are obtained for lists in ascending order, followed by those for the random.

The third group contains all other predicates. We avoided reporting execution times, since, even for 100K lists, the former are less than a quarter of a second, across all predicates in the group, yielding no interesting (or safe) results for comparison. Instead we opted to measure *number of inferences per list element*, just to give an indication how close in terms of performance versions are. Results averaged between all tests, for each predicate are presented in Fig. 1. Finally, list_min8 is not included in the figure, since setof is implemented at a lower level, so the exact number of inferences is not correctly reported by SWI-Prolog.

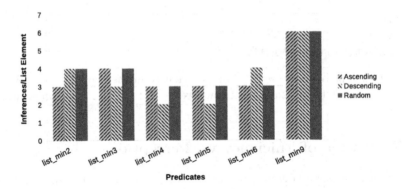

Fig. 1. Results showing Inferences/List Element on the third group of predicates.

All predicates we tested (most of them recursive) scan the whole list once no matter the type of list. So, with minor deviations in any of the ascending, descending, or random order, the number of inferences is more or less the same (the extra lines from one predicate to the other cause the extra inferences but play a minor role). Thus, performance is independent of the type of list.

Minor differences among predicates in the figure are attributed to the order of checks. For instance, in list_min2 arithmetic comparisons occur "backwards", whereas in list_min3 occur on the "way down" to the base recursive case, thus showing slightly different behaviour on the extreme cases (ascending/descending order). It should be noted that the assert/retract version seems to be unaffected by the order of elements in the list and yields the higher number of inferences, due to constantly accessing Prolog memory.

Regarding student perception, the definitions of list_min8, list_min2 and list_min7 were among the first three preferences, gathering 72%, 48% and 40% respectively of the students who preferred them in their top-three choices, although the last one requires a considerable number of inferences compared to all the rest. All other versions were roughly equally preferred. It was surprising that 16% of the students declared as a top-three choice list_min1; it takes an enormous amount of cputime to complete which makes it practically useless but it was preferred for its readability. Even more surprising is that 20% included list_min9 in their best three choices; it is extremely complex and far from purity but it may match the programming style that learners have been exposed to in previous courses.

6   Conclusions

We presented the flexibility of Prolog by using a single operation and multiple programming techniques that result in different implementations. Each version of the predicate list_min allows space to discuss all interesting features of Prolog. The code variations gave us the opportunity to discuss declarativeness versus efficiency issues as well as readability, purity and dirty characteristics of the language. As educators, we make use of those examples in our class of novice Prolog learners and we showed their perceptions and evaluations.

References

1. Bratko, I.: PROLOG Programming for Artificial Intelligence, 4th edn. Addison-Wesley Longman Publishing Co., Inc, USA (2012)
2. Brna, P., et al.: Prolog programming techniques. Instr. Sci. **20**(2), 111–133 (1991). https://doi.org/10.1007/BF00120879
3. Clocksin, W.F., Mellish, C.S.: Programming in Prolog, 5 edn.. Springer, Berlin (2003). https://doi.org/10.1007/978-3-642-55481-0
4. Flach, P., Sokol, K., Wielemaker, J.: Simply logical - the first three decades. In: Warren, D.S., Dahl, V., Eiter, T., Hermenegildo, M., Kowalski, R., Rossi, F. (eds.) Prolog: 50 Years of Future, LNAI 13900, pp. 184–193. Springer, Cham (2023)
5. Gegg-Harrison, T.S.: Learning prolog in a schema-based environment. Inst. Sci. **20**(2), 173–192 (1991). https://doi.org/10.1007/BF00120881
6. Hermenegildo, M.V., Morales, J.F., Lopez-Garcia, P.: Some thoughts on how to teach prolog. In: Warren, D.S., Dahl, V., Eiter, T., Hermenegildo, M., Kowalski, R., Rossi, F. (eds.) Prolog: 50 Years of Future, LNAI 13900, pp. 107–123. Springer, Cham (2023)
7. Hogan, A., Blomqvist, E., Cochez, M., D'amato, C., Melo, G.D., Gutierrez, C., Kirrane, S., Gayo, J.E.L., Navigli, R., Neumaier, S., Ngomo, A.C.N., Polleres, A., Rashid, S.M., Rula, A., Schmelzeisen, L., Sequeda, J., Staab, S., Zimmermann, A.: Knowledge graphs. ACM Comput. Surv. **54**(4), 1–37 (2022). https://doi.org/10.1145/3447772
8. Morales, J.F., Abreu, S., Hermenegildo, M.V.: Teaching prolog with active logic documents. In: Warren, D.S., Dahl, V., Eiter, T., Hermenegildo, M., Kowalski, R., Rossi, F. (eds.) Prolog: 50 Years of Future, LNAI 13900, pp. 171–183. Springer, Cham (2023)
9. O'Keefe, R.A.: The Craft of Prolog. MIT Press, Cambridge (1990)
10. Ross, P.: Advanced Prolog: Techniques and Examples. Addison-Wesley (1989)
11. Sekovanić, V., Lovrenčić, S.: Challenges in teaching logic programming. In: 2022 45th Jubilee International Convention on Information, Communication and Electronic Technology (MIPRO), pp. 594–598 (2022). https://doi.org/10.23919/MIPRO55190.2022.9803530
12. Sterling, L., Shapiro, E.: The Art of Prolog (2nd Ed.): Advanced Programming Techniques. MIT Press, Cambridge (1994)
13. Van Someren, M.W.: What's wrong? Understanding beginners' problems with Prolog. Instr. Sci. **19**(4), 257–282 (1990). https://doi.org/10.1007/BF00116441
14. Warren, D.S.: Introduction to Prolog. In: Warren, D.S., Dahl, V., Eiter, T., Hermenegildo, M., Kowalski, R., Rossi, F. (eds.) Prolog: 50 Years of Future, LNAI 13900, pp. 3–19. Springer, Cham (2023)
15. Warren, D.S.: Writing correct prolog programs. In: Warren, D.S., Dahl, V., Eiter, T., Hermenegildo, M., Kowalski, R., Rossi, F. (eds.) Prolog: 50 Years of Future, LNAI 13900, pp. 62–70. Springer, Cham (2023)

A Better Logical Semantics for Prolog

David S. Warren[1]([⊠]) and Marc Denecker[2]

[1] Stony Brook University, New York, UK
warren@cs.stonybrook.edu
[2] KU Leuven, Leuven, Belgium
marc.denecker@kuleuven.be

Abstract. This paper describes a semantics for the language of pure positive Prolog programs that improves on the widely accepted Least Herbrand Model (LHM) semantics. The LHM semantics gives meaning only to complete Prolog programs, and not to components of programs. Yet programmers clearly understand the meaning of a predicate even if not all predicates used in its definition are defined in the program. For example, programmers understand the meaning of the two rules defining transitive closure without having to know the specific graph that it applies to. A semantics for the Prolog language should also provide such a meaning. We motivate the meaning of Prolog rules as inductive definitions by starting with Clark's completion, analyzing its limitations, and then describing how it can be modified to yield a logical theory of inductive definitions.

1 Introduction

This paper describes a Logic of Definitions, which provides a semantics for the Prolog programming language [13]. All the ideas here are more fully presented in [6],[1] which is itself an explication of earlier ideas developed by Denecker and his group in [5]. The primary differences from the presentation in that paper are that here we restrict our models to be Herbrand models and we use the Clark completion semantics to motivate this approach to improved Prolog logical semantics. We eliminate any formalism and focus on the informal motivation and discussion. There is nothing in this paper that is not in that original paper. The hope is that this paper may be more accessible to a wider audience of Prolog programmers, and perhaps provide intuitions that will help in understanding that paper.

2 The Least Herbrand Model Semantics of Prolog

The initial formulation of the logic of positive Prolog was that clauses were Horn clauses and Prolog execution was SLD resolution applied to a set of Horn clauses.

---

[1] Also available at: https://people.cs.kuleuven.be/~marc.denecker/A-PDF/Prolog50.pdf.

© The Author(s), under exclusive license to Springer Nature Switzerland AG 2023
D. S. Warren et al. (Eds.): Prolog: The Next 50 Years, LNAI 13900, pp. 82–92, 2023.
https://doi.org/10.1007/978-3-031-35254-6_7

Prolog evaluators answered "yes" to ground queries for which it could find an SLD proof and "no" when no proof was found. Early Prolog evaluators included an operation called *not*, which was described as *not provable*.[2] This shows the recognition that the failure of a query indicates that it is not provable, and not that it is logically false. But the "yes" response for true queries suggests that the "no" response might be for queries that are false, and many programmers productively interpreted that "no" as logically false. The attempt to make this interpretation logically correct led to a search for a new logic-based semantics for positive Prolog that would indeed imply failing queries are logically false.

Seminal papers in this research effort include:

1. In 1977 van Emden and Kowalski [11] provide a definition of the least Herbrand model (LHM) and its construction, for positive Prolog programs, and showed that the atoms true in the LHM were exactly the atoms for which there is an SLD proof.
2. In 1977 Clark [4] defines the completion of a positive Prolog program (by essentially turning the Horn clause implications into biconditionals) and shows that a (slightly modified) SLD resolution finitely fails for a (ground) query if and only if the program completion logically implies that the query is false.
3. In the mid-eighties, work by Chandra and Harel [3], Apt, Blair, and Walker [2] and Przymusinski [10] built on earlier work on fixpoint logic [9] and contributed to the definition of the perfect model as the generally accepted meaning for stratified programs. The (unique) perfect model of a positive program is its Least Herbrand Model. Since according to this semantics, a positive program has only a single model, an atom false in this model is false in all models and thus is logically false.

This idea of using a single model to provide the semantics for a Prolog program seems to have taken hold when the database community became interested in using the function-free subset of positive Prolog as a logic of deductive databases, later called Datalog.

This semantics, known as the LHM semantics, has become widely accepted by the logic programming community.

A Herbrand structure (see [7]) is a first-order structure for a language in which every ground term of the language names a distinct object (the unique names assumption) and all objects are named (the domain closure assumption). Restricting to Herbrand structures allows programmers to use functions to store and later retrieve data, as it allows arguments to functions to be recovered from their applications. For the remainder of this paper we assume that all structures are Herbrand structures.

For positive Prolog programs (as we consider here), Tarski's fixpoint theorem guarantees that any set of Horn clauses, i.e., any Prolog program, has a unique minimal Herbrand model, its LHM. As shown in [11], it can be constructed in a

---

[2] The form of the *not* operator in most Prologs is \+, which is intended to approximate in ASCII the logical *proves* symbol ⊢ with a slash / through it.

bottom-up fashion by starting with the empty set, and then iteratively adding ground atomic formulas that are heads of ground rule instances that have all body literals in the current set. This continues until nothing more can be added (perhaps to ω). The resulting set of atomic formulas determines the Herbrand structure in which the atomic formulas derived in this process are true, and all others are false. And this structure is a model of the program Horn clauses, satisfying them all. Under this semantics, every (positive) Prolog program has a unique model, so a query is true if it is true in all models, i.e., true in the single LHM, and it is false if it is false in all models, i.e., false in the single LHM.

In [11] it was proved that the atoms true in the LHM of a program are exactly the atoms that SLD resolution proves true. This means that if SLD succeeds on a ground query, it is true in the LHM and thus logically true. If SLD fails on a ground query, it is false in the LHM and thus logically false. Thus a "no" answer to a Prolog query demonstrates that the query is logically false.

But the claim of this paper is that there are problems with the LHM semantics. Specifically, the LHM gives meanings *only* to full programs, but not to program components. No meanings are given to subcomponents of full programs. And this clearly violates the intuitions of Prolog programmers. Prolog programmers undeniably give meaning to program components.

Consider the example of a teacher of introductory Prolog who gives the class an assignment to write a predicate defining "sibling" in terms of a base "childOf" predicate that will work for any definition of "childOf", and then to exemplify it with their own nuclear family. One student submits the program:

```
childOf(tessa,david).
childOf(jonah,david).
sibling(tessa,jonah).
sibling(jonah,tessa).
```

The teacher marks this wrong, so the student responds by asking what a correct answer would be. And the teacher replies:

```
childOf(tessa,david).
childOf(jonah,david).
sibling(X,Y) :- childOf(X,P), childOf(Y,P), X \== Y.
```

To which the student replies that his program has exactly the same meaning, i.e. LHM, as the teacher's program, so it should be accepted as a reasonable alternative correct answer to the problem. The teacher reminded the student that she asked for a definition that would work for all `childOf` relations, as does the rule above. But, replies the student, the meaning of that rule alone, under the LHM, is that `sibling` is the empty relation, since that is the LHM of that rule alone. Clearly there is a problem.

The problem is that the teacher wants a definition of sibling, that holds for every value of the childOf relation, not only for the family of the student. But the LHM semantics has nothing like this to say. It can give meaning only to complete programs, here when `sibling` and `childOf` are both defined. But the teacher gives a meaning, and wants the student to give that same meaning, to a component of the program, the component consisting of the single rule for `sibling`.

3   Clark Completion

An early proposal to provide a semantics for positive Prolog programs that accounted for queries being false was made by Keith Clark in [4]. He said that programs were not made up of individual Prolog clauses, but of Prolog *defini-tions*. That is, the set of clauses that have the same predicate symbol in the head together make up a *definition* of a relation. And that definition for a predicate can be constructed from the rules for that predicate by putting them together into one conditional formula whose head is the predicate with all distinct vari-ables as arguments, and whose body comes from the disjunction of the bodies of the rules. We introduce explicit existential quantifiers and equalities to ensure that this single implication is equivalent to the set of original implications for the predicate. And now, in this single formula, we change the *if* into an *if-and-only-if*, which is intended to turn it into a *definition*.

The `sibling` rule becomes the definition:

$$sibling(X, Y) \iff \exists P(childOf(X, Y) \land childOf(Y, P) \land X == Y) \quad (1)$$

The `childOf` clauses become the definition:

$$childOf(X, Y) \iff (X = tessa \land Y = david) \lor (X = jonah \land Y = david) \quad (2)$$

Here, in this program, the singleton set of rules defining the `childOf` rela-tion expresses the correct definition of the concept of sibling in terms of binary relation of being a child of. A Herbrand structure, whose language includes the two predicate symbols: `sibling/2` and `childOf/2`, is a model of that formula if it makes that formula true. A structure makes it true if for whatever relation it assigns to `childOf`, it assigns the right sibling relation to the `sibling` predicate, i.e., the sibling relation in the family represented by the relation for `childOf`. So this semantics *does* provide a meaning to individual predicate definitions and indeed exactly the meaning we (and our poor teacher) want; that the `sibling` rule gives the correct definition for any possible family.

Since the Clark completion semantics does the right thing for this definition and many, many others, why is it not the dominant semantics for Prolog?

4   So What's Wrong with Clark Completion?

Indeed, there is a fly in the ointment; Clark completion doesn't always work. It works beautifully for the examples we have considered so far, but consider the example of transitive closure:

```
tc(X,Y) :- edge(X,Y).
tc(X,Y) :- edge(X,Z), tc(Z,Y).
```

which becomes under Clark completion:

$$tc(X, Y) \iff edge(X, Y) \lor \exists Z(edge(X, Z) \land tc(Z, Y)) \tag{3}$$

But this formula does not define transitive closure as required. Actually, given an edge relation, this may not *define* a relation at all. To define the `tc` relation, it must be the case that for any particular `edge` relation, this formula uniquely determines the set of tuples that `tc` is true of. But this formula doesn't do that.

Consider the `edge` relation:

```
edge(a,a).   edge(b,a).
```

Consider the two Herbrand structures, described by the set of ground formulas true in them:

```
M1 = {edge(a,a), edge(b,a), tc(a,a), tc(b,a)}.
M2 = {edge(a,a), edge(b,a), tc(a,a), tc(b,a), tc(a,b)}.
```

These are both models of the `tc` if-and-only-if formula above and they have the same interpretation for `edge`. M1 is clearly the transitive closure as intended. So how can the `tc(a,b)` fact be true in M2 and it still be a model of (3)? Consider the instance of (3):

$$tc(a, b) \iff edge(a, b) \lor \exists Z(edge(a, Z) \land tc(Z, b)) \tag{4}$$

The left-hand is true in M2, but also the right hand is true: take Z=a! Hence M2 is a model. Therefore, (3) does *not* (always) define a relation.

For those knowledgeable about FOL this does not come as a surprise. In fact, there is *no* first-order (FO) formula that defines transitive closure. This is a well-known fact (and limitation) of FOL.[3]

5 "Fixing" Clark's Completion

Instead of giving up on Clark's completion and settling for LHM, let's try to understand what went wrong and see if we can fix it without throwing out the baby with the bathwater.

Clark's name for these equivalences, definitions, suggests that such a collection of rules are viewed as a formal expression of a (non-formal) definition of the concept expressed by the head predicate. That accords very well with programmers' intuitions. The problem is however that in general, these equivalences called "definitions" do not correctly formalize the non-formal definitions that programmers understand when interpreting the rules. Let's look more closely at these equivalence formulas and how they work.

The form of a Clark formula for a predicate p is, schematically:

$$p(\overline{X}) \iff \Psi(\overline{X}, p, \overline{q})$$

---

[3] See a footnote in [6] for a proof.

where $\overline{X}$ is a sequence of variables, Ψ indicates some logical formula that contains within it: $\overline{X}$, occurrences of variables in the left-hand-side of the bi-conditional, p, occurrences of atomic formulas with predicate p, and $\overline{q}$, occurrences of atomic formulas with predicates other than p. These $\overline{q}$ predicates are called *predicate parameters* in this context.

If we fix the interpretation of the predicates $\overline{q}$, we see that this equivalence expresses that p is a fixpoint of the right hand side formula.

In fact, we saw that this was the case for the transitive closure example just above. The two models M1 and M2 above are indeed the two fixpoints of its completion definition, when the interpretation of the edge predicate is set to the 2-edged graph $\{edge(a, a), edge(b, a)\}$.

So, we see that the problem with Clark's completion is that the parameterized operators of some definitional if-and-only-if formulas have multiple fixpoints.

For this example, the fixpoint we want for the definition of transitive closure is the *least* fixpoint, the one with the smallest relation, since that is the one that indeed properly captures the transitive closure of the given graph. (The other, larger fixpoint M2, has a "phantom" path, e.g., the "path" from a to b.) The operator defined by a Clark definition is known as the *immediate consequence operator* and is always a monotonic operator for any positive Prolog definition. Every monotonic operator is known to have a least fixpoint. And it is this *least* fixpoint that matches our intuition of what we want to define and is thus the one we want to choose when defining relations.

So, the obvious solution is to use the least fixpoint of these Clark definitions instead of all the fixpoints. But that can't be expressed in FOL, as we've mentioned. So, instead of using $\Longleftrightarrow$, we will extend the logic by introducing a new symbol $\triangleright$ for definitions, which can appear *only* in a formula generated by Clark's completion of a positive program. We next must define when such a $\triangleright$ formula is true in a (Herbrand) model.

Consider a Herbrand structure M that interprets all symbols in the $\triangleright$ formula. (It may include more.) To determine whether this formula is true in M, we need to compute the least fixpoint for this formula and verify if it is equal to the interpretation of the defined predicate in M. If it is, then the formula is true in M; if not, it is false in M. Now to construct the fixpoint, we begin with an initial set of ground atoms obtained from the given structure by taking every atom for any predicate parameter that is true in the structure. Then from this set we iterate adding atomic formulas for the defined predicate that are immediately implied by the right-hand-side of the $\triangleright$ formula. We iterate until there is no change (maybe infinitely many times, in which case we take the infinite union of the intermediate sets). This produces our least fixed point. Indeed this is just the well-known iteration of the T_P operator, but where the values of the parameter predicates are determined by the relations assigned to them by the Herbrand structure.

For example, consider the Herbrand structure:

$$M3 = \{edge(a, a), edge(b, a), edge(c, b), tc(a, a), tc(b, a), tc(c, b), tc(c, a), q(d)\}$$

We want to know whether the ▷ formula:

$$tc(X, Y) \; \triangleright \; edge(X, Y) \vee \exists Z(edge(X, Z) \wedge tc(Z, Y))$$

is true in M3. So we compute the least fixpoint, starting with the parameter predicate facts, those for *edge*, that are true in the structure:

$$\{edge(a, a), edge(b, a), edge(c, b)\}$$

and iterate to add implied *tc* facts:

$$\{edge(a, a), edge(b, a), edge(c, b), tc(a, a), tc(b, a), tc(c, b)\}$$

$$\{edge(a, a), edge(b, a), edge(c, b), tc(a, a), tc(b, a), tc(c, b), tc(c, a)\}$$

$$\{edge(a, a), edge(b, a), edge(c, b), tc(a, a), tc(b, a), tc(c, b), tc(c, a)\}$$

The set is unchanged on this last iteration, so we have reached the fixpoint. Now we check if the four *tc* facts in the fixpoint are exactly those in the structure *M3*. In fact, they are so *M3* makes this ▷ formula true and is thus a model of this formula. Notice that this ▷ formula remains true when we have *any* other additional facts for any predicates other than *tc* and *edge*. For example, *M*3 has $q(d)$ which had no effect on the truth or falsity of the *tc* ▷ formula.

And we can see, by a similar (actually the same) construction, that:

$$\{edge(a, a), edge(b, a), edge(c, b), tc(a, a), tc(b, a), tc(c, b), tc(c, a), t(a, c)\}$$

is *not* a model of this formula.

So, our problem is solved: we have a logic of definitions with a Herbrand model theory that gives the intuitively correct meanings to program components.

The meaning of a large component is the conjunction of the meanings of its components, just as in Clark's completion semantics. Note that the structure *M*3 is also a model of the ▷ formula obtained from the program component defining the **edge** relations:

```
edge(a,a).
edge(b,a).
edge(c,b).
```

So *M*3 is a model of both the *edge* ▷ formula and the *tc* ▷ formula, and so is in the intersection of their respective sets of models.

Thus, the meaning of an entire program is the conjunction of the meanings of its component definitions; i.e., its models are the intersection of the sets of models of its components; and thus agrees with the LHM for complete programs. Notice that a model of a program component may have facts involving predicates that are *not* symbols in the component. So a model of a full program may also have relations for predicates not in the program. However, if we restrict those models to the language of the program, they will all reduce to the LHM of the program. So this semantics is consistent with LHM semantics.

Thus, all is well, except for ...

5.1   Mutually Recursive Definitions

The above story works only for definitions that do not involve mutual recursion. To handle such mutual definitions, we must put the definitions of all mutually defined relations together into one large definition, which will define all the mutually defined relations at the same time with one least fixpoint. (If we don't do this, non-least fixpoints may sneak back in.)

Therefore our ▷ definitional connective must actually connect multiple definitions of mutually defined relations. This is because, were we not to put them together and take a single least fixpoint over all of them, we might again end up with multiple fixpoints, and no definitions. So, to be correct, we must gather all the rules for a given set of mutually defined predicates together, and take the least fixpoint for all of them together. We don't go into the details of this, but it is not too difficult to do, only a bit messy. See [6] for details.

6   So What Have We Got?

Readers who have been paying attention will probably have noticed that what we have done here is essentially to rediscover the notion of inductive definitions of relations. In fact, our use of ▷ formulas to characterize the least fixpoint of definitions is similar to the inductive definition logic introduced in [9]. This logic is the first presentation of fixpoint logic.

Recall the notion of an inductive definition of a set. An inductive definition consists of a set of inductive rules, each of which consists of a set of objects as the condition and an object as the consequent. A set S is closed under an inductive rule if when all the condition objects are in S, then the consequent is also in S. The set defined by a set of such inductive rules is the smallest set closed under all the rules. And that smallest set is the least fixpoint.

Note that the set of atoms true in the LHM of a program P is exactly the set defined by the inductive rules obtained by considering each ground instance of a Prolog rule in P as an inductive rule whose condition is the set of atoms in that Prolog rule body, and the consequent is the head atom in that Prolog rule. This follows directly by noting that the well-known iterated T_P construction exactly constructs the smallest set closed under the inductive rules.

Similarly the least fixpoint of the parameterized operator is exactly the meaning of those rules when they are treated as an inductive rules to define a relation, in terms of its parameter relations. In fact, going to the trouble of combining all the bodies of the various rules defining a particular relation, as Clark does, actually just obscures what started out as a pretty obvious inductive definition. Others have noticed that Prolog definitions look very much like inductive definitions. All we are saying here is that they indeed *are* inductive definitions.

What we end up with is a logic with a Herbrand model theory that incorporates inductive definitions. Others, for example [1] and [8], have studied the logic of inductive definitions. For this paper, for Prolog programmers, we have looked only at Herbrand models. But these structures, and the logic, can be generalized to Tarskian structures, in which case extra assumptions are required to constrain them to be (isomorphic to) Herbrand structures when necessary for Prolog programs. This more general logic is the logic described in [6] and forms the basis of the FO(ID) framework of Denecker, et al. [12].

7   Negation

For 50 years now, the general conviction is that the negation not in Prolog cannot be classical negation $\neg$. This belief stems from the fact that Horn theories do not entail the falsity of atoms. But the definitional view sheds a completely different light on the issue. Indeed, definitions do semantically entail the falsity of any defined atomic formula A that is false in the LHM. Therefore, any program interpreted as an inductive definition semantically entails the truth of the classically negated atomic formula $\neg A$. As such the finite failure inference rule can be understood to infer the falsity of A, and hence, the truth of the classically negated $\neg A$. As such, negation is here classical negation, not negation-by-failure. It is the meaning of the ":-" symbol that has changed; it is not implication but indicates an inductive rule. To conclude, the definitional view on logic programs sheds a different light on the nature of language constructs: negation as failure is indeed classical negation! It is the rule operator that is non-classical: much stronger than a material implication, it is a definitional operator of inductive definitions.

8   Discussion

As a final example of the importance of providing meaning for program components, consider Datalog, a sublanguage of Prolog in which there are no complex data structures, only constants. In Datalog one has a set of stored relations, the extensional database, and then one writes queries (or views) to ask questions of the database. Datalog programmers *must* understand their view definitions and queries independent of any specific extensional database state. The whole point of writing a query is to find out something unknown about the current database state. For example, if we define a view and write a query to it, such as:

```
rich(Emp) :- employee_sal(Emp,Salary), Salary > 300000.

| ?- rich(david).
```

we are trying to get information about an unknown extensional relation employee_sal. We want to know if, in that unknown relation, David's salary is greater than $300,000. That is why we wrote this query. It doesn't make sense to think that the extensional database state, i.e., the contents of the relation employee_sal must be known before we can understand this query, as is done in the original LHM program semantics. That is exactly backwards: we understand the view and query and use that understanding to find out something we don't know about the extensional database. The semantics provided in this paper explains how this actually works.

Some discussions of Prolog semantics include a concept called the "closed world assumption," the intuitive idea being that the only things that are true are in some sense things that one knows are true; everything else is false. And then the choice of the least Herbrand model of the LHM theory is said to follow from this idea. Notice that in our treatment, there is no mention of "closed world." The "closure" in our framework (as in Clark's) is done at the level of the definition, not the "world." And that "closure" is part and parcel of an inductive definition, a notion with a long history in classical mathematics. So, we might summarize this by saying that for symbols appearing in a program the idea of a closed world assumption is unnecessary; the closure we need is at the level of definitions, not the level of the entire theory (or program). Closure at the program level does not allow for the treatment of program components and thus for a compositional semantics. And closure at the level of definitions comes automatically with the idea of inductive definition.

9   Conclusion

We have extended first-order logic by adding a new kind of "formula," the inductive definition using the new connective ▷. And we have described how these inductive definition formulas are true or false in Herbrand models. The only (but it is a big only) change to Clark's completion semantics is that we have changed the idea of definition from first-order definition to inductive definition. One way to think about it is that this semantics now chooses only the least fixpoint as a model of the definition, not *any* fixpoint as Clark's FO definitions do.

This has allowed us to construct a semantics for (positive) Prolog that is compositional, i.e., in which the meaning of a program is a function (here conjunction) of the meanings of its components. This is not only theoretically elegant, it is fundamentally practical. It correctly reflects and models how people write and understand large programs, one piece at a time.

References

1. Aczel, P.: An introduction to inductive definitions. In: Barwise, J. (ed.) Handbook of Mathematical Logic, pp. 739–782. North-Holland Publishing Company (1977)
2. Apt, K.R., Blair, H.A., Walker, A.: Towards a theory of declarative knowledge. In: Minker, J. (ed.) Foundations of Deductive Databases and Logic Programming, pp. 89–148. Morgan Kaufmann (1988)
3. Chandra, A.K., Harel, D.: Horn clauses queries and generalizations. J. Log. Program. **2**(1), 1–15 (1985)
4. Clark, K.L.: Negation as failure. In: Gallaire, H., Minker, J. (eds.) Logic and Data Bases, Symposium on Logic and Data Bases, Centre d'études et de recherches de Toulouse, France, 1977, Advances in Data Base Theory, pp. 293–322, New York (1977). Plemum Press
5. Denecker, M., Ternovska, E.: A logic of nonmonotone inductive definitions. ACM Trans. Comput. Log. **9**(2), 14:1–14:52 (2008)

6. Denecker, M., Warren, D.S.: The logic of logic programming. CoRR, cs.LO/2304.13430, arXiv/2304.13430 (2023)
7. Lloyd, J.W.: Foundations of Logic Programming, 2nd (edn.). Springer, Heidelberg (1987). https://doi.org/10.1007/978-3-642-96826-6
8. Martin-Löf, P.: Hauptsatz for the intuitionistic theory of iterated inductive definitions. In: Fenstad, J.E. (ed.), Second Scandinavian Logic Symposium, pp. 179–216 (1971)
9. Moschovakis, Y.N.: Elementary Induction on Abstract Structures. North-Holland Publishing Company, Amsterdam-New York (1974)
10. Przymusinski, T.C.: Perfect model semantics. In: Kowalski, R.A., Bowen, K.A. (eds.) Logic Programming, Proceedings of the Fifth International Conference and Symposium, Seattle, Washington, USA, August 15–19, 1988, vol. 2, pp. 1081–1096. MIT Press (1988)
11. van Emden, M.H., Kowalski, R.A.: The semantics of predicate logic as a programming language. J. ACM **23**(4), 733–742 (1976)
12. Vennekens, J., Denecker, M., Bruynooghe, M.: FO(ID) as an extension of dl with rules. Ann. Math. Artif. Intell. **58**(1–2), 85–115 (2010)
13. Warren, D.S.: Introduction to prolog. In: Warren, D.S., Dahl, V., Eiter, T., Hermenegildo, M., Kowalski, R., Rossi, F. (eds.) Prolog: 50 Years of Future, LNAI 13900, pp. 3–19. Springer, Cham (2023). https://doi.org/10.1007/978-3-031-35254-6_1

The *Janus* System: A Bridge to New Prolog Applications

Carl Andersen[1][(✉)] and Theresa Swift[2]

[1] Raytheon BBN Technologies, Arlington, USA
carl.andersen@rtx.com
[2] Johns Hopkins Applied Physics Laboratory, Laurel, USA
Theresa.Swift@jhuapl.edu

Abstract. Despite its strengths, Prolog is not widely used in commercial settings, in part due to a lack of external packages and to difficulties integrating Prolog with more popular languages. We describe the *Janus* system, which tightly combines XSB Prolog and Python, and how such a hybrid system helps address these obstacles.

1 Introduction

After 50 years, the state of Prolog exhibits both strengths and weaknesses. Prolog is widely acknowledged as the leading framework for employing logical reasoning in general programming. Even its detractors admit that Prolog represents an important alternative to imperative and functional programming and that many of its features (e.g., unification, representation of object structure via terms, query-based computation) are intriguing. Additionally, Prolog is still a living language, with many actively maintained systems that support extensions to vanilla Prolog such as constraint-based reasoning, tabling, program analysis, multi-threading and probabilistic deduction.

Indeed, one sign of Prolog's health is that, as of this writing, there are numerous actively-maintained Prologs that are (usually) ISO-compliant including SWI [17], SICStus [3], Ciao [8], YAP [12], ECLIPSe [13], GNU Prolog [6], Picat[1] [18], Trealla[2], Tau[3] and XSB [15]. q Several of these Prologs are the results of over a decade of effort, and all have differing strengths. For instance, Picat, SICStus, and Eclipse are excellent for constraint-based reasoning, Ciao is

---

[1] Picat has a non-ISO syntax, but it is based on the B-Prolog engine [19].
[2] https://github.com/trealla-prolog/trealla.
[3] http://tau-prolog.org.

This research was developed with funding from the Defense Advanced Research Projects Agency (DARPA) under contract number FA8750-18-C-0001. The views, opinions and/or findings expressed are those of the authors and should not be interpreted as representing the official views or policies of the Department of Defense or the U.S. Government. Distribution Statement "A" (Approved for Public Release, Distribution Unlimited).

D. S. Warren et al. (Eds.): Prolog: The Next 50 Years, LNAI 13900, pp. 93–104, 2023.
https://doi.org/10.1007/978-3-031-35254-6_8

particularly strong for program analysis and flexible syntax, YAP is especially fast for single-threaded SLDNF, SWI offers a fast and stable multi-threaded engine, and XSB has pioneered a wide array of tabled deduction strategies.

Nonetheless, the authors, who have over 50 years of combined experience in industry, have seldom seen Prolog adopted for projects except at our instigation. One immediate reason for this is developer unfamiliarity: in the U.S. few developers learn Prolog in Computer Science courses, which instead emphasize popular imperative languages. Many developers are reluctant to confront the learning curve associated with resolution, backtracking, unification, and building complex objects from terms and lists.

One avenue for coaxing developers to learn and use logic programming is to make Prolog more powerful and easier to use. We believe that addressing the following issues, although they are not exhaustive, will help Prolog become more widely used in industry. They are listed in what we believe is their increasing importance.

- *Embeddability.* When Prolog is used in industry, it is rarely the main implementation language for projects (Sect. 4.1 describes an exception). Instead, projects are written in Java, Python, C^{++}, $C^{\#}$ or Javascript with Prolog performing specific functionality. As discussed in Sect. 2, although several of the Prologs mentioned above can be called by Java, Python or $C^{\#}$, few Prologs interface to all three, or to newer languages like Rust or Julia. Even when interface frameworks exist, they are often difficult to set up and require unintuitive commands and data transformations.
- *Graphical Interfaces and IDEs.* Contemporary Prologs offer few facilities for development of graphical applications; SWI Prolog's xpce is an exception. In particular, adding web front ends is a pain point for most Prolog applications. A related gap is the dearth of graphical Integrated Development Environments (IDEs) for Prologs, comparable to those for other languages, such as PyCharm/IntelliJ or Visual Studio Code.[4] Of course, many Prologs do include sophisticated command line interpreters (CLIs) that enable rapid code iteration. However, contemporary developers usually prefer graphical IDEs that show execution in the context of the original code files. While plugins for Prolog sometimes exist for major graphical IDEs, they are typically limited in functionality, and rarely offer full graphical debugging, nor associated capabilities such as value inspection and breakpoints.
- *Packages.* The combined number of packages available in Prolog (probably less than 1000) is minuscule compared to those offered by such languages as Python, JavaScript, or Java (well over 100,000 each). In practice, the lack of a large package base often makes development in Prolog uneconomical, preventing its adoption.

Our system, *Janus*, addresses these issues by integrating Prolog and Python into a single system, putting Prolog at a Python programmer's fingertips and

---

[4] Here again, SWI's xpce-based debugger is an exception.

vice-versa. Both languages execute within a singe process: this allows the overhead of calling one language from another to be extremely low, and supports
Janus's fast bi-translation of large, complex data structures between languages.[5]

Janus is automatically configured and available when versions 5.0 or later
of XSB are installed. Alternately, *Janus* also supports configuring and installing
XSB for Python programmers via the Python package manager `pip`.[6] The *Janus*
code is compact and has already been ported to `lvm` Prolog developed by Graph-
Stax, Inc., where it is being used in internal applications.

Although *Janus* is still new, we show that in several projects, it has directly
addressed the package problem by making the huge ecosystem of Python packages usable in Prolog code with little effort. These include a government research
project (DARPA AIDA), along with several industrial research projects (cf.
Sect. 4). The application areas include natural language processing, visual query
answering, geospatial reasoning, and handling semantic web data. *Janus* has
also addressed the embeddability problem by enabling the use of XSB within a
Python-based robotics application (Sect. 4.2). Less progress has yet been made
using *Janus* in IDEs and graphical interfaces, although it has supported XSB use
in Jupyter notebooks and we believe that *Janus* provides a natural foundation
for such work.

This paper focuses on the impact of *Janus* for applications, while a companion
paper [14] covers fully its implementation and performance. Accordingly, our
paper is structured as follows. After presenting related work, we briefly outline
the architecture of *Janus* in Sect. 3.

2   Related Work

Table 1 provides a summary of foreign language interfaces for various Prologs.
Most of the Prologs mentioned in Sect. 1 are written largely in C and, so offer
bi-directional interfaces with C/C++. Exceptions are Tau Prolog written in
Javascript, and Scryer written in Rust. Many Prologs offer two-way Java interfaces, while a few offer interfaces to Python or Javascript, or support for .NET.[7]
Some of these interfaces have proven quite useful: for example in the U.S. Cus-
toms Automated Targeting System[8] Java calls SICStus Prolog millions of times
per day, every day, for name-address standardization [5].

Many interfaces are implemented (e.g. SICStus to .NET, XSB to Java) via
socket connections to a separate process running the other language. This approach is workable for many use cases, but introduces unacceptable latencies for
tightly coupled applications. Also, some interfaces can be non-trivial to set up

---

[5] A separate approach to cobinding Python and Prolog functionality is the `natlog`
interpreter, written in Python [16].

[6] A beta version of the `pip` interface is available through https://test.pypi.org/project/
python-xsb-installer.

[7] SICStus also offers a general-purpose SON-RPC library.

[8] www.dhs.gov/sites/default/files/2022-05/privacy-pia-cbp006%28e%29-ats-
may2022.pdf.

Table 1. Foreign Language Interfaces between Prologs/ Python and other languages. Here, 'f' = 'from', 't' = 'to'.

	C	C++	Java	Javascript	Julia	.NET	Python	Rust
Ciao	f/t		f/t	f/t			f/t	
Eclipse	f/t	f/t	f/t					
GNU	f/t	f/t						
Picat	f/t		f/t					
Scryer								f/t
SICStus	f/t	f/t	f/t			X		
SWI	f/t	f/t	f/t	f/t			f/t	f/t
Tau				f/t				
Treala	t							
XSB	f/t		f/t				f/2	
YAP	f/t	f/t	f/t					
Python	f/t	f/t	f/t	f/t	f/t	X	–	f/t

(e.g. XSB to C, which requires file wrappers) and to use (e.g. Interprolog, which uses a complex type syntax). Finally, many of the interfaces are third-party (not written by the system developers) and so their quality may vary.

Three factors taken together distinguish *Janus* and its use. First, *Janus* tightly combines Prolog and Python into a single process. Second, its automatic bi-translation (Sect. 3) allows large and complex data structures to be communicated from one language to another without requiring special declarations. As will be discussed in subsequent sections, the result of these two factors is that *Janus* is extremely fast. Third, specialized expertise about compilation and linking is handled by the *Janus* configuration process, allowing transparent, on-demand compilation for Prolog and Python modules, and on-demand loading of Python modules when called by Prolog. These features are fully supported for Python modules even when they call other languages, such as C.

3   A Brief Review of the *Janus* API and Performance

This section briefly presents aspects of *Janus* that have been used in applications. The *Janus* API and performance are fully described in [14] and the XSB manual.

Prolog and Python Data Structures. In part because of its dynamic typing, Prolog's data structures are remarkably simple: in addition to base datatypes such as atomic constants, integers and floats, all data structures are logical terms. The base datatypes of Python are similar to those of Prolog, while its constructed types are also simple: lists, sets, tuples, and dictionaries.

The simplicity of data structures in each language enables *Janus* to bi-translate Prolog and Python data structures in a transparent manner. For instance, Python and Prolog lists have the same syntax, while a Python tuple such as `(a,1,[b,c])` is translated to a Prolog term `"(a,1,[b,c])` – i.e., a term with the same arity but whose functor is the empty string. A Python dictionary is recursively translated to a pyDict/1 term whose argument is a list of 2-ary terms, each of which represent a key-value pair. For instance, the dictionary

```
{"name": "Bob", "languages": ["English", "GERMAN"]}
```

is translated to the Prolog term

```
pyDict(['''(name,'Bob'),'''(languages,['English','GERMAN']) ])
```

Prolog Calling Python. The advantage of bi-translation can be seen from the following *Janus* library example.

Example 1. The Python `wikidataIntegrator` package[9] provides a wrapper to access Wikidata via the MediaWiki API. It returns (sometimes copious) information about a Wikidata concept (Qnode or Pnode) as a JSON structure or Python dictionary. Within *Janus* the XSB goal:

```
pyfunc(xp_wdi,get_wd_entity(Qnode),Json)
```

executes several steps. First, *Janus* automatically loads if needed the Python `xp_wdi` and`wikidataintegrator` modules along with their supporting Python packages. Once loaded, `wikidataintegrator` calls the Wikidata REST server, and creates a large Python dictionary out of the Json returned from the server. *Janus* then translates the Python dictionary to a Prolog term that can be searched in a manner analogous to how Python dictionaries are searched.

Although the `xp_wdi` package uses a small amount of Python for the interface, the code is included simply for ease of use. In fact, the `wikidataintegrator` package could be used without writing *any* Python code, although this would require slightly more sophistication on the Prolog side.

Python Calling Prolog. The bi-translation sketched in Sect. 3 is also used when Python calls Prolog, where several additional features need to be addressed.

Non-determinism. Calls to a non-deterministic goal G are handled by building a Python list or set in a manner that resembles list or set comprehension to a Python programmer.

Logical Variables. Since Python does not support logical variables, *Janus* calls are structured as a sequence of ground arguments followed by a sequence of uninstantiated arguments for return values.

Truth Values of Answers. In systems like XSB or SWI that support the well-founded semantics, a given answer to a goal G may have the truth value *true* or *undefined*. As a result answers can be returned with their explicit truth values.

---

[9] https://github.com/SuLab/WikidataIntegrator.

Example 2. Janus is initialized from Python by a directive such as `import janus`, which in addition to importing Python code for `px` dynamically loads and initializes XSB within the Python process. For brevity we show an example using `jns_qdet()`, a function specialized to call deterministic goals.

```
Ans,TV = jns_comp('basics','reverse',[1,2,3,('t1','t2'),{'a':{'b':'c'}}])
```

which is translated to Prolog to call

```
?- basics:reverse([1,2,3,''(t1,t2),pyDict([''(a,pyDict([(b,c)])]))
```

Once `jns_qdet()` returns the Python command `print(Ans + ' / ' + TV)` prints out the list comprehension

```
[{'a': {'b': 'c'}}, ('t1', 't2'), 3, 2, 1] / 1
```

Since TV is 1, this means that the answer is true in the well-founded semantics.

3.1 Performance

In the implementation of *Janus*, low-level C-APIs are used both for Python and XSB, so that a terms on Prolog's heap are quickly translated to objects on Python's heap and vice-versa. The translation is very fast – an element in a list, set, tuple or dictionary is translated and created in 30–90 ns on a moderate-speed server. Tests show that translation scales linearly with data structures containing millions of elements translated and copied in under a second. The use of bi-translation makes the C code for calls simple and their overhead low. When only a small amount of data is transferred between systems close to a million round-trip calls can be made from Prolog to Python. Round-trip calls from Python to Prolog are more expensive, with around a hundred round-trip calls possible per second.

4   Applications Using *Janus*

4.1   DeepContent: Automated Question Answering for DARPA AIDA

BBN used XSB and *Janus* extensively in its work on DARPA's Active Interpretation of Disparate Alternatives (AIDA) project. AIDA focused on two Natural Language automation tasks: Question Answering and Answer Summarization. After extracting semantic knowledge graph content from thousands of textual and video news reports, AIDA performers assembled *hypotheses* from the graph. Each hypothesis explained some real-world event of interest by answering standard (who, where, when, why, and how) questions. Here, the AIDA program addressed contemporary themes of information conflict by asking performers to identify conflicting hypotheses. For example, in explaining the 2014 crash of an airliner over Ukraine, systems often identified two competing hypotheses (among many) in the data. The first was that Ukrainian separatists mistakenly shot down the airliner using Russian-supplied missiles. The second was that the plane was destroyed by the Ukrainian Air Force.

The BBN team used Prolog as its primary programming language for *Deep-Content*, its data analysis and hypothesis assembly pipeline. Despite the size of AIDA's knowledge graphs (hundreds of millions of triples), the graphs were maintained in XSB, which executed a series of complex analytics scalably and in comparable runtime (1–2 h) to imperative approaches used by other performers. A full description of the pipeline is found in [1,2]; we focus here on *Janus*' contributions.

Prolog was the choice for AIDA's semantic search and analytics because of Prolog's integration of backtracking search (made efficient by tabling), query-oriented processing, and imperative (side-effect) functions. Our experience is that Prolog is far more agile and requires many fewer lines of code than, for example, a Java+SPARQL approach to writing software processing Semantic Web data. This is particularly true when an application requires advanced reasoning. For AIDA, BBN quickly implemented a Prolog meta-interpreter performing fuzzy query processing that we estimate would have required 5X effort and code lines in an imperative language.

Janus enabled key capabilities at several points in BBN's AIDA pipeline. *Janus*' first use was in inter-document co-reference resolution of the many entities mentioned in AIDA documents. Here, *Janus* enabled low-latency direct calls to a variety of Python-based NL packages and interfaces. These included Elasticsearch (for text indexing and geo-queries), fastText, MUSE, BERT, and Faiss (for text embeddings), and SpaCy (for parse trees), among others.

All these packages have sophisticated capabilities that our team could not have efficiently replicated in Prolog (or in Python!). Integration of these capabilities significantly boosted the accuracy of our co-reference code. Importantly, *Janus* enabled tight integration of these Python calls within larger Prolog-based query processing routines executing thousands of times per second. In this context, a loose Prolog-Python integration via shell calls or sockets would have slowed the overall pipeline unacceptably.

Additionally, *Janus*' ease of use, requiring only an import and the use of specialized calls, made it easy to develop in both languages and generally preserved Prolog's conciseness and readability. Usually, the time required to integrate some new Python package was dominated by learning and understanding the package itself. Developing and testing associated *Janus* code often took only 1–2 h.[10]

Later in the pipeline, our team required a simple priority queue supporting insertion/deletion of arbitrary keys as part of the meta-reasoner mentioned earlier. In our experience, one weakness of Prolog is the difficulty of implementing standard data structures requiring indexing and destructive assignment so that they are scalable and efficient. In this case, we explored a series of Prolog-based priority queue implementations. SWI's heaps.pl (implementing a classic pointer-oriented algorithm) required logarithmic to linear time for arbitrary inserts/deletes, causing unacceptable slowdown of the larger application.

---

[10] About a dozen *Janus* package libraries are included in the XSB distribution.

We then augmented the heaps package with XSB's trie package, which achieved efficient indexing required for inserts/deletes, but also introduced unacceptable copying of the large terms we needed to index. When further Prolog elaborations failed to achieve acceptable speeds, we very quickly stood up a *Janus* call to a Python priority queue package, which performed acceptably. Team members still disagree about whether a scalable priority queue is possible in Prolog, but the team is in agreement that using *Janus* can save time in solving prosaic problems.

In the late stages of AIDA, DARPA added a requirement that users leverage Wikidata as a background knowledge base, and we describe the *Janus* library for this as a case study. Wikidata is an enormous knowledge base (>13B triples in 2021) that is challenging to load, even on capable servers with terabytes of RAM. After failing to load Wikidata using more conventional relational database methods, BBN used *Janus* to solve the problem. We successfully loaded Wikidata using `rdflib_HDT`, an addon to the popular Python-based `rdflib`[11] triple store. The addon leverages the HDT compression system, which in turn allows query access to RDF knowledge bases compressed to a 10X factor. The library `jns_wd` allowed our Prolog application to efficiently call Wikidata through `rdflib_HDT` at a negligible performance penalty.[12]

The basic `jns_wd` query is: `wd_query(?Arg1,?Arg2,?Arg3,?Lang)`. This query allows Prolog to backtrack through Wikidata triples using various argument instantiation patterns, potentially filtering the `Arg3` results using a language designator, `Lang`. Internally, Wikidata uses URLs for non-literals, but ensuring a query uses the correct URL is tedious and error-prone. Accordingly, the library performs transformations that enable queries to use short abbreviations of the URLs (e.g., `Q144` for http://www.wikidata.org/entity/Q144).

4.2 RAACE, a BBN Autonomy Project

DeepContent's architecture was unusual in that XSB not only performed reasoning, but orchestrated a variety of Python libraries. Users more familiar with Python may choose to employ the reverse architecture, in which XSB performs an inference function within a larger Python-based system. The recent addition to *Janus* for supporting Python-to-Prolog calls, made this possible.

BBN used such an architecture in Resource Aware Autonomy for Collaborative Effects (RAACE), a recent internal research project exploring autonomous agents. Here, Prolog was used to perform Situational Awareness (SA), planning and plan monitoring functions within a larger agent autonomy architecture written in Python. This architecture builds upon Robot Operating System (ROS) [11], a widely used autonomy framework supporting both Python and C++ development and offering many capabilities, including sensing, navigation, simulation, and testing, among others. Here, the advantages of conforming to existing Python autonomy code bases mandate that Prolog be a supporting player.

---

[11] https://rdflib.readthedocs.io/en/stable.

[12] WikidataInegrator, mentioned in Sect. 3 augmented the Wikidata-HDT snapshot.

As with DeepContent, a low-latency Python-Prolog interface is advantageous for autonomy, in this case because an agent may need to update seen its SA and plan many times a second. Janus-px achieves the needed latency and enables a concise codebase as seen in DeepContent. Our XSB Prolog reasoner initially performs SA by updating its knowledge base with the latest sensor inputs. Here, *Janus'* translation of arbitrary Python data structures into intuitive Prolog terms enables straightforward use of incoming Python data with little effort. In this case, we convert incoming Python multi-level dicts (hash tables) to semantic graphlets referencing an in-house autonomy ontology representing observations, events, platform capabilities, world objects, and plan constructs.

One important *Janus* feature that we used here was making round trip calls, i.e. Python calling Prolog calling Python. This feature allowed our Prolog code to leverage Python packages with the same benefits seen in DeepContent.

We believe that XSB Prolog is an ideal language for autonomy programming when supplemented with *Janus*. Prolog's semantic reasoning model easily represents and manipulates evolving, declarative sensor data streams and naturally performs sophisticated SA reasoning and organized planning. In addition to *Janus*, XSB has attractive autonomy capabilities such as rigorous negation, tabling, and Hilog-based metareasoning. While many autonomy engines already use Prolog as a core component [9], the addition of *Janus* to fill Prolog capability gaps is likely to greatly increase Prolog use in this area.

4.3 Understanding Visual Information

Visual Query Answering (VQA), i.e., answering questions about image or video data, is an actively researched topic. Probably the leading approach to this problem uses *scene graphs* [10], a type of knowledge graph that represents both images and objects within each image as nodes; and image and object relations as edges, Typically, the images themselves are related by spatial or temporal measures. Objects within an image have relations that may be *global*, based on non-intersecting bounding boxes, or *local* if the bounding boxes intersect. The problem of *Scene Graph Generation (SGG)* is also a highly active topic. The generation of local relations within an image is usually performed by specialized neural models that analyze the intersections or unions of bounding boxes. Global relations are often generated by a mixture of neural models and knowledge-driven relations [4].

Along with neural models, XSB and Python are used in an ongoing commercial proof of concept project that involves both SGG and VQA. A mixture of Python and Prolog is used in SGG to generate spatial global object relations. For the VQA, an English query is analyzed by SpaCy using trained models for entity and relation extraction. The extracted entities and relations together with information about their textual spans effectively form a small graph, which is translated by XSB into an executable query. Currently, the query is executed by XSB, which makes use of Python geospatial and other packages.

Although this project only recently began, the use of *Janus* has so far allowed development work in Python and Prolog to be performed largely independently.

Ongoing development work aims to allow SGG and VQA functionality to be invoked either by Python or Prolog so that development and testing of the integrated system can be performed by developers in their preferred language.

4.4 A Demonstration of Intelligent Orchestration

A smaller R&D project funded by a large defense contractor used the $\mathcal{E}$rgo system (based on XSB) [7] and Python together to 1) interpret simple natural language statements about changing situations; 2) understand the significance of the changes to concrete plans to achieve a high-level goal; and 3) use geospatial data to reason about how to achieve the goal in an altered situation. For this, $\mathcal{E}$rgo used *Janus* to interpret the output of SpaCy on the natural language statements and to query Google Maps for directions and other information. $\mathcal{E}$rgo then devised new concrete plans to achieve the high-level goal.

5 Discussion

The preceding sections show how similarities between Python and Prolog – their implementation in C, dynamic typing, and the simple recursive nature of their data structures – support a fast, powerful interface resulting in new applications and use cases for Prolog. In this section, we revisit the three issues introduced in Sect. 1 and review the extent to which *Janus* mitigates each.

Janus has the most impact upon the *Packages* problem, by enabling easy use of the vast Python package ecosystem in Prolog. Over a dozen Python packages for natural language analysis, vector similarity search, geospatial information, access to Wikidata, and interfaces to semantic web data all proved key to the Prolog applications described in Sect. 4; libraries for most of these packages are now included in the XSB distribution and repo. In addition to XSB applications, the very recent port of *Janus* to a commercial Prolog is being used for customer demos. Large package bases are commonly found in languages with robust frameworks for classes and complex object definition. It is surprising that the availability of LogTalk across many different Prologs has not, to our knowledge, led to a vibrant Prolog class and package ecosystem.

Mitigation of the *Embeddability* problem was shown in Sect. 4.2, where Prolog is used for specialized reasoning within a larger autonomy application. In addition, the Python-Prolog interface is planned to support the multi-language development approach to VQA discussed in Sect. 4.3. However, *Janus* has not yet been used to construct an interface from a language such as Rust or Julia.

Janus has had less impact upon the problems of *Graphical Interfaces and IDEs* thus far. We have enabled Jupyter notebooks to directly call XSB, a functionality available in the XSB distribution. However, while XSB calls to Python graphics libraries like `TkInter` and `plotty` are occasionally found in the projects of Sect. 4, we have not yet developed a major application fronted by Python graphics or developed Python graphics-centric XSB libraries. We are hopeful that such libraries will be developed over the next year. We believe these libraries can in turn be leveraged to create a powerful Prolog IDE. The need for a graphical IDE is particularly pressing for Prolog due to the well-known learning curve imposed by core Prolog features such as backtracking, unification, and cuts – not to mention tabling, constraint satisfaction and other advanced features.

In summary, *Janus* provides a viable solution to the package problem, has begun to address the embeddability problem, but has so far had less impact on the problem of graphical interfaces and IDEs. Although work remains to address these problems, without *Janus* the applications of Sect. 4 either would have been less reliant on Prolog or would not have used Prolog at all.

Disincentives for using Prolog in industry—lack of native packages, lack of IDEs, lack of proficient programmers – hamper all but the most popular languages. However Prolog's strengths are unique, and steadily accumulate as new research results move into Prolog systems year after year. A recent panel at a logic programming conference had the title *"No Logic is an Island."* We believe that building bridges from Prolog to hugely popular languages like Python will contribute to Prolog still thriving in its hundredth year.

References

1. Andersen, C., Swift, T., Ki, A., Gerken, M., Carroll, D., Harless, C.: Improved entity resolution and relaxed query hypothesis generation using SAMSON-2020. In: 2020 NIST Text Analysis Conference on Streaming Multimedia Knowledge Base Population (SM-KBP) (2020)
2. Andersen, C., et al.: KB construction and hypothesis generation using SAMSON. In: 2019 NIST Text Analysis Conference on Streaming Multimedia Knowledge Base Population (SM-KBP) (2019)
3. Carlsson, M., Mildner, P.: SICStus Prolog - the first 25 years. Theory Pract. Logic Program. **12**(1–2), 35–66 (2012)
4. Chen, V., Varma, P., Krishna, R., Bernstein, M., Re, C., Fei-Fei, L.: Scene graph prediction with limited labels. In: International Conference on Computer Vision, pp. 2580–2590 (2019)
5. Cui, B., Swift, T.: Preference logic grammars: fixed-point semantics and application to data standardization. Artif. Intell. **138**, 117–147 (2002)
6. Diaz, D., Abreu, S., Codognet, P.: On the implementation of GNU Prolog. Theory Pract. Logic Program. **12**(1–2), 253–282 (2012)
7. Grosof, B., Kifer, M., Swift, T., Fodor, P., Bloomfield, J.: Ergo: a quest for declarativity in logic programming. In: Warren, D.S., Dahl, V., Eiter, T., Hermenegildo, M., Kowalski, R., Rossi, F. (eds.) Prolog: The Next 50 Years. LNCS (LNAI), vol. 13900, pp. xx–yy. Springer, Cham (2023). https://doi.org/10.1007/978-3-031-35254-6_18
8. Hermenegildo, M.V., et al.: An overview of Ciao and its design philosophy. Theory Pract. Logic Program. **12**(1–2), 219–252 (2012)
9. Ingrand, F., Ghallab, M.: Deliberation for autonomous robots: a survey. Artif. Intell. **247**, 10–44 (2017)
10. Johnson, J., Krishnan, R., Stark, M., Li, L., Shamma, D., Bernstein, M., Fei-Fei, L.: Image retrieval using scene graphs. In: International Conference on Computer Vision, pp. 3668–3678 (2015)

11. Quigley, M., et al.: Ros: an open-source robot operating system. In: ICRA Workshop on Open Source Software (2009)

12. Santos Costa, V., Damas, L., Rocha, R.: The YAP Prolog system. Theory Pract. Logic Program. **12**(1–2), 5–34 (2012)

13. Schimpf, J., Shen, K.: ECLiPSe - from LP to CLP. Theory Pract. Logic Program. **12**(1–2), 127–156 (2012)

14. Swift, T., Andersen, C.: The Janus system: multi-paradigm programming in Prolog and Python. In: Proceedings of the International Conference on Logic Programming. EPTCS (2023)

15. Swift, T., Warren, D.S.: XSB: extending the power of Prolog using tabling. Theory Pract. Logic Program. **12**(1–2), 157–187 (2012)

16. Tarau, P.: Natlog: a lightweight logic programming language with a neuro-symbolic touch. In: ICLP (2021)

17. Wielemaker, J., Schrijvers, T., Triska, M., Lager, T.: SWI-Prolog. Theory Pract. Logic Program. **12**(1–2), 67–96 (2012)

18. Zhou, N., Kjellerstrand, H., Fruhman, J.: Constraint Solving and Planning with Picat. Springer Briefs in Intelligent Systems. Springer, Cham (2015). https://doi.org/10.1007/978-3-319-25883-6

19. Zhou, N.F.: The language features and architecture of B-Prolog. Theory Pract. Logic Program. **12**(1–2), 189–218 (2012)

Teaching Prolog

Some Thoughts on How to Teach Prolog

Manuel V. Hermenegildo[1,2]($\boxtimes$), Jose F. Morales[1,2], and Pedro Lopez-Garcia[2,3]

[1] Universidad Politécnica de Madrid (UPM), Madrid, Spain
[2] IMDEA Software Institute, Madrid, Spain
{manuel.hermenegildo,josef.morales,pedro.lopez}@imdea.org
[3] Spanish Council for Scientific Research (CSIC), Madrid, Spain

Abstract. Prolog, and (Constraint) Logic Programming in general, represent a unique programming paradigm. Prolog has many characteristics that are not present in other styles of programming, and this is one of the reasons why it is taught. At the same time, and precisely because of this uniqueness, teaching Prolog presents some special challenges. In this paper we present some lessons learned over many years of teaching Prolog, and (C)LP in general, mostly to CS college students, at several universities. We address how to show the beauty and usefulness of the language, and also how to avoid some common pitfalls, misconceptions, and myths about it. The emphasis of our discussion is on how, rather than what. Despite some focus on CS college students, we believe that many of the ideas that we propose also apply to teaching Prolog at any other education level.

Keywords: Teaching Prolog · Prolog · Prolog Myths · Prolog Beauty · Prolog Playgrounds · Active Logic Documents · Logic Programming · Constraint Logic Programming

1 Introduction

(Constraint) Logic Programming, (C)LP, and Prolog in particular, represent a unique programming paradigm with many characteristics that are not present in other styles of programming, such as imperative, object-oriented, or functional programming. Most notably the paradigm is based on logic and includes search as an intrinsic component, as well as the use of unification, generalizing pattern matching. This brings about other interesting and also different aspects, such as for example reversibility of programs or being able to represent knowledge and reason about it, including formulating specifications and algorithms within the same formalism. It is thus not only a unique *programming* paradigm, but also a modeling and reasoning tool.

Partially funded by MICINN projects PID2019-108528RB-C21 *ProCode*, TED2021-132464B-I00 *PRODIGY*, and FJC2021-047102-I, by the Comunidad de Madrid program P2018/TCS-4339 *BLOQUES-CM*, and by the Tezos foundation. The authors would also like to thank the anonymous reviewers for very useful feedback on previous drafts of this paper.

D. S. Warren et al. (Eds.): Prolog: The Next 50 Years, LNAI 13900, pp. 107–123, 2023.
https://doi.org/10.1007/978-3-031-35254-6_9

These unique characteristics, coupled with its usefulness in many application areas, are fundamental reasons why Prolog is taught, certainly in many top institutions. Quite simply, a CS graduate is not complete without knowledge of one of the handful of *major* programming paradigms that we have come up with in CS to date. However, precisely because it is a quite different paradigm, teaching Prolog presents some particular challenges. Our first and perhaps most important consideration about teaching Prolog is that if it is done *it definitely should be done right*. Learning a programming paradigm that is quite different from what students have typically seen before and have already adapted to cannot be done lightly, in a few days, and certainly not in the same way that one moves from one imperative programming language to another. Fortunately, very good material exists (books, slides, web sites, exercises, videos) for the task. Our objective in this paper is to present a few complementary lessons learned over many years of teaching Prolog, and (C)LP in general, mostly to CS college students, at several universities, including T.U. Madrid, U. of New Mexico, and U.T. Austin.[1] In this context, the students have typically already been exposed to other programming languages, as well as hopefully some concepts of logic and proofs, at the point in time in which they are exposed to Prolog and (C)LP. An important objective in this scenario is then to make the material attractive, intriguing, and challenging to such an audience. We offer some ideas on how to show the beauty and usefulness of the language, and also to how to avoid some common pitfalls, misconceptions, and myths about it. Our emphasis is more on methodological issues, rather than, e.g., on syllabus design, for which there is comparatively more material available. We also make no attempt to cover all aspects of how to teach Prolog, which would of course require a book onto itself, but rather provide a few ideas that we have found useful. Despite some focus on CS college students, we believe that most of the ideas that we propose also apply to teaching Prolog at any other education level.[2] Finally, while our discussion centers primarily around Prolog, given the theme of this volume, we believe many of the considerations and ideas are applicable to the (constraint) logic programming paradigm in general.

2   Showing the Beauty of the Language and the Paradigm

Perhaps the most important objective when teaching Prolog is to succeed in showing the great beauty of the (C)LP paradigm in general and of Prolog in particular. To this end, we believe that it is important to transmit (already in the first class) the original *motivations* behind the language. The following approach has worked well for us in our courses:

---

[1] See https://cliplab.org/logalg for a collection of our teaching materials. We would like to thank the many contributors to these materials which have influenced this paper, including Francisco Bueno, Manuel Carro, Isabel García Contreras, Daniel Cabeza, María José García de la Banda, David H. D. Warren, Ulrich Neumerkel, Michael Codish, and Michael Covington.

[2] See also other papers in this volume, which address the subject of teaching Prolog to school children [2,3,19].

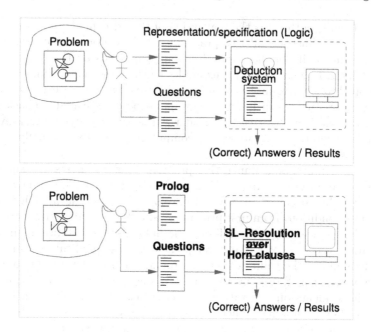

Fig. 1. A motivational view of (C) LP and Prolog.

1. Prolog, an acronym of *Programming* and *Logic*, represents an answer to the fundamental question of what is the best way to *program* computers, in order to get them to solve problems and do what we need, and in particular of how *logic* can help us in this task.
2. There are many standard ways in which logic is used in the context of programming, e.g., as a means for defining the semantics of programs, writing specifications, and proving properties of programs with respect to those specifications. But here we are concerned with using logic *directly as the programming language*.
3. Now, time for the real *overall vision*: if we assume we have an *effective deduction procedure*, i.e., a mechanical proof method that, given a description of a problem written in logic, can provide answers to questions about this problem (prove theorems about it), then *a different view of problem solving and computing is possible* (Fig. 1, top):
   (a) First, we program once and for all this *automated deduction procedure* in the computer;
   (b) then, for each problem we want to solve, we find a suitable *representation* for the problem in logic (which would be just the specification of the problem);
   (c) and, to obtain solutions, we simply ask questions and let the deduction procedure do the rest.

Prolog (Fig. 1, bottom) is the realization of this "dream."[3]

4. Time now to illustrate all this practically with one or more examples. The level of complexity of these initial examples depends on the background of the students. In general, simple examples (such as the classic family relations or, more broadly, examples with bounded search tree), are good starters. However, for students with some programming and mathematical background we have found it motivating to consider the task of specifying precisely what a simple imperative program should compute, in order to eventually prove its correctness.

5. E.g., consider a simple imperative program that calculates the squares of the first five naturals. After looking at the imperative code and how remote it is from the specification, we will develop gradually the intended semantics (post-condition) from first principles using Peano arithmetic, encoded as Horn clauses, starting with defining the naturals, then addition, then multiplication, etc. (Fig. 2).[4] We develop each of these predicate definitions by reasoning about the (infinite) set of (ground) facts that we want to capture (introducing thus informally the notion of declarative semantics), and work with the students on generating the definitions by generalization from the tables of facts, thinking inductively, etc.[5] Finally, we show that, by loading these definitions into an LP system, one can use this specification by itself, not only to do the task specified (generate the squares of the naturals < 5), but also to subtract using the definition of addition, or even compute square roots. I.e., the specification can be explored and debugged! And, since the logic is executable, one does not need to prove that the imperative program adheres to the specification, or in fact to write the imperative program at all.

6. This presentation should be motivating, but at the same time it is also a good moment for expectation management. We discuss (informally) for what logics we have effective deduction procedures, and the trade-offs between expressive power and decidability, justifying the choice of first-order logic and SLD-resolution in classical LP, and giving at least the intuition of what semi-decidability entails.[6]

---

[3] A historical note can be useful at this or a later point, saying that this materialization was done by Colmerauer (with colleagues in Marseilles and in collaboration with Kowalski and colleagues in Edinburgh) [4,14], and was made possible by the appearance of Robinson's resolution principle [18], Cordell Green's approach to resolution-based question answering [7], the efficiency of Kowalski and Kuhnen's SLD resolution [12], Kowalski's combination of the procedural and declarative interpretations of Horn clauses [11], and the practicality brought about by Warren et al.'s Dec-10 Prolog implementation [17,23].

[4] The `:- use_package(sr/bfall).` directive (an expansion) activates breadth-first execution, which we find instrumental in this part of the course; see also the discussion in Sect. 3.

[5] See also [21], in this same volume, for an ample discussion of how to build programs inductively.

[6] See also the discussion in Sect. 3 on termination, the shape of the tree, search strategies, etc.

```
:- use_package(sr/bfall).                                        run ▶

natural(0).
natural(s(X)) :- natural(X).

less(0,s(X)) :- natural(X).
less(s(X),s(Y)) :- less(X,Y).

add(0,Y,Y) :- natural(Y).
add(s(X),Y,s(Z)) :- add(X,Y,Z).

mult(0,Y,0) :- natural(Y).
mult(s(X),Y,Z) :- add(W,Y,Z), mult(X,Y,W).

nat_square(X,Y) :- natural(X), natural(Y), mult(X,X,Y).

output(X) :- natural(Y), less(Y,s(s(s(s(s(0)))))),
    nat_square(Y,X).
```

Fig. 2. Horn-clause specification (and program) for squares of naturals < 5 (click on run to load).

7. Having shown this *declarative* view of logic programs, it is of course important to also show the operational semantics, i.e., unification, resolution, etc. Some members of the LP community have argued that only the declarative semantics are important,[7] but this is clearly not so in our view. Instead, we believe that it is important to present Kowalski's declarative/procedural duality, i.e., that (constraint) logic programs are, at the same time, logical theories (that thus have a declarative meaning) and procedural programs that can be debugged, followed step by step, etc. like any other language. How could we otherwise reason about complexity (or, going further, even memory consumption, etc.)? To say that these things don't matter does not make sense in the world of programming languages. In other words, without an operational semantics, we do not (also) have a programming language, but rather just a specification and/or knowledge representation formalism – the beauty of Prolog is that it is *both*. And the argument for the procedural interpretation goes further: natural language also involves procedural forms of expression. Thus, elimination of the ability to represent procedures also eliminates the ability to represent some types of knowledge.

8. Finally, it is of course important to relate the declarative and procedural views, explaining that the declarative meaning of a set of rules is a (possibly infinite) set of ground facts and that these constitute precisely the set of ground literals for which, when posed as queries, Prolog (possibly needing a fair search rule) answers yes.

---

[7] And even some LP languages have been proposed that explicitly did not have an operational semantics, such as, e.g., the Goedel language.

Once motivation is established, and we can understand programs both declaratively and operationally, we can show other unique aspects that contribute to the elegance and beauty of the language:

1. We can show with examples (and benchmarking them) how in Prolog it is possible to go from executable specifications to efficient algorithms gradually, as needed. For example:[8]

   (a) The mathematical definition (i.e., the specification) of the modulo operation, $\boxed{\texttt{mod(X,Y,Z)}}$ where Z is the remainder from dividing X by Y, i.e., $\exists Q s.t.\ X = Y * Q + Z \wedge Z < Y$, can be expressed directly in Prolog:

   ```
   mod(X,Y,Z) :- less(Z, Y), mult(Y,Q,W), add(W,Z,X).        run ▶
   ```

   This version is clearly correct (since it is directly the specification) and (using breadth-first search) works in multiple directions, always finding all solutions:

   ```
   ?- op(500,fy,s).
   yes
   ?- mod(X,Y, s 0).
   X = s 0,
   Y = s s 0 ? ;
   X = s 0,
   Y = s s s 0 ? ;
   X = s s s 0,
   Y = s s 0 ? ;
   ...
   ```

   but it can be quite inefficient.

   (b) At the same time we can write a version such as this one:

   ```
   mod(X,Y,X) :- less(X, Y).                                 run ▶
   mod(X,Y,Z) :- add(X1,Y,X), mod(X1,Y,Z).
   ```

   which is much more efficient, and works well with the default depth-first search rule. One can time some queries or reason about the size of the proof trees to show this.[9]

2. It is also important to show the power and beauty of unification, not only as a generalization of pattern matching, but also as a device of *constructing and accessing (parts of) complex data structures* and passing them and returning them from predicates. This can be illustrated to students by building data structures piecemeal in the top level, as illustrated in Fig. 3, which shows graphically the process of building some data structures in memory via unifications, just before performing a call to the **p/4** procedure. The idea is to

---

[8] Clicking on the run ▶ links is perfectly safe!.

[9] See also [1], in this same volume, for another interesting example which can be used similarly.

```
?-  X=f(K,g(K)),
    Y=a,
    Z=g(L),
    W=h(b,L),
    %
    p(X,Y,Z,W).
```

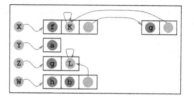

Fig. 3. Using unification to build data structures with declarative pointers.

illustrate that logical variables can be seen as "declarative pointers" [9]. I.e., in the same way a set of Prolog clauses constitute at the same time statements in logic and a program, the data structures of Prolog can be seen at the same time as (Herbrand) terms of the logic and as traditional data structures with (declarative, i.e., single assignment) pointers. We have found that explaining this duality is also very enlightening.

There are of course many other beautiful and elegant aspects to show (e.g., higher-order, meta-interpretation, or types and program properties in general, all of which in (C)LP once more can be covered within the same language), but our space here is limited. As a compelling example, in (C)LP, types (and properties in general) can be defined as (runnable) predicates. E.g., the *type* natlist can be defined as:

```
natlist([]).                                    run ▶
natlist([H|T]) :- natural(H), natlist(T).
```

and this predicate can be used to check that an argument is a list of naturals (dynamic checking) or "run backwards" to generate such lists (property-based testing for free!). Some of these aspects are covered in other papers in this volume [10].

3   Dispelling Myths and Avoiding Misconceptions

In addition to showing the beauty of the language, another aspect that we believe is important to cover during the course is to dispel the many *unfounded myths and misconceptions* that still circulate about Prolog and the (C)LP paradigm in general, and to which students may be exposed. While some of these views may have been at least partially true of early implementations of Prolog, both the language and its implementations have come a long way over many years (actually decades) of evolution, and it is easy to show how the shortcomings of early Prologs have been addressed in most current systems. The following is an incomplete list of some of these perceived shortcomings and some suggested dispelling facts or actions:

Explaining Termination. As mentioned in the previous section, it is certainly a good idea to start teaching the declarative view, i.e., using the logical reading

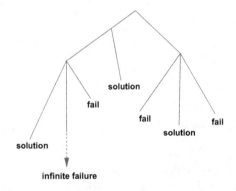

Fig. 4. Possible cases in the search.

when writing and reading clauses. In this view of the language, if the logic that we write is correct the system will answer any question. As mentioned before, here examples with bounded search tree are great starters (e.g., using only constants or avoiding recursion). However, trouble begins at the very beginning once structures and recursion are introduced: students soon run into termination problems. This is true of course of any programming language or proof system. However, non-terminating executions are likely to discourage beginners if their origins are not explained well and no remedies provided.

For example, let us define a pair of natural numbers in Peano representation:

```
natural(0).                                              run ▶
natural(s(X)) :- natural(X).

pair(X,Y) :- natural(X), natural(Y).
```

A query such as `?- pair(X,Y),X=s(0).` will hang with the standard Prolog depth-first rule, because the search never progresses beyond `X=0`, since there are infinite possible solutions for `Y` that will be explored first. In contrast, if the program is executed with a breadth-first strategy (which explores all branches fairly), it produces the expected solutions quickly.

A solution that has worked well for us is the following:

1. Provide students with a means for *selectively* switching between search rules, including in particular at least one that is fair. E.g., being able to run programs in breadth-first, depth-first, iterative deepening, tabling, etc. This comes built-in in certain Prologs[10] but it is in any case easy to implement in any Prolog for example via a meta-interpreter.

---

[10] E.g., in Ciao Prolog, in which we have added over time a number of features to facilitate teaching Prolog and (C)LP, one can for example use `:- use_package(sr/bfall).` to run all predicates breadth-first. Also, many Prologs have tabling nowadays.

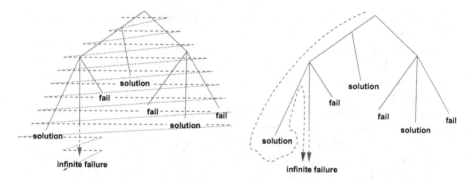

Fig. 5. Breadth-first (left) and depth-first (right) exploration.

2. Without giving too many details, start by running all predicates in breadth-first mode - all examples work great! This will allow students to gather confidence with recursion, search, and the power of a logic-based programming language (specially if they have already taken an introductory logic course), by simply thinking logically and/or inductively.
3. After students have been exposed to and written a few examples, we have found figures such as Figs. 4–5 useful to introduce them in a graphical way to the basic theoretical results at play, i.e., the soundness and (refutation-)completeness of the SLD(NF)-resolution proof procedure used by Prolog. The practical implication to convey is that the search tree has the shape of Fig. 4, i.e., that all solutions and some failures are at finite depth, but that there are branches leading to failure that may be infinite and that it is not always possible to detect this. This summary depiction makes it easy to explain why breadth-first (or iterative deepening, or any other fair search rule) is guaranteed to produce all solutions if they exist in finite time (Fig. 5, left), and why depth-first sometimes may not (Fig. 5, right). Of course, neither one of them is guaranteed to always finish after producing the positive answers.
4. At the same time, one should discuss the advantages and disadvantages of these search rules in terms of time, memory, etc. I.e., that the price to pay for breadth-first execution's advantages is very large (potentially exponential) memory and time consumption, while depth-first can be implemented very efficiently with a stack, with iterative deepening representing an interesting middle ground. This can be shown very practically by benchmarking actual examples, motivating the practical choices made for Prolog, which bring in great efficiency at the (reasonable) price of having to think about goal and clause order.
5. For example, simply changing the goal order (in this case in the query) to `?- X=s(0),pair(X,Y).` modifies the search space and the program can produce all the answers with the standard Prolog search. This leads naturally to discussing how one needs to reason about the behavior (cost and termination)

of predicates depending on the different *modes* (see [20]) in which they will be called.

6. And it can also be pointed out that there exist other techniques like delays and, specially, tabling, which helps detect some of the infinite failures in finite time, and avoid repeated answers (even infinite ones), in addition to changing dynamically the goal order.

7. More generally, while using small examples, sophisticated Prolog implementations, and modern fast computers can create the misconception that Prolog provides solutions effortlessly, it should be stressed that, as a Turing complete language, also Prolog programmers eventually need to care about algorithmic time and memory complexity of both their programs and the libraries/features they utilize, and, at the limit, termination.

8. Thus, this is also a good moment to introduce informally the notion of *undecidability* and the *halting problem* and relate them to the graphical depictions of the search tree. Some students may not be aware that there exist *decision problems* that admit no algorithmic solution. One should underline that this is of course not a particular problem of Prolog, but rather the essence of computability, and no language or system (Prolog, logic, nor any other Turing-complete programming language) can provide a magic formula that guarantees termination.

9. Needless to say it is also important to explain how to control search, via clause order and literal order, as well as pruning (see cut later). And, if time permits, it is important to discuss the use of the constraint systems built into most current Prolog systems (Q, R, fd, ...), and how they can bring about many other improvements to search (e.g., generate and test vs. constrain and generate), arithmetic (see below), etc.

Showing that Prolog Arithmetic can also be Reversible. The opposite of course is true if the discussion is limited to the ISO-Prolog arithmetic built-ins. However, this is far from the only answer in modern Prolog systems. The approach that we take is:

1. Present all the initial examples using Peano arithmetic (as shown in the `nat/1` example and in Sect. 2): it is beautiful and reversible (if run with a fair search rule of course). Although obviously inefficient and slow for number crunching, Peano arithmetic is an excellent tool for the first steps in writing numeric and recursive programs.

2. Then, the ISO-Prolog arithmetic built-ins can be introduced, explaining that they were added for practical efficiency, but at the cost of losing some reversibility. For example, using `Y is X+1` instead of `Y=s(X)` is no longer always reversible.

3. Then, (arithmetic) constraint domains can be introduced showing that they can represent the best of all worlds: at the same time beautiful, powerful, and efficient! For example, in the case of CLP{Q,R} (or CLP(fd)) our simple increment becomes `Y .=. X+1` which is both reversible and efficient. An alternative that we have also used is to start from the beginning using constraint-based arithmetic instead of Peano, but it can be more cumbersome because

for the student to fully understand what is really going on one should really discuss the workings of the constraint solver. In that sense Peano is simpler because with only unification and Horn clauses all operations are fully defined. Still, both approaches are fine.

The Occur Check is Available (If Needed). A misconception is that Prolog must be unsound because there is no occur check.

1. First, it is important to explain why the decision to leave out the occurs check was made in the first place: in addition to reducing the cost of general unification, removing the occurs check allows the complexity of the *variable-value* unification case to be constant time (instead of linear, since there is no need to check that the left hand side does not occur in the value), which is arguably a basic requirement for a practical programming language.
2. It is also important to point out that the lack of occurs check is rarely an issue in actual applications, and that, furthermore, there is in any case a built-in for unification with occurs check. In most cases, including e.g., implementation of theorem provers, one can selectively use the unification with occurs check built-in only when needed. It can also be useful to provide a package (easy to implement in most Prologs with a term expansion) that calls unification with occurs check by default for all unifications. This can also be provided in some systems via an engine/compiler flag.
3. Furthermore, it should be mentioned that many Prolog systems in fact now support infinite tree unification (stemming all the way back to Prolog II) as the default. In this extension to unification (actually, a constraint domain), infinite terms are actually supported and the unifications that would be the subject of the occurs check produce such terms. For example, the answer to `?- X = f(X).` is simply `X = f(X)`, and the system does not go into a loop when performing such unifications or printing such infinite terms.

Prolog Can be Pure (Despite Cut, Assert, etc.)

1. In the same way that we start with a powerful yet not necessary efficient search rule such as breath-first, it is convenient to restrict the discussion initially to *pure* fragments of Prolog without side-effects, cuts, or the dynamic manipulation of database.
2. In this phase it can be convenient to have a mechanism to enable a *pure mode* in the Prolog implementation where impure built-ins simply are not accessible. However, this is not strictly necessary and the objective can also be achieved by simply not allowing the use of impure built-ins, or, in fact, any built-ins, initially. Peano arithmetic is again handy here.
3. Later, the ISO-Prolog built-ins can be introduced. Here, it is convenient to treat each kind of *impurity* separately:
   (a) Cuts: a first consideration is that using if-then-else is often preferable. Then, regarding cuts, it is important to explain at least the difference between (green) cuts added as optimizations to discard unnecessary choice

points (but which do not alter the declarative semantics) from (red) cuts that are only meaningful for some calling modes and whose removal would make the program incorrect. Explain that argument indexing makes many green cuts unnecessary.

(b) Assert/retract: some programming patterns using dynamic program manipulation, like explicit memoization or algorithms that explicitly interleave phases of database modifications with pure deductions, do not sacrifice declarativeness. The classic Fibonacci program with a double recursion, implemented with and without memoing, is a good example here. Assert and retract in modern Prolog systems are module-aware, which makes it easier to encapsulate their effects. Also, it should be noted that there are other approaches, such as mutables or condition-action rules, that offer more structured ways to express state change; see, e.g., [6,13].

4. It is also useful to develop pure libraries (e.g., implicit states *ala* DCGs, monad-like styles), built-ins, or semantics where effects and actions are properly captured.

5. Finally, it is also important to point out that sometimes impurity is just necessary, but one should strive to keep it encapsulated as much as possible as libraries or program expansions.

Negation. Explain negation as failure, possibly from the theoretical point of view (least-Herbrand-model semantics, see also [20,22]) and through its classical implementation using Prolog built-ins. And devote time to discussing the limitations, either at a simple level (avoid calling negation on non-ground goals) or delving more deeply into stratification, etc. A good idea is to suggest to the students that they guard themselves from mistakes by defining their own negation that performs some checks, for example that the negated goal is ground:

```
not(G) :- ground(G), !, \+ G.                              run ▶
not(_) :- throw(error).
```

In an advanced course one can also go into more complex topics, commenting on the alternatives that Prolog systems offer nowadays (such as the very interesting s(CASP) approach [8]) and on ASP.

Prolog is in Many Ways as Other Languages, But Adds Unique, Useful Features.

1. It is interesting to show that Prolog is not a "strange" language, and is in fact completely "normal" when there is only one definition per procedure which is called in one mode. But that at the same time it can also have several definitions for the same procedure, and can thus support natively search, several modes, running "backwards," etc.

2. Moreover, Prolog (and specially modern Prolog systems) actually *subsume* both functional and imperative programming. At least theoretically, this is well known since functions can be easily encoded as relations and since mutable variable changes can be declaratively encoded by state-threading or other

means. (And that this idea is very useful in practice for analysis of other languages using Horn clauses!)

In practice, translating functional or imperative constructs to Prolog is relatively easy, specially when using special syntactic extensions (such as *logical loops* or *functional notation*). Performance-wise, most Prolog implementations are optimized enough to execute recursions as efficiently as loops (e.g., *last-call optimization*), use *logical mutable variables* (equivalent to implicit arguments), or as a last resort store mutable states via the dynamic database.

3. For students that have some notions of programming language implementation, it helps to explain that, when running "forward", Prolog uses a stack of activation records for local variables, and return addresses (forward continuations), as every language, that allow knowing where to return when a procedure returns (succeeds). Then, Prolog also has a stack of *backwards continuations*, to know where to go if there is a failure (previous *choice point*), and this (coupled with other memory and variable binding management techniques) implements Prolog's backtracking semantics very efficiently.

4. College students that are already familiar with younger languages (Erlang, Haskell, or even Rust) often recognize striking similarities in syntax and semantics with Prolog (e.g., "pattern matching"). Most of them tend to be amazed by Prolog simplicity and expressive power and recognize that Prolog is still unique.

Prolog has Many Applications/Uses/...

1. Show some of the many examples of great applications that Prolog has. There are great collections on line, and some new ones have been gathered for the Prolog 50th anniversary, but in particular there are some really excellent examples in the volume in which this paper appears. An excellent example is ProB, winner of the first Colmerauer Prize [15]. See also the excellent related discussion[11] on the advantages of using Prolog.

2. Give the students as homework real, challenging, and interesting projects where they can experience the power and elegance of the language.

3. Another thing to perhaps point out in this context is that modern applications are almost never written in a single language and some Prolog implementations can be easily embedded as part of more complex systems, and this is done routinely.

Prolog Can also Have "Types" (If Needed). Prolog is in principle a dynamically typed language, and this is not without its advantages –the success of Python attests to this. Second, as mentioned before, types and many other properties can indeed be defined very elegantly within the same language of predicates, and used as both run-time tests and generators. Furthermore, there are Prolog systems that also check these types and properties statically (again, see [10] in this volume).

---

[11] https://prob.hhu.de/w/index.php?title=Why_Prolog%3F.

And, to end this section on myths and misconceptions, a final mention is due to the **Fifth Generation (FG) project**. It is probably unlikely for current students to be aware of this project, but since the subject of its success or failure does comes up with some periodicity, e.g., in online forums, it suffices to say that one hand there were many interesting outcomes of this project (and there is ample literature on the subject) and on the other the fate of the FG Project is in any case quite unrelated to Prolog and (C)LP, simply because, contrary to widespread belief, the FG did not use Prolog or "real LP" anyway! It used flat committed choice languages,[12] which arguably did not contribute to make the FG as successful as it could have been.

4   Some Thoughts on Systems

Some thoughts regarding the different types of Prolog systems that we fortunately have currently freely available for teaching. This includes:

1. The classical systems with traditional installation, which in general are most appropriate for more advanced users and intensive use. In the context of teaching, they have the advantage that the best implementations portray a serious language which is competitive with the most popular languages in performance, features, environment, libraries, embeddability, small executables, etc. The drawback is of course that this type of system requires installation, but that should not be any hurdle for college students (or at least not for those in CS).
2. At the same time, there are now fortunately also very good Prolog playgrounds and notebooks that require no installation. Examples are, e.g., the Ciao Playgrounds and Active Logic Documents, SWISH, τ-Prolog, s(CASP) playground, etc. These no-installation alternatives can be very attractive for beginners, young students, or simply casual users, and they are in all cases very useful for supporting executable examples in manuals and tutorials, as done here. These systems can be server-based or browser-based, each having advantages and disadvantages. A good discussion on this topic can be found in [16] and [5], within this same volume.
3. As far as functionality, ideally the system (or systems) to be used should allow covering ISO-Prolog and some constraint domains –most current Prolog systems are capable of this. Other desirable features in our opinion are the possibility of restricting programs to pure LP (and supporting several search rules and tabling), modern forms of negation (such as, e.g., ASP/s(CASP)), functional syntax, extended support for higher-order and libraries, etc. Again, many current Prolog systems provide at least some of these characteristics.

---

[12] An interesting topic that is however out of our scope here –let's just say for this discussion that they used "something similar to Erlang."

5   The Programming Paradigms Course

So far, we have generally assumed that a reasonable number of lectures are available for teaching the language. However, a particularly challenging case is the standard "programming paradigms" course, now quite widespread in CS programs, where each programming paradigm, including often (C)LP and Prolog, is devoted perhaps two or three weeks. This scenario has some risks, and in extreme cases could even be counter-productive. A first risk, mentioned before, is that it is simply not easy, even for experts, to, in just very few classes, teach Prolog and the (C)LP paradigm well enough that the students really "get it." Other potential pitfalls in practice include, for example, that in some cases a "logic programming" library from a non-LP language (e.g., emulating Prolog in Scheme) may be used instead of a "real" Prolog system, which will have much more competitive speed and memory efficiency (plus an advanced programming environment, being capable of generating efficient executables, etc.). Shortcuts such as these, coupled with a superficial presentation in a few classes, can run the risk of leading to misconceptions about the language, its capabilities, applications, performance, and ultimately, its beauty. All this brings about the obvious and important question of what to do if the programming paradigms course is really the only slot available in the curriculum to teach Prolog. This is in our opinion a topic that deserves more attention from the (C)LP community. While, as mentioned before, quite good material exists for full-size Prolog courses, this is arguably less so for the (C)LP part of a programming paradigms course. So, in parallel with arguing for the presence of specific full courses devoted to (C)LP, it would be very useful to develop material (slides, notes, a short book, etc.) aimed specifically at teaching this "programming paradigms slot" well. In addition, we hope that the reflections in this paper can also help in this challenging context.

6   Conclusions

We have presented some lessons learned from our experience teaching Prolog, and (C)LP in general, over the years. We have covered some methodological issues that we feel are important, such as how to show the beauty and usefulness of the language, and also to how to avoid some common pitfalls, misconceptions, and myths about it. However, teaching Prolog and (C)LP is an extremely rich subject and there are of course many other aspects that we have not been able to address for lack of space. We still hope that at least some of our suggestions are of use to other instructors that are teaching or plan to teach Prolog. For a more complete picture, as mentioned before, much of our experience over the years is materialized in a) the courses that we have developed, for which, as pointed out before, the material is publicly available[13], and b) the many special features that we have incorporated over time in our own Ciao Prolog system in order to aid in this important task of teaching logic programming. Again, we have touched upon some of them, such as being able to choose different search

---

[13] https://cliplab.org/logalg.

rules, the playground, or active logic documents, but there are many others. We hope that all the ideas present in these materials and systems are helpful and inspiring to both Prolog instructors and students.

References

1. Bassiliades, N., Sakellariou, I., Kefalas, P.: Demonstrating multiple prolog programming techniques through a single operation. In: Warren, D.S., Dahl, V., Eiter, T., Hermenegildo, M., Kowalski, R., Rossi, F. (eds.) Prolog: The Next 50 Years. LNCS (LNAI), vol. 13900, pp. 71–81. Springer, Cham (2023). https://doi.org/10.1007/978-3-031-35254-6_6
2. Cecchi, L.A., Rodríguez, J.P., Dahl, V.: Logic Programming at Elementary School: why, what and how should we teach Logic Programming to children. In: Warren, D.S., Dahl, V., Eiter, T., Hermenegildo, M., Kowalski, R., Rossi, F. (eds.) Prolog: The Next 50 Years. LNCS (LNAI), vol. 13900, pp. 131–143. Springer, Cham (2023). https://doi.org/10.1007/978-3-031-35254-6_11
3. Cervoni, L., Brasseur, J., Rohmer, J.: Simultaneously teaching mathematics and prolog in school curricula: a mutual benefit. In: Warren, D.S., Dahl, V., Eiter, T., Hermenegildo, M., Kowalski, R., Rossi, F. (eds.) Prolog: The Next 50 Years. LNCS (LNAI), vol. 13900, pp. 124–130. Springer, Cham (2023). https://doi.org/10.1007/978-3-031-35254-6_10
4. Colmerauer, A.: The birth of prolog. In: Second History of Programming Languages Conference, pp. 37–52. ACM SIGPLAN Notices (1993)
5. Flach, P., Sokol, K., Wielemaker, J.: Simply logical - the first three decades. In: Warren, D.S., Dahl, V., Eiter, T., Hermenegildo, M., Kowalski, R., Rossi, F. (eds.) Prolog: The Next 50 Years. LNCS (LNAI), vol. 13900, pp. 184–193. Springer, Cham (2023). https://doi.org/10.1007/978-3-031-35254-6_15
6. Genesereth, M.: Dynamic logic programming. In: Warren, D.S., Dahl, V., Eiter, T., Hermenegildo, M., Kowalski, R., Rossi, F. (eds.) Prolog: The Next 50 Years. LNCS (LNAI), vol. 13900, pp. 197–209. Springer, Cham (2023). https://doi.org/10.1007/978-3-031-35254-6_16
7. Green, C.C.: Application of Theorem Proving to Problem Solving. In: Walker, D.E., Norton, L.M. (eds.) Proceedings IJCAI, pp. 219–240. William Kaufmann (1969)
8. Gupta, G., Salazar, E., Arias, J., Basu, K., Varanasi, S., Carro, M.: Prolog: past, present, and future. In: Warren, D.S., Dahl, V., Eiter, T., Hermenegildo, M., Kowalski, R., Rossi, F. (eds.) Prolog: The Next 50 Years. LNCS (LNAI), vol. 13900, pp. 48–61. Springer, Cham (2023). https://doi.org/10.1007/978-3-031-35254-6_4
9. Hermenegildo, M.: Parallelizing irregular and pointer-based computations automatically: perspectives from logic and constraint programming. Parallel Comput. 26(13–14), 1685–1708 (2000)
10. Hermenegildo, M., Morales, J., Lopez-Garcia, P., Carro, M.: Types, modes and so much more - the prolog way. In: Warren, D.S., Dahl, V., Eiter, T., Hermenegildo, M., Kowalski, R., Rossi, F. (eds.) Prolog: The Next 50 Years. LNCS (LNAI), vol. 13900, pp. 23–37. Springer, Cham (2023). https://doi.org/10.1007/978-3-031-35254-6_2
11. Kowalski, R.A.: Predicate logic as a programming language. In: Proceedings IFIPS, pp. 569–574 (1974)

12. Kowalski, R., Kuehner, D.: Linear resolution with selection function. Artif. Intell. **2**(3), 227–260 (1971)
13. Kowalski, R., Sadri, F., Calejo, M., Dávila-Quintero, J.: Combining prolog and imperative computing in LPS. In: Warren, D.S., Dahl, V., Eiter, T., Hermenegildo, M., Kowalski, R., Rossi, F. (eds.) Prolog: The Next 50 Years. LNCS (LNAI), vol. 13900, pp. 210–223. Springer, Cham (2023). https://doi.org/10.1007/978-3-031-35254-6_17
14. Kowalski, R.A.: The early years of logic programming. Commun. ACM **31**(1), 38–43 (1988)
15. Leuschel, M.: ProB: harnessing the power of prolog to bring formal models and mathematics to life. In: Warren, D.S., Dahl, V., Eiter, T., Hermenegildo, M., Kowalski, R., Rossi, F. (eds.) Prolog: The Next 50 Years. LNCS (LNAI), vol. 13900, pp. 239–247. Springer, Cham (2023). https://doi.org/10.1007/978-3-031-35254-6_19
16. Morales, J., Abreu, S., Hermenegildo, M.: Teaching prolog with active logic documents. In: Warren, D.S., Dahl, V., Eiter, T., Hermenegildo, M., Kowalski, R., Rossi, F. (eds.) Prolog: The Next 50 Years. LNCS (LNAI), vol. 13900, pp. 171–183. Springer, Cham (2023). https://doi.org/10.1007/978-3-031-35254-6_14
17. Pereira, L., Pereira, F., Warren, D.: User's Guide to DECsystem-10 Prolog. Dept. of Artificial Intelligence, Univ. of Edinburgh (1978)
18. Robinson, J.A.: A machine oriented logic based on the resolution principle. J. ACM **12**(23), 23–41 (1965)
19. Tabakova-Komsalova, V., Stoyanov, S., Stoyanova-Doycheva, A., Doukovska, L.: Prolog education in selected high schools in Bulgaria. In: Warren, D.S., Dahl, V., Eiter, T., Hermenegildo, M., Kowalski, R., Rossi, F. (eds.) Prolog: The Next 50 Years. LNCS (LNAI), vol. 13900, pp. 144–153. Springer, Cham (2023). https://doi.org/10.1007/978-3-031-35254-6_12
20. Warren, D.S.: Introduction to prolog. In: Warren, D.S., Dahl, V., Eiter, T., Hermenegildo, M., Kowalski, R., Rossi, F. (eds.) Prolog: The Next 50 Years. LNCS (LNAI), vol. 13900, pp. 3–19. Springer, Cham (2023). https://doi.org/10.1007/978-3-031-35254-6_1
21. Warren, D.S.: Writing correct prolog programs. In: Warren, D.S., Dahl, V., Eiter, T., Hermenegildo, M., Kowalski, R., Rossi, F. (eds.) Prolog: The Next 50 Years. LNCS (LNAI), vol. 13900, pp. 62–70. Springer, Cham (2023). https://doi.org/10.1007/978-3-031-35254-6_5
22. Warren, D.S., Denecker, M.: A better logical semantics for prolog. In: Warren, D.S., Dahl, V., Eiter, T., Hermenegildo, M., Kowalski, R., Rossi, F. (eds.) Prolog: The Next 50 Years. LNCS (LNAI), vol. 13900, pp. 82–92. Springer, Cham (2023). https://doi.org/10.1007/978-3-031-35254-6_7
23. Warren, D.: Applied logic-its use and implementation as programming tool, Ph. D. thesis, University of Edinburgh (1977), also available as SRI Technical Note 290

Simultaneously Teaching Mathematics and Prolog in School Curricula: A Mutual Benefit

Laurent Cervoni[1]([✉]), Julien Brasseur[1], and Jean Rohmer[2]

[1] Talan Research and Innovation Centre, Paris, France
{laurent.cervoni,julien.brasseur}@talan.com
[2] Institut Fredrik Bull, Paris, France

Abstract. Created in the 1970s, Prolog has its roots in mathematical logic. Its use to model logic problems is natural, but beyond logic, we suggest that using and learning Prolog for most of the topics in the high school math curriculum (probability, algebra, analysis or geometry) allows for a better assimilation of the course concepts. We argue that using Prolog is helpful in that it asks to properly model a problem, which is essential to develop problem-solving skills since it is often the key for finding a solution. At the same time, high school students discover a programming language that is easier to learn than imperative languages since the syntax is close to natural language and the language specification is more synthetic than traditional imperative languages.

Keywords: Prolog · Teaching · Mathematics · Education

1 Introduction

Based on predicate logic, Prolog is particularly well suited for expressing relationships between objects, checking properties about these relationships, validating the consistency of logical rules or for its intrinsic database capabilities.

However, the (re)introduction of Prolog into the educational system at the secondary school level, and its use as a complement to traditional school subjects, provides a new and enriching form of learning that may prove to facilitate the acquisition of certain knowledge.

There have been many examples in the past of the use of Prolog in mathematical analysis (derivative), geometry (Géometrix [6]) or chemistry [7,8]. Various papers [1–4], some going back to the 1980s, have illustrated, through a few examples, the pedagogical interest of Prolog in the teaching of elementary mathematics, or more advanced mathematics (such as the learning of recursion via fractals [5], or related to graphs [9,10]). Its educational potential in the history classroom [11] has also been considered.

Supported by Talan Research Center.

This collection of work shows the interest of exploring the usefulness of Prolog in a pedagogical context. The experiments we have conducted in 2022 with senior High School students seem to confirm its relevance. In this paper, we gather some of the case studies which were proposed to the students.

2   Prolog and Mathematics: A Natural Fit

An important step in solving mathematical problems is to correctly describe and express the problem. That is, being able to identify the givens of the problem and its assumptions. The intellectual process of breaking down the problem into simpler sub-problems is often an essential step towards the solution. Then, the expression of the different components of the problem and its links with the knowledge acquired in class make it possible for the student to devise a process to solve the problem.

Many mathematics teachers (especially, but not only) seem to encourage students to proceed to this "decomposition" of a problem which allows them to better understand how to solve it.

Transcribing a problem into Prolog is a relevant and efficient way to perform the analysis and the elementary decomposition of a problem. Indeed, it involves identifying all the elements of a problem and putting them into factual form. Then, the student must identify the givens of the problem and write them down as rules and facts. (Re)introducing Prolog into mathematics education thus has the double advantage of giving students the keys to a rigorous method for approaching problem solving with an initiation to declarative programming.

The experiments we conducted in a French high school, during the year 2022, with Senior Year students show that it is not necessary to use complex terms (unification, recursion, resolution, for example) to make students understand the concepts. In three sessions of 3 h, they were able to understand the basic principles of writing Prolog programs and to prepare a presentation for middle school students by themselves.

On the other hand, the declarative approach will facilitate the expression of the problem and the solution in "natural language", will invite to make clear sentences, which is an important skill to train. To describe certain problems, they will have to write or express sentences such as:

1. An empty list has a length of zero
2. The last element of a list containing only one element is the element itself
3. The parents of my ancestors are my ancestors.

More generally, writing in Prolog allow to articulate both natural language, drawing (of genealogical relationships for example) and writing an imperative program. Prolog thus allows to "navigate" between abstract and concrete, or between modelling and experimental verification. In order to do this, it is essential to take time with the students, and, above all, not to rush into absorbing the Prolog reference manual.

3   Some Examples

The intrinsic qualities of Prolog justify its implementation in high schools (not an intention to apply it artificially out of context). As we will illustrate with a few examples, its use has the potential to allow students to assimilate the elements of the course and to manipulate them and exploit them easily during exercises.

As we shall illustrate, its use has the potential to allow students to assimilate the elements of the course and to manipulate them easily during the exercises. When solving problems or doing exercises, Prolog may give students a way to understand the flow and application of certain theorems. Let us now consider a few examples.

3.1   Counting Triangles

A classic mathematical puzzle is to count how many triangles there are in a geometric figure made of line segments.[1]

First of all, one has to find a suitable formalism to describe the figure, and another to express the definition of a triangle. This is very easy in Prolog.

It is only needed to give a name to each line, for example by choosing two distinct points through which it passes: AB, AC, DE, DF, ... (in general it will pass through more points than the two chosen to name it). Then, we describe the membership of points to lines:

```
line_point(ab,a).
line_point(ab,b).
line_point(ef,a).
```

and so on. Finally, we express the knowledge of what a triangle is:

```
triangle([A,B,C]):-
      line_point(AB,A),
      line_point(AB,B),
      line_point(BC,B),
      line_point(BC,C),
      line_point(CA,C),
      line_point(CA,A).
```

One can now experiment with this first try in Prolog on a case study, and see that it is not totally satisfactory: Prolog will tell us that a point is a triangle (the three vertices being in coincidence), that a segment line is a triangle (the three vertices being aligned), and, finally, it will find that with three vertices, we can name six triangles $[A, B, C]$, $[A, C, B]$, ..., which is not of much relevance, as these "six" triangles are nothing but one.

---

[1] See, for example: https://www.rd.com/article/triangle-puzzle/.

These experiments, and the modifications to our Prolog program that they may require (specifying that the vertices and segments must be distinct, e.g. by defining a new *ad hoc* predicate), are an excellent ground to encourage careful, precise exploration of the relationships between concepts, models, experiences, real world, and human perception.[2]

3.2   Polynomials

In early mathematics course, second-degree polynomials are defined as follows:

a second-degree polynomial function P is a function defined on $\mathbb{R}$ *by:* $P(x) = ax^2 + bx + c$, *where* $a, b, c \in \mathbb{R}$ *are real numbers with* $a \neq 0$.

In Prolog, this polynomial in the x variable can be written as:

```
quadPolynomial(A*x^2+B*x+C)  :- A=\=0, number(A),
                                number(B), number(C).
quadPolynomial(A*x^2+B*x) :- A=\=0, number(A), number(B).
quadPolynomial(A*x^2+ C) :- A=\=0, number(A), number(C).
```

By writing these three clauses, the pupil becomes aware of different, more or less complete forms of polynomials (the teacher then guides him/her in this). They may start with only the first rule and find that it is not very precise. They can then move on to the standard application exercises of the course, where the aim is to check whether a function is a second degree trinomial or not, for example:

```
quadPolynomial(7). FALSE
quadPolynomial(12*x^2+1*x+0). TRUE
```

The advantage of using Prolog is that the student can transcribe the course definition exactly with a minimum of learning. In the same way, if he has to represent the solution of a second degree polynomial, the course is also written directly in Prolog. Introducing the concept of the undefined variable "_", this can be written as follows:

```
solvePoly(A*x^2+B*x+C, Discriminant, _, _) :-
   Discriminant is B*B - 4*A*C,
   Discriminant $<$ 0.
   /* The discriminant is negative, no solutions to display */
solvePoly(A*x^2+B*x+C, Discriminant, X1, X1) :-
   Discriminant is B*B - 4*A*C,
   Discriminant = 0,
   A =\= 0,
```

---

[2] More details can be found at: https://fr.slideshare.net/Jean_Rohmer/compter-les-triangles-en-prolog.

```
    X1 is -(B/(2*A)).
    /* The discriminant is zero, X1 is the only solution */
solvePoly(A*x^2+B*x+C, Discriminant, X1, X2) :-
    Discriminant is B*B - 4*A*C,
    Discriminant > 0,
    A =\= 0,
    X1 is (-B-sqrt(Discriminant))/(2*A),
    X2 is (-B+sqrt(Discriminant))/(2*A).
```

Then, "solvePoly(1*x^2+2*x+1,D,A,B).", will give A=B=-1 and D=0. This ability to directly represent the course concepts in the form of Prolog facts and clauses contributes to a reinforcement of the learning of the course basics (the student appropriates the concepts and retranscribes them after assimilating a few writing rules, to begin with). Progressively, he also acquires the fundamentals of logic programming (unification, resolution, etc.).

3.3   Euclidean Geometry

These same principles can be applied to various areas of mathematics. Thus, for example, a simple geometry exercise allows the students to express the different stages of the problem but also to describe the elements at their disposal.

We give below an illustration where we "translate" two elementary geometry theorems into Prolog.

```
/* a triangle ABC is right-angled at B,
   if it is inscribed in a circle of which AC is a diameter */
rightTriangle(B, [A,B,C], Circle) :-
     diameter([A,C], Circle),
     inscribed([A,B,C], Circle).
/* AB is perpendicular to EF if there are 2 triangles
   ABE and ABF, both right-angled at B */
perpendicular([A,B],[E,F]) :-
     rightTriangle(B,[A,B,E], Circle1),
     rightTriangle(B,[A,B,F], Circle2).
```

If, now, a student is asked to verify the following property:

> Let A, B, E and F be four points in the plane. Suppose that the segment [B, E] is a diameter of a circle C_1, that [B, F] is the diameter of another circle C_2 and, finally, that the triangles BAE and BAF are inscribed in the circles C_1 and C_2, respectively. Show that the segments [B,A] and [E,F] are perpendicular.

It will suffice, then, to describe the problem to Prolog, by writing that:

```
diameter([a,e],c1).
diameter([a,f],c2).
```

```
inscribed([a,b,e],c1).
inscribed([a,b,f],c2).
```

For example, the student can easily check that $[B, A]$ and $[E, F]$ are perpendicular by asking whether "`perpendicular([a,b],[e,f]).`" is true, and Prolog will return "TRUE".

Although Prolog is not a substitute for learning how to solve a problem, it is a valuable tool for learning how to understand and structure a problem, which is the first step towards solving it. Learning to pose a problem correctly is sometimes enough to trivialise its solution.

Pythagoras, Thales or midpoint theorems can be expressed just as simply in the form of Prolog clauses and, with the use of the traditional trace when executing a Prolog program, the student can see the solution of an exercise step by step.

In a first step, the teacher can show the students how to express theorems in Prolog, with the learners having to describe the exercises as facts (as in the example above). Then, in a second step, the students write all the case studies (theorems or propositions and descriptions of the exercises) themselves.

4   Conclusion

Solving a problem in Prolog means describing it. As we have seen from a few examples, no matter how you describe the problem, no matter how diverse the description, Prolog will always return an answer. The main interest of Prolog for mathematics education is that it learns to understand, express and structure a problem. This step alone often makes it possible, if not to solve the problem, at least to identify possible lines of attack opening the way to its resolution. It seems to us that this step is fundamental in the problem solving process and that Prolog, by its nature, is adapted to its learning.

The interrelationship between the modelling of theorems or course principles in Prolog and the progressive learning of the language seems to us to be more relevant than in traditional imperative languages where an algorithm must first be imagined. With Prolog's native solving principle, the student discovers the mechanisms that allow him to solve an exercise. The trace helps him to better understand which theorems apply or why some descriptions he may have made are incorrect or incomplete.

However, by calling the Prolog interpreter, the student will get the information that the property can be derived, but not how. The sequence of predicates is essential, and can be obtained by using the trace which, beyond debugging, also allows to understand the "reasoning" implemented and its relevance. Moreover, the solution obtained is relative to the known and described knowledge. A Prolog answer confirms that the knowledge domain is sufficient to reach a satisfactory conclusion, whereas a failure does not show that the requested objective cannot be reached. It does not show that the objective cannot be reached, but rather that the knowledge expressed (in the form of rules and facts) is sufficient.

Finally, it is important to note that languages evolve rapidly and are likely to move from widespread use to more moderate use; therefore, while it is good to introduce students to a computer language, it should not necessarily be chosen on the basis of its popularity, but rather its educational potential.

References

1. Ball, D.: PROLOG and mathematics teaching. Educ. Rev. **39**(2), 155–161 (1987)
2. Bensky, T.: Teaching and learning mathematics with Prolog. arXiv preprint arXiv:2108.09893 (2021)
3. Buscaroli, R., Chesani, F., Giuliani, G., Loreti, D., Mello, P.: A Prolog application for reasoning on maths puzzles with diagrams. J. Exp. Theor. Artif. Intel. 1–21 (2022)
4. Connes, A.: Micro-Prolog et géométrie élémentaire. Bulletin de l'EPI (Enseignement Public et Informatique) **44**, 125–137 (1986)
5. Elenbogen, B. S., O'Kennon, M. R.: Teaching recursion using fractals in Prolog. In Proceedings of the nineteenth SIGCSE technical symposium on Computer science education, 263–266 (1988)
6. Géométrix website, http://geometrix.free.fr/site. Accessed 9 Feb 2023
7. Kleywegt, G. J., Luinge, H. J., Schuman, B. J. P.: PROLOG for chemists. Part 1. Chemom. Intel. Lab. Syst. **4**(4), 273–297 (1988)
8. Kleywegt, G. J., Luinge, H. J., Schuman, B. J. P.: PROLOG for chemists. Part 2. Chemom. Intel. Lab. Syst. **5**(2), 117–128 (1989)
9. McGrail, R. W., Nguyen, T. T., Granda, M. S.: Knot Coloring as Verification. In: 2020 22nd International Symposium on Symbolic and Numeric Algorithms for Scientific Computing (SYNASC). pp. 24–31. IEEE (2020)
10. Volk, A. C.: Graph Algorithms in PROLOG, CPS 499/592 Emerging Languages, University of Dayton, Spring (2016)
11. Weissberg, D.: Micro-prolog en classe d'histoire: Montségur au risque de l'informatique. Bulletin de l'EPI (Enseignement Public et Informatique) **39**, 115–120 (1985)

Logic Programming at Elementary School: Why, What and How Should We Teach Logic Programming to Children?

Laura A. Cecchi[1]([✉]) [ID], Jorge P. Rodríguez[1] [ID], and Verónica Dahl[2] [ID]

[1] Grupo de Investigación en Lenguajes e Inteligencia Artificial Facultad de Informática, Universidad Nacional del Comahue, Neuquén, Argentina
{lcecchi,j.rodrig}@fi.uncoma.edu.ar
[2] Computer Sciences Department, Simon Fraser University,Burnaby, Canada
veronica_dahl@sfu.ca

Abstract. In this paper, we argue that Logic Programming(LP) is a viable and desirable paradigm choice for elementary school children. We consider we can fruitfully introduce Computer Science and develop Logical and Computational Thinking skills through LP to children.

We analyse the need of educational methodological approaches and suitable teaching resources to make these ideas sustainable over time. We introduce some proposals of different complexity for teaching LP conducted as an initial effort to make this type of knowledge accessible to elementary school students. The proposal is defined within the frameworks of project-based learning, collaborative learning and projects for social good.

We present a description of a pilot experience carried out for children aged from 8 to 10 years in two public elementary schools in Argentina.

Keywords: Logic Programming Education · Prolog · Computational Thinking · Logical Thinking · Elementary School · Game-based approaches

1 Introduction

At present, there is an international consensus on the importance of Computational Thinking (CT) [30] in developing general-purpose problem solving skills. Hence, countries have begun to incorporate CT into their curriculum since elementary school. However, there is no complete agreement regarding the concepts that should be addressed. In this respect, some works [4,24,27] recognise that the following concepts should be covered: algorithm design, abstraction, decomposition, generalisation and evaluation. Elementary school curricula include some or all of these concepts, in different complexity levels selected according to children's ages [3,22].

There is much research explaining how to introduce CT to children through Imperative Programming, supported by a variety of teaching resources that

D. S. Warren et al. (Eds.): Prolog: The Next 50 Years, LNAI 13900, pp. 131–143, 2023.
https://doi.org/10.1007/978-3-031-35254-6_11

collaborate in this process. The majority of these initiatives use visual programming languages, where students build programs using graphical objects and drag-and-drop interfaces. Examples of these tools are Scratch, Alice and Open Roberta. Compared to text-based programming, these visual languages significantly reduce the challenges for students to learn syntax and avoid the inconvenience of syntax errors.

The Logic Programming paradigm is not represented enough within the paradigms habitually covered in introductory Computer Science (CS) courses and developing children's CT skills.

Similarly, in the literature there is no consensus regarding how to define logical thinking (LT) [32]. In this article we consider that *LT mainly focuses on the abilities needed to identify entities (e.g. objects, concepts) and relationships between them, and to understand, incorporate and soundly use the rules of logical inference relevant to deriving new, implicit ideas in everyday activities, and to reason about and judiciously choose among different logical formulations of the same problem.*

In this paper, we argue that Logic Programming (LP) is a viable and desirable paradigm choice for elementary school children, even for those with no previous programming knowledge. Some research has been done to introduce CS and to develop CT skills through LP for high school children [2,29,31,33]. Similarly, we consider we can fruitfully introduce CS and develop CT and LT skills through LP to children. In addition to this discussion, in this paper we also address the problem of determining what and how we should teach LP, analysing teaching activities we consider suitable to face this challenge. For our proposals we describe some game-based, unplugged and social good projects. Finally, we describe an experience carried out in Argentina with children from 8 to 10 years old, detailing what results are being obtained in the pilot project.

2   Computational Thinking and Logic Programming

Computational Thinking has its origin in the constructionist work of Seymour Papert [23]. Jeannette Wing then introduced the expression in her seminal essay [30] as follows: *"computational thinking involves solving problems, designing systems, and understanding human behaviour, by drawing on the concepts fundamental to computer science"(p.33)*. Thus CT highlights the need to develop the abilities to understand how to solve problems using CS concepts and being an active participant in a digital society [20].

In [14], an algorithm is represented symbolically by

$$\text{Algorithm} = Logic + Control$$

The logic component specifies the knowledge to be used in solving problems, and the control component determines the problem-solving strategies by means through which that knowledge is used.

Regarding algorithm design, in LP the logic component is specified by facts and rules, which represent certain knowledge about the problem we want to solve.

LP and particularly the Prolog control component, which is domain independent, include recursion, backtracking, backward chaining and unification. Hence, we can distinguish *what we want to achieve* from *how we can fulfill our goals.*

Abstraction can generally be characterised as the conceptual process of eliminating specificity by ignoring certain features. Logic as a modelling tool and the emphasis on the essence of the problems are LP key characteristics for students to achieve abstraction.

Decomposition deals with breaking down a complex problem into smaller, more manageable components where each component can be managed independently. A rule in LP is expressed by A if B_1 and ... and B_n which reduces problems of form A to subproblems of the form B_1 and ... and B_n. Thus, we can specify a problem by describing smaller problems that may be more easily solved. These subproblems can then be understood, solved, developed and evaluated separately.

CT is associated with pattern recognition and generalisation in solving problems where repeatable patterns can be observed. In this sense, we wonder if any of the problems or solutions that we have found in the past can be applied to solve the new problem. Students can be introduced to different problems, such as puzzles or scheduling problems, to infer solution patterns.

Finally, we can consider evaluation as the process of ensuring that an algorithmic solution is a good one: that it fits for purpose [5]. Declarative semantics and proof theory of Horn clauses play a crucial role in understanding logic programs and in determining whether the goal is achieved.

LT involves the child's ability to properly utilise these skills as needed [32]. Furthermore, we consider that LT develops other skills as well. It helps us to distinguish good arguments from bad ones, e.g. through identifying fallacies and contradictions. In addition, it allows the child to establish connections between arguments through reasoning, so that they can interpret available evidence and derive new implicit facts, useful to explain a conclusion. Thus, the way we program in LP develops different LT skills, since modelling in LP allows us to focus on a problem's essence. Furthermore, logic programs can be built by translating simple sentences in natural language to a logic subset. Thus, to specify and represent knowledge, students are introduced to logic and consequently to formal reasoning. Two interesting approaches presented in [15,19] address how to relate logic, computation and human thinking through LP in order to best develop some of the mentioned skills, such as problem solving and communication.

Therefore LP can be viewed as a pedagogical device used for teaching to program, in a different way from how we do it in Imperative Programming: a way that promotes computational, logical and creative thinking. These ideas can be transposed into other disciplines, modelling specific situations and solving problems in those domains in a natural way.

3   Proposals for Teaching Logic Programming

This analysis provides useful background for anyone wishing to present a proposal for teaching LP and in particular Prolog to elementary school children.

To the best of our knowledge, no proposal to teach LP to a student population of the age range from 8 to 10 years old has been made in the last 20 years. In the 1980s,s, educational experiences with LP were carried out with elementary school students [8,18]. Taking inspiration from these works, we currently consider it interesting to rescue these ideas, given the importance of this kind of abstract thinking, through bringing this paradigm closer to children in their education.

One of the key considerations is to identify the core of LP concepts that can be learned by children. In this direction, we consider that we must focus on the declarative aspects of LP and restrict the use of procedural aspects of LP to a minimum. The first group of concepts to be taught involves ground knowledge representation and ground querying: constants, ground relationships with just one argument, ground binary relationships and ground atomic queries. A second group includes variable, non-ground binary relationships, non ground atomic queries and non-recursive rules. A third group of concepts covers n-ary relationships, conjunctive queries and simple recursive rules. In an advanced level, we can deal with negation as failure, possibly introduced through rules with exceptions [16,17] or through querying in the negative, as in "Who does not sing?" [6].

In order to make teaching LP viable, we argue that there is a need for suitable teaching resources: Prolog visual implementation and web tools. Using block-based language[1,2] avoids teaching and handling Prolog's textual syntax. A web environment allows collaborative work, in addition to avoiding the inconvenience of installing the software. Furthermore, programming tools must meet certain characteristics [9,10,23,25]: *low floor* (easy to get started), *high ceiling* (opportunities to create increasingly complex projects over time) and *wide walls* (supporting many different types of projects so people with many different interests and learning styles can all become engaged). At present, available environments fulfill some of the requirements, but there is no tool satisfying all of them.

Furthermore, educational methodological approaches should be developed in order to teach LP and reach children of different ages in various scenarios. Regarding methodologies, while there will not be a one-size-fits-all solution to implementing LP education for developing LT and CT skills and for introducing CS to students, we consider that incorporating elements of interaction through fun and games is a great starting point, setting up an appropriate approach for teaching LP to children [11,28]. Moreover, we also consider interesting to work on project-based learning, which is a form of instruction that has been explored in different scenarios of elementary education [26].

We present a set of projects of different complexity for teaching LP. Students participating in these projects do not require prior knowledge in CS. Furthermore, these proposals can be implemented with the usual available resources of the school, not requiring extra equipment.

---

[1] Blockly for Prolog Homepage https://guppy.eng.kagawa-u.ac.jp/~kagawa/Members/Sano/prolog.html.

[2] Blockly Prolog Homepage http://www.programmierkurs-java.de/blocklyprolog/.

Playing Detective: The proposed game is based on detective fiction story-telling in which the goal is to solve several robberies that occurred at different times and points in the city. The game is structured into stages. At each stage, students must face different challenges that, when solved, enable them to advance to the next stage. A set of clues in natural language will be given to the detectives, showing certain situations that will allow them to circumscribe the suspicious persons. Students must code the clues in Prolog and finally query the logic program on *who is the thief*. We strongly recommend to use a block-based environment for codifying the clues in a logic program.

Initially, we explain to students that we are in a problematic situation where the detectives have to identify important data, object and relations to be represented, and useless data that should be discarded.

Below we present concepts and examples that students are able to recognise, remember, recall and use well enough for the purposes of the experience. In each item we present the clue in Spanish and some Prolog code, which can be enlarged pressing the **Load Clue** button. The full code in textual Prolog corresponding with each clue in Spanish can be found in the Appendix A.

- Constant concept and ground relationships with just one argument. Students receive the Clue 1 in natural language: *Hay 7 personas involucradas en el robo: Juan, Ana, Romualdo, Alicia, José, Rosa and Pedro.*
  ```
  involucrado(juan). involucrado(ana). ...          Load Clue 1
  ```
- Ground binary relationships. In this case, the following relationships are used to introduce the concept: to wear, to like and to know (the corresponding words in Spanish are usar, gustar, saber). Some examples are: *Ana y Romualdo usan lentes. A Alicia le gusta pescar. Juan sabe leer.*
  ```
  usa(ana,lentes).    usa(romualdo,lentes).
  sabe(juan, leer).   gusta(alicia, pescar).       Load Clues 2 to 6
  ```
- Ground atomic queries: ¿Juan usa lentes?¿A Rosa le gusta nadar?
  ```
  (Clues 4 to 6) ?- usa(juan lentes).        %% Does Juan wear a hat?
  ?- gusta(rosa,nadar).                       %% Does Rosa like to swim?
  ```
- Atomic queries with variable: Clues 4 to 10. ¿Quién sabe soldar? ¿Quién es el culpable del robo?
  ```
  ?- sabe(Y,soldar).              %% Who does know how to weld?
  ?- culpable(X).                 %% Who is to blame for the robbery?
  ```
- Conjunctive queries: ¿A quién le gusta dibujar y cocinar? (Clues 4 to 6)
  ```
  ?- gusta(Y, dibujar), sabe(Y, cocinar).
                          %% Who likes to draw and knows how to cook?
  ```
- Rules: In this case, the following relationships are used to introduce the concept: a doubtful person, a mysterious person, a suspicious person and a guilty person. Every class of person is defined in function of the previous one. Initially, rules have just one predicate in the body. Some examples are: *una persona es dudosa si usa lentes (a person is doubtful if this person wears glasses); una persona es misteriosa si es dudosa y sabe cocinar (a person is mysterious if this person is doubtful and they know how to cook).*
  ```
  dudosa(X):- usa(X,lentes).                  Load Clues 7 to 10
  misteriosa(X):- dudosa(X),usa(X,sombrero).
  ```

Note that natural language phrases representing conditions are written so that its translation to a rule (Head, Body) is unambiguous and understandable for children.

– Recursive rules: we present recursion (Clue 8) through an example inspired by Kowalski in [13]: *A José le gusta todo lo que le gusta a Rosa (José likes everything Rosa likes)*.

```
gusta(jose,X):-gusta(rosa,X).
```

During the game, students receive four rewards according to what they have learnt: constants and facts; variables and queries; rules; and finally, recursive rules. We address the following CT and LT dimensions all over the game: algorithm design, generalisation, abstraction and decomposition in human communication in order to formalise knowledge; logical deduction when new implicit conclusions are obtained from the rules useful to explain this conclusion; and decomposition when facing rule formalisation with and without recursion.

It is interesting to remark that students must build a large knowledge base with several facts. The goal is to show that even if they can find out the thief without a computer, they can do it faster with Prolog. This idea is to emphasise the point of LP.

Moreover, in several stages the clues seem to be repetitive, in order to reinforce the concept, so that students build a model for the construction of new facts (generalisation).

As an alternative to the way in which the experience was presented and in order to promote collaborative learning, student groups could be provided with pieces of information that, when put all together, form a large knowledge base.

Unplugged Activities Covering Recursion: There exist several off-line activities suitable for elementary school students to introduce the powerful concept of recursion, such as the travel example (one is travelling trough intermediate stops to reach a final city) or the sorting algorithm [1,12]. Below, we present a new unplugged activity we designed, which has been tested. Similarly to most of those existing in the literature, it was designed for easing facilitation by non-specialist teachers.

We propose a simple game which arose spontaneously from an example to introduce children to recursion. We asked a group of children who used the same colour of pen to write their homework, what colour is the pen they use? Since they all used pens of the same colour, we asked them to express this in terms of their neighbour's pen's colour. The first child should say they use a pen of the colour of the second child pen's colour and so on. The key point is that the last child in the sequence has to realise that if they express the colour based on the colour of the first child's pen, then they start all over again. Thus, the need to identify the case base is motivated naturally.

Language/Physical Enactment Games: Several natural language based games can support Prolog teaching as they help students drill on other themes, e.g. grammatical concepts. Vocabulary, for instance, can be enriched by playing tipoteo, where a team wins by guessing a verb the opponent team has secretly chosen, from questions it can pose around the verb's arguments, like: *How do you "tipoty"?, When?, With whom?, Why?.* Initial help from ready-made knowledge bases or grammars can evolve into students writing their own, perhaps from clues they get from previous rounds of playing. Games of physical enactment (e.g. hopscotch-like search space descriptions chalked on the ground, with students representing constituents cloning themselves through others to pursue other avenues upon a branch's failure) can help them embody concepts such as execution strategies, sentence recognition vs. generation, backtracking, etc.; the consciousness that children already master recursion can be brought out through games around embedded relative clauses, and expanded using Russian dolls and the idea of a "genie" that can be conjured to solve simpler forms of (a recursive) problem; songs like "the song that never ends" (or deliberately misplacing the base case for relatives) can illustrate/ warn about looping; and so on.

Social Good Project: Inspired on [7,34] we propose to combine social good, scientific inquiry and LP. Elementary school teachers choice curricular themes focusing on our ecological crises (such as climate catastrophe, ozone depletion, land conversion) and our societal crises (such as inequity, hunger, war), or any other topic of interest involving how to improve quality of life and/or the environment. Students must find out relevant information about the topics (initial status, desired goal, possible actions and their impact) and represent this knowledge as a (syntactically sugared) logic program. Elementary school teachers and students could be given pre-programmed open tools (e.g. piece of Prolog code or grammars) that facilitate open-minded analyses of the topics.

Rules about global impact on human and ecological well-being of the chosen topic and possible measures to tackle it are expected to be part of the logic program. Thus, they can experiment with possible solutions around real data and consequently suggest rationally justified improvements of the current situation in their neighbourhood, province, and beyond. Teachers can thus motivate students to deduce implicit facts about the topic from logic programs, focusing on critical discussion about ecological and societal implications and encouraging children to become, in time, pro-active and responsible citizens and stakeholders of technology.

It is expected that this interdisciplinary project will become known when empowered students interact with their schoolmates, parents and with their community in general, showing the logic programs they have developed and promoting the use of Prolog as a valuable tool for programming.

Finally, to make these ideas sustainable over time, teachers must be instructed in LP and its methodological approaches, showing its advantages related to computing education (abstraction and logical reasoning among others) and the utility of LP to facilitate the achievement of educational goals. Thus, both LP educational packages for teachers and for children would be welcome.

4 Experience

In the context of this proposal's formulation, an experience based on the game Playing Detective was designed, implemented and assessed. This experience focused on fundamental CT and LT concepts such as abstraction, generalisation, decomposition and reasoning. Furthermore, the concepts of Constant, and Ground relationships with just one argument, Binary relationships, Atomic ground queries, Atomic queries with variables, Conjunctive queries, Rules and Simple recursive rules were worked on from the logic programming perspective.

The age of the students who were part of the experience ranged from 7 to 9 years old at the beginning of the school year and from 8 to 10 years old at the end of it. Both students and elementary school teachers had no knowledge about programming, so Prolog was the students' first exposure to a programming language. We worked in two public elementary schools in the city of Neuquén, Argentina, with 33 students ranging from 9 to 10 years old and 23 students ranging from 8 to 10 years old, respectively. Out of the 56 participants, 29 were boys and 27 were girls. Computer Science is not an established discipline in the schools' curricula.

For the purposes of this experience, the following actions were carried out: First, institutional and jurisdictional authorities were informed about the purposes of the experience and they agreed to fulfill the project. Second, elementary school teachers were trained to teach LP, introducing them to LP basic topics and to the Prolog block-based environment. Third, university teachers and students were trained to teach LP using the game "Playing Detective": 16 facilitators, 14 university students and 2 professors, participated in the experience.

The children were put together into groups from 2 to 4 members. A facilitator was assigned for each group to help and encourage the group to solve the challenges. Each group performed either 7 or 8 clues and all managed to solve the final challenge in three hours of work with a break in between. Each clue involves concepts that are related to both LP and the game.

Each LP concept was explored in two or three clues, each challenge was designed to help children apply the problem solving skill. When the last clue was solved, a reward was granted to connect experience with formal knowledge and, in that way, acquire comprehension. It was observed that throughout this process, the teachers' guidance dropped from strong to minimal.

The groups received a card from the teacher, in which they found a clue written in colloquial language. The students' joint work continued until the group reached a consensus on how to analyse and decompose the problem to describe relationships, rules and queries. Then, from the results of this task, the group developed and tested Prolog programs using the block-based environment Blockly Prolog. Figure 1 shows a group of students solving Clue 4. The complete code in textual Prolog can be accessed in https://swish.swi-prolog.org/p/PlayDetective.pl or

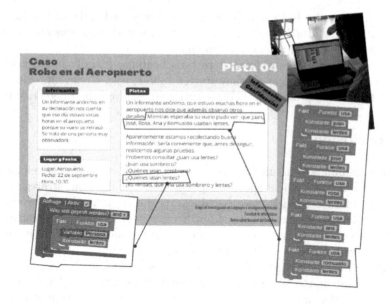

Fig. 1. Group of students solving Clue 4 - Playing Detective

this link to Ciao Prolog Playground. PlayingDetectiveBlocks.xml[3] can be loaded at Blockly Prolog to access to the complete block-based Prolog code.

Regarding recursion teaching, the students initially solved the recursion clue (Clue 8), expressing the recursion rule without difficulties. Afterwards, we carried out one of the proposed unplugged activities, in order to strengthen the concept. After programming the recursive clue, we asked a group of four 9 year olds *which colour is the pen they use* and we asked to express this in terms of the neighbour's colour pen. They did not face problems expressing it. Every child expressed their pen's colour in relation to the same their neighbour's. Finally, the last one realised that if they expressed the colour based on the pen colour the first child was using, they should start all over again. So they said, *Uso una lapicera azul (I use a blue pen)*, finding out the base case.

During these experiences, the facilitators take records of the degree of autonomy, efficiency, and interest for the task. These records show a satisfactory degree of interest, especially during the early phases of the activity. The autonomy degree of the students increases as each concept of LP is explored, it decreases when beginning to explore the next concept, only to grow again shortly afterwards, and so on. The efficiency degree is acceptable and remains the same throughout the entire experience, showing only minimal variations.

After the experience, we consulted the elementary schools' teaching team. They described the task as a transforming experience, emphasising that the boys

---

[3] https://drive.google.com/file/d/1X0vtYx7PUfJK5DH1pvUDqLdbxviH1MEZ/view?usp=sharing.

and girls had remained attentive for longer than expected and that this had been a great achievement of the activity and, at the same time, it was interesting to observe some aspects of the group dynamics.

The teaching team considered it to be a beginner-friendly initial course to CS for the children. Soon after, they started talking with a relevant lexicon and, without feeling the pressure of being scrutinised, enjoyed their detective roles.

5   Conclusion

Logic Programming is a suitable programming paradigm choice for elementary school children. We consider the development of CT skills as one strategy dimension, in order to bring LP close to educators during introductory courses for children. However, in the context of our work we are interested in teaching CS through LP, since our end goal is to encourage the inclusion of LP in the elementary school curriculum all over the world.

In this direction, we analysed the need of teaching resources and educational methodological approaches and we presented different proposals for children. We carried out a pilot project and our results show that children were able to solve problems in a natural way with LP, focusing on key concepts of CS including abstraction, knowledge representation and reasoning. We highlight how early in the education process we can introduce CS, solving problems through declarative programming paradigm.

Regarding "Why", "What" and "How" LP should be taught to children, this work provides, as a starting point, a framework that set guidelines for elementary school curriculum design and implementation, showing a new possible way to engage children in STEM.

Even though the preliminary results are encouraging, further efforts should be done to set how elementary school teachers can be trained to provide LP literacy education. An educational agenda that includes introductory courses for teachers to fill this gap will complete the learning progression and will make the framework sustainable over time.

It is also necessary to make sustained efforts to develop new technological environments that allow the consolidation of LP in primary school increasing and strengthening the initiatives carried out. In this direction, some educational resources are currently being developed to engage children, create customised lessons and increase classroom participation, e.g. in [21] the authors present an interactive web environment based on browser-side Ciao Playground to guide students in learning to program by way of Prolog.

Acknowledgements. The authors would like to thank the anonymous reviewers for their very useful feedback on previous drafts of this paper. We are also grateful to all the participants of Prolog'50's Education Committee meetings for their fruitful, encouraging and inspiring discussions on teaching Prolog to students at all levels. Support from Veronica Dahl's NSERC grant 31611021 is also gratefully acknowledged.

A   Appendix

Run on ![Prolog playground logo] Prolog playground or on ![SWISH logo] SWISH

```
 1  Prolog for Kids: Playing  Detective
 2  Code in textual  Prolog corresponding  to the block-based
 3  Prolog  code developed by 8 to 11 years old children
 4  October 2022
 5
 6  %%    Clue 1: Estela nos indica que en el lugar  se encontraban 7 personas
          involucradas en el hecho:  Juan, Ana, Romualdo, Alicia, Jose, Rosa y
          Pedro.
 7  involucrado(juan).          involucrado(ana).          involucrado(romualdo).
 8  involucrado(alicia).        involucrado(jose).         involucrado(rosa).
 9  involucrado(pedro).
10
11  %%    Clue 2: Laura nos indica que en ese  momento, estaban en el salon
          principal tres personas  que usan  sombrero Juan, Ana y Pedro.
12  usa(juan,sombrero).      usa(ana,sombrero).      usa(pedro,sombrero).
13
14  %%    Clue 3:Roberto nos cuenta que  ese dia habia dos personas mas que usaban
          sombrero: Romualdo  y Alicia.
15  usa(romualdo,sombrero).             usa(alicia,sombrero).
16
17  %%    Clue 4: Un informante anonimo mientras esperaba su vuelo pudo ver  que
          Juan, Jose, Rosa, Ana y Romualdo usaban lentes.
18  usa(juan,lentes).        usa(jose,lentes).        usa(rosa,lentes).
19  usa(ana,lentes).         usa(romualdo,lentes).
20
21  %%    Clue 5:Cristian  nos cuenta que a Rosa le gusta nadar; a Alicia le gusta
          bailar y pescar; a Juan le gusta ver TV y bailar; y a Romualdo le gusta
          pescar, ver TV y bailar.
22
23  gusta(alicia,bailar).       gusta(alicia,pescar).        gusta(rosa,nadar).
24  gusta(juan,verTV).          gusta(juan,bailar).          gusta(romualdo,verTV).
25  gusta(romualdo,bailar).     gusta(romualdo,pescar).
26
27  %%    Clue 6: De  los formularios que anoto Veronica podemos conocer que Ana y
          Juan saben leer. Por otra parte, Ana sabe soldar y cantar. Tambien
          sabemos que Romualdo sabe cocinar y Alicia sabe dibujar.
28  sabe(juan,leer).            sabe(ana,leer).            sabe(ana,soldar).
29  sabe(ana,cantar).           sabe(romualdo,cocinar).    sabe(alicia,dibujar).
30
31  %%    Clue 7: Julio, basado en su enorme experiencia, nos dice que  debemos
          dudar de algunas  personas. Una persona es dudosa si usa lentes. Por otra
          parte, tambien  nos informa que  una persona  es  dudosa si sabe
          dibujar.
32  dudosa(X):- usa(X,lentes).
33  dudosa(X):- sabe(X,dibujar).
34
35  %%    Clue 8: Emma, nos aclara que a Jose le gusta hacer algo si eso le que
          gusta hacer a Rosa.  Ademas, nos informa que resulta misteriosa una
          persona si sabe leer y le gusta nadar. Tambien resulta misteriosa una
          persona si dudamos de ella y ademas esa persona usa sombrero.
36  gusta(jose,X):-gusta(rosa,X).                    %%Recursive Rule
37  misteriosa(X):- sabe(X,leer), gusta(X,nadar).
38  misteriosa(X):- dudosa(X),usa(X,sombrero).
39
40  %%    Clue 9:Nahuel, nos indica que una  persona  es sospechosa si es
          misteriosa  y le gusta pescar.Tambien nos  informa que una  persona es
          sospechosa si es  misteriosa,  sabe soldar y  le gusta nadar.
41  sospechosa(X):- misteriosa(X), gusta(X,pescar).
42  sospechosa(X):- misteriosa(X), sabe(X,soldar), gusta(X,nadar).
43
44  %%    Clue 10: Ayelen, nos indica que la persona culpable es  una persona que
          esta involucrada,  que es sospechosa y  que sabe cocinar.
45  culpable(X):-involucrado(X),sospechosa(X),  sabe(X,cocinar).
```

References

1. Bell, T.C., Witten, I.H., Fellows, M.: Computer Science Unplugged: off-line activities and games for all ages. Computer Science Unplugged (2015)
2. Beux, S., et al.: Computational thinking for beginners: a successful experience using prolog. In: CILC, pp. 31–45 (2015)
3. Bocconi, S., et al.: Reviewing computational thinking in compulsory education. Tech. rep, Joint Research Centre (Seville site) (2022)
4. Bubnic, B., Kosar, T.: Towards a consensus about computational thinking skills: identifying agreed relevant dimensions. In: Psychology of Programming Interest Group (2019)
5. Curzon, P., Dorling, M., Ng, T., Selby, C., Woollard, J.: Developing computational thinking in the classroom: a framework. Project report, Computing at School (June (2014)
6. Dahl, V., Cecchi, L.A.: Introducing prolog in language-informed ways. In: Warren, D.S., Dahl, V., Eiter, T., Hermenegildo, M., Kowalski, R., Rossi, F. (eds.) Prolog - The Next 50 Years. No. 13900 in LNCS, Springer (2023)
7. Dahl, V., Moreno-Navarro, J.J.: Doughnut computing in city planning for achieving human and planetary rights. In: Ferrández Vicente, J.M., Álvarez-Sánchez, J.R., de la Paz López, F., Adeli, H. (eds.) Bio-inspired Systems and Applications: from Robotics to Ambient Intelligence. IWINAC 2022. Lecture Notes in Computer Science, vol. 13259, pp. 562–572. Springer, Cham (2022). https://doi.org/10.1007/978-3-031-06527-9_56
8. Ennals, R.: Logic as a computer language for children: core materials. Tech. rep, Imperial College of Science and Technology Department of Computing (1982)
9. Grover, S., Pea, R.: Computational thinking in k-12: a review of the state of the field. Educ. Res. **42**(1), 38–43 (2013)
10. Guzdial, M.: Programming environments for novices. In: Fincher, S., Petre, M. (eds.) Computer Science Education Research, pp. 137–164. Taylor & Francis (2005)
11. Hallström, J., Elvstrand, H., Hellberg, K.: Gender and technology in free play in Swedish early childhood education. Int. J. Technol. Des. Educ. **25**, 137–149 (2015)
12. Huang, W., Looi, C.K.: A critical review of literature on "unplugged" pedagogies in K-12 computer science and computational thinking education. Comput. Sci. Educ. **31**(1), 83–111 (2021)
13. Kowalski, R.: Logic for problem solving. Edinburgh University, Department of Computational Logic (1974)
14. Kowalski, R.: Algorithm= logic+ control. Commun. ACM **22**(7), 424–436 (1979)
15. Kowalski, R.: Computational logic and human thinking: how to be artificially intelligent. Cambridge University Press (2011)
16. Kowalski, R., Datoo, A.: Logical English meets legal English for swaps and derivatives. Artif. Intell. Law **30**(2), 163–197 (2022)
17. Kowalski, R., Dávila, J., Sator, G., Calejo, M.: Logical english for law and education. In: Warren, D.S., Dahl, V., Eiter, T., Hermenegildo, M., Kowalski, R., Rossi, F. (eds.) Prolog - The Next 50 Years. No. 13900 in LNCS, Springer (2023)
18. Kowalski, R.A.: Logic as a computer language for children. In: ECAI, pp. 2–10 (1982)
19. Levesque, H.: Thinking as computation: a first course. The MIT Press (2012)
20. Lodi, M., Martini, S.: Computational Thinking, Between Papert and Wing. Sci. Educ. **30**(4), 883–908 (2021)

21. Morales, J.F., Abreu, S., Hermenegildo, M.V.: Teaching prolog with active logic documents. In: Warren, D.S., Dahl, V., Eiter, T., Hermenegildo, M., Kowalski, R., Rossi, F. (eds.) Prolog - The Next 50 Years. No. 13900 in LNCS, Springer (2023)
22. Ottestad, G., Gudmundsdottir, G.B.: Information and communication technology policy in primary and secondary education in Europe. Second Handbook of Information Technology in Primary and Secondary Education, pp. 1–21 (2018)
23. Papert, S.A.: Mindstorms: children, computers, and powerful ideas. Basic books (1980)
24. Prottsman, K.: Computational thinking meets student learning: extending the ISTE standards. International Society for Technology in Education (2022)
25. Resnick, M., Maloney, J., Monroy-Hernández, A., Rusk, N., Eastmond, E., Brennan, K., Millner, A., Rosenbaum, E., Silver, J., Silverman, B., et al.: Scratch: programming for all. Commun. ACM **52**(11), 60–67 (2009)
26. Saad, A., Zainudin, S.: A review of project-based learning (pbl) and computational thinking (ct) in teaching and learning. Learn. Motiv. **78**, 101802 (2022)
27. Shute, V.J., Sun, C., Asbell-Clarke, J.: Demystifying computational thinking. Educ. Res. Rev. **22**, 142–158 (2017)
28. Stables, K., et al.: Critical issues to consider when introducing technology education into the curriculum of young learners, vol. 8(2) (spring 1997) (1997)
29. Tabakova-Komsalova, V., Stoyanov, S., Stoyanova-Doycheva, A., Doukovska, L.: Prolog education in selected high schools in bulgaria. In: Warren, D.S., Dahl, V., Eiter, T., Hermenegildo, M., Kowalski, R., Rossi, F. (eds.) Prolog - The Next 50 Years. No. 13900 in LNCS, Springer (2023)
30. Wing, J.M.: Computational thinking. Commun. ACM **49**(3), 33–35 (2006)
31. Yuen, T.T., Reyes, M., Zhang, Y.: Introducing computer science to high school students through logic programming. Theory Pract. Logic Program. **19**(2), 204–228 (2019)
32. Yunus, Y.S.: Features of logical thinking of junior schoolchildren. Middle European Scientific Bulletin 10 (2021)
33. Zhang, Y., Wang, J., Bolduc, F., Murray, W.G.: LP based integration of computing and science education in middle schools. In: Proceedings of the ACM Conference on Global Computing Education, pp. 44–50 (2019)
34. Zhang, Y., Wang, J., Bolduc, F., Murray, W.G., Staffen, W.: A preliminary report of integrating science and computing teaching using logic programming. Proceed. AAAI Conf. Artif. Intell. **33**(01), 9737–9744 (2019)

Prolog Education in Selected Secondary Schools in Bulgaria

Veneta Tabakova-Komsalova[1,2]([envelope]) [ID], Stanimir Stoyanov[1,2] [ID],
Asya Stoyanova-Doycheva[1,2] [ID], and Lyubka Doukovska[2] [ID]

[1] University of Plovdiv "Paisii Hilendarski", Plovdiv, Bulgaria
{v.komsalova,stani,astoyanova}@uni-plovdiv.bg
[2] Institute of Information and Communication Technologies, Bulgarian Academy of Sciences,
Sofia, Bulgaria
lyubka.doukovska@iict.bas.bg

Abstract. This article presents our activities for introducing the training of Prolog programming to the secondary school. The beginning was the development of an appropriate curriculum. The results of an experiment conducted with a group of selected students are summarized in this paper. A project is briefly presented, the purpose of which is to provide an opportunity to share knowledge and experience about Prolog programming and at the same time help build a community of interested students. In the conclusion, we have tried to summarize our experience which would possibly help to introduce Prolog programming in secondary school in other conditions.

Keywords: Education · Prolog · Logic Programming · Artificial Intelligence

1 Introduction

Recently, more and more efforts have been made worldwide to introduce the study of artificial intelligence (AI) in secondary schools. European countries strive to take a leading position in the technological development in the field of AI and take care of the rapid and comprehensive adoption of AI in their economy. Bulgaria is no exception to this trend. A strategy for the development of artificial intelligence in Bulgaria until 2030 was published, including artificial intelligence in education and science. In 2019, Bulgaria's Ministry of Education and Science prepared a National Program for Innovations in Secondary Education. The program addresses three types of innovation: innovative curricula involving new subjects, new teaching methods, and innovative learning spaces (STEM centres).

Implementing the program, the heads of schools from the region of the city of Plovdiv contacted our team for the joint development of a curriculum for the introduction of the discipline "artificial intelligence" in their schools. We have proposed a curriculum including logical programming based on the Prolog language [1] as one of the main topics (Fig. 1).

D. S. Warren et al. (Eds.): Prolog: The Next 50 Years, LNAI 13900, pp. 144–153, 2023.
https://doi.org/10.1007/978-3-031-35254-6_12

№	Topic
Section 1: Introduction to Artificial Intelligence (AI)	
1.	Definition of AI. Origin and history.
2.	Modern AI. Artificial intelligence and logic programming
Section 2: Knowledge	
4.	Knowledge in the field of artificial intelligence. Specialized and general knowledge.
5.	Presentation of knowledge. Representation of knowledge through rules.
Section 3: Logic	
9.	Logic. Basic concepts of mathematical logic. Deductive logic – basic concepts, syntax and semantics.
10.	Predicate logic. Presenting knowledge with common sense.
Section 4: Logic programming language Prolog	
11.	Logic programming and Prolog. Why Prologue? History. Applications.
12.	Theoretical foundations of the Prolog language. Facts, rules and goals.
13.	Getting to know SWI-Prolog. Examples
14.	Introduction to the Prolog programming language. Unification.
15.	Introduction to the Prolog programming language. Resolution.
16.	Return mechanism. Operator cut (!).
17.	Arithmetic expressions and operators.
18.	Working with data structures in the Prolog language. Lists.
19.	Lists. Basic operations.
20.	Predicates that handle lists. Examples.
21.	Knowledge-based systems. Knowledge base. Inference machines.
22.	Development of an independent project. Main stages.

Fig. 1. Programming in Prolog curriculum.

One of the ideas embedded in the program is to emphasize and demonstrate that the Prolog language is a convenient means of representing and processing knowledge in various subjects, studied in secondary school. For this reason, the course included examples from subjects such as history, geography, literature, cultural and historical heritage, etc. In this sense, one of the main approaches in the conducted experimental training is the creation of a system of learning tasks related to the students' knowledge both in the other school subjects and in their everyday life [2]. The conclusion that can be drawn from our observations is that students like this type of learning. Moreover, there is an increase in interest in the subjects covered by the examples.

A total of 115 students participated in the training during the two years. In the course of the training, we carried out several surveys related to the attitude of the students toward the training being conducted. Survey results [3] show that over 70% of students believe that studying AI is useful for their future development and are willing to study it in the future. Only 8% of the surveyed students answered that this training has no relevance to their future life. The results show that the students have mastered the learning material at a very good level. However, a number of difficulties are also observed. According to the students, the use of the Prolog language is appropriate and motivating.

Our observations show that Prolog programming can be efficiently studied in different forms and with different age groups of students [4]. Our secondary education legislation allows for the use of different forms of learning. We mainly used one of the eligible forms of training known as "interest-based activities" which means extra-curricular activities that take place outside the normal curriculum and are voluntary. In this way, interest-based education supports the development of students' key competencies in the fields of mathematics, informatics, natural sciences, and technology. The experience accumulated so far allows us to say that the interest and motivation of students are constantly growing and logic and Prolog programming can be successfully introduced in school education to different degrees, in various forms, and in different volumes. The approved curriculum and the associated teaching material can be used to train students in different professional, profiled, or innovative classes, as well as in different age groups.

Although we have prepared three books, our experience shows that there is a lack of well-developed and suitable textbooks for secondary school students. Our plans are to complete the process of creating textbooks and manuals with additional exercises and teaching material while expanding the reach of schools in different regions and cities in Bulgaria.

Interesting results for the introduction of logic programming in school are presented in various publications. In [5] the introduction of logic programming in elementary school for students aged 8 to 10 years is demonstrated. An approach for an effective and natural introduction of Prolog and logical thinking in school is discussed in [6]. In [7] it is argued that using Prolog requires proper problem modelling, while developing skills for solving a variety of problems, including mathematical problems. In addition, students are introduced to a programming language that is easier to learn than imperative languages because the syntax is close to natural language. The article [8] presents the key features of Logical English as the syntactic sugar of logic programming languages. Furthermore, an application of Logical English for teaching logic as a computer language for children is also demonstrated.

2   The Project "Digital Bulgaria in Prolog"

Based on our two-year experience of introducing artificial intelligence in some secondary schools, and especially on the good results of the programming approach applied to the presentation and processing of knowledge from different school subjects, our future plans are to expand the forms of learning logic programming and more specifically, Prolog programming. We find the inclusion of STEM centres a suitable opportunity. Furthermore, the time is very appropriate as the Recovery Plan of Bulgaria provides significant funding for the establishment of a national network of STEM centres so the interest of secondary schools in the opportunities offered by the project has been greatly increased. The creation of STEM canters is aimed at schools with innovative practices and those with the potential to develop innovations in the field of natural sciences, digital technologies, engineering thinking, and mathematics. The canters in the schools with which our team cooperates have the following focus: digital/video games, mobile applications, media products, digital marketing, graphics and design, etc. Artificial intelligence is also introduced as an innovation. A regional STEM centre is under construction, which will operate as a link between school STEM centres. Our project is an additional opportunity for such kind of interaction and in this way, it will be deployed in the regional STEM centre. Therefore, we propose a project called "Digital Bulgaria in Prolog". Bulgaria is a country with ancient history, remarkable cultural and historical heritage, folklore, and natural attractions. The idea of the project is to select interesting artefacts, events, and traditions from our cultural and historical heritage, folklore, and history and these artefacts are to be modelled in a formal way with the means of logic programming and specifically with the logic programming language Prolog.

The implementation of the project includes different types of activities, for example, it is necessary to develop an appropriate curriculum. The current program, according to which we started the training, is given in Fig. 1.The establishment of a network of school centres that will be involved in the implementation of the project has started. A key factor in the success of the project is the training of the teachers who will be working with the students – substantial efforts are being made to prepare various forms of training for them (e.g., in a specialized program in the Teacher Training Department at the university or on-site at the school itself). At the same time, the preparation of appropriate teaching materials has begun. Workshops are held periodically to promote the objectives of the project.

We have chosen "project-oriented training" as a form of teaching for the students participating in the project. Project-oriented training allows for the implementation of individual projects or in a team, with students being individually assessed. In this way, along with the activities listed above, the project work program includes the development of a knowledge-based system. The system's general architecture includes the components that will be briefly presented. The general architecture of the system that will be developed within the project consists of two major components – a distributed knowledge base and a personal tourist guide. The distributed knowledge base consists of separate thematic modules that store knowledge about the corresponding topics, which can be, for example, cultural and historical heritage, folklore, history, geography, etc. The modules will be structured in separate thematic areas, for instance, folklore may include areas such as national costumes, folk songs and folk singers, and needlework. Each module can be developed independently of other modules. One such module will be implemented in each school STEM centre. Thus, a parallel structure of the knowledge base can be implemented. The system will be implemented in SWI-Prolog [9].

The knowledge base will be implemented mainly by students. Individual groups of students can specialize in a topic of their choice. To help them, teachers prepare appropriate templates. Templates are relatively small executable programs or program segments that can be used as demonstration tools to develop the elements of digital libraries. Templates can be extended by learners to build knowledge and develop complete applications. They can also be adapted for other domains, but they shouldn't be modified or deleted by learners. Teachers can use existing templates to develop new ones. Each template consists of the following three parts:

- Artefact Description – a brief textual description of the specific artefact presented by the template.
- Student Assignment – a textual statement of the student assignment related to this artefact.
- Sample Code fragment – optional; a short sample Prolog code representing factual information and knowledge about this artefact can be added.

Teachers prepare the templates as comments that students leave at the beginning of their program code (as shown in Figs. 3 and 4).

The main function of a personal tourist guide is to act as a specific user interface. The tourist guide will be able to initiate a dialogue with the user (student, tourists) and accept requests to the system, taking into account the preferences and wishes of the specific tourist.

3 An Experiment

The regular education of students from selected schools will start the next academic year with the curriculum proposed in Fig. 1. We are currently conducting training with teachers who will be involved in teaching the students. At the same time, we are carrying out an experiment with a group of students, the purpose of which is to check how successful our approach is by implementing conditions close to real teaching. In this section, we would like to demonstrate the results of the experiment with three examples from different school subjects. The following examples were prepared by secondary school students who studied imperative programming as a mandatory form of education.

The first example deals with kinship relationships, one of the most exploited introductory examples in Prolog programming books. Figure 2 shows the solutions of two students: the first one created a Prolog program by changing the school subject (the Krum dynasty from the history of Bulgaria), and the second presented the genealogical relationships between the characters of a large patriarchal family from a famous Bulgarian novel, studied in the subject of Bulgarian literature.

In Student1's solution, the template was adapted for the royal dynasty from Bulgarian history while Student2's solution adapted the template for family relationships described in a famous Bulgarian novel. In both cases, the students used one-position axioms man/1 and woman/1. The first student used additional two-position axioms for son/2 and daughter/2 by which (s)he defined a predicate for a parent. The second student introduced the parent relationship as a two-position axiom parent/2. The learners used a different representation of the constants. Students easily learn to construct rules by describing kinship relationships such as father/2 and mother/2. In this case, the teacher set a template without a sample code and the students gave different definitions. They used variables in the rules to describe generally valid definitions. After that, they moved on to building more complex logical kinship relationships (grandfather/2, brother/2, uncle/2, etc.), as described in [10]. In this sense, if the logic we write is correct, Prolog will answer any question related to the described knowledge base. Our experience shows that after mastering this basic example, students easily adapt it to similar tasks from other disciplines (history, geography, biology, chemistry, etc.).

The second example (Fig. 3) demonstrates a game template described in its Artefact Description section. A student presented an adaptation for the subject of geography in the form of a game named "Guess the city".

Various exercises presented as games are used to increase the interest of students. This example is also interesting because we believe that games are an effective way to introduce children to computers. This view can also be seen for example in [11]. In this case, the students have to create a game that tests their knowledge of characteristic sights of Bulgarian cities. The program in the above example initiates a dialog with the user. Depending on the answers, it tries to guess the city the player has in mind. If confirmation of a given hypothesis is found, the program should not continue looking for another solution. The user dialog uses the control predicate -> /2 from SWI-Prolog to mark positive and negative answers.

We would like to briefly comment on the solutions given in Fig. 3. We are of the opinion that the problem of declarative and imperative style is a sensitive issue. Our experience shows that we should approach it very carefully. On the one hand, students

```
% %%%%%%%%%%%%%%
% Pattern "Family relations"
% Student1 - Khan Krum dinasty
man("Krum"). man("Omurtag"). man("Malamir").
man("Persian"). man("Boris-Mihail").
man("Vladimir"). man("Gavirl"). man("Simeon").
man("Qkov"). man("Doks").
man("Tudor"). man("Mihail"). man("Petur").
man("Ivan"). man("Veniamin").
% We describe all the women in the family tree
woman("UnknownWife"). woman("UnknownWife2").
woman("Zvinica").
woman("Maria"). woman("Evraksiq").
woman("Anna"). woman("Maria-Irina").
% We describe all the sons in the family tree
son("Omurtag","Krum"). son("Enravota","Omurtag").
son("Malamir","Omurtag"). son("Persian","Zvinica").
son("Boris-Mihail","Presian"). son("Doks","Presian").
son("Gavril","Presian"). son("Vladimir","Boris-
Mihail").
%.......
% We describe all the daughters in the family tree
daughter("Evraksiq","Boris-Mihail").
daughter("Anna","Boris-Mihail").
daughter("Zvinica","Omurtag").
% We describe all the marriages the family tree
married("Krum","UnknownWife").
married("UnknownWife","Krum").
married("Omurtag","UnknownWife2").
married("UnknownWife2","Omurtag").
married("Zvinica","UnknownMan").
married("UnknownMan","Zvinica").
%....
```

```
/*We describe the logic of all relationships in the
family tree*/
parent(A,B):-son(B,A);daughter(B,A).
father(A,B):-parent(A,B),man(A).
mother(A,B):-
parent(A,B),woman(A),married(C,A),parent(C,B).
grandfather(A,B):-parent(A,C),parent(C,B),man(A).
grandmother(A,B):-
parent(A,C),parent(C,B),woman(A).
brother(A,B):-parent(C,A),parent(C,B),man(A).
sister(A,B):-parent(C,A),parent(C,B),woman(A).
aunt(A,B):-sister(A,C),parent(C,B).
uncle(A,B):-brother(A,C),parent(C,B).
cousin(A,B):-uncle(C,B),parent(C,A).

/* Student2 - Family relationships in the novel "The
Iron Cresset" */
parent(stoyan,kocho). parent(stoyan,lazar).
parent(stoyan,manda). parent(stoyan,nona).
parent(stoyan,katerina). parent(sultana, kocho).
parent(sultana, lazar). parent(sultana, manda).
parent(sultana,nona). parent(sultana, katerina).
man(stoyan). man(kocho). man(lazar).
woman(sultana). woman(manda). woman(nona).
woman(katerina).
successor(Y, X) :- parent(X, Y).
mother(X, Y) :- parent(X, Y), woman(X).
father(X, Y) :- parent(X, Y), man(X).
brother(X,Y):- parent(Z,X), parent(Z,Y), man(X),
X \== Y.
brother(X,Y):- parent(Z,X), parent(Z,Y), man(X),
man(Y), X \== Y.
```

Fig. 2. Example "Family relationship"

study imperative programming languages as mandatory subjects. Accordingly, teachers of these subjects are supporters and followers of this style. In our meetings with students and teachers, the question is always asked: why not Java, C++, C#, or Python? On the other hand, logic programming in Prolog is taught in elective courses and mainly within STEM education. In these conditions, we cannot afford to put one style against the other. Our strategy is to convince and demonstrate that, depending on the problem to be solved, the appropriate means are chosen. For this example (Fig. 3), we believe that regardless of the imperative style of the dialogue with the user, the main task is to search for verification of hypotheses, for which Prolog is a suitable tool. For this purpose, we offer examples mainly from cultural and historical heritage, history, and geography, and we think we succeed because students like these examples very much. We will allow ourselves to indicate an illustrative case. A teacher and some students from one of the schools decided to create a program for the classification and properties of chemical elements. After a lot of effort, they managed to write the program in C++. After our Prolog training, they developed a new program written in Prolog by using much easier and much shorter code. This teacher is now our biggest supporter and enjoys teaching students in Prolog. Our findings confirm those detailed in [12]. A combination of logic programming and imperative programming is discussed in [13].

```
% %%%%%%%%%%%%%%%%
% Pattern "Guess the animal" ...
/* Artefact Description: This is a game that
encourages deductive solutions and creativity. It
originated in the USA in the 19th century but its
popularity soared in the 1940s when it began to be
widely played on radio quizzes. The most popular
versions of this game are called "Guess the plant,
fruit, mineral, ...". In our case, the story is "Guess the
animal"; by activating a dialogue, the game tries to
guess the animal the player means by pointing
familiar characteristics to him/her... */
go :- hypothesis(City),
    write('I guess the city is: '),
    write(City), nl, undo.
/* hypotheses to be tested */
hypothesis(plovdiv) :- plovdiv, !.
% hypothesis(sofia) :- sofia, !.
%...
hypothesis(unknown).
/* identification rules */
plovdiv:- south_central_region,
    verify(is_an_ancient_theater),

verify(bishops_Basilica_of_Phlippopolis),
    verify(there_are_seven_hills).
% sofia:- ...
% follow rules for Sofia and other cities in Bulgaria
/* classification rules */
south_central_region:-
verify(is_located_in_central_southern_Bulgaria), !.
south_central_region:- verify(maritza_river).
%...
ask(Question) :- % user interface ....
write('Does the city have the following landmark: '),
    write(Question), write('? '), read(Answer), nl,
    ( (Answer == yes ; Answer== y) ->
assert(yes(Question)) ;
        assert(no(Question)), fail).
:- dynamic yes/1,no/1.
/* How to verify something */
verify(S) :- % answers: yes -> true, no -> false
    (yes(S) -> true ;   (no(S) -> fail ;     ask(S))).
/* undo all yes/no assertions */
undo :- retract(yes(_)),fail.
undo :- retract(no(_)),fail.
```

Fig. 3. Example "Guess the city"

The third example is from Bulgarian folklore and more specifically, embroideries. The template is prepared as a logical problem. The task to solve is given in the Artefact Description part of the template. Figure 4 presents one of the solutions provided by the students.

The program in Fig. 4 is relatively advanced for beginners. It is a constraint problem to find a linear arrangement of four coloured shapes that satisfy a set of constraints on how they can be arranged. The student uses a generate and test strategy. Shape_color/1 is true for satisfying a condition represented as a list of shape-colour pairs, where the shapes and colours are given in the shape/1 and color /1 predicates. Five specified constraints are identified by integers 1–5. The first 6 subgoals in the shape_color/1 definition non-deterministically generate all possible states, essentially using permutation1/2. The last subgoal, check_rules/2, checks that the generated state satisfies all 5 constraints. The constraint is checked by the r/2 clause. Each constraint is checked using select/3 and append/3 to verify that the positions of the coloured figures in the state list do indeed satisfy the specified requirement.

The solution to the third example was provided by a student with a very good mathematical background. Unlike most students, he demonstrates a good understanding and use of list structures and recursion. Also, the solution uses its own predicates (permutation, select, member, append) instead of the built-in ones.

```
% %%%%%%%%%%%%%%%%%%%
/* Pattern " The Bulgarian embroideries"
Artefact Description: The embroideries are an
essential part of the Bulgarian folklore heritage. Let's
assume that four shapes lie next to each other in
embroidery: a triangle, a parallelogram, a circle, and a
square (they are listed in any order). The colors of
these shapes are green, yellow, blue, and red. The red
shape lies between the green and blue (may not be
right next to it), the circle lies to the right of the
yellow shape, the square lies to the right of the
parallelogram and the circle, and the parallelogram is
not at the end, and the blue shape does not lie next to
the yellow shape...
Student Assignment: The student has to determine
what color each of the shapes is...    */

shape(['triangle', 'parallelogram', 'circle', 'square']).
color(['green', 'yellow', 'blue', 'red']).
s([1, 2, 3, 4, 5]).
shape_color(FC) :-
    shape(F), color(C), s(S),
    permutation1(F, F1),
    permutation1(C, C1),
    by_pairs(F1, C1, FC),
    check_rules(S, FC).
by_pairs([], [], []).
by_pairs([H1 | T1], [H2 | T2], [H1-H2 | R]) :-
    by_pairs(T1, T2, R).
check_rules([], _).
check_rules([H | T], FC) :-
    r(H, FC),
    check_rules(T, FC).
% The red figure lies between the green and blue:
r(1, FC) :-
    select1(C1, [_-'green', _-'blue'], [C2]),
    append1(_, [ C1 | R1], FC),
    append1(_, [_-'red' | R2], R1),
```

```
    member1(C2, R2).
% The circle lies to the right of the yellow figure:
r(2, FC) :-
    append1(_, [_-'yellow', 'circle'-_ | _], FC).
% The square lies to the right of the rectangle and the
circle:
r(3, FC) :-
    select1(F1, ['parallelogram'-_, 'circle'-_], [F2]),
    append1(_, [F1, F2, 'square'-_ | _], FC).
% The square lies to the right of the rectangle and the
circle:
r(4, FC) :-
    \+ FC = ['parallelogram'-_ | _],
    \+ append1(_, ['parallelogram'-_], FC).
% The blue figure does not lie next to the yellow
figure:
r(5, FC) :-
    \+ append1(_, [_-'yellow', _-'blue' | _], FC),
    \+ append1(_, [ _-'blue', _-'yellow' | _], FC).
permutation1([], []).
permutation1(List, [First | Perm]) :-
    select1(First, List, Rest), permutation1(Rest,
Perm).
select1(Elem, [Elem | Tail], Tail).
select1(Elem, [Head | Tail], [Head | Rest]) :-
    select1(Elem, Tail, Rest).
member1(Elem, [Elem | _]).
member1(Elem, [_ | Tail]) :- member1(Elem, Tail).
% if the left list is empty then the resulting list is the
same as the right list,
append1([], RightList, RightList).
% otherwise, we take the head from the left list and
transfer it to the head of the final list,
append1([LeftHead|LeftTeil], RightList,
[LeftHead|RightPart]) :-
    append1(LeftTeil, RightList, RightPart). % continues
for the tail of the left list
```

Fig.4. Example "Bulgarian embroideries"

4 Conclusion

This article presents our activities for introducing the training of Prolog programming
to the secondary school. Our two-year relatively successful experience motivates us to
improve the training approach and look for new educational forms. For this purpose,
we conducted an experiment which is presented in this article. From this experiment,
we have selected three distinctive examples. The first one shows the type of examples
that students do well and enjoy working on. The second one demonstrates a blending of
imperative and declarative programming styles. The third one shows that students with
a good mathematical background can also cope with more difficult tasks for beginners.

One main conclusion we can draw is that it is of utmost importance that computer
science teachers are consistently convinced step by step that the "peaceful coexistence" of
declarative and imperative styles is not only possible but even useful and can bring many

benefits. We are currently running an extensive teacher training campaign. In teaching, we try not to contrast the two styles, taking into account that computer science teachers are usually trained in, support, and actually teach an imperative style of programming. At the same time, it is worth explaining to students that the two styles are different from each other. For this reason, an effective approach is a conviction that it is essential to choose an adequate style depending on the problem to solve. In this context, the selection of suitable examples is of paramount importance.

We know from experience that students like examples from domains such as cultural heritage, history, geography, and literature. In order to maintain and strengthen this interest, we started the implementation of a project called "Digital Bulgaria in Prolog". This project provides a shared, ever-growing repository of various Prolog writing examples. In addition to the disciplines typical of STEM canters, examples from Bulgarian folklore, historical facts, natural landmarks, and others can also be developed under the umbrella of artificial intelligence. In addition, the project contributes to the fact that students from different schools can easily share knowledge and experience and feel like they belong to one community – that of friends of logic programming in Prolog. In this way, our project will contribute to sharing experiences between students from different schools.

On the other hand, the project enables teachers to work in a team – usually, the teacher of informatics collaborates with the teacher of the specific subject (history, geography, chemistry, physics, and others). Teachers of these disciplines (unlike computer science teachers) are not tempted by the imperative style. They very quickly adopt the declarative style.

We hope that these conclusions will be useful for the introduction of Prolog programming in other countries and under other conditions.

Acknowledgment. The research is supported by the project KP-06-M62/2 "Modeling of knowledge in the field of Bulgarian folklore" funded by the National Research Fund and by the Bulgarian Ministry of Education.

References

1. Kowalski, R.: Predicate logic as programming language. In: Proceedings IFIP Congress, pp. 569–574. North-Holland Publishing Co., Stockholm (1974)
2. Glushkova, T., Stoyanov, S., Tabakova-Komsalova, V., Grancharova-Hristova, M., Krasteva, I.: An approach to teaching artificial intelligence in School. In: Smyrnova-Trybulska, E. (ed.) Innovative Educational Technologies, Tools and Methods for E-learning, 12, Katowice–Cieszyn 2020, pp. 257–267. https://doi.org/10.34916/el.2020.12.22
3. Tabakova-Komsalova, V., Glushkova, T., Krasteva, I., Stoyanov, S.: AI training – approaches, results, analyses and conclusions. In: Smyrnova-Trybulska, E. (ed.) E-learning in the Time of COVID-19 , 13, Katowice–Cieszyn 2021, pp. 176–186. https://doi.org/10.34916/el.2021. 13.15
4. Tabakova-Komsalova, V., Glushkova, T., Grancharova-Hristova, M., Krasteva, I.: Learning tasks in artificial intelligence education. Educ. Technol. **11/2020**(1), 15–22, 233–240. ISSN 1314–1791 (PRINT), ISSN 2535–1214 (ONLINE) (2020) https://doi.org/10.26883/2010. 201.2292

5. Cecchi, L., Rodrıguez, J., Dahl, V.: Logic programming at Elementary School: why, what and how should we teach logic programming to children?. In: Warren, D.S., Dahl, V., Eiter, T., Hermenegildo, M., Kowalski, R., Rossi, F. (eds.) Prolog - The Next 50 Years. No. 13900 in LNCS, Springer, July 2023

6. Dahl, V., Cecchi, L.: Introducing prolog in language-informed ways. In: Warren, D.S., Dahl, V., Eiter, T., Hermenegildo, M., Kowalski, R., Rossi, F. (eds.) Prolog - The Next 50 Years. No. 13900 in LNCS. Springer, July 2023

7. Cervoni, L., Brasseur, J., Rohmer, J.: Simultaneously teaching Mathematics and Prolog in school curricula: a mutual benefit. In: Warren, D.S., Dahl, V., Eiter, T., Hermenegildo, M., Kowalski, R., Rossi, F. (eds.) Prolog - The Next 50 Years. No. 13900 in LNCS, Springer, July 2023

8. Kowalski, R., Dávila, J., Sartor, J., Calejo, M.: Logical English for Law and Education, In: Warren, D.S., Dahl, V., Eiter, T., Hermenegildo, M., Kowalski, R., Rossi, F. (eds.) Prolog - The Next 50 Years. No. 13900 in LNCS, Springer (July 2023)

9. SWI-Prolog. https://www.swi-prolog.org/

10. Warren, D.S.: Introduction to Prolog. In: Warren, D.S., Dahl, V., Eiter, T., Hermenegildo, M., Kowalski, R., Rossi, F. (eds.) Prolog - The Next 50 Years. No. 13900 in LNCS, Springer, July 2023

11. Genesereth, M.: Dynamic Logic Programming. In: Warren, D.S., Dahl, V., Eiter, T., Hermenegildo, M., Kowalski, R., Rossi, F. (eds.) Prolog - The Next 50 Years. No. 13900 in LNCS, Springer, July 2023

12. Hermenegildo, M.V., Morales, J.F., Lopez-Garcia, P.: Some thoughts on how to teach Prolog. In: Warren, D.S., Dahl, V., Eiter, T., Hermenegildo, M., Kowalski, R., Rossi, F. (eds.) Prolog - The Next 50 Years. No. 13900 in LNCS, Springer, July 2023

13. Kowalski, R., Sadri, F., Calejo, M., Dávila, J.: Combining logic programming and imperative programming in LPS. In: Warren, D.S., Dahl, V., Eiter, T., Hermenegildo, M., Kowalski, R., Rossi, F. (eds.) Prolog - The Next 50 Years. No. 13900 in LNCS, Springer, July 2023

Introducing Prolog in Language-Informed Ways

Verónica Dahl[1] and Laura A. Cecchi[2]

[1] Simon Fraser University, Burnaby, Canada
veronica_dahl@sfu.ca
[2] Grupo de Investigación en Lenguajes e Inteligencia Artificial Facultad de
Informática, Universidad Nacional del Comahue, Neuquén, Argentina
lcecchi@fi.uncoma.edu.ar

Abstract. We argue that using students' conscious and unconscious language and grammar proficiency, plus applying what we know about language acquisition, can make Prolog learning much more accessible. This strategy could increase our potential to extend its influence widely, simultaneously helping develop computational, logical and subject-specific concepts and skills. Our position elicits a nontraditional -and in our view, more pedagogical and efficient- ordering of themes and tools.

Keywords: Prolog and LP Education · Logical thinking ·
Computational Thinking · Applied Linguistics · Regenerative and
Redistributive AI

1 Introduction

In acquiring language, humans unconsciously acquire many of the skills and notions that are also needed in general for logical thinking and for computational thinking, and also for understanding, using, and creating Prolog programs in particular[1]. For instance, the concept of a **list** is implicit in the linguistic competence of even toddlers, owing to their naturally acquired proficiency with lists of sounds. Of course, this competence rests on their also naturally acquired understanding of **symbols**: sequences of sounds in a given order are recognized as pointing the mind to something other than themselves, just from humans becoming exposed to language. Typically, children younger than 2 years old already recognize the meaning of many sentences, even if they reproduce them in ways only grammatical to their own personal dialect. For instance, they might omit the determiner "the" when asking for a door to be opened, or pronounce "opi" rather than "open".

We argue that using students' conscious and unconscious language and grammar proficiency, plus applying what we know about language acquisition, can make Prolog much more accessible, consequently maximizing our potential to

---

[1] In the remainder of this article, we highlight sample notions in bold type as we relate them to language.

D. S. Warren et al. (Eds.): Prolog: The Next 50 Years, LNAI 13900, pp. 154–167, 2023.
https://doi.org/10.1007/978-3-031-35254-6_13

extend its influence widely, while simultaneously helping develop computational, logical and subject-specific concepts and skills. This position elicits a nontraditional (and in our view, more pedagogical and efficient) approach to learning Prolog: through giving language and grammars a central role.

Grammar-based introductions to Prolog can simultaneously help teach and drill on **linguistic-oriented concepts**, making **parts of speech** fun to learn, e.g. through consulting made-up funny lexicons in generation and in analysis mode; and raising consciousness about **ambiguity** naturally, e.g. around words that serve more than one function. Grammars can also serve to drill on **other disciplines** (e.g., on the languages of DNA [2]), with mutually reinforcing effects between both fields.

2   Motivation

Human language is, arguably, one of the most complex, intricate and subtle abstract systems ever invented. Yet natural language skills and notions are among the first, best learned and most universally and assiduously practised human skills and notions.

At the same time, much of the (largely unconscious) linguistic competence of even small children relates directly to concepts also needed to learn Prolog, logic thinking [28] and computational thinking [35].

This motivates us to explore the reaches of a) taking language anchored approaches to learn or solidify Prolog concepts as our pedagogical pivot, and b) counting Prolog grammars among our main tools. We shall substantiate this position through a series of discussed examples.

Preliminary empirical evidence for our position was provided by several initial experiences in teaching Prolog to children [6]. This approach was also successful with university students of humanistic careers taught by Dahl over the years[2].

3   Spoken Languages as Pedagogical Pivots

Many Prolog, Logical and Computational-Thinking concepts, including several often judged "difficult" to teach, are already in the (unconscious) linguistic competence of even small children, ready to be transposed from linguistic realms into other subjects. Examples are **recursion**, which can be brought to focus e.g. through games or programs around embedded structures such as noun phrases containing others, as in "the mother of the groom"; **loops**, as in "the song that never ends"; **meta-programming**, teachable e.g. in analogy with sentences about sentences, such as ""Greta loves Gaia" has three words", or **ambiguity**, as in "Only convicted criminals can view short sentences as the only good ones"[3].

---

[2] At universities of La Coruña, Nice, Rovira e Virgili, Simon Fraser: a single semester's course allowed them to implement NLP programs in Prolog and even motivated several of them to change career as a result, into Computing Sciences. One of them, Kimberly Voll, even completed a PhD in CS at SFU.

[3] Example inspired by Ursula Le Guin's book "Steering the Craft", p. 23.

We next discuss and exemplify how logic grammars, owing to their close relationship to language, are particularly well-suited to make those unconscious concepts more explicit and easily relatable to programming concepts.

3.1 Grammars as a Prelude to Prolog, and More

The success of nature's methods for language acquisition might inspire us to first expose students, through simple and age-appropriate grammars, to small fragments of what they have first acquired when learning to speak: syntax and lexicon intertwined [9], with a heavy noun bias[4]. A first, lexico-syntactic Prolog grammar that exploits this bias follows.

Example 1. A first logic grammar for (super-controlled) English [5].

```
say --> do , what.
do --> open; close; paint.
what --> door; box; bottle; window.
```

Students can become familiar with this grammar's role as *sentence recognizer*, by typing at the Prolog prompt, e.g.:

```
say ''open door''.
```

or with its role as *sentence generator*, e.g. by querying Prolog with

```
say Something.
```

Such drills will familiarize students with the versatility of Prolog/Prolog grammars, and naturally elicit further concepts such as that of **variables**, such as "Something" above; that of **constants**, exemplified by object words, that of **data structures**, exemplified through **lists** (of words) and through **terms** (such as those represented by drawing derivation trees, and later, through terms constructed to represent meaning); the notion that **declarative specifications have procedural interpretations**, through showing that languages can be described or specified through (sequence-sensitive) rewriting rules and that querying a grammar makes it directly executable; the notion of a (logic) **grammar** itself, as describing a language using its words (called terminal symbols), special words about them serving to group them (called meta-, or non-terminal symbols), and rewriting rules that do so; the notion of **existential variables** as those in queries, which "ask" for desired values for them that satisfy the query;

---

[4] Whether a language has a noun or verb bias appears to be culture and activity dependent [33], but our same argument applies transposed to any other first-learned constituents.

[5] We freely use syntactic sugar throughout the paper for readability because it is easy to guarantee through compilation into more cumbersome but "legal" forms, e.g. by automatically adding square brackets around terminal symbols. Full notational details are explained in [34], pp. 13–14.

the notion of **versatility** from changeable input/output argument roles determining various modes of running a grammar (generation, recognition or later, analysis or translation); the notion of **execution strategy** (try several on a derivation tree); of **modularity** that propitiates easy adaptations (have students change the lexicon into that of some domain of their interest, some second language they speak, even some nonsense imaginative vocabulary to have fun with, or have them add more sentence forms, questions, etc.).

Procedural notions can also be taught, when desired, from minimalistic grammatical examples, as we discuss next around the example of recursion.

Recursion is often considered difficult to teach, partly because it is usually taught around mathematical examples, of which not all people are fans. Yet children already use and understand recursive examples easily in natural language, delighting for instance in songs such as "The song that never ends" or "José se llamaba el padre". Examples that follow the general form of such songs (i.e., those containing a text that repeats indefinitely) are therefore more universally accessible. One such example follows.

Example 2. A recursive grammar for Sheep Language.
We can view sheep language as having sentences conformed by the sound "b" followed by any number of "a" sounds:

```
baaing --> b, as.
as --> a.
as --> a, as.
```

Teachable moments here, such as finding out why reversing the order of the last two rules might leave our sheep speechless, could alert students about the need to judiciously place end-of-recursion rules (and clauses) first, and generally become aware of the practical implications of **left-to-right, top-down** orderings in Prolog as well as in (logic) grammars. Since Prolog's strategy is already second-nature to creatures whose language and life events, similarly, follow sequential temporal orderings, we feel such an awareness could productively be elicited as soon as the opportunity arises.

How explicitly we present the procedural aspects, how "proper" a terminology we introduce, and how much syntactic sugar we make available is, in our opinion, the teacher's choice, to be made in function of their audience's needs and background. The wonderful thing is that Prolog's modularity and versatility allow us, whenever desired, to focus only the declarative parts of a grammar or program. For instance, students of literature with no computer background need not scrutinize any of the utilites that handle input/output, and are thus free to only learn (at first) how to consult it for their various specific purposes.

3.2   From Syntax to Semantics

We have seen how to elicit/drill on many notions and skills that pertain to Prolog, using purely syntactic descriptions of small subsets of language, or as they are also called, controlled languages. Augmented with appropriate arguments in their non-terminal symbols, grammars can also morph into **producers and consumers of structure**, be it semantic or other, related to the target language.

For instance, to obtain the term command(open(door)) as the meaning representation for the utterance "open door" (e.g. because we want to command a robot through natural language, as in [12]), all we have to do is complete the grammar of Example 1 with semantic structure building arguments[6], and call it in analysis mode (i.e., by specifying a concrete sentence as input and a variable as output).

Example 3. A syntactico-semantic grammar

```
say(command(Action(Thing))  --> do(Action),  what(Thing).

do(Thing,Action(Thing))  --> Action = open;  close.

what(Thing)  --> Thing = door;  box;  bottle;  window.
```

Grammar rules can now be seen as progressive producers and consumers of (semantic representation) structure, e.g. command(open(door)) results from the first rule producing its general structure, with values still unspecified, and from the rules for "do" and "what" producing those concrete values. This dynamic understanding of (grammatical) data structures rejoins the view of logical variables as traditional structures with declarative, i.e. single-assignment pointers, and of unification as a device for "constructing and accessing (parts of) complex data structures" stated in [24].

Adding semantic-building arguments will elicit a host of other concepts, such as that of **conditional rules**, through covering simple examples such as "Every bird sings" or "Dogs bark"; that of **semantic types**, such as *bird* or *dog*, or of **implicit vs. explicit constituents**, as exemplified in these last two sentences, where the use of plural makes the quantifier implicit. **Negation-as-default** can be motivated through testing e.g. "who doesn't sing?", and **semantic types** can be motivated from, e.g. "which birds don't sing?".

If desired, we can enact a smooth passage from grammars into Prolog by either discussing Prolog equivalents of already introduced sample grammars (i.e., the result of their compilation into Prolog), or by teaching Prolog by example. The latter can be done through having students observe and discuss the behaviour of (already developed) grammars that generate Prolog clauses as meaning representations of Natural Language (NL) sentences in some appropriate (i.e., sufficient for our purposes while still natural) NL subset.

A minimalistic such grammar is shown in https://swish.swi-prolog.org/p/ DBcreation.pl. Its affirmative, elementary sentences (formed around relational words and proper names) translate to Prolog facts, allowing students to create simple knowledge bases entirely through language. They can then consult the

---

[6] We abuse notation here again, for readability: variables are not legal, in most Prologs, as function names. Again we assume a compiler that "legalizes" our more human-readable notations.

resulting information also through NL, for further drilling. Sample output for a knowledge base creation grammar that admits a larger coverage of English [14] is shown in SampleOutput.pdf[7].

3.3 Semantics Vs. "The Other Syntax"

In themselves, the meaning representations we may assign to language utterances are no more than what linguists have called "the other syntax": a different, yet still syntactic way of expressing the same idea. What gives them meaning is the underlying logic system we are explicitly or implicitly using to make syntactic expressions correspond to elements in, and utterances about, the world that our sentences represent.

Making such logic systems explicit, as our community has been doing for many decades (ever since [10, 16, 17]), is what makes NLP results verifiable, hence accountable. It is therefore important, when processing human language subsets, to formally define the logical system underlying their syntax and semantics, in order to have more clarity than a simple "other syntax" would allow us.

A similar clarity is also due, and often lacking, in modern NLP and AI systems. Some of them are designed to make semantically unsubstantiated guesses from syntax alone, by optimizing word prediction methods and counting on the human reader to complete the meaning in their head [3].

Further sources of non-overtly acknowledged human help that contribute to hide the crying need for semantics have been researched for instance in [22]. The resulting lack of transparency tends to lend undue credibility to still unreliable or even unsafe systems, which are being released onto the public prematurely, with often quite harmful societal effects [5, 29].

3.4 Targeted vs General-Purpose Controlled Languages

Statistical AI could benefit from being complemented with semantics. Here LP could play a major role. There is in fact ongoing such work, e.g. [23] shows that machine learning methods can advantageously exploit default rules in logic programming; [32] uses Natlog[8] to make text-to-text or text-to-image generators easy-to-customize, thus readily providing impressive, NL friendly extensions which are as well amenable to formal definitions of their syntax and semantics. As LP (or any other effective means) of endowing current AI with meaning becomes more mainstream, there should be a welcome increase in transparency, explainability and accountability, as well as a badly needed decrease in current AI's exorbitant carbon footprint [1]. Another possible tack is to develop completely logical alternatives to machine learning which do not resort to statistics; this is being done for instance in the NLP field of grammar induction [15].

---

[7] https://drive.google.com/file/d/1miCb6A21qZbO2wXKqu-QB4WpaCcoXPS7/view?usp=sharing.

[8] Natlog modifies the syntax of Prolog's clauses to make them closer to NL.

An interesting and fairly general approach for leading from language into Prolog is that of Logical English [26], where users express sentences as close paraphrases of Prolog clauses, to in particular minimize ambiguities, e.g. for creating legal and educational databases.

It may not always be practical to use NL for *generating* more involved Prolog programs than those defining moderately straightforward knowledge bases, but interesting subsets of NL will often be useful for *consulting* more complex systems implemented in Prolog, such as those in robotics or planning. For such applications, we favour developing parsers tailored to application-appropriate NL subsets.

Query languages for Prolog systems are, appropriately, quite varied, since they are designed so that a query's evaluation with respect to the underlying logic system directly produces its answer, even when the logic system involved is richer than Prolog, e.g. multi-valued.

In [12], for instance, the NL subset we chose for queries mostly comprises imperative sentences of a certain form, whose intended recipient (a given robot) is often implicit, and whose "meaning" is evaluated into instructions necessary to command mini-robots at Sophia Antipolis University, from natural language commands such as "Go to point P taking care that the temperature remains between X and Y degrees.". In [13], instead, we evaluate the meaning of a user's query (e.g., "A system that has the optional processor MTS05 and the memory module SMX08, and whose memory size is different from 12 K words") through first mapping it into a first-order-logic meaning representation of it, whose (co-routined) execution yields descriptions of a computer system satisfying the user's query. In another application, e.g. if we want students to learn/drill on first-order logic, just the first-order logic expression of an input phrase might be considered to be its meaning.

Such targeted parsers, while giving up generality, can provide natural-sounding human language interfaces to even sophisticated Prolog systems, without the user having to resort to contrived paraphrases. Moreover, we have observed that using NL front ends for a variety of sophisticated Prolog applications can go a long way towards making Prolog engaging and interesting to learn. Automatic disambiguation capabilities can often be included, as usual, taking advantage of context specificities[9].

3.5   Learning Concepts from Varied Disciplines

We have already shown that, because of their sequence-sensitive nature, grammatical notions pertaining to spoken languages are most naturally expressed in terms of grammar rules, such as as "a sentence is a noun phrase *followed by* a verb phrase".

---

[9] Note, however, that not all NL ambiguities will be resolvable even by humans, e.g. the ambiguity of "sentence" may remain even when a legal context is assumed (consider for instance "This judge is famous for their kilometric sentences)".

But this is also true of many other curricular disciplines' definitions, cf. for instance the molecular biology definition "a tandem repeat is a DNA sequence followed by the same sequence, any number of times". Specialized controlled languages can help students learn such concepts both informally (as expressed in words) and formally (as translated automatically from words into Prolog grammars or programs), as well as providing opportunities to drill.

Even the simplest of grammars can help children become acquainted not only with linguistic concepts they understand but have not yet made conscious or named, but also with a variety of other subject-matter concepts. For instance, the philosophical concept of **"meta"** can be introduced by helping children distinguish words in the **object language** (such as "works") vs. in the **meta-language** of grammatical constituent names (such as "verb"). Most helpfully, Prolog's grammatical notation itself, once introduced, will clearly help them distinguish object language words explicitly through square brackets.

4   A Case Study: Exploring Possible Solutions to Quantifiable Problems

Besides centering language competence and using adequate pedagogical orderings for introducing logical/computational concepts, we stand to get best results if we also adapt the examples we use, whenever possible, to what the students are keenly interested in or affected by.

Among the issues that most stand to affect contemporary children in particular, and in which children have already shown keen interest by unprecedentedly organizing worldwide for climate change action, our interlocking societal and ecological crises stand out.

4.1   Doughnut Computing for Societal and Ecological Remediation

Inspired by Kate Raworth's "Doughnut Economics" (DE) [30], which provides visual measures of the distance from where we are to where we want to be with respect to various societal and earth sciences sustainability indicators, we have developed a Prolog grammar that can be used to explore societal and ecological breakdown remediation (see https://swish.swi-prolog.org/p/CO2.pl) .

Doughnut Economics' *ecological indicators* measure how dangerously we are overshooting planetary boundaries. They are taken from Earth Sciences and include: climate change, ocean acidification, chemical pollution, nitrogen and phosphorous loading, freshwater withdrawals, land conversion, biodiversity loss, air pollution and ozone layer depletion. Its *societal indicators* measure the proportion of people worldwide that fall short of life's basics. These include food, health, education, income and work, peace and justice, political voice, social equity, gender equity, housing, networks, and energy.

DE proposes to use these indicators at every level of societal and ecological organization (e.g. cities, provinces, countries) to calculate how to shift our present economic goal away from perpetual "growth" in a finite planet, into the

explicit goal of *meeting the needs of all within planetary limits*. Many municipalities, such as Portland, Quebec, and Amsterdam, have already adopted this
goal and are trying to implement it.

Our grammar, intended as a computational enabler for DE, presents users
with possible solutions to a (quantifiable) problem in either an ecological or a
social area. Users must enter the quantity (in percentages or in units of measurement) representing the present status and goal status, plus a name and number
for each of the those actions that would contribute, if taken, to solve it, as well
as the quantity. Quantities must, consistently, be stated in percentages or units
of measurement by which the action, if taken, would contribute to the problem's
solution. For instance, for reducing carbon emissions in Canada from a current
level of 15 tonnes per capita to zero, sample actions (numbered from 1 to 6, and
respectively contributing CO_2 decreases of 8, 7, 6, 4, 3 and 1 units of measurement) might be:

```
action(1,reduce_fossil_extraction, 8).
action(2,reduce_military_spending, 7).
action(3,ration_air_and_car_travel, 6).
action(4, reduce_waste, 4).
action(5, end_planned_obsolescence, 3).
action(6, limit_plastics, 1).
```

The complete grammar can be accessed and tested here: https://swish.swi-
prolog.org/p/CO2.pl. It is easy to transform it to a Prolog program proper if
preferred, but then we would lose the automatic concatenation of actions that
the grammar does invisibly. We next show (modulo notation) the first four solutions, or "sentences" (out of the 8 possible solutions), that result from running
this grammar for the above sample input data, for an idea of results obtained:
solutions with least number of sufficient actions are printed first. This heuristic could, of course, be changed. It results from having ordered our numbered
actions from most to least impactful. These solutions are: reduce fossil extraction
and military spending; or reduce fossil extraction and ration air and car travel
and reduce waste; or reduce fossil extraction and reduce waste and end planned
obsolescence; or reduce fossil extraction and ration air and car travel and limit
plastics- with respective total gains or 15, 18, 17 and 15.

Initially, students could just play with and discuss the effects of entering as
input different actions for different problems, in any of their social or earth sciences curricular themes. Section 4.2 discusses ideas on how this framework could
be applied to, for instance, equity issues. Later they could start inspecting and
modifying the grammar itself, with endless possibilities, all the way up to developing, in university, action evaluators for the Doughnut Economics model [30]
that can be useful in their cities, provinces, countries [11], tending to the creation
of a new field of AI: Regenerative, Redistributive.

A possible version for teenagers might introduce constraints so that we can see
the effects of actions in one area of the Doughnut over actions in another area, be it

social or ecological, and propose remedies to possible bad side effects. For example, those left unemployed by reducing a high emitting sector could be retrained into care work or green jobs. Initial prototypes have been explored through extending the grammar shown in https://swish.swi-prolog.org/p/CO2.pl into including, in the description of a possible action, also its (quantifiable) side effects on any eco-logical or social indicator, plus including a calculation of how these side effects might interact for overall balance. CLP alternatives are being explored as well, in joint work by V. Dahl and S. Abreu.

4.2   Truth and Logic-Literate Kids, Good Uses of Statistics, Regenerative and Redistributive AI

Accurate data, on which our Doughnut Computing game obviously relies, is not always readily available or even collected. Over-reliance on social media manufactured reality, where disinformation is rampant and often toxic, greatly compromises our access to trustworthy information. Teachers these days are therefore keen on helping their students develop narrative and investigative lit-eracy skills needed to not fall prey to fake news, unverified rumour, hate prompts and feeds, etc. [18,25]. Statistically-based AI often contributes to our informa-tion landscape's toxicity through its tendency to mistake agreement for truth and form for meaning. But safe uses of statistics, on the other hand, can usefully complement logically-based AI, allowing us for instance to express data on a given situation in terms of percentage of occurrences.

Games are also important in teaching, as exemplified in [21]. Regenerative and redistributive games can be created around Doughnut Computing, prompt-ing students to research what data is relevant, investigate how it was collected and in this light gauge the accuracy of the ensuing results. When necessary, they may be prompted to demand that missing data be collected (at their municipal-ities, in reliable websites, etc.).

Since almost any problem that is quantifiable e.g. through statistics, can be amenable to analysis through Doughnut Computing, we can apply it to the most varied themes. A crucially important example for children in particular and society as a whole is the widespread practice, puzzling in its specificity to the human species, of incesting children. While measures of its prevalence vary widely across regions (from 6 to 62% of girls and from 3 to 31% for boys) and only represent a lower bound [10], even this lower bound is intolerably high, e.g. in North America as in France, incest affects around 10% of girls younger than 12 and between 2 and 4% of boys, and seems to have remained constant over more than half a century [19].

Anthropological studies conclude that incest is a method of inculcation of domination, since it greatly increases the capacities of domination of some and

---

[10] These numbers do not include the many more cases either never reported, unprovable or "mild" (with degree of "mildness" assessed from the incestor's, not the victim's perspective, since legal systems and social order throughout the world tend to protect the (typically male) incestors rather than their victims.

submission of others, through destroying the (typically female) victims' sense of agency and self while increasing the incestors' sense of entitlement to appropriating women and children's bodies already present in other expressions of global male hegemonic order [19]– an order violently imposed millennia ago which "continues to influence our beliefs, behaviours, and brains, even threatening our survival" [20].

Social studies curricula might fruitfully apply Doughnut Computing to address the roots of such systemic violence in age-appropriate forms. For example, Ontario's Ministry of Education has developed age-adjusted materials for its personal safety project[11], which addresses gendered violence through education. Possible solutions to such problems could be described for their automatic exploration just like we saw in Sect. 4.1 for CO_2. For instance, the inequity issue that 75 % of unpaid care work is imposed on women is a major cause of women's and children's vulnerability to violence. Actions that can be automatically combined towards the goal of reducing that inequity can be conceived, just as we did for CO_2[12]. Simultaneously, psychologically and practical relevant information could be given to students and parents on actions that could protect students around the age when they are most likely to become victims of incest (typically, in six or seven cases out of ten, the victim is a female aged 10 or less, and the aggressor is an older male) [19]. Combinations of possible protective actions might more clearly be considered with the help of the school's team of experts. Such evidence-based initiatives would help the young counteract the misleading effects of early exposure to stories that "warn" them against "witches", wicked stepmothers and wicked old women wanting to kidnap them and eat them, rather than about the real, life devastating danger they are in fact in.

Help with detecting fallacies is paramount for protection through education. While we have no space here for a full analysis of how to complement the activities we have proposed with e.g. Prolog-based games that can help detect fallacies, it is clear that logical thinking and hence training in Prolog can play an important role. Fallacy detectors would be especially useful to deconstruct the illogical "truths" and "common sense" notions encoded in language [27] which both result from, and insidiously enforce, societal domination patterns [20]. Even drills around a simple Prolog dictionary of fallacy forms and/or misnomers (e.g. around gendered or racialized insults) could powerfully train students into logical thinking, further strengthening the road to Prolog while giving them reasoning tools they badly need.

Empowering children with awareness of the usually unspoken ways in which different types of violence against them are societally normalized could tip the scale for entire generations, helping us move once and for all from domination-based into solidarity-based societies. Hopefully we can achieve this on time.

---

[11] https://www.safeatschool.ca/resources/resources-on-equity-and-inclusion/sexism/tool-kits-and-activities.

[12] For instance, redistributing unpaid/paid work; a basic universal income; a basic equity income; professional daycare, etc.

5   Conclusion

We have discussed how Prolog and logical/computational thinking can be introduced most naturally and efficiently by tapping into students' pre-existing human language proficiency, if possible around themes that deeply concern or affect them. Related research which also stresses language in teaching computational thinking for beginners suggests the optimal timing is before imperative programming [4] –i.e., as soon as possible. We believe our proposed tack stands to also help move AI into more than just "ethical" concerns, into a regenerative and redistributive new phase. But in any case, it can provide a useful umbrella and/or complement to other interesting Prolog teaching approaches and initiatives, some of which are described in this same volume ([6–8,21,24,26,31,32]) or discussed in our closely related Prolog 50 Education initiative[13].

Last but not least, a heartfelt appeal to the Prolog community: *please join our efforts!*

Acknowledgements. The authors are most grateful to all participants of Prolog'50's Education Committee meetings, for their inspiring weekly discussions on how to best support Prolog teaching internationally and accessibly. We are also grateful to the anonymous reviewers for their very useful feedback on this paper's previous drafts, as well as to Henri Prade, for our interesting discussions on some of its topics. Support from Veronica Dahl's NSERC grant 31611021 is also gratefully acknowledged.

References

1. Bannour, N., Ghannay, S., Névéol, A., Ligozat, A.L.: Evaluating the carbon footprint of NLP methods: a survey and analysis of existing tools. In: Proceedings of the Second Workshop on Simple and Efficient Natural Language Processing. Association for Computational Linguistics, Virtual (Nov 2021)
2. Bavarian, M., Dahl, V.: Constraint-based methods for biological sequence analysis. J. Univ. Comput. Sci. (2006)
3. Bender, E.M., Koller, A.: Climbing towards NLU: on meaning, form, and understanding in the age of data. In: Proceedings ACL, pp. 5185–5198. Association for Computational Linguistics (2020)
4. Beux, S., et al.: Computational thinking for beginners: a successful experience using prolog. In: CILC - Italian Conference on Computational Logic, vol. CEUR 1459, pp. 31–45 (2015)
5. Birhane, A.: Algorithmic injustice: a relational ethics approach. Patterns **2**(2), 100205 (2021)
6. Cecchi, L.A., Rodríguez, J.P., Dahl, V.: Logic programming at elementary school: why, what and how should we teach logic programming to children? In: Warren, D.S., Dahl, V., Eiter, T., Hermenegildo, M., Kowalski, R., Rossi, F. (eds.) Prolog - The Next 50 Years. No. 13900 in LNCS, Springer (July 2023)
7. Cervoni, L., Brasseur, J.: Teaching prolog and python: the perfect match for artificial intelligence. In: Warren, D.S., Dahl, V., Eiter, T., Hermenegildo, M., Kowalski, R., Rossi, F. (eds.) Prolog - The Next 50 Years. No. 13900 in LNCS, Springer (July 2023)

---

[13] https://prologyear.logicprogramming.org/Education.html.

8. Cervoni, L., Brasseur, J., Rohmer, J.: Simultaneously teaching mathematics and prolog in school curricula: a mutual benefit. In: Warren, D.S., Dahl, V., Eiter, T., Hermenegildo, M., Kowalski, R., Rossi, F. (eds.) Prolog - The Next 50 Years. No. 13900 in LNCS, Springer (July 2023)

9. Clark, E.V., Casillas, M.: First language acquisition. In: The Routledge handbook of linguistics, pp. 311–328. Routledge (2015)

10. Dahl, V.: Un système déductif d'interrogation de banques de données en espagnol. Ph.D. thesis, Universite Aix-Marseille II (1977)

11. Dahl, V.: Doughnut computing: aiming at human and ecological well-being. In: 6th International Conference on the History and Philosophy of Computing (HAPOC-6) (2021)

12. Dahl, V., Fall, A., Thomas, M.C.: Driving robots through natural language. In: 1995 IEEE International Conference on Systems, Man and Cybernetics. Intelligent Systems for the 21st Century, vol. 2, pp. 1904–1908 vol 2 (1995)

13. Dahl, V., Sambuc, R.: Un système de bases de données en logique du premier ordre, en vue de sa consultation en langue naturelle. Universite Aix-Marseille II, Tech. rep. (1976)

14. Dahl, V.: From speech to knowledge. In: Information Extraction: Towards Scalable, Adaptable Systems, vol. 1974, pp. 49–75. LNAI (Lecture Notes in Artificial Intelligence (1999)

15. Dahl, V., Bel-Enguix, G., Tirado, V., Miralles, E.: Grammar induction for underresourced languages: the case of ch'ol. In: Gallagher, J., Giacobbazzi, R., Lopez-Garcia, P. (eds.) Analysis, Verification and Transformation for Declarative Programming and Intelligent Systems. No. 1316 in LNCS, Springer, Cham (2023). https://doi.org/10.1007/978-3-031-31476-6_6

16. Dahl, V.: Logical design of deductive, natural language consultable data bases. In: Proceedings V International Conference on Very Large Data Bases, pp. 24–31 (1979)

17. Dahl, V.: Quantification in a three-valued logic for natural language question-answering systems. In: Proceedings IJCAI'79, pp. 182–187 (1979)

18. Dillon, S., Craig, C.: Storylistening: Narrative Evidence and Public Reasoning. Routledge, Oxford (2021)

19. Dussy, D.: Le berceau des dominations: Anthropologie de l'inceste, livre 1. Maury Imprimeur, France (2022)

20. Eisler, R., Fry, D.P.: Nurturing Our Humanity: How Domination and Partnership Shape Our Brains, Lives, and Future. Oxford University Press, Oxford (2019)

21. Genesereth, M.: Dynamic programming. In: Warren, D.S., Dahl, V., Eiter, T., Hermenegildo, M., Kowalski, R., Rossi, F. (eds.) Prolog - The Next 50 Years. No. 13900 in LNCS, Springer (July 2023)

22. Gray, M., Siddharth, S.: Ghost Work: How to Stop Silicon Valley from Building a New Global Underclass. Houghton Mifflin Harcourt (2019)

23. Gupta, G., et al.: Logic-based explainable and incremental machine learning. In: Warren, D.S., Dahl, V., Eiter, T., Hermenegildo, M., Kowalski, R., Rossi, F. (eds.) Prolog - The Next 50 Years. No. 13900 in LNCS, Springer (July 2023)

24. Hermenegildo, M.V., Morales, J.F., Garcia, P.L.: Some thoughts on how to teach Prolog. In: Warren, D.S., Dahl, V., Eiter, T., Hermenegildo, M., Kowalski, R., Rossi, F. (eds.) Prolog - The Next 50 Years. No. 13900 in LNCS, Springer (July 2023)

25. Kashmiri, Z., Masram, A.: Elements of research based pedagogical tools for teaching science. Educ. Quest- Int. J. Educ. Appl. Soc. Sci. 11(3), 189–192 (2020)

26. Kowalski, R., Davila, J., Sator, G., Calejo, M.: Logical english for law and education. In: Warren, D.S., Dahl, V., Eiter, T., Hermenegildo, M., Kowalski, R., Rossi, F. (eds.) Prolog - The Next 50 Years. No. 13900 in LNCS, Springer (July 2023)
27. Lakoff, R.: The Language War. University of California Press, California (2020)
28. Levesque, H.: Thinking as Computation: A First Course. The MIT Press, Cambridge (2012)
29. McQuillan, D.: Resisting AI. Bristol University Press, Bristol (2022)
30. Raworth, K.: Doughnut Economics: Seven ways to think like a 21st-Century Economist. Chelsea Green, White River Junction, Vermont March (2017)
31. Tabakova-Komsalova, V., Stoyanov, S., Stoyanova-Doycheva, A., Doukovska, L.: Prolog education in selected high schools in Bulgaria. In: Warren, D.S., Dahl, V., Eiter, T., Hermenegildo, M., Kowalski, R., Rossi, F. (eds.) Prolog - The Next 50 Years. No. 13900 in LNCS, Springer (July 2023)
32. Tarau, P.: Reflections on automation, learnability and expressiveness in logic-based programming languages. In: Warren, D.S., Dahl, V., Eiter, T., Hermenegildo, M., Kowalski, R., Rossi, F. (eds.) Prolog - The Next 50 Years. No. 13900 in LNCS, Springer (July 2023)
33. Tardif, T., Gelman, S.A., Xu, F.: Putting the "Noun Bias" in context: a comparison of English and Mandarin. Child Development 70(3), 620–635 (1999)
34. Warren, D.S.: Introduction to Prolog. In: Warren, D.S., Dahl, V., Eiter, T., Hermenegildo, M., Kowalski, R., Rossi, F. (eds.) Prolog - The Next 50 Years. No. 13900 in LNCS, Springer (July 2023)
35. Wing, J.M.: Computational thinking. Commun. ACM 49(3), 33–35 (2006)

Tools for Teaching Prolog

Teaching Prolog with Active Logic Documents

Jose F. Morales[1,2], Salvador Abreu[3], Daniela Ferreiro[1,2],
and Manuel V. Hermenegildo[1,2(✉)]

[1] Universidad Politécnica de Madrid (UPM), Madrid, Spain
[2] IMDEA Software Institute, Madrid, Spain
{josef.morales,daniela.ferreiro,manuel.hermenegildo}@imdea.org
[3] NOVA LINCS/University of Évora, Evora, Portugal
spa@uevora.pt

Abstract. Teaching materials for programming languages, and Prolog in particular, classically include textbooks, slides, notes, and exercise sheets, together with some Prolog programming environment. However, modern web technology offers many opportunities for embedding interactive components within such teaching materials. We report on our experiences in developing and applying our approach and the corresponding tools to facilitating this task, that we call Active Logic Documents (ALD). ALD offers both a very easy way to add click-to-run capabilities to any kind of teaching materials, independently of the tool used to generate them, as well as a tool-set for generating web-based materials with embedded examples and exercises. Both leverage on (components of) the Ciao Prolog Playground. Fundamental principles of our approach are that active parts run locally on the student's browser, with no need for a central infrastructure, and that output is generated from a single, easy to use source that can be developed with any editor. We argue that this has multiple advantages from the point of view of scalability, low maintenance cost, security, ease of packaging and distribution, etc. over other approaches.

Keywords: Active Logic Documents · Prolog Playgrounds · Teaching Prolog · Prolog · Ciao-Prolog · Logic Programming · Web · Literate Programming

1 Introduction

Teaching programming languages traditionally relies on an array of dispersed materials, such as textbooks, class notes, slides, or exercise sheets, as well as

Partially funded by MICINN projects PID2019-108528RB-C21 *ProCode*, TED2021-132464B-I00 *PRODIGY*, and FJC2021-047102-I, by the Comunidad de Madrid program P2018/TCS-4339 *BLOQUES-CM*, by FCT under strategic project UIDB/-04516/2020 (NOVA LINCS) and by the Tezos foundation. The authors would also like to thank the anonymous reviewers for very useful feedback on previous drafts of this paper.

D. S. Warren et al. (Eds.): Prolog: The Next 50 Years, LNAI 13900, pp. 171–183, 2023.
https://doi.org/10.1007/978-3-031-35254-6_14

some programming environment(s) for students to run programs. Teaching Prolog is of course no exception. More recently, web-based technology has been facilitating the combination or embedding of interactive components into such teaching materials. This, however, poses a number of challenges, since there are multiple possible approaches to this end, and new technologies are constantly appearing that offer different trade-offs and capabilities. In this paper we report on our experiences in developing and applying two approaches and the corresponding tools in order to facilitate this task, that we collectively call *Active Logic Documents* – ALD, and which we believe offer interesting advantages over other approaches.

Mixing text and code has long been a topic of research and development, largely stemming from Knuth's seminal Literate Programming [10] concept. However, packaging and distribution of hybrid text and code systems has traditionally been complicated by dependencies on specific working environments, such as, for instance, the need for a specific operating system or even a specific version thereof, the availability of specific support software, library dependencies, etc. Because of this, over the years, several efforts have been made to provide online learning platforms such as the Khan Academy [13] which also strives to present teaching materials in a game-like form, and the idea has more recently materialized in web-based platforms, as exemplified by Jupyter notebooks[1]. This modern web technology affords dynamic and multimedia components, which clearly make teaching materials more palatable. In the Prolog world, SWISH provides a web-based platform for producing notebook-like sites that has been used to create online courses and exercises for logic-based programming languages [15]. Flach et al. [3] offer a very interesting account of their efforts to create progressively more interactive versions of their book, including combinations with Jupyter notebooks and with SWISH. Independently, Brecklinghaus et al. [2] implement a Jupyter kernel for SICStus Prolog and SWI-Prolog.

All these systems, however, rely on a server-side platform. Although this is in principle convenient to the end user, server-centric architectures also have drawbacks, e.g.: they introduce a dependency on the server; maintaining a server-side infrastructure can represent a significant burden; the user content built on such a platform is tied to the availability and reachability of such platform; the approach may also affect other aspects, such as scalability or privacy; etc.

In contrast, the fundamental principles of our ALD approach are that the reactive parts of the materials (the Prolog code written by the course developer or the student and all the related functionality) run locally on the student's web browser, with no need for a central infrastructure, and that the output is generated from a single, easy to use source that can be developed with any editor. We argue that this approach has multiple advantages from the point of view of scalability, low maintenance cost, security, independence from unconventional tools, etc. over other approaches. Our tools, described in the following sections, are meant to help course developers in at least two basic scenarios:

---

[1] https://jupyter.org/.

Fig. 1. The Ciao Playground

- Some course developers prefer to develop (or have already developed) their teaching materials with their own tools (such as, e.g., LaTeX, PowerPoint, Pages, Word, etc.), which have been stable for a long time, and may be reluctant to port these materials to a bespoke platform. For this case we offer a "click-to-run" methodology, based on the Ciao Prolog playground, which we describe in Sect. 2. This provides a very easy way to incorporate click-to-run capabilities in any kind of teaching materials, independently of the tool used to generate them or the generated format (pdf, html, etc.), and with no dependencies on any central server.
- For course developers that are willing to port their materials, we offer a tool (an extension of the LPdoc documenter) that greatly facilitates generating, using any conventional editor, web-based materials with embedded examples and exercises. These will run locally on the student's browser, again with no dependencies on any central server. We describe this part of our approach in Sect. 3.

2   Embedding Runnable Code in Documents via Browser-Based "Click-to-Run"

A common method for adding interactivity to teaching materials is the *"click to run"* approach. Code blocks in such materials become *clickable* elements that load the code into a suitable environment for online execution. This functionality has been traditionally supported by server-side playgrounds or notebooks, where the code is run on a server and the examples need to be loaded and saved on that server. In contrast, our approach incorporates two aspects that depart from these classical methods: the first one is that, as mentioned before, code execution is performed fully on the browser; the second one is that examples are stored in the documents[2] themselves, with no need to previously upload them or have them stored in remote servers.

The main component providing such functionality in our approach is the Ciao Playground[3] [4,5] which allows editing and running code locally on the user's web browser (See Fig. 1). To this end, the playground uses modern Web

---

[2] By "document" we mean the actual document (in pdf, or XML, etc.) which has been produced by the course writer and which is being read by the student.

[3] https://ciao-lang.org/playground.

technology (WebAssembly and Emscripten, see Sect. 5) to run an off-the-shelf Prolog engine and top level *directly in the browser*, able to fully access browser-side local resources. The main advantage of this general architecture is that it is easily reproducible and significantly alleviates maintenance effort and cost, as it essentially eliminates the server-side infrastructure.

In addition to the previously mentioned functionality, the playground provides an easy way to embed short code snippets (or links to larger source code) in web links themselves. These links can then be stored within documents and passed on as Prolog code to the playground, to be locally executed on the student's browser. This approach makes it very easy to include runnable code in manuals, tutorials, slides, exercises, etc., provided they are in a format that has support for HTML links, such as pdf files, and also Google Docs, Jupyter notebooks, Word, PowerPoint, LaTeX, Pages, Keynote, Org mode, or web site generators. Additionally, links can be easily shared by email or instant messaging applications.

For example, assume that we would like to include in the teaching materials being developed the classic append program:

```
1  app([],X,X).
2  app([X|Y],Z,[X|W]) :- app(Y,Z,W).
```

We will start by opening the playground in our browser (which, as mentioned before, will run locally), and pasting the program into the playground editor pane (as in Fig. 1). After perhaps testing the program to make sure it has the functionality that we would like to illustrate, we will use the playground ⟨Share!⟩ button to generate and copy into the clipboard a link that *contains the program encoded within the link itself.* Then we can add this link in any LaTeX, Word, PowerPoint, HTML, etc. document to produce a clickable area such as this one[4] which, when accessed, starts a new instance of the Playground in the browser, with the program preloaded. For LaTeX in particular, some macros are provided with the system as a "**prologrun**" LaTeX style file that simplifies the task even more. For example, the following simple LaTeX source code (where `https://ciao-lang.org/playground/...` represents the link obtained from the playground):

```
1  \codelink{https://ciao-lang.org/playground/...}
2  \begin{prologrun}
3  app([],X,X).
4  app([X|Y],Z,[X|W]) :- app(Y,Z,W).
5  \end{prologrun}
```

is rendered as follows (including the "**run**" button):

```
1  app([],X,X).                              run ▶
2  app([X|Y],Z,[X|W]) :-
3       app(Y,Z,W).
```

---

[4] The reader may safely follow this link!

The Playground is essentially a fully-fledged Prolog environment which includes much other functionality such as running tests, generating documentation, verifying program assertions, or specializing code, some of which will become instrumental in the following steps. In addition, specialized instances of the Playground can be easily created, an example of which is the s(CASP) playground [5][5]. More information on the implementation of the Ciao WebAssembly back end and the Playground architecture can be found in Sect. 5 and in [5] (and for the s(CASP) system in [1]).

3   Active Logic Documents

While click-to-run functionality is convenient and highly portable, we have also developed a more comprehensive tool (as an extension of the LPdoc documenter) that greatly facilitates the generation of web-based materials with *embedded* examples and exercises, using any conventional editor. These full-fledged *Active Logic Documents* are web pages with embedded Prolog programs, all sharing a common environment. The examples run on the pages themselves, in an embedded version of the playground, without the need for a separate playground tab.

Creating Documents with Editable and Runnable Code using LPdoc. The basis of our approach is LPdoc [7,8], which pioneered automatic program documentation in the context of Logic Programming and (C)LP.[6] Its main application is the generation of reference manuals directly from the actual code (including any assertions used to formally describe predicates), as well as from comments in the .pl source files or dedicated .lpdoc documentation files. However, LPdoc is often also used to generate other kinds of documents, such as tutorials, and also web sites and other kinds of on-line linked documents. Like many other tools, such as LaTeX, or the Web itself, LPdoc uses a human-oriented *documentation format*[7] for *typesetting* and does not impose the use of a particular WYSIWYG editor.[8] In particular, LPdoc supports writing rich-text documents in *markdown* syntax, with standard features like the inclusion of *verbatim* text and code blocks, syntax highlighting, and more, which allows for the inclusion of code segments in the midst of fairly flexible structured text, with hyperlinks. The use of documentation generation systems to write whole reference manuals, books, and teaching materials has become quite widespread in the past years.

To realize the ADL approach, the key step was to enhance LPdoc with the possibility of embedding Prolog environments, based on the Ciao Playground,

---

[5] https://ciao-lang.org/playground/scasp.html.

[6] Written in Prolog of course!.

[7] Editors like MS-Word use non-human oriented document formats: bloated with metadata, often binary encoded and undocumented, almost impossible to modify and maintain without the original tools, and really hard to integrate with code-oriented version control systems.

[8] However, note that once the *markup* language is stable and well defined, it is perfectly possible to implement rich WSIWIG front-ends that can save documents in this format. See for example Lyx, TeXmacs, etc. or rich-editors for Markdown.

which opens up a wide degree of possibilities for interaction. With this step, documents with *embedded* editable and runnable examples can be generated easily using LPdoc. The source that the developer of the course, tutorial, etc. works with is one or more LPdoc source files, in, e.g., markdown format. LPdoc processes these files and generates html pages in which the code fragments in the source are automatically rendered as editable panes that can be run in place in an embedded playground (as well as loaded into the standalone playground as before). The generated pages can then be published easily as any other web pages, e.g., in a course web site, in a personal `public_html` area, etc. Everything needed, including the runnable examples, queries, etc., is contained in the pages themselves. When students visit these pages with their browser, all executions occur locally in their browser.

Interaction facilities for Self-assessment. Especially in the context of a self-taught Logic Programming course, the embedded playground approach allows for very rich interactions. That is, code can be evaluated and edited directly in the same document. This enables direct support for self-evaluation and testing mechanisms. For example, code examples allow automated "semantic" evaluation of user input, e.g., by running code tests on the solution provided by the student. Document-level dependencies between examples, topics, and sections, allow "gamification" (e.g., evaluating your progress, obtaining *points* and trophies, hiding/showing tasks, un-blocking levels, etc.) of the learning activities, ensuring that the reader can acquire the necessary confidence on basic topics before going on to more advanced concepts.

Moreover, the Prolog top-level loop which underlies the Playground can interpret terms which result from solutions to goals in more ways than just printing them out. Similarly to Prolog's `display/1` predicate, some terms may be interpreted as giving rise to graphical or other user-interface components.

4   A Simple Example: Coding Factorial

We now illustrate through a concrete, worked-out example, the process of creating documents with editable and runnable examples using LPdoc. We will develop an exercise where we present the student with a simple task: given a factorial program which uses Peano arithmetic, to rewrite it using Prolog's `is/2`. We will show piecemeal how to put together the source for this example. We will first show the part of the output that we want LPdoc to produce and then the source that produces that particular output. The full source and output can be found in Fig. 3 in the appendix, and in the Ciao playground manual [4].[9]

We start the exercise with a title and recalling the code for factorial using Peano arithmetic:

---

[9] https://ciao-lang.org/ciao/build/doc/ciao_playground.html/.

Exercise: factorial using ISO-Prolog arithmetic

Consider again the factorial example, using Peano arithmetic:

```
1    factorial(0,s(0)).                                              ✔ ↗
2    factorial(s(N),F) :-
3        factorial(N,F1),
4        times(s(N),F1,F).
```

This first part of the output is generated by the following code:

```
1    \title Exercise: factorial using ISO-Prolog arithmetic
2
3    Consider again the factorial example, using Peano arithmetic:
4    '''ciao_runnable
5    :- module(_, _, [assertions,library(bf/bfall)]).
6    %! \begin{focus}
7    factorial(0,s(0)).
8    factorial(s(N),F) :-
9    factorial(N,F1),
10   times(s(N),F1,F).
11   %! \end{focus}
12
13   nat_num(0).
14   nat_num(s(X)) :- nat_num(X).
15
16   times(0,Y,0) :- nat_num(Y).
17   times(s(X),Y,Z) :- plus(W,Y,Z), times(X,Y,W).
18
19   plus(0,Y,Y) :- nat_num(Y).
20   plus(s(X),Y,s(Z)) :- plus(X,Y,Z).
21   '''
```

We first note that, in addition to text in markdown format, code between `'''ciao_runnable` and `'''` produces a panel in the output containing the code, which is editable and runnable. The code can be in modules and/or in 'user' files. We also note that it is possible to specify that only some parts of the code should appear in the output, by placing those parts between **begin focus** and **end focus** directives. This makes it possible to hide boilerplate lines (such as, e.g., module declarations, imports, auxiliary code, etc.) when they are not useful for the discussion. In this case we have hidden the auxiliary predicates that we assume have already been seen by the student in another lesson.

The arrow in the code pane allows loading the code in the playground, but we can also run the code in place within the document. One way to do this is to add one or more queries:

Some facts to note about this version:

- **It is fully reversible!**

```
?- factorial(X,s(s(s(s(s(s(0)))))).                                  ▶
```

This can be easily achieved with the following markdown with embedded Prolog code:

```
1   Some facts to note about this version:
2     - It is fully reversible!
3   '''ciao_runnable
4   ?- factorial(X,s(s(s(s(s(s(0))))))).
5   '''
```

In the resulting panel, the query may be edited and pressing on the triangle executes it in place:

```
?- factorial(X,s(s(s(s(s(s(0))))))).                    ▶

X = s(s(s(0))) ?

Next   Stop
```

Regarding scoping, there is essentially one Ciao Prolog top level per page: all programs in the page are loaded into this Ciao Prolog top level and all queries in the same page are executed in that top level, against all the code (possibly separate modules) that has been loaded into the top level up to that point. Code can be (re)loaded anytime by clicking on the green tick mark in the top left of the pane; this facility could be used, for example, to reset the state of the program.

After perhaps mentioning that the Peano approach is elegant but inefficient, we could propose an actual exercise, which is to rewrite the code using Prolog's is/2 (or constraints!):

```
Try to encode the factorial program using is/2 :

1    % TASK 1 - Rewrite with Prolog arithmetic            😐 ? ↗
2
3    factorial(0,s(0)).      % TODO: Replace s(0) by 1
4    factorial(M,F) :-       % TODO: Make sure that M > 0
5        M = s(N),           % TODO: Compute N from M using is/2 (note that N is
6        factorial(N,F1),    %       unbound, so you need to compute N from M!)
7        times(M,F1,F).      % TODO: Replace times/3 by a call to is/2 (using *)
8
9    % When you are done, press the triangle ("Run tests") or the arrow
10   % ("Load into playground").

★ Show solution

Note that wrong goal order can raise an error (e.g., moving the last call to is/2 before
the call to factorial).
```

Here the pane is again editable and contains the original (Peano) code adorned with comments, all of which act as hints or instructions on how to proceed. Of course, this description could also be somewhere else, e.g., in the surrounding text. Clicking on the yellow face will perform the evaluation, in this case running some (hidden) *unit tests* [11], on the code in order to give feedback to the student. Other evaluation methods (e.g., running a program analysis or a mere syntactic comparison) can also be useful. It is also possible for the student to give up and ask for the solution, in which case the proposed solution will be shown and can be executed.

All this functionality can be generated using the following code:

```
1   Try to encode the factorial program using 'is/2':
2
3   '''ciao_runnable
4   :- module(_, _, [assertions]).
5
6   :- test factorial(5, B) => (B = 120) + (not_fails, is_det).
7   :- test factorial(0, 0) + fails.
8   :- test factorial(-1, B) + fails.
9
10  %! \begin{hint}
11  % TASK 1 - Rewrite with Prolog arithmetic
12
13  factorial(0,s(0)). % TODO: Replace s(0) by 1
14  factorial(M,F) :- % TODO: Make sure that M > 0
15  M = s(N), % TODO: Compute N from M using is/2 (note that N is
16  factorial(N,F1), % unbound, so you need to compute N from M!)
17  times(M,F1,F). % TODO: Replace times/3 by a call to is/2 (using *)
18
19  % When you are done, press the triangle ("Run tests") or the arrow
20  % ("Load into playground").
21  %! \end{hint}
22
23  %! \begin{solution}
24  factorial(0,1).
25  factorial(N,F) :-
26  N > 0,
27  N1 is N-1,
28  factorial(N1,F1),
29  F is F1*N.
30  %! \end{solution}
31  '''
32
33  Note that wrong goal order can raise an error (e.g., moving the last
34  call to 'is/2' before the call to factorial).
```

The included unit tests are the ones that will be run to test the student's code (a small subset has been included for brevity). The segment within hint directives behaves similarly to the focus segments but represents a hint or instructions, and will be replaced by the solution, should it be asked for. The solution, if provided, is marked with the corresponding directives.

The appendix provides a complete example of a class exercise based on the code fragments above, showing the full source and the full output. The resulting, working Active Logic Document can be found, as mentioned before, as an example in the Ciao playground manual [4].[10]

5   The Technical Approach

From a technical point of view the Ciao playground requires devising a means for running Prolog code directly in the browser.

---

[10] https://ciao-lang.org/ciao/build/doc/ciao_playground.html/.

Our first attempt at this was the Ciao Prolog JavaScript compiler back-end [12], that enabled the use of Prolog and, in general, (constraint) logic programming to develop not just the server side, but also the client side of web applications, running fully on the browser. Tau Prolog [14] and the tuProlog playground[11] are recent Prolog interpreters written in JavaScript which also make it easy to run Prolog in a web page, serverless. While these JavaScript-based approaches are attractive, they also have drawbacks. *Compilation* to JavaScript was a good option at the time, since it was a client (i.e., browser)-based solution and the resulting speed made it useful for many applications. However, performance does suffer with respect to native implementations (see [12]). This is even more pronounced in the case of the Prolog *interpreters* written in JavaScript mentioned above. It is precisely this performance impact that has led to the development of the WebAssembly virtual machine [6][12], which is currently supported by all major browsers.

WebAssembly and the supporting compilation toolchains, such as Emscripten [16], enable programs written in languages supported by LLVM to be compiled to a form which can be executed entirely in the browser, i.e., without any server-side intervention at runtime, all with very reasonable efficiency. This is the approach used by the Ciao playground in order to be able to run Prolog code in the browser. The playground uses the standard Ciao engine, compiled to WebAssembly using the Emscripten C compiler and the Ciao library for C, which offers functions for term creation, type conversions, term checks, queries, and calls. The result is that in the playground Prolog code runs with performance that is competitive with native Prolog implementations. Additionally, the Ciao environment is comprised of several independent bundles (collections of modules) which can be compiled independently and demand-loaded from WebAssembly. The WebAssembly port of Ciao Prolog thus supports most of the system's software tools, such as LPdoc, CiaoPP (including the testing framework), etc., all of which are written in Prolog.

6   Conclusions and Outlook

We have described the Active Logic Documents (ALD) approach and toolset, that we have developed and been applying for embedding interactive Prolog components within teaching materials. ALD offers on one hand, support for easily adding click-to-run capabilities to any kind of teaching materials, independently of the tool used to generate them, and on the other hand a tool for generating web-based materials with embedded examples and exercises, based on the LPdoc documenter and the embedded version of the playground. We have also justified the fundamental principles of our approach which are that active parts run locally on the student's browser, with no need for a central infrastructure, and that the whole active document (tutorial, manual, exercise, etc.) is generated from a single, easy to use source that can be written and modified

---

[11] https://pika-lab.gitlab.io/tuprolog/2p-kt-web.
[12] https://webassembly.org/.

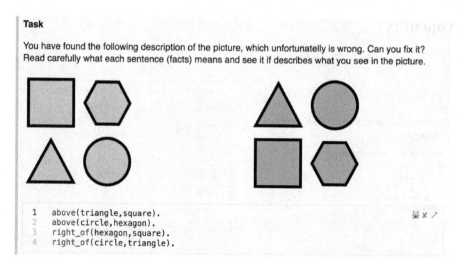

Task

You have found the following description of the picture, which unfortunatelly is wrong. Can you fix it?
Read carefully what each sentence (facts) means and see it if describes what you see in the picture.

```
1   above(triangle,square).
2   above(circle,hexagon).
3   right_of(hexagon,square).
4   right_of(circle,triangle).
```

Fig. 2. Adding gameplay functionality in a course for children. This task is accompanied with introductory text (not shown here) that carefully explains that `above(X,Y)` must be read as *X is above Y*, etc. Rather than introducing *infix* operators at this very early stage, the course begins with trivial formalization tasks to get familiar with syntax and abstraction.

with any editor. We argue that this approach has multiple advantages from the point of view of scalability, maintenance cost, security, ease of packaging and distribution, etc.

Our tools evolved as a side-effect of the development of our own materials over the years for teaching logic programming[13], embedding runnable code and exercises in tutorials[14], slides[15], manuals, etc., and they are currently being used in other projects, such as for example in the development of a Programming course for young children (around 10 years old) within the Year of Prolog initiatives. The latter effort has implied the inclusion of additional useful features in the toolset, such as a "gameplay" which progressively discloses more advanced parts of the course while striving to keep the interaction interesting and challenging (see Fig. 2). The JavaScript interface provided by the tools and the access to Web technology enable endless possibilities for richer Web-based interaction (e.g., SVG visualization of facts), media rich interactions, touch/click inputs, audio, graphics or videos, etc.

---

[13] See also [9] in this same book.

[14] E.g., Interactive CiaoPP tutorials https://ciao-lang.org/ciao/build/doc/ciaopp_tutorials.html/.

[15] E.g., Course material in Computational Logic: https://cliplab.org/~logalg.

182   J. F. Morales et al.

Appendix

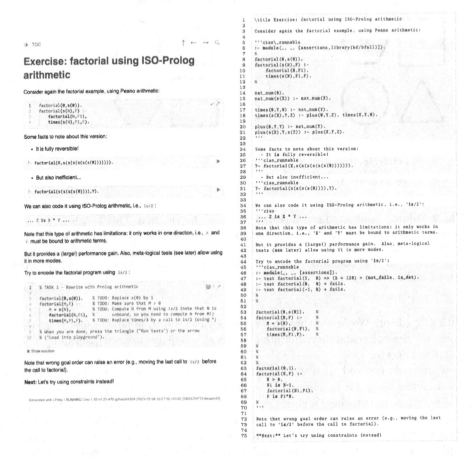

Fig. 3. The full source and LPdoc output for the Active Logic Document for the simple factorial exercise.

References

1. Arias, J., Carro, M., Salazar, E., Marple, K., Gupta, G.: Constraint answer set programming without grounding. Theory Pract. Logic Program. **18**(3–4), 337–354 (2018). https://doi.org/10.1017/S1471068418000285
2. Brecklinghaus, A., Koerner, P.: A Jupyter kernel for Prolog. In: Proceedings 36th Workshop on (Constraint) Logic Lrogramming (WLP 2022). Lecture Notes in Informatics (LNI), Gesellschaft für Informatik, Bonn (2022)
3. Flach, P., Sokol, K., Wielemaker, J.: Simply logical - the first three decades. In: Warren, D.S., Dahl, V., Eiter, T., Hermenegildo, M., Kowalski, R., Rossi, F. (eds.) Prolog: The Next 50 Years. LNCS (LNAI), vol. 13900, pp. 184–193. Springer, Cham (2023). https://doi.org/10.1007/978-3-031-35254-6_15

4. Garcia-Pradales, G., Morales, J., Hermenegildo, M.V.: The Ciao Playground. Tech. rep., Technical University of Madrid (UPM) and IMDEA Software Institute (2021). http://ciao-lang.org/ciao/build/doc/ciao_playground.html/ciao_playground_manual.html
5. Garcia-Pradales, G., Morales, J., Hermenegildo, M.V., Arias, J., Carro, M.: An s(CASP) In-browser playground based on Ciao prolog. In: ICLP2022 Workshop on Goal-directed Execution of Answer Set Programs (2022)
6. Haas, A., et al.: Bringing the web up to speed with webassembly. In: Cohen, A., Vechev, M.T. (eds.) Proceedings of the 38th ACM SIGPLAN Conference on Programming Language Design and Implementation, PLDI 2017, Barcelona, Spain, 18–23 June 2017, pp. 185–200. ACM (2017). https://doi.org/10.1145/3062341.3062363
7. Hermenegildo, M.: A documentation generator for (C)LP systems. In: Lloyd, J., et al. (eds.) CL 2000. LNCS (LNAI), vol. 1861, pp. 1345–1361. Springer, Heidelberg (2000). https://doi.org/10.1007/3-540-44957-4_90
8. Hermenegildo, M.V., Morales, J.: The LPdoc documentation generator. Ref. Manual (v3.0). Tech. rep., UPM (2011). http://ciao-lang.org
9. Hermenegildo, M., Morales, J.: Some thoughts on how to teach Prolog. In: Warren, D.S., Dahl, V., Eiter, T., Hermenegildo, M., Kowalski, R., Rossi, F. (eds.) Prolog: The Next 50 Years. LNCS (LNAI), vol. 13900, pp. 107–123. Springer, Cham (2023). https://doi.org/10.1007/978-3-031-35254-6_9
10. Knuth, D.: Literate programming. Computer J. **27**, 97–111 (1984)
11. Mera, E., Lopez-García, P., Hermenegildo, M.: Integrating software testing and run-time checking in an assertion verification framework. In: Hill, P.M., Warren, D.S. (eds.) ICLP 2009. LNCS, vol. 5649, pp. 281–295. Springer, Heidelberg (2009). https://doi.org/10.1007/978-3-642-02846-5_25
12. Morales, J.F., Haemmerlé, R., Carro, M., Hermenegildo, M.V.: Lightweight compilation of (C)LP to JavaScript. Theory and Practice of Logic Programming, 28th International Conference on Logic Programming (ICLP2012) Special Issue 12(4–5), pp. 755–773 (2012)
13. Morrison, B.B., DiSalvo, B.J.: Khan academy gamifies computer science. In: Dougherty, J.D., Nagel, K., Decker, A., Eiselt, K. (eds.) The 45th ACM Technical Symposium on Computer Science Education, SIGCSE 2014, Atlanta, GA, USA, 5–8 March 2014, pp. 39–44. ACM (2014). https://doi.org/10.1145/2538862.2538946
14. τProlog – an open source Prolog interpreter in javascript. http://tau-prolog.org (2021). Accessed 16 May 2023
15. Wielemaker, J., Riguzzi, F., Kowalski, R.A., Lager, T., Sadri, F., Calejo, M.: Using SWISH to realize interactive web-based tutorials for logic-based languages. Theory Pract. Log. Program. **19**(2), 229–261 (2019). https://doi.org/10.1017/S1471068418000522
16. Zakai, A.: Emscripten: an LLVM-to-Javascript compiler. In: Proceedings of the ACM international conference companion on Object oriented programming systems languages and applications, pp. 301–312. SPLASH 2011, ACM, New York, NY, USA (2011). https://doi.org/10.1145/2048147.2048224

Simply Logical – The First Three Decades

Peter Flach[1]([⊠])[iD], Kacper Sokol[1][iD], and Jan Wielemaker[2][iD]

[1] Intelligent Systems Laboratory, University of Bristol, Bristol, UK
{peter.flach,k.sokol}@bristol.ac.uk
[2] SWI-Prolog Solutions b.v., Amsterdam, The Netherlands
jan@swi-prolog.org

Abstract. This paper charts the evolution of the Prolog textbook *Simply Logical – Intelligent Reasoning by Example* from print with runnable programmes on a 3.5-inch diskette published in 1994, via various intermediate online versions, to the fully interactive online edition available today. Our aim is to investigate – from both the writer's and the reader's perspectives – the potential impact of technology on educational materials. The three authors of this paper present three distinct and complementary points of view, which come together to shape an interactive online book that offers an immersive learning experience. Peter describes the philosophy behind the original book and experiences teaching from it. Jan demonstrates how contemporary web programming has enabled a fully interactive realisation of the book's philosophy. Kacper reports how different technologies can be adopted to build a versatile authoring toolkit that underpins the interactive online edition of the book. Collating these distinct yet coherent perspectives allows us to reflect on future opportunities for interactive Prolog teaching materials arising from the continuous development of web technologies. The insights we offer should be of interest to teachers of Prolog as well as those wanting to find out about the latest educational technologies.

Keywords: Education · Learning · Textbook · Interactive · Prolog · SWI-Prolog · SWISH · Artificial Intelligence · Logic Programming

1 The Paperback $\hfill$ *(Peter Flach)*

As a beginning lecturer at Tilburg University in the early 90s of the previous century I started teaching a module on Artificial Intelligence (AI), then an emerging specialist topic within the still young discipline of computer science. Initially using a general AI textbook [10] I started devising practical exercises and coursework assignments in Prolog, which I had come across a couple of years before. These grew into a set of lecture notes that eventually became the *Simply Logical – Intelligent Reasoning by Example* book [7]. I ended up publishing with John Wiley after I had a chat with a representative at a conference; they were very helpful and even suggested the title. I was fortunate in finding Bob Kowalski willing to write a foreword, in which he very graciously wrote that my book

© The Author(s), under exclusive license to Springer Nature Switzerland AG 2023
D. S. Warren et al. (Eds.): Prolog: The Next 50 Years, LNAI 13900, pp. 184–193, 2023.
https://doi.org/10.1007/978-3-031-35254-6_15

relieved him of the temptation to write a revised edition of his own book, *Logic for Problem Solving* [9].

Rather than trying to cover all of AI, which even then had grown into a diverse field, I decided to focus on reasoning in various forms: deductive, inductive, reasoning with natural language, reasoning with incomplete information, etc., which approach is captured by the "intelligent reasoning" part of the book's title. The "by example" moniker reflected the didactic philosophy: teaching by showing, learning by doing. Every AI technique discussed was accompanied by a Prolog programme implementing it. These programmes served two didactic purposes. By running them, the student could get a feeling what a particular technique is all about. But perhaps more importantly, the declarative reading of each programme was an integral part of the explanation of the technique it implemented. For the more elaborate programmes, special attention was paid to their stepwise development, explaining key issues along the way. My hope was that the reader would mount the accompanying 3.5" diskette into their computer, and try out the Prolog programmes alongside reading the book. While this was perhaps optimistic back then, the online format available today integrates the "showing" and "doing" sides of the educational coin very well, as will be demonstrated below.

I still use *Simply Logical* in my lectures as an introduction to both logic programming and AI. Treating the subjects side by side allows for some pretty powerful examples, such as a resolution prover for full clausal logic as a demonstrator for breadth-first search. Rather than modernising the text I have opted for modernising the demonstrators and programming assignments. For example, the natural-language question-answering programme described in Chapter 7 of the book, which nowadays we would call a chatbot, was developed into an Amazon Alexa skill. This demonstrates the power of a hybrid system consisting of speech-to-text and text-to-speech components enabled by deep learning, and a logical engine in the middle capable of explainable logical reasoning. Other material developed over the years includes a Prolog-driven agent that needs to solve a logical puzzle while moving around in a grid world and a Reveal.js slide deck that can be used for self-study and trying out Prolog programmes without leaving the browser. The latter is based on SWISH, which Jan introduces in the following section.

2   Interactive Prolog in the Browser   *(Jan Wielemaker)*

Crucial for realising the fundamental philosophy behind *Simply Logical* is the ability to run code interactively in the browser. Modern browser and service technology allows for several designs:

1. Have Prolog in a sandbox (such as a virtual machine or container) on a server and provide ways to submit a programme and view its output. An example of this approach can be found at Coding Ground.

2. Have a web service with dedicated support for Prolog that offers a sandboxed Prolog execution environment. SWISH[1] – *SWI-Prolog for SHaring* [16] – is implemented based on this paradigm.
3. Execute Prolog in the browser. Some Prolog systems are written directly in JavaScript, thus enabling them to be run in the browser, e.g., Tau-Prolog. Another solution is to compile Prolog to JavaScript [13]. Alternatively, Web Assembly (WASM) offers a low-level virtual machine for the browser, which allows running more traditional C-based Prolog implementations; for example, Emscripten provides a Clang-based compiler suite that targets WASM, underpinning implementations such as the Ciao Playground and SWI-Prolog WASM port.

The first category typically provides a batch-style interaction, making it difficult to adapt for (online and interactive) educational resources; the latter two approaches are more suitable in this respect.

SWISH, originally developed by Torbjörn Lager, is based on Pengines – an architecture to access Prolog on a remote server – and consists of a monolithic multi-threaded SWI-Prolog server. Its user interface is written in JavaScript with server-side assistance for semantic highlighting, feedback on predicates, template insertion and other user-focused features. Pengines underlies Prolog execution, which takes place in a sandboxed environment that consists of a Prolog thread and a temporary module. Executing a query (1) transfers the code and query to the server; (2) starts a thread and creates a temporary module; (3) loads the code into the module; and (4) executes the code. This operationalisation allows for rich interaction with the client, e.g., "read" from the client, ask for alternative solutions or trace through the programme in a manner similar to traditional Prolog tracers. Other noteworthy features of SWISH include:

- The ability to store programmes on the server under Git-style version management. Programmes can either be private or visible to the public, and may *include* each other.
- Availability of *render plugins* that allow rendering Prolog terms – e.g., as tables or graphics that represent chess boards, charts and graphs – using modern web browser technology.
- An R Project interface offering access to R's algorithms and chart outputs.
- *Notebook* format allowing for rich interactive pages that provide a sequence of HTML, Markdown, programme and query cells.

SWISH has proved to be an invaluable resource for the Prolog community, including educators. It facilitates (Prolog) learning, code discussion and exchange as well as shared access to data for data science. After its launch in 2014 the system quickly gained popularity as an alternative to local installations of Prolog systems used for exercises in Prolog classes at schools worldwide. As of December 2022, it hosts over 150,000 programmes and nearly 15,000 notebooks, many of which in several versions. It sustains on average hundreds of concurrent users, peaking at over one thousand users, usually towards the end of each

---

[1] https://swish.swi-prolog.org/.

academic cycle. Notably, teachers started adapting their educational materials and course workflows to SWISH for more than just a convenient online Prolog execution environment. Some wrote course material as SWISH notebooks. Others use SWISH notebooks for exercises; they organise the content as questions, background data, example queries and, sometimes, skeleton or partial solutions. A student then *forks* the notebook, completes it, saves it and sends the link with the completed notebook to the teacher.

As interactive in-browser programming exercises were gaining in popularity, I began to wonder whether we could do something similar to teach Prolog as a programming language. With *Learn Prolog Now!* [2] being one of the more popular online (and later paperback [3]) Prolog books, I experimented with making it interactive. *Learn Prolog Now!* is written in LATEX, which is then converted to an *unintelligible* HTML code used to publish the online version. Because of that, I built the interactive version [4] by using a *rewriting proxy server*. This is a Prolog programme that:

1. uses SWI-Prolog's HTML parser and generator to parse the original pages;
2. identifies the code blocks that represent programmes and queries;
3. re-writes the programme fragments into new HTML elements that connect each programme to relevant queries, allowing these pairs to be transformed into an embedded SWISH instance; and
4. inject JavaScript into the page to make the page – specifically, the code boxes – interactive.

While side-stepping the need to manually edit the book source, this automation is far from perfect. Observing this particular use case of SWISH, nevertheless, motivated Peter and Kacper to make *Simply Logical* similarly interactive. They decided to manually identify the programmes and queries as it was clear that given the available technology it is impossible to do so programmatically with acceptable precision.

3   The Online Edition(s)   *(Kacper Sokol)*

The book was first made freely available in 2007, when the copyright reverted back to Peter, who decided to release its PDF and associated programmes online through a dedicated web page. In 2015, as a pilot, most of the original book source – written in a now obsolete version of MS Word – was ported to a collection of messy HTML files replete with superfluous markup; the figures were extracted as non-standard EMZ files and later converted to the more modern Scalable Vector Graphics (SVG) format. This provided a canvas for transforming a static web page into an online, interactive resource using SWI-Prolog's SWISH platform.

From then on, the manual process of identifying Prolog code listings and their associated queries took place, with appropriate HTML code being embedded by hand to display interactive SWISH code boxes. Each SWISH box initially renders the programme as text, as in the original book. Opening the box reveals

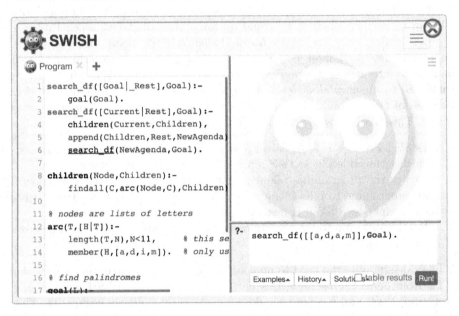

Fig. 1. Interactive SWI-Prolog code box based on SWISH. A code listing (top) can be turned into an interactive code box (bottom) by pressing the "play" button in its top-right corner.

a tripartite widow with an editable code listing (pulling in additional code as required), pre-populated Prolog queries, and an answer pane as shown in Fig. 1. Two decades after publication of the original book, technology had caught up sufficiently to support the envisaged didactic philosophy, which was an almost revelatory experience. The *first* release had thus seen the light of day.

The script responsible for rendering SWISH code boxes was elaborate enough to streamline certain tasks. Prolog queries displayed in the text were assigned unique IDs, which allowed them to be dynamically imported into relevant code boxes upon launch. Both interactive programmes and static code listings could also be tagged, providing an opportunity to import code into interactive boxes at run time. To give the book a fresh look and feel and prepare its presentation for a range of modern devices – desktop and laptop computers, tablets and mobile phone screens – the HTML content was adapted to the Bootstrap framework. The book was split into four HTML files: Part I, Part II, Part III and Appendix, complemented with an index page, with the source hosted on GitHub[2]. The *second* release of the book's online version was built with Jekyll to generate static web pages, which were hosted on GitHub Pages under the dedicated https://book.simply-logical.space/ domain.

However, the main text was now written in HTML, which was still fairly limiting, especially when it comes to authoring (new or derived) content. With Markdown being much simpler to write, edit and maintain as well as more human-readable and covering all of the markup needs, I started porting and cleaning the source. In the process, the diversity of the book's building blocks – text, figures and code listings – sparked an idea for a bespoke content generation system where the resources are split into prime elements that can be reused to compose new material. Initially, this novel workflow relied on Jekyll, which proved to be limiting and prompted me to embark in late 2018 on developing a bespoke content generation platform. Its prototype, while versatile, required the source documents to be extensively annotated, making the authoring experience overly complicated and stalling the project.

When Jupyter Book [6] arrived in early 2020 it rekindled my hope for a modular version of *Simply Logical*. The platform allowed composing content from diverse building blocks and offered nearly all of the required functionality, apart from support for SWISH code boxes. While based on the Sphinx Python documentation generation engine, it nonetheless could be extended with a custom plugin. This encouraged me to finalise the separation, conversion and cleaning of the book content, and to begin developing the necessary Jupyter Book extensions. The result is a highly modular design, where the book is split into a collection of files based on their type: text, exercise, solution, code and figure. All of these materials are published on GitHub under the permissive Creative Commons (BY-NC-SA) licence, which allows easy reuse, incorporating into bespoke courses, or adapting into alternative educational resources such as practical training sessions. This release marked the *third* instalment of the online edition [8].

From a technical perspective, the latest version is realised through a collection of bespoke Jupyter Book plugins (that also work with Sphinx) spanning functionality specific to SWI-Prolog [17]. These extensions were later adapted to be compatible with the cplint [14] and ProbLog [5] probabilistic programming languages. Specifically, I developed and released sphinx-prolog[3], which among other things allows to embed interactive SWI-Prolog and cplint code boxes based on their respective SWISH implementations. The sphinx-problog[4] extension offers analogous functionality for ProbLog facilitated by the online execution environment underpinning the code examples published as part of the ProbLog website.

---

[2] https://github.com/simply-logical/simply-logical/.
[3] https://github.com/simply-logical/sphinx-prolog/.
[4] https://github.com/simply-logical/sphinx-problog/.

```
 1  ```{swish} swish:0.1
 2  ---
 3  query-text: ?-linked(a,b,X). ?-linked(a,X,b).
 4  query-id: swishq:1.1.1 swishq:1.1.2 swishq:1.1.3
 5  inherit-id: swish:4.5.6 swish:4.5.7 swish:4.5.8
 6  source-text-start: 4.5.6-start
 7  source-text-end: 4.5.6-end
 8  hide-examples: true
 9  ---
10
11  optional :- content.
12
13  /** <examples>
14  ?-linked(X,a,b).
15  */
16  ```
```

Listing 1. Example of SWISH code box syntax.

Including a SWISH code box is as simple as writing a specially-formatted Markdown code block, an example of which is shown in Listing 1. This element is assigned a unique ID (`swish:0.1`), and its content can either be provided verbatim (`optional :- content.`) or loaded from a file. Through its optional parameters it is possible to:

- explicitly provide the query (`query-text`) and/or import it from a tagged block (`query-id`);
- inject a programme from another code box through its ID (`inherit-id`);
- prepend (`source-text-start`) or append (`source-text-end`) code from external Prolog files; and
- if Prolog queries are included directly in the code via a specially-formatted query block (lines 13–15 in Listing 1), hide them from the users prior to launching the code box (`hide-examples`).

To streamline the process of creating new online interactive educational resources, I published a suite of templates for Prolog[5], cplint[6] and ProbLog[7] content. By *forking* any of these repositories one can adapt static resources or build new teaching materials in a matter of minutes.

4 Discussion and Outlook

Developing Jupyter Book plugins and building authoring environments for interactive Prolog content set us on a path to further explore alternative technologies

---

[5] https://github.com/simply-logical/prolog-book-template.

[6] https://github.com/simply-logical/cplint-book-template.

[7] https://github.com/simply-logical/problog-book-template.

for composing diverse (interactive) training resources. As a proof of principle we created a prototype of a new publishing workflow in which multiple artefacts such as online documents, slides and computational notebooks can be generated from a unified collection of source materials [15]. This contrasts with much of current practice, where authoring environments are limited to individual publishing artefacts, for example, LaTeX or MS Word documents, and PowerPoint or Keynote slide decks. While in its early stages of development, Quarto [1] is a notable departure from this paradigm and a substantially more powerful realisation of the envisaged workflow. It is a scientific and technical publishing system that allows to author content as Markdown files or Jupyter Notebooks, and publish it as articles, reports, presentations, websites, blogs and books in formats such as HTML, PDF, MS Word or EPUB. Quarto supports scientific features – e.g., equations, citations and cross-referencing – and inclusion of dynamic content created with various programming languages.

Regardless of the underlying technology, our ideal scenario is an authoring environment in which the author can concentrate on producing content without much (initial) regard for the delivery format. Similar ideas have been around for a long time – e.g., Luhmann's Zettelkasten [11] – but were lacking the technology to support them and make them efficient. While we hope that the next 50 years of Prolog will see these ideas and opportunities come to full fruition, numerous challenges need to be overcome. One particular bottleneck is limited interactivity of the educational resources published on the Internet, which in part is due to the need for compute resources. Without access to a dedicated machine – however it is implemented in the physical world – interacting with code examples remains constrained.

For example, up until recently SWISH used to run on a single server hosted by the Vrije Universiteit Amsterdam (VU). The single process and single hardware placed in a single network made the system highly vulnerable. This could be addressed by migrating the server to a set of *federated services*; while currently SWISH runs on two servers in different locations, *load balancing* is still missing. The concept of server-side execution, nonetheless, remains problematic because it concerns a complex, non-standard service that requires significant compute resources which are in need of continuous maintenance and a sustained stream of funding. An alternative approach is to move towards Prolog systems running in the browser of each individual user.

Among other things, the browser-based approach lifts the need for sandbox containment because this security feature is already provided by the browser. Currently, SWISH rejects programmes it cannot *verify* to be safe, which includes scripts that perform *intractable* meta-calling. In the future, this could be resolved by using a process rather than a thread for implementing Pengines, and isolating this process using an operating system sandbox. Additionally, as it stands, SWISH is *stateless*, i.e., executing a query against a programme does not change the server state, since new queries are executed in a fresh environment. This implies that we cannot interactively call `assert/1` in one query and use the asserted clauses in the following queries. Instead, we must both assert and use the clauses in the same query. One big advantage of avoiding permanent state, nonetheless, is making all queries fully reproducible.

As noted in Sect. 2, there are JavaScript-based Prolog systems that explicitly target the web browser, in addition to more versatile WASM implementations. The ideal scenario would be for the Prolog community to come up with a "standard" embedding interface to enable designing interactive web pages using multiple Prolog backends. However, the browser control flow is inherently incompatible with traditional single-threaded Prolog systems since one cannot wait *synchronously* for input in a browser (e.g., call `read/1`). Instead, one must return control to the browser and when the input becomes available as an *event*, only then Prolog may resume. There are two ways to achieve that. One is to run Prolog in a *WebWorker* (roughly, a browser task without a window) and make it communicate with the browser task associated to a normal browser window. The other is to *yield* from the Prolog virtual machine and *resume* Prolog when the data become available. This leads to at least two interface designs:

- with a WebWorker we get interaction with a Prolog process that is not very different from Prolog running on a remote server; whereas
- using a pure JavaScript or Prolog with *yield* allows running Prolog on the same page and having bi-directional calls between Prolog and JavaScript, which facilitates managing the browser directly from Prolog.

Running Prolog in the browser rather than remotely on a server solves several problems. With Prolog being served as a static file, storage and chat services – which are currently part of SWISH – can be offloaded to existing cloud services. This creates a reliable distributed infrastructure that can be sustained by several Prolog implementations. Such diversification is important as due to the use of many features that are unique to SWI-Prolog, SWISH is practically not portable to other Prolog implementations.[8]

All of these observations lead us to conclude that an in-browser solution is probably the future of Prolog on the web, especially for educational use. The SWISH design is good for offering a collaborative, interactive coding environment and (programmatic) access to (large) shared data sets, but its limitations affect the design and capabilities of tools and resources that rely on it. When combined with the envisaged authoring suite, both SWISH and in-browser Prolog implementations to come (such as the Active Logic Documents described in Chapter 14 of this volume [12]) will offer immersive and engaging Prolog teaching as well as learning materials.

Acknowledgements. The development of the sphinx-prolog and sphinx-problog Jupyter Book plugins was supported by the TAILOR Network – an ICT-48 European AI Research Excellence Centre funded by EU Horizon 2020 research and innovation programme, grant agreement number 952215.

---

[8] Note that when Pengines is realised through processes rather than threads, implementing Pengines based on other Prolog systems becomes much easier.

References

1. Allaire, J., Teague, C., Scheidegger, C., Xie, Y., Dervieux, C.: Quarto (2022). https://doi.org/10.5281/zenodo.5960048, https://github.com/quarto-dev/quarto-cli
2. Blackburn, P., Bos, J., Striegnitz, K.: Learn Prolog Now! http://www.let.rug.nl/bos/lpn/index.php (2001)
3. Blackburn, P., Bos, J., Striegnitz, K.: Learn Prolog Now! (Texts in Computing, Vol. 7), College Publications, London (2006)
4. Blackburn, P., Bos, J., Striegnitz, K.: Learn Prolog Now! https://lpn.swi-prolog.org/ (2014)
5. De Raedt, L., Kimmig, A., Toivonen, H.: ProbLog: A probabilistic Prolog and its application in link discovery. In: IJCAI. vol. 7, pp. 2462–2467. Hyderabad (2007)
6. Executable Books Community: Jupyter Book (2020). https://doi.org/10.5281/zenodo.4539666, https://github.com/executablebooks/jupyter-book
7. Flach, P.: Simply Logical – Intelligent Reasoning by Example. John Wiley & Sons, Inc. (1994)
8. Flach, P., Sokol, K.: Simply Logical – Intelligent Reasoning by Example (Fully Interactive Online Edition). https://book.simply-logical.space/ (2022)
9. Kowalski, R.: Logic for problem solving. Edinburgh University, Department of Computational Logic (1974)
10. Luger, G., Stubblefield, W.: Artificial Intelligence: Structure and strategies for complex problem solving. Benjamin/Cummings (1993)
11. Luhmann, N.: Zettelkasten, https://zettelkasten.de/introduction/
12. Morales, J.F., Abreu, S., Ferreiro, D., Hermenegildo, M.V.: Teaching prolog with active logic documents. In: Warren, D.S., et al. (eds.) Prolog: The Next 50 Years. LNAI, vol. 13900, pp. 171–183. Springer, Switzerland (2023). https://doi.org/10.1007/978-3-031-35254-6_14
13. Morales, J.F., Haemmerlé, R., Carro, M., Hermenegildo, M.V.: Lightweight compilation of (C)LP to JavaScript. Theory Pract. Log. Program. **12**(4–5), 755–773 (2012). https://doi.org/10.1017/S1471068412000336
14. Riguzzi, F.: Foundations of Probabilistic Logic Programming. River Publishers, New York (2018)
15. Sokol, K., Flach, P.: You only write thrice: Creating documents, computational notebooks and presentations from a single source. In: Beyond static papers: Rethinking how we share scientific understanding in Machine Learning – ICLR Workshop (2021). https://doi.org/10.48550/arXiv.2107.06639
16. Wielemaker, J., Lager, T., Riguzzi, F.: SWISH: SWI-Prolog for sharing. In: Proceedings of the International Workshop on User-Oriented Logic Programming (IULP 2015); 31st International Conference on Logic Programming (ICLP 2015), pp. 99–113 (2015). https://doi.org/10.48550/arXiv.1511.00915
17. Wielemaker, J., Schrijvers, T., Triska, M., Lager, T.: SWI-Prolog. Theory Pract. Logic Program. **12**(1–2), 67–96 (2012). https://doi.org/10.1017/S1471068411000494

Prolog-Based Languages and Systems

Dynamic Logic Programming

Michael Genesereth[(✉)]

Computer Science Department, Stanford University, Palo Alto, USA
genesereth@stanford.edu

Abstract. Dynamic Logic Programming (DLP) is an extension to logic programming designed to support the representation of knowledge about dynamic worlds. It combines the strengths of safe, stratified, side-effect-free logic programming in defining relations with the power of simultaneous transition rules for defining dynamic operations. Because relation definitions in DLP are safe and stratified and side-effect-free, dynamic logic programs are simpler than general Prolog programs and they allow for efficient implementation. At the same time, defining operations using simultaneous transition rules adds expressive power without compromising the conceptual simplicity of logic programming. DLP is the basis for the logic programming language Epilog (aka Dynamic Prolog) [10].

1 Introduction

In Dynamic Logic Programming, the states of the application environment are modeled as sets of ground atomic sentences (here called *datasets*), and definitions are written in the form of *rules* that can be applied to these instances. *View definitions* define higher level *view* relations in terms of lower level *base* relations, and *operation definitions* specify how the world state changes in response to external inputs (such as the actions of agents or the passage of time).

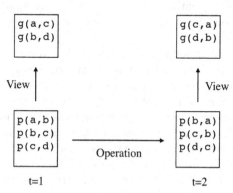

Views are defined by writing Prolog-style rules. For example, the rule below says that g is true of x and z if there is a y such that p is true of x and y and p is also true of y and z. (This is the view used in the preceding figure.)

```
g(X,Y) :- p(X,Y) & p(Y,Z)
```

© The Author(s), under exclusive license to Springer Nature Switzerland AG 2023
D. S. Warren et al. (Eds.): Prolog: The Next 50 Years, LNAI 13900, pp. 197–209, 2023.
https://doi.org/10.1007/978-3-031-35254-6_16

Operations are defined using transition rules. For example, the following rule says that when the action a is performed in any state, for any y such that p holds of x and y, then p will be false of x and y in the next state and p will be true of y and x. (This is the operation used in the preceding figure.)

```
a :: p(X,Y) ==> ~p(X,Y) & p(Y,X)
```

This paper provides technical detail about the syntax and semantics of Dynamic Logic Programming. Section 2 describes the concept of datasets; Sect. 3 gives details of view rules; and Sect. 4 covers transition rules and shows how they are used in formalizing dynamic behavior. Section 5 gives an example of the use of Dynamic Logic Programming in defining the game of Tic Tac Toe.

2 Datasets

A *vocabulary* is a collection of *object constants*, *function constants*, and *relation constants*. Each function constant and relation constant has an associated *arity*, i.e. the number of *arguments* allowed in any expression involving that constant.

A *ground functional term* is an expression formed from an n-ary function constant and n ground terms. In this paper, we write functional terms in traditional mathematical notation - the function constant followed by its *arguments* enclosed in parentheses and separated by commas. For example, if f is a unary function constant and a is an object constant, then f(a), f(f(a)), and f(f(f(a))) are all ground functional terms. A *ground term* is either an object constant or a ground functional term.

A *ground atom* (or *factoid*) is an expression formed from an n-ary relation constant and n ground terms. In analogy with functional terms, we write factoids in traditional mathematical notation - the relation constant followed by its *arguments* enclosed in parentheses and separated by commas. For example, if r is a binary relation constant and a and b are object constants, then r(a,b) is a factoid.

The *Herbrand universe* for a given vocabulary is the set of all ground terms that can be formed from the constants in the vocabulary. In the absence of function constants, the Herbrand universe for a vocabulary is just the set of all object constants. In the presence of function constants with arity greater than 0, the Herbrand universe is necessarily infinite, as it includes not just object constants but also functional terms nested arbitrarily deeply.

The *Herbrand base* for a database is the set of all factoids that can be formed from the constants in its vocabulary. For example, for a vocabulary with just two object constants a and b and a single binary relation constant r, the Herbrand base is {r(a,a), r(a,b), r(b,a), r(b,b)}.

A *dataset* is any subset of the Herbrand base, i.e. an arbitrary set of the factoids that can be formed from the vocabulary of the database. The factoids in a dataset representing a state are assumed to be true in that state, and all other factoids in the Herbrand base are typically assumed to be false.

3   View Definitions

A *static logic program* is a set of rules that define new relations in terms of existing relations. Such view definitions take the form of Prolog-like rules with the constraint that the rules are safe and stratified and side-effect-free.

The vocabulary of a static logic program is a superset of the vocabulary of any dataset to which it is applied. It includes the object, function, and relation constants used in the dataset, but it can include additional object, function, and relation constants as well.

Static logic programs can also include a new type of symbol, called a *variable*. Variables allow us to state relationships among objects without naming specific objects. In what follows, we write variables as strings of alphanumeric characters beginning with a capital letter, e.g. X, Y, Z, Mass, Speed, and so forth.

Atoms are analogous to dataset factoids except that they can optionally contain variables as well as object constants. For example, if r is a binary relation constant, if a is an object constant, and if X and Y are variables, then r(a,X) is an atom, as is r(a,Y) and r(X,Y) and r(X,X).

A *literal* is either an atom or a negation of an atom (i.e. an expression stating that the atom is false). A simple atom is called a *positive* literal, The negation of an atom is called a *negative* literal. In what follows, we write negative literals using the negation sign ~. For example, if p(a,b) is an atom, then ~p(a,b) denotes the negation of this atom.

A *rule* is an expression consisting of a distinguished atom, called the head, and zero or more literals, together called the body. The literals in the body are called *subgoals*. The following expression is an example of a rule. Here, r(X) is the head, the expression p(X,Y) & q(Y) is the body; and p(X,Y) and ~q(Y) are subgoals.

    r(X) :- p(X,Y) & ~q(Y)

Intuitively, a rule is something like a reverse implication. It is a statement that the conclusion of the rule is true whenever the conditions are true. For example, the rule above states that r is true of any object x *if* there is an object y such that p is true of x and y and q is not true of y. For example, if we know that p(a,b) is true and q(b) is false, then, using this rule, we can conclude that r(a) is true. See the end of this section for a more formal treatment of semantics.

A *logic program* is a set of facts and rules of the form just described. Unfortunately, the language of rules, as defined above, allows for logic programs with some unpleasant properties (ambiguities and potentially infinite answer sets). To eliminate these problems, we concentrate exclusively on logic programs where the rules have two special properties, viz. safety and stratification.

A rule in a logic program is *safe* if and only if every variable that appears in the head or in any negative literal in the body also appears in at least one positive literal in the body. A logic program is safe if and only if every rule in the program is safe.

The rule shown below is safe. Every variable in the head and every variable in the negative subgoal appears in a positive subgoal in the body. Note that it is okay for the body to contain variables that do not appear in the head.

```
r(X,Y) :- p(X,Y,Z) & ~q(X,Z)
```

By contrast, the two rules shown below are not safe. The first rule is not safe because the variable Z appears in the head but does not appear in any positive subgoal. The second rule is not safe because the variable Z appears in a negative subgoal but not in any positive subgoal.

```
s(X,Y,Z) :- p(X,Y)
t(X,Y) :- p(X,Y) & ~q(Y,Z)
```

(Note that this condition is stronger than necessary. We do not need every rule to be safe; we just require that the program as a whole is safe. The definition of this broader notion of safety is a little complicated and the distinction is unnecessary here, so we skip over this subtlety in the interests of simplicity.)

We say that a set of view definitions is *stratified with respect to negation* if and only if its rules can be partitioned into *strata* in such a way that (1) every stratum contains at least one rule, (2) the rules defining relations that appear in positive goals of a rule appear in the same stratum as that rule *or* in some lower stratum, and (3) the rules defining relations that appear in negative subgoals of a rule occur in some *lower* stratum (not the same stratum).

As an example, assume we have a unary relation p that is true of all of the objects in some application area, and assume that q is an arbitrary binary relation. Now, consider the ruleset shown below. The first two rules define r to be the transitive closure of q. The third rule defines s to be the complement of the transitive closure.

```
r(X,Y) :- q(X,Y)
r(X,Z) :- q(X,Y) & r(Y,Z)
s(X,Y) :- p(X) & p(Y) & ~r(X,Y)
```

This is a complicated ruleset, yet it is easy to see that it is stratified with respect to negation. The first two rules contain no negations at all, and so we can group them together in our lowest stratum. The third rule has a negated subgoal containing a relation defined in our lowest stratum, and so we put it into a stratum above this one, as shown below. This ruleset satisfies the conditions of our definition and hence it is stratified with respect to negation.

```
s(X,Y) :- p(X) & p(Y) & ~r(X,Y)

r(X,Y) :- q(X,Y)
r(X,Z) :- q(X,Y) & r(Y,Z)
```

By comparison, consider the following ruleset. Here, the relation s is defined in terms of p and the negation of r, and the relation r is defined in terms of p and the negation of s.

```
r(X,Y) :- p(X) & p(Y) & q(X,Y)
s(X,Y) :- r(X,Y) & ~s(Y,X)
```

There is no way of dividing the rules of this ruleset into strata in a way that satisfies the definition above. Hence, the ruleset is *not* stratified with respect to negation.

The problem with unstratified rulesets is that there is a potential ambiguity. As an example, consider the rules above and assume that our dataset also included the facts p(a), p(b), q(a,b), and q(b,a). From these facts, we can conclude r(a,b) and r(b,a) are both true. So far, so good. But what can we say about s? If we take s(a,b) to be true and s(b,a) to be false, then the second rule is satisfied. If we take s(a,b) to be false and s(b,a) to be true, then the second rule is again satisfied. The upshot is that there is ambiguity about s. By concentrating exclusively on logic programs that are stratified with respect to negation, we avoid such ambiguities.

View definitions in static logic programs are required to be both safe and stratified with respect to negation. This is a departure from view definitions in Logic Programming languages like Prolog, which permit rules that are unsafe and logic programs that are not stratified.

The semantics of view definitions in static logic programs can be formalized by defining the result of applying a static logic program to a dataset. The resulting *extension* is the set of all facts that can be"deduced" from the dataset on the basis of the rules in the static logic program.

An *instance* of an expression (atom, literal, or rule) is one in which all variables have been consistently replaced by terms from the Herbrand universe. For example, if we have a language with object constants a and b, then r(a) :- p(a,a), r(a) :- p(a,b), r(b) :- p(b,a), and r(b) :- p(b,b) are all instances of r(X) :- p(X,Y). (To be clear here, we use the word *instance* here to refer exclusively to *ground* expressions.)

Given this notion, we can define the result of a single application of a single rule to a dataset. Given a rule r and a dataset Δ, we define $v(r, \Delta)$ to be the set of all ψ such that (1) ψ is the head of an arbitrary instance of r, (2) every positive subgoal in the instance is a member of Δ, and (3) no negative subgoal in the instance is a member of Δ.

Using this notion, we define the result of repeatedly applying the rules in a single stratum Σ to a dataset Δ of factoids in the vocabulary of the stratum below. Consider a sequence of datasets defined recursively as follows. $\Gamma_0 = \Delta$, and $\Gamma_{n+1} = \cup v(r, \Gamma_n)$ for all r in Σ. Finally, we define the closure of Σ on Δ to be the union of the datasets in this sequence, i.e. $C(\Sigma, \Delta) = \cup \Gamma_i$.

Finally, we define the *extension* of a static logic program Ω on dataset Δ as follows. Our definition relies on a decomposition of Ω into strata $\Sigma_1, \dots, \Sigma_n$. Let $\Delta_0 = \Delta$, and let $\Delta_{n+1} = \Delta_n \cup C(\Sigma_{n+1}, \Delta_n)$. Since there are only finitely many rules in a static logic program and every stratum must contain at least one rule, there are only finitely many sets to consider (though the sets themselves might be infinite).

It can be shown that there is only one extension for any static logic program applied to any dataset. Although it is sometimes possible to stratify the rules in more than one way, this does not cause any problems. So long as a program is stratified with respect to negation, the definition just given produces the same extension no matter which stratification one uses.

Note that the extension of any function-free static logic program on a finite dataset must be finite. Also, the extension of any non-recursive static logic program applied to a finite dataset must be finite. In both cases, the extension can be computed in time that is polynomial in the size of the dataset.

In the case of recursive programs without function constants, the result must be finite. However, the cost of computing the extension may be exponential in the size of the data, but the result can be computed in finite time.

For recursive programs with function constants, it is possible that the extension is infinite. In such cases, the extension is still well-defined; but in practice it may be necessary to use a different algorithm to compute whether or not a given atom is in the extension. There are multiple ways this can be done. See Ullman's book on Database Systems and Knowledge Base Systems for a discussion of some usable approaches.

4   Operation Definitions

The syntax of operation definitions is analogous to the syntax for view definitions. The various types of constants are the same, and the notions of term and atom and literal are also the same. However, to these, we add a few new items.

To denote operations, we designate some constants as *operation constants*. As with function constants and relation constants, each operation constant has a fixed arity - unary, binary, and so forth.

An *action* is an application of an operation to specific objects. In what follows, we denote actions using a syntax similar to that of atomic sentences, viz. an n-ary operation constant followed by n terms enclosed in parentheses and separated by commas. For example, if f is a binary operation constant and a and b object constants, then f(a,b) denotes the action of applying the operation f to a and b.

An *operation definition rule* (or, more simply, an *operation rule*) is an expression of the form shown below. Each rule consists of (1) an action expression, (2) a double colon, (3) a literal or a conjunction of literals, (4) a double shafted forward arrow, and (5) a literal or an action expression or a conjunction of literals and action expressions. The action expression to the left of the double colon is called the *head*; the literals to the left of the arrow are called *conditions*; and the literals to its right are called *effects*. The following rule is an example.

```
click(a) :: p(a,b) & ~q(a) ==> ~p(a,b) & q(a) & click(b)
```

Intuitively, the meaning of an operation rule is simple. If the conditions of a rule are true in any state, then executing the action in the head requites that we execute the effects of the rule.

For example, the rule above states that in any state in which p(a,b) is true and q(a) is false, then executing click(a) requires that we remove p(a,b) from our dataset, add q(a), and perform action click(b).

As with rules defining views, operation rules may contain variables to express information in a compact form. For example, we can write the following rule to generalize the preceding rule to all objects.

```
click(X) :: p(X,Y) & ~q(X) ==> ~p(X,Y) & q(X) & click(Y)
```

As with view rules, *safety* is a consideration. Safety in this case means that every variable among the effects of a rule or in negative conditions also appears in the head of the rule or in the positive conditions.

The operation rules shown above are both safe. However, the rules shown below are not. The second effect of the first rule contains a variable that does not appear in the head or in any positive condition. In the second rule, there is a variable that appears in a negative condition that does not appear in the head or in any positive condition.

```
click(X) :: p(X,Y) & ~q(X) ==> ~p(X,Y) & q(Z) & click(Y)
click(X) :: p(X,Y) & ~q(Z) ==> ~p(X,Y) & q(X) & click(Y)
```

In some operation rules there is no condition, i.e. the effects of the transition rule take place on all datasets. We can, of course, write such rules by using the condition true, as in the following example.

```
click(X) :: true ==> ~p(X) & q(X)
```

For the sake of simplicity in writing our examples, we sometimes abbreviate such rules by dropping the conditions and the transition operator and instead write just the effects of the transition as the body of the operation rule. For example, we can abbreviate the rule above as shown below.

```
click(X) :: ~p(X) & q(X)
```

An *operation definition* is a collection of operation rules in which the same operation appears in the head of every rule. As with view definitions, we are interested primarily in rulesets that are finite. However, in analyzing operation definitions, we occasionally talk about the set of all ground instances of the rules, and in some cases these sets are infinite.

The semantics of operation definitions is more complicated than the semantics of updates due to the possible occurrence of views in the conditions of the rule and the possible occurrence of operations in its effects. In what follows, we first define the expansion of an action in the context of a given dataset, and we then define the result of performing that action on that dataset.

Suppose we are given a set Ω of rules, a set Γ of actions (factoids, negated factoids, and actions), and a dataset Δ. We say that an *instance* of a rule in Ω is *active* with respect to Γ and Δ if and only if the head of the rule is in Γ and the conditions of the rule are all true in Δ.

Given this notion, we define the *expansion* of action γ with respect to rule set Ω and dataset Δ as follows. Let Γ_0 be $\{\gamma\}$ and let Γ_{i+1} be the set of all effects in any instance of any rule in Ω with respect to Γ_i and Δ. We define our expansion $U(\gamma, \Omega, \Delta)$ as the fixpoint of this series. Equivalently, it is the union of the sets Γ_i, for all non-negative integers i.

Next, we define the positive updates $A(\gamma, \Omega, \Delta)$ to be the positive base factoids in $U(\gamma, \Omega, \Delta)$). We define the negative updates $D(\gamma, \Omega, \Delta))$ to be the set of all negative factoids in $U(\gamma, \Omega, \Delta)$.

Finally, we define the result of applying an action γ to a dataset Δ as the result of removing the negative updates from Δ and adding the positive updates, i.e. the result is $(\Delta - D(\gamma, \Omega, \Delta)) \cup A(\gamma, \Omega, \Delta)$. (Note that, if a factoid appears in both the positive and negative update sets, the resulting dataset contains the disputed factoid. Ideally, actions should not lead to such contradictions; and, arguably, an interpreter should throw an error in such situations. However, programmers seem to prefer this resolution; it allows them to write simpler programs without causing any major problems.)

To illustrate these definitions, consider an application with a dataset representing a directed acyclic graph. In the sentences below, we use object constants to designate the nodes of the graph, and we use the edge relation to designate the arcs of the graph.

```
edge(a,b)
edge(b,d)
edge(b,e)
```

The following operation definition defines a binary operation copy that copies the outgoing arcs in the graph from its first argument to its second argument.

```
copy(X,Y) :: edge(X,Z) ==> edge(Y,Z)
```

Given this operation definition and the dataset shown above, executing copy(b,c) adds edge(c,d) and edge(c,e), resulting in the following dataset.

```
edge(a,b)
edge(b,d)
edge(b,e)
edge(c,d)
edge(c,e)
```

The following rule defines a unary operation invert that reverses the outgoing arcs of the node specified as it argument.

```
invert(X) :: edge(X,Y) ==> ~edge(X,Y) & edge(Y,X)
```

Executing invert(c) removes the previous outgoing arcs from c and turns them into incoming arcs, as shown below.

```
edge(a,b)
edge(b,d)
edge(b,e)
edge(d,c)
edge(e,c)
```

Finally, the following operation rules define a binary operation that inserts a new node into the graph (the first argument) with an arc to the second argument and arcs to all of the nodes that are reachable from the second argument.

```
insert(X,Y) :: edge(X,Y)
insert(X,Y) :: edge(Y,Z) ==> insert(X,Z)
```

Now consider the action insert(w,b). The first rule adds edge(w,b) to the expansion. The second rule adds insert(w,d) and insert(w,e). On the next round of expansion, the first rule adds edge(w,d) and edge(w,e), and the second rules adds insert(w,c). On the third round, we get edge(w,c). At this point, neither rule adds any items to our expansion. Applying the changes to our dataset, we get the dataset shown below.

```
edge(a,b)
edge(b,d)
edge(b,e)
edge(d,c)
edge(e,c)
edge(w,b)
edge(w,d)
edge(w,e)
edge(w,c)
```

Note that it is possible to define insert in other ways. We could, for example, define a view of edge that relates each node to every node that can be reached from the node; and we could then use this view in a non-recursive definition of insert. However, this would require us to introduce a new view into our vocabulary; and, for many people, this is less clear than the definition shown above.

5   Example - Tic Tac Toe

As an example of a dynamic logic program, consider the task of formalizing the rules for the game of Tic Tac Toe (also called Noughts and Crosses, Xs and Os). In what follows, we show how to represent game states as datasets; we show how to define properties of states using view definitions; and we show how to define "moves" in the game using operation definitions.

Tic Tac Toe is a game for two players (the X player and the O player) who take turns placing their marks in a 3 × 3 grid. The first player to place three of his marks in a horizontal, vertical, or diagonal row wins the game. The figure below shows one state of play in Tic Tac Toe.

In our definition of Tic Tac Toe, states are characterized by the contents of the cells on the Tic Tac Toe board and control (whose turn it is to play). (It is true that control can be defined in terms of the contents of cells; but making control explicit costs little and simplifies the description.) In what follows, we use the ternary relation constant cell together with a row m and a column n and a mark w to designate the fact that the cell in row m and column n contains w where w is either an x or an o or a b (for blank). We use the unary relation constant control to state that it is that role's turn to mark a cell. The dataset shown below uses this vocabulary to characterize the game state show above.

```
cell(1,1,x)
cell(1,2,o)
cell(1,3,b)
cell(2,1,b)
cell(2,2,x)
cell(2,3,o)
cell(3,1,b)
cell(3,2,b)
cell(3,3,b)
control(x)
```

Our first step is to define legality of moves. A player may mark a cell if that cell is blank. Otherwise, it has no legal actions.

```
legal(M,N) :- cell(M,N,b)
```

Next, we define the *physics* of the world - how it changes in response to the performance of legal actions. If a player has control and marks a cell, the cell is then marked. Also, control switches to the other player.

```
mark(M,N) :: control(Z) ==> ~cell(M,N,b) & cell(M,N,Z)
mark(M,N) :: control(x) ==> ~control(x) & control(o)
mark(M,N) :: control(o) ==> ~control(o) & control(x)
```

Finally, to complete our game description, we define some properties of game states - rows, columns, diagonals, lines - and we must say when the game terminates.

A row of marks means that there are three marks all with the same first coordinate. The column and diagonal relations are defined analogously.

```
row(M,Z) :- cell(M,1,Z) & cell(M,2,Z) & cell(M,3,Z)
column(M,Z) :- cell(1,N,Z) & cell(2,N,Z) & cell(3,N,Z)
diagonal(Z) :- cell(1,1,Z) & cell(2,2,Z) & cell(3,3,Z)
diagonal(Z) :- cell(1,3,Z) & cell(2,2,Z) & cell(3,1,Z)
```

A line is a row of marks of the same type or a column or a diagonal.

```
line(Z) :- row(M,Z)
line(Z) :- column(M,Z)
line(Z) :- diagonal(Z)
```

A game is over whenever either player has a line of marks of the appropriate type or if there are no cells containing blanks. We define the 0-ary relation open here to mean that there is at least one cell containing a blank.

```
terminal :- line(x)
terminal :- line(o)
terminal :- ~open
open :- cell(M,N,b)
```

Our rules specify the states and physics of the game. They do not specify how to play the game effectively. In order to decide this, a player needs to consider the effects of his legal moves in order to decide a course of action that will lead to a line of his marks while considering the possible moves of the other player.

6   Comparison to Other Languages

Over the years, various LP researchers, have developed extensions to deal with dynamics, e.g. assert and retract in standard Prolog [1], production systems, active databases, transactions in Transaction Logic [2,7], constraint handling rules in CHR [8], evolving logic programs in EVOLP [17], and reactive rules in DALI [5] and LPS [15]. The references give details of these various approaches. We describe just three below.

Prolog's assert and retract provide one way to model dynamics. The key is a conceptualization of dynamics as destructive change of state - states are modeled as sets of stored facts, and changes to state are modeled as applications of assert and retract to these sets of facts. Unfortunately, the semantics of logic programs involving assert and retract is unsatisfying because of the way the execution of these actions gets mixed up with query evaluation in the standard Prolog interpreter. Dynamic logic programming cleans things up by separating the formalization of dynamics from the definition of relations using Prolog rules.

Production systems are another way of expressing dynamics. The transition rules used to define operations in DLP are similar, but there are some important differences. In most production systems, only one rule is applied at a time. (Many rules may be "triggered", but typically only one is "fired".) In dynamic logic programs, all transition rules are executed simultaneously, and all updates (both deletions and additions) are applied to the dataset before the rules fire again. This simplifies the specification of dynamics in many cases, and avoids many problems endemic to sequential update systems, such as unintended race conditions and deadlocks.

Finally, Carro and Hermenegildo [3] introduce a notion of "concurrent data facts" to (Ciao) Prolog [4] which are used primarily for communication among concurrent threads, but also to represent (possibly timestamped) changes in (or to) the external world. This, by itself, is still 'mixed up with query evaluation'. But, by using, e.g., time stamps as an argument in the facts, the reasoning system can be kept monotonic and sound. More relevantly perhaps, the paper also mentions that these concurrent facts facilitate the implementation of reactive condition-action rules, i.e. the part that reacts and exerts the changes on the facts can be encoded within condition-action rules, and these can be implemented within the Prolog system with these building blocks. The reactivity comes from the synchronization provided through the concurrent facts, i.e. execution can wait for concrete facts to be present.

7   Conclusion

In practice, it is common to extend the simple version of Dynamic Logic Programming described here to include "built-in" relations (e.g. arithmetic) and other operators (e.g. aggregates). The syntax and semantics of such extensions are a little messy. Luckily, they pose no significant theoretical challenges; and, in the interest of brevity, they are not covered here.

The intent of this article is to provide a concise but reasonably rigorous account of the syntax and semantics of Dynamic Logic Programming. For motivation and examples of all of these concepts, see the textbook Dynamic Logic Programming.

References

1. Clocksin, W.F., Mellish, C.S.: Programming in Prolog, 4th edn. Springer-Verlag, New York (1994)
2. Bonner, A.J., Kifer, M.: Transaction logic programming, international conference on logic programming (ICLP) (1993)
3. Carro, M., Hermenegildo, M.: Concurrency in prolog using threads and a shared database (1999). International Conference on Logic Programming, pp. 320–334, MIT Press, Cambridge, MA, USA, November (1999)
4. Cabeza, D., Hermenegildo, M.: Distributed www programming using (Ciao) Prolog and the pillow library. Theory Pract. Logic Program. $1(3)$, 251–282 (2001)
5. Costantini, S., Tocchio, A.: The DALI logic programming agent-oriented language. In: Alferes, J.J., Leite, J. (eds.) JELIA 2004. LNCS (LNAI), vol. 3229, pp. 685–688. Springer, Heidelberg (2004). https://doi.org/10.1007/978-3-540-30227-8_57
6. Flesca, S., Greco, S.: Declarative semantics for active rules. Theory Pract. Logic Program. $1(1)$, 43–69 (2001)
7. Fodor, P.: Practical reasoning with transaction logic programming for knowledge base dynamics, PhD Thesis, Stonybrook University (2011)
8. Fruehwirth, T.: Constraint Handling Rules. Cambridge University Press. ISBN 9780521877763 (2009)
9. Genesereth, M., Love, N., Pell, B.: The international game playing competition. AAAI Magazine (2005)
10. Genesereth, M.: Epilog. http://epilog.stanford.edu
11. Genesereth, M., Chaudhri, V.: Logic Programming. Synthesis Lectures on Artificial Intelligence and Machine Learning, February (2020). https://doi.org/10.2200/S00966ED1V01Y201911AIM044
12. Hayes, P.: Computation and deduction. In: Proceedings Second Symposium on Mathematical Foundations of Computer Science, Czechoslovakian Academy of Sciences, Czechoslovakia, pp. 105–118 (1973)
13. Kifer, M., Liu, A.: Declarative logic programming, ACM Books (2018)
14. Kowalski, R.: Algorithm = Logic + Control. In: Communications of the ACM, vol. 22, No. 7, July (1979)
15. Kowalski, R., Sadri, F.: LPS-A logic-based production system framework (2009)
16. Kowalski, R., Sadri, F.: Integrating logic programming and production systems in abductive logic programming agents (2009)
17. Slota, M., Leite, J.A.: EVOLP: an implementation. In: Computational Logic in Multi-Agent Systems, 8th International Workshop, CLIMA VIII, Porto, Portugal, September 10–11 (2007)
18. Warren, D.S.: Programming in tabled prolog. https://citeseerx.ist.psu.edu/viewdoc/download?doi=10.1.1.49.4635
19. Zhou, N.-F.: The language features and architecture of B-Prolog. Theory Pract. Logic Program. $12(1-2)$ (2011). https://doi.org/10.1017/S1471068411000445

Combining Logic Programming and Imperative Programming in LPS

Robert Kowalski[1]([⊠]), Fariba Sadri[1], Miguel Calejo[2], and Jacinto Dávila[3]

[1] Imperial College London, London, UK
rak@doc.ic.ac.uk
[2] Logicalcontracts.Com, Lisbon, Portugal
[3] Universidad de Los Andes, Mérida, Venezuela

Abstract. Logic programs and imperative programs employ different notions of computing. Logic programs compute by proving that a goal is a logical consequence of the program, or by showing that the goal is true in a model defined by the program. Imperative programs compute by starting from an initial state, executing actions to transition from one state to the next, and terminating (if at all) in a final state when the goal is solved.

In this paper, we present the language LPS (Logic Production Systems), which combines the logic programming and imperative programming notions of computing. Programs in LPS compute by using beliefs, represented by logic programs, to model the changing world, and by executing actions, to change the world, to satisfy goals, represented by reactive rules and constraints.

Keywords: Logic programming · Imperative programming · LPS · Reactive rules

1 Introduction

On the one hand, it can be argued that logic programming (LP) is a Turing-complete model of computation, which is well-suited for all computing tasks. It can also be argued that the procedural interpretation of LP gives LP the computational capabilities of an imperative computer language. On the other hand, despite such arguments, conventional imperative languages dominate computing today.

In this paper, we take the position that, to have wider applicability, LP needs to be extended with the ability of imperative languages, to generate actions to satisfy an agent's goals. Without this ability, LP can represent only an agent's beliefs. The beliefs can be queried, to determine whether they hold at a point in time. But without extension, LP cannot represent persistent goals that need to be satisfied over the course of time. For truly general-purpose computing, LP needs to be extended to include persistence goals and a treatment of time that is compatible with destructive change of state.

To support this position, we present the language LPS (Logic Production Systems) [15–22], which combines the use of LP, to represent an agent's beliefs, with the use of reactive rules and constraints, formalised in first-order logic, to represent the agent's

© The Author(s), under exclusive license to Springer Nature Switzerland AG 2023
D. S. Warren et al. (Eds.): Prolog: The Next 50 Years, LNAI 13900, pp. 210–223, 2023.
https://doi.org/10.1007/978-3-031-35254-6_17

goals. Computation in LPS generates actions, to satisfy goals in a model determined by the agent's beliefs.

Production Systems. LPS was inspired in large part by trying to understand the difference and relationship between rules in LP and condition-action rules (CA rules) in production systems [27]. We were motivated by the fact that both kinds of rules were used in the 1980s for implementing expert systems, and that production systems were also being used as a cognitive model of human thinking.

Moreover, we were provoked by Thagard's claim in his popular Introduction to Cognitive Science [34] that "Unlike logic, rule-based systems can also easily represent strategic information about what to do". He gives as an example the rule *IF you want to go home for the weekend, and you have the bus fare, THEN you can catch a bus.* He does not observe that the rule incorporates the use of backward reasoning to give a procedural interpretation to the LP rule *you go home for the weekend if you have the bus fare and you catch a bus.* Viewed in this way, his example is not an argument against logic, but an argument for the procedural interpretation of logic programs.

In contrast, Russell and Norvig in their textbook, Artificial Intelligence: A Modern Approach, [31] characterise production systems as systems of logic that perform forward reasoning with rules of the form *if conditions then actions*, which "are especially useful for systems that make inferences in response to newly arrived information". But they do not take into account that production systems have several features that do not accord well with such a logical interpretation. In particular, production systems destructively update a "working memory" of facts, and they use "conflict resolution" to choose between mutually incompatible actions.

For example, given a state in which you are both hungry and sleepy, and given the CA rules:

If you are hungry then eat.

If you are sleepy then sleep.

instead of deriving the logical consequence that you eat *and* sleep at the same time (assuming that to be impossible), production systems use conflict resolution to choose between eating *or* sleeping. One of the aims of LPS is to give such behaviour a logical interpretation by associating times with actions, and by allowing, in this case, eating *and* sleeping to occur at different times.

Integrity Constraints. In addition to giving CA rules a logical interpretation, LPS also gives them a logical status as *goals,* distinct from the logical status of LP rules as *beliefs.* Our understanding of this distinction between the logic of LP rules and the logic of CA rules was influenced by Gallaire and Nicolas' [28] work on deductive databases in the late 1970s. They distinguished between two kinds of general laws in deductive databases: general laws that are used (like logic programs) to derive implicit (or intensional) data from explicit (or extensional) data, and general laws that are used as integrity constraints to restrict and maintain database updates.

For example, the assumption that it is not possible to eat and sleep at the same time could be represented by the integrity constraint:

not(you are eating and you are sleeping).

where *you are eating* and *you are sleeping* are "facts", which are added to the database when the actions of eating and sleeping are initiated respectively.

This distinction between two kinds of general laws in databases inspired our work [32] on integrity checking for deductive databases, combining backward reasoning using LP rules with forward reasoning using integrity constraints, triggered by database updates. This combination of forward and backward reasoning is reflected in the operational semantics of LPS today.

External Events and Actions. However, integrity checking in traditional database systems only prevents database updates from violating integrity. It does not actively change the database, to ensure that integrity is maintained. Active databases [37] remedy this omission by using *event-condition-action* rules (ECA rules), to perform database-changing *actions* triggered by *events*, when the corresponding *conditions* hold. But, although it is natural to write such rules in the seemingly logical form *if event and condition then action*, ECA rules, like CA rules, do not have a logical interpretation as logical implications.

LPS gives CA and ECA rules a logical interpretation, not only by associating times with events, conditions and actions, but also by generating actions to make goals true. In this respect, LPS can be viewed as a special case of abductive logic programming (ALP) [12], which combines logic programs and integrity constraints with candidate assumptions, which can be used to satisfy the integrity constraints. Whereas in the philosophy of science abduction is used to generate assumptions to explain external observations, abduction in LPS generates actions to make goals true.

Change of State. The final step in the logical development of LPS was to decide how to represent and reason about change of state. It is common in AI to represent such knowledge by means of frame axioms, such as those in the situation calculus [25] and event calculus [23], reasoning, for example, that:

> *if a fact is true in a given state,*
> *then it continues to be true in a later state,*
> *unless it is terminated by an event (either an external event or action)*
> *that occurs between the two states.*

But reasoning with frame axioms is not practical for large scale computer applications. To develop LPS as a practical system, we needed to replace the use of frame axioms by destructive change of state. But we were committed to do so within a logical framework.

Models Instead of Theories. This last problem, of justifying destructive change of state within a logical framework, was solved by abandoning the theoremhood view of LP and replacing it with a model-theoretic view. The theoremhood view regards logic programs as axioms, and regards computation as proving that an answer to a query is a theorem. The model theoretic view regards logic programs as defining a unique, intended model, and regards computation as showing that the model satisfies the query, viewed as a goal.

To employ destructive change of state within a theorem-proving approach, it would be necessary to destructively change the axioms in the middle of a proof. But this would also destroy the justification for arguing that the theorem is a logical consequence of the axioms, because the axioms would not be well-defined. This problem does not arise with the model-theoretic view, because there is no such restriction on the way in which a model is defined.

We were influenced and encouraged in this model-generation view of computation by its use in such LP languages as XSB Prolog [30], Transaction Logic [4] and Answer Set Programming [24], as well as by the treatment of computation as model-generation in the modal temporal language MetaTem [2].

2 Logic Programs for Representing Change of State

Computation in LPS follows the imperative paradigm of generating a sequence of states and events, to make goals true. However, unlike states in imperative programming languages, which are collections of computer memory locations named by "variables", states in LPS are sets of facts (called *fluents*) that change with time. In this respect, states in LPS are like relations in a relational database.

LPS, like relational databases and Datalog, distinguishes between extensional fluents, which are stored explicitly, and intensional fluents, which are defined in terms of extensional fluents and other intensional fluents. These definitions are like view definitions in relational databases.

Change of state in LPS also follows the imperative paradigm of destructive updates, maintaining only a single current state. However, whereas imperative programs update variables by means of assignment statements, LPS updates fluents by means of events, whose effects are defined by logic programs. Events directly affect only the status of extensional fluents. They affect the status of intensional fluents indirectly, as ramifications of changes to the extensional fluents.

LP clauses in LPS are written in the form *conclusion if conditions*, where the *conclusion* is a simple atomic formula, and the *conditions* can be an arbitrary formula of first-order logic [21]. However, in the current implementation of LPS in SWISH [38], *conditions* are restricted to conjunctions of atomic formulas and their negations.

As a simple example, consider the following LP clauses in LPS syntax, where *lightOn* is an extensional fluent, *lightOff* is an intensional fluent, and *switch* is an event, which can be an external event or an internally generated action.

> *initially lightOn.*
> *observe switch from 1 to 2.*
> *observe switch from 3 to 4.*
> *lightOff if not lightOn.*
> *switch initiates lightOn if lightOff.*
> *switch terminates lightOn if lightOn.*

The first clause defines the initial state at time 1, in which the fluent *lightOn* is *true*. The clause is shorthand for the sentence *holds(lightOn, 1)*, written in the syntax of the event calculus [23].

The second and third clauses define observations of the external event *switch*, which occurs instantaneously both in the transition between the state at time 1 and the next state at time 2, and between the state at time 3 and the next state at time 4. The clauses are shorthand for *happens(switch, 1, 2)* and *happens(switch, 3, 4)* in a syntax similar to that of the event calculus.

The fourth clause defines the intensional fluent *lightOff* in terms of the extensional fluent *lightOn*. The clause is shorthand for *holds(lightOff, T)* if not *holds(lightOn, T)*.

The fifth and sixth clauses are *causal laws*, which specify, in effect, that a *switch* event turns the light on if the light is off and turns the light off if the light is on. The two clauses are shorthand for:

$$initiates(switch, \ lightOn, \ T + 1) \ \ if \ holds(lightOff, \ T).$$
$$terminates(switch, \ lightOn, \ T + 1) \ if \ holds(lightOn, \ T).$$

Given these clauses, the general command go(Timeline) in the SWISH implementation displays the history of states and events generated by computation in LPS. Notice that "times" are actually periods of time during which no change of state takes place. Events, on the other hand, are instantaneous and take place between time periods.

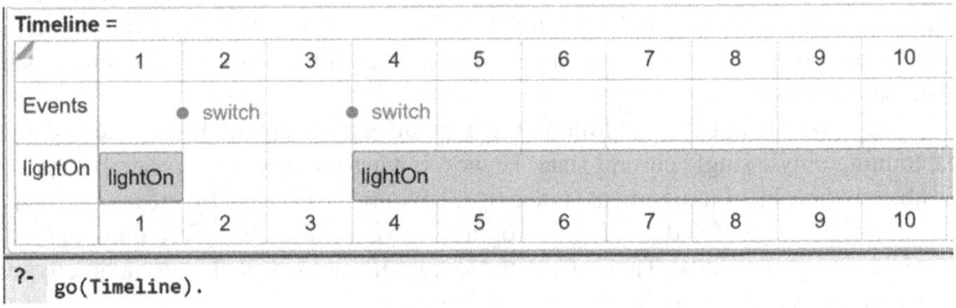

Fig. 1. An initial history of states and events, displayed as a Gantt chart. https://demo.logicalcontracts.com/p/basic-switch.pl

The SWISH implementation of LPS includes other general predicates that display other views of the computation. For example, the command state_diagram(Graph) generates the more abstract display in Fig. 2.

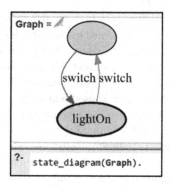

Fig. 2 A state diagram for the example in Fig.1.

Logically, the history computed by LPS determines a model that *satisfies* the program, by making all the sentences in the program true. It makes extensional fluents true or false, by using causal laws, to initiate and terminate extensional fluents. It makes intensional fluents true or false (as ramifications of changes to extensional fluents), by using intensional fluent definitions.

In Fig. 1, the occurrence of the *switch* event between times 1 and 2 terminates the truth of the extensional fluent *lightOn*, so that it is no longer true at time 2. As a consequence, according to both negation as failure (NAF) and the classical meaning of negation, *not lightOn* becomes true at time 2, and consequently *lightOff* also becomes true at time 2.

The sentences *not lightOn* and *lightOff* remain true at time 3, simply because they are not made false by the occurrence of any terminating events. Similarly, the fluent *lightOn* that becomes true at time 4 remains true indefinitely, unless and until some terminating *switch* event occurs.

In general, computation in LPS satisfies an event-calculus-like *causal theory*:

$holds(Fluent, T + 1)$ *if* $happens(Event, T, T + 1)$ *and* $initiates(Event, Fluent, T + 1)$.
$holds(Fluent, T + 1)$ *if* $holds(Fluent, T)$ *and there does not exist Event such that*
$$\big[happens(Event, T, T + 1) \ and \ terminates(Event, Fluent, T + 1)\big].$$

Here the second sentence is a *frame axiom,* which asserts that a fluent that holds at a time T continues to hold at the next time $T + 1$, unless an event that terminates the fluent occurs between T and $T + 1$.

It is important to note that LPS does not reason explicitly with such frame axioms. Forward reasoning with the frame axiom would entail the computational cost of reasoning that, for every fluent that holds at a time T and that is not terminated by an event that occurs between T and T + 1, the fluent continues to hold at time T + 1. Backward reasoning is only marginally better. Backward reasoning, to determine whether a fluent holds at a given time, entails the cost of chaining backwards in time until the time the fluent was initiated, checking along the way that the fluent was not terminated in between times. Both kinds of reasoning are intolerably inefficient compared with destructive change of state.

Instead, in LPS, when an event occurs, then any fluent initiated by the event is added to the current state, and any fluent terminated by the event is (destructively) deleted from the current state. However, although the causal theory is not used to reason explicitly whether any fluents hold, the causal theory and its frame axiom are *emergent properties* that are true in the model generated by the computation. This is like the way in which the associativity of the append relation is used neither to generate a model of append, nor to compute instances of append, but it is an emergent property, which is true in the model generated by the recursive definition of append.

Notice that the logical interpretation of destructive change of state, as generating extensional fluents in a timestamped model-theoretic structure, provides a logically pure alternative to the logically impure use of assert and retract in Prolog, which is one of the ways many Prolog programmers avoid the inefficiencies of the frame axiom in practice.

Unlike models in modal logic, which are collections of possible worlds connected by accessibility relations, models in LPS are single models in which fluents are stamped with the times at which they hold, and events are stamped with the times between which they happen. In this example, the *Herbrand model*, which consists of all the facts that are true in the model, is:

> {*happens(switch*, 1, 2), *happens(switch*, 3, 4), *initiates(switch, lightOn*, 3),
> *initiates(switch, lightOn*, 4), *terminates(switch, lightOn*, 2),
> *terminates(switch, lightOn*, 5), *terminates(switch, lightOn*, 6), ..., *holds(lightOn*, 1),
> *holds(lightOff*, 2), *holds(lightOff*, 3), *holds(lightOn*, 4), *holds(lightOn*, 5), ...}

3 Reactive Rules as Goals

In addition to logic programs, which can be regarded as an agent's *beliefs,* LPS also includes reactive rules of the form *if antecedent then consequent* and constraints of the form *false conditions*, which can be understood as an agent's *goals*. LPS can also generate *actions* to help an agent satisfy its goals.

For example, the reactive rule *if lightOff then switch*, which is shorthand for:

> For all $T1$ [*if holds(lightOff*, $T1$) *then*
> there exists $T2$ such that [*happens(switch*, $T2$, $T2 + 1$) *and* $T1 \leq T2$]].

represents the goal of switching the light whenever the light is off.

An LPS agent uses its beliefs to determine when the antecedent of a rule becomes true, and then it performs actions to make the consequent of the rule true. If time is unbounded, then the model determined by the resulting history of states and events can be infinite, and the computational process might never end.

The timeline in Fig. 3 displays an initial portion of the infinite model generated when the reactive rule above is added to the previous example.

Here, instead of the intentional fluent *lightOff* persisting, as before, from state 2 to state 3, the reactive rule recognises that *lightOff* is true at time 2 and generates the goal of performing a *switch* action in the future. The *switch* action can be performed at any time

Timeline =

	1	2	3	4	5	6	7	8	9	10
Events		● switch		● switch						
lightOn	lightOn		lightOn		lightOn					
Actions			● switch		● switch					
	1	2	3	4	5	6	7	8	9	10

```
?- go(Timeline).
```

Fig. 3 https://demo.logicalcontracts.com/p/simple%20switch.pl

after time 2. However, in practice, LPS generates models in which goals are satisfied as soon as possible. So, in this case, it performs the action immediately, between times 2 to 3.

Whereas, without the reactive rule, the second *switch* external event turned the light on, now the same external event turns the light off. So, again, the reactive rule is triggered and turns the light back on, as soon as possible.

Of course, leaving it to the LPS implementation to make reactive rules true as soon as possible is a risky business. However, it is possible to specify the time at which the consequent of the rule is made true explicitly, in this example by using any one of the following equivalent notations:

> *if lightOff at T1 then switch from T1 to T2.*
> *if lightOff at T then switch from T to T+1.*
> *if lightOff at T then switch from T.*

At the time of writing, we do not have a syntax for representing this temporal relationship without writing time explicitly.

In general, both the *antecedent* and *consequent* of a reactive rule can be a conjunction of (possibly negated) timeless predicates, such as the inequality relation $\leq$ and (possibly negated) fluents and events. All variables, including time variables, in the *antecedent* are universally quantified with scope the entire rule. All other variables are existentially quantified with scope the *consequent* of the rule. All times in the *consequent* are later than or at the same time as the latest time in the *antecedent*.

Goals in LPS can also include constraints of the form *false conditions*, which restrict the actions that an agent can perform. In the current implementation, they also restrict the external events that the agent will accept. For example, adding the constraint *false lightOn, switch,* which is shorthand for:

> *not(holds(lightOn, T) and happens(switch, T, T + 1)).*

to the current example, results in the timeline in Fig. 4.

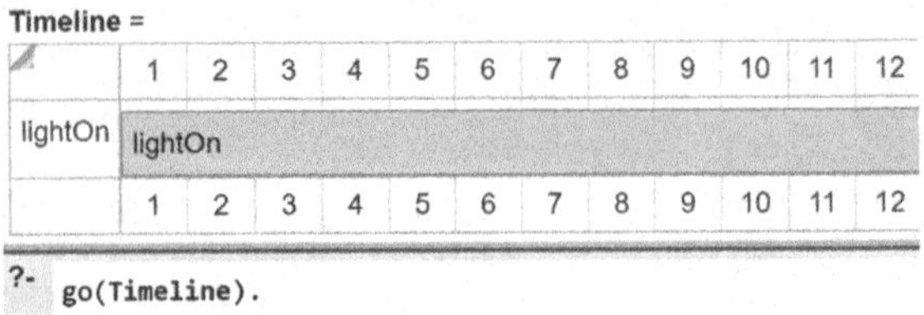

Timeline =

	1	2	3	4	5	6	7	8	9	10	11	12
lightOn	lightOn											
	1	2	3	4	5	6	7	8	9	10	11	12

?- go(Timeline).

Fig. 4. https://demo.logicalcontracts.com/p/simple%20switch.pl with the constraint.

4 Logic Programs for Representing Complex Events

The *antecedents* and *consequents* of reactive rules can also include complex events defined by LP clauses of the form *complex-event if conditions,* where the *conditions* have the same syntax as the *antecedents* and *consequents* of reactive rules. The start time of the *complex-event* is the earliest time in the *conditions* of the clause, and the end time of the *complex-event* is the latest time in the *conditions*.

For example, the following two LP clauses define a complex event, *sos*, which is a simplified distress signal of a light flashing three times in succession. Each flash of light takes place over two time steps and is separated from the next flash by one time step. At the time of writing, we do not have a shorthand syntax without time for such clauses:

*sos from T*1 *to T*4 *if lightOff at T*1, *flash from T*1 *to T*2,
$\qquad$ *flash from T*2 *to T*3, *flash from T*3 *to T*4.
*flash from T*1 *to T*3 *if lightOff at T*1,
$\qquad$ *switch from T*1 *to T*2, *switch from T*2 + 1 *to T*3.

LPS can use the definition of the complex *sos* event both to recognise and to generate distress signals. Moreover, it can both recognise and generate them at the same time using a reactive rule such as:

if sos to T then sos from T+2.

Figure 5 displays a scenario in which LPS recognises an initial *sos* signal and acknowledges it by generating an *sos* in response. But then it recognises its own response as another *sos* signal, and responds to it as well, *ad infinitum*.

Timeline =

	3	4	5	6	7	8	9	10	11	12	13	14	15	16	17	18	19	20	21	22	23	24	25	26	27	28	29	30	31
Events		switch		switch		switch																							
	switch		switch		switch																								
Composites	sos							flash		flash		flash		sos															
		flash		flash		flash			sos											flash		flash		flash					
lightOn	lightOr		lightOr		lightOr			lightOr		lightOr		lightOr			lightOr		lightOr		lightOr										
Actions										switch		switch		switch			switch		switch		switch								
											switch		switch		switch			switch		switch		s						
	3	4	5	6	7	8	9	10	11	12	13	14	15	16	17	18	19	20	21	22	23	24	25	26	27	28	29	30	31

Fig. 5. Here the command go(Timeline, [composites]) displays the timeline together with complex (composite) events. https://demo.logicalcontracts.com/p/new%20sos.pl

5 Prolog Programs for Defining Animations

In addition to the timeline visualisations, the SWISH implementation of LPS includes animations which display one state at time. See for example the program in Fig. 6, in which dad chases around the house turning off the lights which bob turns on. Notice that the switch predicate has arguments to indicate the agent of the action, the location of the switch and the state of the light immediately following the action.

```
10 if       location(bob, Place) at T, light(Place, off) at T
11 then     switch(bob, Place, on) from T.
12
13 if light(Place, on) at T, location(dad, Place) at T
14 then switch(dad, Place, off) from T.
15
16 if light(Place, on) at T, not location(dad, Place) at T
17 then goto(dad, Place).
18
```

Fig. 6. https://demo.logicalcontracts.com/example/badlight.pl.

The animation is generated using purely declarative Prolog clauses that define the rendering of fluents as two-dimensional objects, as shown in Fig. 7.

```
39 display(Location(P,L),[type:ellipse,label:P,point:[PX,PY],size:[20,40],fillColor:green]) :-
40    locationXY(L,X,Y), PY is Y+10, (P=dad -> PX is X + 25 ; PX is X+50).
```

Fig. 7. The Prolog code for visualizing the locations of bob and dad.

6 Related Work

In the Introduction, we focused on the historical development of LPS. But as we developed LPS, along the way we discovered many related, parallel developments, leading in a similar direction. For example, David Harel, in his famous paper on Statecharts [11], argues that there are two kinds of systems: transformational systems and reactive systems. Transformational systems specify a transformation, function, or input/output relation, as in LP and functional programming. Reactive systems, "which present the more difficult cases", describe dynamic behaviour, which "takes the general form 'when event Y occurs in state A, if condition C is true at the time, the system transfers to state B". This behaviour is a special case of the way reactive rules are executed in LPS. Although Harel draws attention to these two kinds of systems, he does not consider how they might be related and be combined.

Several other authors have also identified similar distinctions between different kinds of systems or rules, and they have developed more comprehensive systems or logics to combine them. For example, SBVR (Semantics of Business Vocabulary and Rules) [29] combines alethic modal operators, representing structural business rules, with deontic modal operators, representing operative business rules. Input-output logic [3] combines constitutive norms, representing an agent's beliefs, with regulative norms, representing an agent's goals. FO(ID) [8] combines first-order logic with definitions, similar to the way in which ALP combines integrity constraints with logic programs. Formally, an FO(ID) theory is a set of FO axioms and definitions. A model of such a theory is a (2-valued) structure satisfying all FO axioms and being a well-founded model of all definitions.

Other authors have also recognized the need to extend LP in similar ways. CHR [9] extends LP with propagation rules, which behave like production rules. The original semantics of CHR was given in terms of linear logic, which justifies destructive updates. EVOLP [1] extends the syntax of LP rules, so that their conclusions update the rules of the extended logic program. The semantics is given by the resulting sequence of logic programs. Like LPS, DALI [6] extends LP by means of reaction rules. However, in DALI, reaction rules are transformed into ordinary LP rules, and the semantics of a DALI program is given by a sequence of logic programs, which is similar to the semantics of EVOLP. Epilog [10] extends LP with operation rules of the form *action:: conditions* ⇒ *effects*, which means that if the *conditions* of the rule are true in a state, then the *action* is performed by executing the *effects* of the rule to generate the next state. The semantics of Epilog is given by the sequence of state transitions generated by executing all applicable operation rules in parallel. Ciao includes a facility to timestamp data predicates, which can be used in combination with concurrency, to implement condition-action rules [5].

The majority of the above systems and languages specify only one state transition at a time. In contrast, Transaction Logic (TL) [4] extends LP with clauses that define transactions (or complex events), which use destructive updates to generate sequences of state transitions. Unlike models in LPS, which include all states in a single model by associating explicit state (or time) parameters with events and fluents, models in TL are like possible worlds in the semantics of modal logic, where each state is represented by a separate Herbrand interpretation. However, unlike modal logics, where truth is defined relative to a single possible world, truth (of a transaction fact) in TL is defined relative to a path from one state to another. The TL semantics has been used to give an alternative semantics for CHR [26]. TL was also one of the inspirations for complex events in LPS.

In addition to related work in computer science, logic and AI, we have been encouraged by related work in cognitive psychology, initiated by Stenning and van Lambalgen [33]. They consider a variety of psychological tasks which seem to show that people do not reason logically with rules expressed in natural language, and they argue that the data can be explained by assuming that there are two kinds of rules, and that people have trouble deciding between them. In the case of the Wason selection task [36], the most widely cited psychological study of human reasoning, they claim that "by far the most important determinant of ease of reasoning is whether interpretation of the rule assigns it descriptive or deontic logical form". In [13], this distinction between different interpretations of a rule is reinterpreted as a distinction between LP rules representing beliefs and first-order logic rules representing goals.

7 Future Prospects

The current implementation of LPS in SWISH is merely a proof of concept. Nonetheless, even in its current form, it has proved to be useful for several trial commercial applications, including one in the area of smart contracts[1] and another in the context of SCADA (Supervisory Control And Data Acquisition).

There is much scope for improving the current implementation, not only to make it more efficient, but also to improve its decision-making strategy, when there is more than one way to satisfy a collection of goals. We would also like to extend the Logical English syntax [14] that we have developed for LP to include the whole of LPS. A particular challenge in this regard is to develop a natural language syntax for temporal relationships in LPS. See, for example, the English representation of the rock-paper-scissors game in LPS [7].

References

1. Alferes, J.J., Brogi, A., Leite, J.A., Pereira, L.M.: Evolving logic programs. In: Flesca, S., Greco, S., Ianni, G., Leone, N. (eds.) JELIA 2002. LNCS (LNAI), vol. 2424, pp. 50–62. Springer, Heidelberg (2002). https://doi.org/10.1007/3-540-45757-7_5
2. Barringer, H., Fisher, M., Gabbay, D., Owens, R., Reynolds, M.: The imperative future: principles of executable temporal logic. John Wiley & Sons, Inc. (1996)
3. Boella, G., der Torre, L.V.: Regulative and constitutive norms in the design of normative multiagent systems. In International Workshop on Computational Logic in Multi-Agent Systems, pp. 303–319, Springer (2005)
4. Bonner, A., Kifer, M.: Transaction logic programming. In: Warren D.S. (ed.) Logic Programming: Proc. of the 10th International Conf., pp. 257–279 (1993)
5. Carro, M., Hermenegildo, M.: Concurrency in Prolog Using Threads and a Shared Database. 1999 International Conference on Logic Programming, pp. 320–334, MIT Press, Cambridge (1999)

---

[1] https://demo.logicalcontracts.com/example/fintechExamples.swinb.

6. Flesca, S., Greco, S., Ianni, G., Leone, N. (eds.): JELIA 2002. LNCS (LNAI), vol. 2424. Springer, Heidelberg (2002). https://doi.org/10.1007/3-540-45757-7

7. Davila, J.: Rock-Paper-Scissors (2017). https://demo.logicalcontracts.com/p/rps-gets.pl

8. Denecker, M., Vennekens, J.: Building a knowledge base system for an integration of logic programming and classical logic. In: Garcia de la Banda, M., Pontelli, E. (eds.) ICLP 2008. LNCS, vol. 5366, pp. 71–76. Springer, Heidelberg (2008). https://doi.org/10.1007/978-3-540-89982-2_12

9. Schrijvers, T., Frühwirth, T. (eds.): Constraint Handling Rules. LNCS (LNAI), vol. 5388. Springer, Heidelberg (2008). https://doi.org/10.1007/978-3-540-92243-8

10. Genesereth, M.: Dynamic Logic Programming. In: Warren, D., Dahl, V., Eiter, T., Hermenegildo, M., Kowalski, R. and Rossi, F. (eds.) Prolog - The Next 50 Years. LNCS, vol. 13900. Springer (2023)

11. Harel, D.: Statecharts: A Visual Formalism for Complex Systems. Sci. Comput. Programming **8**, 231–274 (1987)

12. Kakas, A., Kowalski, R., Toni, F. : The Role of Logic Programming in Abduction. In: Gabbay, D., Hogger, C.J., Robinson, J.A. (eds.) Handbook of Logic in Artificial Intelligence and Programming 5, pp. 235–324. Oxford University Press (1998)

13. Kowalski, R.: Computational logic and human thinking: how to be artificially intelligent. Cambridge University Press (2011)

14. Kowalski, R., Dávila, J., Sartor, G., Calejo, M.: Logical english for law and education. In: Warren, D., Dahl, V., Eiter, T., Hermenegildo, M., Kowalski, R., Rossi, F. (eds.) Prolog - The Next 50 Years. LNCS, vol. 13900. Springer (2023)

15. Kowalski, R., Sadri, F.: Logic Programming towards multi-agent systems. Ann. Math. Artif. Intell. **25**, 391–419 (1999)

16. Kowalski, R., Sadri, F.: Integrating logic programming and production systems in abductive logic programming agents. In: Polleres, A., Swift, T. (eds.) RR 2009. LNCS, vol. 5837, pp. 1–23. Springer, Heidelberg (2009). https://doi.org/10.1007/978-3-642-05082-4_1

17. Kowalski, R., Sadri, F.: An agent language with destructive assignment and model-theoretic semantics. In: Dix, J., Leite, J., Governatori, G., Jamroga, W. (eds.) CLIMA 2010. LNCS (LNAI), vol. 6245, pp. 200–218. Springer, Heidelberg (2010). https://doi.org/10.1007/978-3-642-14977-1_16

18. Kowalski, R., Sadri, F.: Abductive logic programming agents with destructive databases. Ann. Math. Artif. Intell. **62**(1), 129–158 (2011)

19. Kowalski, R., Sadri, F.: A Logic-based framework for reactive systems. In: Bikakis, A., Giurca, A. (eds.) RuleML 2012. LNCS, vol. 7438, pp. 1–15. Springer, Heidelberg (2012). https://doi.org/10.1007/978-3-642-32689-9_1

20. Kowalski, R., Sadri, F.: A logical characterization of a reactive system language. In: Bikakis, A., Fodor, P., Roman, D. (eds.) RuleML 2014. LNCS, vol. 8620, pp. 22–36. Springer, Cham (2014). https://doi.org/10.1007/978-3-319-09870-8_2

21. Kowalski, R., Sadri, F.: Model-theoretic and operational semantics for Reactive Computing. N. Gener. Comput. **33**(1), 33–67 (2015)

22. Kowalski, R., Sadri, F.: Programming in logic without logic programming. Theory Pract. Logic Program. **16**(3), 269–295 (2016)

23. Kowalski, R., Sergot, M.: A Logic-based Calculus of Events. In: New Generation Computing, Vol. 4, No.1, 67--95 (1986). Also in: Inderjeet Mani, J. Pustejovsky, and R. Gaizauskas (eds.) The Language of Time: A Reader, Oxford University Press (2005)

24. Lifschitz, V. Answer set programming. Springer (2019)

25. McCarthy, J., Hayes, P.J.: Some philosophical problems from the standpoint of artificial intelligence. In: Readings in artificial intelligence, pp. 431–450. Morgan Kaufmann (1981)

26. Meister, M., Djelloul, K., Robin, J.: Unified semantics for Constraint Handling Rules in transaction logic. In International Conference on Logic Programming and Nonmonotonic Reasoning, pp. 201–213. Springer (2007)
27. Newell, A., Simon, H.A.: Human problem solving vol. 104, No. 9. Prentice-Hall, Englewood Cliffs, NJ (1972)
28. Nicolas, J.M., Gallaire, H.: Database: Theory vs. Interpretation. In: Gallaire, H., Minker, J. (eds.) Logic and Databases, Plenum, New York (1978)
29. OMG. (Object Management Group): Semantics of Business Vocabulary and Rules (SBVR), OMG Standard, v. 1.0. (2008)
30. Rao, P., Sagonas, K., Swift, T., Warren, D.S., Freire, J.: XSB: a system for efficiently computing well-founded semantics. In: Dix, J., Furbach, U., Nerode, A. (eds.) LPNMR 1997. LNCS, vol. 1265, pp. 430–440. Springer, Heidelberg (1997). https://doi.org/10.1007/3-540-63255-7_33
31. Russell, S.J., Norvig, P.: Artificial intelligence: a modern approach, 2nd edn. Prentice Hall, Upper Saddle River, NJ (2003)
32. Sadri F., Kowalski R.: A Theorem-Proving Approach to Database Integrity. In: Minker, J. (ed.) Foundations of Deductive Databases and Logic Programming, Morgan Kaufmann, pp. 313–362 (1988)
33. Stenning, K., van Lambalgen M.: Human Reasoning and Cognitive Science. MIT Press (2012)
34. Thagard, P.: Mind: Introduction to Cognitive Science. Second Edition. MIT Press (2005)
35. Warren, D. S., Denecker, M.: A better semantics for prolog. In: Warren, D., Dahl, V., Eiter, T., Hermenegildo, M., Kowalski, R. and Rossi, F. (eds.) Prolog - The Next 50 Years. LNCS, vol. 13900. Springer, Heidelberg (2023)
36. Wason, P.C.: Reasoning about a rule. Q. J. Exp. Psychol. **20**(3), 273–281 (1968)
37. Widom, J., Ceri, S. (eds.) Active database systems: Triggers and rules for advanced database processing. Morgan Kaufmann (1995)
38. Wielemaker, J., Riguzzi, F., Kowalski, R.A., Lager, T., Sadri, F., Calejo, M.: Using SWISH to realise interactive web-based tutorials for logic-based languages. Theory Pract. Logic Program. **19**(2), 229–261 (2019)

Ergo: A Quest for Declarativity in Logic Programming

Benjamin Grosof, Michael Kifer[(✉)], Theresa Swift[(✉)], Paul Fodor,
and Janine Bloomfield

Coherent Knowledge, Mercer Island, USA
{benjamin.grosof,michael.kifer,theresa.swift,paul.fodor,
janine.bloomfield}@coherentknowledge.com
http://coherentknowledge.com

Abstract. $\mathcal{E}$rgo is a higher-level logic programming system developed by Coherent Knowledge Systems as a successor to Flora-2 [39]. From the start, Flora-2 and $\mathcal{E}$rgo were designed with the explicit requirement of declarativity and usability using novel technologies developed over the years by the authors and their colleagues. Although $\mathcal{E}$rgo programs are compiled into XSB [29] and they adopt many Prolog features, $\mathcal{E}$rgo is altogether a different language. For instance, $\mathcal{E}$rgo's core execution strategy is not the SLDNF of Prolog, but is instead based on the Well-Founded Semantics [31] and its core syntax is a combination of HiLog [6] and F-logic [20]. $\mathcal{E}$rgo supports object-oriented modeling, logical meta-reasoning, defeasible reasoning, fully semantic update operators as in Transaction Logic [2,3], explanations, and a variety of other features not found in Prologs. In this paper, we describe some of these novel features of $\mathcal{E}$rgo with special emphasis on their relation to Prolog and how they contribute to the high degree of declarativeness of $\mathcal{E}$rgo.

1 Introduction

Declarativity has been a quest in Logic Programming since its inception. This quest is shared by the $\mathcal{E}$rgo language, which tries to make the declarative semantics (what a program means) and the operational semantics (how a program derives its results) as transparent as possible.

$\mathcal{E}$rgo [7], or $\mathcal{E}$rgoAI Reasoner, is part of the recently open-sourced $\mathcal{E}$rgoAI suite of tools developed by Coherent Knowledge Systems, LLC.[1] The other tools include an IDE and connectors to major programming languages and data sources. $\mathcal{E}$rgo is the successor of and a replacement for the well-known Flora-2 [19] system, developed at Stony Brook University, NY. Although modern Prologs have developed far beyond Prolog's original ISO specification [17], and although

---

[1] http://coherentknowledge.com/.

M. Kifer—Supported in part by NSF grant 1814457.
P. Fodor—Stony Brook University, USA.

D. S. Warren et al. (Eds.): Prolog: The Next 50 Years, LNAI 13900, pp. 224–236, 2023.
https://doi.org/10.1007/978-3-031-35254-6_18

$\mathcal{E}$rgo is compiled into XSB, $\mathcal{E}$rgo differs substantially from Prolog. First, while $\mathcal{E}$rgo supports predicate definitions using a syntax similar to Prolog, it also fully supports HiLog [6] and the F-logic frame syntax [20] along with rule id's, Skolem symbols and much else. Second, like some Prologs, including XSB [29] and SWI [37], $\mathcal{E}$rgo supports the well-founded semantics (WFS) [31] along with SLDNF-style resolution. But WFS is the *core* semantics of $\mathcal{E}$rgo. Furthermore, $\mathcal{E}$rgo supports defeasible reasoning, explicit negation, and quantifiers. Third, $\mathcal{E}$rgo draws from deductive databases default support for reactivity and transactionality. We refer to languages and systems like $\mathcal{E}$rgo and Flora-2 that are based on the well-founded semantics as *WFS-based Logic Programming*, (WFSLP) to distinguish them from Prolog-based systems and from Answer Set Programs (ASP), which is based on the stable model semantics (SMS)). In order to leverage WFSLP, $\mathcal{E}$rgo makes heavy use of tabling in ways that are discussed throughout the paper. Due to space limitations we cannot provide an introduction to tabling, but a short overview of tabling can be found in the introduction to this volume [36], while a much more detailed tutorial can be found in [30].

We believe that WFSLP is important for programmers who wish to program at a high but computationally clear level; that systems such as $\mathcal{E}$rgo serve as a means to make available Logic Programming research results such as explicit negation, HiLog, F-Logic; and that successes and failures of WFSLP systems can inform the community of Prolog developers. Although $\mathcal{E}$rgo is still evolving, it has been used in commercial and research projects in financial compliance, legal reasoning, healthcare, and battlefield assessment.

This paper describes some aspects of $\mathcal{E}$rgo that we believe are both significant and of potential interest to the Prolog community. Sections 3, and 4 describe a few aspects of $\mathcal{E}$rgo's approach to declarativity. Section 5 discusses explainability. Section 6 briefly describes interfaces and applications. The final Sect. 7 discusses $\mathcal{E}$rgo features that could, versus could not, be adopted by Prolog systems, as well as summarizes current and future work.

2   Ergo Syntax

HiLog. $\mathcal{E}$rgo has a rich syntax that includes HiLog predicates [6] and F-logic frames and classes [20]. In forming either type of construct, variables and constants in $\mathcal{E}$rgo are denoted slightly differently than in Prolog. For instance p('John',goes,Where) is a Prolog term in which the first two arguments are constants and the third a variable. The same term in $\mathcal{E}$rgo is written as p(John, goes,?Where). Variables in $\mathcal{E}$rgo thus begin with the ? symbol, while capitalized strings such as John are constants, rather than variables as in Prolog.

Unlike a Prolog term, which has the form: $p(t_1, ..., t_n)$ where p is a function symbol and $t_1, ..., t_n$ are logical terms, a HiLog term has the form $t_0(t_1, ..., t_n)$ where $t_0, ..., t_n$ are also HiLog terms. For example,

```
closure(?Graph)(?From,?To)
```

is a well-formed $\mathcal{E}$rgo term. Although HiLog terms are syntactically higher-order, the term above is translated by $\mathcal{E}$rgo to a first-order term that uses long, synthesized function symbol names that are highly unlikely to be ever needed by a user and whose uniqueness is enforced. As a result unification and resolution can be performed on HiLog terms in a manner similar to Prolog-style terms.

F-logic Frames. F-logic frames differ significantly from Prolog and Hilog predicates, and there is not enough space to fully describe frames in this paper. To get a taste of F-logic frames, consider the frame *molecule*:

```
John:person[age->?A>30, child->Bob,
            phone->?P \in ['111-222-3456','123-456-7890']]
```

which has the same meaning as these frame atoms:

```
John:person, John[child->Bob], John[age->?A], ?A>30,
John[phone->?P], ?P \in ['111-222-3456','123-456-7890']]
```

These frame facts say that John is a person, whose child is Bob, and whose age is constrained to be greater than 30, and who has two particular phone numbers. Frame rules may also make use of monotonic and non-monotonic (property-overriding) inheritance. An $\mathcal{E}$rgo rule can contain any HiLog term or F-logic frame as a subgoal. $\mathcal{E}$rgo also has support for user-defined functions and other extensions, that cannot be discussed here due to space limitation.

3   Ergo and Declarativity

Flora-2 and then $\mathcal{E}$rgo were the result of a long series of efforts by us and other researchers to develop technologies that could serve as building blocks for truly declarative LP systems in the resolution-based computational paradigm. This section and the next briefly discuss some of these building blocks.

The Well-Founded Semantics (WFS) in $\mathcal{E}$rgo. WFS provides clear semantics for Prolog-style LP, although when implemented in Prolog systems like XSB and SWI, obtaining this semantics requires tabling declarations. $\mathcal{E}$rgo's strategy is different: WFS is supported by default, making the first key step towards declarativity, since termination and logical semantics are then assured for many types of programs. For instance, in $\mathcal{E}$rgo transitive closure may be written as:

```
reachable(?X,?Y):- reachable(?X,?Z),edge(?Z,?Y).
reachable(?X,?Y):- edge(?X,?Y).
edge(1,2). edge(2,3). edge(3,1).
```

$\mathcal{E}$rgo depends on WFS in a critical way because the rules that arise from the use of F-logic and HiLog (Sect. 2), and defeasible reasoning (Sect. 4.2), are often non-stratified.

Object-oriented modeling and meta-operations. F-logic [20] was developed with the explicit purpose of bringing object-oriented concepts (classes, complex objects, inheritance) into LP in a semantically clear and logical way. Hitherto object orientation was widely considered to be inherently procedural and incompatible with LP. HiLog [6], on the other hand, was developed in order to eliminate much of the need for extra-logical meta predicates in Prolog. Both F-logic and HiLog raise the level of abstraction in LP and can greatly improve its declarativeness.

Termination in $\mathcal{E}$rgo. $\mathcal{E}$rgo's default use of tabling for WFS ensures termination for programs in which all subgoals and answers have a finitely bounded size. Such a termination class includes all of Datalog and is far larger than the termination class of Prolog using SLDNF. Moreover, $\mathcal{E}$rgo further expands this class by allowing use of tabling methods that use types of term abstraction sometimes called **restraint**, which we describe by examples.

First, consider the simple $\mathcal{E}$rgo program P_{FinMod} consisting of the single rule:

```
p(?X) :- p(f(?X))
```

It is easy to see that P_{FinMod} has a finite (empty) model. However in the default WFS tabling of $\mathcal{E}$rgo (as well as of Prolog) the query ?- p(?X) will not terminate since an infinite number of subgoals will be created: p(?X), p(f(?X)), p(f(f(?X))) and so on. $\mathcal{E}$rgo can address this via *subgoal abstraction* [26], in which subgoals are abstracted once they reach a maximum size. In P_{FinMod}, abstraction with subgoal depth 2 or more would rewrite p(f(f(?X))) to p(f(?X)) ensuring a finite number of subgoals. In fact, it can be shown than when subgoal abstraction is added to WFS, any program with a finite model (i.e., a finite number of true and undefined answers) will terminate. Second, consider the program P_{InfMod}, whose model is infinite:

```
p(f(?X)) :- p(?X).
p(a).
```

$\mathcal{E}$rgo addresses this problem by providing a declaration that abstracts answers in a manner similar to how subgoals are abstracted above. When using such *answer abstraction* at term depth greater than or equal to two, the goal ?- p(?Y) to P_{InfMod} would produce answers p(a), p(f(a)), both as true answers, along with p(f(f(X)) with truth value undefined. In this way, an informationally sound approximation to the goal p(?Y) is provided: all true answers obtained by $\mathcal{E}$rgo are semantically true and all false subgoals are false, but some *true* answers and some false subgoals are considered as *undefined*. In this manner $\mathcal{E}$rgo supports a fully semantic kind of bounded rationality termed *restraint* [13]. In addition, $\mathcal{E}$rgo supports many other kinds of restraint, such as for: external predicate calls that do not return; allowing only a maximal number of answers to subgoals of a certain type; and skipping of rule instances that are in the distant future.

The bounded rationality in $\mathcal{E}$rgo has proven useful, particularly for evaluating queries to programs created by, e.g., natural language analysis. Moreover, the computational mechanism behind bounded rationality is also used for debugging: via a method called *tripwires*. A user may set a tripwire on, say, the maximal number of interdependent subgoals in a computation or on the elapsed time a computation uses. If this number is exceeded, the program will suspend execution and $\mathcal{E}$rgo will provide a command line to examine the suspended execution.

In sum, the above mentioned features, exploiting WFS, give $\mathcal{E}$rgo a considerable degree of declarative control over the termination of queries.

Transactionality and Reactivity in $\mathcal{E}$rgo. Although $\mathcal{E}$rgo supports changes to code by Prolog-like asserting and retracting, it also supports transactional changes based on Transaction Logic [3,24]. This logic was developed in order to provide a declarative, completely semantic theory of update operations in LP. To see this, consider the two sequences of goals ($\mathcal{E}$rgo uses\for various reserved keywords):

1. insert{p(a)},\false.
2. t_insert{p(a)},\false.

After Sequence 1 is executed, p(a) will have been inserted into $\mathcal{E}$rgo's store and will become true. In contrast, p(a) is not true after Sequence 2 in which the *transactional* insert, t_insert/1, was used. This is because a transactional insert in $\mathcal{E}$rgo is not "committed" if it is part of a larger goal that fails (and similarly for transactional deletes). As with relational databases, integrity constraints can be added, to prevent committing changes that violate an integrity constraint.

Deductions performed by $\mathcal{E}$rgo react to change: by default, changes to the underlying data are **reactive** (although $\mathcal{E}$rgo provides a separate **passive** mode). In **reactive** mode, if there is change to a fact or rule ϕ upon which $\mathcal{E}$rgo's tables change, those tables that depend on ϕ and only on ϕ will change as necessary in order to preserve correctness using XSB's incremental tabling [28]. $\mathcal{E}$rgo also provides alerts that can notify or perform other actions if the alert condition is violated. Common uses of alerts include monitoring whether an atom A and its explicit negation \neg A are both derived, thereby making the facts inconsistent.

Delay Quantifiers. The delay quantifiers wish/1 and must/1 cause dynamic reordering of subgoals that do not fulfill argument binding requirements. These quantifiers check conditions on variables in a subgoal and delay that subgoal if these conditions fail. For example, evaluation of the subgoal must(ground(?X) or nonvar(?Y))^?X[foo->?Y] delays evaluation of ?X[foo->?Y] until either ?X is ground or ?Y is partially instantiated. If the desired instantiation is unachievable, a runtime error results. With the wish/1 quantifier, the subgoal is executed after the delay anyway, without issuing errors.

4   Negation: Still Not a Simple Matter

Users of other Logic Programming systems based on the well-founded variety of negation tend to suffer from a number of difficulties that have partly to do with insufficiently expressive syntax and partly with implementation decisions that force the user to face the bare metal of the execution mechanism. By contrast, in $\mathcal{E}$rgo, explicit use of negation can be avoided by working at higher conceptual levels. One such level is *inheritance with overriding* in F-logic [38] and the other is *Defeasible Reasoning*. Since the basic idea of inheritance with overriding is well known, we will briefly explain only the idea of defeasibility here.

4.1   Negation, Quantifiers, and Delay

One major problem with negation in LP is that the lack of explicit quantifiers makes the precise meaning of well-founded negation obscure to the user. Consider, for instance the following rule in XSB:

```
answer(M)  :- man(M), tnot(play(M,G)), game(G).
```

Does `answer/1` mean "all men who play no games" or "all men who don't play some game"? Neither it turns out, and this results in an error because `''tnot''`, the WFS negation of XSB, takes only ground calls. But if `game(G)` is moved leftwards then `answer/1` would mean "all men who don't play some game," i.e.,

```
answer(M)  :- man(M), ∃G(game(G),tnot(play(M,G))).
```

In a logic system, why should syntactic reordering make that be the case? And how do we write "men who play no games"? Maybe like this?

```
answer(M)  :- man(M), tnot((game(G),play(M,G))).
```

No, this also ends up with an error due to the non-ground G. Instead, one must use a different operator in XSB:

```
answer(M)  :- man(M), not_exists((game(G),play(M,G))).
```

It collects all the variables in `game(G),play(M,G)` and implicitly quantifies them with ∃ in the scope of `tnot`. This, however, means that

```
answer(M)  :- not_exists((game(G),play(M,G))), man(M).
```

would give a different answer, so both `not_exists` and `tnot` have non-declarative aspects and their semantics depends on the context where they occur. In contrast, $\mathcal{E}$rgo allows explicit quantifiers `\exist` and `\forall`, which lets one express the intent clearly and unambiguously. In addition, in the scope of negation, subgoals that have unquantified unbound variables are automatically delayed, so the semantics does not depend on the order of the subgoals.

4.2   Defeasible Rules

As mentioned earlier, a very promising approach is to hide complex uses of negation inside high-level concepts that most users understand intuitively because they use similar reasoning in their daily life. Here we illustrate the idea that conclusions of some rules may conflict with conclusions of other rules and, if the former rules have *strength* (or *priority*) at least as high as the latter rules then the former conclusions may "defeat" the latter ones. In other words, inferences made via some rules may be undone by other inferences. We will illustrate the idea via an example from the U.S. tax code, simplified for didactic purposes. We give, next, an informal syntax, partly in italics; then, later, actual $\mathcal{E}$rgo code.

Default rule:
```
deductible(Expense) :- work_related(Expense).
```
But (exception):
```
nondeductible(Expense) :- lobbying(Expense).
```
Nevertheless (exception to exception):
```
deductible(Expense):-lobbying(Expense),state_permitted(Expense).
```
Constraint: can't be both deductible and not.
```
false :- deductible(Expense), nondeductible(Expense).
```
Facts:
```
work_related(expense123). lobbying(expense123).
state_permitted(expense123).
```
Query: Is expense123 deductible?
```
?- deductible(expense123).
```
The above rules imply both `deductible(expense123)` and `nondeductible(expense123)`, which is inconsistent with the constraint. The inconsistency problem could be repaired using negation:

```
deductible(Exp) :- work_related(Exp), not nondeductible(Exp).
nondeductible(Exp) :- lobbying(Exp), not state_permitted(Exp).
```

but the number of exceptions, exceptions to exceptions, exceptions to exceptions to exceptions, etc., in a real situation can be large, making it hard to manage the complexity of the rules and get them right.

Defeasible reasoning takes a different approach. Rather than piling up negation upon negation as above, we instead keep the original simple form of the rules — pretty much pulling their formulation right out of the tax code — but organize the rules according to a "priority" or "overriding" relationship, which, again, is pulled out of the same tax code. Typically, this priority relation is acyclic but it does not have to be. A rule inference can be *defeated* if inferences made by higher priority rules contradict the lower priority inference. Defeat may have different forms, like rebuttal, refutation, and others. What that means exactly is specified via an *argumentation theory* and the version of defeasible reasoning implemented in $\mathcal{E}$rgo is called *Logic Programming with Defaults and Argumentation Theories* (LPDA) [33]. $\mathcal{E}$rgo comes with a dozen of different (mostly experimental) argumentation theories, but we are aware of only 3 or 4 actually being employed by the users. Note that an $\mathcal{E}$rgo program can engage different argumentation theories in different modules. Here is our tax code in the actual $\mathcal{E}$rgo language:

```
:- use_argumentation_theory.
@default_rule1 deductible(?Expense) :- work_related(?Expense).
@exceptn1    nondeductible(?Expense) :- lobbying(?Expense).
```

```
@exceptn_to_exceptn1  deductible(?Expense) :-
                      lobbying(?Expense), state_permitted(?Expense).
\overrides(exceptn1, default_rule1).           // rule 2 beats rule 1
\overrides(exceptn_to_exceptn1, exceptn1).  // rule 3 beats rule 2
// ?X can't be both deductible & not
\opposes(deductible(?X), nondeductible(?X)).
work_related(expense123).   lobbying(expense123).
```

Here the first statement tells $\mathcal{E}$rgo to use the default argumentation theory. The syntax @default_rule1 and the like is used to assign *tags* to rules, and these tags are then used to define the rule overriding relation. The \opposes relation specifies facts that contradict each other and thus cannot be true in the same consistent knowledge base. With the above program, we get that

expense123 is deductible because:

   it is derived by default_rule1, and

   default_rule1 is not defeated by exceptn1 because

     exceptn1 is defeated by exceptn_exceptn1.

These defeated/not-defeated conclusions hold in the default argumentation theory, and all other argumentation theories, in $\mathcal{E}$rgo.

LPDA is not the only theory for defeasible reasoning proposed over the years. Here is just a small sample of other approaches: $[1, 4, 5, 8-11, 15, 22, 23, 27, 35, 40]$. LPDA, however, distinguishes itself by its simplicity, flexibility, and declarativity. It can simulate several other approaches to defeasibility and is available both in the WFS and SMS versions [33,34], each being a natural extension of the corresponding semantics in standard LP.

5   Explanations

Explainability of how a system reaches its conclusions and decisions is an important capability, especially for AI. It aids the productivity and reliability of system development, especially testing and debugging, for developers, domain subject matter experts, executives who sponsor development and operations, customer/IT support, and regulatory/legal compliance. In some high-value application arenas, such as defense, finance, and healthcare, explainability is a critical requirement for trust in the system, across the lifecycle.

For every query answer, $\mathcal{E}$rgo automatically generates and makes available a full explanation for that particular answer, justified as *proof* in *natural deduction* (a.k.a. intuitionistic) style [16]. The structure of the justification is a set of chained reasoning steps (each corresponding to an instantiated rule). The overall collection of steps forms a directed graph, in which literals are nodes. The (potentially cyclic) digraph is also available as a tree, including in graphical human-computer interaction (HCI) via an expansible/collapsible tree metaphor for presentation and navigation. $\mathcal{E}$rgo has a capability for restricted natural language processing (NLP), based on templates that map between logical syntax and natural language sentences. Using this capability, $\mathcal{E}$rgo automatically makes available explanations in natural language, e.g., English.

Because even non-programmers are already familiar with natural deduction style proofs (e.g., from high school geometry) and with expansible/collapsible trees in HCI (e.g., on webpages), $\mathcal{E}$rgo's explanations can be understood easily.

6   Interfaces and Applications

An important feature of $\mathcal{E}$rgo is its ability to interact with other languages and systems through interfaces, interoperating in both directions (out from $\mathcal{E}$rgo, and in to $\mathcal{E}$rgo). $\mathcal{E}$rgo can call external libraries and systems. Conversely, other languages and systems can call $\mathcal{E}$rgo. As part of all this, $\mathcal{E}$rgo supports interoperation with common forms of data.

For example, the $\mathcal{E}$rgo-Python interface allows Python programs to query $\mathcal{E}$rgo knowledge bases, and lets $\mathcal{E}$rgo call specialized Python libraries, e.g., scikit-learn and PyTorch for machine learning (ML), spaCy for natural language processing (NLP), matplotlib for data science visualization, and the Google Maps API for geo-spatial. $\mathcal{E}$rgo can interact, including over the Web: through its data connectors for JSON, DSV, XML, HTML, RDF and OWL; through its SPARQL interface to query RDF triple stores; and through its RESTful interfaces with Web services. Other interfaces include to relational databases (e.g., to query through SQL), MiniZINC-based constraint solving systems, etc.

These $\mathcal{E}$rgo interfaces are important tools for extending the capabilities of $\mathcal{E}$rgo and for building sophisticated applications, including for tax and financial regulations, configuration, defense, and healthcare. Below we will briefly discuss two applications in tax and financial regulations. In many of such applications the explanation facility of $\mathcal{E}$rgo is particularly useful.

Section 162 of the Internal Revenue Code (IRC) allows taxpayers (e.g., corporations) to deduct certain "trade or business expenses". There are many different types of expenses that may be deductible under Sect. 162, including: rent or lease payments for business property, salaries, interest, etc.

To be deductible under Sect. 162, an expenditure must be *"ordinary and necessary"* for the business, but there are limitations e.g., for contributions to political campaigns, lobbying, entertainment expenses, and capital expenditures.

Our implementation of Sect. 162 used $\mathcal{E}$rgo to represent and reason about the different kinds of expenditures and their deductibility, including object-oriented modeling, defeasible reasoning, and explanations. A simplified example of defeasible reasoning used in this application was discussed in Sect. 4.2.

Regulation W is a U.S. Federal Reserve banking regulation, issued in the aftermath of the 2008 financial crisis. It aims to prevent conflicts of interest between banks and non-bank affiliates, such as securities firms or insurance companies, by imposing restrictions on risk-transferring transactions, including requirements for reserving additional capital and quick reporting. An application for compliance with Regulation W was developed using Ergo as a highly successful Proof of Concept by the Enterprise Data Management Council (EDMC), a major financial industry consortium, in conjunction with EDMC's larger overall Proof of Concept on its Financial Industry Business Ontology (FIBO), which was so successful that FIBO became an industry standard.

The regulation was captured in $\mathcal{E}$rgo via a corpus of defeasible rules that also mapped between logical syntax and English phrases. Ergo automatically inferred answers to decision/analytics questions about compliance with Regulation W, and automatically provided an explanation for every answer. These questions were asked in English and explanations were presented in English. This showed that $\mathcal{E}$rgo can be used *directly by domain experts* to encode, query and obtain answers with justifications in natural language, in cooperation with knowledge engineers, instead of the longer traditional process of developing an expert system (where the domain expert is repetitively interviewed by the knowledge engineer who constructs and validates the expert system). Ergo was particularly useful in this application for providing fully detailed explanations of compliance decisions, that constituted audit trails, and for analyzing relationships between affiliates. Non-programmer compliance officers were able to understand these explanations, straightforwardly and with confidence, including to validate rules and conclusions as correct, incorrect, or missing – i.e., to help debug knowledge.

7   Discussion and Future Work

$\mathcal{E}$rgo *and Prolog: A Symbiosis.* Prolog has proven to be a remarkably adaptable language. Modern Prolog systems incorporate constraint-based reasoning, probabilistic reasoning, multi-threading, syntactic extensions, external interfaces and other features. Informal standards have emerged: a given Prolog may follow SWI's multi-threading API, Ciao's API for program analysis, or XSB's API for tabling. $\mathcal{E}$rgo has also incorporated many of these features, including constraint-based reasoning and trie data structures among others.

Although $\mathcal{E}$rgo freely borrows from Prolog, some $\mathcal{E}$rgo features are difficult for Prolog systems to adopt, including the default use of WFS, HiLog and F-logic, and its ability to adjoin defeasibility theories. These difficulties may relate to the different orientations. Prolog is oriented towards programmers who want a fast system with good procedural control that is reasonably declarative. $\mathcal{E}$rgo is geared to programmers who may want to represent knowledge using object-oriented modeling and to enforce the consistency of this knowledge through mechanisms such as defeasibility, reactivity, and transactionality.

In contrast, other features of $\mathcal{E}$rgo can be incorporated by Prolog systems relatively easily. Subgoal and answer abstraction are two such features, already implemented in XSB and SWI, both of which support WFS. $\mathcal{E}$rgo's transactionality and integrity constraints are another two such features: they mainly depend on an undo mechanism that is invoked when a goal containing an assert fails ($\mathcal{E}$rgo supports both transactional and non-transactional versions of update predicates). Another such feature is $\mathcal{E}$rgo's ability to dynamically reorder goals based on the status of variable bindings. Explicit quantification could, perhaps, be adopted as well. Our experience also shows that a simple bidirectional $\mathcal{E}$rgo-to-Prolog interface is beneficial to both languages.

Support for Machine Learning. A key area for current and future work is to combine $\mathcal{E}$rgo more tightly with machine learning (ML) and with natural language processing (which is largely based on ML). In one example of current work for battlefield assessment, $\mathcal{E}$rgo calls SpaCy [21], an NLP suite, to process natural language statements about a given situation which $\mathcal{E}$rgo assembles into a coherent whole for decision support. In another, $\mathcal{E}$rgo processes natural language questions via SpaCy to answer questions about a collection of scene graphs [18] of visual images. Conversely, there are also important opportunities for ML and NLP to leverage $\mathcal{E}$rgo. ML training might call $\mathcal{E}$rgo as part of a constraint in a loss function. Such a setup would make heavy use of XSB's efficient Python interface, as well as $\mathcal{E}$rgo's nearly linear scalability.[2] .

Uncertainty. The value of combining $\mathcal{E}$rgo with ML will increase as $\mathcal{E}$rgo incorporates uncertainty more fully. A starting point is the integration of XSB's packages for uncertainty, PITA [25] and its extension PLOW [14]. These formalisms handle not only full probabilistic reasoning, which has a high computational complexity, but also T-Norm (a.k.a. fuzzy) style reasoning whose complexity is much lower. As a use case of uncertain reasoning, the use of $\mathcal{E}$rgo within loss functions will often depend on the differentiability of $\mathcal{E}$rgo's inferences. Alternately, for $\mathcal{E}$rgo to say, resolve ambiguous natural language parses, it must be able to weigh uncertainties arising out of a neural model. Unfortunately, this is not always straightforward because neural models often have a topmost softmax layer, which can artificially reduce the entropy of a result and its alternatives (cf. e.g., [32]). More discussion on directions for future work appears in [12].

References

1. Baader, F., Hollunder, B.: Priorities on defaults with prerequisites, and their application in treating specificity in terminological default logic. J. Autom. Reason. **15**(1), 41–68 (1995)
2. Bonner, A., Kifer, M.: Transaction logic programming. In: Int'l Conference on Logic Programming, pp. 257–282. MIT Press, Budapest, Hungary (June 1993)
3. Bonner, A., Kifer, M.: An overview of transaction logic. Theor. Comput. Sci. **133**, 205–265 (1994)
4. Brewka, G., Eiter, T.: Preferred answer sets for extended logic programs. Artif. Intell. **109**, 297–356 (1999)
5. Brewka, G., Eiter, T.: Prioritizing default logic. In: Intellectics and Computational Logic - Papers in Honour of Wolfgang Bibel, pp. 27–45. Kluwer Academic Publishers (2000)
6. Chen, W., Kifer, M., Warren, D.S.: HiLog: a foundation for higher-order logic programming. JLP **15**(3), 187–230 (1993)
7. Coherent Knowledge Systems: ErgoAI. A Website (2023). https://github.com/ErgoAI
8. Delgrande, J., Schaub, T., Tompits, H.: A framework for compiling preferences in logic programs. Theory Pract. Logic Program. **2**, 129–187 (2003)

---

[2] in the size of the *ground* program; a consequence of being based on the well-founded semantics, plus the design of $\mathcal{E}$rgo's expressive extensions (e.g., HiLog).

9. Dung, P., Son, T.: An argument-based approach to reasoning with specificity. Artif. Intell. **133**(1–2), 35–85 (2001). https://doi.org/10.1016/S0004-3702(01)00134-5

10. Eiter, T., Faber, W., Leone, N., Pfeifer, G.: Computing preferred answer sets by meta-interpretation in answer set programming. Theory Pract. Logic Program. **3**(4), 463–498 (2003)

11. Gelfond, M., Son, T.C.: Reasoning with prioritized defaults. In: Dix, J., Pereira, L.M., Przymusinski, T.C. (eds.) LPKR 1997. LNCS, vol. 1471, pp. 164–223. Springer, Heidelberg (1998). https://doi.org/10.1007/BFb0054795

12. Grosof, B.: Logic programming in AI: some directions. In: Programming with High-Level Abstractions. Proceedings of the 3rd Workshop on Logic and Practice of Programming (LPOP), pp. 66–70 (2022)

13. Grosof, B., Swift, T.: Radial Restraint: a semantically clean approach to bounded rationality for logic programs. In: Proceedings of AAAI (2013)

14. Grosof, B., Swift, T.: PLOW: probabilistic logic over the well-founded semantics. In: AAAI Spring Symposium on Combining Machine Learning with Knowledge Engineering (AAAI-MAKE) (2019)

15. Grosof, B.: A courteous compiler from generalized courteous logic programs to ordinary logic programs. Tech. Rep. Supplementary Update Follow-On to RC 21472, IBM (July 1999)

16. IEP: Natural deduction. In: Feiser, J., Dowden, B. (eds.) Internet Encyclopedia of Philosophy. IEP (2023), a Peer-Reviewed Academic Resource. https://iep.utm.edu/natural-deduction

17. ISO working group JTC1/SC22: Prolog international standard ISO-IEC 13211–1. Tech. Rep., International Standards Organization (1995)

18. Johnson, J., et al.: Image retrieval using scene graphs. In: Conference on Neural Information Processing Systems, pp. 3668–3678 (2015)

19. Kifer, M.: Knowledge representation & reasoning with Flora-2. The Flora-2 Web Site (2022). http://flora.sourceforge.net

20. Kifer, M., Lausen, G., Wu, J.: Logical foundations of object-oriented and frame-based languages. J. ACM **42**, 741–843 (1995)

21. Montani, M.H.I.: spaCy 2: natural language understanding with Bloom embeddings, convolutional neural networks and incremental parsing (2017). https://spacy.io

22. Nute, D.: Defeasible logic. In: Handbook of logic in artificial intelligence and logic programming, pp. 353–395. Oxford University Press (1994)

23. Prakken, H.: An argumentation framework in default logic. Ann. Math. Artif. Intell. **9**(1–2), 93–132 (1993)

24. Rezk, M., Kifer, M.: Transaction logic with partially defined actions. J. Data Semantics **1**(2), 99–131 (2012)

25. Riguzzi, F., Swift, T.: The PITA system: Tabling and answer subsumption for reasoning under uncertainty. Theory Pract. Logic Program. **11**(4–5), 433–449 (2011)

26. Riguzzi, F., Swift, T.: Terminating evaluation of logic programs with finite three-valued models. ACM Transactions on Computational Logic 15(4) (2014)

27. Sakama, C., Inoue, K.: Prioritized logic programming and its application to commonsense reasoning. Artif. Intell. **123**(1–2), 185–222 (2000)

28. Swift, T.: Incremental tabling in support of knowledge representation and reasoning. Theory Pract. Logic Program. 14(4–5) (2014)

29. Swift, T., Warren, D.: XSB: extending the power of prolog using tabling. Theory Pract. Logic Program. **12**(1–2), 157–187 (2012)

30. Swift, T., Warren, D., et al.: The XSB Programmer's Manual: Volume, Version 5.0 (2022). http://xsb.sourceforge.net

31. van Gelder, A., Ross, K., Schlipf, J.: Unfounded sets and well-founded semantics for general logic programs. J. ACM **38**(3), 620–650 (1991)
32. Vickram Rajendran, W.L.: Accurate layerwise interpretable competence estimation. In: Conference on Neural Information Processing Systems (2019)
33. Wan, H., Grosof, B., Kifer, M., Fodor, P., Liang, S.: Logic programming with defaults and argumentation theories. In: International Conference on Logic Programming (July 2009)
34. Wan, H., Kifer, M., Grosof, B.: Defeasibility in answer set programs with defaults and argumentation rules. Semantic Web J. (2014)
35. Wang, K., Zhou, L., Lin, F.: Alternating fixpoint theory for logic programs with priority. In: Lloyd, J., Dahl, V., Furbach, U., Kerber, M., Lau, K.-K., Palamidessi, C., Pereira, L.M., Sagiv, Y., Stuckey, P.J. (eds.) CL 2000. LNCS (LNAI), vol. 1861, pp. 164–178. Springer, Heidelberg (2000). https://doi.org/10.1007/3-540-44957-4_11
36. Warren, D.S.: Introduction to prolog. In: Warren, D.S., Dahl, V., Eiter, T., Hermenegildo M., Kowalski, R., Rossi, F. (eds.) Prolog - The Next 50 Years. No. 13900 in LNCS, Springer (July 2023)
37. Wielemaker, J., Schrijvers, T., Triska, M., Lager, T.: SWI-prolog. Theory Pract. Logic Program. **12**(1–2), 67–96 (2012)
38. Yang, G., Kifer, M.: Inheritance in rule-based frame systems: semantics and inference. J. Data Semantics **2800**, 69–97 (2003)
39. Yang, G., Kifer, M., Zhao, C.: Flora-2: A rule-based knowledge representation and inference infrastructure for the Semantic Web. In: International Conference on Ontologies, Databases and Applications of Semantics (ODBASE-2003), pp. 671–688 (2003)
40. Zhang, Y., Wu, C., Bai, Y.: Implementing prioritized logic programming. AI Commun. **14**(4), 183–196 (2001)

Prolog Applications: Finalists for the Colmerauer Prize

PROB: Harnessing the Power of Prolog to Bring Formal Models and Mathematics to Life

Michael Leuschel[✉][iD]

Institut für Informatik, Universität Düsseldorf, Universitätsstr. 1,
40225 Düsseldorf, Germany
michael.leuschel@hhu.de

Abstract. PROB is an animator, model checker and constraint solver for high-level formal models. It has been developed for over 20 years and has built on the power of Prolog to help users develop safe systems, by bringing their formal mathematical models to life and uncovering unexpected behaviour. Almost all of PROB's features require constraint solving for an undecidable mathematical language with existential and universal quantification, higher-order sets, functions and relations and unbounded variables. PROB has been used by many academics in teaching and research. It has been used at the heart of a considerable number of academic and industrial tools. In particular, PROB has been used by several companies to validate the safe configuration of train systems around the world. In this setting PROB has been certified according to the European norm EN 50128. The long-term vision is to be able to routinely use formal mathematical models as runtime artefacts and make a larger subset of mathematics itself executable.

1 Tools for Formal Methods

Formal methods provide a mathematical approach to software and systems development. Before developing software or building a system, one develops a formal model which is analysed for correctness using a variety of tools:

- *provers* to prove properties interactively or automatically,
- *animators* to enable a user to interactively explore the behaviour of a formal model,
- *simulators* to automatically analyse a (random) set of behaviours,
- *explicit state model checkers* to automatically generate the state space of a formal model and check temporal properties,
- *symbolic model checkers* to check properties symbolically via constraint-solving,
- *test case generators* to derive test-cases for an implementation from the model, or
- *code generators* to derive an implementation that is correct by construction.

Many formal methods are rooted in logic. As such Prolog is an ideal candidate language to develop a formal methods tool. PROB is such a tool with a

© The Author(s), under exclusive license to Springer Nature Switzerland AG 2023
D. S. Warren et al. (Eds.): Prolog: The Next 50 Years, LNAI 13900, pp. 239–247, 2023.
https://doi.org/10.1007/978-3-031-35254-6_19

foundation in Prolog. PROB is an animator, model checker and constraint solver for high-level formal models. On the practical side, it can be used to ensure the safety of critical systems. On the theoretical side, it strives to bring formal models and mathematics to life.

2   PROB for State-Based Formal Methods

State-Based Formal Methods and Applications. State-based formal methods contain an explicit representation of the state of a model, and encompass languages like B [1], Event-B [2], Z [32] and TLA$^+$ [21]. All these languages build on logic and set theory to enable convenient modelling of many safety critical systems and algorithms.

Their use is not confined to the academic world; in particular for railway applications the B method has been used for many industrial applications over the last twenty-five years [7,23]. The initial industrial use of B was for the driverless metro line 14 in Paris [10], whose CBTC (Communication-Based Train Control) product has since then been adapted by Siemens for many other metro lines worldwide such as the recent installation for metro line 4 in Paris. Alstom's U400 CBTC product uses the B-method in a similar fashion. The product is running on over 100 metro lines and has 25% of the worldwide market share [7].

Executable Formal Models. Within the B-method high-level models are transformed into executable software using a combination of proof, manual refinement and low-level automatic code generation. Early validation of such models used to be a challenge though and some researchers used to argue that high-level models should not be executable [16].

This was the initial motivation for the development of PROB [24,25], a tool to make high-level formal models executable, thus enabling early inspection and validation.

The side bar on the right shows a small example B predicate and the challenges involved. In B, such predicates can appear as invariants over variables, assertions, guards and preconditions

Example: In B one can express that two graphs g_1, g_2 are isomorphic in B by stipulating the existence of a structure preserving permutation p as follows:

$$\exists p . p \in 1..n \rightarrowtail 1..n \wedge \forall i . (i \in 1..n \Rightarrow \quad p[g_1[\{i\}]] = g_2[\{p(i)\}])$$

Here, $1..n \rightarrowtail 1..n$ is the set of all permutations over the set of integers $1..n$, and $g_k[\{x\}]$ stands for the relational image of g_k for $\{x\}$, i.e., the set of a all successor nodes of x in the graph g_k. This predicate is typical of the kind of predicates that appear in high-level B specifications. PROB is capable of solving such predicates for reasonably sized graphs.

of operations, conditions within statements, and many more. As such, animation or execution of high-level B models is challenging, in particular since for high-level models operation preconditions and guards can be arbitrarily complex.

This challenge was overcome using the power of Prolog,[1] in particular Prolog's co-routining and constraint solving capabilities (see the discussion on constraints in [34] in this book). PROB thereby enables users to bring their formal models to life, making it possible to detect issues very early in the development process. In particular, PROB enables domain experts—with no education in formal methods—to inspect a B model and provide feedback based on their unique expertise.

Evolution and Industrial Uses of PROB. Initially PROB supported animation and explicit state model checking [24]. Over the years, PROB's underlying Prolog constraint solver has been improved, enabling further uses like *symbolic model checking* [20] or *test-case generation*. Many other features, like domain specific *visualisation* [35] or probabilistic *simulation* [33] have been added on top of PROB's core.

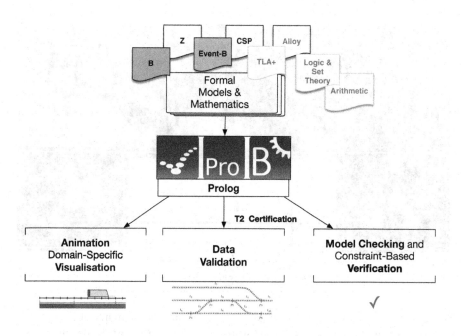

Fig. 1. High-Level View of Typical Uses of PROB

Over the years, the performance of PROB has continually been improved. This enabled the use of PROB for data validation, i.e., verifying properties of large data sets [22]. For this use, PROB has been certified [5] for use in safety-critical applications according to the European norm EN 50128. In particular,

---

[1] The letters "Pro" in the name PROB also makes allusion to its reliance on Prolog.

PROB has been used by companies like Siemens, Alstom, ClearSy and Thales, to validate the safe configuration of train systems all over the world (e.g., Paris metro line 1, São Paulo, Alger, Barcelona, Mexico, Toronto) [7]. The surveys [11] and [4] provide some interesting feedback about PROB's use in the railway domain.

In another new direction, PROB was used in [15] for the first time to execute a high-level formal B model in real-time to control trains (cf., Fig. 2). In this case, a mathematical model was directly used as a runtime artefact, without the need for code generation, be it manual or automated.

PROB has also been used by many academics in teaching and research. Notably, it is itself being used within several other tools, ranging from domain specific modeling tools (Meeduse [17], Coda [6]), university course planning (Plues [30]), railway validation (SafeCap [18], RDV [26], DTVT [22], Olaf, ClearSy Data Solver, Dave, Ovado [3]), security analyses (B4MSecure, VTG [29]), UML modeling (iUML and UML-B [28], UseCasePro), to test case generation (BTestBox, Cucumber-Event-B [31]).

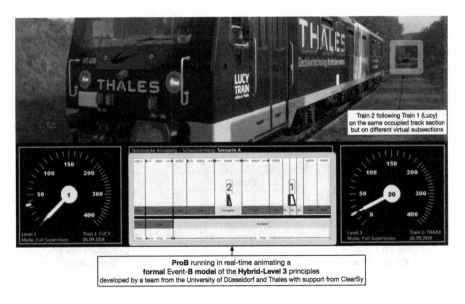

Fig. 2. A frame of a video of DB https://www.youtube.com/watch?v=FjKnugbmrP4 with PROB running a formal B model in real-time to control two trains and demonstrate the ETCS (European Train Control System) Hybrid Level 3 concepts [15]. The visualisation in the lower middle part is generated from PROB. The formal model was linked to the outside world via PROB2-JAVA-API [19].

3   Implementation

PROB has been developed over around 20 years and was initially developed in SICSTUS Prolog [8]. The core of PROB consists of about 400 Prolog files containing over 150,000 lines of code along with a large test suite of almost 7 000 unit tests and more than 2 000 integration tests. This strict testing regime is important for certification. For end users, PROB provides multiple user interfaces: a command-line interface (PROBCLI) for batch verification and data validation, a Jupyter kernel [12] for notebook usage, a Java API, and a set of graphical user interfaces (Tcl/Tk, JavaFX) for interactive animation, visualisation, and verification. All of these interfaces share the same Prolog core.

Although development began over 20 years ago, PROB is still actively developed. It is certainly a challenge to keep an academic tool in development for that amount of time; but the task was eased by the support of many students and researchers, the robustness of Prolog and the excellent support provided by SICSTUS.

PROB has recently [13] been made compatible with SWI-Prolog and we are working to make it compatible with Logtalk and other Prolog systems like Ciao Prolog.

Table 1. PROB source code statistics from [13]

	Files	Code lines	Comment lines
Core (Prolog)	165	85 680	15 651
Extensions (Prolog)	237	59 358	10 570
Extensions (C, C++)	84	78 784	1 691
GUI (Tcl/Tk)	23	32 803	2 753

(as of PROB 1.11.1, released 2021-12-29)

4   Challenge

Almost all of PROB's features, from animation to verification, require constraint solving at the level of the underlying formal language, i.e., for an undecidable mathematical language with existential and universal quantification, higher-order sets, functions and relations and unbounded variables. Moreover, PROB generally needs not just to find *one* solution for a predicate, but *all* solutions, e.g., when evaluating a set comprehension. Similarly, for model checking it needs to find all possible transitions to ensure that the complete state space is verified.

Below we illustrate this with a few small examples evaluated using PROB's Jupyter notebook interface [12] (which is also useful within teaching; see also the chapter [27] in this book).

First, we define the infinite set of primes and compute the intersection with a finite set of candidate values:

```
In [19]:  Primes={x|x∈ℕ ∧ ∀y·(y∈2..x-1 ⇒ x mod y > 0)} ∧
          P50 = Primes ∩ 1..50
```

Out[19]: *TRUE*

Solution:

- $P50 = \{1, 2, 3, 5, 7, 11, 13, 17, 19, 23, 29, 31, 37, 41, 43, 47\}$
- $Primes = /*@symbolic*/\{x \mid x \in \mathbb{N} \wedge \forall y \cdot (y \in 2 .. x - 1 \Rightarrow x \bmod y > 0)\}$

Observe how the intersection is computed explicitly, while the set of all primes is automatically kept symbolic. In a similar fashion, the variable f is automatically recognised in the next example as a (higher-order) infinite function and kept symbolic. Again, the set comprehension *res* of all square roots of 100 is computed explicitly. Also note that $f(2)$ denotes the (also infinite) squaring function and that all solutions for *res* are computed, even though no finite bounds were provided for x.

```
In [26]:  f = λe.(e∈ℕ | λbase.(base∈ℤ | base**e)) ∧ res={x|f(2)(x) = 100}
```

Out[26]: *TRUE*

Solution:

- $res = \{-10, 10\}$
- $f = /*@symbolic*/\lambda e \cdot (e \in \mathbb{N} \mid /*@symbolic*/\lambda base \cdot (base \in \mathbb{Z} \mid base^{\wedge}e))$

The core of PROB solves these challenges by using Prolog's co-routing feature (i.e., building on the independence of the computation rule of logic programming) to build a constraint solver on top of CLP (FD) [9]. In particular, the kernel of PROB contains various specific solvers, e.g., for booleans, integers, sets, relations, functions, sequences, which communicate via reification and co-routines (see [14]).

Below is another example, encoding the famous Send-More-Money puzzle in B's mathematical language (i.e., finding distinct digits S,E,N,D,M,O,R,Y so that the sum SEND+MORE equals MONEY):

```
In [17]:  :table {S,E,N,D, M,O,R, Y |
          {S,E,N,D, M,O,R, Y} ⊆ 0..9 ∧  S > 0 ∧ M > 0 ∧
          card({S,E,N,D, M,O,R, Y}) = 8 ∧
          S*1000 + E*100 + N*10 + D +
          M*1000 + O*100 + R*10 + E =
          M*10000 + O*1000 + N*100 + E*10 + Y }
```

Out[17]:

S	E	N	D	M	O	R	Y
9	5	6	7	1	0	8	2

The above examples demonstrate that formal languages like B, especially when using Unicode syntax, are very close to the way we write mathematics in text books and scientific articles. This makes it possible to copy parts of, e.g., theoretical computer science books into Jupyter enabling students to bring the mathematical definitions to life with PROB [12].

5   Conclusion

PROB is an animator, model checker and constraint solver for high-level formal models. It has been developed over around 20 years and has harnessed the power of Prolog to help users develop safe systems. PROB takes away tedious choices, automatically detects subtle bugs, but still leaves users in control to interactively validate their models. A friendly user experience was always more relevant for PROB than raw benchmark figures. For example, PROB will catch overflows, deal with divisions by zero, and keep track of source level information to visualise and explain errors to end users.

We hope that we can keep on improving PROB and that we have not yet reached the limit of what Prolog and formal methods have to offer. Indeed, we want to drive the idea of formal models as runtime artefacts further (see Fig. 2). The capabilities of the constraint solver of course could still be improved; maybe we can one day reach a state of a human friendly "executable mathematics" language which can be used by novice and expert alike. Safety will also play a crucial role in the future, in particular with the increased use of artificial intelligence in autonomous systems.

Acknowledgements. The first version of PROB was written by Michael Leuschel while in Southampton. During that time Michael Butler, Edd Turner and Laksono Adhianto provided valuable contributions. The first article on PROB was published with Michael Butler at FM'2003 [24] (its journal version is [25]). In 2005 the development moved to Düsseldorf and the STUPS group.

Over the years many people from the STUPS have contributed to PROB. In alphabetical order these persons are: Jens Bendisposto, Carl Friedrich Bolz-Tereick, Joy Clark, Ivaylo Dobrikov, Jannik Dunkelau, Nadine Elbeshausen, Fabian Fritz, Marc Fontaine, David Geleßus, Stefan Hallerstede, Dominik Hansen, Christoph Heinzen, Yumiko Jansing, Michael Jastram, Philipp Körner, Sebastian Krings, Lukas Ladenberger, Li Luo, Thierry Massart, Daniel Plagge, Antonia Pütz, Kristin Rutenkolk, Mireille Samia, Joshua Schmidt, David Schneider, Corinna Spermann, Fabian Vu, Michelle Werth, Dennis Winter.

References

1. Abrial, J.R.: The B-Book. Cambridge University Press (1996). https://doi.org/10.1017/CBO9780511624162
2. Abrial, J.R.: Modeling in Event-B: System and Software Engineering. Cambridge University Press (2010)
3. Badeau, F., Chappelin, J., Lamare, J.: Generating and verifying configuration data with OVADO. In: Dutilleul, S.C., Haxthausen, A.E., Lecomte, T. (eds.) Proceedings RSSRail, pp. 143–148. LNCS, vol. 13294, Springer (2022). https://doi.org/10.1007/978-3-031-05814-1_10

4. ter Beek, M.H., et al.: Adopting formal methods in an industrial setting: the railways case. In: ter Beek, M.H., McIver, A., Oliveira, J.N. (eds.) FM 2019. LNCS, vol. 11800, pp. 762–772. Springer, Cham (2019). https://doi.org/10.1007/978-3-030-30942-8_46

5. Bendisposto, J., Krings, S., Leuschel, M.: Who watches the watchers: Validating the ProB validation tool. In: Proceedings of the 1st Workshop on Formal-IDE. EPTCS XYZ, 2014, Electronic Proceedings in Theoretical Computer Science (2014)

6. Butler, M.J., et al.: Modelling and refinement in CODA. In: Derrick, J., Boiten, E.A., Reeves, S. (eds.) Proceedings Refine@IFM 2013, Turku, Finland, 11th June 2013. EPTCS, vol. 115, pp. 36–51 (2013). https://doi.org/10.4204/EPTCS.115.3

7. Butler, M., Körner, P., Krings, S., Lecomte, T., Leuschel, M., Mejia, L.-F., Voisin, L.: The first twenty-five years of industrial use of the B-Method. In: ter Beek, M.H., Ničković, D. (eds.) FMICS 2020. LNCS, vol. 12327, pp. 189–209. Springer, Cham (2020). https://doi.org/10.1007/978-3-030-58298-2_8

8. Carlsson, M., Mildner, P.: SICStus Prolog - the first 25 years. Theory Pract. Log. Program. **12**(1-2), 35–66 (2012). https://doi.org/10.1017/S1471068411000482

9. Carlsson, M., Ottosson, G., Carlson, B.: An open-ended finite domain constraint solver. In: Glaser, H., Hartel, P., Kuchen, H. (eds.) PLILP 1997. LNCS, vol. 1292, pp. 191–206. Springer, Heidelberg (1997). https://doi.org/10.1007/BFb0033845

10. Dollé, D., Essamé, D., Falampin, J.: B dans le transport ferroviaire. L'expérience de Siemens Transportation Systems. Technique et Science Informatiques **22**(1), 11–32 (2003)

11. Ferrari, A., et al.: Survey on formal methods and tools in railways: the ASTRail approach. In: Collart-Dutilleul, S., Lecomte, T., Romanovsky, A. (eds.) RSSRail 2019. LNCS, vol. 11495, pp. 226–241. Springer, Cham (2019). https://doi.org/10.1007/978-3-030-18744-6_15

12. Geleßus, D., Leuschel, M.: ProB and Jupyter for logic, set theory, theoretical computer science and formal methods. In: Raschke, A., Méry, D., Houdek, F. (eds.) ABZ 2020. LNCS, vol. 12071, pp. 248–254. Springer, Cham (2020). https://doi.org/10.1007/978-3-030-48077-6_19

13. Geleßus, D., Leuschel, M.: Making ProB compatible with SWI-Prolog. Theory Pract. Log. Program. **22**(5), 755–769 (2022). https://doi.org/10.1017/S1471068422000230

14. Hallerstede, S., Leuschel, M.: Constraint-based deadlock checking of high-level specifications. Theory Pract. Log. Program. **11**(4–5), 767–782 (2011)

15. Hansen, D., et al.: Validation and real-life demonstration of ETCS hybrid level 3 principles using a formal B model. Int. J. Softw. Tools Technol. Transfer **22**(3), 315–332 (2020). https://doi.org/10.1007/s10009-020-00551-6

16. Hayes, I., Jones, C.B.: Specifications are not (necessarily) executable. Softw. Eng. J. **4**(6), 330–338 (1989). https://doi.org/10.1049/sej.1989.0045

17. Idani, A.: Meeduse: a tool to build and run proved DSLs. In: Dongol, B., Troubitsyna, E. (eds.) IFM 2020. LNCS, vol. 12546, pp. 349–367. Springer, Cham (2020). https://doi.org/10.1007/978-3-030-63461-2_19

18. Iliasov, A., Lopatkin, I., Romanovsky, A.: The SafeCap platform for modelling railway safety and capacity. In: Bitsch, F., Guiochet, J., Kaâniche, M. (eds.) SAFECOMP 2013. LNCS, vol. 8153, pp. 130–137. Springer, Heidelberg (2013). https://doi.org/10.1007/978-3-642-40793-2_12

19. Körner, P., Bendisposto, J., Dunkelau, J., Krings, S., Leuschel, M.: Integrating formal specifications into applications: the ProB Java API. Formal Methods Syst. Des. **58**(1-2), 160–187 (2021). https://doi.org/10.1007/s10703-020-00351-3

20. Krings, S., Leuschel, M.: Proof assisted bounded and unbounded symbolic model checking of software and system models. Sci. Comput. Program. **158**, 41–63 (2018). https://doi.org/10.1016/j.scico.2017.08.013

21. Lamport, L.: Specifying Systems, The TLA+ Language and Tools for Hardware and Software Engineers. Addison-Wesley (2002)

22. Lecomte, T., Burdy, L., Leuschel, M.: Formally checking large data sets in the railways. CoRR abs/1210.6815 (2012), proceedings of DS-Event-B 2012, Kyoto

23. Lecomte, T., Deharbe, D., Prun, E., Mottin, E.: Applying a formal method in industry: a 25-year trajectory. In: Cavalheiro, S., Fiadeiro, J. (eds.) SBMF 2017. LNCS, vol. 10623, pp. 70–87. Springer, Cham (2017). https://doi.org/10.1007/978-3-319-70848-5_6

24. Leuschel, M., Butler, M.: ProB: a model checker for B. In: Araki, K., Gnesi, S., Mandrioli, D. (eds.) FME 2003. LNCS, vol. 2805, pp. 855–874. Springer, Heidelberg (2003). https://doi.org/10.1007/978-3-540-45236-2_46

25. Leuschel, M., Butler, M.J.: ProB: an automated analysis toolset for the B method. STTT **10**(2), 185–203 (2008)

26. Leuschel, M., Falampin, J., Fritz, F., Plagge, D.: Automated property verification for large scale B models with ProB. Formal Asp. Comput. **23**(6), 683–709 (2011). https://doi.org/10.1007/s00165-010-0172-1

27. Morales, J., Abreu, S., Hermenegildo, M.V.: Teaching prolog with active logic documents. In: Warren, D.S., Dahl, V., Eiter, T., Hermenegildo, M., Kowalski, R., Rossi, F. (eds.) Prolog - The Next 50 Years. No. 13900. LNCS. Springer (July 2023)

28. Said, M.Y., Butler, M., Snook, C.: A method of refinement in UML-B. Softw. Syst. Modeling **14**(4), 1557–1580 (2013). https://doi.org/10.1007/s10270-013-0391-z

29. Savary, A., Frappier, M., Leuschel, M., Lanet, J.-L.: Model-based robustness testing in EVENT-B using mutation. In: Calinescu, R., Rumpe, B. (eds.) SEFM 2015. LNCS, vol. 9276, pp. 132–147. Springer, Cham (2015). https://doi.org/10.1007/978-3-319-22969-0_10

30. Schneider, D., Leuschel, M., Witt, T.: Model-based problem solving for university timetable validation and improvement. In: Bjørner, N., de Boer, F. (eds.) FM 2015. LNCS, vol. 9109, pp. 487–495. Springer, Cham (2015). https://doi.org/10.1007/978-3-319-19249-9_30

31. Snook, C., et al.: Behaviour-driven formal model development. In: Sun, J., Sun, M. (eds.) ICFEM 2018. LNCS, vol. 11232, pp. 21–36. Springer, Cham (2018). https://doi.org/10.1007/978-3-030-02450-5_2

32. Spivey, J.M.: The Z Notation: a reference manual. Prentice-Hall (1992)

33. Vu, F., Leuschel, M., Mashkoor, A.: Validation of formal models by timed probabilistic simulation. In: Raschke, A., Méry, D. (eds.) ABZ 2021. LNCS, vol. 12709, pp. 81–96. Springer, Cham (2021). https://doi.org/10.1007/978-3-030-77543-8_6

34. Warren, D.S.: Introduction to Prolog. In: Warren, D.S., Dahl, V., Eiter, T., Hermenegildo, M., Kowalski, R., Rossi, F. (eds.) Prolog - The Next 50 Years. No. 13900. LNCS. Springer (July 2023)

35. Werth, M., Leuschel, M.: VisB: a lightweight tool to visualize formal models with SVG graphics. In: Raschke, A., Méry, D., Houdek, F. (eds.) ABZ 2020. LNCS, vol. 12071, pp. 260–265. Springer, Cham (2020). https://doi.org/10.1007/978-3-030-48077-6_21

Pacioli: A PROLOG System for Financial Report Processing

Miguel Calejo[(✉)] and Charles Hoffman

auditchain.finance, Zug, Switzerland
mc@logicalcontracts.com, Charles.Hoffman@me.com

Abstract. Financial information is reported by public companies to regulators worldwide using a standard rich structured data format, the "Extensible Business Reporting Language", or XBRL An XBRL report typically comprises two pieces: a file with instance data, made of financial facts contextualised with dates and hypercube dimensions, plus its background ontological information: potentially dozens of files with data element schema and hypercube definitions, hierarchical presentation directives, assertions - a tree graph of XML schema and linkbase resources published on the web.

Pacioli takes all that and converts it into a PROLOG representation, evaluates XBRL formulas, derives new facts, detects higher level patterns, executes diverse types of validation rules, and produces a validation report in multiple formats. It works both as a standalone web application server, and as part of a massive blockchain-coordinated network of validation engines.

Keywords: financial reporting · XBRL · blockchain

1 Introduction

Financial information is reported by public/listed companies to regulators worldwide using a standard rich structured data format, the "Extensible Business Reporting Language", or XBRL [1]. For example, in the United States public companies submit XBRL-based financial reports to the Securities and Exchange Commission (SEC). In Europe listed companies submit XBRL-based financial reports to the European Single Market Authority (ESMA).

XBRL is an open standard, with specifications freely available and freely licensed. XBRL is supported by a strong software development community that has created a range of products, both free and commercial, covering the needs of both end users and developers of XBRL-based reporting solutions and products. For additional information about XBRL, please refer to the XBRL technical specifications [2].

An XBRL report typically comprises two pieces:

- **Report**: A single XML (*or alternatively "inline XBRL"*, *iXBRL* [3] file with instance data: fact values for financial concepts – such as sales or inventory

© The Author(s), under exclusive license to Springer Nature Switzerland AG 2023
D. S. Warren et al. (Eds.): Prolog: The Next 50 Years, LNAI 13900, pp. 248–259, 2023.
https://doi.org/10.1007/978-3-031-35254-6_20

– contextualized with dates and multiple dimensions – such as sales per territory, product, and salesperson; the instance data depends on:
- **Report model**: Background ontological information, in the form of a "Discoverable Taxonomy Set" – potentially dozens of files with data element schema and hypercube (dimensions) definitions, hierarchical presentation directives, assertions - a tree graph of XML schema and linkbase resources published on the web.

Pacioli[1] is a logic and rules engine and toolkit that is purpose built and understands global standard XBRL-based digital financial report models and reports. Both API and GUI interfaces are available for Pacioli. Pacioli provides:

- Loading of XBRL reports and their Discoverable Taxonomy Sets into a self-contained Prolog representation.
- Prolog-based XBRL formula processor, adding auditing and explanation capabilities.
- Combination of a report model with user alterations of formulas and facts, as well as additional XBRL linkbases.
- Fact mapping and derivation, thus providing an "ontology mapping" mechanism to align diverse facts into the same financial concepts for a report, making it more easily comparable to others
- Detection of higher-level logical "blocks" of information, beyond XBRL, such as roll ups, roll forwards, adjustments, disclosures, etc.
- Processing of XBRL and extra-XBRL rules for report validation, including type-subtype associations, disclosure mechanics rules, reporting checklist rules, report model structure rules, and "Fundamental Accounting Concepts" continuity crosscheck rules; this is described by the Seattle Method [4] of processing XBRL-based financial reports;
- All rule outcomes are persisted to the Pacioli model on IPFS[2], anchored to a Merkle-like cryptographic hash of all the above ingredients, thus ensuring immutability and reproducibility for posterity
- Multiple report rendering interfaces

So for example, given Apple's 10K for 2021 inline XBRL filing[3], Pacioli produces an analysis[4]; one information block of which is shown in the pivot table below:

---

[1] Auditchain, *Pacioli Logic and Rules Engine*, https://docs.auditchain.finance/auditchain-protocol/pacioli-logic-and-rules-engine.

[2] https://ipfs.io, the "InterPlanetary File System", a decentralized, redundant, robust file storage service.

[3] https://www.sec.gov/Archives/edgar/data/320193/000032019321000105/aapl-20210925.htm.

[4] Pacioli Technical Analysis report saved to IPFS, https://auditchain.infura-ipfs.io/ipfs/QmSuMTNG1W98U3xTsJRX2cs1LxKQqGKqM9iq2w1HhsaCZB/.

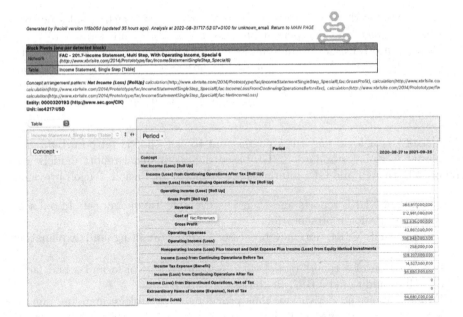

The indentation denotes aggregation (summing) of values. If you follow the link in the previous footnote and navigate to MAIN PAGE/Derivations Graph, you can see how the facts above were derived from the filed data.

PROLOG lovers can add a suffix to the URL of any Pacioli report and obtain its "PacioliModel"[5] in this case 36k PROLOG facts (reported or derived) for the Apple report and analysis. Searching in there for the fac:'Revenue' fact in the pivot table above, you'll find that it was not reported by the XBRL filer, but actually derived (by a simple mapping) from another, reported fact, defined for a us-gaap [5] concept:

```
mappedFact(...,
    fac:'Revenues',
    'i55e5364a9af5491886caee077afe8d44_D20200927-20210925',
    usd,
    null,-6,
    365817000000,
    'http://accounting.auditchain.finance/2022/fac/Rules_Mapping/...-definition.xml' +
        ('us-gaap':'RevenueFromContractWithCustomerExcludingAssessedTax') +
        reported
).
```

The above gory representation boils down to: we know that sales (as defined in the "Fundamental Accounting Concepts" taxonomy [6]) is USD 365817000000 because that value was reported for US-GAAP taxonomy [7] concept 'us-gaap': 'RevenueFromContractWithCustomerExcludingAssessedTax'.

---

[5] "Model" being used here in the broad sense of representation, NOT of Herbrand model. For the above example, https://auditchain.infura-ipfs.io/ipfs/QmSuMT NG1W98U3xTsJRX2cs1LxKQqGKqM9iq2w1HhsaCZB/ReportAndModel.pl.gzip.

For more examples, see the Pacioli batch report[6] for recent Dow Jones top 30 company filings.

2 System Architecture

Pacioli has been available since early 2021 as a web application at http://pacioli.auditchain.finance to support debugging, rule development and training. Advanced users (developers, accountants) interact with SWISH [8] notebooks[7]: they submit financial report URLs and obtain report validation analyses from Pacioli, as self-contained HTML mini sites generated by SWI-Prolog's "termerized" HTML templates [9], using Javascript frameworks[8] for browser client-side data rendering. The report analysis output includes machine-readable (Prolog and JSON) files, all stored on IPFS:

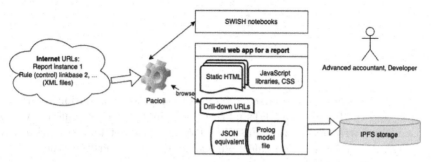

But its main use case is embedded in "Pacioli nodes", constituting the decentralized Auditchain validator network, anchored over the Polygon blockchain and monetary currency:

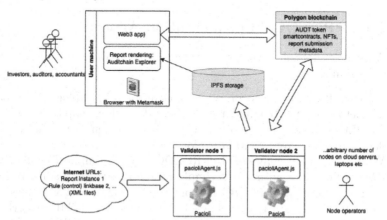

---

[6] https://auditchain.infura-ipfs.io/ipfs/QmaATb3njmXgbbZVuUPuJweukyHNk2Wb xGVJCSEUgqRt3o/.

[7] For exemple https://pacioli.auditchain.finance/tools/PowerUserTool.swinb.

[8] Namely https://pivottable.js.org/examples/ and http://tabulator.info, in addition to SWISH-generated https://graphviz.org graphs.

Pacioli coordination is performed by an Auditchain nodejs agent, and most users interface via Auditchain's Web3 app:

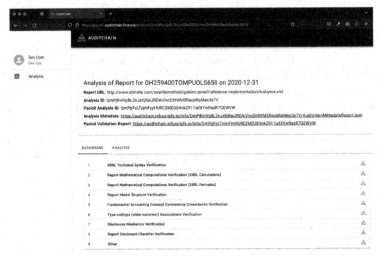

The AUDT token acts as currency for user fees, network operation and ruleset rewards, and the future rule NFTs marketplace: financial report rulesets will be (in late 2023) wrapped as Non Fungible Tokens; a ruleset may comprise (say) mapping rules and derivation rules, plus value assertions verifying the result of some unique financial analysis.

Since late 2021 this network went through alpha and beta programs with a dozen validators across the planet, with (Polygon) mainnet deployment imminent.

3   Some PROLOG Implementation Aspects

Since April 2020, Pacioli development indulged us on a gourmet feast of PRO-LOG programming[9]:

- XBRL to PROLOG conversion is a perfect fit for SWI-Prolog's XML parser: at the meta level, XBRL standard "legalese" definitions map to internal Pacioli PROLOG clauses; at the object level, XML elements are translated into Prolog terms, and stored within Prolog facts.
- CSV tabular files are converted to PROLOG terms, to support loading report SBRM specifications authored in simple Excel sheets; after loading it, Pacioli can generate the equivalent XBRL report, comprising several XML files... each rendered by the same DCG mechanism used below for HTML rendering.
- To save development time, we opted to delegate detailed XBRL conformance tests of the financial report to a reference XBRL (pre)processor[10]; the preprocessor is invoked as a PROLOG subprocess.

---

[9] Open sourcing of Pacioli is still under discussion, hence no code URL yet.
[10] https://github.com/Arelle/Arelle.

- Powerful ad-hoc querying over multiple "PacioliModel" files with PROLOG[11], to empower future financial research use cases not yet explored
- XBRL formula evaluation, including variable binding, is done by the straight execution of a Prolog goal generated from the formula; XBRL search over report facts[12] and multidimensional contexts in a XML document maps straight into PROLOG backtracking over their relational representation, with expressions evaluated by a simple PROLOG interpreter
- Simplified syntax for representing XBRL formulae as PROLOG terms, using custom operators, as opposed to the complex original XML linkbase. See 4.5.
- Block detection via declarative clauses. See 4.2
- Report rendering: "termerised HTML" [9] galore; Pacioli puts this "inverted Definite Clause Grammar" HTML template engine to use, including embedding of external Javascript objects, namely for pivot and interactive tables.

Although mainstream language such as Python or Javascript would provide some of the above capabilities, PROLOG is arguably the only covering all.

4   Diving into an Example Report

Rather than use a full report which can be quite large and challenging to explain in detail, a smaller example report[13] is used to illustrate Pacioli's capabilities.

4.1   Report Verification Summary

The following is a summary of the results of execution of all rules, summarised by rule kind; green icons denote compliance to all rules:

#	Verification Category	Result
1	XBRL Technical Syntax Verification	♨
2	Report Mathematical Computations Verification (XBRL Calculations)	♨
3	Report Mathematical Computations Verification (XBRL Formulas)	♨
4	Report Model Structure Verification	♨
5	Fundamental Accounting Concept Consistency Crosschecks Verification	♨
6	Type-subtype (wider-narrower) Associations Verification	♨
7	Disclosure Mechanics Verification	♨
8	Report Disclosure Checklist Verification	♨
9	Other	♨

---

[11] Potentially replacing the XULE expression language by PROLOG: https://pacioli. auditchain.finance/example/XULE.swinb.

[12] XBRL reports and rules translate into PROLOG unit clauses: the formula rule facts are meta-interpreted.

[13] Pacioli Analysis Summary, https://auditchain.infura-ipfs.io/ipfs/QmNUY15G1dhT XYCpyUyvqYWZ33Nc6mKRUDz7GDgLFonaPs/.

4.2 Blocks of Information

To render a financial XBRL report for a human, one needs to consider first the presentation structure imparted by its author: a big tree of "XBRL presentation links" with a root for the report itself, then all its XBRL networks as children, each with a sub-tree of presented XBRL concepts. This hierarchical structure of XBRL concepts, plus the time dimension, provide a basic scaffold for "hanging" facts in context.

But within that massive XBRL structure and facts lie smaller "blocks"[14] of information, fact chunks comprising something meaningful for an analyst or accountant, such as a "rollUp" (where one fact aggregates others, say over a quarter or year). These higher level pieces of information are not part of XBRL, and are instead detected by Pacioli, using "concept arrangement pattern detection" meta-rules, determining the blocks list[15]:

#	Network	Hypercube	Block	Pattern	Disclosures
1	01-Balance Sheet	Balance Sheet [Hypercube]	Assets	RollUp	disclosures:AssetsRollUp, disclosures:BalanceSheet
2	01-Balance Sheet	Balance Sheet [Hypercube]	Liabilities and Equity	RollUp	disclosures:BalanceSheet, disclosures:LiabilitiesAndEquityRollUp
3	02-Net Assets	Net Assets [Hypercube]	Net Assets	RollUp	disclosures:NetAssetsRollUp
4	03-Income Statement	Comprehensive Income Statement [Hypercube]	Net Income	RollUp	disclosures:IncomeStatement
5	04-Income Statement (Alternative)	Comprehensive Income Statement [Hypercube]	Net Income	RollUp	disclosures:IncomeStatementAlternative
6	05-Comprehensive Income	Comprehensive Income Statement [Hypercube]	Comprehensive Income	RollUp	disclosures:ComprehensiveIncome
7	06-Cash Flow	Cash Flow [Hypercube]	Net Cash Flow	RollUp	disclosures:CashFlowStatement, disclosures:NetCashFlowRollUp
8	06-Cash Flow	Cash Flow [Hypercube]	Assets, Beginning Balance	RollForward	disclosures:AssetsRollForward, disclosures:CashFlowStatement
9	07-Prior Period Errors	Prior Period Errors [Hypercube]	Equity, Originally Stated	Adjustment	disclosures:PriorPeriodError
10	08-Prior Period Errors (Alternative)	Prior Period Errors [Hypercube]	Prior Period Errors [Adjustment]	Set	disclosures:PriorPeriodErrorAlternative

As an example of block detection, take rollUps. This is the main PROLOG clause detecting them:

```
1   rollUp(R,Network,_ArrFather,PathedLabelledConcepts,Path, % input args
2       [Rule],PLCsublist, SupportingFacts,[roles:[items:Items,total:[Total]]] % output args
3       ) :-
4       Rule=calculation(Network,Sum), aRule(R,Rule),
5       memberchk(_/_/Sum,PathedLabelledConcepts), calculationParcelConcepts(R,Rule,Parcels),
6       % Check that the calculation uses only concepts in the above list, and obtain their sublist:
7       coveredPLC(PathedLabelledConcepts,[Sum|Parcels],PLCsublist),
8
9       % get rid off the labels:
10      findall(Concept, member(_/_/Concept,PLCsublist), Concepts),
11      first(PLCsublist,Path/_/_),
12
13      length(Concepts,N), length(Contexts,N), length(AspectModels,N),
14
15      % Construct logical goal to find the satisfying facts:
16      sameElements(Contexts,_),
17      sameDimensions(AspectModels,_SomeDimensions),
18      samePeriod(AspectModels,_SomePeriod),
19      sameUnit(AspectModels,_SomeUnit),
20      arrangementGoal(R,true,Network,Concepts,Contexts,AspectModels,FactBinder,SupportingFacts),
21
22      % bind and remove duplicate factsets:
23      findall(SupportingFacts, doBind(FactBinder,SupportingFacts), SupportingFactsL_),
24      sort(SupportingFactsL_,SupportingFactsL),
25      member(SupportingFacts,SupportingFactsL),
26
27      SupportingFacts = [_ExternalConcept/Total|Items_],
28      findall(SF,member(_/SF,Items_),Items).
```

---

[14] "Blocks" emerged from professional practice and are informally explained in Sect. 3.3 of http://accounting.auditchain.finance/framework/LogicalTheoryDescribingFinancialReport.pdf.

[15] Full list for this report in https://auditchain.infura-ipfs.io/ipfs/QmNUY15G1dhTXYCpyUyvqYWZ33Nc6mKRUDz7GDgLFonaPs/blocks.html.

This ain't pretty because of all the details involved, but basically a PROLOG goal query is generated and then queried over the report facts:

- A calculation rule is picked (on line 4)
- The Sum (total) of the calculation must be in the presented concepts for the given Network (line 5) and the "Parcels" (added terms in Portuguese...) too (line 7)
- After setting up a couple of unbound lists, these are constrained via simple unification (lines 16–19)
- Then a fact binder goal generator predicate is called (line 20), applying XBRL fact binding principles
- All solutions are found, and returned one by one on backtracking (line 23–25)

The detected block is identified by path of its root concept in the XBRL presentation tree, by the rule supporting it, and has associated a set of financial report SupportingFacts. The last (output) argument returns the internal block structure, identifying in this case a total and a list of items.

4.3 Rendering of a Block

By considering its intrinsic meaning, a block can be rendered in a manner more suitable for accountants, with pivoting controls and underlined totals, as shown below[16]. Numbers in green violate no rules, and have been validated by at least one:

Block Pivots (one per detected block)

Network	11-Variance Analysis (Main pattern that was detected) (http://www.xbrlsite.com/seattlemethod/report/role/VarianceAnalysis)
Table	Variance Analysis [Hypercube]

Concept arrangement pattern: *Net Income [RollUp]* calculation(http://www.xbrlsite.com/seattlemethod/report/role/VarianceAnalysis, proof:NetIncome)
Entity: GH259400TOMPUOLS65II (http://standards.iso.org/iso/17442)
Unit: iso4217:USD

Concept	Period 2020-01-01 to 2020-12-31		
	Actual [Member]	Budgeted [Member]	Variance [Member]
Variance Analysis [Roll Up]			
Revenues	7,000	6,000	1,000
(Expenses)	(3,000)	(2,000)	(1,000)
Gains	1,000	750	250
(Losses)	(2,000)	(1,000)	(1,000)
Net Income	3,000	3,750	(750)

4.4 Associations Between Blocks of Information

Blocks have associations between them, which can be visualized in a graph[17], where links are defined by the facts shared by several blocks:

---

[16] Rendering of information block, https://auditchain.infura-ipfs.io/ipfs/QmNUY15G1 dhTXYCpyUyvqYWZ33Nc6mKRUDz7GDgLFonaPs/01ecbc0ceca6b093c221.html #0fb66fa8527c7cb7ec08.

[17] Blocks Graph, https://auditchain.infura-ipfs.io/ipfs/QmNUY15G1dhTXYCpyUyv qYWZ33Nc6mKRUDz7GDgLFonaPs/blocksGraph.html.

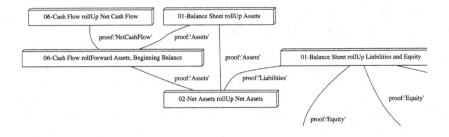

4.5 Rules

Most rules define assertions on facts[18], for example:

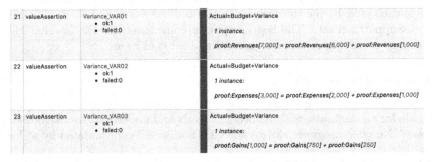

Pacioli supports different rule kinds:

- The above rules are XBRL "value assertions", checking some arithmetic relationship, which must hold true for all facts in the report
- XBRL calculations are conceptually a specific subtype of value assertions, where a total must be equal to a sum of terms
- Mapping rules are simple pairs, mapping one concept in one XBRL taxonomy (such as a regulatory standard like US-GAAP) into its equivalent in another taxonomy (such as a custom taxonomy for analysis, such as "Fundamental Accounting Concepts".
- Derivation rules compute one fact from others, and are encoded as XBRL Formulas; they're useful to align a financial report that uses its own taxonomies, to some other taxonomy framework for comparison with others.
- Disclosure rules, together with reporting checklist rules, identify blocks of information which must be present (reported) in the financial report; these typically express regulatory obligations

A major driver for the development of Pacioli was the need to analyze financial reports from multiple perspectives. The same report can be validated against different rules and even concept taxonomies: for example, an analyst may wish to evaluate a company's performance not in terms of the facts it reported

---

[18] Full value assertions list in https://auditchain.infura-ipfs.io/ipfs/QmNUY15G1dhT XYCpyUyvqYWZ33Nc6mKRUDz7GDgLFonaPs/valueAssertions.html.

directly, but instead with her own rules defined over a custom taxonomy of XBRL concepts. Hence the need for mapping and derivation rules (effectively solving financial reporting's "ontology mapping" problem), while applying specific value assertions to check the facts.

Following is a fragment for the example report's "Derivation Graph", showing mapping and derivation rules at work:

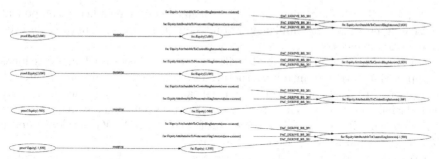

Nodes represent facts, with a XBRL concept (including its taxonomy prefix) together with a value. Links denote rule instances. 'proof' (the XBRL taxonomy of the financial report in question) facts are mapped to some 'fac' (Fundamental Accounting Concepts, another XBRL taxonomy) facts, and complemented by some other derived 'fac' facts further to the right.

4.6   Pacioli Rules vs. PROLOG

Each Pacioli rule is represented as a PROLOG term, comprising an expression with (PROLOG) variables and a list of variable declarations. Here are two examples:

The second example has simple variable declarations, indicating just their XBRL concept.

The first example however is more complex, as it also refers an hypercube defining a dimension for reported vs. corrected values: two of its variables are for the same concept (Equity), but intended to be bound to different facts, positioned elsewhere in the hypercube. The full rules list for this example report can be found here.

Rules are evaluated by a small interpreter, following the XBRL principles regarding fact binding: a single variable assignment must use fact values from the same context dimensions, same date, etc.

5   Significance – Present and Future

In the past, PROLOG application projects usually contained a heavy component of research: new language implementation techniques, new system tools, or even theoretical advances.

On the contrary, projects built with mature, mainstream languages focus on application rather than infra structure development. Thanks to the present maturity of PROLOG environments (specifically, SWI-Prolog), such is the case with Pacioli, a project that was driven straight from business requirements, as reflected in the core team: a senior professional PROLOG developer and a domain guru – no present academics onboard.

Up to now a dozen Pacioli instances, operated by different entities around the world, have already validated thousands of financial reports in different jurisdictions. Arguably, one of the most significant PROLOG applications to date, both in scale and global social impact.

As for the significance of financial reporting and its independent validation... recent events seem to indicate, again, how insufficient scrutiny leads to global financial problems. Cf. discussion on Pacioli analysis of Silicon Valley Bank [10].

Acknowledgement. To Jason Meyers and the Auditchain early investors, for betting Auditchain on Pacioli; to Jacinto Dávila for help with Pacioli and for his Auditchain Explorer UI; to Bogdan Fiedur for the blockchain agent and Auditchain smartcontracts; to Christopher Jastrzebski for all the support, and his Auditchain Web3 UI; to Fuad Begic for the complementary Luca report editor under development; to Andrew Noble and Dudley Gould for encouragement and suggestions. To Jan Wielemaker and associates, for a software stack that finally made PROLOG feasible for business applications. And finally, to Bob Kowalski: for his vision half century ago, and all the personal support in recent years.

References

1. XBRL International, Introduction to XBRL. https://www.xbrl.org/introduction/
2. XBRL International, XBRL Specifications. https://specifications.xbrl.org/specifications.html
3. XBRL International, iXBRL, https://www.xbrl.org/the-standard/what/ixbrl/
4. Charles Hoffman, CPA, Seattle Method. https://xbrlsite.com/seattlemethod/SeattleMethod.pdf
5. US Generally Accepted Accounting Principles. https://www.cfainstitute.org/en/advocacy/issues/gaap#sort=%40pubbrowsedate%20descending
6. Fundamental Accounting Concepts. https://accounting.auditchain.finance/fac/Index.html
7. US-GAAP taxonomy. https://accounting.auditchain.finance/reporting-scheme/us-gaap/documentation/Index.html

8. SWISH: SWI-Prolog for Sharing source repository. https://github.com/SWI-Prolog/swish

9. Tutorial - Creating Web Applications in SWI-Prolog. https://github.com/Anniepoo/swiplwebtut/blob/master/web.adoc#termerized-html-syntax

10. Jason Meyers, personal communication, Auditchain's. https://www.linkedin.com/feed/update/urn:li:activity:7044740816300351489?updateEntityUrn=urn%3Ali%3Afs_feedUpdate%3A%28V2%2Curn%3Ali%3Aactivity%3A7044740816300351489%29 LinkedIn page

Logic Model Processing

Pierre Dissaux[✉]

Ellidiss Technologies, 24 Quai de la Douane, 29200 Brest, France
`pierre.dissaux@ellidiss.com`

Abstract. Model Driven Engineering (MDE) refers to the use of software models to represent System or Software conceptual, logical, or physical abstractions, aiming at standardizing and easing industrial engineering processes. MDE is more and more applied in various domains of application and brings foundations for the digitalization of the industry. The avionics and Space software industry started the move several decades ago, which stimulated the emergence of many innovative technologies to improve the elaboration of these models and their exploitation. Logic Model Processing (LMP for short) is one of them.

Logic Model Processing is an adaptation of Logic Programming to Model Driven Engineering using standard Prolog language. The LMP framework consists of a methodology, a set of tools and Prolog libraries. This technology has been progressively and continuously developed during the last thirty years and produced many actionable outcomes, mostly under the form of tools that have been deployed worldwide for industrial usages and a few non-academic publications.

This paper introduces the origin of the LMP solution, provides an overview of its implementation, and gives a few examples of its practical use and of its most recent developments.

Keywords: Model Driven Engineering · Logic Model Processing · Prolog

1 Genesis of LMP

The Hierarchical Object-Oriented Design (HOOD) [1] method was elaborated in the nineties under the sponsorship of the European Space Agency, to master the increasing complexity of large real-time embedded software, most of them written in Ada. Although Model Driven Engineering was not a common term at that time, HOOD was already providing a strong support for pre-coding architectural and detailed design phases of software development life cycles. Indeed, HOOD provides software modelling abstractions thanks to dedicated graphical and textual notations and a methodology enforcing early verifications as well as synchronized automatic code and documentation generation.

© The Author(s), under exclusive license to Springer Nature Switzerland AG 2023
D. S. Warren et al. (Eds.): Prolog: The Next 50 Years, LNAI 13900, pp. 260–270, 2023.
https://doi.org/10.1007/978-3-031-35254-6_21

Practical use of such solutions on real scale industrial projects required the development of efficient Computer Aided Software Engineering (CASE) tools providing both model edition and model processing features. One of the possible solutions that were studied to implement these model processing features was Prolog [19]. The outcome of this almost 30-year-old experiment was later called Logic Model Processing.

The first realization of a HOOD model processing feature using Prolog was the development of a HOOD Rule Checker. This is required to verify that the software architecture (HOOD Design) is really compliant with the rules defined by the HOOD standard. An illustrative subset of this feature is explained below.

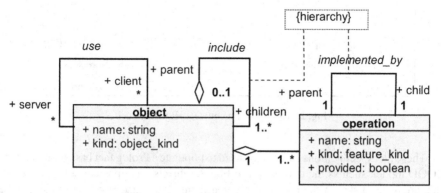

Fig. 1. Fragment of the HOOD meta-model

Figure 1 shows a fragment of the HOOD meta-model. The main building blocks are the HOOD Objects that are characterized by their Name, their Kind and the name of their parent Object in the decomposition hierarchy. With LMP, such an abstraction is handled by the Prolog fact specification isObject(Name,Kind,Parent)..

Each Object has a Provided Interface containing a list of provided Operations that are characterized by their own Name and the one of the Object where they are located. This can be represented by the other Prolog fact specification, isProvided(Name,'OPERAT ION',Object)..

In a similar way, connection lines can also be described by means of Prolog facts. In particular, the implemented_by links between Operations of a parent Object and the ones of a child Object are described by facts of the form isImplementedBy(Op1,'OPERATION',Parent,Op2,Child,1)..

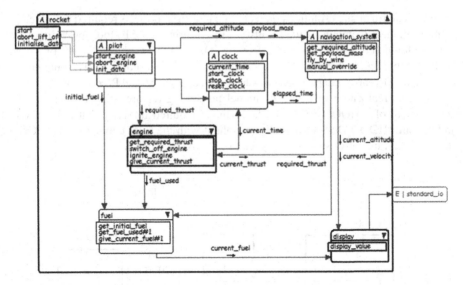

Fig. 2. Example of a concrete HOOD model

These fact specifications can thus be used to populate a Prolog fact base for a concrete HOOD model, such as the one shown in Fig. 2. Objects are represented by boxes and Operations are listed in their top-left compartment. `Implemented_by` links can be identified on the diagram by the three arrows starting from the outer box Operations. A fragment of the corresponding populated fact base is:

```
isObject('rocket','ACTIVE','NIL').
isObject('pilot','ACTIVE','rocket').
isProvided('start','OPERATION','rocket').
isProvided('start_engine','OPERATION','pilot').
isImplementedBy('start','OPERATION','rocket',
'start_engine','pilot',1).
```

Figure 3 provides a typical example of a design rule that is defined by the HOOD Reference Manual and must be verified to ensure that the model shown in Fig. 2 is correct.

I-6	*Each OPERATION provided by a PARENT shall be IMPLEMENTED_BY one OPERATION provided by one of its CHILDren.*

Fig. 3. Example of a HOOD design rule

This can easily be translated into a Prolog rule where model elements can be directly referenced using the facts described above.

```
/* HRM 4 rule I6:
Each OPERATION provided by a PARENT shall be
IMPLEMENTED_BY one
OPERATION provided by one of its CHILDren. */

errI6(X,U)  :- isProvided(U,'OPERATION',X),
  not(isImplementedBy(U,'OPERATION',X,_,_)).

checkI :- isNotTerm(X), errI6(X,U),
  write('ERROR : Operation : '), write(U),
  write(' provided by not terminal object : '), write(X),
  write(' should be implemented by a child object !
(I6)'), nl.
checkI :- printlf('---> rule I6 checked...').

/* utility rules */
isTerm(Y)  :- hoodObject(Y,_,_), not(hoodObject(_,_,Y)).
isNotTerm(Y) :-  hoodObject(Y,_,_), isParent(Y).
isParent(Y) :- hoodObject(_,_,Y), !.
```

A similar approach was followed to implement the complete set of HOOD rules, as well as other advanced model processing features such as an automatic Ada code generator and various documentation generators. This solution has been included into the Stood [2] product and distributed to major aerospace industrial companies over several decades. It is still actively supported and maintained.

2 Overview of LMP

After this first successful application of Logic Programming to implement processing tools for the HOOD software modeling language, LMP has been continuously improved and applied to a variety of other languages and processing goals to the present day. Based on this practical feedback and assuming that any modeling language can be defined by a meta-model, either strongly formalized or not, the LMP methodology can be summarized as follows:

- Each class of the meta-model defines a Prolog fact specification whose parameters correspond to the attributes of this class. Different strategies may be used to cope with attributes inherited from super classes.
- An application model (instance of the meta-model) is represented by a populated Prolog fact base, where fact parameter values correspond to meta-class attribute values.
- The model processing program is expressed by a set of Prolog rule bases, referring to other rules or the fact base representing the model. Note that several fact bases from various origins can be referenced by the same processing rules [14].

- To execute a LMP program, it is necessary to instantiate the fact base associated with the current state of the model(s) to be processed, to merge it with the rule base associated with the processing to be performed and to run a query with a standard Prolog engine. This step is illustrated by Fig. 4. Note that LMP mainly uses sbprolog [3] although it may be adapted to any other Prolog environment.

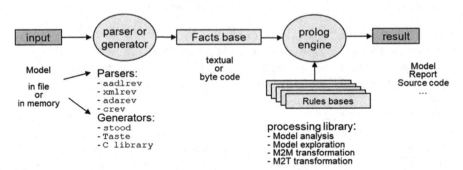

Fig. 4. Logic Model Processing

The input modeling languages that have been addressed are either token-based languages (i.e., defined by a textual grammar), such as software programming languages (Ada, C,...) or software architecture description languages (HOOD, AADL [4],...), or tag-based languages (i.e., defined by an XML structure), such as UML [5], SysML [6] and Domain Specific Languages (DSL).

The processing goals that have been developed until now, cover a large spectrum of model verification and exploitation tools in a homogeneous way, whereas different ad-hoc technologies are usually required with alternate implementations (e.g., Object Constraint Language [7], Atlas Transformation Language [8], Query View Transformation [9], Acceleo [10], ...). Typical LMP processing goals are:

- Model explorations or queries.
- Model verifications or rule checkers.
- Model transformations into other models, source code or documentation.

Two options are possible to convert an input model into the corresponding fact base. If the input model has been serialized and stored into a file, a parser tool is required to perform a syntactic translation between the original syntax into a list of Prolog facts. On the other hand, if the model is stored in a data structure within a CASE tool, the best solution consists in developing a Prolog facts generator.

3   Examples of Application

3.1   HOOD Processing Tools

Stood is a software design tool supporting the HOOD methodology that was presented in Sect. 1. It intensively uses LMP to implement the design rule checkers, the various code and documentation generators as well as a few reverse engineering tools. It has been deployed on many projects, and especially to support the development of embedded software for the Airbus family of civilian aircraft (A340, A350, A380). Table 1 gives the list of the LMP applications that have been customized or specifically created by Airbus to support their software development process [13]. Moreover, as such software requires proper certification by aviation authorities like DO 178 recommendations [11], some of these tools have been qualified. The good characteristics of the Prolog language added to the flexibility of the LMP framework made these realizations possible.

Table 1. LMP applications at Airbus

LMP rule base	Tool	DO 178 Qualification (verification tools)
HOOD to Ada	Stood	No
HOOD to C/Asm	Stood	No
HOOD Checker	Stood	Yes
HOOD to Document	Stood	No
HOOD to Frama-C	Stood	Yes

The more generic LMP tools that are included in the off-the-shelf "Stood for HOOD" distribution have been used by many other industrial programs, such as military helicopters, driverless metro, railways signaling and a collection of spacecrafts. In particular, they were used for the development of the control software embedded into the European Robotic Arm that is docked at the International Space Station.

3.2 AADL Processing Tools

The Architecture Analysis and Design Language (AADL) is a standard of the SAE [4] for the design of real-time software and its hardware execution platform. It defines a rich component-based textual and graphical description language with strong semantic specifications enabling the development of advanced analysis and verification tools. Several tools have been developed to support AADL modeling and processing activities.

Among them, "Stood for AADL" is a variant of "Stood for Hood", still enforcing the HOOD methodology, but including an AADL graphical editor associated with AADL text export and import features. Another tool called AADL Inspector [12] has been specifically designed and uses the LMP technology to manage AADL processing tools, including exploration, verification, and transformation tools [14]. Table 2 gives a summary of the main LMP programs that have been developed for AADL. The two tools are commercially supported and distributed worldwide.

Except for the last one, the model processing features that are listed in Table 2 require that a set of Prolog rules is prepared at tool design time (offline) and embedded into the tool package in advance. In these cases, the end user cannot modify the processing rules at model design time (online). To offer such capabilities, an online Prolog processing feature has been implemented in AADL Inspector.

Table 2. LMP applications for AADL

LMP rule bases	tool	category
AADLinstance builder	AADL Inspector	model exploration
AADL semantic rules	AADL Inspector	model verification (static analysis)
AADL ARINC 653 rules	AADL Inspector	model verification (static analysis)
AADL to Cheddar	AADL Inspector	model verification (timing analysis)
AADL to Marzhin	AADL Inspector	model verification (simulation)
AADL to OpenPSA	AADL Inspector	model verification (safety analysis)
HOOD to AADL	Stood	model transformation
AADL to HOOD	Stood	model transformation
UML MARTE to AADL	AADL Inspector	model transformation
SysML to AADL	AADL Inspector	model transformation
Capella to AADL	AADL Inspector	model transformation
FACE to AADL	AADL Inspector	model transformation
AADL printer	AADL Inspector	model unparser
LAMP checker	AADL Inspector	online model processing

The Prolog rules can thus be embedded inside the model to be processed and potentially modified by the designer at any time. This variant of LMP is called LAMP [15] (Logical AADL Model Processing) and allows for Prolog code to be directly inserted inside AADL as annexes and processing goals to be executed as Prolog queries. LAMP comes with a library of reusable Prolog model exploration, verification, and transformation rules that helps the user to set-up complete assurance case solutions.

4 Related Work

This section presents three related projects mentioning the use of the Prolog language in the context of Model Driven Engineering. Other related work could be found in the area of representing and processing ontologies with Prolog. This has not been explored here.

4.1 D-MILS

The D-MILS European FP7 project [16], ended in October 2015, was focused on extending MILS (Multiple Independent Levels of Security) for use with distributed systems. The similarities with LMP are that a) it addressed multi-domain assurance cases of distributed real-time architectures using a specific variant of the AADL language (MILS-AADL) as input and b) one of its processing tools, the Configuration Compiler, was written in Prolog and used the SWI Prolog constraint logic programming feature.

However, D-MILS is much more specific than LMP due to the use of a non-standard modelling language and requires the set-up of a complex tool chain to operate. In particular, the Prolog facts representing the input model are not directly derived from the MILS-AADL description but from the output of another intermediate model transformation.

4.2 PTL

Prolog based Transformation Language (PTL) [17] addresses the development of model transformations in a Model Driven Engineering context using the Prolog language. It is not specific to any application domain but relies on an existing transformation language (Atlas Transformation Language: ATL) and a particular modeling environment (Eclipse Modeling Framework: EMF).

Compared to LMP, the scope of PTL appears to be much more restrictive, as it only targets model transformations and not the other kinds of model processing. Moreover, it is presented as a hybrid approach which mixes Prolog and ATL languages, whereas everything is expressed in Prolog with LMP. Finally, the need for PTL to operate within the Eclipse platform brings another limitation that LMP does not have.

4.3 Multiprocessor Scheduling Analysis

In this article [18], a Prolog based framework is proposed to allow engineers to verify the consistency between a software application running on a multiprocessor platform and scheduling analysis feasibility tests. The software and hardware architectures are represented by Prolog facts, and the inference engine checks whether these facts conform to one of the design patterns associated with the feasibility tests.

Although it focuses on the resolution of a very specific problem, the implementation of the design pattern checking algorithm applied to multicore systems relies on the same general principles as LMP. The main differences come from the choice of an input model and corresponding transformation into Prolog facts, that are both specific to the Cheddar tool, and the use of a richer Prolog environment.

5   Exploitation and Dissemination

As said before, the LMP technology has been embedded in several commercial off-the-shelves Computer Aided Software Engineering tools that have been distributed and supported worldwide for several decades. These tools are namely Stood and AADL Inspector, both edited and distributed by Ellidiss Technologies. Please refer to Tables 1 and 2 for the list of LMP features that are provided by these two products.

Two kinds of metrics can be used to evaluate the dissemination of the technology. The first one is the number of end user licenses and support contracts that have been sold. This number reaches a few hundred units. The second one is the number of free downloads of evaluation copies of the products from the Ellidiss website [2, 12], which represents the most important dissemination means of the technology. It is important to note that although these products are never downloaded without having a good reason in mind, there is no way to confirm that the software has been properly installed and used. Moreover, the same user may have downloaded the products several times or with different identifiers. On the other hand, a single download may sometimes correspond to multiple users, like a full college lab class.

For the Stood product, the total number of free downloads during the last 17 years reaches 2500 units. Its repartition over time is shown on Fig. 5.

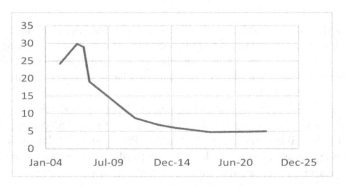

Fig. 5. Average number of Stood downloads per month.

AADL Inspector is a more recent product for which the free download metrics are more precise and include an indication of the user location. Over the period 2011–2022, more than 900 individual downloads of the product have been tracked. Figure 6 provides more details about the location and date of these downloads.

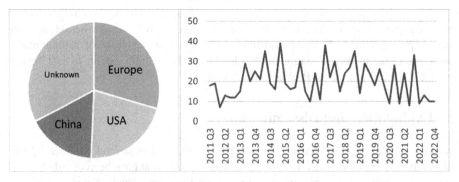

Fig. 6. Location and date of AADL Inspector Downloads

In summary, we can conclude that the LMP technology has been disseminated indirectly to more than 3000 people over the world during the two last decades.

6   Conclusion

Taking advantage of the intrinsic good properties of the Prolog language and augmented by a well-defined implementation approach, the benefits of the LMP solution are multiple:

- Generic solution for various model processing functions.
- Standard Prolog language (ISO/IEC 13211–1).
- Independent: compatible with all meta-modelling formats.
- Interpreted: supports both off-line and online processing (e.g., LAMP).
- Declarative: fits well with multi-steps incremental development processes.
- Modular: multiple separate fact and rule bases.
- Explainable: appropriate for tool qualification.
- Flexible:

  - Support of heterogeneous models.
  - Support of incomplete models (subsets).
  - Support of erroneous models (debugging).

- Industrial return of experience from commercially supported tools.
- Sustainable project, started almost 30 years ago, and still relevant and efficient.

After several decades of continuous development and deployment within the industry, where it is often not directly visible to the end users, the LMP technology is still commercially supported worldwide. Moreover, several new applications are currently under study to continue to contribute to the improvement of future Model Driven Engineering tool thanks to the power of the Prolog language.

References

1. HOOD: Hierarchical Object Oriented Design. http://www.esa.int/TEC/Software_engine ering_and_standardisation/TECKLAUXBQE_0.html
2. Stood. http://www.ellidiss.com/products/stood/
3. Sbprolog. Stony Brook Prolog. https://www.cs.cmu.edu/afs/cs/project/ai-repository/ai/lang/ prolog/impl/prolog/sbprolog/0.html
4. AADL: SAE AS-5506D, Architecture Analysis and Design Language. https://www.sae.org/ standards/content/as5506d/
5. UML: Unified Modeling Language. http://uml.org/
6. SysML: Systems Modeling Language. http://sysml.org/
7. OCL: Object Constraint language. http://www.omg.org/spec/OCL/
8. ATL: Atlas Transformation Language. http://www.eclipse.org/atl/
9. QVT: Query View Transformation. http://www.omg.org/spec/QVT/
10. Acceleo. https://www.eclipse.org/acceleo/
11. DO178. https://www.rtca.org/?s=DO+178
12. AADL Inspector. http://www.ellidiss.com/products/aadl-inspector/
13. Dissaux, P., Farail, P.: Model verification: return of experience. In: ERTS Conference Proceedings (2014)

14. Dissaux, P., Hall, B.: Merging and processing heterogeneous models. In ERTS Conference Proceedings (2016)
15. Dissaux, P.: LAMP: a new model processing language for AADL. In: ERTS Conference Proceedings (2020)
16. D-MILS project. http://www.d-mils.org/page/related-links
17. Almendros-Jimenez, J., et al.: PTL: a model transformation language based on logic programming. J. Logical Algebraic Meth. Program. **85**, 332–366 (2016)
18. Rubini, S., et al.: Specification of schedulability assumptions to leverage multiprocessor Analysis. J. Syst. Archit. **133** (2022)
19. Warren, D.S., et al.: Introduction to Prolog. In: Warren, D.S., Dahl, V., Eiter, T., Hermenegildo, M., Kowalski, R., Rossi, F. (eds.) Prolog: 50 Years of Future, LNAI 13900, pp. 3–19. Springer, Cham (2023)

Symbium: Using Logic Programming to Streamline Citizen-to-Government Interactions

Tristan Krueger[1], Abhijeet Mohapatra[1(✉)], and Michael Genesereth[2]

[1] Symbium Corp., California, USA
`{tristan,abhijeet}@symbium.com`
[2] Stanford University, California, USA
`genesereth@stanford.edu`

Abstract. Symbium is a US company launched in 2019. Its primary offering is a web-based service, called the Citizen's Dashboard, that helps homeowners, architects, and contractors comply with the regulatory aspects of residential construction. A distinguishing feature of the service is its use of Logic Programming to facilitate and, in some cases, automate regulatory processes involving permits, inspections, and rebates or refunds. The Citizen's Dashboard represents a significant improvement over traditional, manual approaches to regulatory compliance and has the potential to save individuals and governments billions of dollars per year.

Keywords: logic programming · computational law · government relationship management

1 Introduction

A recent study on replacement of home appliances (e.g., refrigerators, dishwashers, air conditioners etc.) in the United States suggests that billions of hours are lost each year (7.5 billion hours in 2021) [2,10] due to inefficiency in permitting processes. More than 40% of available rebates or refunds for energy-efficient appliances go unclaimed, \$350M in 2021 [7,17], due to the complexity of regulations and the associated rebate processes. Problems in securing permits and inspections for appliance replacements frequently cause significant delays in completing projects (in many cases more than 100 days). And the numbers are much larger when one looks beyond appliances to other types of home improvement.

Citizen's Dashboard. Symbium's solution to this problem is a service called the *Citizen's Dashboard* [9,15] - a web-based service that facilitates interactions between citizens (e.g., homeowners, architects, and contractors), governmental agencies (e.g., municipalities, counties, states) and other organizations (e.g., utility providers, insurance providers). The initial focus of the service is residential construction, with projects ranging from simple appliance replacements to the addition of accessory dwelling units (ADUs).

Symbium's implementation of the Citizen's Dashboard is organized into three pillars. (1) It provides its users with comprehensive data about residential properties and buildings (e.g., zoning, tax assessments, and building permit history). (2) It allows its users to describe proposed changes and automatically evaluates those changes for compliance with applicable regulations. (3) It manages transactions with governmental agencies and other organizations (e.g., applying for building permits, scheduling inspections, and obtaining rebates).

A distinctive feature of the Citizen's Dashboard is its focus on citizens rather than governmental agencies. Other companies sell their products and services to individual government agencies, and, as a result, citizens are forced to use different systems to interact with different agencies. Symbium's customer is the citizen. The Citizen's Dashboard provides integrated interaction with multiple government agencies, making it easier for citizens to manage the various regulatory aspects of construction projects.

2   Role of Logic Programming

Technologically, the key to Symbium's deployment of the Citizen's Dashboard is its use of Logic Programming technology in codifying rules and regulations. This approach is similar to the one used in [8] to represent the British Nationality Act as a logic program.

The Symbium team formalizes zoning and building regulations as rules in Dynamic Prolog (also known as Epilog [4,5]); and the Symbium platform uses these rules to assess regulatory compliance of proposed projects. In this way, the system is able to provide instantaneous feedback on project plans, circumventing the manual evaluation process in common use today.

Symbium's analysis of laws begins with the encoding of base facts. In the following, facts about a property of interest, e.g., zoning designation of the property, area of new units, are codified in Epilog.

```
property(property1)
property.zone(property1,"RH-1(D)")
project(project1)
project.property(project1,property1)
project.new_unit(project1,new_unit1)
project.new_unit.size(project1,new_unit1,800)
```

The example below is typical of rules encountered in municipal planning codes. It states that an accessory cottage violates the city's size restriction if it is built in the RH-1(D) zoning district and the area of the construction exceeds 900 square feet.

```
violation(Property,size) :-
    project.property(Project,Property) &
```

```
property.zone(Property,"RH-1(D)") &
project.new_unit.size(Project,Unit,NewUnitSize) &
greater_than(NewUnitSize,900)
```

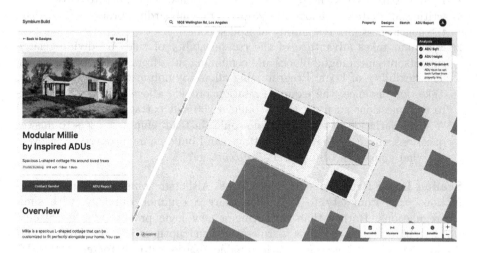

Fig. 1. Violation pinpointing in Symbium's Citizen's Dashboard

Symbium uses a similar approach to codify the rules involved in applying for permits, rebates, and tax incentives. Symbium uses both view definitions and operation definitions to manage the transactions between citizens and governmental agencies. The use of Epilog instead of Prolog to model dynamics is justified as it enables a clear separation of the formalization of dynamics from the definition of relations [3,4], allowing for a more organized and flexible approach to modeling complex systems.

The sample rule below describes what happens when the system receives a notice of code violation for a property from the city. Such a notice restricts new buildings from being built on the property.

```
message(Jurisdiction,code_violation(Property)) : :
    project.property(Project,Property) &
    property.jurisdiction(Property,Jurisdiction) &
    project.submittable(Project)
    ==> ¬project.submittable(Project)
```

One of the main challenges which Symbium faces in the building and maintenance of the Citizen's Dashboard is the large number of rules which affect residential construction projects. San Francisco's zoning code, for instance, has thousands of regulations and is updated up to six times per month. Furthermore, the regulations applicable to a project may stem from multiple regulatory bodies, e.g., environmental designations, state law, and national restrictions, and the interactions between these regulations may increase the combinatorial complexity of a project's analysis. Symbium uses Logic Programming to solve the above challenges in three ways.

1. Domain experts with no programming experience are trained to assist in the writing and editing of logic programs. This onboarding process is aided by the conciseness and readability of Epilog code.
2. Symbium takes advantage of the composability of rules by dividing large rulesets into meaningful blocks and combining rules from overlapping sources.
3. The flexibility of Logic Programming allows Symbium to reuse regulations. Take, for instance, the example relation provide above, which allows users to ask questions such as "Can I build a 900 sqft cottage on my property?" A slight variation of this same rule could, instead, empower users to answer questions such as "What size of cottage can I build on my property?" or, even, "In what zones can I build a 900 sqft cottage?"

Scaling Logic Programs Across Cities. Although zoning and building regulations vary from city to city, they share a common ontology, with similar regulations. Rather than authoring a new logic program for every city, the Symbium team develops a ruleset which captures the regulations that broadly apply to every city, with tunable relations to characterize the difference in regulations from city to city. In the following rule, the relation `jurisdiction.zone.max_size` characterizes the maximum cottage size regulations of a city.

```
project.noncompliant(Project) :-
    project.property(Project,Property) &
    property.jurisdiction(Property,Jurisdiction) &
    property.zone(Property,Zone) &
    project.new_unit.size(Project,Unit,NewUnitSize) &
    jurisdiction.zone.max_size(Jurisdiction,Zone,MaxSize) &
    greater_than(NewUnitSize,MaxSize)
```

To complete the logic program for a city, the above ruleset is supplemented with Epilog facts and rules to encode the city-specific zoning and building code regulations.

```
jurisdiction.zone.max_size("San Francisco","RH-1(D)",900)
jurisdiction.zone.max_size("Oakland","R1",1200)
```

The above authoring process enables the Symbium team to efficiently build and scale logic programs.

3   Citizen's Dashboard: Coverage and Reception

The Citizen's Dashboard is currently available in select California cities, and Symbium is working to make the service available across the state in the coming year. Subsequently, Symbium plans to expand the service nationwide.

This service has received favorable reviews from multiple journalists, with articles appearing in Forbes [1], Government Technology [9], Builder Online [11], and so forth. The company is also the recipient of multiple awards. In 2019, Symbium was named a Hive 50 honoree [6]. In 2020, it won the prestigious Ivory Prize for Housing Affordability [12]. In 2021, it received the American Bar Association Women of Legal Tech award [13]. And, in both 2021 and 2022, it was listed as a GovTech 100 company [16].

In the long term, the company aspires to apply the Citizen's Dashboard to other areas of regulatory compliance, such as property taxes, licenses, interstate commerce, and so forth. The Citizen's Dashboard is a technology that can facilitate many types of interactions between citizens and government agencies, all part of a Government Relationship Management (GRM) [14].

4   Broader Impact of Logic Programming

Symbium recently deployed a feature of the Citizen's Dashboard that verifies whether a specific instance of a home appliance replacement qualifies for a rebate. This feature not only allows users to access and apply for rebates more easily but also significantly reduces the time required for verification, from four weeks to a few seconds. This example illustrates how Symbium's implementation of automated legal automated legal reasoning represents a significant improvement over traditional, manual approaches to managing regulatory compliance, and it has the potential to save individuals and governments billions of dollars per year. The key to the success of the Citizen's Dashboard is the use of Logic Programming in codifying rules and regulations. Municipal regulations in the US are updated regularly - in some cases as frequently as 6 times per month. As such, Logic programming is a reliable approach to codify and maintain these regulations.

The discipline of codifying rules and regulations as logical statements by the Symbium team has led to the revelation of open texture issues, e.g., *what is the backyard of a building?* and the identification of inconsistencies between municipal and state codes. These issues were subsequently resolved by the municipalities in collaboration with the Symbium team. Symbium's interactions with municipal and state governments in the US indicate that Logic Programming has begun to affect the very process of policy making itself.

References

1. Castenson, J.: Platform digitizes painful planning process to provide greater access to affordable housing. https://www.forbes.com/sites/jennifercastenson/2022/03/21/platform-digitizes-painful-planning-process-to-provide-greater-access-to-affordable-housing/?sh=361fcaff171e (2022)
2. City of Oakland: average permit processing turnaround times. https://www.oaklandca.gov/resources/average-permit-processing-turnaround-times (2021)
3. Genesereth, M.R.: Dynamic logic programming. Tech. rep., Stanford University (2022). http://logicprogramming.stanford.edu/miscellaneous/dlp.html

4. Genesereth, M.R.: Dynamic logic programming. In: Warren, D.S., Dahl, V., Eiter, T., Hermenegildo, M., Kowalski, R., Rossi, F. (eds.) Prolog - The Next 50 Years. No. 13900 in LNCS, Springer (2023)

5. Genesereth, M.R., Chaudhri, V.: Introduction to logic programming. Synthesis Lectures on Artificial Intelligence and Machine Learning, Morgan & Claypool Publishers (2020). https://doi.org/10.2200/S00966ED1V01Y201911AIM044

6. McManus, J.: Symbium: the permitter. https://www.builderonline.com/recognition/symbium_o (Nov 2019)

7. Rewiring-America: High-Efficiency Electric Home Rebate Act (HEEHRA). https://www.rewiringamerica.org/policy/high-efficiency-electric-home-rebate-act (2022)

8. Sergot, M.J., Sadri, F., Kowalski, R.A., Kriwaczek, F., Hammond, P., Cory, H.T.: The british nationality act as a logic program. Commun. ACM **29**(5), 370–386 (1986). https://doi.org/10.1145/5689.5920

9. Staff, N.: Symbium creates property info lookup portal for California. https://www.govtech.com/biz/symbium-creates-property-info-lookup-portal-for-california (2021)

10. Statista: Household Appliances - United States. https://www.statista.com/outlook/cmo/household-appliances/united-states (2021)

11. Strong, S.: Tech Innovator Symbium launches new property and Permit Information Portal. https://www.builderonline.com/design/technology/tech-innovator-symbium-launches-new-property-and-permit-information-portal_o (2021)

12. Symbium: Symbium wins the ivory prize for housing affordability. https://symbium.com/press/symbium-wins-the-ivory-prize-for-housing-affordability (2020)

13. Symbium: Symbium CEO and co-founder Leila Banijamali honored with ABA LTRC. https://symbium.com/press/leila-banijamali-nominated-for-2021-women-of-legal-tech-award (2021)

14. Symbium: Symbium's vision of Government Relationship Management. https://symbium.com/blog/symbiums-vision-of-government-relationship-management (2021)

15. Symbium: How Complaw will revolutionize the public's experience of property data for cities and counties. https://symbium.com/blog/how-complaw-will-revolutionize-the-publics-experience-of-property-data-for-cities-and-counties (2022)

16. Symbium: Symbium is named a GovTech 100 company for the second consecutive year. https://symbium.com/press/symbium-is-named-a-2022-govtech-100-company-for-the-second-consecutive-year (2022)

17. Todorova, A.: Goodbye, Mail-In Rebates. https://www.wsj.com/articles/SB115663801471546598 (2006)

PROLEG: Practical Legal Reasoning System

Ken Satoh[(✉)]

National Institute of Informatics, 2-1-2, Hitotsubashi, Chiyoda-ku, Tokyo, Japan
ksatoh@nii.ac.jp

Abstract. This paper introduces a legal knowledge representation language, PROLEG. PROLEG rules are general rules in the form of Horn clauses and special meta-prediate expressing exceptions. Exceptions are introduced to express negative information in stead of "negation as failure". It is because reasoning pattern of general rules and exceptions fits lawyers' reasoning and therefore lawyers understand PROLEG easily. We firstly give the definition of syntax and semantics of PROLEG and show an application for legal reasoning.

Keywords: PROLEG · Logic Programming · Legal Reasoning

1 Background

After many years of theoretical research on logic programming and nonmotonic reasoning, I sought practical applications of my theoretical research and I entered law school in 2006 and learned "Japanese presupposed ultimate fact theory" (we write "JUF theory" for short in this paper) which was developed in lawyers training center in Japan at the law school. This theory is to help judges to make reasonable conclusions even under incomplete information environment due to lack of evidence. I immediately understood the aim of this theory is exactly same as nonmonotonic reasoning and am sure that I can implement the reasoning in JUF theory [10].

My understanding of JUF theory is as follows:
In a litigation, the truth values of some facts which contribute to the judgement might be unknown due to the sufficient evidence. Then, from the deductive reasoning, the correct logical condition for the judgment is "unknown" as well. However, judges are not allowed to give such unknown judgement but have to give decisive answer. To solve this problem, JUF theory attach a default truth value to every condition in Japanese Civil Code and let judges use the default value when the condition is unknown in the litigation. Then all the conditions are determined by real truth values or default truth values and therefore conclude the decisive judgement. Actually, an attached default value is closely related with the burden of proof. Since if the default value is favorable to the plaintiff (the defendant, respectively), the defendant (the plaintiff, respectively) must prove the negation of the default value otherwise the defendant (the plaintiff, respectively) lose the litigation.

D. S. Warren et al. (Eds.): Prolog: The Next 50 Years, LNAI 13900, pp. 277–283, 2023.
https://doi.org/10.1007/978-3-031-35254-6_23

2   PROLEG

We firstly started to write legal rules in PROLOG [10] reflecting burden of proof in a similar way to the British Nationality Act in PROLOG [13]. However, we found that lawyers have difficulty to understand negation as failure in PROLOG so we changed the syntax from negation as failure into a framework of general rules and exceptions which is a common reasoning pattern among lawyers to create PROLEG (PROlog based LEGal reasoning support system) [7].

Our main aim is to make lawyers to use legal reasoning system by providing a minimum legal language sufficient for the reasoning so that lawyers understand the behavior of the system. Our approach is quite opposite with academic trends in AI and law in that researchers introduce many subtlty to express detailed deontic modality. As far as pratical legal system is concerned, however, the legal systems which usual AI and Law researchers provide is too complicated for lawyers who do not have a background of logic and thus the lawyers do not use them.

Although we have not conducted any psychological experiments, we had experiences on PROLEG with law school graduates who write PROLEG solution for Japanese bar exams for each year from 2009 to 2022 (total more than 60 graduates) in that they can start to make a program in PROLEG after a few weeks training of programming in PROLEG. I believe that PROLEG is the most familiar legal knowledge representation language for lawyers and has a potential to be a de fact standard.

Now, we introduce PROLEG. PROLEG system consists of a rulebase and a fact base.

– A PROLEG rulebase consists of the following expression.
  • A rule of the form of Horn clauses (without negation as failure):

$$H \Leftarrow B1, ..., Bn.$$

  • An exception is an expression of the form:

$$exception(H, E).$$

  where H, E are atoms each of which is the head of a rule.
– A PROLEG factbase consists of the truth value of related facts in a case. We use an expression for a fact P in a case as:

$$fact(P).$$

The intuitive meaning of PROLEG rules is that if the conditions of general rules are satisfied, its conclusion is satisfied in general but if the exception E is satisfied the conclusion is no longer true. Note that E of $exception(H, E)$ is the head of a rule so there is a general rule whose head is E. Then we could write an exception E of exception E' by representing as $exception(E, E')$.

The semantics of PROLEG program is defined as follows [7]. We make a program to be grounded by the constants in the program and name it as P.

Let M be a set of atoms. We define a set of applicable rules w.r.t. M, P^M, as follows:

$$\{R \in P | \text{there is no } E \text{ s.t. } exception(head(R), E) \text{ and } E \in M\}$$

This means that if some exception is found for a conclusion H of rule R, we do not allow such a rule R to participate in a derivation. The semantics of P (called an extension of P) is given as a set of atoms M s.t. $M = min(P^M)$ where $min(T)$ is the minimum model of T.

It is analogous to answer set definition and actually, PROLOG and PROLEG is mathematically equivalent in the sense that there is a one-to-one translation from PROLEG to PROLOG and vice versa. Here, we reproduce the equivalence translation according to [9].

Suppose that we have a program whose general rules are as follows:

$C \Leftarrow B_{11}, ..., B_{1n_1}.$
$C \Leftarrow B_{21}, ..., B_{2n_2}.$
$\vdots$

$C \Leftarrow B_{k1}, ..., B_{kn_k}.$
and excetions are as follows:
$exception(C, E_1).$
$\vdots$

$exception(C, E_m).$

Then, we can traslate the above PROLEG program into the following program:

$C : -B_{11}, ..., B_{1n_1}, \text{ not } E_1, ..., \text{ not } E_m.$
$C : -B_{21}, ..., B_{2n_2}, \text{ not } E_1, ..., \text{ not } E_m.$
$\vdots$

$C : -B_{k1}, ..., B_{kn_k}, \text{ not } E_1, ..., \text{ not } E_m.$
Note that rules with the same head has the same negative literals. If we add some facts in PROLEG and PROLOG, we can show that derived literals are equivalent.

On the other hand, suppose that we have the following PROLOG program:
$C : -B_{11}, ..., B_{1n_1}, \text{ not } E_{11}, ..., \text{ not } E_{1m_1}.$
$C : -B_{21}, ..., B_{2n_2}, \text{ not } E_{21}, ..., \text{ not } E_{2m_1}.$
$\vdots$

$C : -B_{k1}, ..., B_{kn_k}, \text{ not } E_{k1}, ..., \text{ not } E_{km_k}.$
Then, we can translate a PROLOG program into the following PROLEG program using additional predicate C_i.
$C \Leftarrow C_1.\quad C_1 \Leftarrow B_{11}, ..., B_{1n_1}.$
$C \Leftarrow C_2.\quad C_2 \Leftarrow B_{21}, ..., B_{2n_2}.$
$\vdots$

$C \Leftarrow C_k.\quad C_k \Leftarrow B_{k1}, ..., B_{kn_k}.$
$exception(C_1, E_{11}). \quad \cdots \quad exception(C_1, E_{1m_1}).$

$$exception(C_2, E_{21}). \qquad \cdots \qquad exception(C_2, E_{2m_2}).$$
$$\vdots$$
$$exception(C_k, E_{k1}). \qquad \cdots \qquad exception(C_k, E_{km_k}).$$

If we add some facts in PROLEG and PROLOG, we can show that derived literals except additional predicate C_i's are equivalent.

It is interesting that even two languages are mathematically equivalent but understandability of lawyers is different.

Moreover, this way of writing rules explicitly reflects a burden of proof in litigation. The burden of proof for the conditions of a general rule resides in the party who wants its conclusion to be satisfied whereas the burden of proof for exceptions resides in the party who wants to deny the conclusion. Therefore, it is useful for lawyers in civil litigation to decide which evidence should be collected to win the case. Here is an example of PROLEG rules in contract law. We omit detailed arguments in each predicate for the sake of explanation.

```
right_to_ask_payment(Seller,Buyer,Object,Price)<=
    purchase_contract_establishment( Seller,Buyer,Object,Price).
% A seller has a right to force a buyer to make an payment
% over the object if a purchase contract is established.

purchase_contract_establishment(Seller,Buyer,Object,Price)<=
    purchase_agreement(Seller,Buyer,Object,Price).
% A purchase contract is established if there is an agreement
% of purchase of the object.

exception(right_to_ask_payment(Seller,Buyer,Object,Price),
          payment(Buyer,Seller,Object,Price)).
% There is an exception about sellerÂ\fs right to ask payment
% if buyer made payment.

payment(Buyer,Seller,Object,Price)<=
    payment_fact(Buyer,Seller,Object,Price).
% Payment is made if there is a fact of payment.
```

And here is a case description using PROLEG facts

```
fact(purchase_agreement(bob,alice,television,1000  euro)).
% Bob sold the television from Alice at the price of 1000 euro.

fact(payment_fact(alice,bob,television,1000 euro)).
% Alice paid 1000 euro to Bob for television.
```

PROLEG provides an explanation of the reasoning process to a judgement using a block diagram. We show a block diagram for the above case in Fig. 1. The explanation of block diagram is as follows:

– Right-handside top-most block expresses a judgement.

- A bottom item of each block expresses the result of evaluation of conclusions/conditions; o: success, x: fail
- A solid line between blocks expresses conclusion-condition relation for a general rule.
- A dotted line shows exception of the conclusion of a general rule.

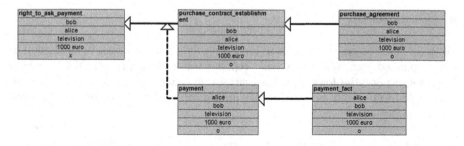

Fig. 1. PROLEG block diagram

3 Current Status of PROLEG and Its Applicability and Possible Extensions

We have been constructing a large rule base of 2500 rules and exceptions consisting of civil code and supreme court case rules since 2009. As far as we know, it is the largest legal rule base in the world. We checked the correctness of the rulebase to solve the multiple-choice part of Japanese bar exams by the law school graduates from University of Tokyo which is one of the best law school in Japan for 2009–2022. To manage such a large database, debugging tools are essentially necessary so we have investigated such legal debugging [1] as well. Regarding the efficiency of legal reasoning in civil litigation, a judge must provide a decisive decision so the structure of rule base in PROLEG is a stratified logic programming to guarantee a binary decision so that efficient implementation is possible. As a direct application of PROLEG in civil code litigation, PROLEG can be used to check a missing arguments which should be made by lawyers and as an educational tool, for law school students to enhance their understanding on legal reasoning based on burden of proof. We extend PROLEG into an interactive system to arrange issues [11][1]. We have been developing ODR (Online Dispute Reasoning) system more intelligent than E-Bay ODR system by enhancing man/machine interface of PROLEG system [6]. We have also been investigating a combination of natural language processing and PROLEG so that a lay user can write a case description in natural language and NLP

---

[1] You can see the demo video at
http://research.nii.ac.jp/~ksatoh/PROLEGdemo/IssueArrangmentDemo.mp4.

extracts necessary information for an input to PROLEG so that a lay user can find out an outcome of his/her problem by PROLEG block diagram [2–4].

There are various directions for extension. Since PROLEG is a framework to write legal rules in terms of general rules and exceptions so we could formalize statutory laws in general [9]. We have investigated an application to criminal law [5], GDPR [12] and an application to Private International Law [8].

4 Conclusion

We have described our activities of logic programming paradigm in legal domain and explained our legal knowledge representation language PROLEG, which has a lot of potential for supporting various legal activities. We strongly believe that PROLEG would be one of the prominent practical application in logic programming.

Acknowledgements. This research was supported by JSPS KAKENHI Grant Numbers, JP17H06103, JP19H05470 and JP22H00543, and JST, AIP Trilateral AI Research, Grant Number JPMJCR20G4, Japan.

References

1. Fungwacharakorn, W., Tsushima, K., Satoh, K.: On the legal debugging in PROLEG program. In: Advances in Intelligent Systems and Computing, vol. 1357, pp. 25–36 (2021). https://doi.org/10.1007/978-3-030-73113-7_3
2. Navas-Loro, M., Satoh, K., Rodríguez-Doncel, V.: ContractFrames: bridging the gap between natural language and logics in contract law. In: Kojima, K., Sakamoto, M., Mineshima, K., Satoh, K. (eds.) JSAI-isAI 2018. LNCS (LNAI), vol. 11717, pp. 101–114. Springer, Cham (2019). https://doi.org/10.1007/978-3-030-31605-1_9
3. Nguyen, H.T., Fungwacharakorn, W., Nishino, F., Satoh, K.: A multi-step approach in translating natural language into logical formulas. In: Proceedings of the 35th International Conference on Legal Knowledge and Information Systems (JURIX 2022), pp. 103–112 (2022). https://doi.org/10.3233/FAIA220453
4. Nguyen, H.T., Nishino, F., Fujita, M., Satoh, K.: An interactive natural language interface for PROLEG. In: Proceedings of the 35th International Conference on Legal Knowledge and Information Systems (JURIX 2022), pp. 294–297 (2022). https://doi.org/10.3233/faia220484
5. Nishigai, Y., Satoh, K.: Programming of "Japanese presupposed ultimate fact theory" in criminal law using PROLEG (in Japanese). Inf. Network Law Rev. **19**, 81–120 (2021). https://doi.org/10.34374/inlaw.19.0_81
6. Nishioka, S., Satoh, K., Mori, Y.: Consumer dispute resolution system based on PROLEG. In: Proceedings of the 35th International Conference on Legal Knowledge and Information Systems (JURIX 2022), pp. 298–301 (2022). https://doi.org/10.3233/FAIA220485
7. Satoh, K., et al.: PROLEG: an implementation of the presupposed ultimate fact theory of Japanese civil code by PROLOG technology. In: Onada, T., Bekki, D., McCready, E. (eds.) JSAI-isAI 2010. LNCS (LNAI), vol. 6797, pp. 153–164. Springer, Heidelberg (2011). https://doi.org/10.1007/978-3-642-25655-4_14

8. Satoh, K., Giordano, L., Baldoni, M.: Implementation of choice of jurisdiction and law in private international law by PROLEG meta-interpreter. In: Baroni, P., Benzmüller, C., Wáng, Y.N. (eds.) CLAR 2021. LNCS (LNAI), vol. 13040, pp. 60–75. Springer, Cham (2021). https://doi.org/10.1007/978-3-030-89391-0_4

9. Satoh, K., Kogawa, T., Okada, N., Omori, K., Omura, S., Tsuchiya, K.: On generality of PROLEG knowledge representation. In: Proceedings of the 6th International Workshop on Juris-informatics (JURISIN 2012), pp. 115–128 (2012a)

10. Satoh, K., Kubota, M., Nishigai, Y., Takano, C.: Translating the Japanese presupposed ultimate fact theory into logic programming. In: Proceedings of the 22nd Annual Conference on Legal Knowledge and Information Systems (JURIX 2009), pp. 162–171 (2009). https://doi.org/10.3233/978-1-60750-082-7-162

11. Satoh, K., Takahashi, K., Kawasaki, T.: Interactive system for arranging issues based on PROLEG in civil litigation. In: Proceedings of the Eighteenth International Conference on Artificial Intelligence and Law (ICAIL 2021), pp. 273–274 (2021). https://doi.org/10.1145/3462757.3466096

12. Sawasaki, T., Troussel, A., Satoh, K.: A use case on GDPR of Modular-PROLEG for private international law. In: Proceedings of the 3th International Workshop on Artificial Intelligence Technologies for Legal Documents (AI4LEGAL 2022), pp. 1–11 (2022)

13. Sergot, M.J., Sadri, F., Kowalski, R.A., Kriwaczek, F., Hammond, P., Cory, H.T.: The british nationality act as a logic program. Commun. ACM **29**(5), 370–386 (1986). https://doi.org/10.1145/5689.5920

Contributed Prolog Applications

Logical English for Law and Education

Robert Kowalski[1]([⊠]), Jacinto Dávila[2], Galileo Sartor[3], and Miguel Calejo[4]

[1] Imperial College London, London, UK
rak@doc.ic.ac.uk
[2] Universidad de Los Andes, Merida, Venezuela
[3] University of Turin, Turin, Italy
[4] Logicalcontracts.Com, Lisbon, Portugal

Abstract. In this paper we present the key features of Logical English as syntactic sugar for logic programming languages such as pure Prolog, ASP and s(CASP); and we highlight two application areas, coding legal rules, and teaching logic as a computer language for children.

Keywords: Logical English · Prolog · Law · Education

1 Introduction

Logical English (LE) [6–11, 15] exploits the unique feature of Prolog-like logic programming (LP), that LP is the only programming paradigm based on the use of logic for human thinking and communication. By exploiting this feature, LE becomes a wide-spectrum computer language, which can be understood with only a reading knowledge of English and without any technical training in computing, mathematics or logic.

LE is not only a Turing-complete computer programming language. It has the potential to represent and reason with a broad range of human knowledge, as shown by its ability to codify the language of law. In an educational setting, it can be used to introduce both computational and logical thinking across the whole range of subjects taught in school, bridging STEM and non-STEM subjects alike.

Basic Syntax. LE differs from pure Prolog primarily in the syntax for atomic predicates. In LE, predicates and their arguments are declared by means of templates, as in:

a person likes *a thing*

where asterisks delimit the argument places of the predicate. In the simplest case, an argument place can be filled by a constant or a variable. For example:

© The Author(s), under exclusive license to Springer Nature Switzerland AG 2023
D. S. Warren et al. (Eds.): Prolog: The Next 50 Years, LNAI 13900, pp. 287–299, 2023.
https://doi.org/10.1007/978-3-031-35254-6_24

Ordinary English:	Alice likes anyone who likes logic.
Logical English:	*Alice likes a person if the person likes logic.*
Prolog:	likes(alice, A) :- likes(A, logic).

A *variable* is a noun phrase ending with a common noun, such as "person" or "thing" and starting with a determiner such as "a", "an" or "the". The indefinite determiner, "a" or "an", introduces the first occurrence of a variable in a sentence. The same noun phrase with the indefinite determiner replaced the definite determiner, "the", represents all later occurrences of the same variable in the same sentence. Any other string of words in the position of an argument place is a constant. Unlike in Prolog, upper and lower case letters have no significance. Here is another example:

Templates:	*a person* is a parent of *a person*, *a person* is the mother of *a person*.
Logical English:	A person is a parent of an other person if the person is the mother of the other person.
Prolog:	is_a_parent_of(A, B) :- is_the_mother_of(A, B).

These examples illustrate some of the following characteristics of the basic syntax of LE, which are inherited from LP:

- Sentences in LE have the form of facts or rules. *Facts* are atomic sentences, whereas *rules* are sentences of the form *conclusion if conditions*, where the *conclusion* is an atomic sentence and the *conditions* are a combination of atomic sentences, typically connected by *and*.
- All variables are implicitly universally quantified with their scope being the sentence in which they occur. This means that variables in different sentences have no relationship with one another, even if they have the same name.
- The basic version of LE is untyped, like Prolog, and variable names are purely mnemonic. So, the first example sentence above has the same translation into Prolog as the meaningless sentence *Alice likes a hat if the hat likes logic*. We are developing an extended version of LE in which types are represented by common nouns, and the arguments of predicates are checked for compatibility with types that are declared in the templates.
- LE is designed so that sentences in LE have a unique translation into pure Prolog. But LE is also designed to be as unambiguous as possible, when understood by a human reader. For this purpose, LE deliberately eliminates the use of pronouns, which are a major source of ambiguity, as in the sentence *A person is a parent of an other person if she is the mother of her.*
- The current, basic syntax of LE does not include relative clauses, as in *Alice likes anyone who likes logic*. This is another deliberate choice, because relative clauses are another source of ambiguity. For example, the relative clause *which breathe fire*

is ambiguous in the sentence *All dragons which breathe fire are scary*. The relative clause can be understood restrictively as meaning that *a dragon is scary if the dragon breathes fire*. Or it can be understood non-restrictively, as meaning that, not only are all dragons scary, but they also breathe fire.

Logically, restrictive relative clauses add extra conditions to a sentence, whereas non-restrictive relative clauses add extra conclusions to the sentence. There are syntactic conventions for distinguishing between restrictive and non-restrictive relative clauses (such as the use of commas), but not everyone uses them correctly and consistently, and they differ between American and British English.

```
18   A meeting is prohibited
19       if a person attends the meeting
20       and the person is unvaccinated
21       and it is not the case that
22           the meeting is excused.
23
24   A person has an obligation that the person pays £100
25       if the person attends a meeting
26       and the meeting is prohibited
27       and the person is notified that the meeting is prohibited.
28
29   An arrest warrant is issued for a person
30       if the person has an obligation that the person pays an amount
31       and it is not the case that
32           the person pays the amount.
33
34   scenario one is:
35       Boris attends christmas party.
36       Novak attends christmas party.
37       Novak is unvaccinated.
38       Novak is notified that christmas party is prohibited.
39       Novak pays £100.
40
41   scenario two is:
42       Boris attends christmas party.
43       Novak attends christmas party.
44       Novak is unvaccinated.
45       Boris is notified that christmas party is prohibited.
46       Novak pays £100.
47       Boris pays £1000.
48
49   query one is:
50       which person has an obligation that which eventuality.
51
52   query two is:
53       An arrest warrant is issued for which person.
54
```

Fig. 1. An LE program together with alternative scenarios and queries, displayed in a VS Code editor. The editor provides syntax highlighting, predictive text, and a simple form of static type checking. https://le.logicalcontracts.com/p/unvaccinated.pl.

2   The SWISH Implementation of LE

The current implementation of LE in SWISH [20] translates LE programs and queries into Prolog or s(CASP) [15]. The implementation uses Prolog or s(CASP) to answer queries, and it translates answers and explanations into LE syntax. Figure 1 displays an example in a VS Code editor. The example illustrates some important additional features, which are not in the basic syntax of LE.

Negation as Failure for Rules and Exceptions. LE uses negation as failure to cater for exceptions, as in the negative condition on lines 21 and 22 of Fig. 1. In contrast, ordinary natural language often omits such explicit negative conditions for exceptions, and it relies instead on stating separately that the conclusion of a rule does not apply, as in Proleg [16, 17]. For example, instead of stating that *a meeting is excused if the meeting is a meeting of the cabinet ministers*, it may be more natural to state that *it is not the case that a meeting is prohibited if the meeting is a meeting of the cabinet ministers.* We are exploring the possibility of extending LE, to include such a treatment of exceptions for legal applications.

Metapredicates for Propositional Attitudes. LE inherits the feature of Prolog that sentences can occur as arguments of meta-predicates. LE uses this to represent deontic modalities (obligation, prohibition, permission) and other propositional attitudes (notification, belief, desire, dislike), introduced by the keyword *that*. For example, in line 24 of Fig. 1 the keyword *that* introduces the proposition *the person pays £100* as an argument of the meta-predicate *A person has an obligation.* Similarly, the keyword *that* in line 27 introduces the proposition *the meeting is prohibited* as an argument of the meta-predicate *the person is notified.*

The implementation of LE translates the sentence on lines 24–27 into the Prolog rule:

```
has_an_obligation_that(A, pays(A, '£_100')) :-
    attends(A, B), is prohibited(B), is_notified_that(A, is_prohibited(B)).
```

It translates the sentence on lines 29–32 into the Prolog rule:

```
'An_arrest_warrant_is_issued_for'(A) :-
    has_an_obligation_that(A, pays(A, B)), not pays(A, B).
```

Notice that the sentence expresses the deontic character of an obligation by representing the less-than-ideal consequence of violating the obligation.

Scenarios and Queries. Figure 1 also includes a number of scenarios and queries, which can be combined and posed to the system, as shown in Fig. 2.

In the combination of query one and scenario one, Novak is obligated to pay £100, but Boris is not, because, although both have attended a prohibited party (thanks to Novak), only Novak has been notified of the prohibition.

In the combination of query one and scenario two, Boris is obligated to pay £100, but Novak is not, because this time it is Boris, rather than Novak, who is notified of the prohibition.

In the combination of query two with scenario one, no arrest warrant is issued, because Novak, the only person obligated to pay £100, pays the required amount.

In the combination of query two with scenario two, Boris is issued an arrest warrant, because he pays an incorrect amount. An explanation for issuing the arrest warrant to Boris is displayed in Fig. 3.

Fig. 2. A log of combined queries and scenarios together with their answers.

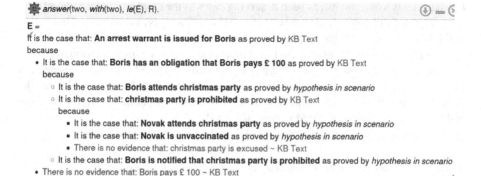

Fig. 3. An explanation for the answer to query two with scenario two.

3   Logical English for Legal Applications

We have been using LE to explore the representation of a wide range of legal texts, helping to identify ambiguities, explore alternative representations of the same text, and compare the logical consequences of the alternatives. The texts include portions of loan agreements, accountancy law, Italian citizenship, EU law on criminal rights, International Swaps and Derivative contracts, and insurance contracts.

The Italian Citizenship Example. We are also developing analogues of LE for other natural languages, such as Italian and Spanish. Figure 4 shows both an LE and a Logical Italian (LI) representation of Article 1 of Act No. 91 of 5 February 1992:

> E' cittadino per nascita: a) il figlio di padre o di madre cittadini; b) chi e' nato nel territorio della Repubblica se entrambi i genitori sono ignoti o apolidi, ovvero se il figlio non segue la cittadinanza dei genitori secondo la legge dello Stato al quale questi appartengono.

Both representations in Fig. 4 were generated manually. In contrast with the manually generated LE representation in Fig. 4, google translate gives the following translation of the original Italian text into English:

> Citizen by birth: a) the child of a citizen father or mother; b) who was born in the territory of the Republic if both parents are unknown or stateless, or if the child does not follow the citizenship of the parents according to the law of the state to which these belong.

Both the Italian text and its English translation are ambiguous: In particular, both the English condition "the child does not follow the citizenship of the parents according to the law of the state to which these belong" and its Italian counterpart, taken literally, seem to cover only the case where both parents have the same citizenship. Moreover, both the Italian "ovvero se" and the corresponding English "or if" seem to relate to a separate alternative from the alternatives that precede it. These readings of the natural language texts leave uncovered such deserving cases as the child having one parent who is stateless or unknown, and another parent who cannot pass on its citizenship to its child. It seems doubtful that these omissions would have been intended by the law.

The LE and LI representations in Fig. 4 incorporate only one interpretation of Article 1.1. Of course, other interpretations are possible, and they could also be represented in LE and LI. For comparison, see the similar case of children found abandoned in the UK, covered by the 1981 British Nationality Act, as formulated both in the original English and in an earlier, unimplemented variant of LE [7].

Figure 4 illustrates several features of LE that were not demonstrated earlier:

- LE uses indentation, rather than brackets, to represent the relative strength of binding of the logical connectives *and* and *or*.
- Variables can be given symbolic names, such as A and B in this example.

```
16  the knowledge base italian_citizen_new includes:       16  la base di conoscenza cittadinanza_italiana include:
17                                                          17
18  a person A is an italian citizen                        18  una persona A ha la cittadinanza italiana
19  if the person A is an italian citizen by birth.         19  se A ha la cittadinanza italiana per nascita.
20                                                          20
21  a person A is an italian citizen by birth               21  una persona A ha la cittadinanza italiana per nascita
22  if a person B is the parent of A                        22  se una persona B è genitore di A
23  and B is an italian citizen.                            23  e B ha la cittadinanza italiana.
24                                                          24
25  a person A is the parent of a person B                  25  una persona A è genitore di una persona B
26  if A is the father of B                                 26  se A è madre di B
27     or A is the mother of B.                             27     o A è padre di B.
28                                                          28
29  a person A is an italian citizen by birth               29  una persona A ha la cittadinanza italiana
30  if A is born in italy                                   30  se A è nato in italia
31  and for all cases in which                              31  e per tutti i casi in cui
32     a person B is the parent of A                        32     una persona B è genitore di A
33     it is the case that                                  33     è provato che
34     B is stateless                                       34     B è sconosciuto/a
35        or B is unknown                                   35        o B è apolide
36        or A does not inherit the citizenship of B.       36        o A non segue la cittadinanza di B.
```

Fig. 4. LE and LI representations of Article 1 of Act No. 91 of 5 February 1992. https://le.logica lcontracts.com/p/italian_citizen_new.pl, https://le.logicalcontracts.com/p/cittadinanza_italiana.pl

- Conditions can have the form *for all cases in which conditions it is the case that conclusion*, which are translated into forall(conditions, conclusion).

In Fig. 4, the possibility that a parent is unknown is expressed positively (as a kind of "strong" negation), to reflect the wording of the original legal text. Alternatively, the same possibility could be expressed using negation as failure, to conclude that a parent of a person is unknown if there is no information about the parent. In fact, with the representation in Fig. 4, it is possible to know that a person is born in Italy, but not to know who the parents are. In such a case, the *for-all* condition would be satisfied vacuously, and the person would be an Italian citizen by default.

4   Logical English for Education

By eliminating ambiguity from natural language, LE forces a writer to think more clearly about the relationship between sentences and their meanings. Thinking about meaning is unavoidable when writing sentences for translation into computer-executable code. But it also helps to avoid misunderstandings in communication among humans. Moreover, it helps to bridge the gap between the sciences and the humanities, by showing that clarity of language and thought is important in all academic disciplines.

The Italian citizenship example shows in a simple case how the use of symbolic names, which is associated with STEM disciplines, can be used to improve the clarity of communication in a non-STEM area. But the logical use of natural language, associated with LE and with some non-STEM disciplines, is also an important skill for use in STEM subjects, to make technical information more accessible to a wider audience.

The Definition of Subset. Figure 5 shows both an LE and an LS (Logical Spanish) representation of the definition of subset. Arguably, the definition can be understood by a reader without any training in mathematics or logic, but with only a reading knowledge of English or Spanish. Figure 6 shows all answers to the LE query *which set is a subset of which other set*, first with the scenario named *facts*, and then with the scenario named *lists*.

The subset example illustrates several features that have not been seen earlier:

- Because in the current version of LE variable names are purely mnemonic, the conditions that A and B are sets, on lines 13 and 14, need to be stated explicitly. These conditions would not be necessary if common nouns were treated as types. We plan to extend LE to include such types in the near future.
- The notion of set in lines 12–18 is an abstract notion, which is neutral with respect to how sets are represented concretely. Scenarios one and two employ different concrete representations. Scenario *sets* represents sets by facts that define the *belongs to* relation explicitly. Scenario *lists* represents sets by Prolog-style lists, and the *belongs to* relation is defined in terms of the *is in* relation, which is LE syntax for the Prolog *member* predicate. In both scenarios, there are only two sets. In both scenarios, there is no empty set.

```
12    a set A is a subset of a set B
13        if A is a set
14        and B is a set
15        and  for all cases in which
16            a thing belongs to A
17        it is the case that
18            the thing belongs to B.
19
20    scenario facts is:
21        family one is a set.
22        family two is a set.
23
24        Bob belongs to family one.
25        Alice belongs to family one.
26
27        Alice belongs to family two.
28
29    query subset is:
30        which set is a subset
31        of which other set.
32
33    scenario lists is:
34        [Alice, Bob] is a set.
35        [Alice] is a set.
36
37        a thing belongs to a set
38            if the thing is in the set.
```

```
12    un conjunto A es un subconjunto de un conjunto B
13        si el conjunto A es un conjunto
14        y el conjunto B es un conjunto
15        y en todos los casos en los que
16            una cosa pertenece a el conjunto A
17        es el caso que
18            la cosa pertenece a el conjunto B.
19
20    escenario hechos es:
21        la familia uno es un conjunto.
22        la familia dos es un conjunto.
23
24        Roberto pertenece a la familia uno.
25        Alicia pertenece a la familia uno.
26
27        Alicia pertenece a la familia dos.
28
29    la pregunta subconjunto es:
30        cuál conjunto es subconjunto
31        de cuál otro conjunto.
32
33    escenario listas es:
34        [Alicia, Roberto] es un conjunto.
35        [Alicia] es un conjunto.
36
37        una cosa pertenece a un conjunto
38            si la cosa is in el conjunto.
```

Fig. 5. A definition of the subset relation in LE and LS. https://le.logicalcontracts.com/p/sets%20with%20lists.pl, https://le.logicalcontracts.com/p/conjunto.pl

Reading versus Writing. It is natural to associate teaching computer science with teaching students how to write computer programs. But this overlooks the fact that most people will never need to write computer programs in their adult life. Some people may

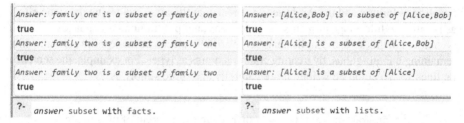

Fig. 6. All subsets with sets represented by facts or by lists.

want to read programs, to convince themselves that the programs meet their requirements. Some may want to understand explanations for answers to queries, and they may want to modify assumptions to obtain better answers. But hardly anyone will need to write programs themselves from scratch.

Focussing on teaching students how to write computer programs also overlooks the fact that learning to write well in any language, whether it be a natural language or a computer language, is much harder than learning to read. In this respect, LE has an advantage over other computer languages, because it can exploit a much wider range of examples requiring only a reading knowledge of natural language.

How to be a Happy Dragon. By focusing on reading rather than writing, examples of programming language constructs that would ordinarily be considered too difficult to teach at an introductory level can be included from the very beginning. Figure 7 illustrates such an example. Here the first sentence uses recursion, the second uses

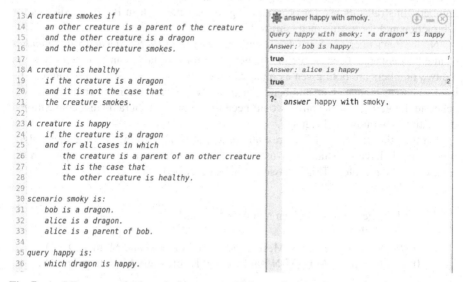

Fig. 7. An LE program for introducing young children to logic and computing. https://le.logica lcontracts.com/p/happy_dragon.pl

negation as failure, and the third uses universal quantification, achieving the same effect as iteration, while-loops or recursion in conventional programming languages.

Although this style of English may seem artificial, it can be made more natural, while remaining unambiguous, by treating common nouns as types. For example, the sentence on lines 13–16 could be written more naturally and more simply as:

> A dragon smokes   if   an other dragon is a parent of the dragon
> and the other dragon smokes.

All the examples we have seen until now can be understood without any knowledge about how LE is executed. Moreover, that understanding can be enhanced by experimenting with different scenarios and queries, and by exploring the logical consequences. In this example, a student can learn that alice is happy, because her only child, bob, is healthy; bob is healthy because he does not smoke; and bob does not smoke, because his parent alice does not smoke. It might be harder to convince a student that bob is a happy dragon too. But at least it shows that Logic and Computing can be introduced to children at an early age without having to use examples, such as controlling a robot or manipulating images on a screen, which can be implemented just as well, or maybe even better, in an imperative programming language.

The Euclidean Algorithm. As a computer language, LE combines in one language the features of a programming language, database language, and knowledge representation and problem-solving language. All the examples we have seen so far are examples of its use for knowledge representation and problem solving. The representation in Fig. 8 of the Euclidean algorithm for computing the greatest common divisor (gcd) of two numbers illustrates its use for programming. It uses the built-in Prolog predicates for subtraction and for testing inequalities.

Notice that a query such as *which number is the gcd of 1946 and which other number* cannot be answered, because the Prolog predicate for inequality can be used only when the two numbers are both given as input. On the other hand, the same program can be used both to test that a given number is the gcd of two other given numbers, as well as to generate the gcd. This capability would need two separate programs in a conventional imperative programming language.

On the other hand, the LE representation is not an algorithm. The Euclidean algorithm is the behaviour obtained by using the LE representation to reason top-down (or backward), as in Prolog. This behaviour can be described imperatively:

> To find the gcd D of two given numbers N and M:
> If N = M, then D = N.
> If N > M, replace N by N-M, find the gcd D' of N-M and M, then D = D'.
> If M > N, replace M by M-N, find the gcd D' of N and M-N, then D = D'.

One of the advantages of the declarative representation is that it is written in the same logical style as the natural definition (or specification) of gcd, illustrated in Fig. 9. Compared with the imperative representation, the LE representation in Fig. 8 makes it

```
10   a number N is the gcd of  N and N.
11
12   a number D is the gcd of a number N and a number M
13      if N > M
14      and a number smallerN is N-M
15      and D is the gcd of smallerN and M.
16
17   a number D is the gcd of a number N and a number M
18      if M > N
19      and a number smallerM is M-N
20      and D is the gcd of N and smallerM.
```

Fig. 8. The Euclidean algorithm represented in LE. https://le.logicalcontracts.com/p/Euclid.pl

much easier to reason that the Euclidean algorithm correctly computes the gcd. As David Warren points out [19], this can be done by using mathematical induction, exploiting the fact that the bottom-up (inductive) interpretation of the program in Fig. 8 computes the same gcd relation as the top-down (algorithmic) interpretation.

Notice that the specification of gcd, illustrated in Fig. 9, is also executable, although it is much less efficient than the Euclidean algorithm.

```
12   a number D is the gcd of a number N and a number M
13      if D divides N
14      and D divides M
15      and for all cases in which
16         an other number divides N
17         and the other number divides M
18         it is the case that
19         the other number =< D.
20
21   a number D divides a number N
22      if D is between 1 & N
23      and 0 is N mod D.
```

Fig. 9. The definition of gcd. https://le.logicalcontracts.com/p/gcd.pl

5   Related and Future Work

LE can be regarded as a controlled natural language, which is similar in spirit to ACE [3] and PENG [18], which are also implemented in Prolog. But, whereas LE is syntactic sugar for pure Prolog, ACE and PENG are syntactic sugar for first-order logic. PENG[ASP] [4], on the other hand, which is syntactic sugar for ASP, is closer to LE, but also closer to natural English.

LE inherits the wide spectrum use of LP as a computer language for programming, program specification, databases and knowledge representation and reasoning. However, in its current form, it is not entirely general-purpose. It lacks the ability of imperative languages to represent an agent's goals and the ability of an agent to satisfy goals by executing actions in reaction to external events.

To remedy this disability, we developed the language LPS (Logic Production System) [12–14] as an extension of LP. In fact, the earliest implementation of LE was for a smart contract using the rock-paper-scissors game [2] written in LPS. We plan to extend LE to include the reactive rules and causal laws of LPS. Other proposed extensions include a more natural representation of rules and exceptions, following the approach of [16, 17], as well as natural language analogues of object-oriented types and embedded functions and relations as in Ciao [1, 5].

In the meanwhile, the current version of LE and its natural language cousins, such as LI and LS, indicate the future potential of logic-based computer languages with a natural language syntax. In this paper, we have highlighted legal applications and education as two major areas in which the benefits of such languages can be exploited already today.

References

1. Casas, A., Cabeza, D., Hermenegildo, M.V.: A syntactic approach to combining functional notation, lazy evaluation, and higher-order in LP systems. In: Hagiya, M., Wadler, P. (eds.) FLOPS 2006. LNCS, vol. 3945, pp. 146–162. Springer, Heidelberg (2006). https://doi.org/10.1007/11737414_11
2. Davila, J.: Rock-Paper-Scissors (2017). https://demo.logicalcontracts.com/p/rps-gets.pl
3. Fuchs, N.E., Schwitter, R.: Attempto controlled English (ACE). arXiv preprint cmp-lg/9603003 (1996)
4. Guy, S.C., Schwitter, R.: The PENGASP system: architecture, language and authoring tool. Lang. Resourc. Eval. **51**, 67–92 (2017)
5. Hermenegildo, M., Morales, J., Lopez-Garcia P., Carro, M.: Types, modes and so much more – the Prolog way. In: Warren, D., Dahl, V., Eiter, T., Hermenegildo, M., Kowalski, R., Rossi, F. (eds.) Prolog - The Next 50 Years. LNAI, vol. 13900, pp. 23–37. Springer, Cham (2023)
6. Kowalski, R.: English as a logic programming language. N. Gener. Comput. **8**(2), 91–93 (1990)
7. Kowalski, R.A.: Legislation as logic programs. In: Comyn, G., Fuchs, N. E., Ratcliffe, M. J. (eds.) LPSS 1992. LNCS, vol. 636, pp. 203–230. Springer, Heidelberg (1992). https://doi.org/10.1007/3-540-55930-2_15
8. Kowalski, R.: Logical English. In: Proceedings of Logic and Practice of Programming (LPOP) (2020)
9. Kowalski, R., Datoo, A.: Logical English meets legal English for swaps and derivatives. Artif. Intell. Law **30**(2), 163–197 (2021). https://doi.org/10.1007/s10506-021-09295-3
10. Kowalski, R., Dávila, J., Calejo, M.: Logical English for legal applications. In: XAIF, Virtual Workshop on Explainable AI in Finance (2021)
11. Kowalski, R., Dávila, J., Sartor, G., Calejo, M.: Logical English for law. In: Proceedings of the Workshop on Methodologies for Translating Legal Norms into Formal Representations (LN2FR), JURIX (2022)
12. Kowalski, R., Sadri, F.: Reactive computing as model generation. N. Gener. Comput. **33**(1), 33–67 (2015). https://doi.org/10.1007/s00354-015-0103-z
13. Kowalski, R., Sadri, F.: Programming in logic without logic programming. Theory Pract. Logic Program. **16**(03), 269–295 (2016)

14. Kowalski, R., Sadri, F., Calejo, M., Dávila, J.: Combining logic programming and imperative programming in LPS. In: Warren, D., Dahl, V., Eiter, T., Hermenegildo, M., Kowalski, R., Rossi, F. (eds.) Prolog - The Next 50 Years. LNAI, vol. 13900, pp. 210–223. Springer, Cham (2023)

15. Sartor, G., Dávila, J., Billi, M., Contissa, G., Pisano, G., Kowalski, R.: Integration of logical English and s(CASP). In: 2nd Workshop on Goal-directed Execution of Answer Set Programs (GDE'22) (2022)

16. Satoh, K., et al.: PROLEG: an implementation of the presupposed ultimate fact theory of Japanese civil code by PROLOG technology. In: Onada, T., Bekki, D., McCready, E. (eds.) JSAI-isAI 2010. LNCS, vol. 6797, pp. 153–164. Springer, Heidelberg (2010). https://doi.org/10.1007/978-3-642-25655-4_14

17. Satoh, K.: PROLEG: practical legal reasoning system. In: Warren, D., Dahl, V., Eiter, T., Hermenegildo, M., Kowalski, R., Rossi, F. (eds.) Prolog - The Next 50 Years. LNAI, vol. 13900, pp. 277–283. Springer, Cham (2023)

18. Schwitter, R.: English as a formal specification language. In: Proceedings of 13th International Workshop on Database and Expert Systems Applications, pp. 228–232. IEEE (2002)

19. Warren, D.S.: Writing correct prolog programs. In: Warren, D., Dahl, V., Eiter, T., Hermenegildo, M., Kowalski, R., Rossi, F. (eds.) Prolog - The Next 50 Years. LNAI, vol. 13900, pp. 62–70. Springer, Cham (2023)

20. Wielemaker, J., Schrijvers, T., Triska, M., Lager, T.: SWI-Prolog. Theory Pract. Logic Program. **12**(1–2), 67–96 (2012)

Exploiting Logic Programming for Runtime Verification: Current and Future Perspectives

Davide Ancona, Angelo Ferrando, and Viviana Mascardi[(✉)]

University of Genova, Genova 16146, Italy
{davide.ancona,angelo.ferrando,viviana.mascardi}@unige.it

Abstract. In this paper we discuss how Logic Programming can be exploited for Runtime Verification, an activity where a monitor is in charge for checking whether an observed event is allowed in the current state. If this is the case, the monitor moves to the successive state, observes another event, and so on, until either a violation is detected, or the stream of events ends. If the system emitting events is expected to run forever, so does the monitor.

Being a semi-formal method, Runtime Verification must rely on a formal specification of the states of the observed system, and on a precise, formal description of the monitor's behavior. These requirements, and the raising need to deal with partial observability of events, make the adoption of Logic Programming in the Runtime Verification domain extremely suitable, flexible and powerful.

Keywords: Runtime Verification · Logic Programming · RML

1 Introduction

In order to gently introduce Runtime Verification, let us suppose that a multiagent system, namely a software system consisting of many autonomous, 'intelligent' interacting entities [80], works well if once the seller agent sends the invoice for the service agreed upon, the buyer agent sends a proof of the payment to the seller, and the seller acknowledges the reception. Alice is a seller and Bob is a buyer. We expect that the messages they exchange meet the pattern

$$P1 \; = \; A \overset{invoice(G)}{\Longrightarrow} B \; : \; B \overset{payProof(G)}{\Longrightarrow} A \; : \; A \overset{okPay(G)}{\Longrightarrow} B \; : \; \epsilon$$

where $ag_1 \overset{msg}{\Longrightarrow} ag_2$ means that agent ag_1 sends a message with content msg to agent ag_2 – these components could be variable or partially instantiated –, the symbol : is a prefix operator used to specify sequences of event types, and ϵ is the empty sequence of event types. The pattern $P1$ represents a translation of the "system working well" rule given in natural language into a simple, but formal language. Let us now suppose that a piece of software M placed outside the

© The Author(s), under exclusive license to Springer Nature Switzerland AG 2023
D. S. Warren et al. (Eds.): Prolog: The Next 50 Years, LNAI 13900, pp. 300–317, 2023.
https://doi.org/10.1007/978-3-031-35254-6_25

multiagent system can observe messages exchanged among agents, and observes the trace

$$S1 \;=\; < alice \overset{invoice(20KgApples)}{\Longrightarrow} bob, alice \overset{okPay(20KgApples)}{\Longrightarrow} bob >$$

If M can recognize that the first event in the trace has type $A \overset{invoice(G)}{\Longrightarrow} B$, and the second has type $A \overset{okPay(G)}{\Longrightarrow} B$, M can reason on $S1$ and on the expected pattern $P1$, and it can derive that Alice should have waited for Bob sending the proof of payment for the apples, before sending an acknowledge to him. Hence, M can warn either the agents or a (human) controller that a violation of the commercial transaction rules took place.

This toy example includes all the main building blocks of Runtime Verification, RV. RV [63] dynamically checks that event traces like $S1$ in our example, generated by single runs of a System Under Scrutiny (SUS, the multiagent system consisting of Alice and Bob in our example) are compliant with the formal specification of its expected correct behavior, $P1$ in our example. The external observer M is named monitor: it is in charge for monitoring what is going on, and for taking actions when needed. The formal specification $P1$ corresponds to the expected initial state of the SUS, and can be seen as the initial state of the monitor. If the first observed event meets the first expected event, the monitor moves to the successive expected state, that is

$$P1' \;=\; B \overset{payProof(G)}{\Longrightarrow} A \;:\; A \overset{okPay(G)}{\Longrightarrow} B \;:\; \epsilon$$

The monitor behavior is driven by a transition relation involving representations of states and observed events.

As we recently observed [15] "*RV is complementary to other verification methods: as formal verification, it is based on a specification formalism, but scales well to real systems and complex properties, by forgoing exhaustiveness as software testing*".

In order to be usable and useful, a RV system needs (i) a language for expressing the expected properties of the SUS that is powerful but easy to write and (ii) an efficient and formally grounded mechanism to recognize violations of those properties by the observed traces of events. In our example the mechanism is a transition relation between states: if no transition is possible, a violation took place.

We believe that Logic Programming (LP) is the right tool for addressing both challenges above thanks to its ability to represent properties like $P1$ in a compact and understandable way, and to its declarative and operational reading. In this paper we provide a short summary of our achievements in exploiting LP for RV (Sect. 2), we analyse the state of the art (Sect. 3) and we draw some perspectives on "*what kinds of applications is Prolog most suited for*" (Sect. 4).

2 Trace Expressions and RML

Trace expressions [4, 6, 9–11, 23] – previously named 'global types' – are a language for specifying patterns like $P1$. They are based on the notions of *event* (for example, Alice sends an invoice for 20 Kg of apples to Bob) and *event type* (for example, one seller sends an invoice for some service or good to one buyer: event types allow specifications to be more general, compact and readable). $\mathcal{E}$ denotes the fixed universe of events subject to monitoring. An event trace over $\mathcal{E}$ is a possibly infinite sequence of events in $\mathcal{E}$, and a Trace Expression over $\mathcal{E}$ denotes a set of event traces over $\mathcal{E}$. Trace expressions are built on top of event types (chosen from a set $\mathcal{ET}$), each specifying a subset of events in $\mathcal{E}$. A Trace Expression $\tau \in \mathcal{T}$ represents a set of possibly infinite event traces, and is defined on top of the following operators:

- ϵ (empty trace, eps in Prolog notation), denoting the singleton set $\{\epsilon\}$ containing the empty event trace ϵ.

- $\vartheta{:}\tau$ (*prefix*, ET:T in Prolog notation), denoting the set of all traces whose first event e matches the event type ϑ, and the remaining part is a trace of τ. For example, the $P1$ trace expression introduced in Sect. 1 contains prefix operators; the trace $S2 = < alice \stackrel{invoice(20KgApples)}{\Longrightarrow} bob, bob \stackrel{payProof(20KgApples)}{\Longrightarrow} alice, alice \stackrel{okPay(20KgApples)}{\Longrightarrow} bob >$ is compliant with $P1$ (it is a valid trace for the $P1$ specification) because $alice \stackrel{invoice(20KgApples)}{\Longrightarrow} bob$ matches the first event type in $P1$, and hence $P1$ can rewrite into

$$P1' = B \stackrel{payProof(G)}{\Longrightarrow} A : A \stackrel{okPay(G)}{\Longrightarrow} B : \epsilon$$

In a similar way, $bob \stackrel{payProof(20KgApples)}{\Longrightarrow} alice$ matches the first event type in $P1'$, that rewrites in

$$P1'' = A \stackrel{okPay(G)}{\Longrightarrow} B : \epsilon$$

and so on.

- $\tau_1 \vee \tau_2$ (*union*, T1\/T2 in Prolog notation), denoting the union of the traces of τ_1 and τ_2. For example,

$$P2 = A \stackrel{invoice(G)}{\Longrightarrow} B : B \stackrel{payProof(G)}{\Longrightarrow} A :$$
$$((A \stackrel{okPay(G)}{\Longrightarrow} B : \epsilon) \vee (A \stackrel{invalidPay(G)}{\Longrightarrow} B : \epsilon))$$

extends $P1$ to cope with the case that the proof of payment is invalid: once A receives it from B, it may either acknowledge the reception, meaning that the payment was successful, or inform B that the payment was not valid. $S2$ and $S3 = < alice \stackrel{invoice(20KgApples)}{\Longrightarrow} bob, bob \stackrel{payProof(20KgApples)}{\Longrightarrow} alice, alice \stackrel{invalidPay(20KgApples)}{\Longrightarrow} bob >$ are both valid traces for $P2$. Instead, $S4 = < alice \stackrel{invalidPay(20KgApples)}{\Longrightarrow} bob >$ is not. In fact, the first allowed message in $P2$ must match $A \stackrel{invoice(G)}{\Longrightarrow} B$, and $alice \stackrel{invalidPay(20KgApples)}{\Longrightarrow} bob$ does not.

- $\tau_1 \cdot \tau_2$ (*concatenation*, T1*T2 in Prolog notation), denoting the set of all traces obtained by concatenating the traces of τ_1 with those of τ_2. For example, assuming that $P3$ specifies the correct interactions between a seller and a wholesaler, $P4 = P2 \cdot P3$ models the pattern where, after concluding an interaction with a buyer ruled by $P2$, the seller can start interacting with the wholesaler, according to the rules specified by $P3$.

- $\tau_1 | \tau_2$ (*shuffle*, T1|T2 in Prolog notation), denoting the set obtained by shuffling the traces of τ_1 with the traces of τ_2. The fact that the seller can converse at the same time with the buyer and with the wholesaler, freely interleaving steps of the two conversations, can be modeled by $P5 = P2 | P3$.

- $\tau_1 \wedge \tau_2$ (*intersection* T1/\T2 in Prolog notation), denoting the intersection of the traces of τ_1 and τ_2. Such an operator is used to express conjunction of properties, we do not provide examples for it, due to space constraints.

Trace expressions semantics is defined by a δ transition relation that states when a trace expression can be rewritten into another upon observation of an event. The semantics is also implemented in Prolog in a natural and elegant way. Recently, we designed and implemented a Domain Specific Language, RML[1] [15] that allows for the use of trace expressions in an abstract and handy way, and that is compiled down into Prolog.

The most recent version of the Prolog implementation of the trace expressions semantics is available in the RML web site, https://github.com/RMLatDIBRIS/ monitor/blob/master/trace_expressions_semantics.pl. Below we show how a simplified version of this Prolog semantics works.

Given a `match` predicate that checks if an observed event E matches an event type ET, the δ transition for the prefix operator can be implemented by

```
delta(ET:T, E, T) :- match(E, ET).
```

meaning that if the event E matches event type ET (body of the clause, namely the part after the :- symbol[2]), a trace expression ET:T can be rewritten into the trace expression T (head of the clause, where the first argument ET:T of the `delta` predicate represents the trace expression, the second argument E is the observed event, and the third argument T is the result of applying δ).

The clause

```
delta(eps,_,_) :- !, fail.
```

means that no transition is possible from the empty trace expression ϵ. This rule prevents the Prolog interpreter from using other available definitions of

---

[1] https://rmlatdibris.github.io/.

[2] $\mathcal{H}$:- $\mathcal{B}$ should be read as 'if $\mathcal{B}$ holds, then $\mathcal{H}$ holds'.

`delta` (the ! 'cut' symbol in the body) and then forcing the failure of the `delta(eps,_,_)` goal (the built-in `fail` predicate).

Clauses

```
delta(T1\/T2, E, T1r) :- delta(T1, E, T1r).
delta(T1\/T2, E, T2r) :- delta(T2, E, T2r).
```

mean that if T1 can be rewritten into T1r upon observing E (body of the first clause), then also the union T1\/T2 can (head of the first clause). This is true also in case T2 can be rewritten into T2r, when T1\/T2 can be rewritten into T2r (second clause). We should note here that if both T1 and T2 can be rewritten into a new trace expression upon observing E, nondeterminism occurs. The actual implementation available in the RML repository is deterministic [12], and forces the monitor to rewrite T1 and disregard the possibility to rewrite T2.

Clauses

```
delta(T1|T2, E, T1r|T2) :- delta(T1, E, T1r).
delta(T1|T2, E, T1|T2r) :- delta(T2, E, T2r).
```

deal with shuffle: if T1 can be rewritten into T1r, then T1|T2 can be rewritten in T1r|T2 where, differently from union, T2 is kept in the rewritten trace expression (first clause). Other clauses deal with concatenation and intersection[3].

In order to exemplify the `delta` functioning we need to define its transitive closure `closure_delta(T, Evs)` that takes one trace expression T and the list of observed events Evs[4], and prints some messages for informing the user of what is going on[5]:

```
closure_delta(T, []) :-
  write(T), write('\n no more events to consume').
closure_delta(T, [Ev|Evs]) :-
  delta(T, Ev, T1),
  write(T), write(' accepted '), write(Ev), write(' and moved on'),
  closure_delta(T1, Evs).
```

---

[3] The code of this simplified semantics is available from https://github.com/VivianaMascardi/VivianaMascardi.github.io/blob/main/Software/traceExprSimplifiedSemantics.pl.

[4] In the real RV system, these events are generated by the SUS as a possibly infinite stream; the example provided here aims at simulating how the monitor works, assuming that events were previously logged and are hence a finite sequence.

[5] In the first clause we should distinguish the case where the trace expression may halt (for example, it is `eps`), which is fine, from the case where the trace expression expects more events, which is instead a violation since the trace of events is the empty list `[]`. The actual implementation in the RML repository provides a `may_halt` predicate to properly deal with these cases.

```
closure_delta(T, [Ev|_Evs]) :-
  write(T),write(' cannot accept '),write(Ev),write(' *FAILURE*').
```

We provide the following definition for the match predicate, where 20 stands for $20KgApples$

```
match( msg(alice, bob, invoice(20)), msg(A, B, invoice(G)) ).
match( msg(bob, alice, payProof(20)), msg(B, A, payProof(G)) ).
match( msg(alice, bob, okPay(20)), msg(A, B, okPay(G)) ).
match( msg(alice, bob, invalidPay(20)), msg(A, B, invalidPay(G)) ).
```

When we call the goal

```
T = msg(A, B, invoice(G)) :
      msg(B, A, payProof(G)):
      ((msg(A, B, okPay(G)) : eps) \/
       (msg(A, B, invalidPay(G)) : eps)),
Evs = [msg(alice, bob, invoice(20)),
        msg(bob, alice, payProof(20)),
        msg(alice, bob, invalidPay(20))],
closure_delta(T, Evs).
```

where T corresponds to $P2$ and Evs corresponds to $S3$ we obtain the following output where, for readability, we use the same logical variables A, B, G used in the goal above; the actual output of the Prolog interpreter shows different, newly generated ones:

```
msg(A,B,invoice(G)):
msg(B,A,payProof(G)):
( msg(A,B,okPay(G)):eps)\/
  (msg(A,B,invalidPay(G)):eps)
consumed msg(alice,bob,invoice(20)) and moved on

msg(B,A,payProof(G)):
( msg(A,B,okPay(G)):eps)\/
  (msg(A,B,invalidPay(G)):eps)
consumed msg(bob,alice,payProof(20)) and moved on

(msg(A,B,okPay(G)):eps)\/
(msg(A,B,invalidPay(G)):eps)
consumed msg(alice,bob,invalidPay(20)) and moved on

eps
no more events to consume
```

On the other hand, if Evs = [msg(alice, bob, invalidPay(20))] in the goal above, corresponding to $S4$, the output is

```
msg(A,B,invoice(G)):
msg(B,A,payProof(G)):
( msg(A,B,okPay(G)):eps)\/
  (msg(A,B,invalidPay(G)):eps)
cannot accept msg(alice,bob,invalidPay(20))    *FAILURE*
```

because the trace expression $P2$ does not expect $alice \overset{invalidPay(20KgApples)}{\Longrightarrow} bob$ as first exchanged message.

The actual code in the RML repository is much more complex: indeed, trace expressions can support both parameters and recursion, and can model – in a finite way – infinite traces of events. For example

$$P6 \;=\; A \overset{ping(X)}{\Longrightarrow} B \;:\; B \overset{pong(X)}{\Longrightarrow} A \;:\; P6$$

specifies an infinite trace of $ping$ and $pong$ messages, with the same content, exchanged by two agents A and B, while

$$P7 \;=\; A \overset{ping(X)}{\Longrightarrow} B \;:\; B \overset{pong(X)}{\Longrightarrow} A \;:\; (P7 \;\vee\; \epsilon)$$

specifies all the traces that start with $ping$ $pong$, and are followed by zero or more – including infinite – repetitions of $ping$ $pong$. The Prolog representations are

```
    P6 = msg(A, B, ping(X)):msg(A, B, pong(X)):P6
```
and
```
    P7 = msg(A, B, ping(X)):msg(A, B, pong(X)):(P7\/eps)
```
respectively. [6].

Our work on trace expressions started in 2012 and continued up to now without interruptions. Our most recent achievements involve the challenging problem of partial observability of events in the SUS, that we tackled both in a centralized [14] and in a decentralized multiagent setting [13].

Although in this section we took a multiagent system as running example, RV – and RML in particular – can be exploited to monitor any kind of system, from robotics to Internet of Things.

---

[6] In the code available from the RML repository, we re-implemented substitution to manage the scope of a logical variable: hence, we can distinguish between the term `P6` where we want `A, B, X` to be unified with the same values forever, and `P6'` where we want them to remain the same in two consecutive `ping pong` events, but possibly change in the next round. In the RML language we exploit the `let` keyword and curly brackets to define the variable scope, as discussed in https://rmlatdibris.github.io/rml.html, 'Parametric specifications'. The Prolog representation of trace expressions features the implementation of `let`. Given that terms can be cyclic, we used the `coinduction` library of SWI Prolog [75], to recognize when two cyclic terms are the same and manage them properly while applying substitutions, avoiding non-termination.

3   State of the Art

To get an updated picture of the use of LP for RV, on February 2023 we analyzed the literature on RV and LP by issuing queries on Google Scholar[7]. The main inclusion criterion was being in the first 22 answers to one of the following four queries on Google Scholar: "runtime verification" and "logic programming", "runtime verification" and "prolog", "runtime monitoring" and "logic programming", "runtime monitoring" and "prolog". We then carefully filtered the results that did not meet the exclusion criteria "being PhD or Master theses, books or unpublished pre-prints". After removing duplicates we retained the following 62 papers: 1985 [60], 2001 [16], 2005 [76], 2006 [84], 2008 [1,77,78], 2009 [18,29,32,50,53–55,65], 2010 [27], 2011 [3], 2012 [19,24,44], 2013 [49], 2014 [5,22,23,28,30,68], 2015 [7,35,45,67,79], 2016 [8,10,26,37,52,72], 2017 [36,38,51,64] [44,70], 2018 [25,40,42,47,48,61] 2019 [41,46,62,73,81], 2020 [39,82], 2021 [15,71], 2022 [13,14], 2023 [83].

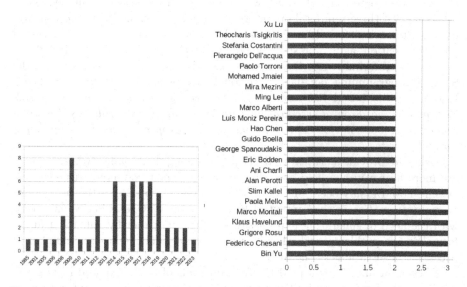

Fig. 1. Distribution of papers over years (left) and co-authors of at least two papers (right).

The distribution of papers over years is shown in Fig. 1 (left), while Fig. 1 (right) shows the authors that co-authored three or two papers among the retrieved ones, excluding papers we were involved in. The words that occur more often in the titles (resp. abstracts) are represented in Fig. 2 (resp. Fig. 3).

Besides RML and Trace Expressions, another work where computational logic is used to monitor traces at runtime is EAGLE [17]. The work by Barringer

---

[7] https://scholar.google.com/.

Fig. 2. Most frequent words in titles.

Fig. 3. Most frequent words in abstracts.

et al. was not returned by the search on Google Scholar but it is mentioned by Havelund in [45], that we analyzed in depth. EAGLE is logic defined and implemented by Barringer et al., it offers a succinct set of primitives supporting recursive parameterized equations, with a minimal/maximal fix-point semantics together with three temporal operators: next-time, previous-time, and concatenation. Prolog is definitely more powerful and expressive, but EAGLE received a lot of attention, as it represents one of the first implemented logics for RV.

In [45], Havelund describes a rule-based RV system implemented in the SCALA programming language[8]. Although not using Prolog, his conclusions hold for Prolog-based RV as well: "*Rule-based systems seem natural for RV and monitoring. From a specification notation point of view, rule-based systems appear quite suitable for expressing the kind of properties the RV community normally writes.*"

Below we provide a critical analysis of two among those papers whose authors are more active in the field according to Fig. 1. Their common feature is discussing how LP has been, or could be, exploited to cope with the problem of *partial information* in the context of RV: the paper by Chesani et al. [27] deals with the need of generating hypotheses, whereas the paper by Alberti et al. [3] formalize the problem of whether it is possible to safely reduce the number of necessary observations of the SUS.

Chesani et al. [27] presented the fundamentals of a reactive and logic-based version of the Event Calculus [59] named $\mathcal{REC}$ for monitoring declarative properties, while maintaining a solid formal background. Monitoring calls for the ability of carrying out 'open' reasoning, i.e., of reasoning upon the *partial and incomplete information* acquired during the execution, extending the inferred results as new events occur. $\mathcal{REC}$ achieves the goal by taking advantage of the SCIFF proof procedure [2], an extension of Fung and Kowalski's IFF proof-procedure for abductive LP [43]. In a paper building on top of [27], Bragaglia et al. [21] studied a Prolog-based axiomatization of $\mathcal{REC}$ and discussed different runtime monitoring application fields including Business Process Management, clinical guidelines, and multiagent systems.

---

[8] https://www.scala-lang.org/.

Alberti et al. [3] showed that speeding up RV by considering *traces with partial information* by reducing the number of observations is possible for the case where the observation space can be modeled as a set of (not necessarily consecutive) natural numbers. They also show that it is possible to draw conclusions about the complete execution trace by observing partial traces when the property to be checked is expressed in Linear Temporal Logics [69], widely used in model checking and RV. Although they have no running Prolog-based implementation of their runtime monitoring tool, Alberti et al. claim that detection of complex events (composed of atomic ones) can benefit from LP techniques, and that tools and techniques developed in the field of LP can be used to guide event detection at a higher level thereby further saving observation effort.

4   Conclusions and Future Perspectives

A logic program is a set of Horn clauses, namely logical implications meeting some constraints on the form of their heads, or consequences, and their bodies, or premises. It has both an operational reading, since Horn clauses can be executed by an interpreter to demonstrate that some goal can be achieved, and a declarative one, when they are seen as a formal specification. When the behaviour of a system that moves from one state to another upon some event taking place can be described by rules in the form of Horn clauses, then the logic program implementing such clauses becomes, at the very same time, a tool for *executing the system transition mechanism*, and a *formal description of the system's operational semantics*. In other words, the implementation of the transition mechanism is coherent with the semantics by design, being expressed in the same LP piece of code.

In this paper we discussed how LP can be exploited for RV. Being a semiformal method, RV must rely on a formal specification of the states of the system observed by the monitor, and on a precise, formal description of the monitor's behavior. Because of these requirements, we found the adoption of LP in the RV domain extremely suitable and powerful.

When observed events are not complete, the RV activity becomes even more challenging. RV in presence of incomplete information requires reactivity, to react to events that have been fully observed and timely emit a verdict on their compliance to the system's specification. It also requires rationality, to reason about events that have been observed only in a partial way or not at all (noisy communication, events sampling due to hardware or software requirements). In these situations, the monitor must make guess on what these events might have been, and if the system's execution is still safe.

LP is well known to integrate reactivity and rationality in an elegant, handy way [20,31,33,34,58]. This is another reason why LP is well suited to implement RV tools, especially under partial observability, and our experience suggests that features like coinduction, meta-reasoning, all-solutions predicates are necessary for development of sophisticated RV engines.

Based on our more than ten years experience in using LP for RV, we believe that RV might become a killer application for LP. The only issue that might affect our forecast is efficiency of logic-based approaches, and a comparison of the efficiency of RML and state of the art RV tools is on its way to explore this possible obstacle. Nevertheless, as stated in the recent paper Fifty Years of Prolog and Beyond [56], *"Prolog is a surprisingly efficient language"*! The authors provide convincing evidences for this claim, including availability of last call optimization, efficient indexing and matching, and fine-tuned memory management with efficient backtracking. As far as our research is concerned, grounding RML and trace expression specifications by exploiting contextual knowledge on the SUS might provide an additional efficiency speed-up, making LP competitive with any other approach.

Developing examples in challenging scenarios would represent a further test of our approach and would make it more understandable also outside the Prolog community. To this aim we will take inspiration by the work by Dal Palù, Dovier, Formisano, and Pontelli for scenarios where the SUS is a model of a biological domain [66], and by the works by Kowalski, Dávila, Sartor and Calejo [57] and Satoh [74] for RV of legal systems.

References

1. Alberti, M., et al.: Expressing and verifying business contracts with abductive logic programming. Int. J. Electron. Commer. **12**(4), 9–38 (2008). https://doi.org/10.2753/JEC1086-4415120401

2. Alberti, M., Chesani, F., Gavanelli, M., Lamma, E., Mello, P., Torroni, P.: Verifiable agent interaction in abductive logic programming: the SCIFF framework. ACM Trans. Comput. Log. **9**(4), 29:1–29:43 (2008). https://doi.org/10.1145/1380572.1380578

3. Alberti, M., Dell'Acqua, P., Pereira, L.M.: Observation strategies for event detection with incidence on runtime verification: theory, algorithms, experimentation. Ann. Math. Artif. Intell. **62**(3–4), 161–186 (2011). https://doi.org/10.1007/s10472-011-9259-5

4. Ancona, D., et al.: Behavioral types in programming languages. Found. Trends Programm. Lang. **3**(2–3), 95–230 (2016)

5. Ancona, D., Briola, D., El Fallah Seghrouchni, A., Mascardi, V., Taillibert, P.: Exploiting Prolog for projecting agent interaction protocols. In: Giordano, L., Gliozzi, V., Pozzato, G.L. (eds.) Proceedings of the 29th Italian Conference on Computational Logic, Torino, Italy, June 16–18, 2014. CEUR Workshop Proceedings, vol. 1195, pp. 30–45. CEUR-WS.org (2014). http://ceur-ws.org/Vol-1195/long2.pdf

6. Ancona, D., Briola, D., Ferrando, A., Mascardi, V.: Global protocols as first class entities for self-adaptive agents. In: Weiss, G., Yolum, P., Bordini, R.H., Elkind, E. (eds.) Proceedings of the 2015 International Conference on Autonomous Agents and Multiagent Systems, AAMAS 2015, Istanbul, Turkey, May 4–8, 2015, pp. 1019–1029. ACM (2015). http://dl.acm.org/citation.cfm?id=2773282

7. Ancona, D., Briola, D., Ferrando, A., Mascardi, V.: Runtime verification of fail-uncontrolled and ambient intelligence systems: a uniform approach. Intelligenza Artificiale **9**(2), 131–148 (2015). https://doi.org/10.3233/IA-150084

8. Ancona, D., Briola, D., Ferrando, A., Mascardi, V.: MAS-DRiVe: a practical approach to decentralized runtime verification of agent interaction protocols. In: Santoro, C., Messina, F., Benedetti, M.D. (eds.) Proceedings of the 17th Workshop "From Objects to Agents" co-located with 18th European Agent Systems Summer School (EASSS 2016), Catania, Italy, July 29–30, 2016. CEUR Workshop Proceedings, vol. 1664, pp. 35–43. CEUR-WS.org (2016). http://ceur-ws.org/Vol-1664/w7.pdf

9. Ancona, D., Drossopoulou, S., Mascardi, V.: Automatic generation of self-monitoring mass from multiparty global session types in jason. In: Baldoni, M., Dennis, L., Mascardi, V., Vasconcelos, W. (eds.) DALT 2012. LNCS (LNAI), vol. 7784, pp. 76–95. Springer, Heidelberg (2013). https://doi.org/10.1007/978-3-642-37890-4_5

10. Ancona, D., Ferrando, A., Mascardi, V.: Comparing trace expressions and linear temporal logic for runtime verification. In: Ábrahám, E., Bonsangue, M., Johnsen, E.B. (eds.) Theory and Practice of Formal Methods. LNCS, vol. 9660, pp. 47–64. Springer, Cham (2016). https://doi.org/10.1007/978-3-319-30734-3_6

11. Ancona, D., Ferrando, A., Mascardi, V.: Parametric runtime verification of multiagent systems. In: Larson, K., Winikoff, M., Das, S., Durfee, E.H. (eds.) Proceedings of the 16th Conference on Autonomous Agents and MultiAgent Systems, AAMAS 2017, São Paulo, Brazil, May 8–12, 2017, pp. 1457–1459. ACM (2017). http://dl.acm.org/citation.cfm?id=3091328

12. Ancona, D., Ferrando, A., Mascardi, V.: Can determinism and compositionality coexist in RML? In: Dardha, O., Rot, J. (eds.) Proceedings Combined 27th International Workshop on Expressiveness in Concurrency and 17th Workshop on Structural Operational Semantics, EXPRESS/SOS 2020, and 17th Workshop on Structural Operational SemanticsOnline, 31 August 2020. EPTCS, vol. 322, pp. 13–32 (2020). https://doi.org/10.4204/EPTCS.322.4

13. Ancona, D., Ferrando, A., Mascardi, V.: Exploiting probabilistic trace expressions for decentralized runtime verification with gaps. In: Calegari, R., Ciatto, G., Omicini, A. (eds.) Proceedings of the 37th Italian Conference on Computational Logic, Bologna, Italy, June 29–July 1, 2022. CEUR Workshop Proceedings, vol. 3204, pp. 154–170. CEUR-WS.org (2022). http://ceur-ws.org/Vol-3204/paper_17.pdf

14. Ancona, D., Ferrando, A., Mascardi, V.: Mind the gap! Runtime verification of partially observable MASs with probabilistic trace expressions. In: Baumeister, D., Rothe, J. (eds.) EUMAS 2022. LNCS, vol. 13442, pp. 22–40. Springer, Cham (2022). https://doi.org/10.1007/978-3-031-20614-6_2

15. Ancona, D., Franceschini, L., Ferrando, A., Mascardi, V.: RML: theory and practice of a domain specific language for runtime verification. Sci. Comput. Program. **205**, 102610 (2021). https://doi.org/10.1016/j.scico.2021.102610

16. Barnett, M., Schulte, W.: Spying on components: a runtime verification technique. In: Workshop on Specification and Verification of Component-Based Systems (2001)

17. Barringer, H., Goldberg, A., Havelund, K., Sen, K.: Rule-based runtime verification. In: Steffen, B., Levi, G. (eds.) VMCAI 2004. LNCS, vol. 2937, pp. 44–57. Springer, Heidelberg (2004). https://doi.org/10.1007/978-3-540-24622-0_5

18. Bodden, E., Chen, F., Rosu, G.: Dependent advice: a general approach to optimizing history-based aspects. In: Sullivan, K.J., Moreira, A., Schwanninger, C., Gray, J. (eds.) Proceedings of the 8th International Conference on Aspect-Oriented Soft-

ware Development, AOSD 2009, Charlottesville, Virginia, USA, March 2–6, 2009, pp. 3–14. ACM (2009). https://doi.org/10.1145/1509239.1509243

19. Bodden, E., Hendren, L.J.: The Clara framework for hybrid typestate analysis. Int. J. Softw. Tools Technol. Transf. **14**(3), 307–326 (2012). https://doi.org/10.1007/s10009-010-0183-5

20. Bozzano, M., Delzanno, G., Martelli, M., Mascardi, V., Zini, F.: Logic programming and multi-agent systems: a synergic combination for applications and semantics. In: Apt, K.R., Marek, V.W., Truszczynski, M., Warren, D.S. (eds.) The Logic Programming Paradigm - A 25-Year Perspective. Artificial Intelligence, pp. 5–32. Springer, Heidelberg (1999). https://doi.org/10.1007/978-3-642-60085-2_1

21. Bragaglia, S., Chesani, F., Mello, P., Montali, M., Torroni, P.: Reactive event calculus for monitoring global computing applications. In: Artikis, A., Craven, R., Kesim Çiçekli, N., Sadighi, B., Stathis, K. (eds.) Logic Programs, Norms and Action. LNCS (LNAI), vol. 7360, pp. 123–146. Springer, Heidelberg (2012). https://doi.org/10.1007/978-3-642-29414-3_8

22. Briola, D., Mascardi, V., Ancona, D.: Distributed runtime verification of JADE and Jason multiagent systems with Prolog. In: Giordano, L., Gliozzi, V., Pozzato, G.L. (eds.) Proceedings of the 29th Italian Conference on Computational Logic, Torino, Italy, June 16–18, 2014. CEUR Workshop Proceedings, vol. 1195, pp. 319–323. CEUR-WS.org (2014). http://ceur-ws.org/Vol-1195/short3.pdf

23. Briola, D., Mascardi, V., Ancona, D.: Distributed runtime verification of JADE multiagent systems. In: Camacho, D., Braubach, L., Venticinque, S., Badica, C. (eds.) Intelligent Distributed Computing VIII. SCI, vol. 570, pp. 81–91. Springer, Cham (2015). https://doi.org/10.1007/978-3-319-10422-5_10

24. Bugiel, S., Davi, L., Dmitrienko, A., Fischer, T., Sadeghi, A., Shastry, B.: Towards taming privilege-escalation attacks on android. In: 19th Annual Network and Distributed System Security Symposium, NDSS 2012, San Diego, California, USA, February 5–8, 2012. The Internet Society (2012). https://www.ndss-symposium.org/ndss2012/towards-taming-privilege-escalation-attacks-android

25. Búr, M., Szilágyi, G., Vörös, A., Varró, D.: Distributed graph queries for runtime monitoring of cyber-physical systems. In: Russo, A., Schürr, A. (eds.) FASE 2018. LNCS, vol. 10802, pp. 111–128. Springer, Cham (2018). https://doi.org/10.1007/978-3-319-89363-1_7

26. Chesani, F., Masellis, R.D., Francescomarino, C.D., Ghidini, C., Mello, P., Montali, M., Tessaris, S.: Abducing workflow traces: a general framework to manage incompleteness in business processes. In: Kaminka, G.A., Fox, M., Bouquet, P., Hüllermeier, E., Dignum, V., Dignum, F., van Harmelen, F. (eds.) ECAI 2016 - 22nd European Conference on Artificial Intelligence, 29 August-2 September 2016, The Hague, The Netherlands - Including Prestigious Applications of Artificial Intelligence (PAIS 2016). Frontiers in Artificial Intelligence and Applications, vol. 285, pp. 1734–1735. IOS Press (2016). https://doi.org/10.3233/978-1-61499-672-9-1734

27. Chesani, F., Mello, P., Montali, M., Torroni, P.: A logic-based, reactive calculus of events. Fundam. Informaticae **105**(1-2), 135–161 (2010). https://doi.org/10.3233/FI-2010-361

28. Chowdhury, O., Jia, L., Garg, D., Datta, A.: Temporal mode-checking for runtime monitoring of privacy policies. In: Biere, A., Bloem, R. (eds.) CAV 2014. LNCS, vol. 8559, pp. 131–149. Springer, Cham (2014). https://doi.org/10.1007/978-3-319-08867-9_9

29. Costantini, S., Dell'Acqua, P., Pereira, L.M., Tsintza, P.: Runtime verification of agent properties. In: Abreu, S., Seipel, D. (eds.) Proceedings of INAP 2009 18thIn-

ternational Conference on Applications of Declarative Programming and Knowledge Management, pp. 257–271 (2009)

30. Costantini, S., Gasperis, G.D.: Runtime self-checking via temporal (meta-)axioms for assurance of logical agent systems. In: Giordano, L., Gliozzi, V., Pozzato, G.L. (eds.) Proceedings of the 29th Italian Conference on Computational Logic, Torino, Italy, June 16–18, 2014. CEUR Workshop Proceedings, vol. 1195, pp. 241–255. CEUR-WS.org (2014). http://ceur-ws.org/Vol-1195/long16.pdf

31. Costantini, S., Tocchio, A.: A logic programming language for multi-agent systems. In: Flesca, S., Greco, S., Ianni, G., Leone, N. (eds.) JELIA 2002. LNCS (LNAI), vol. 2424, pp. 1–13. Springer, Heidelberg (2002). https://doi.org/10.1007/3-540-45757-7_1

32. Dalpiaz, F., Giorgini, P., Mylopoulos, J.: Software self-reconfiguration: a BDI-based approach. In: Sierra, C., Castelfranchi, C., Decker, K.S., Sichman, J.S. (eds.) 8th International Joint Conference on Autonomous Agents and Multiagent Systems (AAMAS 2009), Budapest, Hungary, May 10–15, 2009, vol. 2, pp. 1159–1160. IFAAMAS (2009). https://dl.acm.org/citation.cfm?id=1558189

33. Dell'Acqua, P., Engberg, M., Pereira, L.M.: An architecture for a rational reactive agent. In: Pires, F.M., Abreu, S. (eds.) EPIA 2003. LNCS (LNAI), vol. 2902, pp. 379–393. Springer, Heidelberg (2003). https://doi.org/10.1007/978-3-540-24580-3_44

34. Dell'Acqua, P., Sadri, F., Toni, F.: Combining introspection and communication with rationality and reactivity in agents. In: Dix, J., del Cerro, L.F., Furbach, U. (eds.) JELIA 1998. LNCS (LNAI), vol. 1489, pp. 17–32. Springer, Heidelberg (1998). https://doi.org/10.1007/3-540-49545-2_2

35. Du, X., Liu, Y., Tiu, A.: Trace-length independent runtime monitoring of quantitative policies in LTL. In: Bjørner, N., de Boer, F. (eds.) FM 2015. LNCS, vol. 9109, pp. 231–247. Springer, Cham (2015). https://doi.org/10.1007/978-3-319-19249-9_15

36. Estivill-Castro, V., Hexel, R.: Deterministic high-level executable models allowing efficient runtime verification. In: Pires, L.F., Hammoudi, S., Selic, B. (eds.) MODELSWARD 2017. CCIS, vol. 880, pp. 119–144. Springer, Cham (2018). https://doi.org/10.1007/978-3-319-94764-8_6

37. Ferrando, A.: Automatic partitions extraction to distribute the runtime verification of a global specification. In: Mascardi, V., Torre, I. (eds.) Proceedings of the Doctoral Consortium of AI*IA 2016 co-located with the 15th International Conference of the Italian Association for Artificial Intelligence (AI*IA 2016), Genova, Italy, November 29, 2016. CEUR Workshop Proceedings, vol. 1769, pp. 40–45. CEUR-WS.org (2016). http://ceur-ws.org/Vol-1769/paper07.pdf

38. Ferrando, A.: RIVERtools: an IDE for RuntIme VERification of MASs, and beyond. In: Mascardi, V. (ed.) Proceedings of the Demonstrations Track of PRIMA 2017 co-located with the 20th International Conference on Principles and Practice of Multi-Agent Systems (PRIMA 2017). CEUR Workshop Proceedings, vol. 2056, pp. 13–26. CEUR-WS.org (2017)

39. Ferrando, A., Cardoso, R.C., Fisher, M., Ancona, D., Franceschini, L., Mascardi, V.: ROSMonitoring: a runtime verification framework for ROS. In: Mohammad, A., Dong, X., Russo, M. (eds.) TAROS 2020. LNCS (LNAI), vol. 12228, pp. 387–399. Springer, Cham (2020). https://doi.org/10.1007/978-3-030-63486-5_40

40. Ferrando, A., Dennis, L.A., Ancona, D., Fisher, M., Mascardi, V.: Verifying and validating autonomous systems: towards an integrated approach. In: Colombo, C., Leucker, M. (eds.) RV 2018. LNCS, vol. 11237, pp. 263–281. Springer, Cham (2018). https://doi.org/10.1007/978-3-030-03769-7_15

41. Franceschini, L.: RML: runtime monitoring language: a system-agnostic DSL for runtime verification. In: Marr, S., Cazzola, W. (eds.) Conference Companion of the 3rd International Conference on Art, Science, and Engineering of Programming, Genova, Italy, April 1–4, 2019. pp. 28:1–28:3. ACM (2019). https://doi.org/10.1145/3328433.3328462

42. Fredlund, L.Å., Mariño, J., Pérez, S., Tamarit, S.: Runtime verification in erlang by using contracts. In: Silva, J. (ed.) WFLP 2018. LNCS, vol. 11285, pp. 56–73. Springer, Cham (2019). https://doi.org/10.1007/978-3-030-16202-3_4

43. Fung, T.H., Kowalski, R.A.: The Iff proof procedure for abductive logic programming. J. Log. Program. **33**(2), 151–165 (1997). https://doi.org/10.1016/S0743-1066(97)00026-5

44. Hamlen, K.W., Jones, M.M., Sridhar, M.: Aspect-oriented runtime monitor certification. In: Flanagan, C., König, B. (eds.) TACAS 2012. LNCS, vol. 7214, pp. 126–140. Springer, Heidelberg (2012). https://doi.org/10.1007/978-3-642-28756-5_10

45. Havelund, K.: Rule-based runtime verification revisited. Int. J. Softw. Tools Technol. Transfer **17**(2), 143–170 (2014). https://doi.org/10.1007/s10009-014-0309-2

46. Havelund, K., Reger, G., Roşu, G.: Runtime verification past experiences and future projections. In: Steffen, B., Woeginger, G. (eds.) Computing and Software Science. LNCS, vol. 10000, pp. 532–562. Springer, Cham (2019). https://doi.org/10.1007/978-3-319-91908-9_25

47. Havelund, K., Roşu, G.: Runtime verification - 17 years later. In: Colombo, C., Leucker, M. (eds.) RV 2018. LNCS, vol. 11237, pp. 3–17. Springer, Cham (2018). https://doi.org/10.1007/978-3-030-03769-7_1

48. Howar, F., Giannakopoulou, D., Mues, M., Navas, J.A.: Generating component interfaces by integrating static and symbolic analysis, learning, and runtime monitoring. In: Margaria, T., Steffen, B. (eds.) ISoLA 2018. LNCS, vol. 11245, pp. 120–136. Springer, Cham (2018). https://doi.org/10.1007/978-3-030-03421-4_9

49. Hu, R., Neykova, R., Yoshida, N., Demangeon, R., Honda, K.: Practical interruptible conversations. In: Legay, A., Bensalem, S. (eds.) RV 2013. LNCS, vol. 8174, pp. 130–148. Springer, Heidelberg (2013). https://doi.org/10.1007/978-3-642-40787-1_8

50. Huang, T., Wu, G., Wei, J.: Runtime monitoring composite web services through stateful aspect extension. J. Comput. Sci. Technol. **24**(2), 294–308 (2009). https://doi.org/10.1007/s11390-009-9225-4

51. Inçki, K., Ari, I., Sözer, H.: Runtime verification of IoT systems using complex event processing. In: Fortino, G., et al. (eds.) 14th IEEE International Conference on Networking, Sensing and Control, ICNSC 2017, Calabria, Italy, May 16–18, 2017, pp. 625–630. IEEE (2017). https://doi.org/10.1109/ICNSC.2017.8000163, https://doi.org/10.1109/ICNSC.2017.8000163

52. Indiono, C., Mangler, J., Fdhila, W., Rinderle-Ma, S.: Rule-based runtime monitoring of instance-spanning constraints in process-aware information systems. In: Debruyne, C., Panetto, H., Meersman, R., Dillon, T., Kühn, O'Sullivan, D., Ardagna, C.A. (eds.) OTM 2016. LNCS, vol. 10033, pp. 381–399. Springer, Cham (2016). https://doi.org/10.1007/978-3-319-48472-3_22

53. Kallel, S., Charfi, A., Dinkelaker, T., Mezini, M., Jmaiel, M.: Specifying and monitoring temporal properties in web services compositions. In: Eshuis, R., Grefen, P.W.P.J., Papadopoulos, G.A. (eds.) Seventh IEEE European Conference on Web Services (ECOWS 2009), 9–11 November 2009, Eindhoven, The Netherlands, pp. 148–157. IEEE Computer Society (2009). https://doi.org/10.1109/ECOWS.2009.15

54. Kallel, S., Charfi, A., Mezini, M., Jmaiel, M., Sewe, A.: A holistic approach for access control policies: from formal specification to aspect-based enforcement. Int. J. Inf. Comput. Secur. **3**(3/4), 337–354 (2009). https://doi.org/10.1504/IJICS. 2009.031044

55. Klose, K., Ostermann, K.: A classification framework for pointcut languages in runtime monitoring. In: Oriol, M., Meyer, B. (eds.) TOOLS EUROPE 2009. LNBIP, vol. 33, pp. 289–307. Springer, Heidelberg (2009). https://doi.org/10.1007/978-3-642-02571-6_17

56. Körner, P., et al.: Fifty years of Prolog and beyond. Theory Pract. Log. Program. **22**(6), 776–858 (2022). https://doi.org/10.1017/S1471068422000102

57. Kowalski, R., Quintero, J.D., Sartor, G., Calejo, M.: Logical English for law and education. In: Warren, D.S., Dahl, V., Eiter, T., Hermenegildo, M., Kowalski, R., Rossi, F. (eds.) Prolog - The Next 50 Years. LNCS, vol. 13900, pp. 287–299. Springer, Cham (2023)

58. Kowalski, R., Sadri, F.: Towards a unified agent architecture that combines rationality with reactivity. In: Pedreschi, D., Zaniolo, C. (eds.) LID 1996. LNCS, vol. 1154, pp. 135–149. Springer, Heidelberg (1996). https://doi.org/10.1007/BFb0031739

59. Kowalski, R.A., Sergot, M.J.: A logic-based calculus of events. In: Mani, I., Pustejovsky, J., Gaizauskas, R.J. (eds.) The Language of Time - A Reader, pp. 217–240. Oxford University Press (2005)

60. LeDoux, C.H., Jr., D.S.P.: Saving traces for Ada debugging. In: Barnes, J.G.P., Fisher, G.A. (eds.) Proceedings of the 1985 Annual ACM SIGAda International Conference on Ada, SIGAda 1985, Paris, France, May 14–16, 1985, pp. 97–108. Cambridge University Press (1985). https://doi.org/10.1145/324426.324385

61. Leotta, M., Ancona, D., Franceschini, L., Olianas, D., Ribaudo, M., Ricca, F.: Towards a runtime verification approach for internet of things systems. In: Pautasso, C., Sánchez-Figueroa, F., Systä, K., Murillo Rodríguez, J.M. (eds.) ICWE 2018. LNCS, vol. 11153, pp. 83–96. Springer, Cham (2018). https://doi.org/10.1007/978-3-030-03056-8_8

62. Leotta, M., et al.: Comparing testing and runtime verification of IoT systems: A preliminary evaluation based on a case study. In: Damiani, E., Spanoudakis, G., Maciaszek, L.A. (eds.) Proceedings of the 14th International Conference on Evaluation of Novel Approaches to Software Engineering, ENASE 2019, Heraklion, Crete, Greece, May 4–5, 2019, pp. 434–441. SciTePress (2019). https://doi.org/10.5220/0007745604340441

63. Leucker, M., Schallhart, C.: A brief account of runtime verification. J. Logic Algebraic Programm. **78**(5), 293–303 (2009). https://doi.org/10.1016/j.jlap.2008.08. 004. https://www.sciencedirect.com/science/article/pii/S1567832608000775, the 1st Workshop on Formal Languages and Analysis of Contract-Oriented Software (FLACOS'07)

64. Majma, N., Babamir, S.M., Monadjemi, A.: Runtime Verification of Pacemaker Functionality Using Hierarchical Fuzzy Colored Petri-nets. J. Med. Syst. **41**(2), 1–21 (2016). https://doi.org/10.1007/s10916-016-0664-5

65. Malakuti, S., Bockisch, C., Aksit, M.: Applying the composition filter model for runtime verification of multiple-language software. In: ISSRE 2009, 20th International Symposium on Software Reliability Engineering, Mysuru, Karnataka, India, 16–19 November 2009, pp. 31–40. IEEE Computer Society (2009). https://doi.org/10.1109/ISSRE.2009.12

66. Palù, A.D., Dovier, A., Formisano, A., Pontelli, E.: Prolog meets biology. In: Warren, D.S., Dahl, V., Eiter, T., Hermenegildo, M., Kowalski, R., Rossi, F. (eds.) Prolog - The Next 50 Years. LNCS, vol. 13900, pp. 318–333. Springer, Cham (2023)

67. Perotti, A., Boella, G., Garcez, A.A.: Runtime verification through forward chaining. In: Bartocci, E., Majumdar, R. (eds.) RV 2015. LNCS, vol. 9333, pp. 185–200. Springer, Cham (2015). https://doi.org/10.1007/978-3-319-23820-3_12

68. Perotti, A., d'Avila Garcez, A.S., Boella, G.: Neural networks for runtime verification. In: 2014 International Joint Conference on Neural Networks, IJCNN 2014, Beijing, China, July 6–11, 2014, pp. 2637–2644. IEEE (2014). https://doi.org/10.1109/IJCNN.2014.6889961

69. Pnueli, A.: The temporal logic of programs. In: 18th Annual Symposium on Foundations of Computer Science, Providence, Rhode Island, USA, 31 October - 1 November 1977, pp. 46–57. IEEE Computer Society (1977)

70. Rabiser, R., Guinea, S., Vierhauser, M., Baresi, L., Grünbacher, P.: A comparison framework for runtime monitoring approaches. J. Syst. Softw. **125**, 309–321 (2017). https://doi.org/10.1016/j.jss.2016.12.034

71. Ricca, F., Mascardi, V., Verri, A.: Test'n'Mo: a collaborative platform for human testers and intelligent monitoring agents. In: Ahrendt, W., Ancona, D., Francalanza, A. (eds.) VORTEX 2021: Proceedings of the 5th ACM International Workshop on Verification and mOnitoring at Runtime EXecution, Virtual Event, Denmark, 12 July 2021, pp. 17–21. ACM (2021). https://doi.org/10.1145/3464974.3468446

72. Rosà, A., Zheng, Y., Sun, H., Javed, O., Binder, W.: Adaptable runtime monitoring for the Java virtual machine. In: Margaria, T., Steffen, B. (eds.) ISoLA 2016. LNCS, vol. 9953, pp. 531–546. Springer, Cham (2016). https://doi.org/10.1007/978-3-319-47169-3_42

73. Sánchez, C., et al.: A survey of challenges for runtime verification from advanced application domains (beyond software). Formal Methods Syst. Des. (2), 1–57 (2019). https://doi.org/10.1007/s10703-019-00337-w

74. Satoh, K.: PROLEG: Practical legal reasoning system. In: Warren, D.S., Dahl, V., Eiter, T., Hermenegildo, M., Kowalski, R., Rossi, F. (eds.) Prolog - The Next 50 Years. LNCS, vol. 13900, pp. 277–283. Springer, Cham (2023))

75. Simon, L., Mallya, A., Bansal, A., Gupta, G.: Coinductive logic programming. In: Etalle, S., Truszczyński, M. (eds.) ICLP 2006. LNCS, vol. 4079, pp. 330–345. Springer, Heidelberg (2006). https://doi.org/10.1007/11799573_25

76. Stolz, V., Huch, F.: Runtime verification of concurrent Haskell programs. Electron. Notes Theor. Comput. Sci. **113**, 201–216 (2005). https://doi.org/10.1016/j.entcs.2004.01.026

77. Tsigkritis, T., Spanoudakis, G.: Diagnosing runtime violations of security & dependability properties. In: Proceedings of the Twentieth International Conference on Software Engineering & Knowledge Engineering (SEKE'2008), San Francisco, CA, USA, July 1–3, 2008, pp. 661–666. Knowledge Systems Institute Graduate School (2008)

78. Tsigkritis, T., Spanoudakis, G.: A temporal abductive diagnostic process for runtime properties violations. In: Roth-Berghofer, T., Schulz, S., Leake, D.B., Bahls, D. (eds.) Explanation-aware Computing, Papers from the 2008 ECAI Workshop, Patras, Greece, July 21–22, 2008. University of Patras, pp. 49–60 (2008)

79. Wenger, M., Zoitl, A., Blech, J.O.: Behavioral type-based monitoring for IEC 61499. In: 20th IEEE Conference on Emerging Technologies & Factory Automation, ETFA 2015, Luxembourg, September 8–11, 2015, pp. 1–8. IEEE (2015). https://doi.org/10.1109/ETFA.2015.7301447

80. Wooldridge, M.J., Jennings, N.R.: Intelligent agents: theory and practice. Knowl. Eng. Rev. **10**(2), 115–152 (1995). https://doi.org/10.1017/S0269888900008122

81. Yu, B., Liu, J., Lei, M., Yu, Y., Chen, H.: Parallel runtime verification approach for alternate execution of multiple threads. In: Miao, H., Tian, C., Liu, S., Duan, Z. (eds.) SOFL+MSVL 2019. LNCS, vol. 12028, pp. 99–109. Springer, Cham (2020). https://doi.org/10.1007/978-3-030-41418-4_8

82. Yu, B., Lu, X., Chen, H., Lei, M., Wang, X.: Runtime verification of ethereum smart contracts based on MSVL. In: Xue, J., Nagoya, F., Liu, S., Duan, Z. (eds.) SOFL+MSVL 2020. LNCS, vol. 12723, pp. 142–153. Springer, Cham (2021). https://doi.org/10.1007/978-3-030-77474-5_10

83. Yu, B., Tian, C., Lu, X., Zhang, N., Duan, Z.: A distributed network-based runtime verification of full regular temporal properties. IEEE Trans. Parallel Distributed Syst. **34**(1), 76–91 (2023). https://doi.org/10.1109/TPDS.2022.3215854

84. Zhao, Y., Oberthür, S., Kardos, M., Rammig, F.: Model-based runtime verification framework for self-optimizing systems. Electron. Notes Theor. Comput. Sci. **144**(4), 125–145 (2006). https://doi.org/10.1016/j.entcs.2006.02.008

Prolog Meets Biology

Alessandro Dal Palù[1], Agostino Dovier[2(✉)], Andrea Formisano[2], and Enrico Pontelli[3]

[1] University of Parma, Parma, Italy
alessandro.dalpalu@unipr.it
[2] University of Udine, 33100 Udine, Italy
{agostino.dovier,andrea.formisano}@uniud.it
[3] New Mexico State University, Las Cruces, NM, USA
epontell@nmsu.edu

Abstract. This paper provides an overview of the use of Prolog and its derivatives to sustain research and development in the fields of bioinformatics and computational biology. A number of applications in this domain have been enabled by the declarative nature of Prolog and the combinatorial nature of the underlying problems. The paper provides a summary of some relevant applications as well as potential directions that the Prolog community can continue to pursue in this important domain. The presentation is organized in two parts: *"small,"* which explores studies in biological components and systems, and *"large,"* that discusses the use of Prolog to handle biomedical knowledge and data. A concrete encoding example is presented and the effective implementation in Prolog of a widely used approximated search technique, large neighborhood search, is presented.

1 Introduction

Since their infancy, Logic Programming (LP) and Prolog have shown their suitability to address problems from the domain of modern Biology and the broader realms of medicine and life sciences. This was already evident in the first edition of the ICLP conference in 1982 [43]; R.A. Overbeek offered a tutorial on LP and molecular analysis during JICSLP 1992 [61]. The use of Prolog-style technologies in the domain of Biology has progressively increased over the years, especially thanks to the introduction of extensions like *Constraint Logic Programming (CLP),* which supports a more effective use of mathematical constraints to guide the search process, and *Inductive Logic Programming (ILP),* which supports learning of rules that represent biological systems from observations. The literature that explores the use of LP technologies to guide computational biology tasks is extensive. For a survey of contributions to computational biology using the framework of *Answer Set Programming (ASP),* we refer the interested reader to [17,23]. In the survey [17], in particular, bioinformatics problems are clustered in three main areas: *Genomics* studies (e.g., *Haplotype* inference, *Phylogenetic* inference), *Structural* studies (e.g., problems associated with *Protein* structure prediction), and *Systems* studies (e.g., reasoning about biological networks).

In this complementary paper, we present a review of applications of Prolog in the realm of computational biology and bioinformatics. We use the term *Prolog* as an

D. S. Warren et al. (Eds.): Prolog: The Next 50 Years, LNAI 13900, pp. 318–333, 2023.
https://doi.org/10.1007/978-3-031-35254-6_26

umbrella that covers both the actual Prolog language as well as related frameworks, like CLP, ILP, and Datalog (see also [81]). After a brief review of some of the older contributions (up to 1995) in Sect. 2, the presentation is structured, in broad strokes, along two major lines. Section 3 explores the use of Prolog to investigate biological components and systems, such as molecular analysis or structure prediction, thus dealing with *"small"* parts of nature. Section 4 explores the use of Prolog to handle biomedical knowledge and data, thus dealing with *"large"* amount of data. This paper also reflects the experience gained by organizing thirteen editions (2005–2018) of the Workshop on Constraint-based methods in Bioinformatics, co-located with the International Conference on Logic Programming and the International Conference on Constraint Programming (http://clp.dimi.uniud.it/wcb). We consider the various proposals presented in such workshops using local search for dealing with optimization problems with extensive search spaces; Sect. 5 explores how approximated local search with large neighborhoods can be implemented in Prolog. Some conclusions and future perspectives are presented in Sect. 6.

2 Early Days

Dating back to 1982, in the first edition of ICLP, Jouvert et al. presented a medical decision system, called *SPHINX*, that makes use of knowledge representation of medical facts to implement first-order logical deductions [43]. This initial work was followed by a number of Prolog-based applications devoted to the investigation of different aspects of Biology. One of the first examples of the use of Prolog as a modeling and query language for protein structure data can be found in [76], as an alternative to the relational database exploited in a protein modeling facility developed at the U. K. Scientific Centre. In 1986, Rawlings et al. modelled the super secondary structure of *proteins* using Prolog facts, in order to enable Prolog query-answering processes to identify admissible arrangements of secondary structure components (i.e., its local sub-structures such as α-helices and β-strands) [65]. The problem of determining protein secondary structure from its primary sequence is addressed by Muggleton et al. [56] using Golem, an ILP system capable of producing Prolog rules that describe topological relations among residues. A Prolog-based representation and the inference of topological properties of proteins (e.g., bonds, secondary structures, spatial positions and angles) are described in various works of Saldanha et al; among them, we mention the GENPRO system [68], that generates Prolog rules from protein structure datasets. The approach has been improved in [69,70], where LP is used to describe the secondary structure of amylin using a combination of knowledge sources. In the proposal of Barton et al. [5], Prolog is used to implement a database of protein data and various functionalities to process and analyze information on secondary structure of proteins, including an interface to TOPOL [64], a system, implemented in Prolog, that enables reasoning about protein topology. An elaborated technique, called *analogy by abstraction* and implemented in Prolog, is proposed in [39] to predict the 3D structure of an unknown protein by heuristically transforming a known protein structure. The same authors propose a Prolog implementation of a technique called *inductive prediction by analogy* [40], applied to the function prediction of proteins' structure from aminoacid sequences.

Kemp et al. [46] implemented in Prolog and C a database called P/FDM, used to store protein data and to enable fast prototyping of Prolog applications. In particular, the problem of identification of hydrophobic micro-domains is considered and solved in Prolog thanks to its suitability in handling lists and tree structures. The advantage of exploiting Prolog in P/FDM is also shown in [33,47] by considering the problem of protein structure analysis for the specific case of antibodies.

In the context of the *Human Genome Project*, various applications of deductive databases and Prolog have been developed. The Prolog expert system *ISCN Expert* [13] is designed to allow declarative representation of human chromosomal data and to mechanize reasoning tasks about chromosomal abnormalities. The parallel capabilities of Prolog have been exploited to determine pseudo-knots of DNA sequences [49]. Wong in 1993 used Prolog to model the *Probed Partial Digestion of DNA*, with the goal of finding genomic maps compatible with experimental data [82]. The DNA-ChartParser system uses the Prolog unification mechanism to implement parting of DNA sequences; in particular, [48] dealt with the specific case of E. coli promoters. One of the first uses of Prolog as a high-level language for representing and querying biochemical data is proposed by Kazic in 1994, to circumvent impedance mismatch of other hybrid systems existing at the time of publication [45]. The same ideas are applied to create a declarative system to model and reason about metabolism of E. coli [44]. Several other applications in the early Nineties focused on logic-based representations of genomic information and rules to describe their relationships have appeared in the literature [30,37,77]. The BIOLOG system [50] is a Prolog implementation to automate the analysis of nucleic acid sequences. BIOLOG features include access to databases, querying, sequence alignment and rearrangement, search for homologies, etc. Yoshida et al. developed Lucy [83], a system that takes advantage of Prolog representation, set operations, and recursion, to organize genomic knowledge and enable querying and reasoning on molecular biological data.

3   Going Small: Dealing with Nature Building Blocks

Almost twenty years before the breakthroughs provided by Deep Learning [2], Prolog has been used to solve the protein tertiary structure prediction problem—i.e., predicting the 3D shape of a protein given its primary structure. Even strong approximations of the problem (with simplified lattice and energy models) are NP-complete [14]. However, an approach combining a Prolog modeling of the problem with learning tools to predict selected fragments of the protein (e.g, helices and sheets) and exploiting a statistical energy function to treat the different aminoacids, is able to fold proteins of length greater than 100 in reasonable time [15]. An idea not very different from what current deep learning tools do is used in [16] where, given as input the collection of possible 4-tuples of consecutive aminoacids, a Prolog program reconstructs minimal-energy shapes of the protein by merging consecutive partially overlapping tuples.

A Prolog expert system is part of the FIGENIX platform [32], designed to automate the pipeline of structural and functional annotation, in particular to detect genes and their location in a biological sequence and predicting the proteins that they encode. The 3D genome reconstruction problem is addressed in [51] by combining Prolog and a solver for mixed integer programming. The system GenePath [84] supports the analysis of genetic data, using user pre-defined patterns, to infer potential genetic networks regulating biological processes, in particular the relations connecting mutations and changes in system's behavior. The core of GenePath is implemented in Prolog.

Logic programming has been used in [3] to implement a toolkit aimed at identifying constrained portion of genes by integrating phylogenetic information and multiple sequence alignments. The approach described in [4] solves the problem of identifying *orthologs* (that is, genes across different genomes with the same function), groups of orthologous genes in close proximity, and gene duplication, by means of a Prolog application. Such system implements features such as access to gene-databases, text processing of gene-data, gene alignment, homolog-pair detection, ortholog gene-groups identification, etc.

The reconstruction of metabolic networks in presence of incomplete information is the goal of the system described in [28]. The Prolog implementation combines a declarative representation of data and algorithms for genome sequence analysis, also exploiting metabolic and phylogenetic information, and handling incompleteness and defaults. The reconstruction process can proceed autonomously or in interaction with the user. A declarative approach to the automation of genome analysis is done with the MAGPIE system which relies on SICStus Prolog, a full description of the system can be found in [27]. BioSim [38] is a simulation environment developed in CLP for qualitative reasoning on biological regulatory processes. The detection of causality relations in metabolic networks is the goal of [6] which present a system developed on top of the SICStus Prolog interpreter. In [74] SWI-Prolog is used in combination with R to determine and analyze signaling pathways and to identify markers of drug sensitivity and resistance in a case study concerning breast cancer cells. Problog is used in [29] to automate a model of gene regulatory networks combining declarative representation and probabilistic/statistical inference. The proposed approach to modeling pathways is validated by learning regulatory networks from time-series gene expression data on Saccharomyces cerevisiae.

Extensions of Prolog capable of dealing with probabilistic inference under distribution semantics have been used for biological applications. The framework, combining logic and probability, enables the identification of genes and other motifs, as proposed in [12,54] using the PRISM system [71]. The interpretation of gene networks in [18] is implemented in Problog [26]. The ILP system Progol [55] has been used for learning biological properties [57] and detecting constraint protein structure [78,79]. The system Cplint [66] is used in [75] to analyze evolution of cancer data.

In Systems Biology, logic programming has been used to analyze and simulate biological networks. For instance, the Biochamm system [8], supports the analysis and simulation of Boolean, kinetic, and stochastic models of biochemical systems (see, e.g., its use in [19]). In [25] CLP is used to infer ranges of parameter values from observations and to perform qualitative simulations in molecular networks.

A Glimpse of a Prolog Encoding. We would like to briefly introduce here a simplification of the protein structure prediction problem and show the expressive power of Prolog (with constraints) for its encoding. A protein is a sequence of aminoacids. For the scope of this section we consider aminoacids as basic components (we do not analyze their internal structure; the interested reader is referred, e.g., to [9]). The linear distance between two consecutive aminoacids is assumed to be constant (3.8Å), while the angles between sequences of two and three aminoacids can change and, thus, even with discrete approximations, the protein might take a number of spatial forms, called foldings, of huge size. Two different aminoacids cannot overlap in a folding. There are 20 different kinds of aminoacids; however they can be clustered in two families: h (for hydrophobic) and p (for polar or hydrophilic). h aminoacids tends to stay internally in a folding and to attract each other. In this presentation we use a very simple lattice spatial model where analyzing the possible foldings: the 2D Cartesian plane where the unit is taken as the linear distance between consecutive aminoacids. Angles admitted are $-90°, 0°, +90°$. Two aminoacids are in "contact" if their distance is the lattice unit. The problem is that of predicting the folding (one of them) that maximizes the number of contacts between non consecutive hydrophobic (h) aminoacids.

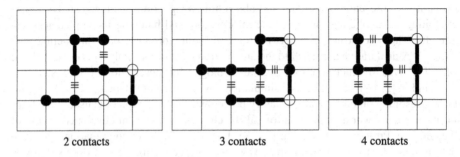

| 2 contacts | 3 contacts | 4 contacts |

Fig. 1. Some foldings of the "protein" $hhphphhhh$ (h/p are represented as ●/○, respectively). Contacts are emphasized using the symbol ≡

Let us see how this problem can be encoded in Prolog. The input is a list `Protein` $= [a_1, \ldots, a_n]$ of constant terms h and p. The output is a list of 2D positions `Folding` $= [X_1, Y_1, \ldots, X_n, Y_n]$ and a variable `Energy` that will store the number of h-h contacts. The length n of the protein is computed from the input list, and the list of $2n$ variables for the folding is generated and the interval $0..2n$ is assigned as domain to them. In order to break symmetries, the first two aminoacids are set in (n, n) and $(n + 1, n)$, respectively. Using the classical constraint & generate programming style of CLP, constraints between the variables, modeling the problem, are added and then the built-in predicate `labeling` that searches for the solutions, with the option of looking for solution(s) maximizing the number of h-h contacts, is called.

```
1  pf(Protein,Folding,Energy) :-
2      length(Protein,N), M is 2*N, length(Folding,M),
3      Folding ins 0..M, N1 is N + 1,
4      Folding = [N,N,N1,N|_],
5      next_constraints(Folding),
6      avoid_self_loops(Folding),
7      contacts(Protein,Folding,Energy),
8      labeling([max(Energy)],Folding).
```

Let us focus on the constraints. We need to constrain consecutive (next) aminoacids to be put at distance 1 in the grid. This is made by the following predicate that implements a for-loop (#= is the equality predicate symbol for numerical terms in CLP)

```
1  next_constraints([_,_]) .
2  next_constraints([X1,Y1,X2,Y2|C]) :-
3       next(X1,Y1,X2,Y2),
4       next_constraints([X2,Y2|C]).
5  next(X1,Y1,X2,Y2):-
6       abs(X1-X2)+ abs(Y1-Y2)  #= 1.
```

To guarantee non overlapping of aminoacids in foldings, we have to impose that different pairs $[X_i, Y_i]$ and $[X_j, Y_j]$ denote different points. This can be forced by saying $X_i \neq X_j \vee Y_i \neq Y_j$. Disjunctions should be avoided in constraint modeling since they introduce an explicit source of non-determinism. Since we know the maximum value for the variables, we can express alternatively the property by saying that $MX_i + Y_i \neq MX_j + Y_j$ where M is a sufficiently big number ($M = 100$ in the following encoding). Then the built-in global constraint all_different forcing the difference of all those terms is exploited.

```
1  avoid_self_loops(Folding)  :-
2       positions_to_integers(Folding, IntList),
3       all_different(IntList).
4  positions_to_integers([],[]).
5  positions_to_integers([X,Y|R],  [I|S]):-
6       I   #= X*100+Y,
7       positions_to_integers(R,S).
```

Finally, we need to express the "energy function" where we count the contacts between pairs of h aminoacids that are at distance 1 in the lattice. The following predicates are the recursive implementation of two nested for-loops. For each pair A, B with $A = 1, \ldots, n - 2$ and $B = A + 2, \ldots, n$ the pairs (XA, YA) and (XB, YB) are considered by the predicate energy: if the aminoacids A and B are both h and their distance is unitary, then the Boolean flag ContactEn is set to 1 else, it is set to 0.

```
1  contacts([_],_,0).
2  contacts([A,B|Protein],[XA,YA,XB,YB|Folding],E)  :-
3       energy_contrib_of_A(A,XA,YA,Protein,Folding,E1),
4       contacts([B|Protein],[XB,YB|Folding],E2),
5       E #= E1 + E2.
6  energy_contrib_of_A(_,_,_,_,[],[],0).
7  energy_contrib_of_A(A,XA,YA,[B|Prot],[XB,YB|Folding],E):-
8       energy(A,XA,YA,B,XB,YB,C),
9       energy_contrib_of_A(A,XA,YA,Prot,Folding,E1),
10      E #= E1 + C.
11 energy(h,XA,YA,h,XB,YB,ContactEn)  :-
12      ContactEn in 0..1,
13      abs(XA - XB)+abs(YA - YB) #= 1   #<==> ContactEn #= 1.
14 energy(_,_,_,p,_,_,0).
15 energy(p,_,_,_,_,_,0).
```

Let us observe that in the arguments of labeling we have imposed to maximize the energy. The presented code runs in SWI Prolog, provided the directive :- use_module(library(clpfd)) that loads the library of the constraint solver for finite domains is added. The solution for the instance in Fig. 1 is found in 0.3s on a common desktop (CPU Intel i7 1.8GHz, Memory 16GB, Windows 10). With minor changes (basically in the syntax of labeling) it runs in B-Prolog and SICStus Prolog.

4   Going Large: Dealing with Biological Databases

Prolog has played a key role in facilitating the development of informatics infrastructures for the management and manipulation of biological data. The rapid growth of computational tools to perform specific steps in biological analyses has raised challenges in the creation of workflows which effectively interoperate such tools to achieve a desired objective. Early work in this direction focused on the challenges derived from the lack of a data format standardization in specific domains of computational biology.

Prolog's definite clause grammars (DCGs) and the ability, with proper care, to derive "reversible" computations, allowed the simple and declarative development of data formats translators. Additionally, the ability to embed computation along with parsing in the DCGs enabled Prolog to handle aspects of data format analysis that are beyond the capabilities of other tools—e.g., dealing with the context-dependent nature of data formats like Nexus [52]. An example of this is represented by the data format translators in phylogenetic inference described in [34], which use a denotational semantics approach to handle complex data formats. Other examples of use of DCGs can be found in [67], which describes a grammar for syntactic recognition of regulatory regions in chromosomes, and in the GenLang system [20], where grammars are applied to the gene structure prediction problem. Prolog is used in [73] to access and query various biological databases and to process retrieved data. The system integrates SWI-Prolog and Java and runs on parallel hardware to efficiently process large amounts of data.

Prolog has provided an effective approach to automate the development of biomedical workflows, as demonstrated for example in the BSIS system [62], which incorporates formal descriptions of biomedical web services and automatically combines them into executable workflows to meet formally specified analysis objectives. Similar studies on the use of Prolog to implement analysis pipelines have been proposed in [1,7]. BSIS makes use of a graphical domain-specific language for the description of partially specified phylogenetic analysis workflows and uses a Prolog planner to complete the workflow and map it to an executable sequence of web service calls. This line of work was expanded with the development of the EvoInfo working group, tasked with the creation of standards for informatics applications in the field of phylogenetic inference.

Various proposals to exploit Prolog in processing phylogenetic data appeared in the literature. We mention here some of the most interesting systems. [59] shows how Datalog can be effectively used to manage the specific tree-shaped structure of data in a phylogenetic database management system, and to process complex phylogenetic queries. PhyloGena [36] is a system for automated phylogenetic processing. The knowledge base of the system is written in Prolog and TUProlog is used as inference engine.

PhyloPattern [31] is a Prolog library, interoperable with Java, implementing function-alities for pattern processing (e.g., representation, recognition, querying) on phyloge-netic tree-shaped structured data. PhyloBase [41,42] defines a data model for phylo-genetic databases and an expressive query language for phylogenetic database, called PhyQL, whose queries are translated into Datalog and executed by a Prolog engine. This stream of works resulted in the creation of a formal ontology for phylogenetic inference (CDAO [63]) and a web services standard (PhyloWS [24]). The primary tools developed to manipulate repositories of CDAO instances have been realized using Pro-log, taking advantage of its database capabilities and the ability to encode ontology's relationships as logical rules, leading to the CDAOStore system [10,11]. CDAOStore also provides the first implementation of the PhyloWS standard, using Prolog to pro-vide manipulation of phylogenetic datasets. These foundations led to a larger effort to promote accessibility and reuse of phylogenetic datasets, captured in the Phylotas-tic project [60], which continues to include several components coded in Prolog and in ASP. The Biological Logic Programming toolkit (Blipkit [58]) is another attempt to data integration and defines a number of Prolog modules implementing various functionali-ties to process gene sequences, RNA structures, evolutionary relationships, phenotypes, biological interactions, etc.

5   Approximate Search in Prolog

In real-life optimization problems, and in biology in particular, the size of the search tree makes any complete search technique practically unfeasible. Therefore a widespread approach is the one of using approximate search techniques, globally referred to as local search, as witnessed by several contributions in the series of workshops WCB (c.f. Sect. 1). These techniques return a "good" solution, the best one found in a given time-out. In this section we show how to implement a very effective technique, Large Neigh-borhood Search (LNS) [72], in Prolog. This was exploited by some Prolog approaches to biology problems (such as [16]) but it can be used for any optimization problem encoded in Prolog.

LNS is a form of local search, where an admissible solution enables the exploration of a "large" neighborhood in the search space. The neighborhood depends on *moves*, that generalize the traditional local search move: here a large number of variables is allowed to change subject to constraints. The basic LNS routine is the following:

1. Generate an initial solution
2. Randomly select a subset of the variables of the problem that will be subject to changes, and maintain previous unifications to the other variables.
3. Look for a new solution that improves the cost function. Go back to step 2.

A timeout mechanism is typically adopted to terminate the cycle between steps 2 and 3. For example, the procedure is terminated if either a general time-out occurs or if k suc-cessive iterations are performed without any improvement in the quality of the solution. In these cases, the best solution found is returned. It is possible to occasionally allow-ing a worsening move—this is important to enable the procedure to abandon a local minimum. This approach is based on programs terminating by timeout, by storing previously found solutions and so on. Since logical variables of Prolog are not suitable for accepting a revised assignment, extra-logical programming Prolog capabilities should be exploited. Specifically, a combination of backtracking, assertions and reassignment procedures are enforced, by using extra-logical features of Prolog to record intermediate solutions in the Prolog database (using the `assert`/`retract` predicates). The loss of declarativity is balanced by enhanced performance in the implementation of LNS.

The main predicate `lns` is defined in three rules. In the first one it launch the main computation after having modeled the problem (in this case by constraining the variables—the reader might consider as an example the simplified protein folding problem as encoded in Sect. 3). It always fail, and the results is given by one of the next rules. Let as assume the our problem has always strictly positive `Cost`, and that we want to minimize this value. After cleaning the facts asserted by previous executions, we assert the initial (out of range) value 0 to two facts, that will store the best solution found so far and the last one. Then, a call of predicate `local` with a `time_out` is made. When the call of the first rule fails (it always fail), the second and, possibly, the third rule will return the best solution.

```
1  lns(+Input, +Time) :-
2      constrain(Input,Solution,Cost),
3      retractall(best(_,_)),        assert(best(_,0)),
4      retractall(last_sol(_,_)), assert(last_sol(null,0)),
5      time_out(local(Input,Solution,Cost), Time,_), fail.
6  lns(_,_) :- best(_,0),
7      write('Insufficient time for the first solution'), nl.
8  lns(_,_) :- best(Solution,Cost), Cost > 0,
9      print_results(Solution,Cost).
```

Let us focus on the rule implementing local search steps. The predicate `local` looks for another solution and loops on that, since `another_sol` always ends with failure. The call with negation does not instantiate the variables (that are however constrained between them by the `lns` definition) and thus a new fresh call is made.

```
1  local(Input, Solution, Cost):-
2      \+ another_sol(Input, Solution, Cost),
3      local(Input, Solution, Cost).
```

Let us focus on the predicate `another_sol` computing the successive solution. The last solution found is retrieved. If it is "null" this means that we have not yet found the first solution and we look for it. If a previous solution exists, we are exactly in the point where we implement LNS. The call to a random generator assigns a random integer, in $[1..10]$, to the variable `Prob` (line 5). Lines 6 and 7 decide the "new" constraint for the variable `Cost`. If `Prob` = 1 (line 6, event with probability 10%) we look for new solutions better than $\frac{5}{6}$ of the last solution found. Thus, we are accepting worsening solutions. This is useful for escaping local minima. If `Prob` > 1 (line 7, event with probability 90%) we look for improving solutions w.r.t. the last solution found.

```
1  another_sol(Input, Solution, Cost) :-
2    last_sol(LastSol, LastCost),
3    (LastSol = null -> labeling(Solution); %%% First sol
4     LastSol \= null ->                    %%% Core of the LNS
5        random(1,11,Prob),               %%% Prob in {1,...,10}
6        (Prob = 1 -> Cost #> 5*LastCost//6;
7         Prob > 1 -> Cost #< LastCost ),
8         large_move(LastSol,Solution),
9         time_out(labeling(Solution), 120000, Flag)),
10   (Flag == success -> true;
11    Flag == time_out -> write('Warning''), nl, fail)),
12    !,
13    retract(last_sol(_,_)),
14    assert(last_sol(Solution,Cost)),
15    best(_,Val),
16    (Val>Energy ->
17       retract(best(_,_)), assert(best(Solution,Cost));
18      true),
19    fail.
```

The predicate large_move (called in line 8) decides randomly which values of the variables of the last solution are maintained in the search and which variables are left unassigned. It is defined simply by a recursion on a list and by a call to random for each variable. If the random value is below a certain threshold k (e.g., 10% as in the example), then the variable is left unbounded and it will be assigned during the new search, otherwise the value from the last solution is assigned to the corresponding variable in the solution list. For instance:

$$\text{LastSol} = [\, 2,\ 34,\ \ 6, 18, 21, 35,\ 31,\ 41, 56, 12, 3,\ \ \ 4,\ \ \ 3, 6, 7, 90\,]$$
$$\text{Solution} = [\, 2,\ X_2, X_3, 18, 21, 35, X_7, X_8, 56, 12, 3, X_{12}, X_{13}, 6, 7, 90\,]$$

Then a new search (with timeout) is invoked (line 9).

The execution of the call of line 9 might end computing a new solution (success) or due a timeout (two minutes in the example). If the timeout is reached (line 11) a message is printed, a failure is forced and a new call to another_sol will be made by local. If the warning is printed many times during the computation, the programmer might consider to change the threshold k.

If a new solution is found (line 10), it is stored (lines 13–14) and, if it is the case, the best solution found so far is updated (lines 16–18).

The rule ends with a forced failure (line 19) that forces local to repeat the call to another_sol for a new attempt. Let us remark that the failure erases any temporary assignments to the variables. The *cut* (!) in line 12 is introduced to avoid the computation of another solution with the same random choices, forcing backtracking to a higher level for the successive new attempt.

SLD and backtracking search or constraint based search implemented by labeling explore the search tree in depth-first search. If the search tree is large and we have a fixed amount of available time, then the search will be limited to a small portion in the left part of the tree. LNS allows us to visit distant subtrees of the search tree. When, by chance, a promising area is found, large moves in that area allow us to improve the computed solution (see e.g., [80]).

6 Conclusions

Prolog has clearly demonstrated over the years its strengths as an ideal paradigm to address a diversity of challenges in bioinformatics. This paper touches on several successful examples of uses of Prolog frameworks in these domains. This line of research is also important as it has led to techniques which have been generalized to other domains—e.g., [16] explored a Prolog implementation of LNS, which has been later applied to totally different contexts (e.g., [53]). The most recent literature in this area has been primarily focused on the use of ASP for modeling a variety of inference problems—surveys can be found in [17,22]. This avails of the clear mathematical properties of ASP to guarantee provable properties of the encodings. Other techniques that have been used and that are close to logic programming are integer linear programming, local search, pseudo Boolean and SAT.

Prolog maintains an important edge for future uses in computational biology, thanks to its ability to interact with numerical constraint solvers for solving complex combinatorial problems arising in biology and with machine learning in inductive logic programming. In particular, a big data analysis based on logic programming might result in a predicted model. This model contains a lot of information that can be analyzed, verified using formal tools developed in the years for logic programming, facilitated by the declarative semantics.

Although for string/substring problems arising in DNA analysis the lack of direct access to vectors is a drawback for pure Prolog, the availability of interfaces with different languages of modern Prolog releases allows the programmers to exploit Prolog as a reasoning for complex distributed and parallel systems (see e.g. [21]). Thus, we share the feeling of Gupta et al. [35] that Prolog and its dialects will maintain their key-role for automated reasoning in the following 50 years.

Acknowledgements. We thank the anonymous reviewers that allowed us to greatly improve the focus and the presentation of the paper. This research is partially supported by INdAM-GNCS projects CUP E55F22000270001 and CUP E53C22001930001, by Interdepartmental Project on AI (Strategic Plan UniUD-22-25), and by NSF grants 2151254 and 1914635.

References

1. Angelopoulos, N., Giamas, G.: Prolog Bioinformatic Pipelines: A Case Study in Gene Dysregulation. In: Workshop on Constraint-Based Methods in Bioinformatics (WCB14). Lyon, France (2014)
2. Baek, M., Baker, D.: Deep learning and protein structure modeling. Nat. Methods **19**, 13–14 (2022)
3. Bansal, A.K.: Establishing a framework for comparative analysis of genome sequences. In: Proceedings of the International IEEE Symposium on Intelligence in Neural and Biological Systems, pp. 84–91 (1995)

4. Bansal, A.K., Bork, P.: Applying logic programming to derive novel functional information of genomes. In: Gupta, G. (ed.) PADL 1999. LNCS, vol. 1551, pp. 275–289. Springer, Heidelberg (1998). https://doi.org/10.1007/3-540-49201-1_19

5. Barton, G.J., Rawlings, C.J.: A Prolog approach to analysing protein structure. Tetrahedron Comput. Methodol. **3**(6 PART C), 739–756 (1990)

6. Bodei, C., Bracciali, A., Chiarugi, D.: On deducing causality in metabolic networks. BMC Bioinform. **9**(S-4) (2008)

7. Burger, A., Davidson, D., Baldock, R.: Formalization of mouse embryo anatomy. Bioinformatics **20**, 259–267 (2004)

8. Calzone, L., Fages, F., Soliman, S.: Biocham: an environment for modeling biological systems and formalizing experimental knowledge. Bioinformatics **22**(14), 1805–1807 (2006)

9. Campeotto, F., Dal Palù, A., Dovier, A., Fioretto, F., Pontelli, E.: A constraint solver for flexible protein model. J. Artif. Intell. Res. (JAIR) **48**, 953–1000 (2013)

10. Chisham, B., Pontelli, E., Son, T., Wright, B.: CDAOStore: a phylogenetic repository using logic programming and web services. In: International Conference on Logic Programming, pp. 209–219 (2011)

11. Chisham, B., Wright, B., Le, T., Son, T., Pontelli, E.: CDAO-Store: Ontology-driven Data Integration for Phylogenetic Analysis. BMC Bioinform. **12**, 98 (2011)

12. Christiansen, H., Have, C.T., Lassen, O.T., Petit, M.: Inference with constrained hidden markov models in PRISM. Theory Pract. Logic Program. **10**(4–6), 449–464 (2010)

13. Cooper, G., Friedman, J.M.: Interpreting chromosomal abnormalities using Prolog. Comput. Biomed. Res. **23**(2), 153–164 (1990)

14. Crescenzi, P., Goldman, D., Papadimitrou, C., Piccolboni, A., Yannakakis, M.: On the complexity of protein folding. In: Proceedings of STOC, pp. 597–603 (1998)

15. Dal Palù, A., Dovier, A., Fogolari, F.: Constraint logic programming approach to protein structure prediction. BMC Bioinform. **5**, 186 (2004)

16. Dal Palù, A., Dovier, A., Fogolari, F., Pontelli, E.: CLP-based protein fragment assembly. Theory Pract. Logic Program. **10**(4–6), 709–724 (2010)

17. Dal Palù, A., Dovier, A., Formisano, A., Pontelli, E.: Exploring life: answer set programming in bioinformatics. In: Kifer, M., Liu, Y.A. (eds.) Declarative Logic Programming: Theory, Systems, and Applications, pp. 359–412. ACM / Morgan & Claypool (2018)

18. De Maeyer, D., Renkens, J., Cloots, L., De Raedt, L., Marchal, K.: PheNetic: network-based interpretation of unstructured gene lists in E. coli. Mol. BioSyst. **9**, 1594–1603 (2013)

19. Degrand, É., Fages, F., Soliman, S.: Graphical conditions for rate independence in chemical reaction networks. In: Abate, A., Petrov, T., Wolf, V. (eds.) CMSB 2020. LNCS, vol. 12314, pp. 61–78. Springer, Cham (2020). https://doi.org/10.1007/978-3-030-60327-4_4

20. Dong, S., Searls, D.B.: Gene structure prediction by linguistic methods. Genomics **23**(3), 540–551 (1994)

21. Dovier, A., Formisano, A., Gupta, G., Hermenegildo, M.V., Pontelli, E., Rocha, R.: Parallel logic programming: a sequel. Theory Pract. Log. Program. **22**(6), 905–973 (2022)

22. Erdem, E.: Applications of answer set programming in phylogenetic systematics. In: Balduccini, M., Son, T.C. (eds.) Logic Programming, Knowledge Representation, and Nonmonotonic Reasoning. LNCS (LNAI), vol. 6565, pp. 415–431. Springer, Heidelberg (2011). https://doi.org/10.1007/978-3-642-20832-4_26

23. Erdem, E., Gelfond, M., Leone, N.: Applications of answer set programming. AI Mag. **37**(3), 53–68 (2016)

24. EvoInfo Working Group: PhyloWS: Phyloinformatics Web Services API. https://evoinfo.nescent.org/PhyloWS (2009)

25. Fanchon, E., Corblin, F., Trilling, L., Hermant, B., Gulino, D.: Modeling the molecular network controlling adhesion between human endothelial cells: inference and simulation using

constraint logic programming. In: Danos, V., Schachter, V. (eds.) CMSB 2004. LNCS, vol. 3082, pp. 104–118. Springer, Heidelberg (2005). https://doi.org/10.1007/978-3-540-25974-9_9

26. Fierens, D., et al.: Inference and learning in probabilistic logic programs using weighted boolean formulas. Theory Pract. Logic Program. **15**(3), 358–401 (2015)

27. Gaasterland, T., Sensen, C.W.: Fully automated genome analysis that reflects user needs and preferences. A detailed introduction to the MAGPIE system architecture. Biochimie **78**(5), 302–310 (1996)

28. Gaasterland, T., Selkov, E.: Reconstruction of metabolic networks using incomplete information. In: Rawlings, C.J., Clark, D.A., Altman, R.B., Hunter, L., Lengauer, T., Wodak, S.J. (eds.) Proceedings of the Third International Conference on Intelligent Systems for Molecular Biology, Cambridge, United Kingdom, 16–19 July 1995, pp. 127–135. AAAI (1995)

29. Gonçalves, A., Ong, I.M., Lewis, J.A., Santos Costa, V.: A Problog model for analyzing gene regulatory networks. In: Riguzzi, F., Zelezný, F. (eds.) Late Breaking Papers of the 22nd International Conference on Inductive Logic Programming, Dubrovnik, Croatia, 17–19 September 2012. CEUR Workshop Proceedings, vol. 975, pp. 38–43. CEUR-WS.org (2012)

30. Goodman, N., Rozen, S., Stein, L.: Requirements for a deductive query language in the mapbase genome-mapping database. In: Ramakrishnan, R. (ed.) Proceedings of the Workshop on Programming with Logic Databases. In Conjunction with ILPS, Vancouver, BC, Canada, October 30, 1993. Technical Report, vol. 1183, pp. 18–32. University of Wisconsin (1993)

31. Gouret, P., Thompson, J.D., Pontarotti, P.: PhyloPattern: regular expressions to identify complex patterns in phylogenetic trees. BMC Bioinformatics **10**, 298 (2009)

32. Gouret, P., Vitiello, V., Balandraud, N., Gilles, A., Pontarotti, P., Danchin, E.G.J.: FIGENIX: intelligent automation of genomic annotation: expertise integration in a new software platform. BMC Bioinform. **6**, 198 (2005)

33. Gray, P.M.D., Paton, N.W., Kemp, G.J.L., Fothergill, J.E.: An object-oriented database for protein structure analysis. Protein Eng. Des. Sel. **3**(4), 235–243 (1990)

34. Gupta, G., et al.: Semantics-based filtering: logic programming's Killer app. In: Krishnamurthi, S., Ramakrishnan, C.R. (eds.) PADL 2002. LNCS, vol. 2257, pp. 82–100. Springer, Heidelberg (2002). https://doi.org/10.1007/3-540-45587-6_7

35. Gupta, G., et al.: Prolog: past, present, and future. In: Warren, D.S., Dahl, V., Eiter, T., Hermenegildo, M., Kowalski, R., Rossi, F. (eds.) Prolog: 50 Years of Future, LNAI 13900, pp. 48–61. Springer, Cham (2023)

36. Hanekamp, K., Bohnebeck, U., Beszteri, B., Valentin, K.: PhyloGena - a user-friendly system for automated phylogenetic annotation of unknown sequences. Bioinformatics **23**(7), 793–801 (2007)

37. Hearne, C., Cui, Z., Parsons, S., Hajnal, S., et al.: Prototyping a genetics deductive database. In: ISMB. vol. 2, pp. 170–178 (1994)

38. Heidtke, K.R., Schulze-Kremer, S.: BioSim: a new qualitative simulation environment for molecular biology. In: Glasgow, J.I., Littlejohn, T.G., Major, F., Lathrop, R.H., Sankoff, D., Sensen, C.W. (eds.) Proceedings of the 6th International Conference on Intelligent Systems for Molecular Biology (ISMB-98), Montréal, Québec, Canada, 28 June - 1 July, 1998. pp. 85–94. AAAI (1998)

39. Ishikawa, T., Terano, T.: Using analogical reasoning to predict a protein structure. Genome Inform. **4**, 339–346 (1993)

40. Ishikawa, T., Terano, T.: How to predict it: inductive prediction by analogy using taxonomic information. In: Proceedings of the Third International Conference on Multistrategy Learning, pp. 285–293. AAAI Press (1996)

41. Jamil, H.M.: A visual interface for querying heterogeneous phylogenetic databases. IEEE ACM Trans. Comput. Biol. Bioinform. **14**(1), 131–144 (2017)

42. Jamil, H.M.: Optimizing phylogenetic queries for performance. IEEE ACM Trans. Comput. Biol. Bioinform. **15**(5), 1692–1705 (2018)
43. Joubert, M., Fieschi, M., Fieschi, D., Roux, M.: Medical decision aid: Logic bases of the system SPHINX. In: Caneghem, M.V. (ed.) Proceedings of the First International Logic Programming Conference, Faculté des Science de Luminy, ADDP-GIA, Marseille, France, September, 14–17, 1982, pp. 210–214. ADDP-GIA (1982)
44. Kazic, T.: Representation, reasoning and the intermediary metabolism of Escherichia coli. In: Proceedings of the Annual Hawaii International Conference on System Sciences, vol. 1, pp. 853–862 (1993)
45. Kazic, T.: Representation of biochemistry for modeling organisms. In: Kumosinski, T.F., Liebman, M.N. (eds.) Molecular Modeling, pp. 486–494. American Chemical Society, Washington, DC (1994)
46. Kemp, G.J.L., Gray, P.M.D.: Finding hydrophobic microdomains using an object-oriented database. Comput. Appl. Biosci. **6**(4), 357–363 (1990)
47. Kemp, G.J.L., Jiao, Z., Gray, P.M.D., Fothergill, J.E.: Combining computation with database access in biomolecular computing. In: Litwin, W., Risch, T. (eds.) ADB 1994. LNCS, vol. 819, pp. 317–335. Springer, Heidelberg (1994). https://doi.org/10.1007/3-540-58183-9_57
48. Leung, S., Mellish, C., Robertson, D.: Basic Gene Grammars and DNA-ChartParser for language processing of Escherichia coli promoter DNA sequences. Bioinform. **17**(3), 226–236 (2001)
49. Lusk, E.L., Overbeek, R.A., Mudambi, S., Szeredi, P.: Applications of the aurora parallel Prolog system to computational molecular biology. In: Workshop on Concurrent and Parallel Implementations (sessions A and B), held at IJCSLP'92, Washington, DC, USA, November 1992 (1992)
50. Lyall, A., Hammond, P., Brough, D., Glover, D.: BIOLOG - a DNA sequence analysis system in Prolog. Nucleic Acids Res. **12**(1), 633–642 (1984)
51. MacKay, K., Carlsson, M., Kusalik, A.: GeneRHi-C: 3D GENomE reconstruction from Hi-C data. In: Proceedings of the 10th International Conference on Computational Systems-Biology and Bioinformatics, CSBIO 2019. ACM (2019)
52. Maddison, D., Swofford, D., Maddison, W.: NEXUS: an extensible file format for systematic information. Syst. Biol. **46**(4), 590–621 (1997)
53. Meneghetti, A.: Exploiting fashion features for floor storage systems in the shoe industry. Int. J. Eng. Bus. Manage. 5, SPL.ISSUE (2013)
54. Mørk, S., Holmes, I.: Evaluating bacterial gene-finding hmm structures as probabilistic logic programs. Bioinformatics **28**(5), 636–642 (2012)
55. Muggleton, S.: Inverse entailment and Progol. N. Gener. Comput. **13**(3–4), 245–286 (1995)
56. Muggleton, S., King, R.D., Sternberg, M.J.E.: Using logic for protein structure prediction. In: Proceedings of the Twenty-Fifth Hawaii International Conference on System Sciences, vol. 1, pp. 685–696 (1992)
57. Muggleton, S., Srinivasan, A., King, R.D., Sternberg, M.J.E.: Biochemical knowledge discovery using inductive logic programming. In: Arikawa, S., Motoda, H. (eds.) DS 1998. LNCS (LNAI), vol. 1532, pp. 326–341. Springer, Heidelberg (1998). https://doi.org/10.1007/3-540-49292-5_29
58. Mungall, C.: Experiences using logic programming in bioinformatics. Lect. Notes Comput. Sci. **5649**, 1–21 (2009)
59. Nakhleh, L., Miranker, D.P., Barbançon, F., Piel, W.H., Donoghue, M.J.: Requirements of phylogenetic databases. In: 3rd IEEE International Symposium on BioInformatics and Bio-Engineering (BIBE) 2003, 10–12 March 2003, Bethesda, MD, USA, pp. 141–148. IEEE Computer Society (2003)

60. Nguyen, T.H., Pontelli, E., Son, T.C.: Phylotastic: an experiment in creating, manipulating, and evolving phylogenetic biology workflows using logic programming. Theory Pract. Logic Program. **18**(3–4), 656–672 (2018)

61. Overbeek, R.A.: Logic programming and genetic sequence analysis: a tutorial. In: Apt, K.R. (ed.) Logic Programming, Proceedings of the Joint International Conference and Symposium on Logic Programming, JICSLP 1992, Washington, DC, USA, November 1992, pp. 32–34. MIT Press (1992)

62. Pan, Y., Pontelli, E., Son, T.: BSIS: an experiment in automating bioinformatics tasks through intelligent workflow construction. In: Chen, H., Wang, Y., Cheung, K.H. (eds.) Semantic e-Science, pp. 189–238. Springer, Cham (2010). https://doi.org/10.1007/978-1-4419-5908-9_6

63. Prosdocimi, F., Chisham, B., Pontelli, E., Thompson, J., Stoltzfus, A.: Initial Implementation of a Comparative Data Analysis Ontology. Evol. Bioinforma. **5**, 47–66 (2009)

64. Rawlings, C.J., Taylor, W.R., Nyakairu, J., Fox, J., Sternberg, M.J.E.: Reasoning about protein topology using the logic programming language Prolog. J. Mol. Graph. **3**(4), 151–157 (1985)

65. Rawlings, C.J., Taylor, W.R., Taylor, W.R., Nyakairu, J., Fox, J., Sternberg, M.J.E.: Using prolog to represent and reason about protein structure. In: Shapiro, E. (ed.) ICLP 1986. LNCS, vol. 225, pp. 536–543. Springer, Heidelberg (1986). https://doi.org/10.1007/3-540-16492-8_101

66. Riguzzi, F., Cota, G., Bellodi, E., Zese, R.: Causal inference in cplint. Int. J. Approx. Reason. **91**, 216–232 (2017)

67. Rosenblueth, D.A., Thieffry, D., Huerta, A.M., Salgado, H., Collado-Vides, J.: Syntactic recognition of regulatory regions in Escherichia coli. Comput. Appl. Biosci. **12**(5), 415–422 (1996)

68. Saldanha, J., Eccles, J.R.: GENPRO: automatic generation of Prolog clause files for knowledge-based systems in the biomedical sciences. Comput. Methods Programs Biomed. **28**(3), 207–214 (1989)

69. Saldanha, J., Eccles, J.R.: The application of SSADM to modelling the logical structure of proteins. Bioinformatics **7**(4), 515–524 (1991)

70. Saldanha, J., Mahadevan, D.: Molecular model-building of amylin and α-calcitonin gene-related polypeptide hormones using a combination of knowledge sources. Protein Eng. Des. Sel. **4**(5), 539–544 (1991)

71. Sato, T.: A statistical learning method for logic programs with distribution semantics. In: Proceedings of the 12th International Conference on Logic Programming (ICLP 95), pp. 715–729 (1995)

72. Shaw, P.: Using constraint programming and local search methods to solve vehicle routing problems. In: Maher, M., Puget, J.-F. (eds.) CP 1998. LNCS, vol. 1520, pp. 417–431. Springer, Heidelberg (1998). https://doi.org/10.1007/3-540-49481-2_30

73. Shu, W., Lan, J.: Design a pathway/genome expert system using a Prolog machine incorporated with a parallel hardware searcher. In: Proceedings of the Asia Pacific Association of Medical Informatics, APAMI, pp. 9–14 (2006)

74. Stebbing, J., et al.: Characterization of the tyrosine kinase-regulated proteome in breast cancer by combined use of RNA interference (rnai) and stable isotope labeling with amino acids in cell culture (silac) quantitative proteomics. Mol. Cell. Proteomics **14**(9), 2479–2492 (2015)

75. Tarzariol, A., Zanazzo, E., Dovier, A., Policriti, A.: Towards a logic programming tool for cancer data analysis. Fundam. Informaticae **176**(3–4), 299–319 (2020)

76. Todd, S., Morffew, A., Burridge, J.: Application of relational database and graphics to the molecular sciences. In: Longstaff, J. (ed.) Proceedings of the Third British National Confer-

ence on Databases (BNCOD) 3, Leeds, UK, July 11–13, 1984, pp. 1–13. Cambridge University Press (1984)

77. Tsur, S., Olken, F., Naor, D.: Deductive databases for genomic mapping (extended abstract). In: Chomicki, J. (ed.) Proceedings of the Workshop on Deductive Databases held in conjunction with the North American Conference on Logic Programming, Austin, Texas, USA, November 1, 1990. Technical Report, vol. TR-CS-90-14. Kansas State University (1990)

78. Turcotte, M., Muggleton, S., Sternberg, M.J.E.: Use of inductive logic programming to learn principles of protein structure. Electron. Trans. Artif. Intell. **4**(B), 119–124 (2000)

79. Turcotte, M., Muggleton, S., Sternberg, M.J.E.: Generating protein three-dimensional fold signatures using inductive logic programming. Comput. Chem. **26**(1), 57–64 (2002)

80. Van Hentenryck, P., Michel, L.: Constraint-Based Local Search. MIT Press, Cambridge (2005)

81. Warren, D.S.: Introduction to Prolog. In: Warren, D.S., Dahl, V., Eiter, T., Hermenegildo, M., Kowalski, R., Rossi, F. (eds.) Prolog: 50 Years of Future, LNAI 13900, pp. 3–19. Springer, Cham (2023)

82. Wong, W.K.C.: Logic programming and deductive databases for genomic computations: A comparison between Prolog and LDL. In: Proceedings of the Annual Hawaii International Conference on System Sciences. vol. 1, pp. 834–843. IEEE Computer Society (1993)

83. Yoshida, K., et al.: Toward a human genome encyclopedia. In: Proceedings of the International Conference on Fifth Generation Computer Systems. FGCS 1992, June 1–5, Tokyo, Japan, pp. 307–320. IOS Press (1992)

84. Zupan, B., et al.: GenePath: a system for automated construction of genetic networks from mutant data. Bioinform. **19**(3), 383–389 (2003)

Prolog in Automated Reasoning
in Geometry

Vesna Marinković[(⊠)] [iD]

Faculty of Mathematics, University of Belgrade, Belgrade, Serbia
vesnap@matf.bg.ac.rs

Abstract. In this paper a brief overview of tools for automated reasoning in geometry developed in Prolog is given. We argue that Prolog is as a good choice for automated reasoning applications and this argument is justified by the example of the tool ArgoTriCS for automated solving of geometry construction problems, developed by the author of the paper. We point out features which made Prolog suitable for development of the tool ArgoTriCS, and illustrate the important aspects of the tool: specification of the underlying knowledge base and the search procedure. The system ArgoTriCS can solve many different triangle construction problems and output formal specification of construction in GCLC language, as well as construction in JSON format which enables generation of dynamic illustrations.

1 Introduction

Over the past several decades, the field of automated reasoning and automated theorem proving has experienced substantial growth, and today many difficult theorems can be proved automatically, without human guidance. Many challenges, however, still remain across the various domains to which it is frequently applied. One such domain is geometry, where automated reasoning is mostly aimed at proving theorems and solving construction problems. There, it finds its applications in mathematical education, both for enriching the teaching process as well as helping students acquiring knowledge on their own, but also in, for example, robot kinematics and computer vision [4].

There are three different approaches to automated theorem proving in geometry: the algebraic approach, based on translating geometry statements into a set of algebraic equations and proving corresponding statements using algebraic techniques [2,22]; the synthetic approach, which tries to automate traditional geometry proofs [5,9]; and the semi-synthetic approach, which involves calculations over some geometric quantities [6]. Algebraic methods are known to be very efficient, but the proofs obtained do not reflect the geometrical nature of the problem being solved and are therefore unsuitable for educational purposes. Synthetic methods, on the other hand, may produce geometry-style, human-readable proofs, even proofs that are similar to proofs made by humans, but

This research is supported by the Serbian Ministry of Education, Science and Technological Development through the University of Belgrade, Faculty of Mathematics (Grant No. 451-03-47/2023-01/s200104).

D. S. Warren et al. (Eds.): Prolog: The Next 50 Years, LNAI 13900, pp. 334–345, 2023.
https://doi.org/10.1007/978-3-031-35254-6_27

are, in general, not very efficient. By using semi-synthetic methods, one does get somewhat readable proofs, but since the proofs are formulated in terms of arithmetic expressions, they are not similar to the ones made by humans.

The goal of this paper is to give a short overview of geometry tools developed in Prolog, with an emphasis on the system ArgoTriCS for automated solving of construction problems, developed by the author.

2 Prolog Tools for Automated Reasoning in Geometry

Ever since its beginnings in the 1970s, Prolog has proved to be convenient for automated reasoning applications for several reasons: it enables rapid system prototyping, which gives the user an opportunity for testing different components of the system in early phases of development; its inference machinery is based on the refinement of the resolution method, known to be well-suited for automation; and it has built-in pattern matching based on unification, facilitating easy drawing of conclusions. In addition, it features rule-based programming, which enables writing code in a form that is more declarative than procedural, and supports automatic backtracking execution, which allows for systematic testing of alternatives. It is, also, suitable for modeling mathematical problems, as well as their structuring in order to solve them more easily [3].

Although automated reasoning in geometry has been actively developing over the past decades and there exists a community actively engaged in automated deduction in geometry[1], there are still not many systems for reasoning in geometry on the whole. The existing ones can be broadly divided into two groups, one focused on theorem proving, and the other on solving construction problems. In the following, we will briefly describe geometry tools developed in Prolog.

Theorem Provers. GEOM [7] is a Prolog program that can solve problems from high-school plane geometry. A problem statement in GEOM contains the hypothesis and the goal of the conjecture being proved, but also optionally a specification of a diagram (in the form of Cartesian coordinates of points appearing in the problem) that illustrates the problem being solved. Providing such a diagram can guide the proving process as well as help it detect counterexamples for pruning unprovable goals. Note that any diagram provided represents just one model, that is, one particular case for which the theorem being proved holds.

QED-Tutrix [8] is an intelligent geometry tutor that helps students prove geometry statements. Its inference engine is implemented in Prolog. The key element of its engine is a graph constructed in a forward-chaining manner [20], developed in Prolog, which contains all possible proofs of the problem being solved.

Geometry theorems can also be proved by theorem provers for first-order logic or its fragments. Coherent logic [1] is a fragment of first-order logic that represents a framework suitable for generation of readable proofs. The first automated

---

[1] There is a conference dedicated to automated deduction in geometry, held every two years: https://adg2023.matf.bg.ac.rs/.

theorem prover based on coherent logic, Euclid [11], was developed in Prolog and its inference system relied on a forward-chaining mechanism. Euclid was able to prove many theorems of lesser difficulty from geometry textbooks.

Geometry Construction Solvers. Progé [18] is a framework implemented in Prolog in which different types of geometry construction problems can be solved automatically. The geometry universe to which the construction problem belongs is specified by the user. In Progé, functional symbols are used to express basic constructions, while relational symbols are used for formulation of constraints that describe the figures. This way, geometric knowledge is described as a set of corresponding axioms.

ArgoTriCS [14, 16] is a system for automated solving of triangle construction problems, and is discussed in more detail in the next section.

3   ArgoTriCS – Automated Triangle Construction Solver

System Description. ArgoTriCS is a system for automated solving of geometry construction problems, primarily used for constructing a triangle given locations of three of its important points listed below and illustrated in Fig. 1 [14]:

- vertices A, B, and C;
- midpoints M_a, M_b, M_c of sides opposite to vertices A, B, and C, respectively;
- feet H_a, H_b, H_c of altitudes from vertices A, B, and C, respectively;
- feet T_a, T_b, T_c of internal angle bisectors at vertices A, B, and C, respectively;
- circumcenter O, centroid G, orthocenter H, and incenter I of a triangle.

These points were considered by Wernick, who listed all 139 non-trivial, significantly different associated problems [21].

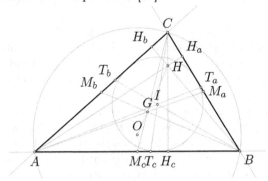

Fig. 1. Important points of a triangle considered by Wernick.

Example 1. Consider the problem to construct triangle ABC, given the locations of its vertex A, the midpoint M_c of its side AB, and the midpoint M_b of its side AC. Since the vertex A is already given, the problem is to construct the other two vertices, B and C. One solution to this problem is straightforward: the vertex B is constructed as a point symmetric to A wrt M_c and, similarly, the vertex C as a point symmetric to A wrt M_b (Fig. 2).

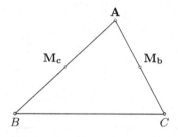

Fig. 2. Construction of triangle ABC given locations of vertex A, and midpoints M_b and M_c of sides AC and AB.

The ArgoTriCS system relies on a geometry knowledge base, identified by a thorough manual analysis of solutions available in the literature, and on a specific, guided search procedure. The system works on fixed set of points, lines, and circles and these are the ones identified as relevant for solving some construction problem. For instance, a line a through points B and C is considered relevant, as it is used for solving many construction problems, however, a line through points T_a and H_c is not considered relevant, since it was not used in solution to any problem. The ArgoTriCS system distinguishes three different pieces of knowledge: definitions, lemmas, and primitive constructions.

Definitions are statements by which objects are uniquely identified, while *lemmas* are additional statements that hold for some set of objects. For instance, the statement that the centroid G of a triangle is an intersection point of its two medians is given as the definition of the point G, while the statement that the centroid of a triangle divides each median in the ratio $2 : 1$ is given as a lemma (Fig. 3). The system supports both instantiated and non-instantiated (i.e. general) definitions and lemmas. For example, as there exist exactly one orthocenter H, one centroid G, and one circumcenter O in any triangle, Euler's theorem, stating that $\overrightarrow{HG} : \overrightarrow{HO} = 2 : 3$, is given as an instantiated lemma, as it holds only for these points. On the other hand, the lemma stating that the center of a circle belongs to the bisector of an arbitrary chord of that circle is applicable to any chord of any circle and is, therefore, general.

Primitive constructions are rules that specify which new objects can be constructed from the already constructed ones: for instance, one can construct a line through any two known points; or one can construct a point symmetric to a known point X with respect to another known point Y.

The points considered by ArgoTriCS do not have fixed coordinates; their positions are instead constrained by definitions and lemmas they are involved in (however, in the associated illustrations in Cartesian plane, all points do get concrete coordinates). While solving a construction problem, one is faced with a huge search space: in each construction step, many different primitive constructions can be applied, possibly in different ways. For instance, in Example 1, instead of constructing a point symmetric to A wrt M_b, one can construct a point symmetric to M_b wrt A or a point symmetric to M_c wrt A, or a line through points M_b and M_c, or a circle centered at A passing through M_b, or a

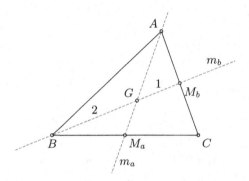

Fig. 3. Centroid of a triangle with its basic properties.

circle over diameter AM_c, or many other objects that are not needed for solving this construction problem (Fig. 4). To achieve a higher level of control over the objects constructed, before the search for a construction begins, general definitions are instantiated by relevant objects and added to the knowledge base. Objects identified as relevant are the ones appearing in some definition or a lemma. Similarly, general lemmas are instantiated by objects that satisfy their hypotheses and their conclusions are added to the knowledge base. However, primitive constructions are kept in non-instantiated form and get instantiated only during the search for the construction (see Example 2, page 8).

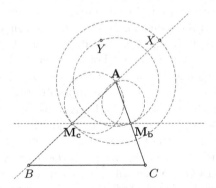

Fig. 4. One can apply many different primitive constructions to the set of known points A, M_b, and M_c, some of them in different ways.

The construction starts from the points given, with the goal of constructing the vertices A, B, and C of a triangle. The search procedure is systematic and iterative: primitive constructions are ordered in a certain way[2] and in each

---

[2] Primitive constructions are ordered so that the ones used more frequently are listed before the ones used rarely. Primitive constructions that are used more often are identified by preliminary experimentation with different possible arrangements on a large corpus of problems and by calculating aggregated statistics on the number of times each one was used.

step ArgoTriCS tries to apply some primitive construction to the objects already constructed or given by the problem specification. If it succeeds, the search for the next applicable primitive construction starts again from the first primitive construction in a waterfall manner. A primitive construction is applicable if we can find an instantiation such that all objects from its hypotheses are already constructed, while the objects from its conclusion are not. Each successful application of a primitive construction produces a new object, which is added to the set of constructed objects maintained during the search. If all three vertices of the triangle are constructed, the search terminates successfully. If at least one vertex of the triangle is not yet constructed and no primitive constructions is applicable, the search terminates unsuccessfully, meaning that this construction problem cannot be solved using identified geometry knowledge. In order to make the search procedure more efficient, additional techniques are employed, such as limiting the objects being constructed to only those appearing in a definition or a lemma involving an object not yet constructed.

Implementation. ArgoTriCS was developed in Prolog[3] and totals around 3500 lines of code, including the specification of the identified knowledge base. Prolog was chosen because of several conveniences, such as straightforward formulation and parsing of definitions, lemmas, and primitive constructions. For instance, the midpoint of an arbitrary segment XY is described by the Prolog term `midpoint([X,Y])`, while the midpoint M_a of the side BC of the triangle is given by `midpoint([b,c])`. Observe the use of variables X and Y in the former and the use of concrete points b and c in the latter.

Objects are defined using a Prolog predicate `def`, which takes three arguments: the object being defined, the list of properties by which it is defined, and its unique label. For instance, the midpoint M_a of a segment BC is defined as a point for which the signed ratio of segments $\overrightarrow{BM_a}/\overrightarrow{BC}$ is equal to $1/2$:

```
def(midpoint([b,c]), [sratio(b,midpoint([b,c]),b,c,1,2)], 'D21').
```

where `sratio` is a relational symbol with six arguments denoting that the signed ratio of the first four (points) is equal to the ratio of the last two (integers). As another example, the median m_a of a triangle ABC at the vertex A, described by the Prolog term `median(a,[b,c])`, is defined as a line incident to the vertex A and the midpoint M_a of the side BC (see Fig. 3):

```
def(median(a,[b,c]), [inc(a,median(a,[b,c])),
                inc(midpoint([b,c],median(a,[b,c])))], 'D17').
```

where `inc` is a relational symbol representing incidence of point to a line.

Instantiated lemmas are given using the predicate `lemma` with two arguments: the statement of a lemma and its label. For instance, the lemma stating that the centroid G of a triangle divides the median m_a in $2 : 3$ ratio (see Fig. 3) is given by the following rule:

---

[3] For our implementation we used SWI-Prolog.

```
lemma(sratio(a,centroid([a,b],c),a,midpoint([b,c]),2,3), 'L55').
```

A predicate for describing primitive constructions is more complex and has seven arguments: the first one is the list of objects given, the second is the list of numbers used by construction[4], the third is the list of objects being constructed, the fourth is the list of the properties that must be satisfied, the fifth specifies the list of non-degeneracy conditions for objects to exist, the sixth the list of determination conditions under which the objects constructed uniquely exist, while the last one is its label. For instance, the construction of a circle C with center O through point A, if points A and O are known, is written like this:

```
cons([obj(point,A), obj(point,O)], [], [obj(circle,C)],
    [center(O,C), inc_circ(A,C)], [not(eq_point(A,O))], [], 'W06').
```

where `inc_circ` is a relational symbol representing incidence of a point to a circle and `center` is a relational symbol stating that a point is a center of a circle.

A simplified version of the Prolog procedure for updating the set of known objects consists of searching for an applicable primitive construction (meaning that all objects from its premises are already constructed, all properties are satisfied by definitions or lemmas, but the object to be constructed is not yet constructed), checking if the object being constructed could be relevant for a construction, extending the set of known objects with newly constructed objects, and adding one more construction step to the construction trace. The inferences performed are limited to ones constructing an object potentially relevant to a construction. Updating the set of known objects terminates once we construct all of the objects sought or when there is no applicable construction.

```
update_known(Known,Unknown,Trace,Trace) :- sublist(Known,Unknown), !.
update_known(Known_old,Unknown,InputTrace,OutputTrace) :-
  cons(Obj_known,Vals,Obj_constr,Props,NDG,DET,RuleId),
  instantiate(Known_old,Obj_known),
  all_defs_or_lemmas(Props,[],Props1),
  relevant_not_constructed_some(Obj_constr,Props,Known_old),
  not_in_list(Obj_constr,Known_old),
  append(Known_old,Obj_constr,Known_new),
  update_known(Known_new,Unknown,
    [(Obj_known,Vals,Obj_constr,Props1,RuleId)|InputTrace],OutputTrace), !.
update_known(_,_,_,_) :- !, write('Construction can not be found'), nl.
```

Advantages of Using Prolog. By using Prolog, we obtain for free the unification and variable instantiation needed for the instantiation of general definitions and lemmas and for the application of primitive construction. Maintaining the partial construction, the set of constructed objects and the knowledge base, is also simple to achieve. Namely, since the number of performed construction steps and the number of constructed objects may vary, partial construction and the set of constructed objects are represented as Prolog lists.

---

[4] As seen for the signed ratio symbol, some symbols require numbers as arguments.

Search tasks, such as the one appearing in the solving of construction problems, are well-handled using Prolog's built-in query-driven search engine. Prolog's automatic backtracking mechanism enables systematic testing of applicability of different primitive constructions to different, already constructed objects. This also makes it easy to obtain all of the solutions to a construction problem.

Output and Evaluation. ArgoTriCS was applied on problems from Wernick's corpus [21], both in the Euclidean and the hyperbolic setting, where it solved 66 out of 74 significantly different solvable problems in the Euclidean case [19], and 39 problems in the hyperbolic setting[5].

The times required to solve the construction problems vary: for most problems from Wernick's corpus it amounted to a couple of milliseconds, but for some problems it took more than an hour. Although only a limited number of objects (potentially relevant for construction) is considered and different techniques that enable early pruning are employed, the search space still remains huge and sometimes the system is not able to give a result in reasonable time.

Found construction traces can be exported to natural language, to a formal description of the construction in the GCLC language [10], and in JSON format that can be used by the ArgoDG library to generate dynamic illustrations [17].

Example 2. Let us consider a construction problem where the task is to construct $\triangle ABC$ given two vertices A and B and its orthocenter H.

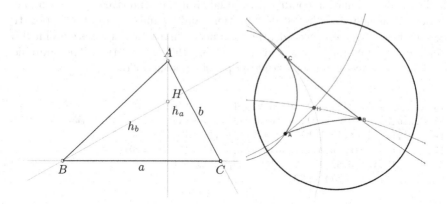

Fig. 5. Construction of $\triangle ABC$ given vertices A and B and orthocenter H, in the Euclidean (left) and the hyperbolic (right) setting.

One of the primitive constructions supported in the system is the construction of a line through two known points:

```
cons([obj(point,P), obj(point,Q)], [], [obj(line,L)],
     [inc(P,L), inc(Q,L)], [], [not(eq_point(P,Q))], 'W02').
```

---

[5] In the case of hyperbolic geometry, there is still no study on how many problems from Wernick's corpus are solvable using a ruler and a compass.

Since there are three known points at the beginning: A, B, and H, three combinations of points are tested for applicability: a line through points A and B, a line through points A and H, and a line through points B and H. Since all three lines considered (line c containing the side AB of a triangle, altitude h_a from vertex A and altitude h_b from vertex B) are the important objects of a triangle, this primitive construction is applicable to all mentioned combinations of points and lines c, h_a and h_b are constructed, respectively. Once we have constructed a line, the primitive construction that constructs a line through a known point perpendicular to some known line is tested for applicability on all possible combinations of known points (A, B, H) and known lines (c, h_a, h_b). However, some lines of this type are not relevant for triangle construction problems, like the line through point H perpendicular to line h_a. The lines constructed are: the line b as a perpendicular to line h_b through point A, the line a as a perpendicular to line h_a through point B, and the line h_c as a perpendicular to line c through point H. At this point, the primitive construction that constructs an intersection point of two lines is tested for applicability and the third vertex C is constructed as an intersection point of lines a and b. At this point the search for a construction terminates, as all three vertices of the triangle are known.

The construction trace automatically generated by ArgoTriCS consists of the steps performed: for each construction step, seven elements are maintained: the list of objects used for performing that step, the list of objects being constructed, the properties that those objects satisfy, the list of non-degeneracy conditions, the list of determination conditions, the label of the primitive construction performed in the step and the list of definitions and lemmas used in the step. If the search for construction succeeds, the obtained construction-trace is simplified by keeping only the steps needed for performing the construction. The simplified construction-trace of this construction problem is the following:

```
[
([A,H],[h_a],[inc(A,h_a),inc(H,h_a)],[],[not(eq_point(A,H))],W02,[D8,D3]),
([B,H],[h_b],[inc(B,h_b),inc(H,h_b)],[],[not(eq_point(B,H))],W02,[D9,D3]),
([A,h_b],[b],[perp(h_b,b),inc(A,b)],[],[],W10,[D9,GD01]),
([B,h_a],[a],[perp(h_a,a),inc(B,a)],[],[],W10,[D8,GD01]),
([a,b],[C],[inc(C,a),inc(C,b)],[not(parall(a,b))],
    [not(eq_line(a,b))],W03,[D8,GD01])
]
```

The above construction trace can be exported to different formats; e.g. construction in natural language, automatically generated by ArgoTriCS, is the following:

1. Construct the line h_a through the points A and H;
2. Construct the line h_b through the points B and H;
3. Construct the perpendicular b to the line h_b through the point A;
4. Construct the perpendicular a to the line h_a through the point B;
5. Construct the intersection point C of the lines a and b.

Figure 5, automatically generated by ArgoTriCS, illustrates the construction in the Euclidean and hyperbolic settings.

The generated construction can be proved correct by proving that if the objects are constructed in this way, then they satisfy the problem specification. In case of the construction considered in Example 2, one should prove that if the triangle ABC is constructed this way, then the initially given point H is indeed its orthocenter. This can be achieved by using OpenGeoProver [12] and provers available within GCLC. Automatically generated compendiums of solutions to problems from Wernick's corpus in Euclidean geometry and hyperbolic geometry are available online [13,15].

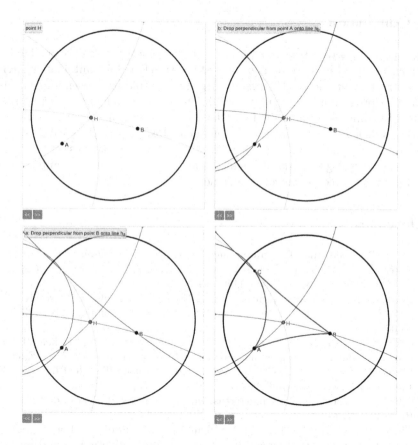

Fig. 6. Dynamic step-by-step illustration of construction of $\triangle ABC$ given two vertices A and B and orthocenter H in hyperbolic setting.

Figure 6 illustrates a dynamic visualisation of the previous construction obtained using ArgoDG library in hyperbolic geometry. The positions of the three given points A, B, and H can be changed and, accordingly, the positions of all other points changes. The construction is performed step-by-step, which makes it suitable for educational purposes.

Currently, ArgoTriCS is being extended with the next-step-guidance feature, which would recommend to the user the next construction step or the objects he/she needs to construct first in order to construct the object required or an important lemma possibly useful for the construction. For instance, if one gets stuck while solving the problem considered in Example 2, the system could suggest to them to construct the altitudes of the triangle first, and then the triangle sides; alternatively, the system could provide the user with lemmas that altitudes are perpendicular to triangle sides.

4 Conclusion

In this paper we gave a brief overview of various geometry tools developed in Prolog and described in more details the system ArgoTriCS for automated solving of construction problems. The system ArgoTriCS could have been implemented in another programming language, but due to many conveniences, such as rapid prototyping and easy maintainability, for us Prolog was an obvious choice.

Despite some beliefs that the golden age of Prolog passed, it still finds various areas of applications. We believe that because of already listed favourable properties of Prolog that makes it suitable for automated reasoning applications, it will keep its place in the years to come.

References

1. Bezem, M., Coquand, T.: Automating coherent logic. In: Sutcliffe, G., Voronkov, A. (eds.) LPAR 2005. LNCS (LNAI), vol. 3835, pp. 246–260. Springer, Heidelberg (2005). https://doi.org/10.1007/11591191_18
2. Buchberger, B.: An algorithm for finding the basis elements of the residue class ring of a zero dimensional polynomial ideal. J. Symb. Comput. **41**(3), 475–511 (2006)
3. Cervoni, L., Brasseur, J., Rohmer, J.: Simultaneously teaching Mathematics and Prolog in School Curricula: a mutual benefit. In: Warren, D.S., Dahl, V., Eiter, T., Hermenegildo, M., Kowalski, R., Rossi, F. (eds.) Prolog - The Next 50 Years. No. 13900. LNCS, Springer (July 2023)
4. Chou, S.C., Gao, X.S.: Automated reasoning in geometry. Handbook of Automated Reasoning 5(1) (2001)
5. Chou, S.C., Gao, X.S., J.Z., Z.: Automated production of traditional proofs for constructive geometry theorems. In: Proceedings of the Eighth Annual IEEE Symposium on Logic in Computer Science LICS, pp. 48–56 (1993)
6. Chou, S.C., Gao, X.S., Zhang, J.Z.: Automated generation of readable proofs with geometric invariants, ii. theorem proving with full-angles. J. Automated Reasoning **17** (1996)
7. Coelho, H., Pereira, L.M.: Automated reasoning in geometry theorem proving with prolog. J. Autom. Reason. **2**, 329–390 (1986)
8. Font, L., Cyr, S., Richard, P., Gagnon, M.: Automating the generation of high school geometry proofs using prolog in an educational context. In: Electronic Proceedings in Theoretical Computer Science, vol. 313, pp. 1–16 (2020)

9. Gelernter, H.: Realization of a geometry-theorem proving machine. Computers & thought, pp. 134–152 (1995)
10. Janičić, P.: Geometry constructions language. J. Autom. Reason. **44**(1–2), 3–24 (2010)
11. Janičić, P., Kordić, S.: Euclid - the geometry theorem prover. FILOMAT **9**(3), 723–732 (1995)
12. Marić, F., Petrović, I., Petrović, D., Janičić, P.: Formalization and implementation of algebraic methods in geometry. In: Proceedings First Workshop on CTP Components for Educational Software. Electronic Proceedings in Theoretical Computer Science, vol. 79, pp. 63–81 (2012)
13. Marinković, V.: Online compendium of problems from Wernick's and Connelly's corpora in Euclidean setting (2015). http://www.matf.bg.ac.rs/~vesnap/animations/compendiums.html
14. Marinković, V.: ArgoTriCS - automated triangle construction solver. J. Exp. Theoretical Artif. Intell. **29**(2), 247–271 (2017)
15. Marinković, V.: Online compendium of problems from Wernick's corpus in hyperbolic setting. http://poincare.matf.bg.ac.rs/~vesnap/animations_hyp/compendium_wernick_hyperbolic.html (2021)
16. Marinković, V., Janičić, P.: Towards understanding triangle construction problems. In: Jeuring, J., Campbell, J.A., Carette, J., Dos Reis, G., Sojka, P., Wenzel, M., Sorge, V. (eds.) CICM 2012. LNCS (LNAI), vol. 7362, pp. 127–142. Springer, Heidelberg (2012). https://doi.org/10.1007/978-3-642-31374-5_9
17. Marinković, V., Šukilović, T., Marić, F.: On automating triangle constructions in absolute and hyperbolic geometry. In: EPTCS 352, Proceedings of the 13th International Conference on Automated Deduction in Geometry, p. 14–26 (2021)
18. Schreck, P.: Constructions à la règle et au compas. Ph.D. thesis, University of Strasbourg (1993)
19. Schreck, P., Mathis, P., Marinković, V., Janičić, P.: Wernick's list: a final update. Forum Geometricorum **16**, 69–80 (2016)
20. Warren, D.S.: Introduction to Prolog. In: Warren, D.S., Dahl, V., Eiter, T., Hermenegildo, M., Kowalski, R., Rossi, F. (eds.) Prolog - The Next 50 Years. No. 13900. LNCS, Springer (July 2023)
21. Wernick, W.: Triangle constructions with three located points. Math. Mag. **55**(4), 227–230 (1982)
22. Wu, W.T.: On the decision problem and the mechanization of theorem-proving in elementary geometry. Sci. Sinica **21**(2), 159–172 (1978)

Logic-Based Explainable and Incremental Machine Learning

Gopal Gupta[⊠], Huaduo Wang, Kinjal Basu, Farhad Shakerin, Elmer Salazar,
Sarat Chandra Varanasi, Parth Padalkar, and Sopam Dasgupta

Department of Computer Science, The University of Texas at Dallas,
Richardson, USA
gupta@utdallas.edu

Abstract. Mainstream machine learning methods lack *interpretability*, *explainability*, *incrementality*, and *data-economy*. We propose using logic programming to rectify these problems. We discuss the FOLD family of rule-based machine learning algorithms that learn models from relational datasets as a set of default rules. These models are competitive with state-of-the-art machine learning systems in terms of accuracy and execution efficiency. We also motivate how logic programming can be useful for *theory revision* and *explanation based learning*.

1 Introduction

Dramatic success of machine learning has led to a plethora of artificial intelligence (AI) applications. The effectiveness of these machine learning systems, however, is limited in several ways:

1. **Lack of Interpretability:** The models learned by machine learning systems are opaque, i.e., they are not comprehensible by humans. This is mainly because these statistical machine learning methods produce models that are complex algebraic solutions to optimization problems such as risk minimization or likelihood maximization.
2. **Lack of Explainability:** These models are unable to produce a justification for a prediction they compute for a new data sample.
3. **Lack of Incrementality:** These methods are unable to incrementally update a learned model as new data is encountered.
4. **Lack of Data Economy:** These methods need large amounts of data to compute a model. Humans, in contrast, are able to learn from a small number of examples.

In this position paper we show that these problems are greatly alleviated if we develop machine learning methods that learn default theories coded in logic programming. The whole field of inductive logic programming (ILP) has been developed in which Horn clauses are learned from background knowledge, positive, and negative examples [7]. Rules with negated goals in the body are also learned in ILP as nonmonotonic logic programs and default rules [10,26]. Representing a

D. S. Warren et al. (Eds.): Prolog: The Next 50 Years, LNAI 13900, pp. 346–358, 2023.
https://doi.org/10.1007/978-3-031-35254-6_28

model as default rules brings significant advantages wrt interpretability, explainability, incremental learning, and data economy. We present LP-based machine learning algorithms that are interpretable and explainable, as well as LP-based reinforcement learning for incremental learning, and LP-based explanation based learning for solving data economy issues.

Default rules are an excellent way of capturing the logic underlying a relational dataset. Defaults are used by humans in their day-to-day reasoning [9, 27]. Most datasets are generated from human-driven activity (e.g., loan approval by bank officials) and our experiments indicate that the rules underlying the model learned from these datasets can be represented quite faithfully and succinctly with default rules. Default rules are used by humans to learn a concept in an elaboration tolerant manner, as they allow humans to constantly adjust the decision boundary. We have developed machine learning algorithms that learn default rules (the *model*) from relational data containing categorical (i.e., discrete) and numerical values that are competitive with state-of-the-art machine learning techniques. These algorithms are *interpretable* and *explainable*.

Once a set of default rules has been learned from data, it is possible that these rules may be wrong (possibly because we over-generalized or under-generalized). When human beings learn from examples (by formulating a rule of thumb in their mind), then when they encounter an example that goes against the learned rule, they revise the rule in light of this new example. For example, suppose we learn the rule that if object X is a fruit, then it goes into the refrigerator. Later, we learn from experience or someone may tell us that pineapples must not go into the refrigerator. In that case, we will revise the rule, changing it to: if X is a fruit, it goes into the refrigerator, except for pineapples. This is a form of *incremental* or reinforcement learning [1]. We will refer it to as logic-based reinforcement learning. Logic-based reinforcement learning can be regarded as theory revision. Logic-based reinforcement learning is elegantly modeled in logic programming using default theories as well.

Traditional machine learning methods need large amounts of data to learn. In contrast, humans can learn from a small number of examples. The problem of learning from a small number of examples has been explored under the topic of explanation-based learning (EBL) [16]. Explanation-based learning can be further developed and applied to practical applications within the framework of logic programming through the use of default theories.

Finally, knowledge expressed as a logic program can be incorporated in the neural learning process. Thus, logic programming can play an important role in neuro-symbolic learning [17, 18, 33]. However, we won't discuss this topic due to lack of space. Logic programming can make a significant difference in this area.

Note that we only give a brief overview of logic-based reinforcement learning and explanation-based learning. These techniques are really important for the field of machine learning, and logic programming can provide excellent solutions. Our hope is that the logic programming community will invest more effort in further developing them.

2   Default Rules

Default Logic [20] is a non-monotonic logic to formalize commonsense reasoning. A default D is an expression of the form

$$\frac{A : \mathbf{M}B}{\Gamma}$$

which states that the conclusion Γ can be inferred if pre-requisite A holds and B is justified. $\mathbf{M}B$ stands for "it is consistent to believe B". If we restrict ourselves to logic programming, then normal logic programs can encode a default theory quite elegantly [12]. A default of the form:

$$\frac{\alpha_1 \wedge \alpha_2 \wedge \cdots \wedge \alpha_n : \mathbf{M}\neg\beta_1, \mathbf{M}\neg\beta_2 \ldots \mathbf{M}\neg\beta_m}{\gamma}$$

can be formalized as the normal logic programming rule:

$$\gamma :\text{-} \alpha_1, \alpha_2, \ldots, \alpha_n, \texttt{not}\ \beta_1, \texttt{not}\ \beta_2, \ldots, \texttt{not}\ \beta_m.$$

where α's and β's are positive predicates and not represents negation-as-failure. We call such rules *default rules*. Thus, the default

$$\frac{bird(X) : M\neg penguin(X)}{fly(X)}$$

will be represented as the following default rule in normal logic programming:
`fly(X) :- bird(X), not penguin(X).`
We call `bird(X)`, the condition that allows us to jump to the default conclusion that X can fly, the *default part* of the rule, and `not penguin(X)` the *exception part* of the rule.

3   Default Rules as Machine Learning Models

Default rules allow knowledge to be modeled in an *elaboration tolerant* manner [12, **baral**]. Default rules are an excellent vehicle for representing inductive generalizations. Humans indeed represent inductive generalizations as default rules [9,27]. Arguably, the sophistication of the human thought process is in large part due to the copious use of default rules [12].

Consider the example about birds above. We observe that bird 1 can fly, bird 2 can fly, bird 3 can fly, and so on. From this we can generalize and learn the default rule that "birds fly." But then we notice that a few of the birds that are penguins, do not fly. So we add an exception to our rule: "birds fly, unless they are penguins". What we are doing is really adjusting our decision boundary, as illustrated in Fig. 1(i) and Fig. 1(ii) (black dots represents normal birds, red dots represent penguins). In logic programming, we can make the exception part of the rule explicit, and code it as:
```
fly(X) :- bird(X), not abnormal_bird(X).
abnormal_bird(X) :- penguin(X).
```

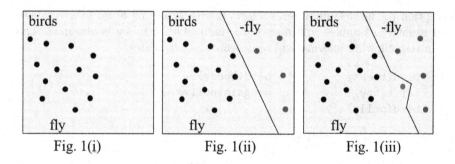

Fig. 1(i)   Fig. 1(ii)   Fig. 1(iii)

Fig. 1. Decision Boundary Refinement

Suppose, we later discover that there is a subclass of penguins (called super-penguins [10]) that can fly. In such a case, we have learned an exception to an exception (See Fig. 1(iii); green dot represents a super-penguin). This will be coded in logic programming as:

```
fly(X) :- bird(X), not abnormal_bird(X).
abnormal_bird(X) :- penguin(X), not abnormal_penguin(X).
abnormal_penguin(X) :- superpenguin(X).
```

Thus, default rules with exceptions, exceptions to exceptions, exceptions to exceptions to exceptions, and so on, allow us to dynamically refine our decision boundary as our knowledge of a concept evolves. This is the insight that the FOLD family of algorithms uses to learn a model underlying a dataset. Figure 1 illustrates the idea.

3.1 FOLD Family of Machine Learning Algorithms

We have developed the FOLD family of algorithms that output a model represented as default rules. Our inspiration is the FOIL algorithm of Quinlan [19]. The FOLD algorithm is a top-down rule-learning algorithm [25]. It starts with the candidate rule

```
p(X,L) :- true.
```

where p(X,L) is the target predicate to learn, and states that record X has the label L (for example, for the Titanic survival dataset, the target predicate will be status(Passenger_Id, S), where S is either survived or perished). It then extends the body with a selected literal (predicate) from among the features so as to cover maximum number of positive examples and avoid covering maximum number of negative examples. The process of selecting a literal to add to the body of the rule relies on heuristics. Traditionally, the Information Gain (IG) heuristic has been used [19,25]. The IG heuristic was pioneered in the FOIL algorithm [19] for learning logic programs and adapted by us for the FOLD algorithm [25] to learn default theories. The FOLD algorithm learns a default theory, so in the next step of learning, it swaps the remaining uncovered positive and negative examples, and recursively applies the literal selection step to learn the exception to the default. Literal selection with swapping of uncovered positive and negative examples continues until reasonable accuracy is obtained. Thus, given the following information, represented as predicates:

```
bird(tweety).          bird(woody).
cat(kitty).            penguin(polly).
bird(polly).
```

and given positive examples:

```
E+: fly(tweety).          fly(woody).
```

and negative examples

```
E-: fly(polly).          fly(kitty).
```

FOLD will learn the default theory:

```
fly(X) :- bird(X), not abnormal(X).
abnormal(X) :- penguin(X).
```

The FOLD algorithm inspired a family of algorithms for learning stratified normal logic programs: LIME-FOLD [23], SHAP-FOLD [24], FOLD-R [22], FOLD-R++ [28], FOLD-RM [31], FOLD-SE [29] and FOLD-TR [30]. Various algorithms in this family differ in the heuristic used for literal selection as well as how efficiently the heuristic is computed. Given a labeled training dataset, these learning algorithms learn a default theory that serves as a model. The default theory is represented as a stratified normal logic program, and hence is *interpretable*. Given a new data record, the model will predict the outcome by executing the logic program. The proof tree generated during execution serves as an *explanation* for the decision reached by the model.

For the FOLD algorithm family, the dataset can have numerical and categorical features, however, the classification label should be categorical. LIME-FOLD is based on using the LIME method [21] for determining the level of contribution of each feature to a prediction [23]. SHAP-FOLD uses Shapley values [15] instead. FOLD-R and FOLD-R++ are binary classifiers that use information gain [19] as the heuristic, where FOLD-R++ uses prefix sums to speed up the computation. FOLD-RM is a multi-class classifier version of FOLD-R++. FOLD-SE is based on a new heuristic called Gini Impurity [14]. This new heuristic leads to a significant reduction in the number of learned default rules and literals. FOLD-SE provides *scalable interpretabilty*, in that the number of default rules learned does not increase with the size of the dataset. The number of rules learned may be as small as 2 for a highly accurate model given datasets of sizes as large as 150,000. FOLD-TR [30] uses the FOLD algorithm to learn to rank.

3.2   Examples and Performance

We next give an example. The Titanic survival prediction is a classical classification challenge, which contains 891 passengers as training examples and 418 passengers as testing examples. The default rule-set learned by our FOLD algorithm is shown below. It captures the underlying logic of the model, namely, that female infant passengers, aged less than 5 in 3rd class who paid fare less than or equal to 10.463 units, perished. Male passengers perished unless they paid a fare in the range 26.25 to 26.387 units inclusive *or* they were younger than 12 with 2 or fewer relatives and were not without parents.

```
status(X,perished) :- class(X,'3'), not sex(X,'male'),
          age(X,N1), N1=<5.0, fare(X,N4), N4=<10.463.
status(X,perished) :- sex(X,'male'), not ab1(X), not ab3(X).
ab1(X) :- fare(X,N4), N4>26.25, N4=<26.387.
ab2(X) :- number_of_parents_children(X,N3), N3=<0.0,
          age(X,N1),N1=<11.0.
ab3(X) :- age(X,N1),N1=<12.0, number_of_siblings_spouses(X,N2),
          N2=<2.0,  not ab2(X).
status(X,survived) :- not status(X,perished).
```

The rules represent a default theory with (nested) exceptions (ab1, ab2, ab3). If a person did not perish, they survived. The model's accuracy is 0.98, precision is 1.0, recall is 0.96, and F1-score is 0.98 [1]. These rules are interpretable by a human.

The learned program can be executed in a Prolog system or an answer set programming system such as s(CASP) [2]. The s(CASP) system can also generate a proof tree that serves as an explanation for a prediction made for a given input. The FOLD-SE system itself also generates an explanation. Explainability is important for understanding the prediction made by a machine learned model. The FOLD family of algorithms are comparable in accuracy to state-of-the-art machine learning systems such as XGBoost [5] and Multi-Layer Perceptrons (MLPs) [1]. XGBoost is a very popular machine learning method based on gradient boosting, while MLPs are neural networks. The FOLD family of algorithms is an order of magnitude faster than XGBoost and MLPs, and, in addition, is explainable. The FOLD family algorithms perform minimal pre-processing of the dataset (no need for one-hot encoding [1], for example). Table 1 shows the performance of FOLD-SE compared to the most prominent rule-based machine learning algorithm called RIPPER [6] on selected datasets (a more extensive comparison can be found elsewhere [29]).

We can see that FOLD-SE outperforms RIPPER on the number of rules generated and execution time. The number of rules may go down from approximately 180 to between 2 and 3 (for rain in Australia dataset, for example). The results reported are an average over 10 runs, so the number of rules reported in the table can be fractional. The scalability of FOLD-SE with respect to interpretability, namely, the number of rules generated is small regardless of the size of the dataset, shows the power of representing inductive generalizations as default rules.

Table 1. Comparison of RIPPER and FOLD-SE on selected Datasets

Data Set			RIPPER					FOLD-SE				
Name	Rows	Cols	Acc	F1	T(ms)	Rules	Preds	Acc	F1	T(ms)	Rules	Preds
acute	120	7	0.93	0.92	95	**2.0**	4.0	**1.0**	**1.0**	**1**	2.0	**3.0**
heart	270	14	0.76	0.77	317	5.4	12.9	0.74	0.77	**13**	4.0	9.1
breast-w	699	10	0.93	0.90	319	14.4	19.9	0.94	0.92	**9**	3.5	6.3
eeg	14980	15	0.55	0.36	12,996	43.4	134.7	0.67	0.68	**1,227**	5.1	12.1
cr. card	30000	24	0.76	0.84	49,940	36.5	150.7	**0.82**	**0.89**	**3,513**	2.0	3.0
adult	32561	15	0.71	0.77	63,480	41.4	168.4	**0.84**	**0.90**	**1,746**	2.0	5.0
rain in aus	145460	24	0.63	0.70	3118,025	180.1	776.4	**0.82**	**0.89**	**10,243**	2.5	6.1

Table 2 compares the performance of FOLD-SE with state-of-the-art machine learning tools XGBoost and Multilayer Perceptrons (MLPs) on training time (in milliseconds). Note that Accuracy and F1-score that are standard metrics [1] are reported. Table dimension is also given (Rows x Columns). The best performer is highlighted in bold. FOLD-SE is comparable in accuracy to widely used machine learning systems such as XGBoost and MLPs, yet it is an order of magnitude faster and is explainable. Thus, the default rule representation of machine learning models is quite effective. Note that the FOLD algorithms have been extensively compared with other ILP methods that learn answer set programs elsewhere [24, 28, 29, 31]. We do not repeat the comparison here due to lack of space. FOLD-SE outperforms Decision Trees [1] in terms of brevity of explanation. For example, for the adult dataset, the tree generated in the Decision Tree method has 4000+ nodes, around half of which are leaf nodes. This translates into 2,000 odd decision rules. Also, the average depth of leaf nodes is 24.7. Therefore, there would be around 50,000 predicates in the decision rule-set. The FOLD-SE algorithm, in contrast, only generates 2 rules with 5 predicates, while achieving greater accuracy.

Table 2. Comparison of XGBoost, MLP, and FOLD-SE

Data Set			XGBoost			MLP			FOLD-SE		
Name	Rows	Cols	Acc	F1	T(ms)	Acc	F1	T(ms)	Acc	F1	T(ms)
acute	120	7	**1.0**	**1.0**	122	0.99	0.99	22	**1.0**	**1.0**	**1**
heart	270	14	**0.82**	**0.83**	247	0.76	0.78	95	0.74	0.77	**13**
breast-w	699	10	0.95	0.96	186	**0.97**	**0.98**	48	0.94	0.92	**9**
eeg	14980	15	0.64	**0.71**	46,472	**0.69**	**0.71**	9,001	0.67	0.68	**1,227**
credit card	30000	24	NA	NA	NA	NA	NA	NA	**0.82**	**0.89**	**3,513**
adult	32561	15	**0.87**	**0.92**	424,686	0.81	0.87	300,380	0.84	0.90	**1,746**
rain in aus	145460	24	**0.84**	**0.90**	385,456	0.81	0.88	243,990	0.82	0.89	**10,243**

Default rules can also be used to make convolutional neural networks (CNNs) explainable as done in the NeSyFOLD system [18], for example (CNNs are neural networks designed for learning from image data).

4   Logic-Based Incremental Learning

The FOLD family of algorithms permits us to learn explainable theories from positive and negative examples. Once a theory is learned, we may encounter further instances (examples) and we may attempt to explain them using this learned theory. If we succeed, our beliefs get stronger, however, if we fail, we update our beliefs to accommodate the new example. For instance, let's say a child drops a glass object on the floor. The object shatters. After a few such mishaps, the child quickly learns the rule "a glass object dropped on the floor will shatter" and will be careful afterwards when holding glass objects. However, later, the child drops another glass object, but the object falls on a soft surface (e.g., carpeted surface), and does not break. The child then updates the prior belief to "a glass object dropped on the floor will shatter, unless the floor is carpeted".

This action/reward-based learning technique of humans closely relates to Reinforcement Learning (RL) [1] in the realm of Machine Learning. In RL, while exploring an environment, an agent gets positive/negative rewards based on its actions. From these rewards, the agent may learn—and subsequently revise—a *policy* to take better actions in its operating environment. The policy can be represented symbolically as a default rule-set, and continuously refined. To achieve this we need a *theory revision framework* that can be applied to default rules. We have developed such an incremental learning framework [4] that we summarize next. This work is distinct from our work on FOLD family of algorithms described earlier. Note that incremental learning is performed by revising the existing theory through the use of the s(CASP) goal-directed answer set programming (ASP) system [2]. With the s(CASP) system, we can obtain a proof tree for any reasoning task performed. This tree can be analyzed and used to update the rules. We illustrate our incremental learning framework through an example.

Consider a house that has sensors installed to protect it from fires and floods. To protect from fire, a fire sensor is installed that will automatically turn on water sprinklers installed in the house if fire is detected. Likewise, a water leak detection sensor in the house will automatically turn off water supply, if water is detected on the floor/carpet and no one is present in the house. The following logic program models these rules:

```
fireDetected :- fire.
turnSprinklerOn :- fireDetected.
sprinklerOn :- turnSprinklerOn.
water :- sprinklerOn.

sprinklerOff :- waterSupplyOff.
```

```
waterSupplyOff :- turnWaterSupplyOff.
turnWaterSupplyOff :- houseEmpty, waterLeakDetected.
waterLeakDetected :- water.

houseFloods :- water, not waterSupplyOff.
houseBurns :- fireDetected, SprinklerOff.
houseSafe :- not houseFloods, not houseBurns.
```

The
program is self-explanatory, and models fluents (sprinklerOn, sprinklerOff, waterLeakDetected, fireDetected, fire, water, houseEmpty) and actuators (turnWaterSupplyOff, turnSprinklerOn). The fluents fire, water, and houseEmpty correspond to sensors. For simplicity, time is not considered. Note that 'fire' means fire broke out in the house and 'water' means that a water leak occurred in the house.

Given the theory above, if we add the fact fire. to it, we will find that the property houseBurns defined above will succeed. This is because the occurrence of fire eventually leads to sprinklers being turned on, which causes water to spill on the floor, which, in turn, causes the flood protection system to turn on, and turn off the water supply. We want houseBurns to fail. To ensure that it fails, we have to recognize that the water supply should be turned off due to a water leak in an empty house *unless* the house is on fire:

```
turnWaterSupplyOff :- houseEmpty, waterLeakDetected,
                      not fireDetected.
```

Therefore, a simple patch to the theory shown above will ensure that houseBurns fails in all situations. By adding *not fireDetected* we are subtracting knowledge preventing houseBurns from succeeding.

Note that to solve the theory revision problem we should be able to analyze the resulting search tree both when a query succeeds or when it fails. The s(CASP) system provides access to the search tree through the justification tree it produces [3]. For a failed query, we obtain the (successful) search tree of the negated query, and analyze its corresponding justification tree. There has been a significant amount of work done on theory revision (or knowledge refinement) in the context of logic [11]. Most of this work assumes that the theory is expressed using Horn clauses. Adding negation-as-failure through answer set programming (along with the ability to obtain proof-trees for queries through s(CASP)) allows for a more powerful theory revision framework [4]. This work is a first step towards building more powerful theory revision frameworks based on using logic programming, specifically, goal-directed answer set programming.

5   Explanation-Based Learning

Machine learning algorithms require large amounts of data to learn a model. Ideally, a small amount of data should be sufficient for learning, including learning or generalizing from just *one example*. In order to do so, however, background (commonsense) knowledge is essential. This aspect is important in machine learning and has been explored under the topic of *explanation-based learning (EBL)*. Logic programming can play an important role in EBL. EBL has been extensively investigated in the past [8,32].

EBL essentially uses prior knowledge to "explain" each training example. An explanation identifies properties that are relevant to a target concept. EBL trades a large number of examples needed in traditional machine learning with background knowledge (called domain theory) for the target concept. The domain theory should be correct (no negative examples entailed), complete (all positive examples are covered), and tractable (each positive example can be explained). It must be noted that EBL has been viewed as a variation of partial evaluation [13]. Traditionally, EBL takes as input a set of training examples, a domain theory expressed using Horn clauses, and operationality criteria that restrict the hypothesis space to a fixed set of predicates, e.g., those needed to directly describe the examples. The goal is to find an efficient definition of the target concept, consistent with both the domain theory and the training examples. Let's consider a very simple example about stacking one object on another. Suppose we have the following specific example involving two objects obj1 and obj2.

```
safeToStack(obj1,obj2).    on(obj1,obj2).     owner(obj1,molly).
type(obj2,endtable).       type(obj1,box).    owner(obj2, john).
fragile(obj2).             color(obj1,red).   color(obj2, blue).
material(obj1,cardboard).  material(obj2, wood).
volume(obj1, 2).           density(obj1, 0.1).
```

and the domain theory explaining why it is safe to stack obj1 on obj2

```
safeToStack(obj1,obj2) :- lighter(obj1,obj2).
lighter(obj1,obj2) :- weight(obj1, W1), weight(obj2,W2), W1 < W2.
weight(X, W) :- volume(X, V), density(X,D),  W =:= V*D.
weight(X,5) :- type(X, endtable).
```

The operational predicates are type, volume, density, on, <, >, =:=. Partially evaluating the predicate call safeToStack(obj1,obj2) against the domain theory while keeping only the operational predicates and generalizing will allow us to learn the general rule:

```
safeToStack(X,Y) :- volume(X,V), density(X,D), WX =:= V*D,
                    type(Y, endtable), WX < 5.
```

Essentially, we have learned a rule that tells us when two objects can be safely stacked, defined in terms of properties of the two objects. While this may appear as simple partial evaluation, more intelligent reasoning can be incorporated by bringing in additional background knowledge. For example, we know that an end-table is similar to a center-table with respect to the stacking property, and so we may further generalize our rule to work for more types of tables. We could generalize it even further to any heavy table-like structure with a flat top, and so on.

EBL can be made more powerful and flexible by representing the domain theory in ASP. For example, constraints can be stated to block simplification along certain evaluation paths during partial evaluation. More general generalizations—represented as default rules—can be made that also account for exceptions. In the example above, while generalizing, we may want to rule out tables that have small-sized surface top, as there is a danger of tipping over upon stacking. We may also want to avoid stacking on tables made of fragile material (another exception). Of course, more knowledge about a table's dimensions, the material it is made of, etc., will have to be added to achieve this. Generalizing to ASP, however, would require developing a partial evaluator for answer set programming under some operational semantics. The s(CASP) system provides one such operational semantics.

6   Conclusion

Default rules are an elegant way to represent knowledge underlying machine learning models. We have developed very efficient machine learning algorithms (e.g., FOLD-SE described above) that are competitive with state-of-the-art methods. Likewise, knowledge represented as default rules can be incrementally updated—via theory revision—as well as generalized/specialized—via explanation-based learning. It is our position that logic-based approaches—centered on representing knowledge as default theories—can lead to the design of machine learning systems that can be competitive with state-of-the-art traditional machine learning systems, while providing advantages of interpretability, explainability, incrementality, and data economy.

Acknowledgements. We are grateful to anonymous reviewers and to Bob Kowalski for insightful comments that helped in significantly improving this paper. Authors acknowledge partial support from NSF grants IIS 1910131, IIP 1916206, and US DoD.

References

1. Aggarwal, C.C.: Neural Networks and Deep Learning - A Textbook. Springer, Cham (2018). https://doi.org/10.1007/978-3-319-94463-0
2. Arias, J., et al.: Constraint answer set programming without grounding. TPLP **18**(3–4), 337–354 (2018)
3. Arias, J., et al.: Justifications for goal-directed constraint answer set programming. In: Proceedings 36th International Conference on Logic Programming (Technical Communications), vol. 325. EPTCS, pp. 59–72 (2020)
4. Basu, K., et al.: Symbolic reinforcement learning framework with incremental learning of rule-based policy. In: Proceedings of ICLP GDE'22 Workshop, vol. 3193. CEUR Workshop Proceedings. CEUR-WS.org (2022)
5. Chen, T., Guestrin, C.: XGBoost: a scalable tree boosting system. In: Proceedings of the 22nd ACM SIGKDD. KDD '16, San Francisco, California, USA, pp. 785–794 (2016). ISBN 978-1-4503-4232-2

6. Cohen, W.W.: Fast effective rule induction. In: Proceedings of ICML, San Francisco, CA, USA, pp. 115–123 (1995)
7. Cropper, A., Dumancic, S.: Inductive logic programming at 30: a new introduction. arXiv:2008.07912 (2020)
8. DeJong, G., Mooney, R.J.: Explanation-based learning: an alternative view. Mach. Learn. **1**(2), 145–176 (1986)
9. Dietz Saldanha, E.A., Hölldobler, S., Pereira, L.M.: Our themes on abduction in human reasoning: a synopsis. In: Abduction in Cognition and Action: Logical Reasoning, Scientific Inquiry, and Social Practice, pp. 279–293 (2021)
10. Dimopoulos, Y., Kakas, A.: Learning non-monotonic logic programs: learning exceptions. In: Lavrac, N., Wrobel, S. (eds.) ECML 1995. LNCS, vol. 912, pp. 122–137. Springer, Heidelberg (1995). https://doi.org/10.1007/3-540-59286-5_53
11. Richards, B.L., Mooney, R.J.: Automated refinement of first-order horn-clause domain theories. Mach. Learn. **19**(2), 95–131 (1995)
12. Gelfond, M., Kahl, Y.: Knowledge Representation, Reasoning, and the Design of Intelligent Agents: the Answer-Set Programming Approach. Cambridge University Press, Cambridge (2014)
13. van Harmelen, F., Bundy, A.: Explanation-based generalisation = partial evaluation. Artif. Intell. **36**(3), 401–412 (1988)
14. Laber, E., Molinaro, M., Pereira, F.M.: Binary partitions with approximate minimum impurity. In: by Dy, J., Krause, A. (eds.) Proceedings of ICML, vol. 80, pp. 2854–2862. Proceedings of Machine Learning Research. PMLR (2018)
15. Lundberg, S.M., Lee, S.-I.: A unified approach to interpreting model predictions. In: Advances in Neural Information Processing Systems, pp. 4765–4774 (2017)
16. Minton, S., et al.: Explanation-based learning: a problem solving perspective. Artif. Intell. **40**(1–3), 63–118 (1989)
17. Mitchener, L., et al.: Detect, understand, act: a neuro-symbolic hierarchical reinforcement learning framework. Mach. Learn. **111**(4), 1523–1549 (2022)
18. Padalkar, P., Wang, H., Gupta, G.: NeSyFOLD: a system for generating logic-based explanations from convolutional neural networks. arXiv:2301.12667 (2023)
19. Quinlan, J.R.: Learning logical definitions from relations. Mach. Learn. **5**, 239–266 (1990)
20. Reiter, R.: A logic for default reasoning. Artif. Intell. **13**(1–2), 81–132 (1980)
21. Ribeiro, M.T., Singh, S., Guestrin, C.: "Why should I trust you?": explaining the predictions of any classifier. In: Proceedings of KDD, pp. 1135–1144. ACM (2016)
22. Shakerin, F.: Logic programming-based approaches in explainable AI and natural language processing. Ph.D. thesis, Department of Computer Science, The University of Texas at Dallas (2020)
23. Shakerin, F., Gupta, G.: Induction of non-monotonic logic programs to explain boosted tree models using LIME. In: Proceeding of AAAI, pp. 3052–3059. AAAI Press (2019)
24. Shakerin, F., Gupta, G.: Induction of non-monotonic rules from statistical learning models using high-utility itemset mining. arXiv:1905.11226 (2019)
25. Shakerin, F., Salazar, E., Gupta, G.: A new algorithm to automate inductive learning of default theories. TPLP **17**(5–6), 1010–1026 (2017)
26. Srinivasan, A., Muggleton, S.H., Bain, M.: Distinguishing exceptions from noise in non-monotonic learning. In: Proceedings of International Workshop on Inductive Logic Programming (1992)
27. Stenning, K., van Lambalgen, M.: Human Reasoning and Cognitive Science. MIT Press, Cambridge (2008)

28. Wang, H., Gupta, G.: FOLD-R++: a scalable toolset for automated inductive learning of default theories from mixed data. In: Hanus, M., Igarashi, A. (eds.) FLOPS 2022. LNCS, vol. 13215, pp. 224–242. Springer, Cham (2022). https://doi.org/10.1007/978-3-030-99461-7_13, isbn: 978-3-030-99460-0
29. Wang, H., Gupta, G.: FOLD-SE: scalable explainable AI (2022)
30. Wang, H., Gupta, G.: FOLD-TR: a scalable and efficient inductive learning algorithm for learning to rank (2022). arXiv: 2206.07295
31. Wang, H., Shakerin, F., Gupta, G.: FOLD-RM: efficient scalable explainable AI. TPLP **22**(5), 658–677 (2022)
32. Wusteman, J.: Explanation-based learning: a survey. Artif. Intell. Rev. **6**(3), 243–262 (1992)
33. Yang, Z., Ishay, A., Lee, J.: NeurASP: embracing neural networks into answer set programming. In: Bessiere, C. (ed.) IJCAI 2020, pp. 1755–1762 (2020)

Reflections on Automation, Learnability and Expressiveness in Logic-Based Programming Languages

Paul Tarau[✉]

University of North Texas, Denton, USA
paul.tarau@unt.edu

Abstract. This position paper sketches an analysis of the essential features that logic-based programming languages will need to embrace to compete in a quickly evolving field where learnability and expressiveness of language constructs, seen as aspects of a learner's user experience, have become dominant decision factors for choosing a programming language or paradigm.

Our analysis centers on the main driving force in the evolution of programming languages: automation of coding tasks, a recurring promise of declarative languages, instrumental for developing software artifacts competitively.

In this context we will focus on taking advantage of the close correspondence between logic-based language constructs and their natural language equivalents, the adoption of language constructs enhancing the expressiveness and learnability of logic-based programming languages and their synergistic uses in interacting declaratively with deep learning frameworks.

Keywords: logic-based programming language constructs ·
automation · expressiveness and learnability · coroutining with logic
engines · definite clause grammars as prompt generators · embedding
of logic programming and in deep learning ecosystems

1 Introduction

Driven by the importance of automation and simplification of coding tasks in a logic programming context, the question we plan to answer is:

What features need to be improved or invented to ensure a lasting ability of logic-based programming languages to compete with languages that have adopted the latest innovations in usability, robustness and easy adoption by newcomers?

Our short answer is that *we need to focus on closeness to natural language, learnability, flexible execution mechanisms and highly expressive language constructs.*

We will elaborate in the next sections on why these features matter, with hints on what language constructs are needed for implementing them.

As an application, we will show the effectiveness of some of our proposed language constructs via definite clause-grammar based prompt generators for today's text-to-text and text-to-image deep learning systems.

2 The Challenges

2.1 It Is Just Automation (Again)

Automation, seen as a replacement of repetitive tasks, has been a persistent theme from which essential computational processes including compilation, partial-evaluation and meta-interpretation have emerged.

Besides competition from today's functional programming languages and proof assistants, all with strong declarative claims, logic-based languages face even stiffer competition from the more radical approach to automation coming from deep learning.

To state it simply, this manifests as replacement of rule-based, symbolic encoding of intelligent behaviors via machine learning, including unsupervised learning among which transformers [11] trained on large language models have achieved outstanding performance in fields ranging from natural language processing to computational chemistry and image processing. For instance, results in natural language processing with prompt-driven generative models like GPT3 [2] or text-to-image generators like DALL.E [7] or Stable Diffusion [12] have outclassed similarly directed symbolic efforts. In fact, it is quite hard to claim that a conventional programming language (including a logic-based one) is as declarative as entering a short prompt sentence describing a picture and getting it back in a few seconds.

We will argue in the next sections that it makes sense for logic-based programming languages to embrace rather than fight these emerging trends.

2.2 The Shifting of the Declarative Umbrella

Logic-based programming languages have shared with their functional counterparts and a few data-base management tools the claim of being "declarative" in the very general sense that the code seen as a specification of *what* needs to be done has clear enough information for the implementation to be able to "automatically" figure out *how* it can be done.

However it is becoming clearer every day that ownership of the declarative umbrella is slowly transitioning to deep neural networks-based machine learning tools that, to state it simply, replace human coding with models directly extracted from labeled and more and more often from raw, unlabeled data. This suggests the usefulness of closely embedding a logic-based language in this fast evolving ecosystem.

2.3   The Importance of Learnability

Learnability is not a crisply definable concept, but it becomes intuitively clear especially as someone gets fluent in several programming languages and paradigms.

Learnability is experienced positively or negatively when teaching or learning a new programming language and also when adopting it as an ideal software development stage for a given project. Good barometers for learnability are the learning curves of newcomers (including children in their early teens), the hurdles they experience and the projects they can achieve in a relatively short period of time. Another one is how well one can pick up the language inductively, simply by looking at coding examples.

When thinking about what background can be assumed in the case of newcomers, irrespectively of age, natural language pops up as a common denominator.

As logic notation originates in natural language there are conspicuous mappings between verbs and predicates and nominal groups as their arguments. Spatial and temporal event streams, in particular visual programming, animations and games relate to logic in more intricate ways and at a more advanced level of mastering a logic-based language.

That hints toward learning methods and language constructs easily mapped syntactically and semantically to natural language equivalents.

2.4   The Importance of Expressiveness

As part of their evolution, programming languages learn from each other. Expressiveness enhancements are contagious. More precisely, language constructs that encapsulate formally clear data objects and their typical usage patterns propagate, often crossing heavily defended programming paradigm border walls.

As Python has been an early adopter of such expressiveness enhancers, it makes sense to consider for adoption some of its language features that one is likely to be impressed even at a first contact, as some of the following:

- ease of defining finite functions (dictionaries, mutable and immutable sequences and sets), all exposed as first class citizens
- aggregation operations (list, set, dictionary comprehensions) exposed with a lightweight and flexible syntax
- coroutining (via the yield statement or async annotations) exposed with a simple and natural syntax
- nested parenthesizing and heavy punctuation avoided or reduced via indentation

Prolog shares some of those but it is usually via separate libraries or semantically more intricate definitions (e.g., setof with care about how variables are quantified as an implementation of set comprehensions). We will explore in the next sections some language constructs covering features where logic-based languages are left behind.

3   A Random Walk in the Space of Solutions

We will next have a glimpse at a "gradient descent" in the space of possible solutions to these challenges with hints about suggested language design and language construct improvements that apply specifically to Prolog and Prolog-like languages and to lesser extent, also to their ASP or Datalog cousins.

3.1   The Testbed: Natlog, a Lightweight Prolog-Dialect Embedded in Python

Our Python-based Natlog system has been originally introduced in [10], to which we refer to for syntax, semantics and low level implementation details. It is currently evolving as a fresh implementation[1], and it will be used as a testbed for the key ideas of this paper.

Prolog's Semantics, but with a Lighter Syntax. While fixing semantics as the usual SLD-resolution, we can keep the syntax and the pragmatics of a logic-based language as close as possible to natural language[2].

We have sketched an attempt to that in the Natlog system's syntax, that we will adopt here. As a hint of its syntactic simplifications, here is a short extract from the usual family program in Natlog syntax:

```
sibling of X S: parent of X P, parent of S P, distinct S X.

grand parent of X GP: parent of X P, parent of P GP.
```

```
ancestor of X A : parent of X  P, parent or ancestor P A.

parent or ancestor P P.
parent or ancestor P A : ancestor of P A.
```

3.2   A Quick Tour of a Few Low-Hanging Expressiveness Lifters

Expressiveness is the relevant distinguishing factor between Turing-complete languages. It can be seen as a pillar of code development automation as clear and compact notation entails that more is delegated to the machine.

A Finite Function API. Finite functions (tuples, lists, dictionaries, sets) are instrumental in getting things done with focus on the problem to solve rather than its representation in the language.

In Natlog they are directly borrowed from Python and in systems like SWI-Prolog dictionaries are a built-in datatype. They can be easily emulated in Prolog but often with a different complexity than if natively implemented.

---

[1] at https://github.com/ptarau/natlog, ready to install with "`pip3 install natlog`".
[2] but *not closer*, as unnecessary verbosity can hinder expressiveness.

In an immutable form as well as enabled with backtrackable and non-backtrackable updates, finite functions implemented as dynamic arrays and hash-maps can offer a less procedural and more expressive alternative to reliance on Prolog's `assert` and `retract` family of built-ins.

Built-Ins as Functions or Generators. Reversible code like in Prolog's classic `append/3` examples or the use of DCGs in both parsing and generation are nice and unique language features derived from the underlying SLD-resolution semantics, but trying to lend reversibility and more generally multi-mode uses to built-ins is often a source of perplexity. Keeping built-ins uniform and predictable, while not giving up on flexibility, can be achieved by restricting them to a few clearly specified uses:

- functions with no meaningful return like `print`, denoted in Natlog by prefixing their Python calls with "#".
- functions of N inputs returning a single output as the last argument of the corresponding predicate with $N+1$ arguments, denoted in Natlog by prefixing their calls with a backquote symbol " ' ". Note that this syntax, more generally, also covers Python's *callables* and in particular class objects acting as instance constructors.
- generators with N inputs yielding a series of output values on backtracking by binding the $N+1$-th argument of the corresponding predicate, denoted in Natlog by prefixing their call with two backquotes " ' ' ".

This simplification (as implemented in Natlog) would also make type checking easier and enable type inference to propagate from the built-ins to predicates sharing their arguments as a convenient mechanism to implement gradual typing.

4   A Step on "The Road Not Taken": First Class Logic Engines

While constraint solvers and related coroutining primitives are present in most widely used logic-based languages, first class logic engines, seen as on-demand reflection of the full execution mechanism, as implemented in BinProlog [9], have been adopted only in SWI Prolog relative recently[3]. Interestingly, similar constructs have been present as far as in [4], where they were efficiently implemented at abstract machine level.

One can think about First Class Logic Engines as a way to ensure the *full meta-level reflection* of the execution algorithm. As a result, they enable on-demand computations in an engine rather than the usual eager execution mechanism of Prolog.

We will spend more time on them as we see them as "the path not taken" that can bring significant expressiveness benefits to logic-based languages, similarly

---

[3] https://www.swi-prolog.org/pldoc/man?section=engines

to the way Python's `yield` primitive supports creation of user-defined generators and other compositional asynchronous programming constructs. To obtain the full reflection of Natlog's multiple-answer generation mechanism, we will make fresh instances of the interpreter first-class objects.

4.1   A First-Class Logic Engines API

A *logic engine* is a Natlog language processor reflected through an API that allows its computations to be controlled interactively from another *logic engine*.

This is very much the same thing as a programmer controlling Prolog's interactive toplevel loop: launch a new goal, ask for a new answer, interpret it, react to it. The exception is that it is not the programmer, but it is the program that does it! We will next summarize the execution mechanism of Natlog's first class logic engines.

The predicate "eng AnswerPattern Goal Engine" creates a new instance of the Natlog interpreter, uniquely identified by `Engine` that shares its code with the currently running program. It is initialized with `Goal` as a starting point. `AnswerPattern` ensures that answers returned by the engine will be instances of the pattern.

The predicate "ask Engine AnswerInstance" tries to harvest the answer computed from `Goal`, as an instance of `AnswerPattern`. If an answer is found, it is returned as (the AnswerInstance), otherwise the atom `no` is returned. It is used to retrieve successive answers generated by an engine, on demand. It is also responsible for actually triggering computations in the engine.

One can see this as transforming Natlog's backtracking over all answers into a deterministic stream of lazily generated answers.

Finally, the predicate "stop Engine" stops the Engine, reclaiming the resources it has used and ensures that `no` is returned for all future queries to the engine.

Natlog's yield operation: a key coroutining primitive Besides these predicates exposing a logic engine as a first class object, the annotation "^Term" extends our coroutining mechanism by allowing answers to be *yielded from arbitrary places* in the computation. It is implemented simply by using Python's `yield` operation. As implemented in Python, engines can be seen as a special case of generators that yield one answer at a time, on demand.

4.2   Things that We Can Do with First Class Logic Engines

We will sketch here a few expressiveness improvements First Class Logic Engines can bring to a logic-based programming language,

Source-Level Emulation of Some Key Built-Ins with Engines. We can emulate at source level some key Prolog built-ins in terms of engine operations, shown here with Natlog's simplified syntax.

```
if_ C Y N : eng C C E, ask E R, stop E, pick_ R C Y N.

pick_ (the C)  C Y _N : call Y.
pick_ no _C _Y N : call N.

not_ G : if_ G (fail) (true).
once_ G : if_ G (true) (fail).

findall_ X G Xs : eng X G E, ask E Y, collect_all_ E Y Xs.

collect_all_ _ no ().
collect_all_ E (the X) (X Xs) : ask E Y, collect_all_ E Y Xs.
```

An Infinite Fibonacci Stream with Yield. Like in a non-strict functional language, one can create an infinite recursive loop from which values are yielded as the computation advances:

```
fibo N Xs : eng X (slide_fibo 1 1) E,  take N E Xs.

slide_fibo X Y :  with X + Y as Z, ^X, slide_fibo Y Z.
```

Note that the infinite loop's results, when seen from the outside, show up as a stream of answers as if produced on backtracking. With help of the library predicate **take**, we extract the first 5 (seen as a Python dictionary with name "X" of the variable as a key and the nested tuple representation of Natlog's list as a value), as follows:

```
?- fibo 5 Xs?
ANSWER: {'Xs': (1, (1, (2, (3, (5, ()))))))}
```

5   Borrowing Some Magic: Logic Grammars as Prompt Generators

With magic wands on a lease from text-to-text generators like GPT3 [2] and text-to-image generators like DALL-E [7] or Stable Diffusion [12] we can introduce Definite Clause Grammars (DCGs) as prompt generators for such systems.

As examples of the natural synergy between declarative constructs of a logic-based language and the declarative features of today's deep learning systems, we will next overview Natlog applications for text-to-text and text-to-image generation. We refer to the Natlog code[4] and its Python companion[5] for full implementation details.

---

[4] see https://github.com/ptarau/natlog/blob/main/apps/natgpt/chat.nat.

[5] see https://github.com/ptarau/natlog/blob/main/apps/natgpt/chat.py.

5.1   Prompt Engineering by Extending GPT3's Text Completion

GPT3 is basically a text completion engine, which, when given an initial segment of a sentence or paragraph as a *prompt*, it will complete it, often with highly coherent and informative results.

Thus, to get from GPT3 the intended output (e.g., answer to a question, elations extracted from a sentence, building analogies, etc.) one needs to rewrite the original input into a prompt that fits GPT3's text completion model.

We will use here Natlog's syntactically lighter Definite Clause Grammars, with one or more terminal symbols prefixed by "@" and "=>" replacing Prolog's "-->". A prompt generator with ability to be specialized for several "kinds" of prompts is described by the DCG rule:

```
prompt Kind QuestText => prefix Kind, sent QuestText, suffix Kind.
```

The predicate **sent** takes a question sentence originating from a user's input and maps it into a DCG non-terminal transforming cons-list Ws1 into cons-list Ws2:

```
sent QuestText Ws1 Ws2 :
   `split QuestText List, to_cons_list List Ws, append Ws Ws2 Ws1.
```

The predicate **query** takes the DCG-generated **prompt** derived from user question Q and converts it back to a string passed to GPT'3 completion API by a call to the function **complete**, implemented in Python, with its answer returned in variable A.

```
query Kind Q A:
   prompt Kind Q Ps (), to_list Ps List, `join List P, `complete P A.
```

Next we will describe specializations to question/answering, relation extraction and analogy invention. An easy way to transform a question answering task into a completion task is to emulate a hypothetical conversation:

```
prefix question =>   @ 'If' you would ask me.
suffix question =>   @ 'I' would say that.
```

Extraction of subject-verb-object phrases can be mapped to completion tasks as in:

```
prefix relation =>  @ 'If' you would ask me what are the subject
                        and the verb and the object in .
suffix relation =>
   @  'I' would say subject is.
```

For analogy invention we will need to create a custom trigger as follows:

```
trigger X Y Z =>
   @ given that X relates to Y by analogy
     'I' would briefly say that Z relates to.

analogy X Y Z A:
   trigger X Y Z Ps (), to_list Ps List, `join List P, `complete P A.
```

We will next show interaction examples for all these use cases. First, question answering:

```
?- query question 'why is logic programming declarative' R?
ANSWER: {'R': 'logic programming is declarative because it expresses the
logic of a problem without describing its control flow. This means that
the programmer does not need to specify the order in which the operations
should  be performed, as the logic programming language will determine
the most efficient way to solve the problem.'}
```

Next, relation extraction. Note that after some preprocessing, the extracted triplets can be used as building blocks for knowledge graphs.

```
?- query relation 'the quick brown fox jumps over the lazy dog' R?
ANSWER: {'R':'"quick brown fox",verb is "jumps" and object is "lazy dog"'}
```

Finally, some examples of analogical reasoning that show GPT3 finding the missing component and explaining its reasoning.

```
?- analogy car wheel bird A?
ANSWER: {'A': 'wing by analogy. This is because both car and wheel
are used for  transportation, while bird and wing are used for flight.'}

?- analogy car driver airplane A?
ANSWER: {'A': 'pilot by analogy. The pilot is responsible for the safe
operation  of the airplane, just as the driver is responsible for the
safe operation of the car.'}
```

5.2   Text-to-Image with DALL.E

To declaratively specify the content of an image to DALL.E [7] or Stable Diffusion [12], Natlog's Definite Clause Grammars work as easy to customize prompt generators for such systems.

As the same OpenAI API (with a slightly different Python call) can be used for text-to-image generation (followed by displaying the generate picture in the user's default browser), the interaction with Python is expressed succinctly by the predicate **paint** that receives as **Prompt** the description of the intended picture from the user.

```
paint Prompt: `paint Prompt URL, #print URL, #browse URL.
```

The query to visualize in the user's browser such a DCG-generated prompts is:

```
?- paint '<text description of intended image>'.
```

with an example of output shown in Fig. 1

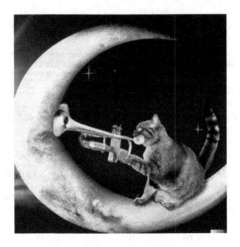

Fig. 1. paint 'photo of a cat playing on the shiny moon with a trumpet'.

The Natlog DCG, in generation mode, will iterate over possible styles and content elements of a desired painting as in the following example:

```
image => style, subject, verb, object.

style => @photorealistic rendering.
style => @a dreamy 'Marc' 'Chagall' style picture.
style => @an action video game graphics style image.

subject => @of, adjective, noun.
noun => @robot.
adjective => @shiny.
verb => @walking.
object => location, @with,  instrument.
location => @on planet 'Mars'.

instrument => @high hills and a blue purse.
instrument => @a sombrero hat.
```

This generates text ready to be passed via the OpenAI Python APIs to DALL.E:

```
?- image Words (), `to_tuple Words Ws, #writeln Ws, nl, fail.
photorealistic rendering of shiny robot walking on planet Mars
  with high hills and a blue purse
photorealistic rendering of shiny robot walking on planet Mars
  with a sombrero hat
. . . . .
```

Besides the expected dependence on the `style` component (photorealistic vs. Chagall-style), as an illustration of GPT3's stereotyping bias, female and respectively male features would be derived from the generated robot pictures depending on the `purse` vs. `sombrero hat` picked by the DCG, as can be seen in the generated images[6].

6 Related Work

An introduction to Natlog, its initial proof-of-concept implementation and its content-driven indexing mechanism are covered in [10], but the language constructs and application discussed in this paper are all part of a fresh, "from scratch" implementation. The semantics of Natlog is the same as Prolog's SLD resolution, and a user familiar with Prolog's syntax and problem solving style [13] will easily adapt to Natlog's syntactic and semantic simplifications. Interoperation with Python has been also used in Janus [1] connecting Python and XSB-Prolog via their foreign language interfaces and systems like DeepProblog [5], in the latter as a facilitator for neuro-symbolic computations. Natlog's focus on keeping the logic component purely declarative is shared with [3] and its closeness to natural language and is shared with [8]. However, similarly to [1] and by contrast to [8] that implements changes via fluents, we rely simply on Python's imperative constructs to represent state changes and more complex interaction with outside computational resources like LLMs.

OpenAI's own `GPT 3.5`-based `ChatGPT`[7] automates the mapping of more queries (e.g., questions, code generation, dialog sessions, etc.) using an extensive Reinforcement Learning With Human Advice process [6]. By contrast, our DCG-supported approach relies exclusively on the pure GPT3 text-completion API on top of which we engineer task-specific prompts.

7 Conclusion and Future Work

We have informally overviewed automation, learnability and expressiveness challenges faced by logic-based programming languages in the context of today's competitive landscape of alternatives from other programming paradigms as well as from neural net-based machine learning frameworks. We have also sketched solutions to the challenges, with some emphasis on coroutining methods and neuro-symbolic interoperation mechanisms. We have illustrated the surprising synergies that emerge when joining declarative logic programming constructs and declarative prompt-driven interactions with Large Language Models based deep learning systems.

Future work, using Natlog as an orchestrator for more complex, multi-agent LLM interactions, where logic reasoning steps are interleaved with goal-driven one-shot LLM queries. We foresee applications to improved multi-step reasoning, bias reduction, fact checking and hallucination detection in LLMs.

---

[6] at https://github.com/ptarau/natlog/tree/main/apps/natgpt/pics.
[7] https://chat.openai.com/chat.

Acknowledgments. These reflections have been inspired by the live and deep-probing Prolog'50 discussions lead by Bob Kowalski and Veronica Dahl with focus on logical thinking and logic-based programming as well as on approaches to make logic-based programming accessible to newcomers, including use cases for a first-contact introduction to computing. I am thankful to the participants of these meetings for sharing their thoughts on both the last 50 years and the next 50 years of logic programming. Finally, many thanks go to the reviewers of the paper for their careful reading and constructive suggestions that helped clarify and substantiate key concepts covered in the paper.

References

1. Andersen, C., Swift, T.: The Janus System: a bridge to new prolog applications. In: Warren, D.S., Dahl, V., Eiter, T., Hermenegildo, M., Kowalski, R., Rossi, F. (eds.) Prolog - The Next 50 Years. No. 13900 in LNCS, Springer (July 2023)

2. Brown, T., et al.: Language models are few-shot learners. In: Larochelle, H., Ranzato, M., Hadsell, R., Balcan, M., Lin, H. (eds.) Advances in Neural Information Processing Systems. vol. 33, pp. 1877–1901. Curran Associates, Inc. (2020). https://proceedings.neurips.cc/paper/2020/file/1457c0d6bfcb4967418bfb8ac142f64a-Paper.pdf

3. Genesereth, M.: Prolog as a knowledge representation language the nature and importance of prolog. In: Warren, D.S., Dahl, V., Eiter, T., Hermenegildo, M., Kowalski, R., Rossi, F. (eds.) Prolog - The Next 50 Years. No. 13900 in LNCS, Springer (July 2023)

4. Hermenegildo, M.V.: An abstract machine for restricted AND-parallel execution of logic programs. In: Shapiro, E. (ed.) ICLP 1986. LNCS, vol. 225, pp. 25–39. Springer, Heidelberg (1986). https://doi.org/10.1007/3-540-16492-8_62

5. Manhaeve, R., Dumancic, S., Kimmig, A., Demeester, T., De Raedt, L.: Deep-problog: neural probabilistic logic programming. In: Bengio, S., Wallach, H., Larochelle, H., Grauman, K., Cesa-Bianchi, N., Garnett, R. (eds.) Advances in Neural Information Processing Systems 31, pp. 3749–3759. Curran Associates, Inc. (2018). http://papers.nips.cc/paper/7632-deepproblog-neural-probabilistic-logic-programming.pdf

6. Ouyang, L., et al.: Training language models to follow instructions with human feedback (2022). https://doi.org/10.48550/ARXIV.2203.02155, https://arxiv.org/abs/2203.02155

7. Ramesh, A., et al.: Zero-shot text-to-image generation (2021). https://doi.org/10.48550/ARXIV.2102.12092, https://arxiv.org/abs/2102.12092

8. Kowalski, R., Fariba Sadri, M.C., Davila, J.: Combining Logic Programming and Imperative Programming in LPS. In: Warren, D.S., Dahl, V., Eiter, T., Hermenegildo, M., Kowalski, R., Rossi, F. (eds.) Prolog - The Next 50 Years. No. 13900 in LNCS, Springer (July 2023)

9. Tarau, P.: The BinProlog Experience: architecture and implementation choices for continuation passing prolog and first-class logic engines. Theory Pract. Logic Program. **12**(1–2), 97–126 (2012). https://doi.org/10.1007/978-3-642-60085-2_2

10. Tarau, P.: Natlog: a Lightweight logic programming language with a neuro-symbolic touch. In: Formisano, A., et al. (eds.) Proceedings 37th International Conference on Logic Programming (Technical Communications), 20–27th September 2021 (2021)

11. Vaswani, A., et al.: Attention is all you need. In: Guyon, I., et al. (eds.) Advances in Neural Information Processing Systems, vol. 30. Curran Associates, Inc. (2017). https://proceedings.neurips.cc/paper/2017/file/3f5ee243547dee91fbd053c1c4a845 aa-Paper.pdf
12. Vision, C.M., at LMU Munich, L.R.G.: Stable Diffusion (2018–2022). https://github.com/CompVis/stable-diffusion
13. Warren, D.S.: Introduction to prolog. In: Warren, D.S., Dahl, V., Eiter, T., Hermenegildo, M., Kowalski, R., Rossi, F. (eds.) Prolog - The Next 50 Years. No. 13900 in LNCS, Springer (July 2023)

Prolog for Scientific Explanation

Jean-Christophe Rohner[1]([⊠]) and Håkan Kjellerstrand[2]

[1] Department of Psychology, Lund University, Lund, Sweden
jean-christophe.rohner@psy.lu.se
[2] Independent researcher, Malmö, Sweden
hkjellerstrand@acm.org

Abstract. Scientific explanations play an important role in most academic disciplines because they give us a fundamental understanding of why things happen or do not happen. In this paper we argue that Prolog has certain properties that make the language ideal for generating scientific explanations. We illustrate these properties in relation to a scientific theory.

Keywords: Abduction · Scientific explanation

1 Introduction

"Explanation" can mean many different things. Here, however, we focus on scientific explanation of the abductive kind. The term "abduction" was originally coined by Charles Sanders Peirce who contrasted this mode of reasoning with deduction and induction. Informally, abduction involves finding a hypothesis, among candidates, that can explain a certain observation [17]. An extensive body of research has developed the theoretical foundations of abduction in logic programs, and to date, there are a number of algorithms that perform this kind of inference (for an overview see [16,26]). More recently, abduction has also been implemented in probabilistic logic programs, enabling inference with uncertain information, e.g. [3,4,9,43].

Scientific explanation, in the traditional sense, employs the same kind of deductive argument as in abductive logic programming, but it involves additional and important qualifications. Simplifying a bit, and barring some tricky philosophical issues, scientific explanation can be characterized as follows, e.g. [1,5,53]:

Definition - Scientific Explanation. Given the tuple (L, C, A, O) where

- L is a set of definite clauses that describe general causal laws which approximately mirror states of affairs (often probabilistically)

- C is a set of atoms that describe initial conditions which are necessary for the occurrence of an effect (in a causal relation)
- A is a set of atoms that define potential candidate explanations (they are abducible by having different possible groundings)
- O is an atom that describes an observation

Finding an explanation of O is finding a set of atoms $\Delta \subseteq A$, such that $L \cup C \cup \Delta \models O$ and $C \cup \Delta \nvDash O$. That is, laws L, initial conditions C, and abduced facts Δ (subsets of A) entail the observation O, and the laws are a necessary part of the explanation. We consider an *explanation* of O a proof tree that encompasses all the steps in the derivation of O from L, C and Δ. Note that this definition omits certain characteristics typically found in abductive logic programming frameworks such as s(CASP), e.g. specific syntax for abducible predicates and the notion of integrity constraints (details can be found in [2,16, 26]; more information about s(CASP) can also be found in [21] in this volume).

A simple example illustrates these ideas. Ignaz Semmelweis was a physician working in a maternity clinic in Vienna. He noted that the incidence of childbed fever was higher in a ward where the staff also performed autopsies. After considering different alternatives, he proposed that the explanation was that the staff in this clinic transmitted "cadaverous particles" to the patients. His observations eventually led to the insight that the use of disinfectants prevents disease [29]. A Prolog program and proof tree for this example is shown in Fig. 1 (we use SWI-Prolog [52]). The include directive loads Theory Toolbox 2 [41], which is a system that defines a set of meta-interpreters for generating proof trees, and CLP(R), which is a system for constraint logic programming with real values [23] (more information about meta-interpreters can be found in [50] in this volume; the advantages of CLP(R) are discussed in Sect. 4.2.).

There is a single causal law L in the predicate disease/2, which says that the probability that person 1 has a disease (X1) depends on the probability that person 2 carries a particle (X2), the probability that person 2 and person 1 have contact (X3), and the probability that the particle is a pathogen (X4). The expression {X1 = X2 * X3 * X4} is a CLP(R) equation representing that disease depends on a conjunction of the causal factors in the body of the clause (assuming independence between events).

The query q then defines the other components of the problem. O represents the observation that a certain patient has a disease with probability 0.8. C1 and C2 represent the initial conditions that a doctor and the patient had contact with probability 0.9 and that the particle is a pathogen with probability 0.9. A defines the set of potential candidate explanations (abducibles): All possible probabilities that the doctor carried the particle (the last argument in the atom is an anonymous variable so it can take on any value). Finally prove/3 and showProof/2 call the meta-interpreter in Theory Toolbox 2 to generate and show any proof trees that entail the observation O. Running the query produces the proof tree to the right in the figure, i.e. the explanation. Here the probability of carrying disease is now known, $\Delta = carry(doctor, cadaverousParticle, 0.988)$, which is a subset of $A = carry(doctor, cadaverousParticle, \_)$. Together with the law L in the disease/2 predicate and the initial conditions in C, Δ entails the observation O.

```
:- include('theoryToolbox2.pl').        PROOF

disease(Person1,X1):-                    disease(patient,0.800)⇐
    carry(Person2,Particle,X2),            carry(doctor,cadaverousParticle,0.988)⇐ true
    contact(Person2,Person1,X3),           contact(doctor,patient,0.900)⇐ true
    pathogen(Particle,X4),                 pathogen(cadaverousParticle,0.900)⇐ true
    {X1 = X2 * X3 * X4}.                   {0.800=0.988*0.900*0.900}⇐ true


q:-
O = disease(patient,0.8),
C1 = contact(doctor,patient,0.9),
C2 = pathogen(cadaverousParticle,0.9),
A = carry(doctor,cadaverousParticle,_),
prove(O,[C1,C2,A],RESULT),
showProof(RESULT,monochrome).
```

Fig. 1. A Hello World Example - Disease Prevention.

Note that a meta-interpreter plays an important role for generating explanations such as the one shown in the figure. In the example we used prove/3 from Theory Toolbox 2. But it would also have been possible to use another system to generate proof trees; s(CASP), for example, has this functionality [2].

Abductive scientific explanation differs from another important kind of scientific explanation: Induction. The goal of induction is to find rules (laws if you will) that describe general relations between classes of objects based on relations that exist between singular objects. For example finding $mortal(X) \leftarrow human(X)$ after observing $mortal(peter)$, $human(peter)$, $mortal(mary)$, $human(mary)$, and so on. In abductive explanation, instead, a law is the starting point, and the goal is to explain an observation. For example, using the general relation $mortal(X) \leftarrow human(X)$ to explain $mortal(peter)$. There is a large body of machine learning research on inductive logic programming, see [10,34,46]. Such algorithms have been successfully applied in organic chemistry [47], molecular biology [33], robotics [28], medicine [7], and anthropology [11].

2   Related Work

The general idea to use abductive logic programming for scientific explanation has been raised by others, e.g. [1,15,18]. Already in the 80's, David Poole and his colleagues saw the similarities between this technical solution and the scientific problem when they were developing the Theorist system [36].

There are a number of practical use cases where abduction from logic programs has been leveraged for scientific explanation, mostly in biology. The Robot Scientist [27] is an autonomous system that conducts genetic research. It generates hypotheses, runs experiments, evaluates data to falsify inconsistent hypotheses, and then repeats this cycle. Abductive inference is used to automatically formulate hypotheses for testing (with a version of Progol [35]). The Gene Path system [54] abduces constraints in genetic networks and explains its answers on the basis of expert knowledge and experimental data. It could be used by a geneticist when planning experiments and reasoning about their outcomes. Similarly, the ARNI system [31] employs abduction from a logical representation of molecular interactions to explain how genes are affected in a causal network. In a related discipline, medicine, [8] show how abductive logic programming can be used to aid physicians to prescribe correct treatments for potential heart failure. More information about Prolog applications in biology can be found in [13] in this volume.

Proof trees play an essential role in our view of scientific explanation, since we suggest that they are explanations. There are a number of technical solutions that produce this kind of output. The s(CASP) system [2], which is available as a SWI Prolog module and on the web with SWISH [51], generates justification trees from answer set programs. The output can even contain natural language. The SLDNF Draw system [19] produces high quality proof trees via LATEX output. SLDNF Draw is also available as a SWI Prolog module and on the web at the CPLINT [39] site. The possibility to obtain proof trees additionally exists in TAU Prolog [48], which is an open-source Prolog interpreter in Javascript.

3   A Theory Example

To facilitate the coming discussion of the advantages of Prolog for scientific explanation we present an example of an actual scientific theory. The program shown in Fig. 2 captures the essential parts of Charles Darwin's theory of natural selection [14, 45] (theories such as this one could be hand crafted or found with inductive logic programming). The set of laws L are encoded in two clauses.

The first clause describes under what conditions children inherit their parents' traits. To keep things general, parent-child generations are represented numerically[1], where $Child = Parent + 1$. The clause then says that the probability that a child has a certain trait (X1) depends on the following probabilities: That their parent reproduces (X2), that their parent has the trait (X3), and that the trait is heritable (X4). Conjunction is represented by a product (assuming independence).

The second clause describes conditions for reproducing. The probability that an individual reproduces (X1) depends on the following probabilities: That they inhabit a certain habitat (X2), that they have a certain trait (X3), and that the trait is adaptive in that habitat (X4). As in the first clause, the product represents conjunction (again assuming independence). Note that the example only provides one explanation for why individuals have certain traits (inheritance), and only one explanation for why individuals reproduce (adaptation). But, of course, there

---

[1] Another way of encoding this would be to have a standard Prolog database where all parent-child relations are enumerated, e.g. parent(a, b), parent(b, c) and so on.

are other potential explanations, such as acquiring traits by imitating others, being in love, and so on. If necessary, such clauses could be added to the theory.

```
:- include('theoryToolbox2.pl').

hasTrait(Child,Trait,X1):-
    Parent is Child - 1,
    Parent > 0,
    reproduces(Parent,X2),
    hasTrait(Parent,Trait,X3),
    heritable(Trait,X4),
    {X1 = X2 * X3 * X4}.

reproduces(Individual,X1):-
    inhabits(Individual,Habitat,X2),
    hasTrait(Individual,Trait,X3),
    adaptiveIn(Trait,Habitat,X4),
    {X1 = X2 * X3 * X4}.
```

Fig. 2. A Theory About Natural Selection

4   Advantages of Prolog for Scientific Explanation

There is a long tradition in philosophy of science of giving logic a central role in the scientific process (even if this is questioned by some philosophers, see for example [22] for a discussion). Some prototypical examples are Hempel's deductive nomological model and Popper's falsificationism [37,53]. We believe that logical description and logical inference are, and should be, important parts of science [42]; not least because the theoretical foundations and the technical tools of logic have developed considerably in recent years, e.g. [1]. It is a big deal, for example, that deduction, induction, and abduction all have a solid formal basis as well as usable technical tools in Prolog, e.g. [26,34,40]. Below we present a set of advantages of Prolog that we believe are important in relation to scientific explanation (additional advantages, with respect to knowledge representation, are discussed in [20] in this volume).

4.1   Multiple Asymmetric Many-One Relations

An important advantage of Prolog is that it naturally represents multiple asymmetric many-one relations. The asymmetry of Prolog clauses is such that $head \leftarrow body$ means that $body$ entails $head$ and that $head$ does not entail $body$. According to the definition, an explanation of O consists of a proof tree that shows the derivation of O from laws L, initial conditions C and abduced facts Δ (subsets of abducibles A). So by having proof trees that involve laws of the form $L = O \leftarrow C_1, C_2, ..., C_n, A_1, A_2, ..., A_m$ we single out the explanandum (O, the thing that we want to explain). In the theory program in Fig. 2 parent traits and parent reproduction explain offspring traits (and not the other way around), because offspring traits is the thing that is being entailed. Compare this to a purely mathematical formalization which, given the description of explanation, can't differentiate between explanandum and explanans (that which explains the explanandum). In $O = C_1 * C_2 * ... * C_n * A_1 * A_2 * ... * A_m$, for example, the value of any one of $O, C_1, C_2, C_n, A_1, A_2, ..., A_m$ is entailed by the remaining values. With this syntax, there is no way of saying that offspring traits is the explanandum and that parent traits and parent reproduction are the explanans.

Another strength of Prolog, besides asymmetry, is that it naturally represents multiple many-one relations. An important insight from the debate on causality, which is essential in scientific explanation, is that things often have multiple causes. John Mackie's take on causality [30], for example, is that any given effect can occur because of several clusters of factors, where multiple factors within a single cluster are jointly necessary and sufficient for the effect to occur, while no individual cluster is, in itself, necessary for the effect to occur. In the natural selection program, for example, one cluster of factors that explains offspring traits consists of parent traits and parent reproduction; within this cluster these factors are necessary and sufficient. But it is possible to come up with other clusters of factors that can explain why individuals have certain traits, e.g. imitating friends that have these traits. Mackie's pattern nicely matches the structure of a Prolog program, where different clauses with the same head correspond to different clusters of factors, and where the literals in the body of each clause correspond to factors within a cluster. So if O is something that we want to causally explain and the Cs and As are conditions that can make O happen, we could have the three clauses $O \leftarrow C_1, C_2, A_1$ and $O \leftarrow C_3, A_2$ and $O \leftarrow C_4, C_5, A_3$.

Before ending this section, we want to make an important remark: Being able to represent this pattern is merely a semantic tool. Establishing cause-effect hinges on empirically showing that the probability of O increases when the probability of the Cs and As increase (everything else being equal) and that the Cs and As precede O [44].

4.2 Relations Between Qualitative and Quantitative Objects and Sets of Objects

Because causal laws play a key role in scientific explanation, it is essential to have a formal language that is expressive enough to fully capture the meaning of the components of such laws. A strength of Prolog is that it is straightforward to represent properties and relations that involve singular objects and sets of objects, where objects can be *either* quantitative or qualitative. Theory representations usually consist of a mix of verbal and mathematical (statistical) information. In the natural selection theory in Fig. 2, for example, traits and habitats are sets of qualitative objects, whereas individuals and probabilities are sets of quantitative objects. In other applications, Prolog has been used to build exact and general representations of atoms, their bonds and charges [47], kinship relations in groups [11], or relations between physical objects, lights and shadows

[12]. Encoding properties and relations that involve qualitative objects is harder in a scheme that only allows large vectors of numbers.

There are specific advantages with using probability equations in a theory (like in the natural selection example). The first advantage is that we can use strong negation (see for example [49]) and distinguish between situations in which a theory entails that O is false, in the sense that O is not the case, and situations in which a theory does not entail O, in the sense that O cannot be deduced from the theory. Consider the second clause in Fig. 2 and suppose we had inhabits(adam, h1, 1), hasTrait(adam, t1, 1) and adaptiveIn(t1, h1, 0) as initial conditions C. With this information the program would entail reproduces(adam, 0); i.e. it is not the case that Adam reproduces. With the same information, however, the query ?-reproduces(eve, X) would yield false (meaning that it is false that the program entails this goal, since the system doesn't know anything about Eve). Being able to describe why things do not happen (in addition to why they do happen) is an important part of scientific explanation. Adding probability equations to a theory complements negation as failure, p is false in the sense that the theory does not entail p, with strong negation, p is false in the sense that the theory entails that p is not the case.

A second advantage, which is specific to CLP(R) and other constraint-based systems (and missing in is/2), is that it is possible to get unique solutions to equations that have multiple unknowns (more information about the advantages of constraint logic programming can be found for example in [24]). In relation to explanation, this means that we can use scientific laws to explain why a phenomenon occurs (or does not occur), even when the probabilities of certain initial conditions are unknown. Consider the second clause in the natural selection example and suppose we had inhabits(adam, h1, _), hasTrait(adam, t1, _) and adaptiveIn(t1, h1, 0). Even if the probabilities of the first two facts are unknown, we get reproduces(adam, 0), because a product that involves zero is always zero. More examples of this technique can be found in the repository for Theory Toolbox 2 [41].

4.3 Homoiconicity

Prolog is a homoiconic language, which means that Prolog programs can perform computations on Prolog programs, including programs that represent scientific theories. There are at least two advantages of homoiconicity with respect to scientific explanation.

The first advantage is that we can write meta-interpreters that yield detailed proof trees for all the steps that lead from laws L, initial conditions C, and abduced facts Δ, to observations O. Because we have suggested that scientific explanations consist of proof trees, this is essential. Let's consider an example observation that we wish to explain. Evidently, most humans are equipped with some form of hair (in addition to several other traits). How can the natural selection theory in Fig. 2 explain this observation? Intuitively it seems that having hair should be a heritable trait that is adaptive. Is this the case? Fig. 3 shows a query q1 with prove/3. The observation O that we want to explain is that

```
q1:-                                    PROOF
0 = hasTrait(3,hair,1),
C = [                                   hasTrait(3,hair,1)⇐
    inhabits(_,humanNiche,1),             2 is 3+ -1⇐ true
    heritable(_,1)                        2>0⇐ true
],                                        reproduces(2,1.000)⇐
A = [                                       inhabits(2,humanNiche,1)⇐ true
    hasTrait(1,endothermic,1),              hasTrait(2,endothermic,1.000)⇐
    hasTrait(1,endothermic,0),                1 is 2+ -1⇐ true
    hasTrait(1,bipedal,1),                    1>0⇐ true
    hasTrait(1,bipedal,0),                    reproduces(1,1.000)⇐
    hasTrait(1,language,1),                     inhabits(1,humanNiche,1)⇐ true
    hasTrait(1,language,0),                     hasTrait(1,endothermic,1)⇐ true
    hasTrait(1,hair,1),                         adaptiveIn(endothermic,humanNiche,1)⇐ true
    hasTrait(1,hair,0),                         {1.000=1*1*1}⇐ true
    adaptiveIn(_,humanNiche,1),             hasTrait(1,endothermic,1)⇐ true
    adaptiveIn(_,humanNiche,0)              heritable(endothermic,1)⇐ true
],                                          {1.000=1*1*1}⇐ true
append(C,A,IN),                           adaptiveIn(endothermic,humanNiche,1)⇐ true
prove(0,IN,RESULT),                       {1.000=1*1.000*1}⇐ true
showProof(RESULT,monochrome).           hasTrait(2,hair,1.000)⇐
                                          1 is 2+ -1⇐ true
                                          1>0⇐ true
                                          reproduces(1,1.000)⇐
                                            inhabits(1,humanNiche,1)⇐ true
                                            hasTrait(1,endothermic,1)⇐ true
                                            adaptiveIn(endothermic,humanNiche,1)⇐ true
                                            {1.000=1*1*1}⇐ true
                                          hasTrait(1,hair,1)⇐ true
                                          heritable(hair,1)⇐ true
                                          {1.000=1.000*1*1}⇐ true
                                        heritable(hair,1)⇐ true
                                        {1=1.000*1.000*1}⇐ true
```

Fig. 3. An Explanation From the Natural Selection Theory

an individual in generation 3 has hair; hence the probability for this is 1 (generation 3 is arbitrary). In the query the initial conditions C are that anybody inhabits a human ecological niche and that any trait is heritable (an anonymous variable unifies with anything). The abducible predicates in the list A describe some things that are relevant to this particular example: Things happen with probability 0 or 1, there are some traits, and a trait might or not be adaptive in the ecological niche. The right part of Fig. 3 shows a proof tree for this goal, which constitutes an explanation according to the theory.

First, note that the probability of each involved causal factor is high (each one is 1). This makes sense given that having a trait was conditional on a conjunction of factors. An interesting and, perhaps, unexpected aspect of this explanation is that the adaptive value of having hair is not involved in explaining why people have hair. Having hair is conditional on reproductive potential, and reproductive potential - in this case - is instead supported by another trait (being endothermic). Incidentally, the explanation in Fig. 3 actually shows that having hair is a so called vestigial trait: A trait that is inherited but that does not have any adaptive value. The query q1 also generates additional proofs; among others, one in which the adaptive value of having hair *is* involved in deducing the observation. The reason for this incoherence will become apparent next.

The second advantage of homoiconicity is that we can write Prolog programs that perform rational theory evaluation, i.e. appraising theories using other criteria than empirical fit. For example, examining if a theory is free of internal contradictions or examining how general it is [37]. In a general Prolog system, such as Theory Toolbox 2 [41], it is fairly straightforward to write predicates that perform such analyses. Let's consider a final query example on the natural selection theory in Fig. 2 that checks if the theory makes conflicting predictions. In the query in Fig. 4 we use the predicate incoherence/7 (from Theory Toolbox 2). This predicate checks if a theory entails different probabilities for a certain goal and, if so, shows explanations for the conflicting answers. As shown in Fig. 4, there is an incoherence, and the explanation is that reproductive potential in the individual in generation 1 can either occur because they have hair or because they are endothermic. In the former case the probability of having hair for the individual in generation 2 is 0; in the latter case the probability is 1. This means that the theory has to be amended somehow. In what way is another matter.

4.4   Transparency

A final advantage of Prolog, and other symbolic approaches to AI, is that knowledge representations in this format are often transparent and, potentially, understandable by humans, e.g. [6]. Clearly, this is an important desideratum for scientific theories, which should be open to introspection and public scrutiny. Scientific theories are often used to make decisions with real life implications, e.g. in medicine, so transparent explanations become even more important. In general, understanding why an argument is an explanation is an important step towards explainable AI, e.g. [25]. Hopefully, Prolog can play an important role in the progress towards achieving this long-term goal.

5   Future Directions and Challenges

It is interesting to speculate about what the future holds for Prolog when it comes to scientific explanation. When thinking about this, it seems that the importance of *induction* often comes up. Because scientific theories are supposed to reflect states of affairs, they should be based on empirical data. So, if we want to be able to enjoy the benefits of Prolog for theory representation, and therefore explanation, high quality algorithms for inducing programs from data are essential.

To date, there are several available systems for inductive logic programming, some of which have achieved important milestones like predicate invention, finding recursive programs, and finding probabilistic programs (for overviews see [10,38]). Certain features of such systems are probably important for wider adoption in the scientific community (outside machine learning). The ability to handle noise, the ability to induce numerical relations, good documentation, and easy

```
q2:-
O1 = hasTrait(2,hair,X1),
O2 = hasTrait(2,hair,X2),
C = [
  hasTrait(1,hair,1),
  hasTrait(1,endothermic,1),
  inhabits(_,humanNiche,1),
  adaptiveIn(endothermic,humanNiche,1),
  adaptiveIn(hair,humanNiche,0),
  heritable(endothermic,1),
  heritable(hair,1)
],
incoherence(O1,O2,C,0.1,X1,X2,R),
showIncoherence(R,monochrome).
```

```
INCOHERENCE

Given inputs:
hasTrait(1,hair,1)
hasTrait(1,endothermic,1)
inhabits(A,humanNiche,1)
adaptiveIn(endothermic,humanNiche,1)
adaptiveIn(hair,humanNiche,0)
heritable(endothermic,1)
heritable(hair,1)

These goals are incoherent at the
threshold 0.1.

PROOFS

hasTrait(2,hair,0.000)⟸
    1 is 2+ -1⟸ true
    1>0⟸ true
    reproduces(1,0.000)⟸
        inhabits(1,humanNiche,1)⟸ true
        hasTrait(1,hair,1)⟸ true
        adaptiveIn(hair,humanNiche,0)⟸ true
        {0.000=1*1*0}⟸ true
    hasTrait(1,hair,1)⟸ true
    heritable(hair,1)⟸ true
    {0.000=0.000*1*1}⟸ true

hasTrait(2,hair,1.000)⟸
    1 is 2+ -1⟸ true
    1>0⟸ true
    reproduces(1,1.000)⟸
        inhabits(1,humanNiche,1)⟸ true
        hasTrait(1,endothermic,1)⟸ true
        adaptiveIn(endothermic,humanNiche,1)⟸ true
        {1.000=1*1*1}⟸ true
    hasTrait(1,hair,1)⟸ true
    heritable(hair,1)⟸ true
    {1.000=1.000*1*1}⟸ true
```

Fig. 4. An Example of Rational Theory Evaluation

installation come to mind. And a dream scenario would be if these features can be combined with predicate invention and recursion.

Another important area for development, towards the goal of using Prolog for scientific explanation, is the integration of inductive logic programming with other machine learning schemes, like deep neural networks. Being able to jointly use neural networks, for encoding unstructured data (e.g. from natural language texts) and inductive logic programming, for learning more complex relations from structured data, leveraging background knowledge, seems very powerful. Especially considering that a large amount of information, besides empirical data, already exists in the form of scientific papers. There is already progress when it comes to integrating neural networks and symbolic learning approaches e.g. [32]. At the same time, we do not think that the importance of neural networks should be overstated; at least not in the context of inducing scientific theories. The primary advantage of neural networks is their ability to deal with unstructured information. But data collection in actual research is usually not ad hoc; instead, it is planned in advance, so it is possible to design studies to generate structured data (directly suitable for inductive logic programming).

6 Conclusions

We have discussed the advantages of Prolog for scientific abductive explanation, suggesting that such explanations are proof trees for the derivation of an observation from a causal theory and initial conditions. Prolog can capture asymmetric many-one relations, represent complex relational concepts that involve qualitative as well as quantitative objects, flexibly reason with both known and unknown information (e.g. probabilities), generate explanations in the form of proof trees and perform rational theory evaluation. And beyond this, Prolog also supports induction and deduction. All in all, our general impression is that all the technical components needed for using Prolog as a great scientific tool are in place. Maybe the keys to wider adoption in the scientific community are easy access, good documentation, and user support. Prolog-on-the-web systems like SWISH and CPLINT, are important steps in this direction.

Acknowledgements. We wish to thank Bob Kowalski, Stassa Patsantzis and three anonymous reviewers.

References

1. Aliseda-Llera, A.: Logics in scientific discovery. Found. Sci. **9**, 339–363 (2004). https://doi.org/10.1023/B:FODA.0000042847.62285.81
2. Arias, J., Carro, M., Chen, Z., Gupta, G.: Justifications for goal-directed constraint answer set programming. Electron. Proce. Theor. Comput. Sci. **325**, 59–72 (2020). https://doi.org/10.4204/EPTCS.325.12
3. Azzolini, D., Bellodi, E., Ferilli, S., Riguzzi, F., Zese, R.: Abduction with probabilistic logic programming under the distribution semantics. Int. J. Approx. Reason. **142**, 41–63 (2022). https://doi.org/10.1016/j.ijar.2021.11.003
4. Bellodi, E., Gavanelli, M., Zese, R., Lamma, E., Riguzzi, F.: Nonground abductive logic programming with probabilistic integrity constraints. Theory Pract. Logic Program. **21**(5), 557–574 (2021). https://doi.org/10.1017/S1471068421000417
5. Bunnin, N., Yu, J.: E. In: The Blackwell Dictionary of Western Philosophy, chap. 5, pp. 197–245. Wiley, Hoboken (2004). https://doi.org/10.1002/9780470996379
6. Caroprese, L., Vocaturo, E., Zumpano, E.: Argumentation approaches for explainable AI in medical informatics. Intell. Syst. Appl. **16**, 200109 (2022). https://doi.org/10.1016/j.iswa.2022.200109
7. Carrault, G., Cordier, M.O., Quiniou, R., Wang, F.: Temporal abstraction and inductive logic programming for arrhythmia recognition from electrocardiograms. Artif. Intell. Med. **28**(3), 231–263 (2003). https://doi.org/10.1016/s0933-3657(03)00066-6
8. Chen, Z., Salazar, E., Marple, K., Gupta, G., Tamil, L., Cheeran, D., Das, S., Amin, A.: Improving adherence to heart failure management guidelines via abductive reasoning. Theory Pract. Logic Program. **17**(5–6), 764–779 (2017). https://doi.org/10.1017/S1471068417000308

9. Christiansen, H.: Implementing probabilistic abductive logic programming with constraint handling rules. In: Schrijvers, T., Frühwirth, T. (eds.) Constraint Handling Rules. LNCS (LNAI), vol. 5388, pp. 85–118. Springer, Heidelberg (2008). https://doi.org/10.1007/978-3-540-92243-8_5

10. Cropper, A., Dumančić, S.: Inductive logic programming at 30: a new introduction. J. Artif. Intell. Res. **74**, 765–850 (2022). https://doi.org/10.1613/jair.1.13507

11. Cunningham, S.J.: Machine learning applications in anthropology: automated discovery over kinship structures. Comput. Humanit. **30**(6), 401–406 (1996). https://doi.org/10.1007/BF00057936

12. Dai, W.-Z., Muggleton, S., Wen, J., Tamaddoni-Nezhad, A., Zhou, Z.-H.: Logical vision: one-shot meta-interpretive learning from real images. In: Lachiche, N., Vrain, C. (eds.) ILP 2017. LNCS (LNAI), vol. 10759, pp. 46–62. Springer, Cham (2018). https://doi.org/10.1007/978-3-319-78090-0_4

13. Dal Palú, A., Dovier, A., Formisano, A., Pontelli, E.: Prolog meets biology. In: Warren, D.S., Dahl, V., Eiter, T., Hermenegildo, M., Kowalski, R., Rossi, F. (eds.) Prolog - The Next 50 Years. LNAI, vol. 13900, pp. 318–333. Springer, Cham (2023)

14. Darwin, C.: On the Origin of Species, 1859. Routledge , London (2004). https://doi.org/10.9783/9780812200515

15. Delrieux, C.: Abductive inference in defeasible reasoning: a model for research programms. J. Appl. Log. **2**(4), 409–437 (2004). https://doi.org/10.1016/j.jal.2004.07.003

16. Denecker, M., Kakas, A.: Abduction in logic programming. In: Kakas, A.C., Sadri, F. (eds.) Computational Logic: Logic Programming and Beyond. LNCS (LNAI), vol. 2407, pp. 402–436. Springer, Heidelberg (2002). https://doi.org/10.1007/3-540-45628-7_16

17. Douven, I.: Abduction. In: Zalta, E. (ed.) The Stanford Encyclopedia of Philosophy. Metaphysics Research Lab, Stanford University (2021)

18. Flach, P., Kakas, A., Ray, O.: Abduction, induction, and the logic of scientific knowledge development. In: Workshop on Abduction and Induction in AI and Scientific Modelling, p. 21 (2006)

19. Gavanelli, M.: SLDNF-draw: visualization of prolog operational semantics in latex. Intelligenza Artificiale **11**, 81–92 (2017). https://doi.org/10.3233/IA-170108

20. Genesereth, M.: Prolog as a knowledge representation language. In: Warren, D.S., Dahl, V., Eiter, T., Hermenegildo, M., Kowalski, R., Rossi, F. (eds.) Prolog - The Next 50 Years. LNAI, vol. 13900, pp. 38–47. Springer, Cham (2023)

21. Gupta, G., Salazar, E., Arias, J., Basu, K., Chandra Varanasi, S.: Prolog: past, present, and future. In: Warren, D.S., Dahl, V., Eiter, T., Hermenegildo, M., Kowalski, R., Rossi, F. (eds.) Prolog - The Next 50 Years. LNAI, vol. 13900, pp. 48–61. Springer, Cham (2023)

22. Hepburn, B., Andersen, H.: Scientific method. In: Zalta, E. (ed.) The Stanford Encyclopedia of Philosophy. Metaphysics Research Lab, Stanford University (2021)

23. Holzbaur, C.: Ofai clp (q, r) manual, edition 1.3.3. Austrian research institute for artificial intelligence. Report, TR-95-09 (1995)

24. Jaffar, J., Maher, M.J.: Constraint logic programming: a survey. J. Logic Program. **19-20**, 503–581 (1994). https://doi.org/10.1016/0743-1066(94)90033-7, special Issue: Ten Years of Logic Programming

25. Jobin, A., Ienca, M., Vayena, E.: The global landscape of AI ethics guidelines. Nat. Mach. Intell. **1**(9), 389–399 (2019). https://doi.org/10.1038/s42256-019-0088-2

26. Kakas, A., Kowalski, R., Toni, F.: Abductive logic programming. J. Log. Comput. **2**, 719–770 (1992). https://doi.org/10.1093/logcom/2.6.719

27. King, R.D., et al.: Functional genomic hypothesis generation and experimentation by a robot scientist. Nature **427**(6971), 247–52 (2004). https://doi.org/10.1038/nature02236

28. Klingspor, V., Morik, K.J., Rieger, A.D.: Learning concepts from sensor data of a mobile robot. Mach. Learn. **23**(2–3), 305–332 (1996). https://doi.org/10.1007/BF00117448

29. Lane, H.J., Blum, N., Fee, E.: Oliver Wendell Holmes (1809–1894) and Ignaz Philipp Semmelweis (1818–1865): preventing the transmission of puerperal fever. Am. J. Publ. Health **100**(6), 1008–1009 (2010)

30. Mackie, J.L.: The Cement of the Universe: A Study of Causation. Clarendon Press (1974). https://doi.org/10.1093/0198246420.001.0001

31. Maimari, N., Broda, K., Kakas, A., Krams, R., Russo, A.: Symbolic Representation and Inference of Regulatory Network Structures, pp. 1–48. Wiley, Hoboken (2014). https://doi.org/10.1002/9781119005223.ch1

32. Manhaeve, R., Dumancic, S., Kimmig, A., Demeester, T., De Raedt, L.: Deepproblog: neural probabilistic logic programming. In: Advances in Neural Information Processing Systems, vol. 31 (2018). https://doi.org/10.1016/j.artint.2021.103504

33. Muggleton, S., King, R.D., Stenberg, M.J.E.: Protein secondary structure prediction using logic-based machine learning. Protein Eng. Des. Sel. **5**(7), 647–657 (1992). https://doi.org/10.1093/protein/5.7.647

34. Muggleton, S.: Inductive logic programming. N. Gener. Comput. **8**(4), 295–318 (1991)

35. Muggleton, S.: Inverse entailment and Progol. N. Gener. Comput. **13**(3), 245–286 (1995). https://doi.org/10.1007/BF03037089

36. Poole, D., Goebel, R., Aleliunas, R.: Theorist: a logical reasoning system for defaults and diagnosis. In: Cercone, N., McCalla, G. (eds.) The Knowledge Frontier: Essays in the Representation of Knowledge, pp. 331–352. Springer, New York (1987). https://doi.org/10.1007/978-1-4612-4792-0_13

37. Popper, K.R.: The logic of scientific discovery. Hutchinson, London (1972). https://doi.org/10.4324/9780203994627

38. Riguzzi, F.: Foundations of Probabilistic Logic Programming: Languages, Semantics, Inference and Learning. CRC Press, Boca Raton (2018)

39. Riguzzi, F., Bellodi, E., Lamma, E., Zese, R., Cota, G.: Probabilistic logic programming on the web. Software: Pract. Exp. **46**(10), 1381–1396 (2016). https://doi.org/10.1002/spe.2386

40. Robinson, J.A.: A machine-oriented logic based on the resolution principle. J. ACM **12**(1), 23–41 (1965). https://doi.org/10.1145/321250.321253

41. Rohner, J.C.: Theory Toolbox 2 (2023). https://github.com/JeanChristopheRohner/theory-toolbox-2

42. Rohner, J.C., Kjellerstrand, H.: Using logic programming for theory representation and scientific inference. New Ideas Psychol. **61**, 100838 (2021). https://doi.org/10.1016/j.newideapsych.2020.100838

43. Rotella, F., Ferilli, S.: Probabilistic abductive logic programming using possible worlds. In: CEUR Workshop Proceedings, vol. 1068, pp. 131–145 (2013)

44. Shadish, W.R., Cook, T.D., Campbell, D.T.: Experimental and Quasi-Experimental Designs for Generalized Causal Inference. Houghton, Mifflin and Company (2002)

45. Shaffner, S., Sabeti, P.: Evolutionary adaptation in the human lineage. Nat. Educ. **1**(14) (2008)

46. Sozou, P.D., Lane, P.C.R., Addis, M., Gobet, F.: Computational scientific discovery. In: Magnani, L., Bertolotti, T. (eds.) Springer Handbook of Model-Based Science. SH, pp. 719–734. Springer, Cham (2017). https://doi.org/10.1007/978-3-319-30526-4_33
47. Srinivasana, A., Muggleton, S.H., Sternberg, M.J.E., King, R.D.: Theories for mutagenicity: a study in first-order and feature-based induction. Artif. Intell. **85**(1), 277–299 (1996). https://doi.org/10.1016/0004-3702(95)00122-0
48. Valverde, R.: Tau Prolog (2022). http://tau-prolog.org/documentation
49. Wagner, G.: Web rules need two kinds of negation. In: Bry, F., Henze, N., Małuszyński, J. (eds.) PPSWR 2003. LNCS, vol. 2901, pp. 33–50. Springer, Heidelberg (2003). https://doi.org/10.1007/978-3-540-24572-8_3
50. Warren, D.S.: Introduction to prolog. In: Warren, D.S., Dahl, V., Eiter, T., Hermenegildo, M., Kowalski, R., Rossi, F. (eds.) Prolog - The Next 50 Years. LNCS, vol. 13900, pp. 3–19. Springer, Cham (2023)
51. Wielemaker, J., Lager, T., Riguzzi, F.: SWISH: SWI-prolog for sharing. In: Ellmauthaler, S., Schulz, C. (eds.) Proceedings of the International Workshop on User-Oriented Logic Programming (IULP 2015), pp. 99–113 (2015)
52. Wielemaker, J., Schrijvers, T., Triska, M., Lager, T.: SWI-prolog. Theory Pract. Logic Program. **12**(1–2), 67–96 (2012). https://doi.org/10.1017/S1471068411000494
53. Woodward, J., Ross, L.: Scientific explanation. In: Zalta, E. (ed.) The Stanford Encyclopedia of Philosophy. Metaphysics Research Lab, Stanford University (2021)
54. Zupan, B., et al.: Discovery of genetic networks through abduction and qualitative simulation. In: Džeroski, S., Todorovski, L. (eds.) Computational Discovery of Scientific Knowledge. LNCS (LNAI), vol. 4660, pp. 228–247. Springer, Heidelberg (2007). https://doi.org/10.1007/978-3-540-73920-3_11

Machines as Thought Partners: Reflections on 50 Years of Prolog

Gregory Gelfond[1(✉)], Marcello Balduccini[1,2], David Ferrucci[1], Adi Kalyanpur[1], and Adam Lally[1]

[1] Elemental Cognition Inc., New York, USA
gregg@ec.ai
[2] Saint Joseph's University, Philadelphia, USA

Abstract. In 1972, Kowalski and Colmerauer started a revolution with the advent of the Prolog programming language. As with LISP, the language enabled us to *think previously impossible thoughts*, and ushered in both logic programming and the declarative programming paradigm. Since that time, a number of descendants of Prolog have been brought into the world, among them constraint logic programming and answer-set prolog. In this paper, we celebrate the 50th anniversary of the Prolog language, and give a brief introduction to a new member of the Prolog family of languages — the logic programming language *Cogent*.

Keywords: Logic programming · Knowledge Representation · Programming Languages · Prolog Anniversary · Cogent

1 Introduction

In his 1972 Turing Award Lecture, Edsger Dijkstra notes that LISP "has assisted a number of our most gifted fellow humans in thinking previously impossible thoughts." Curiously, it was during that same year that Prolog was developed. We do not know if it was felt at that time just how important the discovery of the Prolog language was, but it is not surprising that the name of the language, an acronym for *"Programming in Logic"*, is a homophone for *prologue*. Robert Kowalski's and Alain Colmerauer's language was an introduction to a new way of thinking about programming, one which in some ways is alluded to by an old joke at the language's expense:

> Prolog is what you get when you create a language and system that has the intelligence of a six-year-old - it simply says "no" to everything.

The joke hints at just how revolutionary the language was. For the first time, we now had a language that rather than having a programmer answer the question of *"how"*, we had one that enabled us to answer the question of *"what"*. In other words, the language freed us from thinking about and describing the mechanics of an algorithm, and allowed us to focus on describing the goal, or specification that the algorithm was intended to meet. So, if we come back

D. S. Warren et al. (Eds.): Prolog: The Next 50 Years, LNAI 13900, pp. 386–392, 2023.
https://doi.org/10.1007/978-3-031-35254-6_31

to the notion of a six-year-old child, it turned a programmer into a teacher, and the computer into a student. This shift, to return to Dijkstra's quote on LISP, enabled us to think previously impossible thoughts – and therefore, to ask previously impossible questions.

Two other aspects of the language's nature – its connection to both *Horn clauses* and *context-free grammars* shed light on the kinds of heretofore impossible thoughts we now find ourselves engaged with. SLD and its successor SLDNF resolution enabled us to both simply encode and render computable part of the language of thought itself. This in turn shifted our gaze to the question of: "What kinds of reasoning can be described (i.e., taught) to a machine?" The search for answers to these questions (and others such as uncovering the nature of negation-as-failure) gave rise to other languages and their attendant semantics, such as the *well-founded* [9] and *answer-set semantics* [1,2], advancing our understanding of how we ourselves reason and how the kind of reasoning we carry out can be imparted to a machine. These questions yielded further lines of inquiry into areas such as commonsense reasoning, natural language understanding, reasoning about actions and change, and algorithmics, many of which are part of the foundation of the artificial intelligence technologies in active development here at Elemental Cognition[1].

Elemental Cognition (EC), a company founded by Dave Ferrucci after his success in helming IBM's Watson Project[2] through its landmark success in beating the best humans at the question-answering game of Jeopardy, is a particular beneficiary of the foundations laid by Kowalski and those who followed him. The fields of *knowledge representation, non-monotonic reasoning,* and *declarative programming* can trace part of their ancestry to Kowalski's work, and provide the logical foundations of the work done at EC. In particular, our vision of artificial agents as "thought partners" capable of collaborating with humans, rather than just acting autonomously, depends on numerous developments in these fields.

EC's history with logic programming begins in some respects with Ferrucci's own background, and the IBM Watson project in particular. There, Prolog played a role in the project's natural language pipeline and was instrumental in the detection and extraction of semantic relations in both questions and natural language corpora. Prolog's simplicity and expressiveness enabled the developers to readily deal with rule sets consisting of more than 6,000 Prolog clauses, something which prior efforts involving custom pattern-matching frameworks failed to do. This work in no small part informed the design of EC's neuro-symbolic reasoner, *Braid* [3]. The expressivity and transparency of a Prolog-like language combined with the statistical pattern matching power of various machine learning models enabled a powerful *HybridAI* solution which had been applied to several "real-world" applications. This work in part involved the development of a backward chaining system that can be seen as an extension of Prolog's SLD resolution algorithm by features such as *statistical/fuzzy unification* and *probabilistic rules* generated by a machine learning model. This enabled the system to circumvent

---

[1] https://ec.ai.
[2] https://www.ibm.com/watson.

the knowledge acquisition bottleneck and potential brittleness of matching/uni-fication, while retaining the elegance and simplicity of the declarative paradigm itself. Subsequent work has seen the Braid reasoning system evolve towards the use of the *answer-set semantics* and *constraint logic programming* [7].

All of this enabled a number of high-profile successes, such as our develop-ment of the PolicyPath[3] application which was used during Super Bowl LV in 2021 at the height of the Covid-19 pandemic [4]. The project was built on a declarative, logic-based representation of the related policies, and part of the rea-soning mechanisms developed in the course of the project combined techniques for *reasoning about actions and change* with various flavors of logic programming including *answer-set programming* and *constraint logic programming*. Other suc-cesses include our partnership with the OneWorld Alliance[4] on the development of the virtual agent they employ for scheduling round-the-world travel.

In this paper we give an introduction to a new language called Cogent[5] under development at EC, which carries forward the torch that was lit by the introduc-tion of Prolog.

2   From Prolog to Cogent

As was mentioned previously, the advent of logic programming enabled us to shift our focus from describing the *how* of a computation, to the *what*. In other words, it enabled us to focus our attention on what Niklaus Wirth termed *"the refinement of specification"*. As an example, let's consider the following example: a nurse scheduling program written in *answer-set prolog* (a descendant of Prolog based on the answer-set semantics of logic programs, and one of the elements at the core of EC's internal language known as Cordial).

Listing 1.1. Nurse Scheduling in Answer-Set Prolog

```
1   % The nurses are Andy, Betty, and Chris.
2   nurse(andy; betty; chris).
3
4   % The days are Monday, Tuesday, and Wednesday.
5   day(monday; tuesday; wednesday).
6
7   % The shifts are first, second, and third.
8   shift(1;2;3).
9
10  % We may choose for a nurse to be assigned to a shift on a day.
11  { assigned(N,S,D) }:- nurse(N), shift(S), day(D).
12
13  % A nurse cannot be assigned to more than one shift on the same day.
14  :- nurse(N), day(D), #count{ S : assigned(N,S,D) } > 1.
15
16  % A shift is ''covered" by a nurse on a day if the nurse is assigned to
       the shift on that day.
17  covered(S,N,D):- assigned(N,S,D).
18
```

[3] https://www.billboard.com/pro/super-bowl-halftime-show-covid-safety-coronavirus/.

[4] https://ec.ai/case-travel.

[5] https://ec.ai/cogent-features.

```
19   % Each shift must be covered by exactly one nurse on each day.
20   :- shift(S), day(D), #count{ N : covered(S,N,D) } != 1.
21
22   % A nurse is ''working on'' a day if the nurse is assigned to a shift on
        that day.
23   working(N,D):- shift(S), assigned(N,S,D).
24
25   % Each nurse must be working on at least two days.
26   :- nurse(N), #count{ D : working(N,D) } < 2.
```

The important aspect of the program in Listing 1.1 is that none of the statements describe an algorithm for computing a potential solution. Rather, they encode *the specification itself.* It's worth reflecting and appreciating the power of such a syntactically simple and elegant language. Compare for example this program, against the equivalent programs written in an imperative language using Google's OR-Tools [8]. The difference is stark, and it raises an important question: "Why has the logic programming approach not gained in momentum since its discovery?"

There are many potential answers to this question. One possibility is that in addition to the cognitive load incurred by switching from an imperative to a declarative mindset, there is an additional cognitive load incurred by the close relationship between logic programming languages and the notations of formal logic. This dramatically increases the distance a potential user has to mentally travel in order to get to the current state of the art. Another way to view this, is that logic programming languages on some level, are still at the level of assembly language. The *declarative paradigm* is a higher level paradigm than *imperative programming*, but declarative languages by and large are still on too low a level to be readily adopted. *If* this is true, then a natural question to ask is: "What could a high-level, structured, declarative programming language look like?"

At EC, we believe that one potential answer to this question is *structured natural language*, in particular our own version of this known as *Cogent*. Similar work in this area exists, namely Kowalski's own work on logical English [5,6], but with Cogent we are able to leverage our expertise in both natural language understanding and knowledge representation to build a more flexible, and user friendly representation language. In particular, let's revisit the program from Listing 1.1, only this time in Cogent instead of ASP:

Listing 1.2. Nurse Scheduling in Cogent

```
1    The nurses are ''Andy'', ''Betty'', and ''Chris''.
2
3    The days are ''Monday'', ''Tuesday'', and ''Wednesday''.
4
5    The shifts are ''first'', ''second'', and ''third''.
6
7    A nurse may be ''assigned to'' a shift ''on'' a day.
8
9    A shift may be ''covered by'' a nurse ''on'' a day.
10
11   A nurse may be ''working on'' a day.
12
13   We may choose for a nurse to be assigned to a shift on a day.
14
15   A nurse cannot be assigned to more than one shift on the same day.
16
```

17	A shift is covered by a nurse on a day if the nurse is assigned to the shift on that day.
18	
19	Each shift must be covered by exactly one nurse on each day.
20	
21	A nurse is working on a day if the nurse is assigned to a shift on that day.
22	
23	Each nurse must be working on at least two days.

The reader will notice that with the exception of lines 7, 9, and 11, the text of the program is the same as comments from the ASP encoding in Listing 1.1. Given this program, our reasoning engine is capable of finding solutions *just as efficiently* as the ASP encoding, yet the Cogent program is more accessible to a reader. Not only that, but the fact that the language is a structured form of natural language helps bridge the gap in terms of familiarity to aspiring users. The notion of accessibility to a reader, however is of special importance, since at EC, one of our motivating goals is to help develop *explainable AI*. One important aspect of this is to render the axioms of a domain that an AI system represents both *inspectable* and *clear* to as many users as possible. This kind of transparency enables deeper human and AI partnerships which furthers our vision of artificial agents as "thought partners" capable of collaborating with humans.

Cogent has features that overlap with those found in contemporary logic programming languages, such as *non-deterministic choice, aggregates, recursive definitions, costs, preferences*, a *declarative semantics for negation*, and *contradiction diagnosis*. In addition however, it features numerous advanced term building features that facilitate the construction of clear, concise natural language expressions. Consider the solution to the N-Queens problem given in Listing 1.3

Listing 1.3. N-Queens in Cogent

```
1   # Declarations
2
3   There is exactly one ''board size'', which is a number.
4
5   ''Queen'' is a type.
6   The ''Row'' of a queen can be any integer from 1 to the board size.
7   The ''Column'' of a queen can be any integer from 1 to the board size.
8
9   A queen may be ''attacking'' another queen.
10
11  # Rules of the Domain
12
13  A queen cannot be attacking another queen.
14
15  A queen is attacking another queen if the first queen's row is equal to
        the second queen's row.
16
17  A queen is attacking another queen if the first queen's column is equal
        to the second queen's column.
18
19  A queen is attacking another queen if
20      A - B = C - D
21  where
22      A is the row of the first queen, and
23      B is the row of the second queen, and
24      C is the column of the first queen, and
25      D is the column of the second queen.
26
```

```
27  A queen is attacking another queen if
28     A - B = D - C
29  where
30     A is the row of the first queen, and
31     B is the row of the second queen, and
32     C is the column of the first queen, and
33     D is the column of the second queen.
```

Listing 1.3 demonstrates several term building features of Cogent, as well as a natural encoding of the constraints of the domain. In addition, the language utilizes EC's Braid reasoning engine, making it capable of scaling to advanced production applications, such as the Round-the-World travel application developed for the OneWorld Alliance. While dramatically more complex in scope than the toy examples presented above, the encoding of various rules in Cogent (such as those shown in Listing 1.4) remains not only manageable, but clearly conveys their intention to a reader:

Listing 1.4. Round-the-World Rule Sampling

```
1   At most 4 international transfers can be located in any country.
2
3   At least one selected flight leg must be arriving in each continent group
    .
4
5   A visit is immediately preceding another visit if
6      a selected route is going from the first visit to the second visit.
7
8   At most one selected leg can be arriving in Asia unless
9      the Asia intercontinental arrival exception is in effect.
10
11  At most two selected legs can be arriving in Asia if
12     the Asia intercontinental arrival exception is in effect.
13
14  The Asia intercontinental arrival exception is in effect if
15     a selected leg is traveling from Southwest Pacific to Asia, and
16     another selected leg is traveling from Asia to Europe.
```

In addition to bridging the linguistic gap by being a controlled form of natural language, Cogent is coupled with a powerful AI authoring assistant to help bridge the gap even further, making for a system that we believe is greater than the sum of its parts. It is our belief at EC that Cogent provides a revolution in the arena of declarative programming, and programming at large by elevating the notion of *high-level language* to a new level.

3   Conclusion

In 1972, Kowalski and Colmerauer started a revolution with the advent of the Prolog programming language. The ability to think "previously impossible thoughts", led the community to ask previously unthinkable question, sparking revolutions in natural language understanding, knowledge representation, commonsense reasoning, and other diverse areas. For a time, these fields grew in isolation from each other, and now are coming together rapidly and in profound ways. With the development of Cogent, an ultimate grandchild of Prolog in some sense, we at Elemental Cognition hope to carry forward the tradition and enable a new class of impossible thoughts to be given voice. The community owes a debt to Kowalski, Colmerauer and the Prolog Language, and the great unexplored sea they revealed to us. Happy Birthday.

References

1. Gelfond, M., Lifschitz, V.: The stable model semantics for logic programming. In: Kowalski, R., Bowen, Kenneth (eds.) Proceedings of International Logic Programming Conference and Symposium, pp. 1070–1080. MIT Press (1988). http://www.cs.utexas.edu/users/ai-lab?gel88
2. Gelfond, M., Lifschitz, V.: Classical negation in logic programs and disjunctive databases. N. Gener. Comput. **9**, 365–385 (1991)
3. Kalyanpur, A., Breloff, T., Ferrucci, D.A.: Braid: weaving symbolic and neural knowledge into coherent logical explanations. Proceed. AAAI Conf. Artif. Intelli. **36**(10), 10867–10874 (2022). https://doi.org/10.1609/aaai.v36i10.21333. https://ojs.aaai.org/index.php/AAAI/article/view/21333
4. Kaufman, G.: How the NFL Pulled Off a Safe Super Bowl LV Halftime Show in the Middle of a Pandemic (2 2021). https://www.billboard.com/pro/super-bowl-halftime-show-covid-safety-coronavirus/, non paywalled version. https://www.bioreference.com/how-the-nfl-pulled-off-a-safe-super-bowl-lv-halftime-show-in-the-middle-of-a-pandemic/
5. Kowalski, R., Dávila Quintero, J., Calejo, M.: Logical English for legal applications (11 2021)
6. Kowalski, R., Dávila Quintero, J., Sartor Galileo Calejo, M.: Logical English for law and education. In: Warren, D.S., Dahl, V., Eiter, T., Hermenegildo, M., Kowalski, R., Rossi, F. (eds.) Prolog - The Next 50 Years. No. 13900 in LNCS, Springer (2023)
7. Marriott, K., Stuckey, P.J., Wallace, M.: Handbook of constraint programming, chap. 12. Constraint Logic Programming, pp. 409–452. Foundations of Artificial Intelligence, Elsevier (2006)
8. Perron, L., Furnon, V.: OR-Tools. https://developers.google.com/optimization/
9. Schlipf, J.S., Ross, K.A., Van Gelder, A.: The well-founded semantics for general logic programs. J. Assoc. Comput. Mach. **38**(3), 620–650 (1991)

Author Index

© The Editor(s) (if applicable) and The Author(s), under exclusive license
to Springer Nature Switzerland AG 2023
D. S. Warren et al. (Eds.): Prolog: The Next 50 Years, LNAI 13900, pp. 393–394, 2023.
https://doi.org/10.1007/978-3-031-35254-6

Printed in the United States
by Baker & Taylor Publisher Services